Fairy Tales from Before Fairy Tales

G. Cruikshank fec.t

Fairy Tales *from* Before Fairy Tales

The Medieval Latin Past of Wonderful Lies

Jan M. Ziolkowski

THE UNIVERSITY OF MICHIGAN PRESS ANN ARBOR

Copyright © by the University of Michigan 2007
All rights reserved
Published in the United States of America by
The University of Michigan Press
Manufactured in the United States of America
♾ Printed on acid-free paper

2010 2009 2008 2007 4 3 2 1

A CIP catalog record for this book is available from the British Library.

Library of Congress Cataloging-in-Publication Data

Ziolkowski, Jan M., 1956–
 Fairy tales from before fairy tales : the medieval Latin past of
wonderful lies / Jan M. Ziolkowski.
 p. cm.
 Includes bibliographical references and indexes.
 ISBN-13: 978-0-472-11568-6 (cloth : alk. paper)
 ISBN-10: 0-472-11568-5 (cloth : alk. paper)
 1. Fairy tales—History and criticism. 2. Tales—Classification.
 I. Title.

GR550.Z55 2006
398.209—dc22 2006025452

To students and colleagues in
Folklore and Mythology

Contents

Abbreviations

AT Antti Aarne and Stith Thompson. *The Types of the Folktale: A Classification and Bibliography.* 2nd ed. Folklore Fellows Communications 184. Helsinki: Suomalainen Tiedeakatemia, Academia scientiarum fennica, 1961.

ATU Uther, Hans-Jörg. *The Types of International Folktales. A Classification and Bibliography.* FFC 284–86. Helsinki: Suomalainen Tiedeakatemia/Academia scientiarum fennica, 2004.

BHL *Bibliotheca hagiographica latina antiquae et mediae aetatis.* Ed. Socii Bollandiani. 2 vols. Brussels: Société des Bollandistes, 1898–1901. Supplement, 1911. New Supplement, ed. Henryk Fros, 1986.

BP Johannes Bolte and Georg Polívka. *Anmerkungen zu den Kinder- und Hausmärchen der Brüder Grimm.* 5 vols. Leipzig: Dieterich'sche Verlagsbuchhandlung, 1913–32. Reprint, Hildesheim, Zurich, and New York: Olms-Weidmann, 1992–94.

EM Kurt Ranke, ed. *Enzyklopädie des Märchens: Handwörterbuch zur historischen und vergleichenden Erzählforschung.* 11 vols. to date. Berlin and New York: Walter de Gruyter, 1977–.

F&W *Funk and Wagnalls Standard Dictionary of Folklore, Mythology, and Legend.* Ed. Maria Leach. San Francisco: Harper and Row, 1984.

FFC Folklore Fellows Communications. Helsinki: Suomalainen Tiedeakatemia, Academia scientiarum fennica, 1910–.

Folklore *Folklore: An Encyclopedia of Beliefs, Customs, Tales, Music, and Art.* Ed. Thomas A. Green. 2 vols. Santa Barbara: ABC-CLIO, 1997.

KHM	Jacob Grimm and Wilhelm Grimm. *Kinder- und Hausmärchen, gesammelt durch die Brüder Grimm.*
LdM	*Lexikon des Mittelalters.* 9 vols. Stuttgart and Weimar: J. B. Metzler, 1977–99.
MGH	Monumenta Germaniae Historica inde ab a.C. 500 usque ad a. 1500. Hanover, Munich, and elsewhere, 1819–.
MI	Stith Thompson. *Motif-Index of Folk-Literature: A Classification of Narrative Elements in Folktales, Ballads, Myths, Fables, Mediaeval Romances, Exempla, Fabliaux, Jest-Books, and Local Legends.* 2nd ed. 6 vols. Bloomington: Indiana University Press, 1955–58.
PG	*Patrologiae cursus completus, Series Graeca.* Ed. J.-P. Migne. 167 vols. Paris: J.-P. Migne, 1857–66.
PL	*Patrologiae cursus completus, Series Latina.* Ed. J.-P. Migne. 221 vols. Paris: J.-P. Migne, 1841–64.
TLL	*Thesaurus Linguae Latinae.* Leipzig. B. G. Teubner, 1900–.
VL[1]	Karl Langosch, ed. *Die deutsche Literatur des Mittelalters: Verfasserlexikon.* 1st ed. 5 vols. Berlin: Walter de Gruyter, 1933–55.
VL[2]	Kurt Ruh, Burghart Wachinger, et al., eds. *Die deutsche Literatur des Mittelalters: Verfasserlexikon.* 2nd ed. 10 vols. Berlin and New York: Walter de Gruyter, 1978–99.

Acknowledgments

his book was inspired long ago by Albert B. Lord, who encouraged me to be alert to oral literature and folklore. Its chapters have gained immeasurably from discussions with students in classes at Harvard University. I am also indebted to three undergraduates or erstwhile undergraduates from outside courses. As research assistants during the long gestation of this fairy tale, Lambrina Mileva, Kamila Lis, and especially Emily Vasiliauskas scoured Harvard University's many rich libraries in order to answer my incessant queries. To move to present colleagues and fellow scholars, I am very grateful to Jack Zipes, who produced a reader's report for the University of Michigan Press that was a model of helpfulness in both information and spirit, and to Maria Tatar, whose generous comments after her perusal of the manuscript reassured me that it was ready for the press. To Lino Pertile I give thanks for inspecting and improving my translation of the Italian tale of the peasant Campriano. The Netherlands Institute for Advanced Study in the Humanities and Social Sciences has provided a most tranquil setting in which to see the book into print. Finally, I owe much to Saskia, Ada, and Yetta, who once helped me rediscover fairy tales, and to Liz, who has been magical hands and eyes for me in my study when I have been across the ocean.

For permission to publish revised forms of articles (full details are provided in the bibliography), my warm appreciation goes to the following journals and publishers: to *Viator* for "Folklore and Learned Lore in Letaldus's Whale Poem" (1984); to *Speculum* for "A Fairy Tale from Before Fairy

Tales: Egbert of Liège's 'De puellis a lupellis seruata' and the Medieval Background of 'Little Red Riding Hood'" (1992); to the *Journal of Medieval Latin* for "The Beast and the Beauty: The Reorientation of 'The Donkey,' from the Middle Ages to the Brothers Grimm" (1995) and "The *Rapularius* and 'The Turnip' in *Grimms' Fairy Tales:* A Comparative Study with Translations" (2003); to Rodopi for "A Medieval 'Little Claus and Big Claus': A Fabliau from Before Fabliaux?" (1999); and to SISMEL for "Folktales in Medieval Latin Poetry, 1000–1300" (2005).

Introduction

ifteen years ago I cast about for a topic that would enable me to connect today's culture with the literature in my main field of interest (and please do not put down this book after reading the next three words), Medieval Latin literature. My professional situation prompted me to think of folktales and fairy tales. On the one hand, half of my appointment was in a classics department, where, at that time, the meaning and value of philology were topics of considerable discussion and even tension. In addition, I was trying to find common ground with most of my colleagues in Medieval Latin outside my university, who were predominantly Europeans, who held positions flagged explicitly as Medieval Latin philology, and who devoted much of their research and writing to editing, textual criticism and transmission, and other unquestionably philological pursuits. On the other hand, the remaining half of my salary came from a department in comparative literature, which I subsequently chaired for a number of years. Although comparative literature has never been defined overtly so as to exclude premodern literatures, the understanding of it as "the systematic study of supranational assemblages" tends to diminish the ease of including in it literatures from before when nations existed.[1] Furthermore, comparative literature, which was once bound up with the languages and literatures of different traditions, has become increasingly connected with theoretical approaches, among which the place of philology has been extremely controversial.[2]

Classics and comparative literature differed starkly from each other in the time periods with which they were most often concerned and in the theoretical approaches with which they were associated. A way to elide the differences came to me through one of the happiest serendipities in my intellectual life. Very soon after being hired at Harvard, I had been enlisted by Albert B. Lord (1912–91) to serve on a committee devoted to the study of folklore and mythology. In seeking a confluence between my two or more intellectual identities, I gravitated toward a number of texts written in Medieval Latin that recounted tales that were also documented in later times (especially the Romantic era) in fairy tale collections. Some topics seemed too narrow and specific, others too broad and amorphous, but fairy tales seemed just right: Goldilocks would have been happy.

Upon delving more deeply into these texts and the scholarship that had grown rampant around them, I discovered that the tales had been relatively neglected. Medieval Latinists had edited them and sometimes translated them (particularly into German or Italian), but on the whole they had not grappled in any depth with what the tales might mean, either in their own right or in their significance for the history of folktales and fairy tales. In such interpretations as had been formulated, Medieval Latinists had not been especially troubled about exploring closely the connections of the tales with folk literature in general or the Grimm collection in particular. Although fairy tale scholars of past generations had sometimes noticed the tales and discussed them briefly, by and large the texts had been consigned to the same forlorn and overlooked corner where much of Medieval Latin literature has undeservedly languished. The texts were too unclassical for Medieval Latin philologists, too recherché (and too Latin) for folklorists and fairy tale scholars.

But noticing that the tales recounted in these poems could help me to find an intersection with a general public (and even with my three daughters, who were children when the work began and are now adults), I became ever more convinced that the folktales and fairy tales recorded in Latin could afford one of the few means—and maybe the only one—for putting on display for a broad college audience the materials I study as a specialist. Already a decade and a half ago, it seemed that a professor could canvas twenty-five bright and well-schooled students and find surprisingly few texts, especially from before the twentieth century, that they would have in common. Even the Shakespeare they knew might turn out to be different comedies and tragedies: this one had read *Macbeth* and *As You Like It,* that one *Hamlet* and *A Midsummer Night's Dream.* But to what poems, plays, or novels had they all been exposed? The common store of allusions among them was to be found not in literature and especially not in verse but instead in films, television, and celebrity-oriented current events.

If acquaintance with Anglo-American literature from hundreds of years ago was limited, a collective familiarity with literature from elsewhere in the world and not in English had grown even slighter. Among the many factors that have come into play, both economics and politics of language have been involved.[3] Although it was possible in the aftermath of World War II to hope for the foundation of a "world literature" (*Weltliteratur*) that would draw together the best from everywhere,[4] it has become ever more common for people in the United States in particular to slake their thirst for exoticism by engaging texts produced by ethnic minorities within American culture or literatures written in English in (or translated into English from) outside cultures. I am not faulting this attraction, but I am suggesting that there is much to be gained by remaining open to narratives from other places and times. Being closed to human culture from earlier stretches of history is no different from xenophobia, racism, or other such hostilities, even if it harms no living victims.

While pondering the least common denominators of Western culture as it manifests itself today (at least in North America), I realized that fairy tales could give me an ideal and probably unique opportunity. Fairy tales are one of the few literary genres shared by people of all ages and social classes in all Western countries, from Europe to America and beyond. Virtually the only type of older narrative known to everyone, regardless of age or education, are versions of the fairy tales that were given vintage expression by Charles Perrault (1628–1703), Madame Marie Leprince de Beaumont (1711–80), Hans Christian Andersen (1805–75), and others; and even these tales are most often received not directly with acknowledgment of their authors' names but, rather, as adapted in children's picture books or animated films, without acknowledgment of their ultimate sources. A small subset of the Grimms' fairy tales is known nearly everywhere. Sometimes the tales are familiar from one of the original collections; the first volume of the first edition was published in 1812, but the selection and contents of the collection evolved through the seventh, final edition, published in 1857 (confusingly, the final, 1856, edition of the Grimms' own volume of commentary on their collected fairy tales is the third, not the seventh). Sometimes the tales have won favor separately as retold in individual illustrated children's stories, other times in feature-length Walt Disney animations or other cartoon versions, advertisements, and other minor media (among which may be included scholarship). Because of the ways in which their stories and their collective name have permeated mass culture, the fairy tales of the Brothers Grimm (and not very many in the populace at large are on a footing to know them by their first names, Jacob and Wilhelm) would loom large even if no one read another book.

Being incorrigibly optimistic (if only when it comes to stories), I have faith that people will be inquisitive about ancient and medieval literatures if those literatures can be shown to relate somehow to their present. At the risk of sounding irreparably old-fashioned, I would maintain that past literature contains beauty and wisdom, both of which we can ill afford to jettison. Much older literature has survived a selection process that guarantees it has exercised a strength and depth of meaning over a variety of readers across a long time and wide space. That statement is a long-winded way of saying that much past literature is tried and true, which is why (from the Romantic era down to the present day) fairy tales have so often been viewed—without much examination of the reasons why—as the symbolic expression of a profound wisdom.[5]

Our culture, even our mass culture, could benefit from informed looks at past literature, even so far back as the Middle Ages and beyond. The heroes of comic books, video games, and best-selling children's literature hold the same enormous appeal among popular audiences as do the writings of Joseph Campbell (1904–87), because people have an insatiable desire for stories that hold the promise of deep meaning—of revelation, therapy, life lessons, escape, and entertainment.[6] In addition to building our entertainment and edification upon comic-book heroes and making feature-length films of narrativeless video games or old television serials, why not venture further afield and, in the process, find narratives that have been market tested across hundreds of years and thousands of miles? In the case of the medieval folktales and fairy tales, we have the chance to confront a triple challenge and receive a triple pleasure. Not only are the medieval texts fascinating in their own right, but they enable—and even require—both the exploration of folk literature in the Middle Ages and the study of its later appropriation and conversion, particularly in the Romantic era.

MEDIEVAL VERSIONS OF THE GRIMMS' FAIRY TALES

It took me by surprise to find how thoroughly interwoven some of the Grimms' fairy tales, published in the early nineteenth century, are with tales that were told in truly olden times.[7] In seeking out the nexuses between these so-called classic fairy tales and Medieval Latin literature, I was stunned to encounter tales in which the Brothers Grimm drew directly on narratives they deciphered in Medieval Latin manuscripts. One of these instances induced me to compare *Kinder- und Hausmärchen* 144, "The Donkey" (the German edition of the Grimms' fairy tales is hereafter abbreviated *KHM*), with the Latin *The Donkey Tale* (*Asinarius*) and to compare *KHM* 146, "The Turnip," with the Latin *The Turnip Tale* (*Rapularius*). Both expe-

riences afforded me considerable insights into the working methods of the Grimms and into their presuppositions about the nature of the fairy tale. The two acts of comparison also made me speculate about whether or not information about earlier tellers of fairy tales might not be embedded in the very basics of characters and actions in the surviving tales.

Inspired by such stories, I was encouraged to broaden my purview to embrace medieval texts that stood in different, more oblique relationships to classic fairy tales and well-known folktales. The project quickened my interest even more as I came to examine the Latin texts not just as sources for later expressions of the same tales but also as texts influenced by or even inspired by oral tales that have perished but that can be recovered by reading or, rather, listening between the lines of the text. That process of listening induced me to seek out every scrap I could piece together about the groups that were particularly associated with storytelling in the Middle Ages. This search required taking an approach that bordered on social anthropology, which would ideally lead to a three-step process: first, to study each version in context; second, to know the social position of the teller; and finally, to understand the social circumstances in which the telling of the tale became relevant. The groups that emerged most strongly were travelers, such as Chaucer in his guise of pilgrim in the *Canterbury Tales;* professional entertainers of a humbler sort, since the line between jongleurs, jugglers, and jokers was ever a fine one (as their shared etymology suggests); the old, especially old women, who have often been singled out as the bearers and transmitters of oral traditions; peasants; preachers; and, last but not least, courtiers. Eventually each of these groups would deserve a monograph of its own, devoted exclusively to evaluating what can be discovered about its storytelling activities in the Middle Ages.[8]

As the disparate nature of the aforementioned groups reminds us, it is important to remember that tale-telling took place at all levels of society in the Middle Ages. Tales could originate in one group and migrate very easily into another—either upward or downward, if we wish to conceive of the social order as a vertical hierarchy. Where the tales happened eventually to be recorded does not necessarily indicate anything about where they originated. A tale written in Latin could have taken shape mainly among oral storytellers in the countryside, as the Romantics wanted to believe; contrariwise, a story preserved solely in a chapbook in the early modern period could have begun its life centuries before as elegant courtly entertainment. The Middle Ages was the site of much back-and-forth exchange between the oral and the written, and the rate of exchange between these two media and more only accelerated with the advent of printing. Furthermore, the narrative production, both oral and written, of the Middle Ages enjoyed a

healthy afterlife. In particular, the corpus of "classic" fairy tales owes much to medieval storytelling, since the former absorbed the latter both directly (in the conversion of tales preserved in manuscripts into collections in books) and indirectly (in transmission in and out of texts through many hundreds of years).[9] In dealing with a phenomenon as multifarious and complex as the fairy tale, it is unwise to press too hard for a single origin. Just as many different mouths and hands were involved in the creation of the Bible, so, too, the prophets of the fairy tale—both those who were true to the speech implied by the etymology of the term *prophet* ("one who speaks beforehand") and those who accord better with the image of the quill-bearing Gospel writers—were numberless.

For similar reasons, even with the crutch of earlier scholarship (especially from the first half of the twentieth century), the amount of material is too extensive and the need for work on it too urgent to allow me to adumbrate a history of medieval fairy tales, even just of fairy tales written in Latin. Nonetheless, I hope in this book to use interpretation of a carefully chosen sampling of surviving tales as a means to sketch the complex connections that existed in the Middle Ages between oral folktales and written versions of them, the profundity and variety of uses to which the writers applied the stories, and the diversity of relations that can be documented between the medieval texts and the expressions of the same tales in the "classic" fairy tale collections of the nineteenth century. As the last sentence implies, this book explores a few stories that survive, on the one hand, in versions associated with such greats of the nineteenth-century fairy tale as the Brothers Grimm, Hans Christian Andersen, and Carlo Collodi (pseudonym of Carlo Lorenzini, 1826–90) and, on the other, in Medieval Latin.

Last but not least, I discuss or refer in this book to a number of well-known fairy tales, but at the same time I deal with a subset of tales that have rarely been discussed outside specialist circles. Out of a desire to encourage the reexamination, rereading, and even retelling of these stories, I have calculated my choice of material so as to show the relevance of the Latin Middle Ages by emphasizing material that is still close to being current in mass culture. Accordingly, my final aim is to make accessible texts that were originally written in Latin—a language no longer as easily read as it was in the days of the Brothers Grimm—by offering them in English together with translations of the most relevant and engaging other literary texts (originally in Latin, Italian, German, and Sanskrit) that coincide with them.

Literary records, although they enable only partial views, allow us today our closest approach to the values and ideas of earlier civilizations. Over much longer than a millennium in Western Europe, most of the records were preserved in Latin, a language that is not known to many of the people

who may now have cause to be interested in the past. For those who aspire to keep alive or revivify tales by retelling them today, the appendix may constitute a "happy ending" to this book. Nothing would please me more than to have assisted in giving a new lease on life to the tales and versions of tales there presented. Thanks to the appendix, those who wish to read and compare different literary versions will be able easily to do so. The information there on tale types can be used to reach other literary versions, as well as more recent oral versions.

A special pleasure arises from coming to terms, even if only partially, with the special qualities of each version of a tale within its own context, of fathoming the reasons for the impressive constancy in the basic outlines of many stories across the centuries, and of seeking to account for the equally perplexing variations that can sometimes occur. Abstract arguments can be helpful in disproving the notion that there can be a pure fairy tale form in which no adjustments to immediate cultural needs or pressures have taken place and in which no ulterior motive has prompted the telling and influenced the shaping of the story. But the best support for such reasoning may be to let a variety of tales speak for themselves. They tell us that fairy tales can and should be approached at more than one different angle. They lend weight to the view of the Italian philosopher, historian, and critic Benedetto Croce (1866–1952) that we possess only specific tellings of the tales and that we must analyze these tellings rather than hypothesize about what does not exist. Croce argued strenuously against what he regarded as arbitrary theories about Indian origins, primitive origins, and so forth of fairy tales.[10] In analyzing individual tellings, we need to be as attentive as possible to the particularities of context, since whether a tale is recounted orally or written, it is told by a real person at a particular point in history.[11] These tellers have their own personalities, time periods, sexes, social classes, and multiple communities.[12]

The Romantics turned to the Middle Ages in part out of a wistfulness for a past that they imagined to be in some ways better and more natural than the world in which they lived. Much later, Max Weber (1864–1920) wrote on the disenchantment of the increasingly industrialized world in which he lived.[13] One way of combating the disenchantment or of reenchanting the world has been to resort to the Middle Ages and cultivate fantasy. In such medievalizing, the fairy tale represents one important, formative genre. The actual endless forests and amphibians of the natural world have both been disappearing from causes attributable to human activity. As the dreamlands vanish (at least temporarily) from the real earth, it is solace that at least the impenetrable woods, mutable frogs, and dragons of fairy tales remain; and as a consequence of Romantic (and romantic) preconceptions, the forests

and creatures of fairy tales still bear traces of real or imagined medieval culture. Wonder has migrated out of the general human experience into the more circumscribed realm of childhood, and it bears a medieval or pseudomedieval impress.

THE NATURES OF FAIRY TALES

When did fairy tales begin? Can we pinpoint when this genre or specific stories that belong to it came into being? What did the tales signify when they originated, what do they mean now, and what do the answers to these two questions have to do with each other? It can be proven easily that not all of our favorite fairy tales existed millennia ago or even a mere one thousand years ago, since some of them are known to have been invented by particular modern authors. Yet fairy tales are often considered to be age-old or timeless. Is there any validity in such epithets? Did any stories circulate already in the remote past in forms that have survived and that would make them recognizable to us today as fairy tales?

What qualifies a tale as a fairy tale? Is it features of orality that are etched into it from its folktale beginnings? Is it a particularly literary style? Or does the baseline for a fairy tale have to do not with written or oral style ("once upon a time") but, rather, with content (princesses, frogs, glass slippers)? The last question has a catch, since many fairy tales have no either/or about them. Rather, they are hybrids, often supposedly somehow oral, but at the same time literary. Nowhere is the paradox more salient than in the "classic" manifestations of fairy tale, such as the best-known tales of Charles Perrault, Jacob Ludwig Grimm (1785–1863) and Wilhelm Carl Grimm (1786–1859), and Hans Christian Andersen. But how much heed should we give to a paradox that appears within a paradox? After all, the very expression "classic fairy tale" is an oxymoron. The adjective *classic* implies a hallowed work that has been written and circulated in printed books. Beyond that, a tale is "classic" not just because it relates a story whose general outlines are known to everyone but also because it has a special written style. Yet the term *fairy tale* conjures up the orality of simple folk huddled around the hearth or children intent on bedtime stories. Indeed, these were the vignettes depicted in the frontispieces of the first English translation of Grimms' fairy tales.[14] Although the "classic" fairy tales were not produced by researchers who first lugged recording devices into the field and then transcribed the results, they are felt and judged to be somehow distinct from fully literary tales.

As for the meaning of fairy tales, a plural is in order. No flash of extraordinary insight is required to realize that one and the same tale can hold multiple meanings for us today—or indeed for audiences in any time, since the

odds are that sensitivities to literature, both oral and written, have declined, rather than risen, as the erstwhile dominance of word-based entertainments has yielded to the hegemony of mixed media, such as television, film, and video games. As adults, we may read and study fairy tales partly because they belong to our common childhood experiences, but what do we retain of those childhood memories when we reencounter the same tales later in life? How much does our understanding of them change when we are care-givers, parents, or grandparents reading or retelling them to other children, rather than receiving them as children ourselves? Is it likely that even children all respond identically to the tales, without manifesting differences that reflect the differences in their personalities and in the values and vicis-situdes to which they have been exposed prior to encountering the tales?

When reading or hearing texts that purport to record tales told in a dis-tant past, we may find that the number of possible interpretations only bur-geons. Beyond the meanings that we wrest from the tales to relate to our own life experiences, we may be tempted to quest after other types of sig-nificance. For instance, we could strive to determine the meanings that pre-vailed among the tellers from whom the writers of the texts claimed to have obtained their material, or we could endeavor to isolate the meanings that the writers themselves attempted to highlight in their written versions.

One of the main qualities of the narratives we call fairy tales is their inter-pretability or elasticity. They appear to be fraught with meaning, but (or and) they seem to lend themselves almost equally well to mythological, Indianist, anthropological, ritualist, Freudian, Jungian, Marxist, structuralist, decon-structionist, feminist, postmodernist, and assorted other readings. The pro-liferation of interpretations could point to a flaw in the tales themselves. It could indicate that they have no essential meaning—that they are a clay, eas-ily molded into infinite forms but having no abiding definition. Alterna-tively, the shortcoming (if a multiplicity of meanings is indeed a defect) could rest with the interpreters who have worked on the tales. At one extreme, it could betoken a dearth of rigor that has led to a misguided eclecticism—an openness to a mix-and-match policy that has failed to declare which methods should have primacy on which grounds. At the other, it could betoken an ex-cess of rigidity that has resulted in a hunt for a universalizing approach to the stories.[15] A one-size-fits-all approach ill befits the genre that has given us Cin-derella's slipper. Just as our own contexts, needs, and values change from one stage of life to another, so the meanings that may be uncovered in many fairy tales modulate—horizontally across time; vertically across social strata, ethnic groups, religions, and other such categories.

It could be that none or very few of the approaches to reading fairy tales is wrongheaded but that no single one of them can be applied with equal

effectiveness to all fairy tales and that no individual tale can be fully expli-
cated by any one type of reading. Such an observation hardly seems revolu-
tionary, and it may bode well for the future of the fairy tale. Despite the as-
cendancy of audiovisual media, reading has not dwindled into being an
altogether lost art. In fact, an educated person today may absorb, willy-nilly,
more words and numerals in a typical day than was true a quarter century,
a half century, or a century ago. But many of the letters and numbers are
disjointed and hurried. Graphic signs encircle us, sometimes literally, in
logos on our cars and airplanes, in stickers on our vegetables and fruit, on
the electronic screens that are ever more invasive a part of life, in labels and
trademarks on clothing, and even in tattoos etched into flesh. It is sympto-
matic that in *Sex and the City*—a recent cable-television series (HBO, 1998–
2004) that, by an informal tabulation, alluded more often to fairy tales than
to any other single literary genre—the actual title of the show appears in the
text of an advertisement posted on the side of a bus, while the only other
written words shown on a regular basis glow luridly on a laptop computer,
as words on a screen that is itself seen on a television and as words heard
read aloud in a voice-over.

What has shifted is not the availability of spoken and written words but,
rather, the combinations and guises in which they reach us. In addition, our
time—and maybe our ability—to digest words and other modes for infor-
mation and entertainment have altered. Another development has been the
rapidity with which words, art forms, events, and personages can first be-
come known to everyone and swiftly recede to the liminal status of trivia:
my references to *Sex and the City* may be meaninglessly dated to a reader
who comes of age less than a decade from now, to say nothing of how in-
comprehensible they may be already to nonparticipants of our own day
who ignore mass culture or at least its televised manifestations.

Both the durability and the interpretability of fairy tales are related to
their intrinsic features of being adaptable and portable. By virtue of being de-
ceptively short and simple, fairy tales are not "quick reads" along the order of
fast food. They may be more fairly (or fairily, as the case may be) compared
with rations for hiking and camping. They are light without being lite, sus-
taining without being jejune. If stories are the lifeblood of cultures and indi-
viduals, then fairy tales are a kind of plasma, the shedding of all that is dis-
pensable and the isolation of all that is most basic and sustaining in narrative.
They have survived not because they carry within them single messages that
were encoded in them by all the named and unnamed people who produced
them originally—the people who have been assigned the peculiarly technical
monosyllabic term *folk* (*Volk*)—but because they are capable of being con-
strued in many different (maybe infinitely different) ways. Recognition of

this circumstance does not bestow on us carte blanche to interpret the tales in any which way (even when Snow White, who is known as Blanche Neige in French, is at issue). Rather, it suggests that one must be sensitive to the particularities of the individual expressions that have been given to these plastic forms—the individual tellings and (much more often, when one is examining literature from the past) the individual writings.

ECLECTICISM, HISTORICISM, AND PHILOLOGY

There [is] no short road to the truth about the origin and history of the folktale as a whole. Only by special studies of each story, based always on as large a number of versions as possible, [can] one hope to approach a real knowledge of the facts.[16]

The humanities, like the various branches of philology that are constituents of them, have been criticized for having been rooted in social and political wrongs of the past and for having shared complicity in them. Yet recognizing and acknowledging culpability should not blind us to the multifarious benefits that the combination of the humanities and historicism can confer on their beneficiaries. The humanistic tradition carries within it a presumption that human nature changes, because it requires no great genius to perceive that homo sapiens is endlessly diverse and complicated. Human beings are differentiated by socioeconomic class, education, culture, position in family, temperament, and a myriad of other factors, of which genetics have been the most intriguing, the most dangerous, and the most commonly misrepresented. But whatever differences nature and nurture may engender, people remain enough the same from time to time and place to place that stories and works of scholarship composed by them can be understood (even if only imperfectly) across chronological, geographic, social, religious, and ethnic divides.

The humanities can be represented as sciences—or, at a minimum, fields of knowledge and insight—about human beings. But if they are sciences, they are meant to be sciences for human beings, sciences that can speak to individuals about other individuals and that can humanize. This is not to say that there are not such pitfalls as falsely assuming sameness where it does not exist or misconstruing superficial difference as underlying difference. Rather, it is simply (but not necessarily simplistically) to voice optimism that communication can take place and that experiences can be shared. Our ability to handle language is constrained, as are the bounds of language itself; but even so, both our linguistic ability and our language are marvels. The capacity of individuals to know each other is sadly restricted, yet people

can become impressively attuned to each other despite divides in their natures and backgrounds. The same paradoxes hold in our dealings with the past. Our understandings of the present are already fragmentary; how can we dream of grasping anything about the past two hundred years ago, let alone a millennium before we were born? If the goal is complete comprehension, then we should despair—as we should despair of seeking a total grasp of anything whatsoever. But if the aim is instead as full and firm a grasp as we can achieve, then some sanguineness is in order.

In scholarship as in home decor, personal attire, or taste in almost any category, eclecticism can evince a sense of self-confident identity and simultaneous openness to variety, or it can stand as evidence for a lack of taste, selectivity, coherence, and consistency. The former could be called strong eclecticism, the latter weak eclecticism. The movement toward theory in the literary study of the 1980s coincided with the fateful clash of two different political and economic systems. Although the starkness of the rift between those systems may have been exaggerated, it may have contributed nonetheless to an atmosphere in which people (and scholars are normal people, however hard that is sometimes for them to accept or for others to see) craved universally applicable approaches to the materials and questions that preoccupied them. At the same time, the hunger for a single key or approach that would provide responses to all questions about literature (and history and life) is nothing new. Within folkloristics, Friedrich von der Leyen (1873–1966) is a case in point.[17] At the start of his career, he followed in the footsteps of Theodor Benfey (1809–81), who had proclaimed the Indian origins of folktale in accordance with a migrationist or diffusionist theory. Later von der Leyen fell under the sway of Freudianism, which led him to abandon the idea that folktale originated in India and instead to argue that it had its start in dreams. Eventually he worked his way back to the Indo-European framework of the Brothers Grimm, with modifications.

In debased forms, some of the theories through which von der Leyen made his transit may have contributed to the tragic loss of humane values that occurred in the middle of the twentieth century. But that dehumanization was not healed by subsequent developments in the humanities, which saw attention concentrated ever more on concerns and approaches drawn from the social sciences.[18] Interdisciplinarity is invaluable, but if humanists fail to attend to the human content of history and culture, no one else will take up the task in their stead. They are uniquely positioned to explore knowledgeably, with the help of expertise that they have acquired themselves and that they have received from the toils of their predecessors, the inheritance of the past, which in the present case is the culture of the Latin Middle Ages.

The heady days in which one new approach or set of concerns gave way in quick succession to another may not have ended altogether, but we have entered a time in which more is to be accomplished by synthesizing both the knowledge that has accumulated and the best of a variety of approaches that have been developed. The combinatory approach that I am describing defies a single label, in that it eclectically draws together elements of historicism and philology. The colleagues in the humanities with whom I share buildings and corridors never had all or even most of their texts in common, but they once had much more of a text-based community—based in what used to be called "primary texts"—than is now the case. Now, outside relatively narrow bands of specialization, humanists are not held together any longer through shared basic texts. Rather, they arrive at commonality through approaches and theories. Consequently, it has seemed to me for years as if an eclectic combination of historicism and philology could hold much promise for renewal.

One aim of any renovation in the humanities would be to avoid the once much-touted resistance to theory or to approaches based on social context. But another would be to establish or reinstate a resistance to the totalizing claims for such approaches—to the fetishizing of theory. I stated long ago that for everyone resistant to theory, there is someone resistant to philology; I argued that philology is not without theory but is connected, for better or for worse, with a positivism of which theory has seldom been held culpable.[19] The intersection of philology and folkloristics is a particularly promising locus in which to make an attempt at renovation, since the former has its greatest strengths in specificity of analysis (specific texts), while the latter has achieved wonders in collection of materials and elaboration of general conceptual frameworks (many of them transferred from the social sciences, particularly anthropology). The former has been considered elitist; the latter professes to be connected with popular and even mass culture.

There is a special need for eclecticism in grappling with a culture as varied, complex, and foreign from our own as is European culture in the Latin Middle Ages. Humanism can help us to appreciate the extent to which the past has contributed to present culture, while an idealistic historicism can facilitate a recognition of the sophistication and beauty of the past. It is possible to engage with medieval texts both aesthetically and comparatistically. Once upon a time, when Marxism was still relatively young and certainly not the exclusive province of university-affiliated graybeards, Benedetto Croce took to task Vladimir IAkovlevich Propp (1895–1970), a Russian folklorist, both for his dependence on materialist Marxist concepts and for his treatment of fairy tales according to comparative criteria (in searching for

their origins or inspirations) rather than according to aesthetic or idealistic criteria.[20] Croce saw fairy tales as "poetic organisms" and, accordingly, as the products of individual authors.[21] To him, the same proscriptions apply to fairy tales as to other works of poetry: who can say where its material came from, and who can say which part of it is historic and which is not, when all has passed through emotion and fantasy and has become fantastic and poetic?

In my opinion, Croce was correct in taking issue with the very ambition of formulating and applying a single totalizing approach. Although it would be satisfying to be able, today or any day, to maintain confidently that all folktales can be puzzled out on the basis of a single theory, I believe that it is equally gratifying to accept that there are many right answers and that each tale needs to be studied individually before we can determine which approach or approaches will help us to make the most sense of it. Sometimes the same approach or set of approaches will prove to be equally illuminating across a whole group of tales, which could be a happy event. In any case, the two efforts, generalizing and particularizing, are both necessary components of understanding. It would be easy to fault Propp for having adhered to too rigid a framework for explicating fairy tales and their origins, just as he took issue with von der Leyen for having been too eclectic. The tales differ too much among themselves and are too heterogeneous to submit to a single theory: one approach will not reveal everything about all of them and will probably not reveal everything about any one of them. But their richness of significance does not mean that any approach will do as well as any other in illuminating a given tale. Eclecticism is required, but it must be a careful, strong eclecticism. My compromise is to posit that no single theory (Freudian, Jungian, Marxist, feminist, or the like) will account for all elements of all fairy tales; that sometimes fairy tales can be subsumed in groups for which one or more types of analysis are more illuminating than others; and that sometimes the tales, when juxtaposed to each other, will reveal evolutions that took place across history.

As regards historicism, Propp was heading on the right track when he stated that the interpretative key to the folktale lies not in the present but in the past.[22] I view versions of folktales and fairy tales from the past as constituting not *the* interpretative key but, rather, *an* interpretative key, just as I argue against the assumption that one underlying meaning is inherent in all versions of the story. The meanings that we can find in them may well assist in untangling the meanings of later versions.

The analysis of folktales and fairy tales could be pushed to two extremes. One extreme would be to pursue one meaning immanent in a tale type regardless of the times and circumstances in which different tellings or writings

of the tale were recorded. The other extreme would be to deny that any constant meaning or band of meanings resides in a given tale type. My own experiences suggest that the most realistic approach lies in the middle of these two extremes, and I contend that, wherever possible, it will be a boon to situate tales in a literary historical context and to compare versions from different periods. Such an approach can cast light on any unchanging meanings that may be implicit in the stories. Equally important, it can afford clues about changes that have occurred in the stories as the result of cultural evolution and about the tellers among whom the tales once circulated.

The medieval tales scrutinized in this book are traditional, even if large parts of the tradition have not survived. Each version is a retelling that is never fully independent of earlier tellings, even if those precedents lie beyond our reach. Studying these stories amplifies and refines our understanding of fairy tales that continue to play a large role in our culture. But there is no need for my hunches to dictate to anyone: this work contains ample material to read and appraise, in both interpretations and translations of primary materials.

Folktales in Medieval Latin Poetry

THE BROTHERS GRIMM AND FOLKTALE

Any folklorist who wishes to define the Märchen *in its historic develop-
ment and current existence will somehow relate it to the* Kinder- und
Hausmärchen *of the Grimm brothers. This collection is a landmark,
deeply rooted in sociocultural conditions of nineteenth-century Germany.
But, at the same time, it is also a source for the scrutiny of previous his-
tory of the European folktale, and a point of departure for the study of
its worldwide dissemination.*[1]

The nineteenth century did not invent the folktale, any more
than did either the seventeenth or the sixteenth century.
By the time of the Romantic tellings and writings, many of
these narratives were already hoary and had crossed back and
forth repeatedly for centuries between oral and written states.
One answer to the question of when they originated could be
that they have existed since time immemorial but were not written down
until long afterward. After all, they were not even named until compara-
tively recently. The nineteenth century was the first to designate the folktale
as such, to profess to collect it, to reproduce it in texts that at least claimed
to capture the essence of the oral forms, and to study it. In the identifica-
tion, collection, and study of folktales, the siblings Jacob and Wilhelm
Grimm occupy pride of place, particularly by virtue of the *KHM,* which
they published first in two volumes in 1812 and 1815 and which they (though
more Wilhelm than Jacob) then revised repeatedly until 1857, when the sev-

enth and final edition was published with their "finishing touches" [Ausgabe letzter Hand].

Not all the tales in the *KHM* are (to look at them technically) fairy tales, but the title of the *KHM* is conventionally rendered into English as *Fairy Tales,* which has meant that the boundaries between folktale and fairy tale—or at least the terminology for differentiating them—have been blurred from the beginning. To compound the misfortunes of the English title, it varies between *Grimm's Fairy Tales* and *Grimms' Fairy Tales.* The placement of the apostrophe is no mere grammarian's game, since in the first instance it would implicitly assign one author, Wilhelm Grimm, sole credit for the collection, while in the second it would acknowledge the role of his older brother, Jacob, as well. But there can be no question that the books were collaborative. Whereas much of their scholarly work was done separately (although in close proximity), the Brothers Grimm worked together in laying the foundations for the scientific study of folklore, not only in the *KHM,* but also in their two volumes entitled *German Legends* (in German, *Deutsche Sagen*), which were first published in 1816 and 1818.

Like it or not, the Grimms have been an ineluctable point of reference for folktale scholarship. I say "like it or not" since doubts have been expressed about whether the work done by Jacob and Wilhelm was of a caliber to warrant using their tales in folkloristics. Repeated efforts have been made to discredit the claims of authenticity that the brothers themselves and subsequent scholars advanced on behalf of the *KHM.* But for reaching a broader public, their tales remain not only the best but probably the only feasible alternative to the cartoon world of Walt Disney. The nature of their tales, for better or for worse, has determined what the term *fairy tale* means and what is thought to be a fairy tale, even if the nature of the tales has been transformed in major ways in the migration from Germany to England, the United States, and elsewhere in the Anglophone world.[2]

The nineteenth century was dominated by the *KHM,* both in itself and in reactions to it. Though the effect of the *KHM* on later authors was varied because of their great cultural differences, it was an inspiration and an anxiety of influence already among such authors as the German Friedrich Wolf (pseudonym of Johannes Laicus, 1817–55), the Dane Svend Grundtvig (1824–83), the Germans Ignaz Vinzenz Zingerle (1825–92) and Joseph Zingerle (1831–91), and the Norwegians Peter Christen Asbjørnsen (1812–85) and Jørgen Moe (1813–82), through the Russian Aleksander Nikolaevich Afanasiev (1826–71), to the American Joel Chandler Harris (1848–1908), author of the Uncle Remus stories about Brer Rabbit, Brer Fox, and other animal characters.[3] As these examples indicate, the *KHM* encouraged imitators and emulators throughout the world to record tales

they had heard directly, had been told about, or had perused in one form or another.

Even the observations on sources and analogues that the Brothers Grimm published in their notes to the *KHM* spawned an industry. The collecting of parallels and comparisons (which has yet to cease) culminated in an enormous assemblage of notes on the *KHM*—notes on notes, as it were—by Johannes Bolte (1858–1937) and Jiří Polívka (1858–1933). Bolte was a German literary historian who had been trained in classical philology, while Polívka was a Czech Slavist (his first name was Germanized as "Georg" when he published in that language).[4] Continuing the work begun by the Brothers Grimm, they appended variants (not solely European) for a total of 225 items (the final edition of the *KHM* from 1857 contains 210 tales, with two hundred *Märchen* and ten "children's legends"). The list of variants occupies three large volumes. Beyond that, they published another two volumes of material for the history of fairy tales of different peoples. Their five indispensable volumes (hereafter referenced by the abbreviation BP) came into print over two decades (1913–32), with the first appearing just after the first volume of the *KHM* had celebrated its centenary (1812–1912).

FOLKTALES IN MEDIEVAL LATIN POETRY

The virtual absence of unquestionable fairy tales in Classical and early Medieval literature is not in itself proof of anything.[5]

The very phrase *folktales in Medieval Latin poetry* has an oxymoronic ring to it, in that folktales would seem to be associated in both their creation and their reception with social classes, forms of delivery, and a particular style far removed from the monks or clerics and manuscripts that the phrase *Medieval Latin poetry* conjures up. The most inclusive definition of folktales would characterize them simply as traditional narratives. Yet the adjective *traditional* presumes that the tales are handed down from generation to generation, and such transmission is usually understood to have been oral.[6] Additionally, it is often assumed that the narration of folktales takes place in prose rather than verse, that such narratives are fictional,[7] and that they are told for the sake of entertainment.[8] Ultimately these definitions can be traced back to the times of the German thinker Johann Gottfried Herder (1744–1803) and the Brothers Grimm, when folktale and especially fairy tale came to be understood as based on poetic fantasy, often rooted in a magic world, and welcomed by all strata of society, even if (or because) they were regarded as being improbable and unrealistic.[9]

To bring home the paradox of seeking out such tales in the corpus of

Medieval Latin poetry, I offer two quotations. One is a comment from seventy-five years ago by a folklorist: "This idea, that *Märchen* [folktale] came from the Middle Ages, has no scientific defense."[10] The other is an observation on fairy tales that was made in passing almost a quarter of a century ago by a Marxist critic: "we lack an adequate history of the transitional period between the folk and fairy tales."[11] I respond to these quotations by proposing that if we wish to understand the history of folktales and particularly the complex relationships between oral and written folktales, we would be wise to scrutinize especially closely a phase that has almost universally been overlooked, namely, the two centuries or so that begin around the year 1000. This period sees an early and notable flourishing of verse narratives that can shed light on such later categories as folktales (*Volksmärchen*), "book tales" or "bookish folktales" (*Buchmärchen*), and "artistic" or "literary" fairy tales or folktales (*Kunstmärchen*).[12]

Even by itself, a declaration that folktales can become more intelligible by looking at literature from around 1000 to around 1200 would be controversial, but I here compound the risk by maintaining that during this couple hundred years, we need to pay particular attention to Latin verse texts.[13] I venture further by arguing that we do indeed possess from this period versions of folktales in general as well as of fairy tales in particular, even of the class—known technically as "wonder tales"—that is most often associated with fairy tales.[14] An underappreciated wealth of folkloric material entered European literature during the Middle Ages. This material—above all, the Latin poetry—relates fascinatingly to the so-called classic fairy tales, especially those represented by the Brothers Grimm. In my view, the brothers were on the right track when they incorporated their scaled-down versions of the Medieval Latin poems *The Donkey Tale* (*Asinarius*) and *The Turnip Tale* (*Rapularius*) into their collection: both stories have good call to be considered fairy tales.[15] Other tales that the Grimms included had medieval analogues of which they were not aware. They failed to fold still other medieval tales into their collection, but had they known of them, they could have adapted them to equally good purpose.

EARLY THEORIES ON THE ORIGINS OF FOLKTALES

The nineteenth century generated two main theories to account for the origins and meanings of folktales.[16] The conundrum of when the fairy tale in particular originated was posed for the first time by the Brothers Grimm. In their scattered statements on fairy tales, they propose that the stories contained in fairy tales began as myths but that they evolved or devolved into "true fairy tales" (if I may be allowed a deliberately paradoxical contradiction

in terms) only once the myths had shed their religious meaning.[17] Since the Germanic folktales that most interested the Brothers Grimm bore close resemblances to tales diffused among many other related cultures, they inferred that the tales had taken shape in prehistoric times and had spread with the Indo-European peoples. They stated outright already in 1815 the theory that the Germanic folktales incorporated in the *KHM* were versions of Indo-European myths.[18]

Not long after the middle of the nineteenth century, another German scholar, the Sanskritist Theodor Benfey (1809–81), advanced a different theory—the so-called Indianist theory—about the origins of folktales that were attested internationally.[19] He was less concerned with whether or not folktales had evolved out of another genre than with where folktales had taken shape and begun their spread. In his *Pantschatantra* (1859), Benfey maintained that whereas animal tales (both fable and tales about the trickster, Reynard the fox) had arisen in Europe, most other folktales had come into being in India; from the Indian subcontinent, the tales had been transported, after the advent of Islam, first to Persia and then to the whole of the Arabic-speaking Muslim world. According to Benfey's theory, the tales eventually wended their way to the Latin West, through border zones in Spain and Sicily as well as through the Crusaders. Benfey's view of India as the reservoir of stories from which European folktales derived exercised considerable influence throughout Western Europe in the second half of the nineteenth and early part of the twentieth centuries.[20]

Later a third theory gained prominence. Both the Brothers Grimm and Theodor Benfey implied that most folktales had been born among a single people in a single place at a single time and that they had spread outward and onward from that people, place, and time. In contrast to this model of monogenesis and diffusionism, Joseph Bédier (1864–1938) and others argued for polygenesis, the independent creation of similar tales in different places; polygenesis was a possible explanation that the Grimms had allowed for a minority of folktales. In Bédier's case, polygenesis fitted with his elevation of an individual and elite creator over the idea of collective creation on the part of the *Volk*. Both sides of the seeming dichotomy were Romantic, with, on the one hand, the Romantic image of the individual genius and, on the other, the Romantic notion of art (particularly poetry) as the creation of a whole people, which could mean, in effect, a given social class or ethnic group.[21] The so-called anthropological school associated with England and Scotland—led by, among others, Edward Burnett Tylor (1832–1917), Andrew Lang (1844–1912), and, most famously, James George Frazer (1854–1941)—also left open the possibility of polygenesis.[22] Its exponents maintained that all human cultures developed according to the same course

and that, as a result, they might forge similar or even identical tales in response to similar needs, pressures, and desires.

If the nineteenth century set folktale scholarship on its foundation by identifying and collecting, the twentieth century saw systematization in the establishment of typologies for both tale types and the smaller narrative components (designated "motifs" by folklorists) that give tales their particularity. In 1910 the Finnish folklorist Antti Aarne (1867–1925) cataloged the most important types of tales found in the Western folktale. As printed in 1961 in its second revision and translation by the American folklorist Stith Thompson (1885–1976), Aarne's essential index has often been designated as Aarne-Thompson, AaTh, or (as abbreviated hereafter) AT. Recently it has received further updating and modification by the German folklorist, Hans-Jörg Uther, who has expanded the book to three volumes, abbreviated hereafter as ATU. Ever since Aarne's index of tale types appeared, it has been conventional among folklorists to append a list of tale types to collections of tales; literary scholars, while often willing to express appreciation for the existence of the index and to use it as a resource for locating materials, seldom freight their texts with AT references.

Whether or not it would be hyperbole to label Stith Thompson the father of American folklore, he was without question the folklorist who generated the most basic resources for folktale studies. In addition to his two revisions of AT, he produced by himself the *Motif-Index of Folk-Literature,* which was published in six volumes in a revised edition in 1955–58. The *Motif-Index* (hereafter abbreviated as *MI*) was released in a digitized form in 1993, which is available online in some libraries.

The citizenships of Aarne and Thompson are worth identifying here mainly because their nationalities help to explain the names by which the method associated with their indexes have been designated. In English the method tends now to be called the historic(al)-geographic(al) method, in German geographic-historic; but it is also known as the Finnish or Finnish-American method, after Aarne, Thompson, and their various co-nationals who worked according to similar principles. The method, directed toward determining the origin and distribution of individual tales, was enunciated by Aarne in his guidelines for the comparative study of folktales (1913) and by his fellow Finn Kaarle Krohn (1863–1933) in a more general sense.[23]

Although the Finnish school remains alive and well, knowledge of its procedures (indeed, even of its very existence) has dwindled among literary scholars in general.[24] If the historic-geographic method continues still to be at all widely known among literary scholars, it is owing primarily to its rejection by Vladimir Propp, who, in his widely known and cited *Morphology of the Folktale* (published first in Russian in 1928, then in English initially in

1958 and later in a revised edition in 1968), questioned the correctness of procedures basic to the Finnish school—or rather, he challenged the correctness of the results derived from following these procedures.[25] For one thing, Propp judged as fruitless the attempt of the Finnish school to reach determinations about the regions in which tales originated, since the evidence has not been collected evenly: as an Eastern European, he was acutely aware that tales have been recorded in greater density in some regions of Europe than elsewhere.

Beyond voicing his skepticism about the validity of mapping tales, Propp put his finger on fundamental flaws in the basic principle of the Finnish school, namely, the principle of subdividing the content of the tales into tale types and motifs. In his view, all the types stand in a very close relationship to one another and must be studied in this way.[26] He held that the most profitable route to studying fairy tales is not through examining specific tales but, rather, through considering fairy tales as an ensemble in which all the topics are bound to each other and can be seen to have influenced each other.[27] Although Propp is convincing in his view that scholars cannot isolate research into a given motif and still hope to understand fully the story, it would be equally misguided in an opposite direction to dwell only on the context or the formal characteristics of the narrative without attending to the specifics of the individual tellings.

Finally, in writings of his that are less known than his *Morphology of the Folktale,* Propp displayed a perhaps surprising kinship with nineteenth-century theorists who had attempted to trace fairy tales back to prehistoric societies. Like some of his Romantic predecessors, he drew on his knowledge of early Christian resistance to these stories as one foundation for the argument that they embed within themselves testimony about Stone Age tribal culture, particularly its religious beliefs.[28] There seem to be strong incentives to look carefully at whatever older material can be located, whether it provides help in assessing the geographical distribution and provenance of the tales (as the Finnish method would trust) or corroborates Propp's convictions about the need for caution in drawing conclusions about such matters.

THE BROTHERS GRIMM AND THE MIDDLE AGES

Although neither Jacob nor Wilhelm Grimm spells out precisely when myths lost their religious meaning to become fairy tales, the two imply that the transition occurred in the long and varied era known collectively and probably too simplistically as the Middle Ages. From that implication has arisen an assumption that has been built into many representations of fairy tales since the time of the Brothers Grimm. For instance, a well-known il-

lustration accompanying the first tale in the 1912 edition of the *KHM,* "The Frog King, or Iron Heinrich" (ATU 440), depicts the princess with the frog as it sits on the rim of a well.[29] In the background looms a castle. The tale begins with the words "In olden times, when wishing still helped"; the illustration makes the assumption that these "olden times" were an idealized Middle Ages. Medieval or not, the princess and the frog have been appropriated to many ends in the modern media. Even in the most sexually charged remakings, the medieval setting has been retained: the castle is still in the backdrop.[30] The pattern of medievalizing fairy tales has not been confined to this tale. In the Walt Disney animated feature *Sleeping Beauty* (1959), the title character protests at one point to her father, "Dad, this is the thirteenth century!" Although her exclamation is obviously not drawn from the Grimms' text, the implication that Sleeping Beauty's enchanted castle is medieval would occur naturally to many readers. Less explicitly, the Disney *Beauty and the Beast* (1991) features a stained-glass window at the beginning, fostering the assumption that the events take place in a past when Gothic architecture was the norm—again, the Middle Ages.

How did "Once upon a time" come to equal "In the Middle Ages"? How did the landscape of fairy tales come to be peopled with the princesses, princes, and dwarfs or dotted with the castles that are associated with medieval times? Although Jacob and Wilhelm Grimm are best known among a general audience for their telling of fairy tales, most of their research was rooted in the languages, literatures, and religious beliefs of the Middle Ages. The attraction toward the Middle Ages that the Brothers Grimm manifested had multiple origins, many of which were shared to a degree by other leading figures in the German Romantic movement. Because of the pleasure they took in the Middle Ages and the extent to which they idealized that period, it is not unexpected to find the Grimms instilling a medieval atmosphere in their fairy tales. Like others in the Romantic era, the Brothers Grimm had numerous reasons to feel nostalgic about what they believed—or convinced themselves—that the Middle Ages had represented.

One major impulse was to probe the remains of medieval culture in search of the underpinnings of what were then felt to be present-day national characteristics and culture. Wherever Latin texts survived that could be used in this program, they were taken; but the motivation to resort to Latin materials was nowhere stronger than in Germany. German Romantics and their successors had particularly strong incentives to co-opt Medieval Latin materials as part of their national literary canon, since otherwise their medieval literature risked looking limited and (even worse) derivative from the French. The English had *Beowulf* and an important corpus of other early Old English poetry. The French had troubadour lyrics in Old Occitan

from the south in addition to chansons de geste and romances in Old French from the north. The Italians had much, but above all they had Dante. However rich Old High German and Middle High German may seem to our eyes, these bodies of literature seemed inadequate for the project of determining what the German national character had been in the Middle Ages before the decadence of modernity and for the goal of putting Germany's medieval cultural achievement on a footing comparable with the best anywhere else in Europe.

The turn to the Latin texts of the Middle Ages brought many felicitous consequences, since the Romantics struck a balance between appropriating the past to their own ends and advancing an understanding of the past on its own terms. The co-opting of Latin texts led to the founding of a broadly conceived series of volumes devoted to medieval German history, the Monumenta Germaniae Historica (Historical Monuments of Germany).[31] Indeed, the Brothers Grimm were involved directly in the foundation of the society that eventually developed this series. It is less known but equally relevant that the appropriation of Latin texts as belonging to German literature resulted in the establishment of professorships in Medieval Latin philology in the latter half of the nineteenth century. Although both Jacob and Wilhelm had died more than a decade before Ludwig Traube (1861–1907) was appointed in Munich to the first professorship of Medieval Latin philology in Germany (and in the world), the brothers were caught up in the effort to unearth Medieval Latin texts by German(ic) authors and to enshrine them within the canon of German literature.

Accordingly, they (though much more Jacob than Wilhelm) reached out and added the ninth- or tenth-century epic *Poem of Walter* (*Waltharius*) to the roster of Germanic epics, the twelfth-century epic *Ysengrimus* (usually ascribed to Nivard of Ghent) to the list of texts about Reynard the Fox, the twelfth-century Archpoet to the catalog of medieval lyric poets, and so forth.[32] Since the border between literature and folklore was very porous in the work of the Brothers Grimm, they were consistent in drawing on Latin sources in their folkloric work as well. Thus they tapped the *History of the Lombards* (*Historia Langobardorum*) by Paul the Deacon (ca. 720–99) for a whole series of legends that they intercalated in their *German Legends* (*Deutsche Sagen*).[33]

Maybe more startling is to discover that the Brothers Grimm adapted for inclusion in the *KHM* Medieval Latin poems that they had transcribed directly from manuscripts. The brothers hardly tried to cover their tracks; on the contrary, they identified their sources forthrightly in their annotations. Why, then, has a veil of mystery (or a cloak of ignorance) settled on Latin texts the brothers took as the bases of tales in the *KHM*, others they

edited later out of a recognition that they were folktales, and still others that came to light after their lifetimes?

Part of the reason for the mystery has been that examinations of these Latin texts have been scattered. The poem that is the focus of chapter 2 in the present study was first edited in 1849. Although it has been reedited repeatedly (almost incessantly in the past two decades), the editions have been prepared by philologists for philologists. The very short poem discussed in chapter 3 was not even edited as part of a complete edition until 1889, and it has not been reedited since that date. The extraordinary poem examined in chapter 4 has received its due from philologists but not from folklorists and has been treated in increasing isolation from other texts, whether in Latin or in vernaculars. The two poems dealt with in chapters 5 and 6 have been edited together twice, both times by Medieval Latinists, once flagged as *Märchen* (which means something on the order of "folktales" or "fairy tales") and once as "Latin comedies." Thus the texts are not by any stretch of the imagination unknown, but they have continued to fall between the chairs—in this case, between chairs of Medieval Latin philology and chairs of folkloristics.

Nowhere does the absence of these tales from the bigger picture of fairy tale studies show more glaringly than in their absence from the great anthologies. The fairy tale scholar Albert Wesselski (1871–1939) discussed them here and there in his books, but he omitted them from his short anthology of pre-Grimmian fairy tales in German translations and modernizations. Since, by his own admission, that anthology houses texts that fail to measure up to his criteria for being fairy tales, the reader is left to suspect that the length and difficulty of the Grimms' source texts may have deterred him from translating them. The Medieval Latinist Karl Langosch (1903–92) translated them, but as part of a volume in a series of his Medieval Latin texts and translations. The effect was to flag them as belonging to the canon of Medieval Latin literature rather than as fitting within the context of literary folklore.

Anthologizers in English have been admirably energetic in publishing varied collections of fairy tales. These collections fall into two main groups. One would be compendiums of "classic" fairy tales. The earliest such "classic" collection would be the one by the husband-and-wife team of Iona Opie (1923–) and Peter Opie (1918–82), which pays passing attention to the Middle Ages in its introductory remarks but which includes only materials from the seventeenth century and later. The newer "classics" are by Maria Tatar, who, in beautifully produced anthologies, picks up the tale of fairy tales no earlier than Zoan (Giovan) Francesco Straparola's (ca. 1480–1558), in one case, and Charles Perrault (1628–1703), in the other. Jack Zipes, who deserves gratitude

for his judiciousness and indefatigability in gathering, making available, and interpreting fairy tales, contributed *Beauties, Beasts, and Enchantment: Classic French Fairy Tales* (1991). It goes without saying that this corpus of French materials does not include works in Old French, let alone works in Medieval Latin that may have been composed in French-speaking territories. Zipes's *The Great Fairy Tale Tradition: From Straparola and Basile to the Brothers Grimm*, another very large and useful omnium-gatherum, is similar to the collections of "classics" in starting with Straparola.[34]

The other group of English anthologies looks at first glance to have been conceived on more inclusive principles. Yet Zipes's *Spells of Enchantment: The Wondrous Fairy Tales of Western Culture* contains only two premodern texts in translation, with one being the Cupid and Psyche episode in the *Metamorphoses* (more commonly known as *The Golden Ass*) by Apuleius (born ca. 125 CE) and the other being a tale in the *Deeds of the Romans* (*Gesta Romanorum*), an anonymous, late thirteenth-century collection of preaching exempla drawn from Roman history and legend.[35] An anthology entitled *Folk and Fairy Tales* goes even further in its exclusion of the ancient and medieval, since it offers nothing earlier than a selection from Giambattista Basile's (1575–1632) *The Tale of Tales, or Rather the Entertainment of Little Ones* (*Lo cunto de li cunti overo lo trattenemiento de peccerille* [1634–36], also known as *Pentamerone*).[36] In both anthologies, the real underlying principle is to incorporate texts that command canonical status in fairy tale studies, rather than to strive for inclusion of chronologically diverse materials.

My aim is not to pull a proverbial rabbit out of the equally proverbial hat by proving that all the works in the *KHM* had a single origin or indeed even that most of them can be proven to have originated in the culture that has been called the Latin Middle Ages. In my opinion the history of fairy tale scholarship is shot through with mistakes made on the basis of the fallacy that because the first extant version of a given tale is attested in a particular language at a particular time, therefore the tale itself was first composed or conceived in that language at that time. We need to be vigorous in separating the question of genesis from that of diffusion—and maybe in abandoning altogether the question of genesis. Instead of claiming that the tales arose in the Middle Ages, I hope to cast light on two different sets of phenomena: on the one hand, on the underappreciated and misunderstood wealth of folkloric material that entered the stream of European literature only during the medieval period; on the other hand, on the unacknowledged relationship between this medieval material and the modern literary fairy tale as it took shape in the *KHM* of the Brothers Grimm. My goal is not to imply that all or even most of the tales contained in the famous nineteenth-century collections derive directly from medieval narrative material.

Rather, I seek to demonstrate the complexity of the relationships that can be attested and to suggest that, through comparative analysis, we can determine that the tales should be interpreted not according to a single universalizing method of interpretation but, rather, according to a flexible, eclectic kit of methods.

Incidentally, I hope to demonstrate the undervalued contribution of popular and oral culture (which includes cultures from outside Europe) to medieval literature, as well as to tempt readers of the Grimm collection and admirers of the fairy tale in general to look back to documents as they seek to come to terms with the fairy tale. In the English-speaking world, the toils of the American philologist and ballad scholar Francis James Child (1825–96) have left a lingering awareness of the medieval past that may lie behind a number of the ballads, but as far as fairy tales are concerned, there is a paradox: the tales are often set in a medieval feudal past, with castles and kings; but medieval sources and analogues—perhaps especially in Latin—go unmentioned or undervalued. From the tenth through the thirteenth century, authors writing in Latin made ever more elaborate attempts to use folk narratives as the basis for reworkings that were well on the way to being what we would call fairy tales today. Coming to grips with these phenomena will involve looking both backward, to see what can be divined of the oral literature behind the medieval written evidence, and forward, to compare the medieval texts with what became of them in the "classic" nineteenth-century guise in which they have retained most of their afterlife today.

THE BROTHERS GRIMM AND
NATIONALIST PHILOLOGY

The Brothers Grimm were not only folklorists. Indeed, the field of folklore took shape as such only during their lifetimes. Symptomatically, the English word *folklore* was not coined until 1846, more than a quarter century after the publication of the *KHM*. To state the situation more bluntly, Jacob and Wilhelm Grimm were not so much folklorists as philologists and linguists, and their philology and linguistics played a pivotal role in their fairy tale scholarship. Jacob Grimm's German grammar was the first work of Germanic philology. He developed his linguistic principles on the basis of the Indo-Europeanist theory of his day, and he applied the same theory to the study of fairy tale. In his analysis of fairy tales, the problem of affinities among them is resolved in the same way as the problem of affinities among languages.[37]

The contributions and defects of the philologico-linguistic model that the Brothers Grimm formulated in their folklore and folktale research have

lingered to the present day. As far as shortcomings are concerned, their project was ethnocentric in ways that would today be considered (only partly anachronistically) nationalistic.[38] Yet it would be a gross oversimplification to condemn and consign to the dustbin the Brothers Grimm and the various philologies in which they participated.[39] For all the biases latent in the philologies of the nineteenth century (and beyond), they far outstripped any comparable efforts in other areas of the world either before or after. They furnished dictionaries, grammars, editions, and many worthwhile ideas for interpretations that deserve continued evaluation and application.

In folkloristics, the philology of the Brothers Grimm laid a large part of the foundation for the development of the discipline.[40] The so-called Finnish method owes much to philology. In fact, the AT/ATU system for the designation of tale types within groupings and the practice of assigning sigla to each ethnic group in the establishment of a stemma for the transmission of a tale could be seen as a fusion of biological taxonomy with philology—a close encounter between Charles Darwin (1809–82) and Karl Lachmann (1793–1851).[41] Yet at the same time, the two approaches, folkloristics and philology, have been suspended in constant tension with each other. It would be fair to say that folklore and philology have often tended in exactly opposite directions. Furthermore, it is no accident that the oldest and in many respects most evolved of the philologies—namely, classical philology—has been the most resistant to folkloristics, and vice versa.

For this mutual exclusion to continue would be nothing short of tragic, since we have come to a watershed where the application of close philological analysis to particular texts has never been more exciting (thanks to the availability of tools in the form of printed reference works and electronic databases) and where the past few decades of widespread interest in theory has put us in a position to attain new powers of synthesis. The strengths of philology often lie in the establishment and analysis of individual texts, while those of folkloristics reside in the collection of data and production of overarching theories. Each field needs the other.

The stasis between folkloristics and philology has had a substantial impact on Medieval Latin studies, which has often emphasized—even overemphasized—philological techniques as a way of combating its own inferiority complex vis-à-vis classical philology. As a consequence, it has all too frequently been left to the practitioners of other fields, such as Romance philology in the cases of Ernst Robert Curtius (1886–1956) and Erich Auerbach (1892–1957), to find and point out the relevance of Medieval Latin texts to other medieval and postmedieval literatures and, indeed, to the history of European culture in general. This pattern, in which generalization and broad synthesis have been relegated to outsiders, has not functioned

well when it comes to Medieval Latin materials that have qualities of folk literature. By virtue of being old texts, they have failed to attract the favorable attention of many folklorists; and although pointing out deficiencies in the knowledge of foreign languages can seem belligerent, the mere fact that these texts have been available only in Latin or only in Latin and German or Italian has crimped their accessibility to readers outside the talented but small siblinghood of Medieval Latinists. But a drop in the study of Latin among humanists and folklorists is only one of several causes for which Medieval Latin prose and poetry relevant to the history of fairy tales have languished as they have done.

PROOF OF WHEN FOLKTALES EXISTED, NOT OF WHEN THEY ORIGINATED

One of the most arresting qualities of fairy tales is their apparent timelessness. The collections that have purveyed the basic sense of fairy tales in the English-speaking world and of *Märchen* and the equivalent in the Germanic countries date from the nineteenth century. But it has been recognized—by the Brothers Grimm themselves—that the genre is older than that. How old are the tales?[42] They have the air of being now as they have been for centuries, even millennia. There would appear to be no reason not to assume that they have existed since Neolithic times. Christine Goldberg notes: "Tale telling is undoubtedly as old as humankind, and written examples of folktales begin early."[43] But have the tales always been the same? Has the timelessness been a feature of the stories from the very beginning, or is it a quality that the tales acquired in response to the tastes or needs of a particular period? Moreover, what are we to make of the seeming gulf between the stories as told, which are presumed to be not just hundreds but even thousands of years old, and the stories as written down and collected, which are generally assumed to be far more recent?

Let me hasten to declare my unwillingness to posit that the period from 1000 to 1200 witnessed the origins of the genres of folktale in general and fairy tale in particular as we know them. If to err is human, to seek obsessively after beginnings is equally a trait of the species. Presentations of research and study on many branches of learning have subsections devoted to etiology, which are dedicated to discovering elements of older stages in the evidence of more recent ones.[44] Paleontologists strive to locate, amid the rubble of millions of years ago, the skull that can be pronounced the earliest surviving cranium of the species *Homo sapiens;* astronomers and theoretical physicists endeavor to pinpoint the first rays of the universe; and those "rare birds" we call "philologists," "folklorists," and "literary historians" stalk after

the earliest extant embodiments of particular genres, tales, and motifs. When the quest for origins centers on human beings and their products, the impulse to establish lineage runs many risks, such as overemphasizing the male or female contribution to family resemblances or being based on racist presuppositions. Yet despite recurrent disavowals, despite having been caricatured as the worst of positivism and as a mindless accumulation of facts, the search for beginnings continues, and not all its results have been counterproductive. In fact, "source study" or "source investigation" (the English rendering of the German term *Quellenforschung*) has underpinned much scholarship in the humanities since the nineteenth century. Romanticism, which is ultimately to thank for the elevation of both folkloristics and Medieval Latin philology as autonomous fields, laid the groundwork for the eventual division of linguistic and literary study into national languages and literatures, which entailed the production of histories that had starting points: the hunt was on.[45]

Although the division of studies by language or nation—as in the subclasses within Romance philology and in Medieval Latin philology—makes sense and is essential in helping to foster and maintain expertise, research will inevitably transect fields and disciplines: no quarantine, whether self-inflicted or externally dictated, is possible, and I do not happen to believe it desirable. One drawback to the otherwise often productive symbiosis between the philologies of national languages and literatures, on the one hand, and that of Medieval Latin, on the other, has been an unavowed presumption of a dichotomy between Latin and the vernacular—often viewed simplistically as source and influence, respectively—when instead we have come to realize that such facile dichotomies must be resisted in favor of greater nuance and more gradations. Although distinctions must be drawn, there are also complicated interrelatednesses between such seeming oppositions as oral and written, literacy and illiteracy, moving texts and fixed ones, popular and learned, lay and clerical (or ecclesiastic), classical and nonclassical, and assorted other categories. The interplay is particularly intense in areas where back-and-forth exchange between the various extremes can be shown to have taken place for centuries or even millennia.

Our evidence for the oral, popular, and lay categories is slighter because the classes that controlled textuality had a bias toward the written, learned, and ecclesiastic. But that propensity by no means resulted in complete exclusion. The intensity of the exchanges meant that we can still recover much, and we must seek to do so if we wish to broaden our picture of literature. Within Medieval Latin studies itself, there has been a tendency to envisage medieval culture as exclusively or at least predominantly literate, academic, and eccle-

siastic and to underappreciate other aspects. Yet Medieval Latin was not ar-
cane in its time, no more esoteric than biblical Hebrew or Koranic Arabic are
in Israel or the Islamic world today. Although the parallel is slightly more dis-
tant, Medieval Latin was even less exotic in many places of Latin Christen-
dom than such global languages as Chinese, Spanish, and English are now.

Folktales and fairy tales held a peculiar place in the literary cosmogony:
on the one hand, they were supposed to have existed since time immemo-
rial; on the other, they were held to have national and ethnic features that
could not have preexisted the emergence of the nation or ethnic group as an
independent entity. The development of notions about folktales and fairy
tales played a contributing role in the rise of national identity, nationhood,
and nationalism.[46] In the nineteenth and twentieth centuries, many of the
greatest folktale and fairy tale scholars conceived of the genre along na-
tional-linguistic lines and studied it in accordance with that conception.[47]
Against this backdrop of underlying national divisions, it is understandable
why the Latin material—prenational, supranational, nonnational, or inter-
national, as the case may be—has not been interrogated satisfactorily. For
this reason it is not unexpected to find that even a literary historian and
philologist as simultaneously austere and cosmopolitan as Gustav Gröber
(1844–1911) viewed Latin folktale materials from German-speaking areas as
reflecting national character and virtue—presumably the innocence of the
German peasantry.[48] To take another example, Ernst Tegethoff (1890–),
who put together an anthology with many different medieval folktales in
translation, opened his book with fifteen texts put into German from
Latin. From one perspective, he was giving the Latin prominent billing;
only the section of selections originally in medieval German has as high a
tally. But his preamble reveals his notion that the Latin was only a form,
whereas the content was bound to the national languages, despite their su-
perficial invisibility.

> For no one country or people created folktale [*Märchen*], but rather
> each nation made its little contribution to the folktale [*Märchen*]
> treasure of world literature, one to a greater extent, another to a
> lesser, each according to its ability.[49]

Fairy tales are often researched nation by nation or ethnic group by ethnic
group. Studying by language, when the language cuts across ethnic groups
(as is obviously the case with Latin), has advantages. To make a virtue of
a necessity, it enables us to focus on developments in tale-telling that were
caused by changes in the social class and backgrounds of authors and
audiences.

In examining the literary fairy tale, source seekers have scrabbled relentlessly to unearth the archetypal forms of individual tales and the authors who could be consecrated as the progenitors of the literary folktale and fairy tale.[50] This obsession with origins and original forms is evident in the very word *Urform* in German (slightly nativized in English with the interjection of a hyphen, as *ur-form*). The additional distinction of *urtext* has been introduced to indicate the originary written form.[51]

The Brothers Grimm were convinced that many of the fairy tales they had collected had taken shape in a pre-Christian period of indeterminate date. Their conviction was upheld by the subsequent discovery of the Egyptian version of "The Tale of Two Brothers."[52] This is not to say that they believed most fairy tales had come into being in ancient Egypt. Rather, they located the creation of fairy tales in an undefined primitive time (*Vorzeit*). In their view, these tales had been handed down unchangingly with other traditions for thousands of years. In both creation and transmission the tales were the products not of individuals but of collectivities—the *Volk*.[53] Since they had such faith in the ultimate antiquity of folktales and fairy tales, it stands to reason that they and their followers pored over the texts of earlier times in search of both data about particular narratives and general information about storytellers and storytelling circumstances.

To the Brothers Grimm, the heyday of the "folk" may well have been the Middle Ages—not the Middle Ages of clerics, but the Middle Ages of peasants. The Grimms glorified medieval peasants as noble savages who maintained and transmitted traditions, among which the traditional narratives (folktales) embodied all that was beautiful and true in their culture.[54] This glorification of the peasants found special support, although with different motivations, in the prejudices and predilections of Marxist scholarship, as evidenced most importantly in the oeuvre of Vladimir Propp.

The insistence on the "peasantness" of folktales cast a shadow over almost all information from before the nineteenth century and even over much of it from before the twentieth century. The scholar-collectors were disturbed in the first place that records of storytelling and stories from days of yore survived only in literate reworkings. Beyond that, they recoiled from texts for which specifics on the date and place of recording or on the narrators from whom they had been drawn were not forthcoming.[55]

However tempting it may be to look for testimony that may lead to the origins of this or that tale, we need to accept not only that such quests are often doomed to failure but also that when any search becomes compulsive, it distorts our perception of everything else. The intentness of scholars on studying the origins of tales has come at the expense of analyzing the mean-

ings that tales held in different contexts in different times. Many of the pre-occupations that have been fixtures of literary study since the Romantic era have a questionable basis where Latin poems are concerned, especially such pieces as the very short portion about Little Red Riding Hood in Egbert of Liège's *The Richly Laden Ship* (*Fecunda ratis*), the poem "The Wish-Goat" ("Wunschbock" [app. 2A]), assorted poems of the *Cambridge Songs* (*Carmina Cantabrigiensia* [app. 2C–G]), *One-Ox* (*Unibos* [ATU 1535; app. 3A]), the two versions of *The Turnip Tale* (*Rapularius* [ATU 1689A; app. 4A–B]), and *The Donkey Tale* (*Asinarius* [ATU 430; app. 5A]).[56]

Sleuthing after the origins of fairy tales has attracted the efforts of numerous literary detectives over the years. Although they for a time credited Charles Perrault with the invention of the literary fairy tale, many of them now see its roots in Italy in the sixteenth or seventeenth century, with the publication of Straparola's *Delightful Nights* (*Le piacevoli notti* [1550–53]) or Basile's *The Tale of Tales*.[57] Crediting Basile with inaugurating the literary tradition of fairy tales has hallowed precedent. Particular attention should be drawn to the role that the Brothers Grimm played in the recognition of Basile's originality and special artistic character; Jacob singled out these qualities in a critical appendix that was published in 1822, and his praise led to both German and English translations of Basile. Paradoxically, literary critics emphasize the rhetorical artfulness and literary sophistication of all three of these authors, which they contrast implicitly with the oral tradition of folktales.

The greatest recent exception to the tendency to exclude or, at best, to minimize the medieval has been the work of Jacques Berlioz and collaborators in his group.[58] Before them came Lutz Röhrich.[59] Even farther back was the broadest and most comprehensive effort of all, by Ernst Tegethoff in *Märchen, Schwänke und Fabeln* (1925). But, for better or for worse, outside the highly competent but restricted ambience of Kurt Ranke's *Enzyklopädie des Märchens* (1977–; hereafter referenced by the abbreviation *EM*), the results of such toiling in the vineyard have not had much impact yet on either Medieval Latin studies or folkloristics, particularly (but by no means solely) in North America. Yet if it is legitimate to consider as literary fairy tales the products of vernacular authors who write with artfulness and sophistication, why should it lie beyond the pale to regard any Latin texts as literary fairy tales? To have literary fairy tales (and, by extension, other literary forms of folktale) seems to presuppose an author with writing materials who has heard or read a story of a certain type and who can present it in a certain style. To exclude authors who wrote in Latin solely on the basis of their Latinity betrays narrow preconceptions about the essence of Latin and its possible relations to popular culture.

THE HOMELESSNESS OF MEDIEVAL LATIN AMONG
NATIONAL LITERATURES

The nature of Medieval Latin poems as "wonder tales" has been obscured partly because of a linguistico-cultural paradox that was created by Romanticism itself. A driving force of Romanticism was the recognition (or creation) of national character and culture. Herder in particular maintained that German national character and culture had taken a turn for the worse since the early modern period, and he urged his compatriots to pick up the strands and begin over again, not by returning to the Middle Ages (which, in the absence of time travel, remains an impossibility), but by rediscovering the best elements of that era.[60]

In formulating his own views of the Middle Ages as well as of the folk songs and folk poetry that he believed preserved medieval values, Herder was influenced deeply by Ossianism. This cultural movement was initiated by the alleged discovery and translation of two supposedly ancient poems associated with Ossian (Oisin), a legendary third-century Gaelic warrior and bard, son of Finn or Fingal. James Macpherson (1736–96), a Scottish schoolteacher, purported to have translated Ossian's epics into Modern English in *Fingal, an Ancient Epic Poem* (1762) and *Temora* (1763); Macpherson's poems were partly faithful to oral traditions, but in their main substance they deserve to be regarded as forgeries.[61] *Fingal* was put into German in 1768–69 and French in 1777. Even after the fraud was unmasked and investigators proved that the epic poems were forgeries, Macpherson's poems remained influential.

Partly inspired by the work of Macpherson, Herder called on his fellow Germans to gather the folklore of their regions. He offered them an example by publishing his "folk songs."[62] Among the followers he elicited, the Brothers Grimm figure prominently. The brothers have been labeled "nationalistic folklorists" for having "sought in the stirring events of their nations' pasts a unifying national character, [having] found this character expressed best in folklore, and [having] found in this folklore cause for pride in the past and courage to face the future."[63]

Even more than a century before the concept of the Latin Middle Ages had been articulated, becoming familiar with the Middle Ages required appreciating its Latin elements. Yet the ultimate goal was not to understand those elements in all their own cultural contexts but, rather, to situate them primarily at the origins of what would later become a national history and culture. In most cases, placing elements in such a national context entailed consideration of the national language. To this day, fairy tales are most often scrutinized in groupings demarcated by national linguistic

boundaries: even the structuralist Vladimir Propp recognized this tendency and aimed to abide by it when exploring the Russian folktale.[64] This retrojection onto the Middle Ages of future political boundaries, which in many instances are supposed to separate nations, languages, and cultures simultaneously, has had unhealthy effects on the adequate treatment of Medieval Latin materials.

The Latin of the Middle Ages can be characterized in many ways—as a prestige language, scriptural language, language of the church, imperial language, and so forth—but it cannot be called a national language.[65] On the contrary, its success rested on its supranationality and supratemporality. To state the matter less grandiloquently, Latin was seen to have the virtues of remaining stable across space and time. Whereas the Romance and Germanic languages shaded from dialect to dialect and language to language from one place to another, Latin was, despite regional variations in pronunciation and practice, enough the same in all locales to be understood by its practitioners. It was believed to maintain a similar stability across time.

If Latin texts contained materials that emanated from the predecessors of the future European nations, they contained them despite the Latin language. The Brothers Grimm incorporated stories from Latin manuscripts into their *KHM,* but in the process, they laid the groundwork for a tacit assumption among later scholars that the Latin versions of those stories could not be legitimately considered fairy tales or folktales, because no *Volk* had spoken Latin or told stories in Latin since the fall of ancient Rome. If we approach Medieval Latin texts in the hope of encountering the immediate outpourings of the people, we will be grievously disappointed. What we find is at once less and more.

In folktale scholarship, Latin materials have occupied a strange no-man's-land—maybe a monk's land. For literary scholars, they are too early, not vernacular, and not collected. For folklorists, they are too literary: if literature is in general to be distrusted, Latin is particularly untrustworthy, since it is the most literary and learned of possible written media. Today fairy tales are associated with children, folktales with common folk. Latin would seem far removed from both. But does that mean that authors who wrote in Latin had to have been utterly divorced from folk literature and practices? Were there no Latin authors who were raised in folk settings before obtaining the education to become qualified Latinists? Were there no Latin authors who would have stayed in touch with the spoken languages and entertainments delivered in them? Historians in particular have shown increasing interest in reconstructing the traditional societies in which most people lived during the Middle Ages. The Latin tales should be sources for them—even if sources to be used with care.

LATIN AS THE LANGUAGE OF OFFICIAL CULTURES

Europe has had writing systems for thousands of years. Clay, stone, metal, bark, papyrus, wax, parchment, and paper are only a selection of the materials that have been used for this purpose. Tales have been told during those millennia, but most tellings have not been set down in writing or otherwise recorded. Part of the reason is the sheerly practical one that it has been happily impossible to capture in writing all the words people have spoken. Probably colleagues of mine who grumble that too much is published are right, and yet countless more volumes would exist if every lecture or learned comment had been transcribed. Imagine what would happen if each bedtime story or dirty joke told became the equivalent of a book or article!

Of course, the dearth of premodern folktales results not only from a lack of means for writing but even more from a decision not to record them on the part of the men or, less often, women who controlled those channels. Some types of literature were written down again and again, while others failed to receive the official approval, either explicit or tacit, that was an indispensable prerequisite for being memorialized in literature. Many of the classics were associated with the literate elite. The "golden bough" was wrested from none other than Virgil to become the catchword of literary anthropology in the nineteenth century. Nonetheless, the classics—and maybe particularly the Latin classics—have often been regarded as being antithetical to the folkloric.[66] Homer is the exception that proves the rule: the presence of folktales and even fairy tales in the Homeric epics has long been acknowledged, but perhaps for that very reason, the *Iliad* and *Odyssey* are regarded as being not classical but archaic.[67] Medieval Latinists have tended to be trained to follow and perhaps even to heighten the biases of classical philology against folk material. An emphasis has been laid on studying sources and influences, particularly of texts on texts. The concordances and databases have been aimed at identifying and evaluating the words and phrases that authors use, and even the monumental study of larger building blocks (designated *topoi*) could be censured for having paid insufficient attention to influences of folk literature.[68]

In both the classical and medieval periods, Latin was a language of very special status in a variety of official or hegemonic cultures.[69] In many centuries, only exceptionally did authors breach the resistance—which ranged from prejudices all the way to sanctions—against the recording of stories told by subaltern or subordinate classes. The foremost example among ancient Latin authors may be Apuleius (born ca. 123 CE), whose *Metamorphoses,* known more popularly as *The Golden Ass,* constitutes an elegant filigree of narratives, many of them with strong connections to folk narratives

that both antedated and postdated Apuleius himself.[70] But classical literature features many other folktales and fairy tales, which have become visible to readers who have approached ancient texts with open eyes and minds.[71] There was no absolute dividing line but, rather, a constantly evolving set of reciprocal relationships between the official culture of the intellectual elites and the popular culture of the more numerous others—the folk. Likewise, the literate culture of manuscripts was tied to the oral culture of folklore by bonds of both giving and receiving.[72]

One obstacle to viewing Medieval Latin poems as authentic fairy tales is that the linkage between fairy tales and orality has been very powerful, whereas Medieval Latin has been thought to be un-oral or, at best, to embody "academic orality."[73] The "classic" authors of fairy tales in the vernaculars, such as the Brothers Grimm and Hans Christian Andersen, have been faulted for their unreliability in preserving folktales, but even they betrayed a nostalgia for the orality of the stories they had heard (or pretended to have heard). Accordingly, they insinuated into their tales traits that were meant to recall the act of storytelling, whether those traits took the form of a general stylistic simplicity (as in the case of the *KHM*) or of pointed remarks that create the pretense that the narrator is an actual live storyteller and the reader his audience (in the case of Andersen).[74] Long before the nineteenth-century collectors set to work, such authors as Straparola and Basile followed in the footsteps of John of Alta Silva (Hauteseille), Giovanni Boccaccio (1313–75), and countless other authors of the twelfth century and later by taking advantage of the opportunities that the frame tale offered for textualizing orality.[75] But earlier medieval authors made few gestures in either of these directions. Are their texts therefore disqualified from potentially being fairy tales?

If folklorists have been leery of the taint that literary texts have imposed on the oral traditional material they have transmitted, nowhere has the likelihood of such staining seemed greater than in the case of Medieval Latin, which is associated inherently with literacy, official culture, and resistance to popular culture. The suspicions of folklorists may be well founded for certain times and places. For instance, it has been argued that in the Merovingian period (mid-fifth through mid-eighth centuries), the literate rejected folklore because they feared the dangers that it posed to church culture.[76] Similarly, it has been established that in the prolonged medieval period in Kievan Rus', there were ecclesiastic bans against folktales. Although implying that folktales existed in sufficient abundance as to attract the attention of the religious authorities, these denunciations indicate that the church held storytelling to be sinful, partly because the tales were entertaining rather than edifying and partly because they perpetuated pre- or para-Christian beliefs to

which the leadership was opposed.[77] But does what is known about these two contexts, Merovingian France and ancient Rus', hold true for the rest of the varied phenomena that pass under the name of the Middle Ages—and particularly under the name of the Latin Middle Ages? The close interrelationship between knowing Latin, being literate, and belonging to the clergy has become almost proverbial.[78] It is apparently all very well to use the phrase *homo narrans* to designate the seemingly universal human characteristic of storytelling, but the application of Latin bears witness to, more than anything, the utility of this dead language in taxonomy.[79] The idea of anyone having actually told stories in Latin, at least in the many centuries in which it ceased being a fully living mother tongue, is evidently preposterous.

Furthermore, folklorists have been perplexed at where to fit Latin in the geographical framework that has been practically hardwired into folkloristics since the first half of the twentieth century. This last bafflement has generated truly comic distortions in scholarship. For example, the eighth volume of the extraordinarily useful *EM* contains entries on the *Märchen* of Laotians, Lapps, and Lithuanians but no entry on Latin. Greek is there, but because of the ethnic group, not the language. Perhaps there will be an entry on the *Märchen* of the Romans—but there has been none on *Mittellatein,* and the one on *Mittelalter* is on what would be called "medievalism" in English: the reception of the Middle Ages in modern culture. The same absence can be noted in the two volumes of *Medieval Folklore: An Encyclopedia of Myths, Legends, Tales, Beliefs, and Customs,* which offer entries on English tradition (two of them), French tradition, Hispanic tradition, Hungarian tradition, and so forth but none on Latin.[80] Similarly, *The Oxford Companion to Fairy Tales,* an indispensable resource, incorporates Latin evidence only when it fits with modern ethnic or national conceptions. The most bizarrely anachronistic instance in the companion is in the entry on Italy, whose author states, "The oldest example of an 'Italian' literary fairy tale is the story of 'Cupid and Psyche,' embedded in Apuleius' second-century Latin novel *The Golden Ass.*"[81] Since Apuleius was by birth a North African, the only real ground for labeling his story "Italian" would seem to be that it was written in Latin, by which token we could categorize as "Italian" many narratives by authors who never set foot on Italian soil or spoke a word of Italian.

Such exclusion has ironies to it, one of which is that users of the Medieval Latin language—insofar as generalization about such a long-lived and varied phenomenon is advisable—often strove knowingly for a style of expression that would be comprehensible enduringly across time and space (qualities that eluded most vernacular languages until the twelfth century or later). For this reason, the style of the Medieval Latin narratives examined

here comes closer to the distilled version of fairy tale found in canonical modern collections. It does not contain many of the characteristics that would tie it to a narrow locale, since doing so would have defeated the very purpose of using Latin.

Folkloristics has developed refined techniques for identifying regional and local characteristics in folklore. This preoccupation with the region was given canonical form by Carl Wilhelm von Sydow (1878–1952), who could be called—and would probably have liked to be called—a founder of twentieth-century folkloristics. Influenced by Darwinism, von Sydow transferred from botany to the study of folktales the word *oikotype* (or *oicotype*), a term denoting a plant variety that adapted by natural selection to a specific environment.[82] According to his model, folktales seek to propagate themselves but are stopped by barriers, foremost among which are linguistic barriers, political barriers (which slow the movement of tradition-bearers), and social barriers (by which von Sydow had in mind particularly the animosities between one village and another).[83] It does not take long to realize that this model's emphasis on regionalism, although invaluable in many contexts, is not appropriate to all expressions of traditional popular culture;[84] but old models die hard.

When it comes to folklore studies on the Middle Ages, Latin authors are smuggled (almost as illegal aliens would be across borders) within the entries that pertain to modern European nations. Latin is treated as a mere vehicle—one that at best interferes with the folktales it conveys—rather than as a distinct international or supranational culture that may have had advantages for the collection, preservation, and propagation of fairy tales and related forms. The inconsistency and ambivalence to which all of these examples attest are present already in the wonderful assemblage of information in volume 4 of BP, where most of the divisions are nation by nation but where there are categories in which a nonnational language prevails, as is the case in the volume's occasional discussion of Hebrew texts and in the section titled "Fairy Tale in the Middle Ages" (the latter of which opens with coverage of Medieval Latin). Despite the ever more sophisticated recognition that folklore is an international phenomenon[85] and that folklorists must be comparatists, such divisions have continued to be made. Normally folktale is examined within the confines of national linguistic groups.[86] My study of Medieval Latin represents a departure from this tendency.

The conventional handling of Medieval Latin presupposes that an answer has already been reached on the major question of whether Latin texts from the Middle Ages are useful primarily as sources for information but, where the preservation of folk literature is at stake, are without the same worth as texts written in languages closer to "the people." Although it is

true that, in general, Latin literature, whether classical, medieval, or later, tends to be intensively textual and literarily allusive, not all Latin texts attain (or even strive to attain) the same lofty level of style. Furthermore, there is no reason why a Latin verse narrative should be any further from an oral telling of a folk narrative than would be many vernacular verse forms. For example, it is possible that folktales are strewn throughout the romances of Chrétien de Troyes (ca. 1135–ca. 1183) but that they have been modified even more—in the transition from their putative oral forms into Old French octosyllabic rhyming couplets—than have been the folktales that underlie the Latin elegiac couplets of *The Donkey Tale* and *The Turnip Tale.* The same point would hold for Old French fabliaux, which are closely related to so-called Medieval Latin comedies (*comedie*). In both cases the authors of some texts may have derived the basic content of their stories from oral sources. Even so, that indebtedness in essential content would not predetermine anything about the texts' intended or actual audiences, including the social classes of those audiences.

Regardless of whether the language being examined is Latin or a vernacular, written examples of what could be termed "composition in performance" are rarely forthcoming from the Middle Ages, with the partial exception of sermons and lectures recorded in *reportationes* (transcriptions of sermons or lectures).[87] The stenography was just too difficult. Under normal circumstances it would have been excessively cumbersome, expensive, and disruptive to carry wax tablets or strips of parchment to jot down even summaries of stories as they were told or sung. Before audio recording, folktales were never transcribed verbatim. But during the years from around 1000 to around 1200, an openness to folk literature developed among clerics, writing first in Latin and later in the vernaculars—an openness that may have been unprecedented in scope. These clerics could not engage in a straightforward mechanical rendering of the oral into the written (a process designated in German as *Verschriftung,* "putting into writing"), partly because such a transfer was not technologically feasible but even more because it was not aesthetically desired or even comprehensible. Instead, the clerics aimed at a literarization (*Verschriftlichung,* "putting into literary form") of the narratives they recounted in Latin, a conscious transfer from the medium of the oral text into the very different medium of the literary text.[88]

It has been recognized in a multitude of ways that the Middle Ages witnessed intricate interactions between the oral and the written. Yet to the founders of oral narrative research, the dichotomy between the two was absolute.[89] Folklorists tended to reject written records as hopelessly contaminated. Their assertions are hard to accept, now that the theory of oral traditional composition has been tested in many different medieval literatures

and now that questions of diglossia, orality, and literacy have been plumbed to a depth that was unimaginable even fifty years ago.[90] Rigid distinctions between uneducated and educated, or *litteratus* and *illiteratus,* are now seen not to hold in most of the Middle Ages, and attempts to privilege the oral over the written or vice versa and to determine a priority between the two are regarded as misguided. Texts, for all their complexities and flaws, are understood to have value as evidence (often our sole evidence), and recognition has come that we must bring to bear all the skills that we can muster in reaching inferences about the meanings of texts in their own right and in their relation to both other texts and oral versions that preceded them.

It can be diabolically difficult to pinpoint which medieval texts were genuinely oral traditional, even when the texts in question have been transmitted in vernacular languages. The challenges only mount when the work is in Latin, but the compensation lies in the exciting variations that can be seen in techniques for the literate rendering of orality. It bears remembering that the medium (which could vary as to prose and verse, genre, and even language) in which authors chose to convey stories was not necessarily the one in which they received them. Ten years ago, a mantra of librarians who favored microfilming or microfiching books suffering from acidification was "The medium of preservation is not necessarily the medium of access."[91] This self-evident principle holds true for much supposed "folk" literature in the Western tradition as well as for "art" literature. Latin texts, even ones composed in verse, may have been inspired by oral tellings, which could have been in Latin or in vernaculars. The authors may have attempted to hold true to those tellings in both content and (to the degree that it is conceivable) style. In other words, the medium in which a story survives is not necessarily the medium in which it was transmitted. We may have only a written version of what had been primarily an oral story, or we may have a written version that gives evidence of repeated crossovers between the oral and the written.

Latin is rightly associated with what has been called "official culture." As counterintuitive as the thought may be, an "official language," such as Latin, may have sometimes more easily accommodated adventurous, risqué, or threatening material than could a "popular" vernacular language. Those who had been or were being Latin-educated acquired a formation not solely in a language but also in values and morals. Because the Latin-learned could be relied on to have a common culture that predisposed them to particular types of Christianity as well as to particular views of society, they could be allowed free access to material that might have seemed subversive if it had been readily available to people whose faith in religion or the social structure had been less trustworthy.

This circumstance may help to explain the presence in Latin of two tales that appear first in the famous mid-eleventh-century verse anthology known as the *Cambridge Songs*. In "The Snow-Child" (ATU 1362; app. 2C; labeled "Modus Liebinc" in another manuscript in which it survives), the female lead becomes pregnant from fraternizing (and more) with lowly entertainers while her husband is out of town on an extended business trip.[92] To justify her condition to her spouse upon his return, she claims to have conceived after eating snow. The proximity of this motif to the doctrine of virgin birth is evident in a later English play in which the plausibility of Mary's explanation for her pregnancy is questioned by prosecutors, who actually mention the snow-child story.[93] To turn to the second example, in the first full poem that follows "The Snow-Child" in the *Cambridge Songs* (ATU 852; app. 2D; labeled "Modus florum" in another manuscript), a king offers his daughter in marriage to any man who can move him to call the man a liar.[94] A Swabian tells a tall tale about hunting that concludes with the claim that a charter he found while dismembering a hare proclaimed that he (rather than the king himself) was king. Although from one perspective just a comic tale, from another the account of the Swabian touches implicitly on the revolutionary notion that kings are, despite doctrines of divine anointment, mere men whose claim to power rests only on tatters of parchment. Of these two stories, at least that of the snow-child had a rich afterlife. Around 1200 it was used as a point of departure for school exercises in rhetoric. Such usage offers clear evidence that the old predisposition of pedagogues to incorporate into basic education tales related to preschool nursery tales had not faded.

What should we call the tales that were recast for use in the schools? Should they bear a different name from similar tales that were reworked not for the schools but for the courts? Such twelfth-century authors as Gervase of Tilbury (ca. 1140–1220), Walter Map (ca. 1140–1209), and Petrus Alfonsi (1062–ca. 1140) produced medleys that announce an attentiveness to courts, courtiers, and clerics in their very titles: *Recreation for an Emperor* (*Otia imperialia*), *Courtiers' Trifles* (*De nugis curialium*), and *Scholar's Guide* (*Disciplina clericalis*), respectively.[95] All three of these authors, who are representative of still others, not only permitted but even actively pursued—or, more appropriately, "courted"—inclusion of folklore and folktales (among which were tales from the East) in their writings. Their writings provide ample testimony for the narrative urbanity that courts attained, even before the courts were located in urban areas on a par with those of the early modern period.

The process began considerably earlier than the twelfth century. We find folktales already centrally established in the *Cambridge Songs* (and also in the Wolfenbüttel manuscript closely related to it) in the eleventh century,

very early and clear evidence of courtly song in the Middle Ages.[96] The density of testimony from the eleventh and twelfth centuries distinguishes this part of the Middle Ages as an era in which the fairy tale was brought into high literature on a regular basis—maybe even as the era in which it was first imported into high literature. It was no accident that folktales became established as literature so heavily in Latin. Because Latin was accessible only to those who had passed through an education that shaped not just language but values and intellect as well, it was safer to record popular literature in Latin than in the vernaculars. Just as to this day it has been more permissible to discuss bodily functions and body parts (especially those associated with sex, urination, and defecation) in words derived from Latin rather than in their more colloquial and more Germanic equivalents, so, too, risqué narrative material was at first more acceptable in Latin than in the spoken languages.[97]

When Medieval Latin writers drew on materials that circulated orally in at least part of their transmission, how do we designate the results? Folklorists have distinguished between folklore and "fakelore."[98] Such a distinction is indispensable: the forgeries of Ossian, for example, must not be conflated with the recordings that Milman Parry (1902–35) and Albert B. Lord (1912–91) made in the 1930s and later of Serbian oral traditional singers known as *guslari*. In medieval literature, it seems equally valuable to differentiate between folkloric culture and ecclesiastic culture;[99] but at the same time, it is essential not to present the two as being in binary opposition. The Medieval Latin tales should not be branded as "faketales" merely because of their Latinity. But what should they be called? Are they *Kunstmärchen* (literary folktales or fairy tales) *avant la lettre*?

UNCOLLECTED AS A SYNONYM FOR *NONEXISTENT*

Another cause for the sequestering of Medieval Latin materials is also ultimately the responsibility of the Romantics who laid the groundwork for what fairy tale has become. Before the nineteenth century, fairy tale had had authors (both anonymous and known), manuscripts and books, and publication series. Frame tales had also existed, in which part of the fiction was a teller or tellers whose own circumstances were described and who told the individual tales in their own voices. What the nineteenth century added to the picture as never before were collections that were substantially bigger than those in the past, that dispensed with frames, and that developed a distinctive and consistent form and style. Such collectors as the Brothers Grimm and Aleksander Nikolaevich Afanasiev far outstripped the nine tales that Charles Perrault had assembled in the printed form of *Histoires ou contes*

du temps passé (1697);[100] and Hans Christian Andersen, though not a collector of folk materials, produced a larger number of fairy tales, some of which were based on foktales, than had his French predecessors. Even though probably ever fewer readers peruse any of the nineteenth-century collections in toto, many may assume that the usual originary form of a fairy tale is as a short tale that is embedded in a large volume of other such tales, all of them written in essentially the same style, not varying greatly in length. This assumption is not fair to the nineteenth-century corpora, in which the tales are actually heterogeneous in narrative structure, motifs, beginnings, endings, and other features; and it does not apply to the Medieval Latin poems that are analyzed here, which have been transmitted to us in manuscripts notable for their heterogeneity.

THE RISE OF WONDER AND THE RISE OF THE WONDER TALE

Medieval Latin tales differ from the tales of Basile, Straparola, Perrault, Grimm, Andersen, and others partly in having not been brought together, at least until the rise of the frame tale and the assembling of exempla collections from the late twelfth century on. It is possible that both *The Turnip Tale* and *The Donkey Tale* were composed by the same author, but they are only two tales out of many. John of Alta Silva brings together a generous assortment of folk narratives in his *Dolopathos* (1184; also known as *On the King and the Seven Sages* [*De rege et septem sapientibus*]), including one that was absorbed eventually (and indirectly) into both the Grimms' *KHM* and Hans Christian Andersen's fairy tales.[101] But apart from the structural difference of surviving primarily as individual poems, the Medieval Latin tales contain *in germine* traits of later fairy tales—or, more than seedlings, saplings of what will become eventually the enchanted forest of "wonder tales."

Beyond the coincidence of specific narratives with tales that later become constituents of the "classic" fairy tale collections, it is possible to discern between the tenth and the twelfth centuries a growth of interest in wonder and in wonder tales. The first gradations in this growth are hesitant and closely tied to religious miracle. Accordingly, the line between the non-religious wonder of fairy tales and the religious miracle of saints' legends is hard to calibrate. Furthermore, the authors who chose to recount wonder tales were operating without a how-to manual. The only major literary precedent would have been the tale of Cupid and Psyche in Apuleius's *Metamorphoses* (known more commonly as *The Golden Ass*), but that entire work had only the most tenuous of textual transmissions (two manuscripts, the one copied from the other, both from Montecassino—a paucity quite

possibly owing partly to its nonclassical choice of narrative material). Accordingly, the Medieval Latin authors had to find their own way in figuring out how to bring into literature what we would call folktales, including wonder tales. This process required grappling with some broad, almost universal issues about the nature of wonder as well as about truth and lies, fact and fiction.

Experimentation in Medieval Latin with the materials of folk literature led to only moderately successful results. But the texts composed were copied and read enough to justify concluding that they helped to pave the way for the later vernacular appropriations of folk narrative, in such genres as the fabliau and the *Schwank,* the novella, and the *conte de fées.* Eventually Medieval Latin texts became one of the resources to which the Romantics were obliged—sometimes consciously and sometimes not—for their tales. This indebtedness holds particularly true of the Brothers Grimm.

THE BABEL OF TERMS MEANING "FAIRY TALE"

Even under the best of circumstances, defining literary genres can be a tiresome nuisance: genre classification is notoriously difficult. Nowhere does the possibility for frustration and confoundment loom larger than in the case of what passes in English under the rubric of fairy tale. It would be the meekest of understatements to say that the term *fairy tale* has occasioned much dispute. Probably the longest-lasting generic system that included folktale and fairy tale was that of André Jolles (1874–1947), which has been pervasively influential. Since his book *Simple Forms* (*Einfache Formen*) was published in 1930, it has been translated into French, Italian, Portuguese, Spanish, Croatian, and Japanese.[102] Folklorists, finding Jolles's system more useful for literary scholarship than folkloristics, have devised definitions and systems of their own. Although Wesselski collaborated with Jolles and admired his book, he devised definitions of his own.[103] Lutz Röhrich and Linda Dégh, too, have both developed their own definitions.[104]

Not all tellers and writers have been as preoccupied about defining and classifying the forms they have used in their tellings as have been folklorists and literary scholars. Indeed, part of the appeal that folktale held to the earliest writers of folktales may have been that they could have substantial freedom in experimenting because generic constraints, already fluid in oral folk milieus, allowed for even greater flexibility in written form, where the genre system had not yet been concretized. Our own expectations have been colored inevitably and almost insuperably by what has been called the "Grimm genre" (*Gattung Grimm*), which blurs the boundaries between the oral and the written as well as between the learned and the folk. In the resultant

haze, it is not remarkable that some students of the tales have become so distressed or frustrated as to give up on the effort to define fairy tale or to differentiate between folktale and fairy tale.[105]

The nomenclature has ramified so as to resemble the woods in many fairy tales: a dark and tangled place where heart-wrenching dangers and unwanted confrontations abound. The spectrum of terms across European languages itself tells the story, and right now it is hard to promise that the story will have a fairy-tale ending. It repays the effort to begin with the Romance languages, since the literary activities of Charles Perrault, Marie-Catherine d'Aulnoy (1650–1705), Jeanne-Marie Leprince de Beaumont (1711–80), and many others in the first and second phases of French fairy tale writing (1690–1705) caused the French term *conte de fées* to spread to a number of other languages—especially Romance languages (Italian *racconto di fate*, Castilian *cuento de hadas*, Galician and Portuguese *conto de fadas*)—and even to become the English loan translation *fairy tale*.[106]

The equivalent Danish term is *eventyr* (*æventyr/ äventyr),* the word—corresponding to English *adventure*—that is featured in the title of Hans Christian Andersen's fairy tales. It has come to sound a little quaint. Probably to avoid its archaic flavor and confusing associations, Swedish prefers (*folk*)*saga* or *folksaga* (pl. *sagor* or *folksagor*). In this word the element of talking comes to the fore, since *saga* belongs to the same family as German *sagen* and English *say*.

Even the Romance languages display no unanimity. Galician and Portuguese have the alternative term *história da carochinha* (with its roughly equivalent forms *conto da carochinha* and *estória da carochinha*). The standard collection in Italian uses in its title the word *fiaba*, ultimately a derivative of Latin *fabula*. The last-mentioned word, too, is based on speech. This general notion of talking is salient in English *tale* (which corresponds to the verb *to tell*) and Dutch *sprookje* (which can be matched with the verb *spreken*, "to speak"). Also in this cluster belongs the basic term in German, *Märchen*, used in the title of the foundational collection by the Brothers Grimm. *Märchen* is ultimately the diminutive of the Old High German noun *mâri*, "news, story," which itself derives from the Old High German verb *mâren*, "to announce, to say."[107]

As the connection with talk implies, these terms designated folktale in general before becoming marked as denoting one type of folktale above all others. The special feature of this type is most definitely not the presence of a particular character (the fairy) but, rather, the salience of a particular content (the marvelous and/or the magical). Hundreds of such tales have been indexed by folklorists as ATU 300–749. For this reason, scholars, especially folklorists, often avoid the terms *fairy tale, conte de fées,* and their relatives

and have preferred English *wonder tale* or *magic tale,* Italian *favola* or *fiaba di magia,* French *conte merveilleux,* German *Zaubermärchen,* or Danish *undersaga.* Whereas the term *wonder tale* usually designates an oral folktale, *fairy tale* is likelier to be used to describe a literary fantasy tale.

In turn many of those who work closely with folktales have found or created other terms to describe tales in which the marvelous is less prominent while other features are more so. For example, German employs *Schwankmärchen, Lügenmärchen,* and *Warnmärchen* to designate what may pass loosely as a fairy tale in English because such tales are to be found in *Märchen* collections. The Grimms' *KHM* contains not just the wonder tales that most children and adults regard as fairy tales but more than a half-dozen other subgenres of folktales, such as animal tales, etiological tales, saints' legends, moral tales, jokes and anecdotes, chain tales, and nonsense tales.

WONDER, LIES, LAUGHTER, AND NOVELTY

The texts that will be explored in this book afford a number of clues about the types of tales the authors believed they were presenting to their audiences. To gain insight into the authors' presuppositions about the genres in which they were writing, the best means available are the programmatic statements, at once informative and enigmatic, that they provide. Alongside such mini-manifestos may be put occasional remarks that, from within the poems, shed light on the perspectives of the characters or narrators on the nature of the events described.

What do these passages reveal? Although I will return to them later in greater detail, it is worth making a few observations about them now, since they offer guidance about how we should approach Medieval Latin materials of possible folk origin. In the dedication to his textbook *The Richly Laden Ship* (written 1022–24 CE), Egbert of Liège (born ca. 972) professes that he has drawn heavily on everyday speech of common folk for his materials and that he has tapped "new tales from among the common folk."[108] In the opening lines of what may be regarded as a prototype for one component in the tale of Little Red Riding Hood, Egbert indicates that at least in this particular instance the commoners he has in mind are country folk. He adds further that what he will relate is not a marvel but a true story: "What I have to relate, countryfolk can tell along with me, / and it is not so much marvelous as it is quite true to believe."[109]

In the case of Letaldus of Micy (the earliest author under consideration in the present book), such concern with the marvelous and the miraculous could be taken as an attempt to configure a folktale as sacred legend. Indeed,

his one overt indication that his poem deals with wonder is when he refers to the man's salvation portrayed therein as almost a resurrection and certainly a miracle on the order of Jonah and the whale: "And then the shipwrecked man, like another Jonah, in the middle of the city apprises the astonished people about the miracles of life restored."[110] But elsewhere we seem to be grounded firmly in the same wondrous world with which the beloved fairy tales of the past three centuries have made us conversant. When in *The Donkey Tale* the long-barren queen has given birth to none other than a donkey, the narrator interjects an exclamation that announces to us—if we did not know already from the poem's "Once upon a time" opening—that we are amid the wonders typical of fairy tales: "O what a marvelous, yet rather miserable, thing!"[111] The animal state of the title character in this poem is a source of marvel to those who meet him, such as the doorkeeper of the palace to which the donkey eventually wanders.

> The man does not delay at all: he enters the privy chambers of the king, wishing to reveal the marvels he has seen. Then he said, "Look here, glorious king, I know something hitherto unknown [literally, "something new"] that I will convey to you if you want to know."[112]

Equal wonder that, once again, no longer has any connection (even strained or spurious) with religious miracle is occasioned by the sight of the mammoth turnip in *The Turnip Tale*. The poverty-stricken nobleman who has sown it and grown it is astounded at it, and both he and the king to whom he gives it esteem it for being marvelous.[113]

The opening strophes of the anonymous poem *One-Ox,* written within a few decades of Egbert's verse textbook, bristle with references to the mode of delivery, audience, source, genre, and tone of the poem.

> People's eyes are not satisfied 1
> by seeing the realities of the world;
> their ears are
> fond of novelties.
> At the table of a great prince 2
> is told the account of One-Ox;
> it is presented as a fabliau
> in playful words.
> Banquets come about through foods, 3
> but literary compositions through words;
> in a performance of characters
> let us sing of One-Ox.[114]

The poet asserts that he composed his tale for those who are not satisfied merely with what they see in everyday life but who wish to hear new things. Thus in the first strophe we would seem already to find ourselves once again in the world of the proto-novella, since the very word *novella* can be etymologized as "a new (story)." This world is, the poet would appear to assume, a courtly world, since he presents his poem as being fit for the dinnertime entertainment of a lord. To designate the genre of his poem, the poet relies on *rumor* and *fabula,* words that would be the most natural Latin choices to translate respectively the Old High German noun *mâri* and its diminutive (which eventually became *Märchen*). As he envisages his audience dining, he proffers them the product of his verbal craft, but he specifies that it is not merely a text but a song, and he suggests further that it has a dramatic or at least a mimetic component. It would be going too far to characterize *One-Ox* as a composition in performance, but we would not be reckless in thinking of it as a composition that was designed for performance, probably in response to the poet's own experience in having himself heard the tales within it.

In my opinion, *One-Ox* should not be classified as a wonder tale, since it is rather a concatenation of a trickster's pranks; and yet such novelistic folktales often bear strong resemblances to wonder tales.[115] Whatever generic label we attach to it, *One-Ox* is essential reading for tracking the development of wonder tales from the millennium on. One reason for its importance is that its trickster hero undergoes a rags-to-riches elevation loosely reminiscent of a wonder tale's protagonist. At the start, he lives in the most abject poverty, a butt of contempt even to the other destitute denizens of his country village: "A son of ridiculous sons, / he is a peasant from peasant stock. / Nature made him a man / but fortune a *Wunderkind*" (4.1–4). At the end, he is not only the only one left standing (alive), but in addition he has accumulated substantial other wealth. Yet the ascendancy of One-Ox, however unexpected it may be at the beginning of the story and however much a tribute to his cunning, does not mean that his story operates according to the principles of wonder tales. On the contrary, this peasant trickster receives his start from blind luck but achieves most of his successes by exploiting the credulity about wonder that his antagonists unfailingly display.

In this sense, the poem pillories those who deceive themselves by expecting to find in real life the marvels that can be accepted pleasurably as part and parcel of fiction, such as wonder tales. One-Ox is a showman who stages fairy tales before the eyes of his gullible foes. In their eagerness to believe in a goose that lays a golden egg (in their case, a donkey that defecates money), they cannot restrain themselves from even the foolhardiest action

or expenditure. The provost swallows the story One-Ox has told him about the inflated value of animal hides in the marketplace of a nearby town, and he persuades his two colleagues to join him in slaying their livestock and taking the hides to sell: "I will tell you a miracle, / reveal a wonder, / disclose a most profitable / tip that must be kept secret" (33). Once the priest has joined in the provost's delusion, the mayor is quick to follow suit under the influence of the tale (*fabula*) he has heard: he "belched forth wonderful schemes / that he devised as a result of the tale" (44.3–4). The misguided threesome slaughter their animals, slay their wives, waste their money, and finally kill themselves, all because they are too foolish in their greedy and lustful haste to differentiate between appearance and reality—between wonder tale and workaday reality. After murdering their wives in the mistaken conviction that they will be able to resurrect them by playing a magic horn, the three go to One-Ox's hovel to execute their nemesis; but instead they end up paying him for the privilege of picking through the dung of his mare. What brings about their volte-face in attitude? Their reactions to "the marvelous state of affairs" (123.4) cause them to be "astounded at the new deed" (124.4).

DEFINING FOLKTALE AND FAIRY TALE

In their endeavor to give literary expression to what they purveyed as folk literature, the Brothers Grimm left the future with many unsettling paradoxes. One is that whatever term is used to denote a fairy tale, our sense of this form is conditioned by exposure to literary versions of magic tales, many of which were composed to imitate the magic tales that were supposed to have been transmitted orally. Much of the debate over the origins of fairy tales has been clouded by mutually exclusive preconceptions of what is meant by the German term *Märchen,* which often determines the range of meaning for equivalent *termini technici* in other languages. Because the title of the archetypal collection (the *KHM*) is conventionally rendered as *Grimms' Fairy Tales* in English, it is tempting to read "fairy tale" wherever we encounter *Märchen* or (to take a different approach) to treat fairy tale and folktale as being covalent.[116] But the two categories are not commensurate. With regard to medieval materials, three problems stand out in chiaroscuro.

One problem lies in the unsatisfactoriness of labeling the Grimms' *Märchen* as either oral or literary. What we think of as fairy tale was, in one sense, the discovery or recovery of the Romantics and, in another sense, their creation for middle-class audiences. Although the Grimms collected stories from oral tradition and although they claimed to have solicited written accounts of stories from others "without adding anything and without

so-called touching up" [ohne Zusatz und sogenannte Verschönerung], they did not leave the stories untouched.[117] At the most rudimentary level, they standardized the dialect. Furthermore, they made the stories accord with their idées fixes about what constituted the usual oral fairy tale style. The brothers took pains to differentiate their tales from literary folktales (*Kunstmärchen*) and instead to align them with what they regarded (or longed to regard) as true oral folktales (*Volksmärchen*). Thus when *Märchen* derive from popular oral tradition, they are categorized as *Volksmärchen*.

The term *folktale* carries with it two associations, one of a class ("the folk," which is shorthand for "common folk" or "common people") and the other of a type of transmission (an orality that would be typical of "common folk" who were illiterate). Yet as has long been recognized, the Grimms' tales were not recorded directly from the lips of lower-class informants and were not transcribed from oral tellings. Most of the sources for the brothers were not peasants, but literate and bourgeois women. Furthermore, the tales the Grimms wrote have as one of their strengths a uniformity of style that was imposed by the brothers in imitation of what they found best in oral tale-telling: the texts are at once supremely literary and supremely oral. As this characterization implies, the *KHM* can be viewed as occupying a border zone between folklore and literature—a territory as harshly contested as that between orality and writing in the Western tradition.

One of the most unnerving intricacies that underlie all compounds with the first element *folk*—obviously, the term of greatest concern here is *folktale*—is that they assume the second element to have been a collaborative or group creation. In the late eighteenth and early nineteenth centuries, European intellectuals grew interested in the "folk."[118] Correspondingly, they created many neologisms, usually first in German, to designate the artistic production of the "folk." Analogous words were coined in other languages: the term *folklore* was invented in English in 1846.[119]

The Brothers Grimm enunciated their theory of communal creation, which is summed up in the phrase "Das Volk dichtet" (very roughly, "The folk compose"[120] or "create"). Their theory was intended to encapsulate a fundamental difference that Jacob and Wilhelm believed they detected between the learned or elite cultures and the popular cultures of their day. Whereas the former extolled the role of the individual (Romanticism promoted the ideal of the creative genius in rebellion against society), the latter seemed to put a premium not on the individual but on the tradition, a collectively shared past. The Grimmian dictum became and has remained, even if not always explicitly acknowledged, axiomatic in the historic-geographic method of folktale analysis.

Of course, it is dangerous to put too much credence in a phrase that generalizes so brashly. As close analyses by folklorists in the second half of the twentieth century demonstrated, individuals have played major roles in traditional culture. Singers and storytellers develop distinctive styles of their own and make changes in the content of the traditions they hand down.[121] Furthermore, traditions are not rigid or static. Storytellers keep in mind both their own concerns (asking themselves such questions as "Am I holding the interest of my listeners?" and "Will I have enough to eat tonight?") and the needs and values of their listeners. Last but not least, it has become ever harder to accept the tenet that stories create themselves and that individual tellers and writers did not institute changes.

The needs and values of audiences are far from uniform, since they may reflect differences in ethnic status, social class, gender, age, and the like among subclasses within society as a whole.[122] In other words, the "folk" that is presumed in such terms as *folktale* turns out to be far from monolithic. If the time in question antedates when nation-states existed, it is anachronistic to assume that a "folk" is identical with a "folk nation." Likewise, it is retrojecting modern-day social structures to equate the "folk" with the "underclass" at a time when no clear cultural divide ran between the underclass and the hegemonic class. Although for many Romantics the folk and the peasantry were one and the same, the equivalence does not hold for much of the Middle Ages, when popular culture of folktales, folk dances, folk songs, and so forth belonged to much more of society than merely those who worked the soil.[123]

One paradoxical consequence of the schizophrenic outlook among Romantic "folklorists" is that the anonymity of the purportedly original tales was essential, whereas the canonical form in which the tales reached audiences became ascribed by name to the Romantic and post-Romantic reworkers of them. The Brothers Grimm, Aleksander Nikolaevich Afanasiev, Joel Chandler Harris, and others sometimes identified the tellers from whom they collected their tales, but having specific names was less important than giving the assurance that the tales belonged to a collectivity greater than the individual tellers. In fact, it was an advantage, rather than a disadvantage, to present a story that distilled the features common to multiple tellings. In the end, anonymity guaranteed authenticity, because anonymity was equated with popularity (in the sense of popular or folk origins). The concomitant of this belief was that individual written versions of the tales were regarded as inherently suspect because they impose on the tales the values of the individual writers, who depart as individuals from tradition and as writers from the conventions of oral storytelling. The suspicion of individual texts was endemic among the many adherents of the

Finnish school. The most forceful contrarian view was expressed by Albert Wesselski, who maintained in his 1931 *Versuch einer Theorie des Märchens* (Essay on a Theory of the Folktale) that the "folk" never create; that instead only individual storytellers and especially storywriters create; and that all collections of folktales, from the *KHM* on down, descend directly or indirectly from a long tradition of books.

The "folk" who lurk hidden behind folktales turn out to be a motley crew that includes as tellers women (especially old women), who entertained children at bedtimes and each other while engaged in weaving and preparing foodstuffs; wayfarers; professional entertainers; merchants; preachers; and teachers. The barriers between one group in society and another were not absolutely rigid in the Middle Ages. A simple dichotomy between high and low fails to describe very adequately the situation in the Middle Ages, since, owing to their often shared lack of access to writing, nobles and peasants sometimes resembled each other.[124] Both groups tended to be analphabetic and to live in subhistory, except on the occasions (more isolated in the case of the peasants) when the clerics chose to introduce them into writing. The dividing line between official and unofficial cultures had not been set in concrete.[125] Only in the seventeenth century and later was the gap between the two solidified.

The characteristically Grimmian style of the *KHM* has encouraged regarding their tales as unique. Thus, as I already mentioned, the *KHM* are sometimes qualified as belonging to the "Grimm genre" (*Gattung Grimm*).[126] The chief drawback to putting the Grimms' tales in a class all their own is that it obscures the many similarities between their tales and those of other canonical collections that were assembled after them (and under their influence) in the nineteenth and twentieth centuries. Owing to the extraordinary impact of the *KHM,* most of these later collections were designed to conform (insofar as such conformity was possible within the different linguistic and literary traditions of the later authors) to many of the norms that the Brothers Grimm had fixed in their tales. This process of conformation has been aptly described as "Grimmification."[127]

Accordingly, the term *book tale* (a loan translation from the German *Buchmärchen*) has been introduced to denote the middle or transitional ground between the more fully oral and the more fully literary that is occupied by the Brothers Grimm and other authors of canonical collections, such as those produced by Hans Christian Andersen in Danish, Aleksander Nikolaevich Afanasiev in Russian, and Elek Benedek (1859–1929) in Hungarian or even, astoundingly recently, Italo Calvino's (1923–85) *Le Fiabe* (1956) in Italian. Closely related would be the compendiums of related forms that draw on folk narrative, such as the Uncle Remus stories about Brer Rabbit and

other stories by Joel Chandler Harris (1848–1908), which stand in the same relation to animal folktales as many of the others do to wonder tales. In a similar ambit were the early collections of ballads and folk songs. Some of these were produced before the Grimms, as in the case of Thomas Percy's (1720–1811) *Reliques of Ancient English Poetry* (1765) and Walter Scott's (1771–1832) *Minstrelsy of the Scottish Border* (2 vols., 1802; enlarged edition, 3 vols., 1803). Others appeared concurrently with the early activity of the Brothers Grimm, as in the instance of Vuk Stefanović Karadžić (1787–1864), who published collections of Serbian folk songs (1814 and 1823). A final group came into print under the brothers' influence, with the foremost example being Elias Lönnrot (1802–84), who collected (from 1828 to 1844) the Finnish epico-lyrical songs known as runes and knitted them together as the *Kalevala* (1835–49). All of these men were editors of folk literature, even if their conception of such editing fell far short of what present-day ethnographers, folklorists, and ethnomusicologists would stipulate.

A "book tale" does not seek primarily to be literary (as a *Kunstmärchen*, or "art" fairy tale, would do) but, rather, to satisfy folkloric or pedagogic aims. Despite their ambiguous position vis-à-vis both the oral and the literary, written texts of precisely these sorts have dominated the truly oral in determining what the general public thinks of as fairy tale and also as folktale. Although the folktale has appealed enormously to European audiences over the centuries, it has not yet had a grand success in written form without being adapted at least partially to written aesthetics. These adaptations have existed so long that they have contributed mightily to the picture of folktale that has impressed itself on a general readership. What holds true for the public does even more so for scholars: despite the justified complaints of folklorists, the "art" fairy tales have elicited most of the effort and publications from fairy tale researchers since the early twentieth century. Although there is often a presumption that the genre has a special depth relating to its oral origins and although traces linger of the golden age that extended into the early twentieth century, when researchers have paid much attention to folktales, the stress has been on texts that hover in a gray zone between the oral and the written.

It is very tempting to introduce the corresponding neologism *manuscript tale* (modeled after the German *Handschriftmärchen*) to denote the medieval poetic equivalents of individual Grimms' fairy tales. Systematic investigation of orality and oral literature over the past few decades has highlighted the richly, sometimes bewilderingly transitional nature of much literature in the Middle Ages. We should avoid the reductionism of positing an opposition between a written aesthetic and an oral aesthetic. Especially in the case of experimental literary workings of oral material, we have inter-

mediary—or transitional—forms between the two spectra. The Romantics may have been intuitively attuned to the place of Medieval Latin amid this confusion, since they were attracted to both the orality of the *Volk* and the magic of manuscripts. But they coined no name for the narratives they found in codices. To introduce the term *manuscript tale* and to describe the concomitant "medieval European *Märchen*" (alternatively, "transitional *Märchen*" or "clericized *Volksmärchen*") would together offer an escape from the impasse to which Albert Wesselski led the literary history of folktales in general and fairy tales in particular. Despite having written a 1925 book entitled *Märchen des Mittelalters* (Folktales of the Middle Ages), Wesselski, in a monograph on the theory of *Märchen,* elaborated the idea that true *Märchen* are what could be called fairy tales or wonder tales and that they are distinguished by a particular style of literary narration that probably originated no earlier than the sixteenth century.[128] Wesselski's characterization of fairy tale was bound to exclude medieval evidence: to define true fairy tale as having a modern European style is obviously to restrict true fairy tale to the modern European period. It would seem fairer to label such tales "modern European *Märchen*" and to leave open the possibility that medieval precursors may have existed.

Another sticking point with regard to medieval materials could be called a matter of critical mass. Some theorists have demarcated starkly between, on the one hand, fairy tales that appear singly and, on the other, those that form parts of collections that are devoted exclusively or at least mainly to similar materials, either frame tales (as in Boccaccio's *Decameron*) or less structured assemblings of tales (as with the Grimms or Andersen). Although André Jolles drew this distinction in *Simple Forms* (*Einfache Formen* [1930]) without disqualifying the single tales, recent literary historians have put great weight on the collection as an indicator that fairy tale had achieved a certain standing. By this standard, such Medieval Latin assemblages as John of Alta Silva's *Dolopathos*[129] and the anonymous *Deeds of the Romans* (*Gesta Romanorum*) are excluded, and the first extant collection devoted substantially to fairy tales is either Basile's or Straparola's. Prose Latin texts fail the test in both content (since they encompass many tales that do not pass muster as fairy tales) and style. Even more disturbingly, individual tales in Medieval Latin verse have been shut out of consideration because they have not been transmitted in collections. This exclusion creates anomalies, particularly when the medieval verse versions record, in whole or in part, tales that were incorporated—sometimes explicitly as adaptations of the medieval tales—into later classic fairy tale collections. If we want to seek out early forms of tales along the lines of the *KHM,* we can do no better than to accept the earlier tales—above all, *The Donkey Tale* and *The Turnip*

Tale—that the Grimms themselves regarded as exemplars of the genre in which they wrote.

A third problem pertains to content. How do we resolve which types of tales are folktales? Once again, the genre in which a tale is preserved may not be the genre in which it originated or the genre in which it arrived subsequently. Take, for example, the poem by Letaldus of Micy on a fisherman swallowed by a whale (app. 1B), which is studied in chapter 2. In a programmatic statement, Letaldus presents the story as what a folklorist could consider a legend (German *Sage*); but as a short narrative in hexameters, the poem has been termed an epyllion by more than one Latinist. The story it relates correlates in important elements to the narrative of Jonah in the Hebrew Bible (app. 1A), which would be a myth in terms of folk narrative categories; and in the elements that differ, it bears a resemblance to observations made about Jonah in Hebrew exegesis, which would also be mythic. To enlarge the circumference of parallels still further, the poem of Letaldus shows a remarkable likeness to the story of Pinocchio (and that's no lie). It also bears a resemblance to tall tales, going back to those in Lucian and culminating in the stories of Baron Munchausen (app. 1C).

Another tall tale that is remarkably closely connected with modern legends is "The Wish-Goat" ("Wunschbock" [ATU 1960A "The Great Ox"; app. 2A]), a poem that was written in a ninth-century hand on the final folio of an early ninth-century St. Gall codex.[130] In it, three peasant brothers decide that the one who can describe the largest goat in the world will inherit the goat of their deceased father. Although the poem has been described as being "a little masterpiece in mock-heroic style," characterizing it as a "lying tale" (the German *Lügenmärchen,* which is known in English more euphemistically as a "tall tale") strikes closer to the mark.[131] It belongs to the same world of lies and exaggerations as the legendary logger Paul Bunyan in North American folklore, whose constant companion is the gigantic Babe the Blue Ox. The enormity of this ox is conveyed by "the measurement between the tips of the horns by means of so and so many axe-handles."[132] Likewise, in the Latin poem, the gap between the goat's horns is so great that a bird would apparently need a full day to fly from one to the other.

Beyond the reality that one and the same narrative may be reconfigured—sometimes only very slightly—to serve in different genres, there is the fact that the designations to classify folktales vary in what is used to differentiate among tales. Sometimes the distinguishing feature is the main character. Thus there are trickster tales, with a subclass being animal trickster tales. In a certain sense, the opposite of a trickster tale is a numskull tale. Other types of folktales are designated according to their tone or effect on audiences. Such would be humorous tales, including the comic tales

known as *ridicula* in the *Cambridge Songs* (app. 2C–G), tall tales or lying tales, warning tales (this is where the version of Little Red Riding Hood by Egbert belongs), and, maybe most famously, wonder tales (here fit both *The Turnip Tale* and *The Donkey Tale* [app. 4A–B and 5A, respectively]).

The progression of tale types to which I adhered just now was geared closely to that deployed by Antti Aarne (1867–1925) and Stith Thompson (1885–1976) in their index, the conception and nature of which Stith Thompson presents very readably in his book entitled efficiently *The Folktale* (1946). But the taxonomy and numeration in AT was obviously not one that those who discussed tales in premodern times followed. The ancient and medieval terminology focused instead on the typical settings of tale-telling, whether locations, such as the fireside and nurseries, or occasions, such as winter evenings; the characteristic tellers, foremost among whom were old women or nurses, peasants, professional entertainers, and travelers;[133] the nature of the tales, such as lying or fantasy; and the intended or observed effects of the tales, such as laughter or wonderment.[134]

FABULA

The apparent lack of medieval terms that equates exactly to some modern categories does not militate against the existence of the equivalent genres in the Middle Ages. It is possible to avoid the tempting but unprovable assertion that there have been fairy tales since the dawn of time without slipping into the opposite pitfall of denying that fairy tales existed in a given period, such as the Middle Ages, just because the tales that survive do not measure up exactly to the contours of later fairy tales or because the authors or tellers did not have nomenclature that matches ours precisely. Our terms have developed in earnest only over the past two hundred years and have proliferated impressively, but without a consensus in usages and understandings. Even in the 1920s, which stand out as a heyday of research into medieval folk literature, scholars sometimes drew back consciously and intentionally from imposing nineteenth- and twentieth-century categories on earlier texts.[135] Not surprisingly, the absence of our terminology in the Middle Ages is not evidence that the genres that modern and postmodern words label did not exist then.

It turns out that Latin used the term *fabula* to cover a multitude of narrative forms. In one broad sense, *fabula* encompassed most fiction, embracing not just fable in a narrow Aesopian sense but both myth and folktale. Both the last-mentioned categories could have been intended by Cicero (Marcus Tullius Cicero, 106–43 BCE) in *On Invention,* where he gives an example of *fabula.*[136] Recognizing this breadth, writers of Latin often supplied

additional information to specify the precise meanings they had in mind when they employed *fabula* or kindred words. In discussing what would be called folktale today, they could give particulars about the tellers, such as age and gender or social class and occupation; about the place conventionally associated with the telling of the tales, such as the nursery or fireside; or about the content of the tales and their effect on audiences (for instance, in eliciting wonder or laughter). The writers of the tales that I have in mind were often reticent about the genres in which they themselves were writing, even to the point of not stating whether they were writing in prose, quantitative meter, or accentual rhythm. But they do offer guidance about the natures of the tales on which they drew.

The most promising lead we have today concerning medieval fairy tale genres is the word *fabula,* which was pressed into steady service to designate the sorts of tales under discussion here, folktale in general and wonder tales in particular. Thus it is the term to which Apuleius resorted in his *Metamorphoses* to describe the tale of Cupid and Psyche, which is often considered the first fairy tale in Western literature.[137] Apuleius qualifies the tale, as told by an old woman, as both a *fabula anilis* (which could be loosely translated as "old wives' tale") and a *fabella* (trifling tale).[138] To look at the other end of the chronological continuum, *fabula* is the term that Boccaccio reuses to describe Apuleius's tale of Cupid and Psyche; and he does so in a context that makes clear that he connects it with tale-telling in milieus with which he was himself familiar from his own day and from his own region.[139] To approach the question from a different perspective, *fabula* was the Latin word that was employed to translate the German *Märchen* and its family, and vice versa, in both Medieval Latin and Neo-Latin.[140] Such sources of information give enough pointers toward identifying *fabula* with folktale that folklorists seem fully justified in having devised the title *Fabula* for the international journal for narrative research (*Zeitschrift für Erzählforschung*) that has appeared annually since 1957.

THE NATURE OF MEDIEVAL LATIN LITERATURE

As sharply as the written and the oral differ, to etch too neat a line between them has unfortunate consequences on the appreciation of both literature and oral literature. But that has not been the only obstacle to a fair recognition and appreciation of Medieval Latin folk literature. Apart from the general circumstance that Medieval Latin philology and folkloristics can be as distant from each other as two fraternal-twin fields or disciplines can be (at their closest they are Jacob and Wilhelm, at their most far-removed Cain and Abel or Romulus and Remus), there has been an additional complicating fac-

tor in that the brand of folktale research that held sway for much of the twentieth century had no place for Medieval Latin in its theoretical construct. Even if the so-called historic-geographic method has fallen largely into desuetude, the consequences of its ascendancy remain very much alive.[141]

The Finnish school—or, to give due credit to Stith Thompson, the Finnish-American school—of historical-geographical analysis presumed a deep gulf between true folktales and literary adaptations.[142] The main opposition to this chasm came from Wesselski, who maintained that the efforts to discredit early written versions as contaminated and to exalt the value of much more recent oral versions were misbegotten.[143] From his vantage point, the movements of narrative material between written texts and oral literature have occurred so frequently in Western European literature as to render futile the retrospective imposition of barriers between them. Alternatively, Wesselski allowed that if one of the two "data sets" is to be discredited as contaminated or derivative, it should be the oral, since textual analysis demonstrates that oral versions are more often descended from written versions than vice versa.

As mentioned earlier, Wesselski employed stylistic grounds to exclude Medieval Latin prose texts (let alone Medieval Latin poems) from being fairy tales. The mutual distrust between philologists and folklorists has been most acute in judgments on style and aesthetics. The nineteenth-century mythological school theorized that a kind of entropy caused myth to degrade—like nuclear fuel on its way to being radioactive waste—into fairy tale. To be specific, it regarded folktales as the detritus of Indo-European myth: after myth loses its social function, it degenerates into folktale.[144]

According to the anthropological school, folktales are the remains not narrowly of myth but, rather, of primitive societies in the remote past. By applying a comparative method, members of the anthropological school sought to explain more "advanced" cultures on the basis of more "backward" or "primitive" ones. Edward B. Tylor (1832–1917) introduced the extremely important concept of survivals. A direct continuator of Tylor was Andrew Lang (1844–1912), best known to a general readership for his fairy tale anthologies that were named after different colors. He also translated the *Odyssey,* oversaw English editions of the tales of Charles Perrault and the Brothers Grimm, and supplied the prefaces to all of these works. Lang pointed out the connection of fairy tales with the "primitive" world, while Pierre Saintyves (pseudonym of Émile Dominique Nourry, 1870–1935) signaled the role that initiation rites played in fairy tales.[145] Such efforts persisted through Propp, who maintained in *The Historic Roots of Fairy Tales* (the Russian original has been translated into Italian, as *Le radici storiche dei racconti di fate,* but only in small part into English) that traditions, customs,

and beliefs of primitive peoples are reflected in popular narrative. Propp held that wonder tales contain embedded within them historical remains that document human history in its various phases.[146]

Early in the twentieth century, Hans Naumann (1886–1951) minted the expression *gesunkenes Kulturgut* (sunken cultural materials) to convey the notion that creations and styles in all sorts of realms (including science and art) come into being in the upper reaches of society and "sink" down over time to broader and lower social classes.[147] Ultimately Naumann is indebted in his conception of "sunken cultural materials" to the distinction Herder drew between popular and learned cultures ("Kultur des Volkes" and "Kultur der Gelehrten");[148] but whereas Herder gave the benefit of the doubt always to the former, Naumann came to overemphasize the latter. Although the movement of culture in the opposite direction has been termed *gehobenes Kulturgut* (elevated cultural materials), the concept of elevation has been invoked far less frequently than its more negative opposite.[149]

The thinking associated with *gesunkenes Kulturgut* has led many other scholars, apparently unconsciously, to speak of "residues" (as in "oral residues"). Both metaphors conjure up the poor hygiene of improperly cleaned teeth or porcelain surfaces. In regard specifically to folktales, the conception of "sinking" suggests that they were originally the creative products of the upper stratum and were later co-opted by the lower stratum and that the quality of the tales deteriorated as they seeped into oral popular culture. Wesselski presented the most insistent arguments that the fairy tale tradition of Western Europe was thoroughly dependent on the expression and transmission of the tales in written forms. It is probably a false dichotomy to argue that the influence has always or mainly run in only one direction, since the traffic has flowed heavily in both ways.

To return to the Middle Ages, it is worth entertaining for a moment the possibility that folktales recorded in Latin might be as authentic in content as those written in any other language. In fact, the greatest aesthetic and stylistic leap may occur in the passage from the oral to the written, regardless of whether the written is Latin or vernacular. At the same time, the transition from the oral to the written was not always clear-cut. Emblematic of the provocative unclarity are the opening two lines of *The Donkey Tale,* which was composed around 1200. In one group of manuscripts, the text reads: "Once upon a time there was a king of an unknown region and city, and, what is more, no page [*pagina*] tells the king's name" [Rex erat ignote quondam regionis et urbis, / Sed nomen regis pagina nulla docet].[150] In another set of manuscripts, one crucial word is different: "Once upon a time there was a king of an unknown region and city, and, what is more, no tale [*fabula*] tells the king's name" [Rex erat ignote quondam regionis et urbis, /

Sed nomen regis fabula nulla docet].¹⁵¹ Not quite as starkly wavering, but revealing nonetheless, is the discrepancy between the opening lines of the two versions of *The Turnip Tale:* "A trifling story [*frivola*] reports that there were two brothers" [Fama fuisse duos testatur frivola fratres] and "An extravagant story [*prodiga*] reports that there were two brothers" [Fama fuisse duos testatur prodiga fratres].¹⁵² Whatever misgivings one may have about the concept of "transitional texts" as originally posited in the theory of oral traditional composition (the so-called Parry-Lord theory), the ambivalence of the manuscript traditions in conveying the wording of the openings in *The Donkey Tale* and *The Turnip Tale* speaks volumes about the complex relationship between orality and textuality in the Middle Ages.

THE GENDERED NATURE OF MEDIEVAL LATIN FAIRY TALES

Although reading and writing were a preserve restricted nearly exclusively to men for much of the Middle Ages, there were extraordinary women who overcame the obstacles to write in Medieval Latin. To cite examples that could be the start of an assonating list, one can reel off such names as Hrotsvitha of Gandersheim, Hildegard of Bingen, and Heloise (whose name is almost automatically paired with that of Peter Abelard). Yet throughout the Middle Ages, women remained in a distinct minority in receiving the formal education that was a prerequisite to speaking, reading, and writing Latin. A minority within a minority, female Latin authors were all the more remarkable for being all the more exceptional than their male counterparts. This circumstance of cultural demographics has a bearing on the fate of the tales that are discussed in this book. Indeed, the effects that the predominantly male constitution of the schools, universities, and educated elites in the Middle Ages had on the composition and reception of texts help to explain why the fairy tale nature of various Medieval Latin texts has gone long unappreciated or at least underappreciated.

Schooling in Latin was designed not simply to impart a set of linguistic skills but also, more ambitiously, to shape pupils to become a certain type of adult—most of the time, a certain type of man. Recognition of this demographic reality would be important enough if we were concerned only with how Medieval Latin texts were read, since it would tip us off that the readers would have been even likelier than a general audience to be interested in topics that would appeal to educated men and that they would be imbued in the locker-room-like sex, misogyny, and violence that were—along with classical and late antique Latin poetry, parts of the Bible and liturgy, healthy doses of the verbal arts, and lesser portions of the mathematical arts—mainstays of

medieval education. But the masculinity of the schools in the Middle Ages had additional consequences for the composition of texts. Since one of the main audiences for a prospective author was the school, it would not be surprising to discover that many of the texts were designed with the perspectives, interests, and inclinations of young men in mind.

In 1928 the Russian formalist Alexksandr Isaakovich Nikiforov (1893–1941) published an essay (in Russian) entitled "Towards a Morphological Study of the Folktale."[153] In it he drew a distinction between "masculine" and "feminine" wonder tales or magic tales. Whereas the latter deal with key crises and transitions in the lives of young women, the former present the achievements of male heroes. Nikiforov's distinction received confirmation in the work of Holbek.[154]

A marvelous (to use the fitting adjective) example of a "feminine" wonder tale occurs in Apuleius's *The Golden Ass* or *Metamorphoses*, in the lengthy scene in books 4–6 in which an old woman relates the tale of Cupid and Psyche.[155] Her audience is a young woman who has been kidnapped from her own wedding feast and whom the old woman is seeking to console. The tale itself is a vintage female-oriented fairy tale: it tells about the travails of a young woman who is extraordinarily beautiful, has two jealous older sisters, wins the love of a handsome god, incurs the wrath of her stepmother (who happens to be a goddess), survives (with wondrous help) a set of obstacles, marries, and lives happily ever after. The only reason that this tale can be heard and included within the fiction of *The Golden Ass* is that the male narrator happens to overhear it while he is in the form of a donkey: the story was not meant for the ears of men.

Apuleius's account of Cupid and Psyche finds its correspondent in medieval literature in Chaucer's "The Wife of Bath's Tale," which is told in its literary form by a woman. But such tales are atypical of the Medieval Latin tradition, where (not shockingly, considering the distribution of Latinity across the sexes) no *Märchenfrau* composed narratives. Instead, we find that most of the surviving tales promote male protagonists and are meant to respond to the preoccupations of young men, rather than young women.

Most of the stories that underlie modern conceptions of fairy tale have women as their central figures: consider Cinderella (ATU 510–510A), Beauty of "Beauty and the Beast" (ATU 425C), Sleeping Beauty (ATU 410), and Snow White (ATU 709). Many of them incorporate a rags-to-riches trajectory (or a riches-to-rags-to-riches one). The male equivalents exist, with "The Frog King, or Iron Heinrich" (ATU 440) and "Jack and the Beanstalk" (ATU 328A) being foremost examples. But important differences must be noted between the "masculine" and "feminine" tales. In "The Frog King," the protagonist is not enriched or ennobled by marriage but,

rather, freed from the magic spell that had transformed him into an animal. In many versions of "Jack and the Beanstalk," the hero gains wealth and lives happily ever after, but the former does not result from his marrying—indeed, in many versions his final bliss is not marital but maternal. It may be, as one critic argues, that "[f]airy tales of social elevation through marriage revolve around familiar magic tale building blocks: money, magic, marriage, and a distinct and characteristic reversal of fortune."[156] But an important qualification needs to be added to "fairy tales" in this argument, by specifying "feminine" fairy tales. For marriage to be sometimes an incidental factor and other times an important, but not determining, one in the ascent to wealth and social standing may well be typical of "masculine" fairy tales, whereas it is most definitely a rarity in "feminine" ones.

How is marriage represented in the Medieval Latin recastings of fairy tales? Although "The Snow-Child" offers an example of an adulterous wife, it is the exception rather than the rule. Most male characters benefit from their happy marriages: the wife in Letaldus's poem seeks him out faithfully upon his return from his (mis)adventure at sea; the wife in *One-Ox* assists him in his wiles; the wives of the good brother and the king in both versions of *The Turnip Tale* advise their spouses wisely about crucial decisions. But the major crises and challenges that face the male characters are connected not with the women in their lives but with their own natures or fortunes, and their salvation comes from fortune and from their own cleverness and industry—and, in the case of *The Donkey Tale,* from a father figure. The evidence for the final syndrome could be increased notably by taking into consideration John of Alta Silva's *Dolopathos,* with its transposition into masculine terms of the life-threatening dilemma in the frame of *The Book of One Thousand and One Nights.*

Arguments could be—and have been—made that fairy tales have damaged girls by inculcating in them the belief that their advancement will come through being beautiful and putting up with beasts, through waiting for a Prince Charming, and through other forms of passivity or dependence on men. Women with life experience have long been attracted by the possibilities of communicating their wisdom in stories that deal with such central challenges in women's lives as fathers, husbands, and mothers-in-law. Denigrations and denunciations of old women for their gossip and their stories are rife from antiquity down to the present day and do not address completely empty stereotypes. But they offer a hostile perspective on the role of women as tradition-bearers, a role that shows on a loftier plane in the prominence of women in the boom of fairy tales written in seventeenth-century France and in the credit given to women as informants to the Brothers Grimm when they collected their tales.[157]

For understanding the Medieval Latin materials to be discussed in this book, it is important to realize that the strong feminine associations that fairy tales have developed over the past three centuries or so constitute an important part of the picture but are only that—part of the picture. Among the many possible stories that they could have put into Latin, it is natural that authors writing for all-male audiences gravitated toward materials other than the stories of such characters as Sleeping Beauty and Cinderella. The protagonists of the authors writing for men are men; the goals of these protagonists are prosperity or achievement, as those would have been defined by men of their day. The boys, young males, and men who constituted the primary audience of the Latin tales may have taken as much delight as did girls and women in the ambition for marriage, money, and social elevation; certainly these topics are in the forefront of most of the tales to be considered in this study. But the sequence to be followed by the heroes on whom the men, young and old, modeled themselves varied, in accordance with differences in the realities of their social options.

The chapters that follow will explore tales that survive in both Medieval Latin versions from the tenth through the early thirteenth centuries and later classic fairy tale forms. Sometimes the relationship between these two poles is very direct and immediate. For instance, in two instances, the Brothers Grimm found Medieval Latin tales in manuscripts, transcribed their Latin, and adapted them in German translation to become components in the *KHM*. In other cases, the tales passed back and forth between oral and written forms over the centuries, in a much less direct transmission.

To appreciate the relationship between the medieval and modern versions of the tales requires giving consideration to all sorts of changes—for example, on social, religious, and literary levels—between them. Many of the most important differences that emerge from setting the tales in their sociohistorical contexts relate to the sense of wonder that is fundamental to fairy tales, which indeed are often known technically as "wonder tales." Wonder is the effect that such tales seek to achieve, while magic is the means that they employ to attain this goal. Both the effect and the means will vary from one cultural milieu to another, which guarantees that wonder tales cannot be appreciated fully without being contextualized. The first tale I turn to is a late tenth-century poem that relates to both the biblical book of Jonah and the story of Pinocchio.

Between Sacred Legend and Folktale

A Whale of a Story about a
Tenth-Century Fisherman

THE SWALLOWING IN THE STORY OF PINOCCHIO

n a lifetime that coincided with well more than the first half of the twentieth century, the animator and entrepreneur Walt Disney (1901–66) produced animated films of versions of many "classic" fairy tales. His early films *Little Red Riding Hood* (1922), *The Four Musicians of Bremen* (1922), and *Puss in Boots* (1922), for example, draw on the heritages of both the Brothers Grimm and Charles Perrault. He returned to the story of Little Red Riding Hood in *The Big Bad Wolf* (1934). But it was the enthusiastic reception of his feature-length cartoon *Snow White and the Seven Dwarfs* (1937), also indebted ultimately to the Brothers Grimm, that made feasible a succession of animations based on other folktales and literary fairy tales, including *Cinderella* (1950) and *Sleeping Beauty* (1959); even since Disney's death, the series has continued at a regular pace.

One of the most famous among the cartoons produced directly under Walt Disney himself is *Pinocchio* (1940). Disney's interpretation differs in its general atmosphere, in its roll of characters (especially in its characterization of Pinocchio himself), and even in its basic story line from *The Adventures of Pinocchio: The Story of a Puppet* (*Le avventure di Pinocchio: Storia di un*

burattino), the book published in 1883 on the basis of weekly stories that had been serialized between 1881 and 1883. The author of *The Adventures of Pinocchio* wrote under the pseudonym Carlo Collodi; his real name was Carlo Lorenzini (1826–90).

In its overall framework, *The Adventures of Pinocchio* does not rest on any single oral traditional story, since there is no one folktale of Pinocchio. Instead, the book calls for comparison with such masterpieces of children's literature as *Alice's Adventures in Wonderland* (1865) by Lewis Carroll (pseudonym for C. L. Dodgson, 1832–98) or the Peter Pan stories and plays by J. M. Barrie (1860–1937), rather than with the tale types cataloged by folklorists. Even so, it is commonly regarded as being a literary fairy tale.[1] Since the connection of fairies with fairy tales is purely adventitious, the basis for considering *The Adventures of Pinocchio* a fairy tale is not that it features as a main character a fairy who becomes "the lovely Little Girl with the blue hair."[2] Rather, it is that Collodi employs to good effect a variety of lessons he had learned nearly ten years earlier (1875), when he ventured as his first children's book a volume entitled *Fairy Tales* (*I racconti della fate*). This earlier book incorporated adaptations of French literary fairy tales by Charles Perrault, Madame d'Aulnoy, and Madame Leprince de Beaumont.

The Adventures of Pinocchio may not conform to any one tale type, but it absorbed many techniques and motifs familiar from folktales, both oral and literary. It begins traditionally—"Once upon a time"—but, typically, raises an immediate question about its own apparent traditionality: "Once upon a time there was . . . 'A king!' my little readers will immediately say. No, children you're wrong. Once upon a time there was a piece of wood."[3] One key episode, included in the Walt Disney film as well, has Pinocchio, who has been transformed into a donkey, tossed into the sea. There he is freed, with the help of countless fish, from the donkey skin in which he has been unhappily enveloped. But a sea monster (a frightful shark in Collodi, a furious whale in Disney) swallows him. In the belly of the monster, Pinocchio comes upon his father figure, Geppetto, who has been living there for two years. Eventually Pinocchio escapes. In the Disney version the escape comes about when the boy lights on (so to speak) the idea of setting on fire Geppetto's boat. The smoke and fire cause the sea beast such discomfort that, before long, it belches out Pinocchio, Geppetto, and the cricket Jiminy, who eventually are washed safely ashore.

What sources of inspiration lay behind the portrayal of this scene in either Collodi or Disney may never be fully known, beyond the obvious fact that children's stories are widespread in which the motif of "[v]ictims rescued from swallower's belly" (*MI* F913) is the crucial turning point. The most venerable of these stories would be the Greek myth in which the god

Kronos (youngest son of Uranos and Gaia) devoured five of his children as soon as they were born, so as to avoid the fulfillment of a prophecy that he would be dethroned by one of his own children. His wife (and sister—the family was quite dysfunctional) fled; gave birth to a sixth child, Zeus; and protected him by a ruse so that he could live to free his siblings.

In the most important of these tales in Western culture today, a child (or young anthropomorphized creature) is first swallowed and later delivered from the stomach of the devourer. In the tale "The Wolf and the Kids" (ATU 123), the kids allow the wolf to enter while their mother is absent; although they are eaten by the wolf, they are saved when the old goat cuts open the wolf and rescues them (*MI* K971). In "Little Red Riding Hood" (ATU 333), the wolf gobbles the child and others until they are rescued alive from its belly. What can be investigated in regard to these tales is the earliest full exposition of the folktale that lies at the foundation of both these "classic" versions and many others that are less well known.

THE MONK LETALDUS OF MICY, THE TALE HE HEARD, AND THE TALE HE WROTE

In the late tenth century, Letaldus, a French monk who was attached to the abbeys of Le Mans and Micy and is otherwise known only for prose hagiographical works,[4] wrote a poem to which became attached the quaint title—probably nonauthorial, but nonetheless apt—*About a Certain Fisherman Whom a Whale Swallowed* (*De quodam piscatore quem ballena absorbuit* [app. 1B]). The poem survived into modern times in two manuscripts (one from the late eleventh or early twelfth century, the other from the late twelfth century), although the younger of them was destroyed in 1940.[5] The poem has received many compliments for its gracefulness, has been edited repeatedly, and has begun, over the past two decades, to earn the broad recognition that it deserves.[6] In 208 dactylic hexameters, the piece relates one extraordinary crisis in the otherwise uneventful life of a humble English fisherman named Within, who lives in Rochester (the port in Kent, not far from London). One morning Within sets sail in his coracle or curragh, a small, round boat constructed of leather stretched over a wooden or wicker frame. At first his voyage is entirely routine, but suddenly he and his little vessel are engulfed by a whale. For four days and five nights, Within is engaged in a struggle to free himself. Ultimately, by setting fire to his coracle and plying his trusty sword, he kills the whale. By chance the whale's body washes ashore near Rochester. When Within speaks out to his townsmen as they chop into the carcass in which he is still trapped, they assume it to be possessed and take flight. Only after the local bishop has exorcised the whale with holy water is

Within allowed to tell his story. Soon freed, the fisherman finds himself altered in appearance: his hair has fallen out, his eyes have lost their sight, and his fingernails protrude where the surrounding skin has been eaten away. In celebration of his novel experience, Within is received jubilantly by the clergy, nobility, and commoners of his town; not much later he regains his former looks and returns to a normal life.

Studded with quotations of Virgil and reminiscences of other Latin epic poets, the poem about the fisherman Within has deservedly won admiration for its wit and stylistic elegance. As a result of the attention that has been paid to its style, no one would now deny that the poem contains many artful allusions. To mention only lines and phrases drawn from the *Aeneid,* Within's departure from Rochester (21–22) is described in the words Virgil used of the day when Dido learned of Aeneas's departure (*Aeneid* 4.585); his resignation at not escaping the whale (44) brings to mind the occasion on which Turnus left his battle position to storm the gates of Aeneas's camp (*Aeneid* 9.694); his ingesting of whale meat (95) echoes the scene in which the Trojans prepare the venison that Aeneas brought to them (*Aeneid* 1.212); and his talking from inside the whale (118) occasions in his fellow townsmen the same type of speechlessness Aeneas felt upon seeing the ghost of Creusa (*Aeneid* 2.774).[7] The many borrowings and allusions demonstrate that although Letaldus wrote his poem about a common man, he aimed it at an audience knowledgeable about learned Latin poetry. By applying the lofty language of classical epic poetry to the story of a lowly fisherman, he creates an amusing disjunction while at the same time ennobling his protagonist with the literary trappings of heroism.

Yet the poem about the fisherman Within is not merely a patchwork of words and phrases wrenched from classical Latin poetry. The poem has several dimensions beyond the stylistic one. On account of its style and supposed fancifulness, the poem has elicited tribute as a "fantasy" and as a playful mock epic;[8] but it had not been examined carefully for its content—for the importance of the story it records—until twenty years ago, when attention was first drawn to its special stature as a major monument to the complex interplay between oral tradition and learned lore in the Middle Ages.[9]

It is well known that oral traditional literature left a permanent imprint on poetry composed and performed in the medieval vernacular languages, but the wide-ranging nature of its influence on Latin verse in the Middle Ages is often overlooked. On the one hand, verse techniques in the native tongues of Medieval Latin writers sometimes shaped their Latin styles, as is the case with Aldhelm's highly alliterative poetry.[10] On the other hand, tales transmitted through speech or song now and then suggested the subject matter that Latin authors of the Middle Ages chose to versify, as appears

evident in such masterpieces as the epic *Poem of Walter,* the romance-like *Ruodlieb,* and, last but not least, the folktale *One-Ox,* which will be considered in chapter 4.[11]

In its style, *About a Certain Fisherman* is quite remote from oral poetry, unless Letaldus's use of leonine rhymes reflects a desire to imitate vernacular verse. The rhyming is particularly prominent in the epic scenes in which Within is swallowed (37, 42, 45, 48, 51, 52) and fights free (84, 87, 89–94, 96), as well as in the opening passage (1, 3–4, 6, 9, 11–12, 16, 18, 20).[12] But the leonine hexameters could just as plausibly be a rhetorical flourish owed to school learning.[13]

Whatever the reasons are for the rhymes, the poem begins with Letaldus's intimation that he learned the story of Within by word of mouth: "An elder, commanding respect by his behavior and weighted down by age, whose words are radiant like copper-tinged gold, reported this event" (7–8). In his other writings, Letaldus is scrupulous—or at least makes a strenuous effort to appear to be so—in indicating whether his source of information is his own eyes, the report of other eyewitnesses, a less direct tradition, or actual documents. Unless we assume that he allows himself an altogether different modus operandi (poetic license) because of writing here not in prose but in verse, we should start by evaluating what sort of oral source Letaldus could have had.

The poet's claim of an oral source opens the possibility that the tale is a sailor's tall tale. In such tales collected from sailors in the twentieth century, variants about men being swallowed by great fish and spending time within their bellies are among the most common stories.[14] Furthermore, the narrators of such stories are reported to be in most cases "almost willing to take an oath that their stories are true."[15]

THE GEOGRAPHICAL ORIGINS OF LETALDUS'S SOURCE

The origins of Letaldus's oral story could have been British: the Latin poet not only situates the action of the poem in an English city but even bestows on the hero of the story an unusual name corresponding closely to the Old English adverb and preposition *wiþinnan.*[16] *Within* would be an apt *nom parlant* for a man whose adventure takes place within a whale, and Letaldus may even betray an awareness of the identity between Within's name and the adverb and preposition. At the crucial juncture when the fisherman first calls out to his townsmen from within the whale, in a speech that ends, "It is Within who is held in this belly" [Hac Within servatur in aluo] (115), the poet is at pains to indicate that Within speaks in his native language ("natiue"); and when the woebegone sailor addresses his people for the final

time from inside the belly of the whale, his speech begins, "I am Within" [Within . . . sum] (145).[17] It is hard not to suspect the lingering aftermath of an English pun. When he speaks, the sailor is not only Within but also truly within.

But who would have communicated the original oral traditional tale to Letaldus? Although the argument has been advanced that the elder whose report Letaldus follows in recounting the story was Within himself, it is difficult to imagine when or where the two would have met, and it is even harder to envisage how an unlearned English fisherman could have bridged the language gap between English, on the one hand, and French or Latin, on the other, to communicate directly with a French monk.[18] Whatever the intermediaries, there is no reason to doubt Letaldus's implication that the tale came to him from a source in Britain or to overlook his apparent awareness (15) that the English language of his day played a vital role in ecclesiastic and liturgical life. Stories on the model of *About a Certain Fisherman* would have appealed to the inhabitants of the British Isles, in whose lives and literatures the whale occupied a prominent place.[19]

Whaling took place in both the English Channel and the North Sea.[20] In the very first section of the *Ecclesiastic History of the English People* (*Historia ecclesiastica gentis Anglorum*), the Venerable Bede (673–735) notes that whales are caught in the waters of England. Presumably in part out of interest in whales (which were an extremely valuable catch), an anonymous translator, perhaps with the encouragement of King Alfred the Great (849–99), felt moved in the ninth century to interpolate into his translation of the *Seven Books of Histories, Written against the Pagans* (*Historiarum aduersus paganos libri septem*), by Paulus Orosius (died after 418), the account that the Norwegian nobleman Ohthere gave of his voyage into remote regions where whales and walruses were hunted and caught in astonishing numbers.[21] The importance of the whale in everyday English life emerges in the work of Ælfric (ca. 950–ca. 1010) a century later, in the *Colloquy* (which was written at roughly the same time as *About a Certain Fisherman*), where a timid fisherman confesses that he prefers catching fish to stalking dangerous whales.[22]

Rodulfus (or Raoul) Glaber, a monk who lived from around 990 to 1047, wrote a history for the century and a half from 900 to 1044. In it he describes how, four years before the millennium, "a whale of marvelous size" [cętus mire magnitudinis] was seen to have come by sea to a place named Berneval.[23] In a touch worthy of the most extravagant tall tale, the whale was so large that its transit took several hours. Although this event reputedly occurred in France and not England, it is interesting to observe that Raoul connects the event with a story about St. Brendan, whom he calls "Bendanus" and presents as being East Anglian (rather than Irish). Raoul's angli-

cization of Brendan could be related to Letaldus's awareness of an oral tradition about an English fisherman: both may indicate that as the millennium drew near and apocalyptic anxieties made people hungrier than ever for portents, fishermen's tall tales from across the English Channel took on special salience.[24]

We know from multiple sources that sea creatures washed ashore and were valuable troves. The Old English verses inscribed on the Franks Casket (probably made in eighth-century Northumbria) recount the demise of the whale from whose bone the coffer was made, while the Latin *Canons of Adamnán* (seventh-century Irish) begin with a sentence about the edibility of "sea creatures cast upon the shore" [marina animalia ad litora delata].[25] Whale meat and bones for food and ivory were only two of many parts that provided valuable raw materials;[26] blubber, baleen, ambergris, teeth, and hide could serve as fuel for heat and light, as medicine, and as fabric for textiles.[27] Since the whale was important in a variety of ways to those who lived in Ireland and England, it is no wonder that the whale was chosen by the Old English *Physiologus* poet to represent the creatures of the sea.[28] Confirmation of the importance that whale hunting and whale products held in Britain and Ireland can also be found in written sources from what might seem a surprising origin: Arab travelers to the British Isles and geographers who had received their reports related how the inhabitants of coastal regions hunted whales and worked whale bones.[29] Ash-Sharīf al-Idrīsī (ca. 1100–1165), in a geographical treatise composed (ca. 1154) for King Roger II of Sicily (ca. 1095–1154), includes the following assertion in his treatment of whaling and its purposes in the British Isles:

> There are also sea-animals of such size that the inhabitants of the inner isles employ their bones and vertebrae instead of wood for building houses. They also make from them clubs, lances, spears, daggers, seats, ladders, and other things which elsewhere are made of wood.[30]

Since Muslim wayfarers and writers were the vectors of lore about whales and whaling from the British Isles to the Middle East, it is tantalizing to think that the exchange could have run in both directions—that they could have also carried oral traditions about "great fishes" from the Mediterranean with them. Michael Crichton's novel *Eaters of the Dead: The Manuscript of Ibn Fadlan Relating His Experiences with the Northmen in A.D. 922* may not have been entirely improbable in its depiction of mutual influences between tenth-century Europeans and Muslim visitors, even if his focus was on the experiences of Aḥmad Ibn Faḍlan (flourished ca. 922) in Rus' rather

than on those of one of his fellow Arabs in the British Isles.[31] But such tenuous channels for storytelling would not have been required.

That the whale lore of Ireland and England could have reached the Continent—and Letaldus—seems very plausible in light of the multifarious cultural contacts that took place between the British Isles and France during the tenth century.[32] Even without such conduits, a corpus of whale stories could have been indigenous to northwestern France, since whales were as visible there as in England: not even a hundred years after Letaldus, the French poet Rodulfus Tortarius (also known less Latinately as Raoul Le Tourtier or Raoul Tortaire), of the early twelfth century, portrays in Latin verse the hunting of whales at Bayeux.[33] Indeed, in Normandy the occupation of whale hunting was sufficiently entrenched by the end of the eleventh century and by the early twelfth century as to have made necessary and feasible the use of the Latinized noun *walmannus,* "whale man" (also *waumannus*).[34] Although the equivalent Old English *hwælmann* and Old Icelandic *hvalmaðr* are not attested, other comparable compounds of *hwæl-* and *hval-* exist.[35]

THEORIES ON THE ORIGINAL MEANING OF SWALLOWING STORIES

More important than to conjecture where the story of Within arose is to understand that it stemmed ultimately from oral literature—that is, from a branch of folklore—and to apply this understanding in explicating the poem. Stories in which animals first glut on and later vomit out men are prevalent in folktales, both oral and reworked as literary fairy tales. The most famous of many examples would be the story of Little Red Riding Hood, in which first the grandmother and then the leading lady are eaten by the wolf before being liberated from its belly by a hunter.[36] Given how widespread the general sequence of devouring and regurgitation is, finding an adaptation in Medieval Latin poetry would not in itself be noteworthy. What is striking is that the precise pattern of events in Letaldus's story of a fisherman and a whale recurs in tales found throughout the world as well as throughout time: heroes are ingested by sea monsters, slay the monstrosities only by burning and/or mangling them (especially their livers or hearts) from within, suffer heat or burning, and emerge on land alive (but hairless) after the monsters die.[37]

This intriguing sequence has been explained variously. The most common interpretation of the late nineteenth and early twentieth centuries took stories of this pattern as nature myths or myths of a sun god: the sun, swallowed by the sea as it sets, survives to triumph—*sol invictus* (the sun unvan-

quished)—by cutting and burning its way free with its rays in the morning.[38] This explanation was suggested early, albeit only sketchily, for Letaldus's *About a Certain Fisherman*.[39]

Closely related to solar interpretations are others in which the motivating phenomenon is the moon: after three days of a dark moon, the sickle of the new moon (resembling a scimitar) appears in correspondence to the action of a hero, such as Perseus, who cuts his way out of a dragon.[40] Alternatively, such stories have been construed as being myths referring to a rite of initiation: a novice pretends to descend into an underworld of death but emerges from the temple to be reborn.[41] The notion that the story of Within can be elucidated in terms of an ancient initiation rite has been revived and developed much more recently.[42] Last but not least, these tales have not been left unscathed by psychological explications, that these are sexual myths in which the making of fire symbolizes the act of sex.[43] Otto Rank (1884–1939), a psychologist who began as a Freudian but struck off in a slightly different direction, interpreted such stories as conveying the suppressed memories of birth trauma.[44]

The solar myth would be etiological, to account for what happens to the sun between sunset and sunrise. From the perspective of a person who lives near the sea (particularly on an island or a peninsula jutting into the sea), the phenomenon could be explained as a mythic struggle reenacted daily: the sun is engulfed by a great sea monster but fights free with the sharpness and heat of its rays in the morning. This myth may be attested in a Medieval Latin question-and-answer dialogue (perhaps from the tenth century) between Adrian and Epictetus, where one of the pairings goes as follows: "Where is the sun during the night?—In the belly of the whale that is called Leviathan."[45]

THEORIES ON THE SPREAD OF TALES

In the case of such tales as those about men who are first swallowed and later disgorged by sea beasts, folktale scholars were struck already in the nineteenth century by the wide distribution of evidence. For example, similar forms of a story may be found in Polynesia, among Native Americans, in Africa, in Central Asia, and also in early European texts.[46] Two main theories developed to account for the widespread nature of such tales.[47]

The theory of polygenesis holds that human societies, even when unrelated in their times or places of existence, will share similar environments and experiences and that these similar experiences will prompt them to develop similar tale types and motifs. In other words, similar tale types and motifs are born independently of any source-and-influence process: they

share their resemblances because of polygenesis. In contrast, diffusion theory holds that the distribution of similar tale types and motifs over a broad area indicates their diffusion from a common origin. Such diffusion may result from migration of entire peoples or emigration of individuals, effects of war, religious conversion, commercial trade, travel for pleasure, and other such movements.

STORIES OF MEN SWALLOWED BY SEA MONSTERS IN EUROPEAN LITERATURE

In European literature, the story of a man swallowed by a sea creature can be documented in ancient Greece in at least two myths. One is the myth of Herakles (*Hercules* in Latin), Hesione, and Ketos, recorded in the fifth and third centuries BCE.[48] The mythological background is that Laomedon, king of Troy, betrayed the gods Poseidon and Apollo over the payment due them for constructing the walls of Troy. Thereupon Poseidon dispatched against the city the creature Ketos (the Latin noun *cetus* means "large sea animal, sea monster, whale"). To be liberated from it, the Trojans were obliged to mollify it by offering it Laomedon's daughter, Hesione. At this point, Herakles enters the picture, in one of his mythical deeds that is not subsumed among his famous Twelve Labors. According to the fragments of the story, Herakles enters the mouth of the sea monster sent to consume Hesione and kills it by hacking its sides. He comes out unharmed, except that he has lost his hair because of the intense heat.[49] This last motif, that the "[s]wallowed person becomes bald" (*MI* F921), is widespread in folk literature throughout the world.

The myth of Herakles, Hesione, and Ketos does not survive in a single exposition but must be pieced together with reference to partial accounts. A fragment from the works of Hellanicus of Lesbos (ca. 480–395 BCE) refers to Herakles' first entering the monster through its mouth and then damaging its flanks from inside its belly.[50] Lines 33–37 and 468–78 of the poetic monodrama *Alexandra* by pseudo-Lycophron (Lycophron flourished in the early third century BCE, but pseudo-Lycophron probably composed his poem in the early second century BCE) mention the hair loss that Herakles suffers from the heat within the sea monster.[51] Further partial accounts of the story include a remark in *Against the Professors* (*Adversus mathematicos* 1.255) by Sextus Empiricus (ca. 200 CE?)[52] and scholia on pseudo-Lycophron's lines 33–34 by John Tzetzes (born ca. 1110; died between 1180 and 1185), which John himself sought, later in life, to attribute to his brother, Isaac Tzetzes (died 1138).[53]

The scholia on pseudo-Lycophron are particularly interesting parallels

for their interpretation of the epithet *trihesperos* ("of three evenings" or "of three nights"), which was applied to Herakles.[54] Originally the epithet referred to the three consecutive and unbroken nights Zeus spent with Herakles' mother, Alkmene, in conceiving him; but Tzetzes construed the adjective as signaling the three days that Herakles spent inside the dark belly of the monster. (He reasons that Lycophron refers to the three days as nights because of the darkness that prevailed within the belly of the beast.) Herakles's three days within Ketos affords an obvious parallel to the biblical Jonah's three days and three nights in the stomach of a great fish, which was itself a prefiguration of Christ's three days and three nights in the tomb. The coordination of Herakles and Jonah is attested first by Cyril of Alexandria (died 444) and later by Archbishop Theophylaktos of Ohrid (born ca. 1050; died after 1126), but although these exegetes of the book of Jonah note that the great heat within the sea monster's interior causes Herakles to be hairless when he emerges, neither goes on to propose that Jonah also lost all his hair as a result of his time inside the belly of the whale.[55] Moreover, neither author elaborates a full triangulation of what would have been considered in medieval Christian terms Old Testament, New Testament, and Greco-Roman myth: the middle element is left implicit.

The mythic situation of Herakles pitted against the sea monster Ketos to free Hesione finds a close parallel in the myth of Perseus, who combats the same creature to spare Andromede (Andromeda).[56] Andromede was bound to a rock and offered in sacrifice to placate the monster Ketos (sometimes described as being doglike), who had been dispatched by Poseidon (god of the sea) to lay waste to the country of King Cepheus of Ethiopia after Cassiope (the king's wife and Andromede's mother) had ill-advisedly boasted of being more beautiful than all the Nereids (sea deities) put together. While Andromede is in this plight, Perseus glimpsed her as he was returning from his mission against the Gorgon, fell in love with her, and fought Ketos on the condition that he be allowed to marry Andromede if he prevailed. In one version of the story, Perseus is snatched by the creature and devoured, but he hacks at its liver and kills it. The fantastic nature of this episode may have elicited parody as early as the fifth century BCE: in the *Clouds,* Aristophanes refers in passing to a comedy that burlesqued this part of the myth.[57]

Interestingly, the mythic episode of Perseus's deliverance of Andromede is localized at Joppa (Jaffa), the very harbor where Jonah is reported to have embarked (Jonah 1.3).[58] Flavius Josephus (born 37–38 CE) reports that rocks in the harbor still bore marks where the chains that secured Andromede had been affixed.[59] The ancient travel writer Pausanias (flourished around 150 CE) describes a fountain near Joppa where Perseus is alleged to have washed

off the bloodstains from his battle with the monster; the color of the gore presumably tinged the water of the fountain forever.[60] As for the monster itself, Pliny the Elder (23/24–79 CE) relates how Marcus Scaurus, when aedile (a magistrate in ancient Rome) in 58 BCE, brought its bones from Joppa to put them on display in Rome.[61] Knowledge of the myth, albeit scrambled, persisted through the ages. *Mandeville's Travels,* a text composed in French in the mid-fourteenth century (and later translated into Latin, English, German, and Dutch) and purporting to recount the travels of an English knight named Sir John Mandeville (died 1372?), tells that the site was still shown where an antediluvian giant named Andromeda had been chained and that one of the giant's ribs, forty feet in length, was still to be seen.[62] Although the details were jumbled by either the local tour guides or "Mandeville" himself, the passage makes clear that the myth of Perseus continued to be connected in popular imagination with the whale and to be localized in Joppa. The common association of both Perseus and Jonah with Joppa, which was noted in biblical exegesis as early as Jerome (347–419/420) and Cyril of Alexandria (patriarch of Alexandria from 412 to 444), suggests that the "great fish" of Jonah and the story of Perseus and the sea monster may share a common mythological background.[63]

Other myths in which heroes were swallowed by monsters but later disgorged while still living may have shared additional features with the myths of Herakles and Perseus but have not been preserved in sufficient detail. Such could be the case with an Attic red-figure vase by the vase painter Douris (ca. 475 BCE) that appears to represent Jason, under the watchful eyes of Athena, as he is disgorged by the dragon that guards the Golden Fleece.[64] If we ignore the presence of Athena, this scene comes closer than does the Andromede episode to the stories of Within (and Jonah) in apparently not involving a girl to be fed to a beast who is freed by the hero.

Without referring specifically to any of the myths, Lucian (born ca. 120 CE) employs ludicrous exaggeration to mock tales of improbable swallowings and escapes, in a work entitled antonomastically *A True History.*[65] Expressing himself in the first person (presumably so as better to imitate the sorts of story he is satirizing), he claims to have been engulfed, together with no fewer than fifty companions, ship and all, within a huge whale. For a time, they are content to remain inside the creature, which is sufficiently spacious to be inhabited by warring tribes and to contain an island, a forest, a temple, a cemetery, a farm, and other such features not normally associated with the interiors of great fish. When finally they wish to leave, they dig a shaft hundreds of meters deep into the side of the whale, but to no avail. Then they set fire to the forest, which burns for a full twelve days before the whale succumbs and dies, at which point they drag their ship into

the sea through the mouth of the carcass. Nothing is said about loss of hair or bleaching of skin.

Although Lucian did not make much of a direct mark in twentieth-century mass media, the kind of tall tale he spoofed in *A True History* (a veritable "whale of a story") has not only survived indirectly but even thrived, thanks to its inclusion in one of the best-known modern assemblies of such fanciful tales. The grandiloquently named Karl Friedrich Hieronymus, Freiherr von Münchhausen (1720–97), was a real-life person who took his experiences as a young soldier fighting against the Turks and as traveler in Russia and elsewhere and elaborated them later in his storytelling.[66] By all accounts, his anecdotes transcended the extraordinary to become absurd and impossible. His reputation as a raconteur became such that he himself became a legend, sometimes called simply "the baron of lies" (*der Lügenbaron*). Besides living on in the name of two mental disorders (Munchausen syndrome and Munchausen syndrome by proxy), the baron has the dubious distinction of having named after him an entire subclass of tales in the folktale index (ATU 1889, "Münchhausen Tales").

In the 1780s, Münchhausen suffered a kind of identity theft, as two or more authors writing in German and English brought into print stories that they credited to him.[67] Seventeen tall tales ascribed to him (and known among literary scholars as the Münschhauseniads, with a mock-epic suffix) were published anonymously in German between 1781 and 1783. In 1785 a revised and expanded collection of these tales was published in English under the title *Baron Münchhausen's Narrative of His Marvellous Travels and Campaigns in Russia,* by a German polymath of questionable character named Rudolf Erich Raspe (1737–94), who took up writing in English after he had to leave the Continent to escape criminal charges. In Raspe's book as expanded by yet another author in 1786, Baron Münchhausen, who professes to be two hundred years old, relates his truly unbelievable experiences and travels, which fall into two parts. Whereas the first is built on the seventeen original Münschhauseniads of war and hunting stories, the second taps the tradition of sea stories in Lucian's *A True History.*

Alongside a trip to the moon and a voyage into a volcano is an episode (the third sea story) in which the baron is swallowed by a very large fish while he is swimming one afternoon in the Mediterranean. Münchhausen attempts to secure his escape by causing pain to the fish from within. In keeping with the bizarre, tongue-in-cheek humor of the baron's alleged adventures, the most effective tactic proves to be dancing a hornpipe. Although his motions do not free him directly, they cause the fish to surface (the narrator Münchhausen alleges that it "stood up almost perpendicularly in the water"[68]), at which point it is harpooned by people aboard a nearby

vessel. As they cut into the creature, the baron shouts out and emerges, nude (not owing to any effects of the fish upon him, but because he was swimming naked when he was swallowed). Except for needing to wash himself clean, Münchhausen was unchanged by his four and a half hours inside the whale. After taking refreshment, he swims back to where he left his clothes. This lying tale has been classified—or perhaps typecast—as ATU 1889G, "Man Swallowed by Fish."

In 1786, the collection of stories by Raspe was translated into German in an expanded edition by Gottfried August Bürger (1747–94), which has proven to be the most popular version of Münchhausen's adventures (especially outside the English-speaking world). But there have been other literary recastings of the legendary character and his tales, such as the long novel entitled *Münchhausen: A History of Arabesques* (*Münchhausen: Eine Geschichte in Arabesken* [1838–39]), by Karl Liebrecht Immermann (1796–1840), and the comedy *Münchhausen* by Walter Hasenclever (1890–1940). There have been many other dramatic adaptations. Last but not least, film versions have accorded at least a small niche to both the (in)famous baron and the stories ascribed to him. The first of these, based on a screenplay by Erich Küstner, appeared in 1943. Next came the 1961 Czech film *The Fabulous Baron Munchausen* (also known as *The Original Fabulous Adventures of Baron Munchausen*), directed by Karel Zeman. Most recent, released in 1989, was *The Adventures of Baron Munchausen,* directed by Terry Gilliam. Whether or not most of the authors and directors had any awareness of their ultimate debts, the most important literary and cinematic versions of the cycle all contain the whale episode that goes back to Lucian.

At least two pieces of evidence indicate that the same kind of tale as attested in antiquity (seriously in the myth of Herakles and Ketos and parodically in Lucian) and in modern times (with extravagant fancifulness in Münchhausen) also circulated in Ireland throughout the Middle Ages. The earliest attestation is in the so-called B-text of the notoriously difficult collection of texts known as the *Hisperica famina* (which could be translated roughly as "Irish Talk"), in a section entitled *De gesta re* (meaning "On History" or "About the Exploit Performed").[69] Although it may be that the texts in the *Hisperica famina* were not the work of Irishmen, they seem to have been composed in Ireland (in the seventh century). Rightly or wrongly, their name and the obscurantist "Hisperic" quality of their style have become irrevocably associated with early medieval Hiberno-Latin literature. In any event, the section *De gesta re* relates that a king, not content with the realm he already possesses, organizes a great expedition of conquest. His forces set sail in a fleet, which is swallowed by a gigantic sea monster. The sailors use iron and flint to kindle a fire in the belly of the whale,

and they cut chunks from inside the beast, which they roast and eat. Eventually the whale dies and is washed to the shore, where, to the amazement of the local people, it is beached on the rocks. When the locals set upon the carcass with axes, they discover the sailors inside, still alive.[70] At the end of the section, the poet signifies that the incident became well known.

Although the passage in the *Hisperica famina* B-text shares vocabulary with Letaldus's *About a Certain Fisherman,* none of the overlaps comes close to proving indebtedness by the later poet.[71] Rather, they result inevitably from the circumstance that both poets describe loosely comparable events— events that came to the attention of the two poets through oral tradition: the *Hisperica famina* passage ends with the word *fama,* which denotes a spoken report, and Letaldus, as noted earlier, credits the mouth of an old man as his source of information. The attempt to relate the *Hisperica famina* B-text and Letaldus's *About a Certain Fisherman* as source and influence reflects an overly text-driven conception of medieval literature: it leads one interpreter to qualify the tenth-century poem as being like the Hellenistic *Hecale* by Callimachus, and it leads another to posit improbably that one of Letaldus's main sources was the Greek author Lucian.[72] Not all sources well up from written literature.

Another swallowing story in European literature that replicates the pattern of *About a Certain Fisherman* also comes from an Irish source, albeit one that is not documented until the other end of the Middle Ages from the *Hisperica famina* (and even later). Two versions of a recurrent episode in the Irish Fionn cycle (centering on the exploits of Fionn mac Cumhaill, or Find mac Cumaill) describe how a man kills a sea beast from within by cutting it, frees its other captives, and emerges bald and bereft of clothing.[73] This particular section of the Fionn cycle has been dated on linguistic grounds to the mid-fifteenth century or earlier;[74] but because the Fionn cycle as a whole is considerably older, it is possible that stories like this were being told many centuries earlier. Regardless of when this episode of the Fionn cycle is to be dated, it is possible to state with certainty that the Irish telling of the story arose independently of Letaldus's poetic version, which never circulated widely.[75] Whatever similarities the two versions display are most likely attributable either to coincidence or to shared features of related oral traditions.[76]

With the exception of the Within poem (which has eluded the notice of folklorists), the story of swallowing that concerns us is not attested again securely in European literature until the late thirteenth century, when it occurs in the *Deeds of the Romans* (*Gesta Romanorum*). There, the leading character is a princess who is (together with her ship and its crew) overwhelmed by a whale; members of the crew destroy it by lighting a fire and

stabbing it; she wins her freedom when the animal is washed ashore and cut open by people who hear her crying for help.[77] As in Lucian's *A True History*, this version of the swallowing story lacks the baldness and nakedness often found at the end.

Letaldus's poem merits recognition for providing a wonderfully full Western European version of the swallowing story from the early Middle Ages. It has still greater significance, however, as a model for the ways in which such folklore interacted with learned lore in the Middle Ages.[78] If one inspiration for the tale of Within was a widely disseminated folk story, another must have been the most famous whale story of all time, namely, the book of Jonah. The book of Jonah seems to have been written in the fourth century BCE but to deal with the activities of a prophet who lived in the eighth century BCE. It is unique among the prophetic books in being a narrative rather than a collection of prophecies. It is also unusual in the prominence of the sea within it, since the Hebrews were not a seafaring people.

At the center of the book of Jonah stands a commission handed down by God to the prophet: Jonah is bidden to preach to Nineveh. Instead of doing so, the prophet seeks to flee to Tarshish. He goes to Joppa and sets sail. A storm besets the ship on which he is voyaging. When the sailors draw lots to determine who is the cause of their misfortune, Jonah is found to be the culprit. Eventually he is cast into the sea. This segment of the story has been labeled ATU 973, "Man as Sacrifice to the Storm," "Placating the Storm" (previously AT 973). A man is thrown overboard from a ship to appease the storm (*MI* 264.1).

No sooner is Jonah consigned to the waters than he is rescued by a great fish sent by the Lord: this is the best-known portion of the story. After three days and nights in the belly of the fish, Jonah prays to God for release and is spewed out by the fish upon dry land. Directed once more to preach to Nineveh that it would be destroyed, Jonah does so. At first he is distressed when the city repents and is spared the destruction he foretold, but eventually God shows him the wrongness of this reaction.

Letaldus takes pains to remind us of the Old Testament prophet (as if anyone needed reminding) by characterizing his protagonist explicitly toward the end of his poem (185) as being "like another Jonah" [Ionas uelut alter]. Indeed, Letaldus seems almost to bracket the story between his initial allusions to oral tradition (7–8) and to vernacular poetry in Old English (14–15) and this closing nod to learned Christianity. Throughout the story of the English fisherman, the tenth-century poet interjects remembrances of how the biblical whale story was explicated by Christian exegetes; but he never subordinates one whale story to the other.

Although most texts of the Bible refer vaguely to the monster that swal-

lowed Jonah as a "great fish" [*piscis grandis*] (e.g., Jonah 2.1), Christian commentators were predictably unanimous in following Jesus in assuming that the "great fish" was in truth a whale (*cetus* in the Latin of the Vulgate Bible at Matthew 12.40) and in magnifying its role in the story of Jonah.[79] On the strength of Jonah's own words (see Jonah 2.3), the whale and Leviathan, which were identified with each other, were both felt to represent the Devil or hell.[80] Jesus, when invoking the episode, makes plain that the whale represents the underworld, in which he will abide for three days: "For as Jonas was in the whale's belly three days and three nights: so shall the Son of man be in the heart of the earth three days and three nights" (Matthew 12.40). By extension, the mouth of the whale betokened the entrance to hell.[81] The whale's reputation, unsavory already in antiquity, was only worsened by the vogue of the accounts of its treachery in the *Physiologus* and bestiary.[82] On the authority of these sources, the whale—called *aspidokhelone* (shield tortoise) in Greek, *aspidochelone* (with countless orthographic variations) in Latin—was believed to practice an extremely sly method for bringing men to destruction.[83] It would surface in the middle of the ocean and float motionlessly. Sailors, mistaking the beast for an island, would moor and debark, only to be drowned when the whale suddenly dived after they started a fire for cooking.[84] With similar craft, the whale would emit delightful fragrances to lure tiny fish into his mouth, which he would then close.

Letaldus, since he attempts to place the language of his poem in the tradition of the classical Latin epic,[85] avoids evoking either the unclassical Leviathan or the *Physiologus* whale; yet he manages nonetheless to convey an unmistakable impression that the whale that engulfs Within is evil, even diabolic. He achieves this result through suitably ominous allusions to Scylla (38), Charybdis (38), Etna (73), and the Eumenides (75, 146). Thus we should not be perplexed at the fact that when, near the close of the poem, Within speaks from inside the beached whale, the townspeople of Rochester and their bishop at once assume the whale to be a demon (130) and a *pestis iniqua*, "wicked bane" (129). Rodulfus Glaber, writing less than a half century later about an event that is supposed to have taken place within years of Within's adventures, construed the appearance of a passing whale as a portent of war.[86] A beached whale may have stirred even worse associations. Certainly in the sixteenth and seventeenth centuries a stranded whale was regarded as a sign either of God's power or of the Devil's tireless troublemaking;[87] already in Letaldus's tenth-century poem, the whale carries undertones of the latter sense.

If the whale was associated with satanic forces, its opponent brought to mind Jonah and, through the prophet of the Hebrew Bible, Christ. From

the New Testament (Matthew 12.40) onward, Jonah's confrontation with the whale was considered, in art as well as in literature, a prefiguration of Christ's crucifixion and resurrection.[88] Such an equation is understandable, since both the swallowing by the whale and the entombment can be viewed as temporary deaths. In this loose sense, both events can be compared with fairy tales, in which children are first devoured and later disgorged by animals.[89] But theologians drew much more precise and unusual correspondences between the "great fish" and Jonah, on the one hand, and the crucifixion and the resurrection, on the other. Jesus was seen as the fisherman who answered the demand in Job 40.20: "Canst thou draw out Leviathan with an hook?" [an extrahere poteris Leviathan hamo]. Christ was the fisherman (*piscator*) who made himself the bait (*esca*) and crucified himself on the hook (*hamus*) in order to catch the whale (*cetus*). Once eaten, he was able to force the whale to release the souls it held in bondage.[90] This conception of Christ as a fisherman pervaded Medieval Latin culture. Its most memorable exposition in representational art is in the massive, encyclopedic *Garden of Delights* (*Hortus deliciarum*) that was compiled in the late twelfth century under the direction of Abbess Herrad of Landsberg (Hohenburg).[91] In poetry, Ekkehard IV of St. Gall (ca. 980–ca. 1060), a younger contemporary of Letaldus, started an epitaph with the couplet "After the man born of a virgin had destroyed on the cross and subjugated as victor Leviathan with a hook . . ." [In cruce confregit postquam victorque subegit / Leviathan hamo virgine natus homo . . .].[92]

Letaldus paints Within in similar colors. Like Christ, Within is a fisherman who becomes bait but, in the end, destroys the whale that devours him: "The food produces death; the bait devours the raging devourer; and the prey, the tables now turned, lays low the immense predator" [datque cibus mortem, rabidum vorat esca vorantem, / praedaque praedonem versa vice sternit enormem] (91–92). By drawing our attention to how well his rendition of the swallowing story meshes with learned readings of the book of Jonah, Letaldus moves us to overlook the many conspicuous discrepancies between the tales of Jonah and Within.

As even a summary comparison demonstrates, the texts of the two stories have surprisingly little in common. Jonah is not a fisherman, is deliberately tossed overboard to calm a storm, is swallowed not by a devilish whale but by a helpful fish acting at the behest of God, is freed in response to prayer rather than physical effort, and is unchanged in body by his ordeal. If the stories of Jonah and Within share anything, it is the simple fact that in both tales a man survives being engorged by a large sea creature. Although Jonah's experience may seem to be roughly equivalent to that of Little Red Riding Hood (in that both protagonists are swallowed and in a

sense eviscerated), Within's travails bear a much closer resemblance to the fairy tale; unlike Jonah but like Little Red Riding Hood, Within is not helped but instead threatened with death when he is swallowed, and he is not saved by a divinely induced expectoration but by the slaying of the swallower at human hands.[93] The closest parallel in Greco-Roman myth and legend to Jonah's rescue by the "great fish" is the story that the Greek citharode (player of the cithara, a musical instrument) Arion (ca. 600 BCE) was transported by a dolphin to Taenarum after he had to jump into the sea to save himself from rapacious sailors.[94]

Within's survival forms the core of Letaldus's poem and is no doubt the feature that has prompted readers of *About a Certain Fisherman* to judge it a "fantasy." All the same, there are at least three reasons why Within's victorious encounter with the whale probably seemed less "fantastic" to Letaldus and his audience of tenth-century monks than it does to many people today. In the first place, people in the tenth century may have placed more credence in the possibility that a man (and his small fishing vessel) could not only be swallowed by a whale but even survive the experience. In other words, what happened to Within need not have been, from their perspective, contrary to nature.

Even in the twentieth century, Christians of a fundamentalist bent gathered evidence to prove that there exist whales with the type of jaw, tongue, and gullet capable of accommodating a man and that a man swallowed could survive the heat, gastric juices, and air quality within such a whale. In fact, an article on Jonah published in the *Princeton Theological Review* not a hundred years ago even examined in detail an alleged incident in 1891 in which a whaler named James Bartley was thrown from a boat while hunting a large sperm whale near the Falkland Islands.[95] According to the fullest account of the episode, the whale was caught after Bartley's disappearance.

> The whale was killed and in a few hours the great body was lying by the ship's side, and the crew were busy with axes and spades removing the blubber. They worked all day and part of the night. Next morning they attached some tackle to the stomach, which was hoisted on the deck. The sailors were startled by something in it which gave spasmodic signs of life, and inside was found the missing sailor doubled up and unconscious. He was laid on the deck and treated to a bath of sea water which soon revived him.[96]

Adding to the parallels to Letaldus's poem, the experiences of James Bartley inside the whale are recorded as having coincided closely with those of Within. He experienced great heat:

It finally dawned upon him that he had been swallowed by the whale, and he was overcome by horror at the situation. He could easily breathe; but the heat was terrible. It was not of a scorching, stifling nature, but it seemed to open the pores of his skin and draw out his vitality.

Although his overall health remained good after the episode, his skin was altered permanently by the operation of the stomach acids within the whale.

> During his sojourn in the whale's stomach, Bartley's skin where it was exposed to the action of the gastric juice underwent a striking change: his face, neck, and hands were bleached to a deadly whiteness, and took on the appearance of parchment . . . According to the record, the skin on his face and hands never recovered its natural appearance, but the health of the man did not seem affected by his terrible experience.

This supposedly true account has been demonstrated to be false,[97] but whatever we make of the supposedly veracious account, it is interesting to witness the pains taken by the theologian who examined it to prove that the central event in the book of Jonah was conceivable on scientific grounds and that therefore this book of the Bible could be viewed "as an ordinary historical record."[98] Thus believers are spared the necessity of accepting the Jonah story as truth—one might say "Gospel truth," except that the episode appears first in Hebrew—simply because it is recorded within the canon of the Bible. As Martin Luther (1483–1546) wrote, "Who would not consider it to be a little fantasy [*Märlein*], if it were not in Scripture?"[99]

Whatever Letaldus's tenth-century readers suspected about the anatomy and physiology of whales, they would have had a second, more abstract reason for not finding the tale of Within as improbable as we might do. Medieval and modern views on what a miracle signifies differ distinctly. Owing to the influence of Augustine and his followers, early medieval thinkers held that miracles and commonplace happenings take place on the same plane, for both the ostensibly supernatural and the natural are due to providence; that to God, both types of occurrence are natural.[100] Theologians inferred that miracles are contrary not to nature but, rather, to the order of nature known to humankind in our limited knowledge.[101]

Last but not least, a third reason for which Leraldus's whale story would not have seemed "fantastic" to his monastic confreres is that they were quite likely to have been familiar with a noncanonical version of the Jonah story

similar to it, especially in the vivid final detail of baldness. Christian scholars of the Bible were adamant that Jonah was not altered physically by his stay within the cetacean, since any such change would have undermined construing the episode as a precise prefiguration of the resurrection. Jerome is representative of orthodox opinion on this matter.

> In regard to Jonah matters can be understood in the following way: that he who according to the nature of bodies ought to have been corrupted in the belly of the whale, to have brought benefit to the beast as food, and to have been broken apart and spread throughout its veins and limbs, instead remained safe and intact.[102]

Furthermore, the apocryphal Acts of Paul contains an implicit rejection of stories—in regard specifically to Jonah—in which men are rendered bald and blind after being swallowed by whales.

> [Y]ou know that Jonah the son of Amathios, when he would not preach in Nineveh but fled, was swallowed by a whale, and after three days and three nights God heard Jonah's prayer out of deepest hell, and no part of him was corrupted, not even a hair or an eyelid.[103]

But despite the quandary that a physically metamorphosed Jonah constituted for doctrine, in artistic illustrations of the episode Jonah is often shown entering the whale with a full head of hair and a beard but coming forth both hairless and beardless.[104] In such representations, Jonah has sometimes shed more than his hair; he has lost all of his clothes as well.[105]

In ancient representations where Jonah (and often some of the sailors with him) is nude before being swallowed and disgorged by the "great fish," the explanation may be that doffing clothing was a precaution taken aboard ships in danger of shipwreck.[106] But when Jonah alone is unclothed and only upon emerging from the whale, the motif may well be a reminiscence of the mythical heat within the sea beast. The standard exegetic tradition would have been better served in its doctrine of resurrection by representations of a Jonah who had been left unscathed—untouched in even a single hair on his head (see Luke 21.8)—by his sojourn within the cetacean. But too many other forces were at work in art, literature, and folklore for an alternative view not to make itself felt, as well as heard, seen, and read.

A parallel tradition of a hairless (and naked) Jonah is to be found in various medieval Jewish commentaries on the Bible.[107] Thus the standard *Midrash Tanhuma* (par. Toledot, section 12) states:

And Jonah rose up to flee to Tarshish from before the Lord and he went down to Joppa. Finally, He caused him to endure all the hardships and the fish swallowed him and he called to the Lord from the entrails of the fish, and finally the hair of his head was plucked along with his beard from the heat that he received in the entrails of the fish; and afterward he went off [on a mission] that was still not to his advantage.

Similarly, the midrashic anthology *Yalqut Shim'oni* reports in a gloss on Jonah 4:

Said the Holy One, Blessed Be He, to him [Jonah]: "Just as you have spared my glory and fled from Me to the sea, so have I spared your glory and saved you from the belly of the underworld and from the great heat that was in the fish's entrails." His clothes had been burned and his coat and his hair, and flies and insects and ants and fleas had spread over him and tortured him till he asked his soul to die, as it is said, "And he asked his soul to die" (Jonah 4.8).[108]

Compare the brief commentary of the "Midrash Jonah":

And because of the great heat that Jonah had in the entrails of the fish, his clothes were burned and all the hair of his body and his head, along with his beard, and flies and insects and ants and fleas were spread upon him and tortured him on all sides until he asked his soul to die, as it is said, "And he asked his soul to die." Hence the sages said: anyone who has it within his power to seek mercy on his fellow and does not so seek, or to bring him to repent and does not so bring him, will eventually come into great suffering.[109]

Taken together, the Midrashic evidence amply justifies the speculation that now-lost Jewish representations of a bald and naked Jonah or, even in the absence of such representations, at least Jewish verbal traditions influenced Byzantine painters in their portrayals of the prophet,[110] but theory and proof are of course two different matters. The scattered evidence suffices to encourage theorizing but not to prove any theory conclusively.

How, in any case, could Jewish traditions about the physical effects of Jonah's confinement within the great fish have wended their way to Letaldus, who has never been nominated for inclusion among the so-called Christian Hebraists, the select set of medieval Christian scholars with a working knowledge of Hebrew? The shortest answer would be to take Letal-

dus himself at his word that they came to him through oral tradition, but the fairer reply would be to hypothesize that he had at his disposal a rich brew of traditions, both oral and written—some quite local and nearly contemporary in origin; others from distant, ancient, and indirect sources. For already more than a millennium before Letaldus, stories about swallowings had been circulating among Mediterranean peoples, even among those with as little involvement in seafaring trades as the Jews of biblical times. Related stories can be tracked later in regions of Europe closer to Letaldus, whether because the stories traveled gradually northward from the Mediterranean with the growth of the Roman Empire and the advent of Christianity or because the arrival of writing technology permitted for the first time the recording of tales that had already existed in the northern regions.

Our ability to track definitively the movement of tales from people to people, mouth to mouth, and/or text to text will never suffice—at least where the Middle Ages are concerned—to achieve the pinpoint accuracy of a Global Positioning System. Take, for example, the anonymous, fifteenth-century Middle English sermon *Mirror for Priests* (*Speculum sacerdotale*). This sermon contains, in the midst of an otherwise unexceptionably orthodox account of Jonah, the observation that "owing to the heat of the fish all the hairs on his head were lost and fell off."[111] How the tradition of the bald Jonah reached this sermon writer is a mystery if we expect transmission to have taken place solely from written text to written text, especially from a presumptive Hebrew text to a vernacular English text—and particularly at a time when the Jewish population in England was restricted, to say the least. Here oral tradition seems one likely route (whether involving Jewish informants or not), perhaps in association with an awareness of a pictorial tradition.

Whatever the source or sources of inspiration, Jonah is already textually envisaged as being bald and naked by John the Deacon (825–80; sometimes called Johannes Hymmonides, since he was the son of Hymmo), who in the *Cena Cypriani* (his humorous account in rhythmic verse of the wedding of Cana) uses the epithet *caluus,* "bald," with Jonah twice, once along with the adjective *nudus* (naked) and in the context of a reference to his shipwreck, but in neither case with specific reference to the whale.[112] Meanwhile, in the Greek-speaking world, the nudity of Jonah upon his regurgitation from the whale was included in an anonymous sermon dated earlier than the eighth century, ascribed to pseudo-John Chrysostom.[113] How the paths of sources and influences intersected in these cases, as in so many others connected with tales of men and whales, has not been determined and probably never will be.

John the Deacon was far from the last Christian poet to breach Christian exegetic custom and let slip his acquaintance with the legendary bald

Jonah: the twelfth-century Archpoet tells of the whale that "spews out the poet-prophet who has been rendered bald" (vomet vatem decalvatum).[114] Also striking is the stage description that Jonah should be "bald, wearing an alb" (Ionas, caluus, alba indutus) when he appears in the *Feast of the Asses* (*Festum asinorum*), a fourteenth-century *Ordo Prophetarum* from the cathedral of Rouen; having him clad only in an alb could be as close an approximation to nudity as medieval staging would have allowed.[115]

If the holy man Jonah could take on contours of the hairless hero of the folktale, then there is no reason why the folktale hero could not assume features of Jonah and other holy men. Thus we should not be perturbed to find evidence that Letaldus felt *About a Certain Fisherman* to belong in the same class as his hagiographical prose writings. To him, both his poem of Within and his lives of saints were historical records attesting to the actuality of miracles.

Probably as long as there have been sailors, there have been wild stories about the creatures and adventures they have encountered during their voyages. Some of these reports have been true: the world is large, weather unpredictable, nature abundant and varied. But others have been so greatly embellished as to be preposterous. Baron von Münchhausen, "the baron of lies," had predecessors from millennia earlier. Although direct records of maritime lore from antiquity are limited, indirect evidence survives in books 9–12 of the *Odyssey*, where Odysseus relates his adventures with sea monsters and so forth. Satirists—such as Lucian (ca. 120–190 CE), who wrote in Greek, and Juvenal, who produced his Latin verse satires in the second and third decades of the second century CE—lambasted this part of the *Odyssey* for its unbelievability.[116] But Letaldus betrays no signs of sharing the satirists' contempt for his own unusual tale of a fisherman and the sea.

There are two categories of indications that Letaldus regarded the story of Within as the equivalent of an incident in the life of a saint. To begin with, he unfolded the story according to the procedure followed in his hagiographical works. As in the saints' lives, he established a historical and geographical context by emphasizing the setting of the story in postconversion England (9–16). Gradually narrowing the focus, he soon turned our gaze from the militarily and spiritually laudable inhabitants of England to an outstanding individual of Rochester, Within (17–20).[117] As in his hagiographical works, he stressed the veracity of the source who had supplied him his information (7–8).[118] In a final suggestion that the Within affair should be considered a historical matter, Letaldus posted near the beginning of the poem a quotation from Bede's *Ecclesiastic History of the English People* (*Historia ecclesiastica gentis Anglorum*).[119] His ostentatious connecting of the poem with a work in which English history is presented as a revela-

tion of Christianity was noticed later, for the scribe of one of the two man-
uscripts placed the poem directly after Bede's *Ecclesiastic History* and before
a metrical epitaph for a historically attested personage of the English
church, Lanfranc of Canterbury (ca. 1010–89).[120]

In the past, Letaldus has received high ratings as a historian for the ac-
curacy of his saints' lives.[121] He takes pains to seek out what he regards as
the best possible sources for information (*Liber miraculorum sancti Maxi-
mini,* prologue, *PL* 137.795C):[122] what he saw with his own eyes ("autopsy,"
813C); what he has heard from those, often old men, who were themselves
eyewitnesses to the events he describes (*Liber miraculorum sancti Maximini,*
chap. 16, 804A, 818C; *Miracula sancti Martini Vertavensis,* prologue)[123] or
who could at least provide reliable evidence of a tradition (810B, 784A); and
what he has read in texts, especially old documents (*Miracula sancti Eusicii,*
prologue, "ab antiquis schedulis exceptum" [drawn out from old leaves (of
parchment)]).[124] Others, the hagiographer declares, will engage in falsifica-
tion in order to promote their saints—but not Letaldus.[125] Yet despite this
apparent empiricism, Letaldus actively seeks out what he labels as "what I
am going to call a miracle."[126] He is obliged to make this search, since in his
framework of sanctity, the decisive characteristic of a holy life is, above all,
the miracles that happen before, during, and (especially) after it.[127] Thus he
shows himself to be as predisposed to accept miraculous occurrences in the
saints' lives as he is in the account of Within. The miracles in the saints' lives
carry a symbolic meaning of paramount importance, since miracles are
what lead to belief--the strengthening of credence in those who already be-
lieve, the inception of belief in those who have been nonbelievers.[128] As a re-
sult, the second means of proving the hagiographical quality of *About a Cer-
tain Fisherman* is to find similarities to it in Letaldus's handling of bona fide
miracles.

Although the story of Within seems "fantastic" to modern eyes, Letaldus
lived in an age when the biographies of saints were just as implausible by
today's standards. Saint Brendan, whose legendary travels were growing in
importance in the tenth century, was the first of several saints reputed to
have had confrontations with whales that masqueraded as islands.[129] Since
the events of the *Voyage of Saint Brendan* (*Navigatio sancti Brendani*), pre-
served in an eleventh-century manuscript but perhaps composed in the
ninth or early tenth century, were received with enthusiastic credulity, there
are no grounds for supposing that Letaldus could not have accepted the in-
cident of Within and the whale as true. In fact, Letaldus evinces in his
saints' lives—particularly in his handling of the miracles that they are sup-
posed to have performed posthumously—a ready belief in miracles that
were just as unusual as the swallowing of a man by a whale.

Just as Within kills a whale that is described as having serpentine characteristics (39), the saints in Letaldus's *Life of Saint Julian* (*Vita sancti Juliani*) and *Miracles of Saint Maximinus* (*Liber miraculorum sancti Maximini*) destroy snakes (792AB) and dragons (791CD, 799D, 818B). Just as Within comes forth startlingly hale and hearty from his imprisonment (186), the saints raise men who have died (*Vita Juliani,* passim)—even men who have been buried in an avalanche (817BC). Several of the wonders that Letaldus recounts in his saints' lives take place at sea or in rivers (810C–811B, 811D–813A), for Letaldus accepted the patristic scheme in which the ocean typified the world of danger through which God guides man (see 793C, 798A, 810BC).[130] What is more, the marvels that the saints perform in Letaldus's hagiography arouse the same awe that Within occasions as he issues from the whale. Letaldus often used identical language in his saints' lives and in *About a Certain Fisherman* to describe the aftermath of a miracle: the astonishment (cf. *About a Certain Fisherman* 186 and 202 with *PL* 137.785C), the crowds that gather (cf. 122–24, 137–38, and 175–78 with 787D, 788C, and 792B), the joy of parents and relatives (cf. 202–4 with 789D and 800D), and the quick return to normal life (cf. 205–8 with 801A).

In view of the equation that Letaldus draws between the episode in Within's life and a miracle in a saint's life or afterlife, *About a Certain Fisherman* appears ever less a simple "fantasy." On one level, the poem reveals a great boldness in not absorbing a story from oral literature directly into hagiography (as happened so often in the lives of the saints) but, rather, maintaining within an ornate Latin poem the unpretentious actors and stage of an oral story. On a different level, the poem is stunning in verifying the possibility that miracles, although they occur seldom, can still take place in real life. Letaldus embraces this doctrine in his *Book of Miracles of Saint Maximin* (*Liber miraculorum sancti Maximini*), his major contribution to the vogue for "books of miracles" that evidenced itself in the tenth and eleventh centuries:[131] "Because even though those performing miracles are rare nowadays, all the same there are many in the holy church who by virtue of their lives are not unequal to the miracle-workers."[132] Thus, through the tale of Within, the tenth-century poet disproves once again the mocking objection of pagans (which had evidently occasioned discomfort to both Jerome and Augustine) that the miracle in the book of Jonah is inconceivable, that a man cannot live through three days in the belly of a whale.[133] By sweeping away disbelief of Jonah, Letaldus simultaneously confirms the validity of Christ's resurrection, for Jonah's encounter with the great fish was almost universally interpreted as referring to Christ's three days of death and subsequent liberation. The resurrection of Christ inspired fear, surprise, and utter disbelief, all of which make more understandable why Within's tri-

umph over the whale is greeted first by exorcism and only later by approving marvel.

One part of Letaldus's ingenuity lies, then, not in inventing a story or fashioning a mock epic from a fairy tale but in amplifying an age-old folktale with a threefold learned solemnity: the language of classical Latin epic, the typological framework of biblical commentaries on Jonah, and the faith in miracles of hagiography. Another part of Letaldus's talent consists in retaining intact the aspects of the folktale that an inferior poet would have suppressed or modified.[134] To cite only two examples, Within toils within the whale for four days and five nights rather than the three days expected from the book of Jonah, and he saves himself through his own craft rather than through invocation of God or saints.[135]

An old theory holds that fairy tales are myths that have decayed and lost their meaning and sanctity. No such explanation can account for all of the stories: they have arisen in too many places at too many times and satisfied too many audiences for any one theory to account for their nature or existence. Furthermore, it would be rash to construe the tale of Within first and foremost as an initiation myth that has lost its original, pre-Christian religious signification.[136] Yet the particular tale that Letaldus related, with its ties to a book of the Bible, to a famous piece of animal allegory in the *Physiologus* and bestiary, and to remnants of Greek and Roman myth, has mythic undercurrents that lend it a very special power. By drawing on this tale, Letaldus, for all his air of light-headed and uncomplicated wittiness, demonstrated spectacularly a serious streak that enabled him to make the most of both folklore and learned lore.

Letaldus had, as his contemporary and friend Abbo of Fleury (ca. 940–1005) rightly claimed, "one-of-a-kind knowledge."[137] Just about when Letaldus undertook his first hagiographical work (on Maximin), Abbo went to England (985–87) to serve as *magister* of the school at the abbey of Ramsey; he could have been a conduit, either direct or indirect, for Letaldus's knowledge of an oral tradition about a man swallowed by a whale. Regardless of the truth about this hypothesis, Abbo's judgment of Letaldus's erudition was apt. In the case of *About a Certain Fisherman,* Letaldus showed himself to be singular among his contemporaries by virtue of his ambition to take an oral folktale and reshape it—despite (or maybe because of?) its fantastic elements—within the ambit of the Latin epic tradition, all the while attempting to reconcile it with the more familiar miracles of the Bible and hagiography.

Although Letaldus's effort was probably the most ambitious that has survived between antiquity and his day since the Cupid and Psyche episode in Apuleius's *Metamorphoses,* it was not the last. Authors were only beginning

their quest to convey stories from elsewhere into the written tradition associated with Latin. But they had to find justifications and audiences, and they had to devise forms to accommodate material that had been in many ways anathema within classic literature. Letaldus brought his adaptation of an oral folktale to a fairy-tale conclusion, in which his hero, after travails from which he is miraculously saved, lives happily ever after.

> Then Within returns to his own hearth and his domestic quarters, distinguished by gifts and rich booty. Living happy days over a long, long period of time, he deservedly returned to the attractiveness of his former good looks. (205–8)

Yet Letaldus presents his story not as a fairy tale but, rather, as another genre of oral narrative—as legend. In effect, he attempts to pass off a folktale as a legend and to justify this effort by aligning his tale with sacred legend. Ancient myths of heroes who freed the innocent (especially damsels) from monsters had insinuated themselves into the wilder reaches of sacred legend in apocrypha and hagiography, in stories of St. George and the dragon or St. Michael.[138] Letaldus's achievement was to do the same for the swallowing story that had probably always existed in a parallel universe to that of Jonah. What Letaldus accomplished was spectacular, as a manifestation of a growing fascination with oral literature and of a willingness to test the decorum of classical verse forms by using them for unclassical folk literature.

But Letaldus's accomplishment was not yet a full step into the enchanted world of folktale and fairy tale. Within a few decades of him emerged another Latin poet, readier still to confront the fresh possibilities of oral folktales, but still groping for the most appropriate and appealing literary expression of such new forms. One tale to which Egbert of Liège gravitated, discussed in chapter 3, bears resemblances in its dramatis personae to the tale of Little Red Riding Hood, and like the poem by Letaldus, it represents an attempt to accommodate the wonder and magic of oral literature within a language and a literary tradition that had been honed to serve very different, often even antithetical, purposes.

A Cautionary Tale

Little Red Riding Hood in the 1020s

The tale of Little Red Ridinghood is remarkable both for its extraordinary popularity, and for the fact that no version of the story has been found prior to Perrault's manuscript of 1695.[1]

It is disputed whether Egbert of Liège transmits an early form of the Little Red Riding Hood fairy tale (AT 333).[2]

All knowledge is partial, and the scholarship devoted to "Little Red Riding Hood" demonstrates this again and again.[3]

LITTLE RED RIDING HOOD AND THE EXCLUSION OF THE LITERARY IN FOLKLORISTICS

It has been said that Little Red Riding Hood (known in the earliest French version as *Le petit chaperon rouge,* in the Grimms' tale as *Rotkäppchen*) "is a fairy tale figure as meaningful and widespread as almost no other": "She is the only peasant girl who can claim to be a favorite on a par with famous princesses, and she has been analyzed, modified, parodied, and caricatured as only the Frog Prince has been."[4] She has been drafted into service in most

93

imaginable genres, including not only literature but also music, film, advertising, cartoons, and pornography.[5] Yet despite all the notoriety that has been accorded to this one little girl (admittedly dressed in an attention-grabbing color), her background has a historic dimension that continues to be overlooked. Little Red Riding Hood has a past, a medieval past, that will be explored in this chapter.

One vivid description of folktale research, still applicable although more than a half century old, reads, "Folktale study is like a desert journey, where the only landmarks are the bleached bones of earlier theories."[6] Because theories have proven to be ephemeral in comparison with the tales themselves (although which are more entertaining remains debatable), it might seem prudent to place more stock in the tales and less in the theories or at least to take an eclectic approach toward theorizing so as to hedge bets; but not all contemporary scholars of folktales diversify their theoretical portfolios more than their predecessors did fifty years ago. For example, in *Little Red Riding Hood: A Casebook,* the late Alan Dundes (1934–2005), one of the most influential and productive American folklorists in the second half of the twentieth century, adduced no material dated from before 1697 that is related to the tale of Little Red Riding Hood but (or *and*) managed nonetheless to question sharply the very notion of valuing early written evidence. By scrutinizing a short Latin poem written in the first quarter of the eleventh century, I hope to argue against such dismissal of literary evidence and to underscore the pertinence of studying medieval literature in coming to grips with that beautiful and elusive phenomenon to which English speakers give the name *fairy tale.*

Doubts about literary remains are deeply entrenched in folkloristics.[7] Since its inception as an independent field of study, folklore studies has commonly been the battleground of two factions.[8] One faction comprises literary folklorists, who have focused on folklore in, and through, literature. The other is composed of anthropological folklorists, who have been committed to studying folklore in its cultural context. Fortunately, the lines between the two factions have never been absolute, and prominent members of both have made reasonable proclamations about the need for cooperation; but the distinctions between the two show no signs of disappearing, and it seems that few literary or anthropological folklorists can forbear claiming primacy for their disciplines and materials in attaining a true understanding of folklore.

There is an irony in the fact that the doubts about the value of literary evidence in folkloristics received their fullest and most enduring articulation in the writings of the so-called Finnish school, practitioners of which "seek to reconstruct the history of a tale by tracing, collecting and catego-

rizing all its variants."⁹ The preeminent representative in America of the Finnish historical-geographical method in folktale analysis was Stith Thompson, who received his graduate training from one of the foremost early literary folklorists and who himself advocated careful study of the mutual influence between written and oral tradition.¹⁰ Although to many people in this postmodern age, the very project of reconstruction has become suspect, the reconstructive ambitions of the Finnish school trouble me far less than the prejudice against written evidence that it has sometimes fostered: "all scholars admit some transmission by literature and some by oral variants, but different ones set the proportionate amounts of oral and literary influence at different levels. The Finnish School . . . give[s] the preponderant influence to oral tradition."¹¹ A folklorist trained by Stith Thompson stated the case with specific reference to fairy tale:

> The goal of the Finnish method of research is to discover the complete life-history of a *Märchen*. As a working hypothesis, its workers assume that most motifs originally belonged to particular *Märchen* and then passed over into others. To find this *Urmärchen*, they study very many variants of the oral tale. They hold certain literary documents to be superfluous, such as those the oral sources of which are preserved and those which are copies, translations, or reworkings of older documents.¹²

As will be seen, in the hands of some scholars, the first recordings of the oral sources are even permitted to postdate by centuries the literary documents to which they relate and that they eclipse.

The preference of the Finnish school for oral over literary has not won universal applause among folklorists in either the Old World or the New, but the dissent has taken the form of sporadic guerilla warfare by individual scholars rather than systematic opposition by a well-defined "school." In the first half of this century, the most forceful objections emanated from Albert Wesselski, who challenged proponents of the Finnish method "to abandon their practice of examining oral variants of a not far distant past time and to find and examine old documents"; he asserted "that many of their apparently successful studies would, under such a test, have resulted in failure."¹³ Wesselski remains an estimable figure, both for his energetic reconnoitering of medieval evidence and for his lucid framing of commonsensical objections to the Finnish method; but his quest was doomed to be quixotic, in part because it began at a time when the role of literary scholars in the field of folkloristics was dwindling.

Since Wesselski, relatively few philologists have taken an interest in the

squabble; and among the more numerous literary historians and critics, peace has been bought by (perhaps wisely) begging the question. For example, Jack Zipes, the most prolific of Anglophone (or Anglograph) literary critics to write on fairy tale, carefully sidesteps the controversy by differentiating between folktale as oral and fairy tale as literary. Three quotations illustrate his solution. First, he maintains that whereas folktale "has its roots in the experience and fantasy of primitive peoples who cultivated the tale in an oral tradition," the literary fairy tale "has assumed a variety of distinct and unique forms since the late Middle Ages."[14] Second, he notes that "[j]ust a superficial glance back into history will tell us that fairy tales have been in existence as *oral folk tales* for thousands of years and first became what we call *literary fairy tales* toward the end of the seventeenth century."[15] Third, he argues, "Clearly, fairy tale refers to the *literary* production of tales *adapted* by bourgeois or aristocratic writers in the seventeenth and eighteenth centuries . . . , and the nature of the author's social class, which must be studied in detail, added a new dimension to the folk tale as it was transformed into the fairy tale."[16] Zipes's distinction between folktale and fairy tale works well in the modern period, but it has the unforeseen and no doubt unintended consequence of consigning medieval texts to a limbo, since they are too early to qualify as literary fairy tales but too literary to pass as oral.[17]

Is it advantageous for folklorists and literary scholars alike to develop rationales for disregarding each other's materials and findings, the one group because they deem the evidence superfluous, the other because they scorn it as being primitive? Despite being an old chestnut, the question of the relation between oral and written forms must remain alive, just as ever new formulas for a modus vivendi between the students of oral folklore and philology must be devised. Oral folklore and literary production are often interdependent, as are the scholars who have expertise in these two fields of study.[18] I will return to these issues after wandering through the primeval—or, rather, medieval—forest in search of Little Red Riding Hood and the wolf.

EARLY LITERARY VERSIONS OF "LITTLE RED RIDING HOOD"

The main early records for "Little Red Riding Hood" come in two literary versions. The first is "Le petit chaperon rouge," published in 1697 by Charles Perrault (1628–1703) under the name of his son (P. D'Armancour, who was supposedly only ten but in fact turned seventeen in the year when the manuscript was produced [1695] and was almost nineteen at the time of publication), in a book entitled *Stories of Tales of Bygone Times* (*Histoires ou*

contes du temps passé) and subtitled *Tales of My Mother Goose* (*Contes de ma Mère l'Oye*). The second is "Little Red Cap" ("Rotkäppchen"), published in 1812 by the Brothers Grimm in the first volume of the first edition of their *KHM*. Of markedly less value to folklorists is the 1800 drama *Tragedy of the Life and Death of Little Red Riding Hood* (*Tragödie vom Leben und Tod des kleinen Rotkäppchens*), by Ludwig Tieck (1773–1853).

What weight should we attach to these works of literature as versions of "Little Red Riding Hood?" Alan Dundes left no room for doubt that he preferred oral over written versions. Indeed, in his foreword to his casebook on the tale, he criticized even Antti Aarne and Stith Thompson for their failures to set proper priorities in this regard. According to him, their typing of the tale relied too heavily on Perrault and the Grimms without attending to "*authentic oral versions* of the tale which reveal important details not contained in either Perrault's or the Grimms' accounts." He added: "One of the aims of the present casebook is to demonstrate the nature of the oral folktale from which the Perrault and Grimm versions of the story surely derive."[19] In an essay later in his casebook, Dundes solidified his position: "It is well to keep in mind that fairy tales are first and foremost an *oral* form. So from that point of view, any written version is suspect."[20] His avowed goal was "to illustrate the pitfalls of relying too heavily upon literary, derivative, and bowdlerized renderings of what are wrongly believed to be authentic folktales by considering the case of 'Little Red Riding Hood' (AT 333)."[21]

As these proclamations indicate, Dundes assumed a nearly automatic equivalence: oral versions of fairy tales are presumed to be authentic, written ones most likely inauthentic. He held that disparities between the earlier written versions and certifiably oral versions indicate that the written versions are automatically less trustworthy. His position was exactly opposite (not by coincidence) to that of two literary scholars who averred,

> it is clear that the story of Red Riding Hood has never circulated widely where folk tales are learned orally; practically all versions are based upon Perrault's tale or on that of the Brothers Grimm.[22]

Does either sort of extremism lead to a greater understanding of "Little Red Riding Hood" or, for that matter, of many other tales? In the current state of scholarship, no one would contend that any extant early literary version of "Little Red Riding Hood" represents an accurate transcription of an oral tale; no one would dispute Dundes's contentions that Perrault's tale is a "highly stylized literary retelling";[23] and no one would maintain any longer that the tales of the *KHM* can be considered unadulterated folklore as they once were.

In the case of "Little Red Cap" ("Rotkäppchen"), the Brothers Grimm,

far from being protoscientists of folklore, reworked a tale that they had received from tellers who were anything but illiterate, culturally isolated German peasants. Their informants were Jeanette (Johanna Isabella) and Marie Hassenpflug, highly educated members of a Hugenot family who knew and used stories by Perrault. Jeanette (1791–1860) was twenty-one years old in the fall of 1812 when she furnished Wilhelm with a version based on recollection of the Perrault tale. Her older sister Marie (1788–1856) gave them another version, this one believed to have been based on French oral tradition, which was published as a supplement to the first version in the first edition. Yet we can accept restrictions on the proximity of both Perrault and the Brothers Grimm to oral tradition without needing to deny that both literary versions derive many characteristics from tales that had circulated for centuries before being written down: a folktale does not cease to be a folktale merely because it has been transferred and adapted from an oral to a written medium.[24] In describing the interrelationship of these tales, we are not confined to a harsh dichotomy between literary and oral. As one early commentator on the German *Volksmärchen* summed up, "[t]he relationship between literature and folktale is not a relationship of unilateral dependency."[25] Since the invention of writing, there has been no hard and fast boundary between oral and written: folklore has filtered in and out of literature, literature in and out of folklore.[26] Consequently, under many circumstances and especially under circumstances that involve the multifarious transitional texts and cultures of the Middle Ages, literary historians must work with folklore, folklorists with literature.

Before adopting any general policy, we must evaluate carefully the minutiae of the given tale under examination.[27] Because whatever versions we have at our disposal will have their special textures, the proof in any individual case will be in the telling. As a matter of policy, students of the folktale cannot afford the luxury of bigotry against chronologically far-removed written versions any more than against the records of geographically distant cultures. Just because the ethnographic standards of another time or place differ from our own, we do not need to reject every record produced by that time or place. Granted, we have no direct access to the storytellers of older times. This concession does not mean that we should discount what we do have that is written. Rather, it suggests that we should handle with proper care that which survives.[28]

A middle position that embraces the utility of older written evidence runs counter to the vintage Finnish method as it was refined by Dundes.

In order to understand just how atypical both the Perrault and the Grimm versions of "Little Red Riding Hood" really are, in compari-

son with the original folktale from which they surely derive, one needs to have two important sets of data. First, it is critical to have some idea of what the original oral tale was like. Second, one should be aware of the fact that a probable cognate of the tale is widely distributed in China, Japan, and Korea. It is sad to report that most of the scholars who have written at length about "Little Red Riding Hood" were not in possession of these two crucial data sets. For the most part, the vital information was known to only a few specialists in folktale studies.[29]

Dundes's procedure led to a readily apparent circularity. As a first set of data, he urged us to consider what the original tale was like. But since he dismissed the versions of Perrault and the Grimms as unreliable and since he did not acknowledge the existence of written records for an earlier version, he had no choice but to reconstruct the original tale on the basis of two bodies of much later material. One corpus comprises late nineteenth-century and twentieth-century French versions, especially an 1885 version that folklorists tend somewhat anachronistically to revere as the ancestor of Perrault's seventeenth-century tale.[30] The other encompasses the non-European material to which Dundes referred as his second set of data—material that is both chronologically and geographically distant from Perrault and the Brothers Grimm.

After presenting abbreviated summaries of Chinese, Japanese, and Korean traditions, Dundes concluded that "it should be obvious that the Perrault literary reworking of AT 333 is far from being the most typical version of the tale type."[31] But if one's scope is European—and there is no reason not to have a Eurocentric scope in this case, since Dundes did not argue that Perrault worked within a Chinese, Japanese, or Korean tradition—then perhaps the Perrault tale becomes more typical of "Little Red Riding Hood" as the average Westerner knows it.[32] Indeed, if we opt not to exclude evidence from an older European context, we can find a piece of neglected evidence that helps clarify otherwise baffling aspects of Perrault and the Brothers Grimm. In so doing, we can follow, although not in the sense in which it was intended, the directive with which Dundes capped his introduction.

In future studies of this or other folktales, the reader may realize the importance of consulting all available versions of the tale rather than unnecessarily and arbitrarily limiting the scope of investigation to one or two standard literary versions no matter how important the intellectual niche such literary versions may occupy in Western civilization.[33]

All available evidence should include, besides standard literary versions, not just oral versions but also nonstandard literary versions—literary versions that have been overlooked or accorded insufficient attention.

Since the Finnish school acquired ascendancy in folktale analysis early in this century, common wisdom has held that no traces of "Little Red Riding Hood" survive from before Perrault. In an authoritative study of Perrault that appeared in 1968, Marc Soriano asserted categorically: "This time, no hesitation is possible: the text that we are studying comes directly from oral literature. Before 1697 it never grazed the surface of written literature."[34] In a more recent appraisal of Perrault's sources, Jeanne Morgan betrays equal certainty on this score: "*Le Petit Chaperon rouge* has no known sources or parallels whatsoever. We have only Perrault's word for it that they are indeed 'Contes du temps passé,' in the Preface's allusion to stories 'que nos aïeux ont inventés' [that our ancestors invented]."[35] The complete gap in early literary evidence is all the more surprising in view of the widespread conviction that the number of independent oral folktales with the main elements of "Little Red Riding Hood" attests to a thriving oral tradition in France, probably long before Perrault's version.[36]

EGBERT OF LIÈGE'S "LITTLE RED CAP AND THE YOUNG WOLVES"

Despite the common wisdom, there is a parallel that has been known to philologists since the late nineteenth century, that was even dubbed "Little Red Cap and the Young Wolves" ("Rothkäppchen und die jungen Wölfe") by its first and only editor,[37] and that was quoted in toto in the authoritative source study of the *KHM* that was published in 1913.[38] But the extent of its relevance was never fully appreciated. Whether or not all readers will concur that these few Latin verses are even remotely akin to the later versions that were foundational in written literature, probably most will be astonished that they have not received even passing mention or bibliographic citation in any English-language scholarship on "Little Red Riding Hood" over the past half century.[39]

The Latin verses appear within an extensive poem entitled *The Richly Laden Ship* (*Fecunda ratis*). This verse schoolbook was completed between 1022 and 1024 by Egbert of Liège. A teacher of the trivium (grammar, rhetoric, and dialectic) at the cathedral school of Liège (today in eastern Belgium), Egbert composed *The Richly Laden Ship* for his pupils, dividing its 2,373 unrhymed hexameter verses into two books. In a paroxysm of schoolmasterly inspiration, he entitled the two books respectively the

Prora ("prow" or "bow"; comprising 1,768 lines) and the *Puppis* ("poop-deck" or "afterdeck"; comprising 605 lines). Just as all of creation was loaded two by two onto Noah's ark, so the fundamental elements of learning were supposedly conveyed in the intellectual microcosm of *The Richly Laden Ship*.

The *Prora* encompasses five sections: a prologue (1.1–4), one concatenation of one-line proverbs and sententiae (1.5–596), another of two-line proverbs and sententiae (1.597–1004), an epilogue (1.1005–8), and a medley (added in a second redaction) of longer pieces of fable, satire, and admonition (1.1009–1768). Whereas the *Prora* has a pedagogic bias, the *Puppis* is largely catechistic, with the accent on moral instruction based on the Bible and church fathers (2.1–605). Although *The Richly Laden Ship* is extant in only one manuscript (Cologne, Erzbischöfliche Diözesanbibliothek, Dombibliothek codex 196, 11th century, fols. 1r–63r), the sorts of glosses with which it was outfitted by two of the twelve scribes who participated in its production presuppose that it was employed in schooling.[40] Egbert probably envisaged it as an early eleventh-century competitor for two of the standard primers in the basic school syllabus, namely, the *Distichs of Cato* and the fables of Romulus (in prose) or Avian (in verse).[41]

The Richly Laden Ship has been called "a treasure trove for students of medieval folklore."[42] Although Egbert drew extensively on the Bible and patristic writings, he also relied heavily, by his own admission, on the rich oral traditions that circulated in his region, a border zone between Germanic and Romance language and culture groups. He incorporated into his poem many Latin translations of vernacular proverbs.[43] Because many of the proverbs originated among uneducated countryfolk, Sigebert of Gembloux (ca. 1030–1112) referred to the poem as a book "in metrical style about the sayings of peasants."[44]

In dedicating the poem to his erstwhile schoolmate Bishop Adalbold of Utrecht (ca. 970–1026), Egbert discussed his sources in oral tradition and set forth his pedagogic purpose in exploiting them. As one passage in this dedication makes apparent, Egbert saw oral tradition as a precious resource in teaching, because it was at once familiar from everyday speech in the native language and yet novel when written in the learned language.

> In common speech many people often say many things, and that popular wisdom is expressed in numerous exempla, which are essential to use; I drew upon this material, in the belief that numerous useful things are found in it, and if in some way the clear insights could be retained, they would make neglectful students into attentive listeners

(since they had been written down nowhere, they would be preserved in a more mindful heart). For this reason I gathered into only two little books those things, which I was able to recall over many hours by day and night, committing them to single verses, often to two verses, sometimes to three—as you will see, written in order of length—moreover interlarding some new and popular stories with a few theological matters.[45]

Egbert's rationale for resorting to oral tradition resembles that of ancient grammarians and rhetoricians who commented on the importance of fables in elementary education.[46] Quintilian (ca. 35–ca. 90/100 CE), an ancient author who is unlikely to have been known to Egbert but whose views are typical of the school tradition, noted the value of fables in weaning young children from the nursery tales to which they are exposed before entering grammar school.

> Therefore let pupils learn to paraphrase Aesop's fables, which follow closely upon the stories of the nursery, in plain and unexcessive language; and thereafter to effect the same simplicity of style in writing. [Let them learn] to resolve metrical verses [into prose], next to convey its meaning while changing the words, and then to reshape it more freely in a paraphrase; in this it is permitted both to abridge and to elaborate, so long as the poet's meaning remains intact. This task is difficult even for polished instructors, and the person who handles it well will be qualified to learn anything.[47]

Both Quintilian and Egbert appreciated the advantages of (to resort to terminology that has been in vogue in recent decades) appropriating "low culture" in the early stages of training children in the elements of "high culture."

But whatever he professed in the preface to Adalbold, Egbert obviously did not measure up to a folklore collector in a twentieth-century or twenty-first-century sense, and it would be wrongheaded to judge him so. Most important for our purposes, his terse telling in the *Puppis* (in the forty-eighth of sixty-two episodes) of the story "About a Girl Saved from Wolf Cubs" ("De puella a lupellis seruata") is in a Latin verse form that bears no marks of an oral storytelling. The modern versions of the tale, whether "book tales," literary fairy tales, or oral folktales, revolve around repetition and dialogue (first between the mother and the girl and later between the wolf and the girl); in contrast, the Latin poem is stenographic and contains only one cameo of a speech.

"De puella a lupellis seruata."

Quod refero, mecum pagenses dicere norunt,

2 Et non tam mirum quam ualde est credere uerum:
Quidam suscepit sacro de fonte puellam,

4 Cui dedit et tunicam rubicundo uellere textam; 475
Quinquagesima sancta fuit babtismatis huius.

6 Sole sub exorto quinquennis facta puella
Progreditur, uagabunda sui inmemor atque pericli,

8 Quam lupus inuadens siluestria lustra petiuit
Et catulis predam tulit atque reliquit edendam. 480

10 Qui simul aggressi, cum iam lacerare nequirent,
Ceperunt mulcere caput feritate remota.

12 "Hanc tunicam, mures, nolite," infantula dixit,
"Scindere, quam dedit excipiens de fonte patrinus!"

14 Mitigat inmites animos deus, auctor eorum.[48] 485

["About a Girl Saved from Wolf Cubs"[49]

What I have to relate, country folk can tell along with me,

2 and it is not so much marvelous as it is quite true to believe.
A certain man took up a girl from the sacred font

4 and gave her a tunic woven of red wool;
sacred Pentecost was [the day] of her baptism.

6 The girl, now five years old, goes out[50]
at sunrise, footloose and heedless of her peril.

8 A wolf attacked her, went to its woodland lair,
took her as booty to its cubs, and left her to be eaten.

10 They approached her at once and, since they were unable to harm her,
began, free from all their ferocity, to caress her head.[51]

12 "Do not damage this tunic, mice," the lisping little girl said,
"which my godfather gave me when he took me from the font!"

14 God, their creator, soothes untame souls.]

The differences between Egbert's fourteen hexameters and an oral folktale are indisputable: Egbert's poem is written in the cramped style that typifies *The Richly Laden Ship*,[52] whereas the folktale is oral; Egbert's poem constitutes a permanent lasting text, the folktale a onetime performance; Egbert's poem is for the classroom, the folktale for another sort of social occasion (at which we cannot even hazard a guess). Thus, when Egbert claims that country folk (*pagenses*) can tell the story along with him, he means that they

can do so at the very least in a different language and style. These are major *mutata mutanda*. The educated men of the early modern and Romantic periods saw gulfs of different sorts opening between their own cultures and those of the humble folk, and they viewed the stories, songs, and other cultural expressions of the humble folk as worthy of collection.[53] The motives of medieval recorders of popular culture differed very much. But despite these necessary caveats against anachronistically construing Egbert's aims and results, he remains a folklore collector of the only sort who could have been encountered around the millennium, that is, a male member of the literate class who, to indoctrinate youths, drew on material that had currency among common people.

When evaluating any written text that purports to present a version of an oral tale, the reader must gauge the reliability of the sources and the treatment or use of them. Let us begin with the issue of authenticity. In the case of Egbert's "About a Girl Saved from Wolf Cubs," we have two grounds for judgment: (1) Egbert's avowal to Adalbold in the preface that he used popular traditions and (2) his profession in the first line of the poem that peasants tell the same story. The latter statement admits, albeit obliquely, that Egbert owed a debt to popular sources.[54] Although it is possible that Egbert was lying in the first line of the poem, he would have gained nothing from his audience by so doing. On the contrary, he would have undermined his authority as a teacher, since the boys in his classroom would have realized immediately if the story had not been popular.

The real issue is not authenticity but, rather, the sort of authenticity—not whether or not Egbert appropriated from the peasants, but what he took from them and what he did with it. For all his candor about sources, Egbert turns reticent when it comes to the modifications he introduced. Granted, he altered the style of any prior telling when he translated it into Latin. Did he make equally substantial changes in the content of the story? For want of any unadulterated "peasant version," this question cannot be answered fully; but we can say that he had to have been sufficiently faithful to the folktale for the story still to have been recognizable to his audience. For instance, we can infer that the "original" featured a little girl, for otherwise Egbert would have been free to make the protagonist a little boy—surely a casting that would have made sense for his male audience if they had not been acquainted beforehand with the story in a form that had a girl as the protagonist.

CHRISTIAN IMPLICATIONS OF EGBERT'S TELLING

Sometimes it is posited that the literary fairy tales written in the seventeenth and later centuries "not only obliterated the original folk perspective and rein-

terpreted the experience of the people for them but also endowed the contents with a new ideology."⁵⁵ If, more than a half millennium earlier, Egbert imposed an ideology on a folktale, the ideology would have been that of his literate ecclesiastic culture. In this case, Egbert's version would be an attempt not to re-create an oral folktale in Latin but, rather, to tease out a religiously useful message from the narrative. How easily a Christian ideology can be imprinted on folktales can be seen in twentieth-century adaptations and interpretations of the Grimms' version of "Little Red Riding Hood" by evangelical Christians and anthroposophists. For instance, in one short religious pamphlet, the beginning of the story "is used to tell young children how to avoid the wolf, who is no longer the sexual seducer but rather the Devil himself."

> This short religious pamphlet seeks to point out the dangers of a lack of faith. From the original tale the children were supposed to learn to listen to their mother and to avoid the evil wolf, and it is an easy step to have the wolf represent the Devil and to teach that faith alone can overcome this dangerous enemy.⁵⁶

Such interpretations have jarred on the ears of modern-day academics. Thus, for instance, Dundes characterized the anthroposophical interpretations as "one of the most curious sets of folktale interpretations of all those proposed."⁵⁷ He accorded little space to them, even in comparison with other interpretations with which he disagreed. His resistance to religious interpretations of the tale is noteworthy for two reasons. One is that future generations might find readings generated in our own times just as quaint and dated as the Christian interpretations of earlier times. Is it more bizarre to construe the story as revealing the dangers of the Devil than to follow Michel Foucault (1926–84), who saw "Little Red Riding Hood" as undergoing a "pedagogization of children's sex" as part of a two-century-long war against onanism, or Erich Fromm (1900–1980), who did not hesitate a moment in his Freudian dissection of the story: "Most of the symbolism in this fairy tale can be understood without difficulty. The 'little cap of red velvet' is a symbol of menstruation. The little girl of whose adventures we hear has become a mature woman and is now confronted with the problem of sex"?⁵⁸ It seems fruitless to press these stories for one overarching meaning or to seek any one interpretation that will pertain to all different versions of the story, since each telling can have its own meaning and can demand its own interpretation. Through their very elasticity, fairy tales incite interpretation. Their story lines, both meaningfully pellucid and bafflingly indeterminate, bring out allegorizing tendencies among critics, who strive to fabricate interpretative templates that will be equally valid for all fairy tales.

The other reason for taking note of Dundes's ambivalence toward religious interpretations is that it sheds light on the reluctance of folklorists to give Egbert's poem its due. There seems to be a tacit assumption that a fairy tale version with religious implications could not be "original," that a non-religious folktale is presumably more truly "popular" than a religious one. When the poem has been discussed, either it has been classed as a Christian legend and therefore unrelated to fairy tale, or else its Christian elements have been silently elided, with ensuing damage to its integrity.

What is Christian in Egbert's poem? A first glimpse of Christianization would be in the second line, as Egbert protests that his story is a real miracle and not a fantasy. In this sense, the incident he recounts resembles "numerous hagiographical narratives which portray saintly figures taming a wolf, such as Saint Mungo, bishop of Glasgow, in the sixth century, Saint Austreberthe, Abbess of the Monastery of Parilly in Normandy, who died in 703, Saint Théogonnic, Saint Malo, Saint Hervé, etc."[59] In the words of Hans Robert Jauss (1921–97), "the marvelous in the medieval tale of 'Little Red Riding Hood' is still wholly bound to the supernatural of Christian legend."[60] But it may be an exaggeration to call the marvelous in Egbert's poem "wholly bound to the supernatural of Christian legend." In the very next line of his poem, Egbert perhaps guides us into the indeterminacy of "once upon a time" with the pointed vagueness of the word *quidam* (a certain man). Other less arguably Christian traits are the signaling of baptism in the third, fifth, and thirteenth lines and the moralization in the fourteenth line. The fourteenth line can be omitted without damage to the story, although its excision would deprive the poem of its culminating ambiguity; who is to say whether the untame souls are those of the wolves who menace the girl or those of the baptized, who are brought through the sacrament from an animal into a human state? Apart from the fourteenth line, none of the lines in which baptism is mentioned overtly can be left out without harming the logic of the narrative. Thus the heart of the miraculous truth that Egbert discerns in the story is that no matter how young and helpless the person, no matter how fierce the danger, baptism has the power to protect. With such a message, the story would have made an ideal exemplum in preaching to persuade peasants to accept baptism for their young children. When Egbert wrote, clergy were growing concerned over the souls of infants who died. Because they had not yet progressed to urging the baptism of newborns (canon law permitted the celebration of the sacrament only on the vigils of Easter and Pentecost, except to those in extremis), they must have felt pressure to convince peasants to bring their infants for baptism at the first possible Easter or Pentecost.[61] Whether or not the story ever served as an exemplum, the salience of such features as the godfather, bap-

tism, baptismal gift, and Pentecost justifies the experiment of reading it in Christian terms.

EGBERT'S POEM AND POSSIBLE ANALOGUES

To date, Egbert's poem has been analyzed mainly in accordance with the principles of folklore motif studies, to demonstrate whether or not it belongs to the same complex of stories as the later "Little Red Riding Hood." The story recounted by Perrault and the Brothers Grimm was schematized first by folklorists as follows (AT 333 The Glutton, now ATU Little Red Riding Hood [with a new analysis]):

1. Wolf's Feast. (a) By masking as mother or grandmother, the wolf deceives and devours (b) a little girl (Red Riding Hood) whom he meets on his way to her grandmother's.
2. Rescue. (a) The wolf is cut open and his victims rescued alive; (b) his belly is sewed full of stones and he drowns; (c) he jumps to his death.

A more detailed schema was elaborated by Marianne Rumpf (1921–98), who saw the bare essentials of the story as being the gifts brought by the girl to the grandmother, the encounter with the wolf, the wolf's presence at the grandmother's, the cannibalism, and the questions of the girl to the swallower (about the ears, eyes, nose, teeth, and mouth of the supposed "grandma").[62] Rumpf assigns to her two-page examination of Egbert's story the quizzical caption "The Story in Egbert of Liège's *Fecunda ratis:* An Ur-Form of Little Red Riding Hood?"[63] On the basis of her analysis, Rumpf maintains that Egbert's poem is most definitely not a medieval anticipation of "Little Red Riding Hood" (AT 333), since it lacks the constitutive cannibalistic motif (the swallowing of the grandmother and Little Red Riding Hood by the wolf) and other essential motifs.

If Egbert's poem is not connected with "Little Red Riding Hood," then what is it? In one attempt to resolve this question, Rumpf relates the eleventh-century verses to stories about wolf children.[64] An ancient example would be Romulus and Remus; a more modern, but still exotic, one is Mowgli. The motif is one in which a child who has been carried off by a wild animal grows up and is later saved. Egbert would surely have known the legend that the twin founders of Rome were tended and suckled by a she-wolf when they washed ashore after having been thrown into a river, but similar stories with other protagonists are also widely attested. The most important parallel in medieval Germanic tradition is Wolfdietrich, hero of

the eponymous epic *Wolfdietrich* (ca. 1230), who received his name after being unharmed when left alone as an infant among wolves.[65] An analogue in medieval Irish tradition is the story of Cormac's birth.[66] Last but not least, hagiography contains a number of instances in which future saints are saved from death by exposure when she-wolves adopt and nourish them.[67]

In the language of Stith Thompson's motif index (*MI*), Egbert's poem contains both B771, "wild animal miraculously tamed," and D1442.12, "magic garment tames animal." Rumpf sees the specificity of the latter motif (the redness of the clothing) in Egbert's short tale as being foreign to the later story: in Egbert's tale, it must be understood in the context of Germanic werewolf stories, where it serves an apotropaic function. She does not conjecture whether this apotropaic quality of red is a literary device, a folk belief, or a scientifically observable effect.[68] Certainly red is not known to ward off all animals, such as bulls, although Virgil reported that hunters stretched a cord with scarlet feathers (known as a "scare," Latin *formido*) at the edges of woods to intimidate game as it tried to escape.[69]

The equation of Egbert's story to the Wolfdietrich legend and its congeners has a few flaws, the most striking of which is that the early eleventh-century poet gives no inkling that the little girl stays in the woods to grow up among the wolves. Accounts of children who have been raised by female animals after being lost or abandoned by their human parents have abounded from antiquity to the present. These accounts of feral children range from the purely fictional to the purportedly factual. At the factual end of the spectrum, the taxonomist Carl Linnaeus (1707–78) subsumed wolf children in the tenth edition of his *Systema naturae* (1758) as a subclass of *homo ferus* (wild man): the *Juvenis lupinus Hessianus* (Hessian wolf boy).[70] According to written reports that had been credited for centuries before Linnaeus, the wolf child of Hesse was found running wild in the woods in 1344. He was reputed to have lived for four years with wolves who had excavated a special burrow and outfitted it with leaves for him.[71] Even comparatively recently, serious scholars, such as the psychologist Arnold Gesell (1880–1961), have placed credence in the existence of wolf children, such as the child Kamala whose case attained notoriety in the 1910s and 1920s.[72]

Although these cases of purported zoanthropy are fascinating, they seem irrelevant to "About a Girl Saved from Wolf Cubs." Egbert offers no more hint that the wolf in his story is a surrogate parent (the wolf is a *lupus*, not a *lupa*, and is therefore unlikely to offer much in the way of suckling—a service that a five-year-old girl would not need in any case) than that it is the typical greedy beast of fables, which was standard fare in the elementary textbooks that Egbert's schoolboy audience would have known only too well or of the later Reynard cycle, which may have been spreading through

oral tradition already at this date. Egbert's wolf is in no wise anthropomorphized: it neither nurtures as a wolf mother does nor acts greedy and talks as a typical fabular wolf does.[73] If his beast has any affinities with any conventional wolf, it is with the wolf of Christian symbolism: the diabolic beast that would prey on the faithful flock were it not for the vigilance of both earthly pastors and the heavenly Good Shepherd. Of course, another conventional wolf should not be forgotten: the wolf in "Little Red Riding Hood" is also male, which has provided encouragement for Freudian and other such interpretations. Whatever we make of the wolf and his gender, there is no reason to think that Egbert was at all concerned with or knowledgeable about the realities of the behavior of wolves toward their young.[74]

If one focuses on the situation rather than on the particular animal, an interesting analogue can be found in the account of Daniel in the lions' den (Daniel 6, with a doublet in Daniel 14.30–42): a believer is protected from usually voracious animals through the might of God. One source describes the beasts in this scene as welcoming Daniel like fawning dogs, by licking his hands and wagging their tails.[75] Outside the Bible, there are many other possible comparanda. In *An Ephesian Tale of Anthia and Habrocomes,* Xenophon of Ephesus, a Greek novelist who apparently flourished in the first half of the second century CE, relates how the heroine was thrown into a deep trench with two huge dogs; thanks to the intervention of the well-disposed guard, she was saved from being eaten by the two creatures.[76] Even closer spiritually to Egbert's little girl would be African saints, such as the legendary first-century virgin Thecla of Iconium, a prospective martyr who was sent to the amphitheater to be eaten by beasts but survived. The Roman author Aulus Gellius (born between 125 and 128 CE) records the legend of Androclus (Androcles) and the lion, in which a beast that is supposed to devour a human victim instead licks his feet and hands in return for a much earlier kindness; Androclus had drawn a splinter from its paw.[77] This motif is later ascribed first to St. Gerasimus and then to St. Jerome. Similarly, Gregory the Great recounts in the *Dialogues* (3.11) how a bear that was supposed to martyr Bishop Cerbonius of Populonium instead grew tame, lowered its neck and head, and licked the prelate's feet.[78] Vitae of Irish saints contain several instances in which wild animals or monsters are reduced to licking the feet of the holy men.[79]

A general shortcoming in Rumpf's analysis is that it plays down the contribution of many elements to the distinctive nature of a story: not only narrative motifs, but also themes, settings, and characters, together with their attributes and the functions they serve. Despite a century of struggles toward a scientific narratology of folktales,[80] folktale analysts have not formulated a universally applicable diagnostics for fixing the absolute minimum of

constituents that endue a story of a given type with its distinctive imprint. The complex of features that lend a story its essence will vary from tale to tale, cultural milieu to cultural milieu. This variability does not render the process of analysis futile, but it does recommend that analysts be flexible. If viewed less rigidly, Egbert's poem reveals such significant similarities to "Little Red Riding Hood" as the title character (a little girl with a red riding hood), the main prop (a red riding hood), the lead villain (a wolf), the climactic event (an improbable but safe escape from the lead villain when all seems lost), and two main themes (the dangers of the woods and of being eaten by wolves).

When the poem is seen as an organic whole, Rumpf's explanation of the red clothing as werewolf repellent fails to satisfy. Although in his poem's title, Egbert (if he and not a scribe was responsible for the titles)[81] identifies the heroine only as a little girl, the first attribute singled out within the poem is her tunic woven of red wool. The hooded design of the garment in Egbert's tale would have been more obvious if he had used the Medieval Latin term *cappa* rather than opting for the classical and liturgical connotations of *tunica*.[82] The word *tunica* usually applied to a surcoat and specifically to an outer garment that was white, not necessarily one with a hood that could correspond to a little red riding hood.[83] But a close inspection of lines 11–12 leads to the conclusion that the tunic in Egbert's poem must have a hood: as the wolf cubs begin to nuzzle the girl's head, she warns them not to damage the tunic.[84] In other words, the robe of the girl in Egbert's version must have been a garment with a hood similar to the *coiffure* of her counterpart in the versions of Perrault and the Brothers Grimm—a red hooded cape that the English title "Little Red Riding Hood" was intended to translate.

THE RED RIDING HOOD

Whatever import the cut of the robe had in Egbert's source or sources, he had specifically Christian reasons for stressing the hood.[85] He took pains to convey the presence of the hood, since the covering of the head with a veil was an essential event in the baptismal liturgy with which he was concerned.[86] As this moment in the ceremony was explicated by the ninth-century liturgiologist Amalar of Metz (died after 850), the covering extends the symbolism of the baptismal robe: it signifies the protection of the Lord that is secured through baptism.

> On the covering of the head.
> This too derives from the Old Testament; for thus it is written in Exodus (29.8–9): "You shall bring his sons also" (that is to say, Aaron)

"and shall dress them in linen tunics, and gird them (that is, Aaron and his children) with a sash, and put mitres on them." Now when he has received the grace of sacred baptism, he should not rely on his own strength but he should even pray to be protected by the aid of God and heaven. We wish to understand the renowned protection of the Lord by the linen with which the head is covered.[87]

The garments of the newly baptized, like those of saints and of the clergy, were sometimes felt in the early Middle Ages to possess magical properties against storms and fire.[88] In Egbert's story, the efficacy of the baptismal symbol is such that the wolf cubs, having set out to devour their prey, are reduced instead to performing the equivalent of another event in the baptismal liturgy, the anointment of the head.[89]

The title character of the Little Red Riding Hood story has grown so important that her name has become a common noun, one star in the bright constellation that numbers Cinderella and Bluebeard among its luminaries.[90] Why is the name so important? In part, anyone who remembers the story as it has reached us through the cultural tradition of Perrault, Tieck, and especially the Brothers Grimm remembers it with this chief character and eponymous title: so intimately linked are the two that merely hearing the title or name of the main character suffices to trigger memory of the whole tale.[91] But another part of the explanation is the hermeneutic pressure of a name that seems on an intuitive level to have a meaning, to offer a key that will unlock the true significance of the whole story. The redness emerges as the central mystery of the story, eliciting interpretations that shift with the intellectual vogues of the cultures that produce the interpreters. In the nineteenth and early twentieth centuries, the red was seen as encoding a solar myth;[92] more recently, it has been deciphered as referring to menarchy or lasciviousness among young girls.[93] One critic observes: "Much ado has been made about her fetish of the red hood or cap. Clearly her innocence in the story has been suspect."[94]

Folklorists have been understandably impatient with the welter of wild speculation. In exasperation, Paul Delarue (1889–1956) compared the effects of the red hood on critics with those of the bullfighter's red cape on bulls: "Like the bull that charges the red flag that the toreador presents him and keeps going at an empty casing, folklorists have hurled themselves upon this red headgear that Perrault's version offered them."[95] Delarue went on calmly to argue that far too much attention has been paid to the name and to the color it conveys. In the opinion of most folklorists who have occupied themselves with the story, the appearance in the story of this name, along with both the riding hood and the associated color, was (so to speak)

a red herring, the result of Perrault's whimsy or fraudulence. Delarue noted: "The independent oral versions present a remarkable identity from one extremity of the zone of extension of the tale to the other. They permit one to ascertain that the red headdress of the little girl is an accessory trait peculiar to the Perrault version, not a general trait on which one could base oneself to explain the tale."[96] According to this reasoning, Perrault noticed that folktales were sometimes named after the garments that characters wore, and he decided on this basis to endow his story (his "fakelore") with the air of real folklore by introducing the cap or riding hood. Others have supplemented Delarue's argument with the intimation that Perrault made the hood red because the color "was generally associated at the time with sin, sensuality, and the devil."[97]

The contention that folktales and characters in them were now and then named after features of their clothing is well founded. One pertinent example of both processes can be seen in "The Tale of Rognvald and Raud" ("Rognvalds þáttr ok Rauðs"), an Old Norse short story (þáttr) of the thirteenth or fourteenth century extant in a longer text known as the *Greatest Saga of Olaf Tryggvason* (itself preserved most importantly in the late fourteenth-century *Flateyjarbók* manuscript).[98] In this story, a foundling (originally named "Gunnarr") who has been abandoned by his father is adopted by a childless old couple who call him Raud (Red) after the color of the tunic (*kyrtill*) in which he is dressed; interestingly, this tale shares with Egbert's "About a Girl Saved from Wolf Cubs" a baptismal theme, since it ends in the baptism and reconciliation of Raud and Rognvald. In such stories as this, the garment serves as a token to establish the royalty of the abandoned child.[99] The Middle English *Lay Le Freine* (literally, The Ash-Tree Lay), a Breton lay from the beginning of the fourteenth century, states explicitly that the clothing in which the abandoned heroine is lapped was meant to guarantee that "whoever found her should observe that the child came from a rich family."[100] The coverlet serves at a crucial moment to identify the abandoned daughter to her mother.

Delarue conceded that the redness of the tunic in Egbert and of the riding hood in Perrault lent the two stories about little girls and wolves a similarity, but he saw it as being superficial and coincidental.

> Even if a little girl and a wolf are mentioned in this story, here presented as the account of an actual event that peasants are supposed to have related, it is difficult to see in it a version or the first form of our tale. Without doubt, the dress of the little girl is red, like the headgear of the heroine in Perrault's version. But the "red riding hood" is only an accessory feature, peculiar to this version, not a general feature of the tale.[101]

Rumpf echoed this conclusion.

> It seems to me risky to infer connections with the Little Red Riding
> Hood tale solely from the fact that in the single story from the
> twelfth century [*sic*] a red tunic plays a role as a godparent's gift to a
> little girl.[102]

Striking off in his own direction, Wesselski refused to dismiss the resem-
blances. But even he understated the points of contact between the two
stories.

> Thus apart from the wolf nothing of the story survives in the fairy
> tale (links between them indeed existed) except for the remembrance
> of the red cloak, the only feature that has meaning as a motif in nei-
> ther the story nor the fairy tale, but nevertheless justified the names
> Little Red Riding Hood and Red Cap.[103]

STABILITY AND CHANGE IN TALES

Delarue and most other folklorists who have occupied themselves with Per-
rault's tale have assumed it to be a literary bowdlerization of one "original
oral tale." According to this thinking, Perrault departed from his oral
sources and drew the detail of the red riding hood out of thin air. Thus, one
scholar concludes, "the girl's headgear, the famous red riding hood . . . is a
motif that is characteristic of the Perrault version and is always absent from
the folk versions."[104] Contrarily, versions from oral tradition contain motifs
that are conspicuously absent from Perrault's, with the two most notable
being the choice of roads that the wolf offers the girl upon meeting her
("'What road do you wish to take,' he says to her, 'that of the pins or that
of the needles?'") and the flesh of the grandmother that the wolf invites her
to eat for supper.[105]

But must we accept that the folktale tradition behind Perrault was so
clear and uniform? Must we expect that the story had been elaborated before
him in approximately the form it attained in the late nineteenth century?
Must a story retain complete stability over hundreds of years? Is there not a
paradox or an irony that folktales can be so immutable that an oral tradition
recorded in 1885 should be more faithful to the tradition than a written ver-
sion recorded nearly two hundred years earlier, whereas a folktale known to
cleric and peasant alike in 1022 or thereabouts should disappear without a
trace? Although faith in stability or continuity is one of the premises of the
Finnish method,[106] the transmission of folklore is seen to be subject to at

least two additional principles (variation and selection).[107] Von der Leyen argued long ago: "We cannot always get to the original of these motifs, for many of them have changed greatly. Kaleidoscopic variation takes place in the course of migration."[108] Wesselski went still further in hypothesizing that the oral tradition had no stability except in the proximity of a written text.[109] Indeed, even Dundes declared: "Variation is a key concept in folkloristics. It is variation that in part distinguishes folklore from so-called 'high culture' and 'mass culture.'"[110]

The supposition that the story as we know it was born fully formed—a kind of narrative Athena that surged mature from the head of its creators—must be balanced against the possibility that elements from two or more different stories fused over time. Thus an alternative hypothesis is that "Little Red Riding Hood" originated through both cultural changes and modifications introduced by storytellers. It is conceivable that the apotropaic power of the girl's dress—which could have been apotropaic for one reason in popular tellings (red to deter wolves) and for another in Egbert's account (red to symbolize the salvific capacity of Pentecost and baptism)—was forgotten. Even if it lost its potential to ward off evil, the red hood could have persisted in the story because of its capacity as a storytelling device to attract the attention of children. In literature as in stoplights and clothing, red catches the eye and is felt to warn and protect.[111] The motif of the red hood would have constituted a truly unbroken thread in the history of the narrative or, to press into service Goethe's well-known phrase, *ein roter Faden* (a red thread).[112] But if the red no longer functioned to protect the girl, the storytellers would have been forced to improvise other means of preserving their little heroine—unless they were content, as Perrault was, to watch her become wolf food. Under this impetus, the Grimm brothers, their informants, or the tradition behind them could have amalgamated two stories, one about a red-garbed girl who was carried off by a wolf but later saved from the beast thanks to her clothing and another about a girl either devoured by a wolf or else released from it by a male agent. In other words, the character of Little Red Riding Hood in a tale akin to Egbert's could have been attracted toward another story with a wolf but without a function for the hood. If this conflation took place, one of the results could have been the fairy tale of Little Red Riding Hood as we have it: a prop that was a constitutive element in one story became a frustrating mystery in another.

Before rejecting the idea that Egbert's poem is only one of two or more stories that combined eventually to form "Little Red Riding Hood," we should recall that folklorists have argued for cognate relationships between other, equally dissimilar pairs of folktales. To take an example close to home, it was widely agreed until recently that the Grimms' version of the

Little Red Riding Hood tale grafts an ending from the tale type repre-
sented by the tale "The Wolf and the Kids" (*KHM* 5; ATU 123) onto roots
of the tale type "The Glutton" (AT 333: contrast ATU 333). If elements
from two different tale types could merge so easily and successfully, why
should we rule out that elements from other, lost tale types—with the po-
tential labels "The Red-Garbed Girl" and "Girl Swallowed by Wolf"—
could have coalesced over time?[113] There can be no doubt that much me-
dieval popular literature perished, sometimes surviving only in a brief title
or allusion, sometimes not even receiving such fragmentary immortality.[114]
Only through sheer happenstance may we intuit that there existed in an-
tiquity a folktale of a child pulled out alive from the belly of the Lamia, a
kind of bogeywoman (Horace, *Ars poetica* 340). Although the mention is
too brief to allow for certainty, the motif to which Horace alludes would
seem to be comparable with the removal of the kids from the wolf's belly
in *KHM* 5.

RED AND PENTECOST

To extend this alternative hypothesis, the detail of redness can be shown to
have had a special significance in Egbert's version—a significance that could
easily have sunk into oblivion over the centuries between Egbert and Per-
rault. Here, it is worthwhile pondering Egbert's insistence on Pentecost,
which he touches on in the fifth line (it is not irrelevant that five is ex-
pressed by *quinque* in Latin) and stresses through a sonic architecture of
quod, quam, quidam, and *cui* that culminates in the alliteration of *quinqua-
gesima* with *quinquennis*. The girl, through her age, almost embodies the
day, which is the fiftieth after Easter.[115]

Those of us who are acquainted with British English associate the holi-
day of Pentecost with the color white: the name *Whitsunday* (white Sunday)
recalls the custom of clothing the newly baptized in white baptismal robes
on this day.[116] To be sure, the white baptismal robes must have been a fre-
quent sight on Pentecost, since, except in cases of emergency, baptism could
take place only in the two seasons of Easter and Pentecost.[117] But in most of
the Middle Ages, the predominant liturgical color of the day would have
equally justified the name *Redsunday*. On the holiday, churches contained
many symbolic reminders that Pentecost began with the tongues of red fire
that appeared to the apostles, as a visual equivalent to the glossolalia, or
"speaking in tongues," that ensued.

> And there appeared to them parted tongues as it were of fire, and it
> sat upon every one of them: And they were all filled with the Holy

Ghost, and they began to speak with divers tongues, according as the Holy Ghost gave them to speak. (Acts of the Apostles 2.3–4)[118]

Among the symbolic reminders were the following practices: "red rose leaves were scattered from the roof of the church";[119] the Gospel book was covered in red, to signify the blood of Christ;[120] and, most important, the vestments for that day were red.[121] Thus the red of the surcoat conveys the power of a Pentecostal baptism, as embodied in a red-clothed celebrant. Finally, it bears noting that the *rubicunda tunica* in Egbert's poem does not rule out a white baptismal garment: the red surcoat that the girl was given after being taken from the font could have been placed over the customary white garb of a candidate for baptism.[122]

Whether or not the common people of Egbert's day—the peasants—recounted a girl-and-wolf story in which the liturgical color and baptisms of Pentecost figured prominently is beyond our ken. In much later versions of "Little Red Riding Hood," the heroine brings to her grandmother gifts of bread and wine, which lay a foundation of eucharistic implications that is evident later when the wolf offers the flesh of the old woman to Little Red Riding Hood and presents the woman's blood as wine.[123] It is imaginable that Egbert the cleric Christianized a nonreligious story of a little girl in a red garment who was rescued miraculously from being devoured by a wolf: aware that the redness of the garment was too familiar an element in his sources to allow for its omission, perhaps he made a virtue of a necessity by coordinating the color with the symbolism of the liturgy. If Egbert imposed Christian features in this fashion, then the redness in the story told by the common people could have had a general apotropaic significance that the Latin poet particularized with a religious dimension when he appropriated it.

Egbert's raw material could have been a story much closer to the versions of Perrault and the Brothers Grimm. For instance, Egbert could have deliberately expurgated for children a story with strong sexual implications: he could have made an originally pubescent or adolescent heroine very young (even in times of precocious sexual maturation, the adjective *quinquennis,* "five-year-old," and the noun *infantula,* "very little child," place her securely in childhood), he could have replaced the menstrual associations of red with the religious symbolism of Pentecost, and he could have protected the girl from the sexual implications of being eaten by a wolf (in French, *elle a vu le loup* [literally, "she has seen the wolf"] means "she has lost her virginity") by having her set free earlier in the story.[124] Yet had Egbert made such thoroughgoing changes in the oral tradition, would he still have dared tell his young charges that peasants could tell the story along with him?

Wherever the credit is due, the device of the red hood is integrated

smoothly (seamlessly!) into Egbert's story through the color symbolism. In the scene that Egbert stages, the little girl is protected miraculously from the wolves directly through the virtue of her tunic. The red tunic, which brackets the narrative (at lines 4 and 12) as effectively as it clothes the little girl, can safeguard her precisely because of the liturgical context in which it is bestowed on her—as a baptismal gift on Pentecost from her godfather. The baptismal rites buffer the girl from the wolves within the story, just as, in figurative terms, they shield any Christian from the violence of the infernal wolf, the Devil. Even the motif of head caressing or licking could belong in the same liturgical nexus, since the unction of baptismal candidates on the head with chrism was believed to convey the gift of the Holy Spirit—the gift of tongues![125] What is more, there is evidence that the liturgical anointing of the head had a correspondence in a nonliturgical practice that involved the color red: Guillaume de Lorris, in the first part of the thirteenth-century Old French *Romance of the Rose* (*Roman de la Rose*) refers to the ready and inexpensive availability of rose garlands to be worn on Pentecost.[126]

THE GODFATHER, THE GRANDMOTHER, AND THE WOODCUTTER

In Egbert's tale as in the versions by Perrault and the Brothers Grimm, the red riding hood embodies the affection of a relative for the little girl. Perrault's tale begins:

> Once upon a time there was a little village girl, the prettiest that had ever been seen. Her mother doted on her. Her grandmother was even fonder, and made her a little red hood, which became her so well that everywhere she went by the name of Little Red Riding Hood.[127]

The version of the Brothers Grimm opens similarly.

> Once upon a time there was a sweet little maiden that everyone who even looked at her loved, but most especially her grandmother. She could not think of enough to give the child. Once she presented her with a little cap of red velvet, and because it suited her so well and because afterward she would not wear anything else, she was called nothing but Little Red Cap.[128]

Why do the two authors of the modern fairy tales make the object that gives the title character her name a gift from female relatives, when the garment is presented by her godfather in the medieval story? Here, too, we

may speculate about an alteration in the tale through cultural changes over hundreds of years.

In the Middle Ages, the relationship of godfather and godchild was one of the strongest forms of kinship. At baptism, the parents and godparents were directed to protect the child from fire, water, and all other dangers until the age of seven years. Furthermore, the godparents were enjoined to take part actively in the religious education of the godchild.[129] Finally, they usually gave the godchildren gifts at baptism, not just money, as is sometimes believed, but also jewelry, livestock, and clothing, such as dresses.[130] Before the mid-eleventh century, the level of dye technology in Western Europe restricted the spectrum of principal colors for clothing to variations on white, black, and red. (The fact that dyeing was limited to shades of red is preserved in the use of the English noun and verb *color* to refer to red in the face and in the common application of the Spanish *colorado* to designate red in general; the name of the state Colorado derived from the reddish hue of its main river.)[131] Of these principal colors, red may have been the most appropriate for a baptismal gift, not because it was the preferred color for the female sex (the system of allocating pink to one gender and blue to the other had not yet developed), but because it was a luxurious color that connoted through its very tint the special generosity and affection of its giver.[132]

The godfather is the first and last person mentioned in Egbert's poem; has no identity (he is "a certain man" [quidam]) until after he has performed his godfatherly function of taking his godchild from the font (an action—stressed in lines 3 and 13—that tallies with the actuality of the baptismal ceremony in this era);[133] and, as godfather, exercises the same power over the wolves (10–11) as God, the Father and the Creator, does over souls (12). In many later times and places, the relationship between godparent and godchild has grown ever less important than it was in medieval Western Europe.[134] Therefore the prominence of the godfather could have been as baffling in some societies as it had been immediately comprehensible in the early eleventh century.

Once the reason for the inclusion of the godfather was no longer immediately apparent, the giver of the robe—now no longer comprehensible as a baptismal gift—was replaced by a close relative who could have crafted such an item, namely, a grandmother. This process would have been hastened if oral storytelling was shifting from a particular social class (peasants) back to a particular group designated by sex and age. After an interlude in the Middle Ages when folktales and proverbs were attributed to the social class of peasants, the old women struck back: the old women and nurses who had told *fabulae aniles* in antiquity endured to relate old wives' tales

and Mother Goose rhymes in the early modern period—and to enhance the roles of characters like them in the stories they told.[135]

But the rise of the grandmother meant that the godfather was only displaced or disguised, not completely removed. Because the robe was no longer hallowed by baptism and Pentecost, the male figure who lurked in the background of Egbert's version was drafted for active service in the Brother Grimms' tale and its analogues: if the red riding hood could not control the wolf, the woodcutter could. Consequently, both stories would contain the two opposite forms of male nature that such Freudian interpreters as Bruno Bettelheim have singled out: the dangerous seducer (wolf) who represents the id and the salvational father figure (godfather/hunter) who stands for the ego.[136] Such a psychological construction would have been foreign to Egbert, for whom the rite of baptism (and through it, God) outweighed in importance any human agent in the poem. To him the marvelous truth was not the godfather but the salvational power of baptism.

WARNING WITHOUT TERRIFYING

With the woodcutter we are nearly out of the woods, and yet we still need to discuss the woods themselves. Perrault's version and most of its relatives are usually classified among cautionary tales, designated formally by the German terms *Schreckmärchen* (fright tale) or *Warnmärchen* (cautionary tale)[137] or the French "un récit de mise en garde" (literally, "a tale to put on guard").[138] Among these tales, Perrault's version is unusual in having a bad ending:[139] the tale ends with the unmitigated horror of the sentence "Upon saying these words, the wicked wolf threw himself on Little Red Riding Hood and gobbled her up."[140] This conclusion brings home in particularly brutal form the general danger of being disobedient and careless,[141] alongside the specific one of going out alone in woods.[142] Egbert's tale also shows traces of being admonitory: the girl is snatched when she is wandering "heedless of her peril," apparently near the woods and during the half-light of dawn, the place and time in which wolves were reputed to pose the gravest threat to human beings.[143] But Egbert's tale hews more closely to the usual line of *Warnmärchen* in that it concludes happily. Its ominousness is mitigated to the point where its final line begins with the very word *mitigat*. In this way, Egbert's poem, like the Grimms' version of the Little Red Riding Hood tale, appears designed to win over its audience of schoolchildren by presenting as leading character a child who seems to have a God-given right to be protected.[144]

At the risk of drawing an invidious comparison, Egbert's ending could be said to surpass Perrault's in both its attention to child psychology and its

economy. To start with the issue of child psychology, Egbert's ending warns
children and offers religious instruction, but not at the price of frightening
children out of their wits. Whereas Perrault's tale closes disturbingly with
both the girl and her grandmother entombed within the belly of the wolf,
the story part of Egbert's poem finishes on the lightest of notes, as the little
girl delivers a brief speech that contains the vocative "O mice" [mures] to
designate the wolf cubs. Why does she address the cubs as mice? Unless she
honestly mistakes the wolf cubs for mice because of their small size and un-
wolfishly gentle ways, the girl could be teasing them by calling them mice
when she knows full well that they are actually wolves. *Mus* (mouse) was a
term of endearment in classical Latin, and Egbert, either knowing the clas-
sical usage or else transferring into Medieval Latin a practice drawn from
a spoken language, would not be out of bounds in having a little girl apply
such a word affectionately to her new playmates.[145] Finally, it would be log-
ical for the wolves in this scene to be called mice because, as the etymology
of the noun *rodent* predicts, mice would be the pests most likely to gnaw
at garments.

Whatever the explanation, the girl is faced with progressively less men-
acing creatures: the wolf (*lupus*) gives way to diminutive whelps (*catuli*),
which in turn are scaled down to mice (*mures*). The shift in proportions
from wolf by way of whelps to rodents is related to the bathos that is a com-
mon element in such genres as mock epic and epyllion. The ancient Greek
Battle of the Mice and Frogs (*Batrachomyomachia*), written at the earliest after
Callimachus (third century BCE) and for many centuries falsely ascribed to
Homer, relates in truly classic mock-heroic style a war between the mice
and frogs. Early in the poem, the goddess Athena makes a speech in which
she refuses to intervene on behalf of the mice, on the grounds that in the
past the mice have damaged her temple property in their search for lamp
oil, have chewed holes in her robe, and have made noise that has prevented
her from sleeping.[146] The *Victory of Berenice* by the Hellenistic Greek poet
Callimachus of Cyrene (flourished in the first half of the third century
BCE), contains a scene that operates on almost exactly equal but opposite
principles.[147] This epinician (an ode to commemorate a victory) for Queen
Berenice incorporates a section that deals with one of the Twelve Labors of
Herakles, the myth of the slaying of the Nemean Lion. In the extant frag-
ments of the epinician, Callimachus draws an implicit contrast between the
deadly earnest hunt of Herakles for the dangerous Nemean Lion and the
comically exaggerated search of the old peasant Molorchus (whom Herakles
is visiting in his hovel) for the mice that have been pilfering his pantry,
drinking his lamp oil, keeping him awake at night, and gnawing his clothes,
cloak, and wallet. In Callimachus, mice, which are stereotypically timid

creatures, are presented as being frightening, destructive creatures; in Egbert, wolves, which are usually portrayed as being ravenously dangerous beasts, are reduced to the meekness of mice. Neither the *Battle of the Mice and Frogs* nor the *Victory of Berenice* could have been a source of inspiration for the creator of *The Richly Laden Ship* (*Fecunda ratis*), since neither of the former was available in Latin translation; but both show how readily a reality of life in earlier times—that mice nibble at garments—could wend its way into poetry in mock-heroic and/or parodic contexts.

In Egbert's short poem, the reduction of the wolf cubs to mice brings them down in scale to be on a par with the heroine of the poem, whose own smallness and helplessness are communicated in the choice of the word *infantula* (rather than the earlier *puella*) to describe her.[148] It is easy to imagine her imperative to the young wolves—so effective in its reduction of savage beasts to almost cuddly harmlessness and timorousness—as the final grace note in an oral folktale. As for the economy, unlike the outcome of the versions by Perrault or the Brothers Grimm, that of Egbert's story is linked directly to the name of the character, and the setting of the conclusion in a woodland den of wolves is well suited to a cautionary message about the forest and wolves.[149]

The best-known literary form of the Little Red Riding Hood tale also contrasts a ravening wolf to two embodiments of meekness. In both the Grimms' "Little Red Riding Hood" and Egbert's poem, one embodiment of meekness is a constant (i.e., the title character herself), but the other is different. In Egbert's poem, meekness is embodied in the wolf cubs when they have been rendered miraculously mouselike, capable of harming fabric but otherwise unthreatening. In "Little Red Riding Hood," the icon of harmlessness is the grandmother, a figure who, because of short life spans, would have been less common in the Middle Ages. A key component in the story is the girl's anatomical examination of the wolf as it lies in the grandmother's bed—and in the grandmother's nightclothes and nightcap. This part of the tale features the list of seemingly insouciant exclamations, "Oh, Grandmother, what big ears/eyes/hands/mouth you have," which culminates in the wolf's leaping out of the bed and gobbling up Little Red Riding Hood.

The economy of Egbert's version is perfect: every prop is indispensable and has a meaning. For this reason, if one subscribed to the debatable hypothesis that the original forms of folktales are usually the most logical or coherent,[150] one could build a plausible case that Egbert's "About a Girl Saved from Wolf Cubs" represents a truly original or more nearly original version of one Little Red Riding Hood story. In this prototype, the celebrated garment, the little red riding hood, plays a role more important than simply distinguishing the central character.

We do not know with how many other urtexts "About a Girl Saved from Wolf Cubs" amalgamated or over how long a span of time before becoming ATU 333. No incompatibility exists between the interpretation advanced here and the notion that the tale later took on features and associations that enabled it to serve different, new functions. For instance, the version of the tale that Egbert molded to suit ecclesiastic purposes may have spread and undergone changes before reappearing in oral tradition. To take but one example, a thorough interpretation has been advanced to construe the main modern French form of the folktale as reflecting the specific constant of a sewing ritual that brought together old women and young adolescent girls in northern Italy and southern France.[151]

THE VALUE OF EGBERT'S TRUE WONDER

This reading of Egbert's poem has been too speculative to settle to everyone's satisfaction all questions about the medieval background of the Little Red Riding Hood tale. It is just as true now as it was in 1947 that "the war of the folklorists goes on, with no immediate settlement in sight."[152] But this chapter will have fulfilled its main purpose if it has shaken some widespread complacencies about the worth or worthlessness of written evidence in general and about the origins of the Little Red Riding Hood tale in particular. At the least, this chapter has itself acted as a cautionary tale against the deep pitfall of limiting research only to demonstrably oral literature without taking stock of evidence from earlier times and from written literature. The creed that purely oral versions (which are de facto modern versions) have an intrinsic claim to priority over written versions (whether medieval or from the nineteenth century) is untenable. Literary and oral modes of telling tales have interacted as far back as evidence can be traced, which in most Western traditions means hundreds, if not thousands, of years. Furthermore, the very categories of "oral" or "folk" as opposed to "literary" may well be anachronistic and inappropriate if applied to texts from before the early modern period.

Too few folklorists acknowledge the urgency of locating and holding onto written evidence because it records otherwise irretrievable folklore;[153] and too few bear in mind the principle that Walter Anderson claimed to have enunciated to Kaarle Krohn in 1911: "Every *Märchen* investigator must also be one of literary history."[154] Just as medieval literary scholars would be unwise to shun the methods of the social sciences when serviceable, so folklorists would be foolhardy to convince themselves that they could routinely dispense with the fruits of philology, such as written evidence gathered from earlier cultures. Both philology and folkloristics stand to lose if the two

fields are encouraged to drift further apart. C. W. von Sydow observed acutely:

> [I]t is evident that collaboration between philology and the study of folklore is of supreme importance. Philologists can produce much material of very great value to folklore research . . . But the oral material is no less important for placing the contents of the ancient sources in the living whole to which they belong, and for supplementing their statements, which are often both fragmentary and otherwise corrupted.[155]

Correspondingly, literary folklorism has its limitations but also its values.

Older written versions can be as helpful as newer oral versions in interpreting folktales and in graphing their trajectories across time. In the case of Egbert's "About a Girl Saved from Wolf Cubs," a little piece of Medieval Latin literature that was unearthed more than a century ago has not been exploited by folklorists as it should have been. Egbert's eleventh-century poem raises the possibility that Perrault did not invent out of whole cloth either the character Little Red Riding Hood or her garment, whatever Perrault's other tamperings with the fabric of the story may have been. The poem could be testimony that ATU 333 was anticipated by more than one proto-ATU 333, all but this one of which went unrecorded until Perrault. If so, Egbert's poem should not be regarded as *the* ancestor of Perrault, but it should be registered somewhere on the family tree.[156] Unfortunately, the extremely useful systems of analysis that have been developed for folktale analysis (the typecasting allowed by Aarne and Thompson's tale types, now further rationalized and extended by Hans-Jörg Uther; Thompson's motif indexing; and Propp's morphology) do not accommodate very well the extraordinary diversity, versatility, and variability that sometimes shows through in the patchy, chronologically isolated evidence occasionally available to us.

This analysis of "About a Girl Saved from Wolf Cubs" suggests that if you dismiss the very character and title "Little Red Riding Hood" as hopelessly tainted interventions by literate authors, ignore all early Western written evidence, and define the original tale on the basis of later non-Western material, you lose a lot. If, in examining "Little Red Riding Hood," you exclude European literary versions and reduce the tale to a set of narrative motifs that recur in tales throughout the world, you lose even more. It may be that in 36 percent of the variants, the name *Red Riding Hood* is lacking;[157] but if you take *Red Riding Hood* out of the title "Little Red Riding Hood," what you have left is quite obvious: "Little."

Why Egbert's "About a Girl Saved from Wolf Cubs" has been left entangled in the vast and inadequately explored forest of medieval—especially Medieval Latin—narrative is not hard to see. To return to the osteoskeletal metaphor with which this chapter opened, Egbert's hexameters tell only the bare bones of a story, and even these bones amount to considerably less than the entire skeleton of the Little Red Riding Hood tale as we know it. Beyond that, "Little Red Riding Hood," in all its main expressions, is to be glossed generically not among wonder tales but among cautionary tales.

These concessions seem enormous, far greater than the Big Bad Wolf. Yet two even larger facts remain. One is that Charles Perrault as well as Jacob and Wilhelm Grimm, the authors who have done more than any others (even the most active and clear-thinking scholars) to shape our consciousness of fairy tales, included "Little Red Riding Hood" in their collections. The other is that Egbert himself knew and indicated the nature of the tale. The first two lines of his poem are a chiasmus.

> What I have to relate, country folk can tell along with me,
> and it is not so much marvelous as it is quite true to believe.

In the first half line of the chiasmus, Egbert gives utterance to his own voice, a cleric writing in Latin. In the second, he acknowledges the common people, the *Volk* of his day. In the third, he denies that the tale is marvelous, which he must do because that is what folk say. Instead, he wants the tale to be true, as he concludes in the last half line. Egbert and his fellow clerics were surrounded by wonderful lies, in what they read (the "false figments"[158] of poets) and in what they heard. Egbert tried to stem the tide: although not Dutch, he was a man of the Low Countries who had his finger in the dike of popular literature but pulled it out now and then to see what would happen. As will be discussed in chapter 4, within decades another poet, not far away from Liège, sought actively to facilitate a flow from folk into learned literature.

CHAPTER FOUR

True Lies and the Growth of Wonder

An Eleventh-Century
"Little Claus and Great Claus"

In "Big Claus and Little Claus" Hans Christian Andersen succeeded
in writing one of the most popular of his stories without making any
significant changes in the tradition as he had learned it.[1]

S t may be true that Hans Christian Andersen's tale "Little Claus
and Great Claus" ("Lille Claus og store Claus" in Danish) has
not come close to attaining the hallowed Walt Disney status of
"The Little Mermaid." Indeed, it has not even achieved the
name recognition of "The Princess and the Pea," "The Em-
peror's New Clothes," "The Ugly Duckling," "The Little Match
Girl," or any of a half-dozen other fairy tales and stories among the more
than 150 published by Andersen that have become widely known even to
the general public. But if not in the mass media of the New World, then at
least in the northern climes of the Old World, the tale won a definite pride
of place from being the second tale in Andersen's first pamphlet of four fairy
tales (the others were "The Tinder-Box," "The Princess and the Pea," and
"Little Ida's Flowers") published in 1835 under the title *Tales, Told for Chil-
dren* (*Eventyr, fortalte for Børn*); and in Denmark and Germany, it has not
lost its attractions in the intervening 160 years. "Little Claus and Great

Claus" has been reprinted repeatedly, often illustrated with engravings, in children's books in Danish, German, English, and other languages.[2] Despite the frequency with which the story has appeared in print, the separateness of Danish children's literature and Medieval Latin literature, or of literary folklore and Medieval Latin literature, has meant that the provocative similarities (and equally arresting dissimilarities) between "Little Claus and Great Claus" and the eleventh-century Latin *Verses about One-Ox* (*Versus de Unibove*) have gone underremarked, if not altogether unremarked.[3] Even if *One-Ox* were not affiliated with Andersen's tale, the former would richly repay close examination. It has rightly been called "one of the chefs-d'oeuvre of popular literature, in Latin, of the Middle Ages."[4]

INTRODUCING *ONE-OX*

One-Ox is extant in a single manuscript (Brussels, Bibliothèque royale Albert Ier, MS 10078–10095 [formerly 8176]). In its present form the codex comprises 116 folios, of which there are fourteen quaternions (fols. 1–112) and one binio (fols. 113–16). The text of *One-Ox* is written on folios 38v–42v. The poem could not have been composed any later than the end of the eleventh century, the terminus for when its text was copied. Furthermore, the manuscript we have is hardly the original, although it is not likely to have been written very long after the original. It contains mistakes corrected by the hand that wrote it, in addition to mistakes or perceived mistakes corrected by a second hand. A date in the second half of the eleventh century seems to fit the social circumstances depicted in the poem, such as the fact that the priest who plays a leading role in it is married. One editor has dated the poem in the third quarter of the eleventh century, while another thinks it not inconceivable that the manuscript should be dated in the first half of the eleventh century; other scholars have speculated that the poem could even have been composed in the last quarter of the eleventh century.[5]

Not too long after being copied, the manuscript of the poem probably belonged, in the first decade of the twelfth century, to the library of St. Peter's, the Benedictine abbey in Gembloux. It is often impossible to determine exactly who consulted any given manuscript text. In the case of *One-Ox*, we know that Sigebert of Gembloux used it in the composition of *On Ecclesiastic Authors* (*De scriptoribus ecclesiasticis*), composed around 1111–12.[6]

The unique Latin manuscript, located in what was then the Koninklijke Bibliotheek in Brussels, came somehow to the attention of Jacob Grimm. Shortly after obtaining a transcription from J. F. Willems in 1837, Grimm published the editio princeps of the text in the book *Lateinische Gedichte des X. und XI. Jahrhunderts* (Latin Poems of the Tenth and Eleventh Cen-

turies), produced in collaboration with (Johann) Andreas Schmeller (1785–1852) in 1838.[7]

The poem, 2,841 words and 864 lines in length, comprises 216 strophes, each of four rhythmic octosyllables that are often end-rhymed or at least assonating in couplets to generate the pattern *aabb.* (The rhymes can be as weak or impure as *agricolae/scindere* in 5.3–4; the assonance can be of the type *turgidus/gradum,* as is found in 16.3–4, 130.1–2, 136.1–2, 137.1–2, 138.1–2, 150.1–2, 153.1–2, 156.3–4, and 179.1–2.) Formally the poem stands apart from such presumably earlier (and definitely shorter) poems as "The Song to the Flowers Tune" ("Modus florum" [app. 2D]) and "The Song to the Liebo Tune" ("Modus Liebinc" [app. 2C]), or "The Snow-Child," preserved in the *Cambridge Songs* and elsewhere; these earlier poems were rhymeless and written in a freer strophic structure. *One-Ox* also stands apart from such later compositions in elegiac couplets as *The Turnip Tale* and *The Donkey Tale.*

The metrical form of *One-Ox,* roughly equivalent to an iambic quatrain, is sometimes designated "Ambrosian," after hymns ascribed to St. Ambrose of Milan (ca. 340–97). To move to broader questions of style, the poem is written in a careful, supple, and elaborate, if not always elegant, Latin. The Latinity shows clearly that the poet knew the Bible and biblical exegesis, and his style has such deliberately rhetorical features as alliteration, anaphora, paronomasia, traductio, and oxymoron. At the same time, *One-Ox* is far from being "learned." Rather, it could be compared loosely with the High German writing of the Brothers Grimm—most definitely not written in dialect, but with enough features of popular life and language to imbue the text with a deceptively homespun flavor. Without information about the milieu in which the composer was active, it is impossible to reach an indisputable determination about the associations of the meter and style he elected to employ. Possibly both of them were chosen to match the popular origins of the tales he related.

Much about this Latin poem remains a mystery. So much Medieval Latin literature from the eleventh century is anonymous that it is not unusual for the authorship of *One-Ox* to be unknown. What is tantalizing is to have so long a poem that surrenders so few clues about its social context. It appears to have emanated from the area between the Rhine and the Seine. Arguments have been advanced in favor of its having been composed in Lower Lotharingia, which would correspond to northern France, Belgium, or the Netherlands. According to further speculation, the accentuation of final syllables indicates that the poet's original language may have been a French dialect.[8] The poem makes reference to a border town: One-Ox assures the three townsmen who are his regular antagonists that ox hides sold at a high price in this municipality. Although such towns would have

abounded in the patchwork of different kingdoms, duchies, and counties in the eleventh century, the gullibility of One-Ox's antagonists becomes easier to accept if we assume that this particular town lay across a linguistico-cultural divide—for instance, on the other side of the boundary line between French and Flemish. But such fine explaining is of course not necessary to justify the logic of a folktale, which is after all a story rather than a logical exposition.

I mentioned earlier that the unique manuscript of *One-Ox* seems to have resided in Gembloux. Because of this connection, the hypothesis has been advanced that the poem's use of the biblical noun *musac* (26.1) alluded to the name of Mysach, prior of St. Peter's abbey in Gembloux from 1048 to 1071.[9] Unfortunately it is not possible to extend the resemblance between the noun and the name into any sort of historical allegory that would confirm the supposition. As a result, the explanation could be that mere coincidence was at work.

The real usefulness of drawing attention to *musac* consists in demonstrating that the author, who had considerable versatility in Latin, was deeply conversant with the Vulgate Bible.[10] If not a clerk, he was at least a person who had received a clerical education. Further, his casual use of Hebrew words from the Bible, such as *musac* and *corbanan,* suggests that he expected his audience to recognize and understand such vocabulary as readily as he did. These circumstances are too vague to constitute an additional pointer in the direction of Gembloux, but they certainly underpin the idea that the poet was a monk, a cleric, or at the very least a person who had earned an extensive clerical education and who composed for an audience of his peers.[11] Yet here we run up against an apparent inconsistency. If the composer of *One-Ox* and his audience were probably clergy, how do we explain that the poem portrays—in a vehemently anticlerical tone—the victory of a lone layman over church officials, among whom the priest is the greediest of all?[12]

ONE-OX AND FOLKTALE

Every fairytale must be considered in toto by scholarship, and an analytic method must be combined with synthetic consideration, so as to attain a satisfactory result.[13]

The Latin poem that is designated here as *One-Ox* has been known, from the title given in the single manuscript, as *Verses about One-Ox* (*Versus de Unibove*) or, for short, *One-Ox* (*Unibos*). All these names highlight the plight of the title character as expressed at the beginning of the poem: he is

never able to possess more than a single ox at a time, and eventually even his one ox dies. The term *versus* in the Latin title, which may or may not have been authorial, signifies that the composition is in verse and perhaps that it was sung, but apart from this information about form, the word is not a clear genre marker.[14] From around 1100, *versus* was sometimes applied to Latin rhythmical verse as a way of referring to a new type of song, one related to the *vers* being composed around the same time in the south of France. In *One-Ox* the third strophe ends with the narrator saying (or singing?), "Let's sing of One-Ox" [Uno cantemus de Bove].

The Russian folklorist Vladimir IAkovlevich Propp of the Soviet era once drew an opposition between the genres of song and folktale.

> Just as the expression of the song is singing, so that of the folktale is its narration. The folktale was not created to be read but to be told, and hence to be heard. For the same reasons for which the study of a song is unilateral and insufficient and for a complete understanding it is necessary to study its melody, so too the folktale is studied by analyzing its forms and means of execution. Reading is little expressive; a text receives full resonance only if it is narrated appropriately.[15]

It may be that this contrast made sense in the context of Russian folklore but that such a dichotomy between song and folktale had not been drawn when the composer of *One-Ox* created his composition. Indeed, it may be misleading to individuate *One-Ox* as a song, poem, drama, or mime play alone, since the text features elements of all these genres.

One-Ox harbors within its own programmatic statements terminology that gives further generic hints. Its auditory side is emphasized in the first strophe, but it would be a mistake to conclude that what is heard excludes what is seen: the composer states that just as the eyes are not satisfied by the everyday, so the ears enjoy what is novel. The "rumor" (2.2) of One-Ox is presented as a "fabula", (2.3) a term that could well come as close to meaning "folktale" as was conceivable in eleventh-century Latin. The phrase "per verba iocularia" (2.4) may well refer at once to the joking tone of the tale and the joking profession of those who delivered it, the *ioculatores* as they were known in Latin and the *jongleurs* as they were called in French. Delivery of the tale could have involved miming, recitation in parts, or both: the author is at pains to emphasize, on the one hand, sounds and words and, on the other, whatever he meant by "in personarum drammate" (3.3).

One-Ox has been called "the oldest Western European folktale text"[16] and has been judged to be one of the oldest medieval sources for *Märchen*—presumably in the general sense of "folktale," not in the particular one of

"fairy tale."[17] There is no glossing over the fact that Wesselski was willing to call *One-Ox* a *Schwank* and a *Märlein* but most definitely not a *Märchen*.[18] In his own anthology of pre-Grimmian fairy tales and folktales, Wesselski acknowledged that many of his examples would not pass muster by strict definitions but that all of them would meet the standard of being like tales included in the *KHM*. The case for regarding *One-Ox* as a folktale is even more compelling than for many of the tales with which Wesselski occupied himself. Whatever label is attached to the poem in order to capture its "folk" qualities, *One-Ox* stands out among early texts in which monks, clerics, and other literati appropriated or claimed to appropriate tales that circulated among common people.

Whether or not the assertion that *One-Ox* is the oldest folktale text from Western Europe carries conviction, *One-Ox* is certainly the oldest written expression of a tale type that is attested in hundreds of versions throughout the world, especially in Europe and particularly in Belgium and the Netherlands.[19] (The old Indianist notion that the type of story embodied in *One-Ox* originated in India and entered European literature from there was rebuffed early in the twentieth century.)[20] Stith Thompson observed, "A hasty survey of easily available versions shows 875."[21] The tale type is ATU 1535, which is tagged "The Rich and the Poor Farmer (Unibos)." Although the tale type features the parenthetic *Unibos* in its name, the summary that it includes does not follow the narrative of the eleventh-century Latin poem. Like most other analyses of the tale, Thompson's does not see *One-Ox* as having produced the ur-form of the tale.[22] (Uther's analysis gives the medieval poem more credit.)[23] But how can we possibly get closer to some notional originary form of this or any tale than a version that is clearly recognizable as an expression of the tale, that has markers to declare its popular origins, and that is preserved a half millennium before even the next literary version—and nearly a thousand years before any version recorded directly from an oral source? None of the broad folkloric studies of the tale type make *One-Ox* the point of departure for their comparison of variants, a fact that reflects the bias of much historic-geographic folktale research from the nineteenth and twentieth century against written records in general and literary records in particular, with literary records in Latin being especially problematic and likely to be handled with suspicion.[24]

It is possible that the composer of *One-Ox* heard the story from one or more oral storytellers and adapted it in Latin from this version or these versions in Latin or the vernacular(s). It is less likely that he concocted the story himself. If the story had originated with him, all later versions of the story would have had to have their ultimate inspiration in readings or performances of *One-Ox*. This scenario puts very heavy weight on a text that is ex-

tant in only one manuscript. At the same time, the close correspondences between *One-Ox* and later variants of the story argue that the composer drew heavily and faithfully on a tale stock that was widespread in his time.[25]

The defining features of the tale type are, on the one hand, its consistent opposition between a poor man and one or more richer men whom he outwits and, on the other, a concatenation of three or more subtales that may be found elsewhere as freestanding tales in their own right or as subtales in other larger tales.[26] The opposition is often encoded even in the title of tales, which explains why Thompson identified the tale type (AT 1535) as "The Rich and the Poor Peasant." The linking of subtales occasions acute difficulties in comparing different variants. Thompson explains: "[T]hey are little more than a loose series of single anecdotes. Types of this kind have a natural instability very baffling to the investigator of folktale origins and dissemination."[27] Thompson had observed earlier: "The order in which the incidents occur is also treated with great freedom. Particularly is there a frequent mixture of the elements of this tale with that of Cleverness and Gullibility (Type 1539)."[28] This caveat about mixing could be enlarged, since AT 1535, "The Rich and the Poor Peasant," is related in its final episode also to AT 1525A, "Theft of Dog, Horse, Sheet or Ring. IV. Places Exchanged in Sack."

Thompson's statements give voice to highly problematic revelations about folktale theory. This very tale, so unstable, has been posited repeatedly as the earliest surviving Western European folktale text, yet it conflicts with the doctrine of stability that has been axiomatic in folktale scholarship. Accordingly, it has been acknowledged parenthetically in the name of the tale type, but its real challenges and importance have been downplayed or ignored. Literary variants survive from the eleventh century, as well as from the sixteenth century and beyond. The very existence of these variants and their nature pose problems about the relationship between oral and written transmission, as well as about the inherent stability or instability of folktales (at least of this type) and the kind of genesis that should be imagined for such tales.[29]

The connections among the different tales of this type cannot be schematized nearly so neatly as folklorists of the geographical school posited in the first half of the twentieth century.[30] Josef Müller (1905–)—perhaps not unexpectedly, as a German writing in 1934 in the often nationalistic arena of folklore studies—took the method to an extreme and envisaged the passage of this particular story across Europe as a systematic invasion, a kind of narrative equivalent to the triumphant progress of the Indo-Europeans (or Aryans) across the Continent. According to him, the tale originated in Indo-European antiquity, descended to the Celts in Ireland, and infiltrated the European mainland through Flanders, whence it spread to the south, west, and north.[31] But more interesting to me than constructing a Linnaean

taxonomy of tale types is to probe *One-Ox* and see what its major themes were as well as what kinds of generic expectations and knowledge it assumes on the part of its audience. To come to grips with its themes and genres may be made easier by comparing the Medieval Latin poem with later literary variants of the same story.

Before looking at a few specific motifs in *One-Ox* that will help furnish a background to this larger question, I should give a rapid overview of the poem's contents and structure, because the Latin poem belongs even less to the canon of world literature than does "Little Claus and Great Claus." If the brief prologue (strophes 1–3) and epilogue (216) are excluded, the poem falls into four parts,[32] as follows:

ONE
A. One-Ox discovers treasure (4–29).
The title character is called *Unibos* in Latin (which equates to *One-Ox* in English) because he is unable to afford and keep alive more than a single ox at a time. When eventually even his one ox dies, One-Ox skins it and sells the hide at market. On his return he finds coins while defecating.

B. Sale of the ox skins (30–67).
Accused by the provost of his village of having stolen his new wealth, One-Ox tells him that it derived from the sale of the hide in a neighboring town. The provost, mayor, and priest slaughter their animals and suffer distressing treatment at the market, where they expect instead to receive a warm welcome and high returns for the hides they put up for sale.

TWO
Murder (sham and real) of wives (68–114).
To distract the three dupes from their anger, One-Ox first stages the seeming death of his wife and then pretends to resuscitate her by playing a magic bugle, so as to convince onlookers that she has been rejuvenated and beautified.[33] This appeal to lust succeeds: the priest, provost, and mayor murder their own wives for real and of course are unable to bring them back to life.

THREE
Sale of the mare that supposedly defecates gold (115–58).[34]
In the poem's third episode, One-Ox again sidetracks his three fellow villagers from punishing him. This time he persuades them that his mare shits coins and, in response to their greedy pressure, sells the animal to them. The priest, provost, and mayor find nothing emitting from the anus of the beast except ordure—and one very small coin that had become embedded in a scar in an accident the horse had had as a filly.

FOUR

A. One-Ox escapes death (159–96).

One-Ox escapes death by inveigling a swineherd to take his place inside a barrel that his three foes roll into the ocean. The rascal tells the hapless herdsman that being inside the keg will lead to election as provost.[35]

B. One-Ox tricks his antagonists into killing themselves (197–215).

When he returns not only alive but in possession of a herd of swine, the provost, mayor, and priest are misled into hurling themselves to their death in the ocean, in the belief that the sea contains a paradise filled with swine.

ONE-OX AND FABLIAU

The moral world of *One-Ox* is, to state the case mildly, complex. One couplet in the middle of the poem sums up the complexity well: "There is a popular proverb: / 'There is not an evil that does not bring profit'" [Est vulgare proverbium: / "Quod non prosit, non est malum"] (151.1–2). The undefinable space between not being good and not being evil may be the home of many characters, but in the case of One-Ox, the one who comes to mind most swiftly is the trickster. Tricksters combine within themselves characteristics that would seem to be mutually exclusive, because they are diametrically opposed to each other. One-Ox is surrounded by such oppositions as full and empty, rich and poor, wise and foolish, greed and generosity, money and excrement, beauty and ugliness, friend and enemy, and good and evil.[36] He is regarded as foolish (*stultus*) by other characters but as cunning by the narrator ("artificem versutiae," 118; "callidus," 119). Furthermore, he exploits these oppositions in tricking his antagonists: his habitual modus operandi is to mislead them, which the poet expresses by using the verb *seduco* and its derivatives to describe One-Ox.[37] Such trickster figures embody the paradox that the person who overcomes deceitful, violent, and sinful opponents need not be heroic.

One-Ox has much in common with long biographies of slave or peasant trickster figures—such as the related works about Aesop in ancient Greek, Trubert in thirteenth-century Old French, Pfaffe Amis in Middle High German, Til Eulenspiegel in later German, or Bertoldo in Italian[38]—or even with animal trickster figures, such as Reynard the Fox. Typically, such stories relate the adventures of a lower-class or underclass rascal, a kind of slave or peasant picaro who plays the leading role in a *Schelmenroman* (picaresque novel), *Schwankroman, Schwanknovelle,* or *Schwankbiographie* (respectively, and very approximatively, comic novel, novella, and biography).[39] Although these tales as they come down to us from earlier periods may generally be in

texts composed for the entertainment of the privileged, all these narratives are at the same time safety valves that enable the release of pressures and resentments on the part of the less fortunate.[40] Thus they belong within the domain of the "carnival," as the term was used by the Russian literary scholar Mikhail Mikhailovich Bakhtin (1895–1975) in *Rabelais and His World*.[41] In Bakhtin's framework, carnival is a playful, popular world that exists in tandem with a somber, repressive, and exclusive world. Carnival and the popular life of which it constitutes the essence allow the common people a vent to relieve the stress of repression from the elite, which in the Middle Ages would have been based in the church and feudalism. The tales of slave and peasant trickster figures may have originated orally among these less-fortunate members of society before being recorded in writing for the entertainment of the more fortunate. The trickster figures they present confront the social and religious order, but their challenge is acceptable since the tricksters are presented as being outside reality or at least humanity because of their animal nature. Among Native Americans the animal is named explicitly Coyote. In the Uncle Remus stories the trickster is Brer Rabbit. The medieval equivalent would be Reynard the Fox, so much an animal but also so beloved that his proper name drove the original word meaning "fox" out of the French language. One-Ox is not an animal, but he is named by association with an animal. He is a peasant, in a category between the human and the other.[42] On the whole he bears a family resemblance to Aesop, who was a slave and freedman of inhuman ugliness who told tales about animals.

Yet to reclassify *One-Ox* so drastically when it is nothing approaching book-length would appear unnecessary, since the tale has also been categorized as the first example in Western literature in the genre that eventually gave rise to fabliaux, short, comic tales in verse.[43] The fabliau is a literary form best known in English through Chaucer's "The Miller's Tale" and "The Reeve's Tale" but most numerous in many dozens of Old French poems. There is dispute about how exactly to define fabliau, but by most counts, more than 150 of them survive from the twelfth to the fourteenth century. Rather than having emerged entirely ex nihilo, fabliaux are generally regarded as having been related to two earlier forms of Medieval Latin poetry, first the *ridicula* found in the eleventh-century *Cambridge Songs* and later the *comedie* (*comoediae* in classical orthography, and often not corresponding closely to modern conceptisms of comedy) attested in the twelfth and early thirteenth century. These connections have special relevance, since all of these genres contain materials that are attested later in folktales.

The poem is related in both overall narrative structure and particular motifs to a number of later comic stories, first in Old French fabliaux and then in types of literature in other languages—relationships that may per-

mit further insight into its genre.[44] In structure, *One-Ox* resembles such fabliaux as those in the group *Le Prestre qu'on porte,* which fuses two originally independent clusters of motifs.[45] In motifs, the circumstance in which One-Ox finds treasure while defecating has a parallel in a later fabliau: *The Knights, Clerics, and Peasants (Des chevaliers, des clercs et des vilains)* contains a similar scene.[46]

Although *One-Ox* would appear to violate the principle—enunciated by Per Nykrog in his seminal book—that a fabliau should relate only a single episode,[47] the arrangement of events in *One-Ox* bears a resemblance to the pattern of ascending repetition that is encountered in such fabliaux as *The Three Hunchbacked Minstrels (Des .III. Boçus menesterels).* Indeed, the episode in which each of One-Ox's antagonists kills his wife has very much the casualness about murder and its consequences that is evident in the later Old French story about the three hunchbacks. In addition, it could be mentioned that threesomes, often entailing a threefold repetition of events, were especially favored by fabliau writers: consider the titles *The Three Blind Men of Compiègne (Les Trois Aveugles de Compiegne), The Three Women Who Found the Ring (Les Trois Dames qui trouverent l'anel), The Three Girls (Les Trois Meschines), The Lady Who Walked Three Times around the Church (La Dame qui fist les trois tors entor le moustier),* and so forth.

One-Ox is by no means alone and cut off from fabliaux in its willingness to echo or at least parallel solemn religious motifs in ways we may find very provocative. The sham resuscitation of One-Ox's wife may have called to mind the resurrection of Jesus Christ himself, but it would have been no more theologically distressing to medieval readers than the unholy analogue to the annunciation in the fabliau *The Child Who Was Melted in the Sun (De L'enfant que fu remis au soleil),* in which a woman tries unsuccessfully to convince her husband that she has been impregnated not by sexual intercourse but instead by eating snow. Like the story found in *One-Ox,* the tragicomedy of the snow-child was also recounted for the first time in a Medieval Latin poem of the eleventh century.[48]

In *One-Ox,* the faked resurrection purports to bring about the rejuvenation of an aging wife. Thus it anticipates later popular motifs, such as the fantasized conversion of a loathly old lady to a beautiful young one in "The Wife of Bath's Tale" (and related tales) and the later medieval image of a recycling station, the "Old Wives' Mill," where dissatisfied husbands could take their aging spouses to be refurbished.[49] It finds an even more recent analogue in a joke that made the rounds a few years ago.

An Amish father and son, paying their first visit to a mall, were amazed at all the novelties, especially two silver walls that moved together and

apart. The boy asked, "What are these, Father?" The father answered, "Son, I have never seen anything like them before." As they watched in wonderment, an old lady in a wheel chair rolled up and pressed a circle on the wall. The walls moved apart, the lady rolled into a little room, and the walls moved together again. Small circles with numbers lighted up, one after the other, to higher numbers and then back down again. The walls moved apart again and a beautiful young woman walked out. The father said, "Son, go get your mother."

For better or for worse, the motif lives on.

SOCIAL COMMENTARY

The style of life of some rural nobles and parish priests was not so different from that of the peasants around them. They were also more or less cut off from the great tradition.[50]

The willingness of the poet of *One-Ox* to develop motifs that appear to press against basic tenets of Christianity is matched by his readiness to engage in social commentary that mocks aspects of the social order and economy of his day. He portrays a little world that is characterized by grim poverty. At the center of this world is the hut of One-Ox, where each episode begins and ends.[51] One-Ox is defined by his lowly position in society as a "peasant from peasant stock" [rusticus de rusticis] (4.2), the opposite of the lofty prince who is mentioned in the prologue. From the hut of this base peasant, the poet's disdain radiates out beyond One-Ox himself: satire of a peasant and peasant life is broadened to encompass a kind of rudimentary "estates satire," with criticism of the entire rural establishment, as embodied by the reeve/provost, mayor, and village priest.[52] The three men are identified so intimately with their functions in society that they are described only in terms of their offices (e.g., at 101.1 and 177.1); and even more strikingly, their wives are also.[53] The only one who elicits any sort of positive epithet is the priest, but the poet's designation of him as "celebrated priest of the church" [templi sacerdos inclitus] (30.4) is manifestly ironic.

When One-Ox's three antagonists believe that easy money lies within reach, they dream first of being freed from the onus of tilling the soil to support themselves: "There is no need for us / to plow any longer in rainstorms" [Non est opus sub imbribus / Arare nobis amplius] (39.1–2). It is the prospect of bountiful food that gulls the threesome into drowning themselves at the end. The poverty and hunger do not induce the poet to show any compassion. On the contrary, he voices nothing but scorn for

peasants and manual labor (strophes 4, 53, 56). If the characters represent their offices, then the major events of the poem constitute the harshest of satire: *One-Ox* relates the tale of a poor farmer who outwits, humiliates, punishes, and murders the three potentates of his village.

At least one critic has taken the central preoccupation of *One-Ox* to be the idea of acquiring money and becoming rich.[54] Although this interpretation is exaggerated, it is a small wonder to discover that the very similar "Little Claus and Great Claus" was presented in 1971 as a film by East German State Television.[55] In *One-Ox,* the acquisition of wealth is connected metaphorically with scatology. The conjunction of money and feces reflects a concern about the rise of a money economy.[56] It fits well also with the tendency of fairy tales to express views in favor of the poor and social classes at the very bottom, which are often depicted as being in conflict with classes above them.[57]

In *One-Ox,* two episodes in particular could be subjected readily to a Marxist interpretation but equally well to a Freudian one, since they draw a pungent correspondence between the fecal and the fiscal. In a collaborative work that Sigmund Freud wrote with D. E. Oppenheim, *Dreams in Folklore,* we are told first generally: "Psychoanalysis has taught us that in the very earliest period of childhood feces is a highly prized substance."[58] Later we learn more specifically about the alchemy that causes gold to symbolize feces—and feces to be a mockery of gold: "The most important residue of this former esteem is, however, that all the interest [*sic*] which the child has had in feces is transferred in the adult onto another material which he learns in life to set above almost everything else—gold."[59]

In the first of the two scenes subject to such interpretation, the anonymous poet describes the cloacal circumstances in which One-Ox comes upon his first hoard of money.

> After making the trade 16
> he mounts his mare;
> he is swollen, with distended belly,
> as he turns his steps backward.
> Having a presage of silver, 17
> he enters a frondy grove
> where, as he purges the vessel of his belly,
> he takes a money-filled reward.
> As he strives to wipe his backside, 18
> he hurries to tear off grass;
> but in plucking grass he finds
> that which greedy folk love.

> Soon he stumbles upon three hidden 19
> pint measures of coins
> which he places in a drooping little sack,
> that is soon made swollen.

This first scene stands out from both other episodes in the poem and from almost all other versions of the tale type, since—like the concluding scene, in which a swineherd happens to pass by the barrel in which One-Ox has been placed in preparation for his execution—it involves an act of fortune rather than cunning on the protagonist's part.

In the second scene subject to both Marxist and Freudian interpretation, the poet portrays One-Ox as he dupes his three antagonists into believing that his mare emits coins in its normal bowel movements.

> One-Ox replies cautiously: 127
> "Do you see these silver coins?
> The belly of this mare pours forth
> change instead of base dung.
> Every single night the mare 128
> shoots out such money:
> Ops, queen of money,
> resides in the opening of the anus."
> Upon seeing such things 129
> and hearing these words,
> the foes instantly cast away anger
> and speak thus to One-Ox:
> "If you wish to enjoy good fortune, 130
> sell us this animal;
> the three of us will put aside hate
> if we buy this swollen animal."

As in the case of the faux beautification of One-Ox's wife, the motif of the coin-defecating horse anticipates much later popular iconography.[60] Before the early eleventh century, coins were held in reverence, but with the rise of the profit economy thereafter, coins came to represent wealth and became debased.[61] As a consequence, equations between coins and excrement become more frequent. Against this backdrop, it becomes apparent that the reeve, priest, and mayor demean themselves and their offices by attempting to engage in commerce, which is unfamiliar to them and unfit even for men of such petty authority as they hold. They deserve to be humiliated by the lowest caste in the working class of the neighboring town, namely, one of

the "shabby shoemakers." Their debasement reaches its nadir when they are reduced to digging through an animal's dung in search of the smallest-denomination coin.

As an alternative to a Marxist or Freudian interpretation, a Christian reading of *One-Ox* as a condemnation of greed and lust can easily be imagined. The desire of the priest, provost, and mayor for a swift profit from the hides, for a money-producing horse, and for free herds of swine could be labeled greed, while their hope for their wives to be rendered young and beautiful would equate to lust.[62] Interpreted in this light, *One-Ox* takes on a certain likeness to such fabliaux as *Greed and Envy* (*Le Convoiteux et l'Envieux*) or *The Partridges* (*Les Perdris*), by Jean Bodel (ca. 1165–1210). Such tales may be read as allegories detailing the consequences of gluttony and lust.[63]

THE MORAL OF THE STORY

The moralizing dimension to fabliaux is what has caused many critics to discern a connection with fable that runs deeper than etymology alone.[64] In that regard it is worth paying very close attention to the moral that the poet attaches to the end of *One-Ox*.

But One-Ox in speaking	213
indicates the worst of dangers:	
"Where the shore is steeper,	
where the sea is deeper,	
hasten there swiftly,	214
without fear sink yourselves!	
There are bigger pigs in the water	
than there are on dry land."	
At the advice of One-Ox	215
the three give themselves to the precipices	
in fatal frenzy,	
dying foolishly from the leap.	
This tale shows	216
for ever and ever that	
the sly counsels of an enemy	
must not be believed.[65]	

The actions that precede the poem's last strophe have not appeared to all readers to lead logically or harmoniously to the final moral there provided. Indeed, it could be reasoned that *One-Ox* is meant to entertain through satire, not to instruct;[66] that it turns moral only at the end; and that the rest

of the poem is amoral or even immoral.[67] According to this way of think-ing, the moral at the end would be a late addition, slapped out when the composer realized abruptly that the story needed to have a moral in order to reach closure.[68] Incongruity between narratives and concluding morals is hardly unique in literary fairy tales, with Perrault's eleven tales affording the most famous examples.

But is the moral of *One-Ox* so out of step with what precedes it? In warning against credulousness, the moral responds precisely to the stupidity and gullibility of various characters. One-Ox is himself the first to behave foolishly (21.2), but he learns swiftly from his mistake and is later character-ized by his cleverness ("calliditas," 119). His foes regard One-Ox as dim-wit-ted (76), but it is they who behave unwisely (47, 60.3–4, 68, 102, 211, 215) and even insanely (47, 69, 94, 99.2, 102.3, 105, 114.1, 215.3).

Since *One-Ox* is billed at the beginning as a *fabula,* it is altogether ap-propriate that it be capped with a proverb—even though this closing moral is not equally applicable to all five episodes that precede it. But whether or not the last strophe is integrated with what led up to it, an alternative would be to see the moral as being superficially simple when in reality it was added to comment slyly and complexly on One-Ox and his deeds.[69] It sits well with the dichotomies that are a fundamental and recurring constituent of the poem. Just as the peasant who is thought to be a fool turns out to be cleverer than the vain and silly priest, the greedy mayor, or the equally greedy reeve, so, too, it is wise for all of us to weigh cautiously any advice that we receive and to be sure that following it is to our advantage and does not exploit any weaknesses of ours.

The moral universe of *One-Ox* bears a resemblance to that of "The Snow-Child" ("Modus Liebinc" [app. 2C]), in which there is a stark tit for tat—a kind of moral physics or naive morality in which no action or im-pulse is without its equal and opposite response. The deceived lose first their oxen and money, then their wives, and finally their lives.[70] Correspondingly, the deceiver triumphs completely. His triumph is totally amoral—but it is not to be regretted, since his opponents are no more moral than he is. In this lack of morality, the story resembles the Reynard cycle.

It would be simplistic to reduce One-Ox himself to being Satan, the supreme opponent, in this poem's universe. He can be diabolic without standing allegorically for the Devil.[71] Rather, the closing moral stands in sym-metry with the opening attempt to appeal to ears that are "fond of novel-ties" [amicae novitatibus] (1.4). The "sly counsels of an enemy" [Inimici consilia / . . . subdola] (216.1–3) may be understood as the contents of the tale itself, which would make the person who purveys such novelties into the *inimicus.* Believing in the fantastic is not always good or advantageous.

THE COURTLINESS OF *ONE-OX*

Per Nykrog's *Les Fabliaux* has become a classic of medieval literary scholarship because of its lucidity and thoroughness in making several major provocative assertions, one of which was that the fabliaux did not emanate from the bourgeoisie, as had been widely held, but rather came from a courtly class. One effect of the present subsection in this chapter may be to undergird this assertion by demonstrating how a fabliau-like text of the eleventh century was itself courtly. The presumptive courtliness of *One-Ox* cries out to be set in a broad literary context, especially in view of recent contentions that the phenomena often considered indicators of courtliness existed already in the eleventh century. Whatever the shortcomings of the conception "courtly love" (and there are many), the phrase is an apt acknowledgment that courts and their cultures proliferated in the Middle Ages. For much of the twentieth century, the courtliness was thought to have arisen in secular courts of southern France and from there radiated to northern France, Sicily and the rest of Italy, and other regions of Europe. Only much more recently have scholars recognized that the courtesy of the secular courts was related intimately to the *curialitas* of ecclesiastic courts. C. Stephen Jaeger made a compelling case that courtliness took shape between 950 and 1150 in both episcopal and noble courts in communities along the Rhine.[72] Gerald Bond amplified this theory, by arguing that courtliness in Latin documents from communities along the Loire in the later eleventh century sometimes antedated that in extant French literature.[73] Although Jaeger makes scant reference to such Medieval Latin literature as the *Ruodlieb,* arguably the first extant medieval romance, Bond pays close attention to courtly lyric in the Latin verse of Baudri of Bourgueil and others. But no one has attempted at any length to situate *One-Ox* within this context, even though Per Nykrog recommended such an attempt in *Les fabliaux* when citing a comment of Gaston Paris on Bédier.[74]

This omission seems very odd, in that the poet of *One-Ox*—who, simply by knowing Latin, would appear almost unquestionably to have been a monk or cleric[75]—claims explicitly in the prologue that at least one audience of his tale is courtly.

People's eyes are not satisfied 1
by seeing the realities of the world;
their ears are
fond of novelties.
At the table of a great prince 2
is told the account of One-Ox;

it is presented as a fabliau
in playful words.
Banquets come about through foods, 3
but literary compositions through words;
in a performance of characters
let us sing of One-Ox.
A son of ridiculous sons, 4
he is a peasant from peasant stock.
Nature made him a man
but fortune a wunderkind.

This programmatic statement, which is studded with terms that come tantalizingly close to earlier and later genre markers, has led to widely divergent interpretations.[76]

The most drastic interpretation of the lines may be the rejection by one scholar of the very idea that the first strophe contains information about the genre of the poem.[77] According to this view, the reference to "novelties" [novitatibus] in the first strophe (1.4) is mere rhetoric, while the word *fabula* in the second strophe (2.3) as well as in the epilogue (216.3) should be translated simply as "poetry" or "poem." Less radical than denying any generic significance to the strophes would be to remain open to seeing the term *novitatibus* (1.4) as loosely anticipating the later Italian term *novelle*—from which the Modern English term *novels* eventually evolved—with the common elements being short fiction with a realistic component. It would also be less radical to understand the term *fabula* as being related distantly to later fabliaux or more proximately to fable. The chief character is, after all, given a name that connects him with a farm animal familiar from both reality and beast fable.

The notion of novelty recurs throughout the poem. The three chief fools (*stulti*) make their principal mistakes out of an infatuation with novelty. Thus they are astounded at the novelty of the mare that produces coins (124.4 "De novo facto stupent"). The poet uses this concept of novelty to criticize not only the *stulti* but also perhaps *fabula* (in the sense of "fairy tale") itself. Ingrained in the Latin language from Roman times is the preconception that innovation is seditious, novelty worthless or even perilous. The foolish foes are too enamored of the unheard of possibilities that One-Ox orchestrates, and they give too much credit to strange sights and words: "Under the canopy of heaven / such things have never been heard / as One-Ox perpetrated" [Infra cæli tentoria / Non sunt audita talia, / Quæ perpetrauit Unibos] (68.1–3). Once again, speeches make up a large part of the poem, and *novitates* that One-Ox's foes hear and see induce them to all their foolish ac-

tions. Could their fate be a warning to the audience of *One-Ox* not to be taken in by the strange tales—the fictions and novels—of their day? *One-Ox* and its genre encourage foolish behavior (44.3). There is a parallel between, on the one hand, One-Ox and his effect on his three foes and, on the other, the poet and his possible effect on his audience. Folktales can be entertaining but must be pondered carefully, lest they seduce into foolishness.

The opening of the second strophe, with its apparent claim that the story contained in the poem was told at the table of a great lord, would seem to point to a courtly setting, but to exactly what type of court it refers is impossible to say. By *princeps* (prince), the poet could designate either a lay lord or a lord in the church.[78] In either case, the purported addressee of the Latin poem could not be more starkly demarcated from the central figure of the fiction within it, whose genealogy emphasizes his peasant origins. As a plowman, One-Ox is representative of an entire class, much like his later coworkers Piers Plowman and the impoverished knight in *The Turnip Tale*. Like both of them, but by very different means, One-Ox could bring hope to an entire class (if the members of that class were told the story in a language or format they could understand). At the same time, the boorish behavior and beliefs of him and his fellow villagers help to fix the nature of the class to which the Latin-using audience of *One-Ox* belonged: the urbane and courtly require the counterpoint of the rustic and boorish to define and legitimate themselves. For One-Ox simultaneously to be a hero to one class and the antihero to another may seem paradoxical, but it is common for stories that convey the concerns and aspirations of one group to be taken to serve less flattering aims of another group. This kind of appropriation and redirection may be detectable in Egbert's handling of "Little Red Riding Hood," and it is certainly to be seen in "The Wish-Goat" (*Wunschbock* [app. 2A]), "The Song to the Flowers Tune" ("Modus florum" [app. 2D]), and *The Turnip Tale* (*Rapularius* [app. 4A–B]).

The third strophe is just as provocative as the first two. Its opening line conjures up the conviviality of a banquet, a reprise of the prince's table that was mentioned in the preceding strophe. The real food of the meal is the verbal entertainment. The intertwining of food metaphorics and textual metaphorics is reminiscent of the fifth-century prose text known as *Cyprian's Banquet* (*Cena Cypriani*), as well as of the eleventh-century centolike *Escape of a Certain Captive, Recounted in Allegorical Fashion* (*Ecbasis cuiusdam captivi per tropologiam*).[79] But the complexity is not solely textual, since—at least in the fiction—the verbal entertainment has a "live" component: it involves the eyes and ears, which suggests performance; it takes place "in personarum drammate" (which smacks of theater, if only on the order of a mime play); and it is delivered as song ("cantemus").[80] The author seems to

have made a deliberate effort to convey as much of the action in dialogue form as he could, a strategy that fits with the idea of performance with the assistance of miming.[81] Further support for the theory that the poem was meant to be accompanied by mime play could come from the fact that at least one scene, that in the barrel (or sack), entered eventually into the tradition of comic theater of the marketplace: one finds it in the second of four farces traditionally ascribed to Tabarin.[82]

Was this fabula a proto-fabliau? It is called a fabula at both the beginning and the end. But the word *fabula* possessed such a vast spectrum of meaning in Medieval Latin that this assumption would be very risky if it rested on the two occurrences of this word alone.

THE WONDER OF *ONE-OX*

Albert Wesselski argued that *One-Ox* is not a fairy tale but, rather, a *Märlein* that applies motifs connected with folly and delusion only so as to mock them.[83] Although the closing observation is part of the truth, a more important realization is that *One-Ox* and other pieces of the tenth and eleventh centuries appear simultaneously to deride and yet to acknowledge belief in wonder, which comprehends not only wonder of a religious sort (what is often tagged as "miracle") but also wonder of a worldlier kind ("marvel").[84] The presence in these texts of miracles that are not really miracles could constitute a parody—possibly entailing a subtle criticism—of literary genres in which miracles occupy a fundamental position.[85] Although the genre of medieval literature that might spring first to mind is hagiography, the wonder tale would have been just as likely a target. In any case, *One-Ox* and its kin lack the serenity that endues fairy tale with its peculiar quality. Instead, they bring realism and fantasy recurrently into juxtaposition—and into tension. They differ from fairy tale as defined by either folklorists or literary historians, but they simultaneously resemble fairy tale so closely that even Wesselski believed that children, who have been intimately associated with fairy tale at the latest since the classic fairy tale collections of the nineteenth century, would draw no distinction between the two tale types.[86]

Letaldus's poem of the fisherman swallowed by the whale is an early (but by no means unique) manifestation of a simultaneous fascination for the wonderful or marvelous and an awareness of the dangers that excessive credulity could pose to the religious and social order. The *Cambridge Songs* offer ample testimony of the schizophrenic outlook that held sway. "The Snow-child" ("Modus Liebinc," or "The Song to the Liebo Tune" [app. 2C]) mocks belief in miraculous conception—of the sort that led to the

birth of Christ. In "The Song to the Flowers Tune" ("Modus florum" [app. 2D]) a cunning Swabian wins the hand of a princess by telling a lie that the king must call a lie, because to do otherwise would allow the irrationality of hereditary rule to be overturned—and with it most of the medieval social order. The lie that the Swabian tells is vaguely reminiscent of the lies that provide the very basis of "The Wish-Goat" (*Wunschbock* [app. 2A]), a poem about three poor sons who are heirs to the single goat of their recently deceased father. They decide that the one of them who tells the most extraordinary lie will win sole possession of the beast. All of these lying stories poke fun at or even more harshly treat belief in wonder.[87]

One of the *Cambridge Songs* is an anecdote about Archbishop Heriger (app. 2E) that mocks a tale of a trip to paradise. Because visions of the otherworld were the stuff of medieval classics long before Dante's *Divine Comedy*, the good bishop cannot reject the notion of such an experience—but he can catch out the alleged visionary in misconduct within his imagined paradisiacal expedition. This is the one earlier tale that seems closely analogous to part of *One-Ox*, since the final episode in the eleventh-century poem sees the foolish threesome commit suicide under the misimpression that they will thereby cross over into a land of Cockaigne, an imaginary paradise where food and other pleasures abound.[88]

There is no need to seek a source in a particular time or place for the mockery of belief in wonder that pervades these various compositions.[89] But it is useful to consider that such derision would seem to presume the prior existence of wonder tales that were once taken seriously. A genre cannot be ridiculed if it does not already exist and if the audience does not have foreknowledge of its nature. Otherwise the parody of its conventions would make no sense.

One-Ox constitutes a summa of the love-hate relationship toward wonder that seems to have taken hold of ever more people after the beginning of the second millennium. It casts doubt on not only belief in wonder but also the fictions that portray wonder. It unmasks as deceptions such stock elements of fairy tale as resuscitation of the dead, gold-producing animals, and messages from paradise that lead to voyages into the otherworld.

Terminology had not yet developed to discriminate readily between wonder and miracle. The provost in *One-Ox* equates "miracle" and "prodigy" when relating to his henchmen the profit to be made in selling hides: "I will tell you a miracle, / reveal a wonder" [Vobis dicam miraculum, / revelabo prodigium] (33.1–2). Later, when the provost and henchmen watch the little scene that One-Ox stages with the mare, they see "a marvelous thing" [causam . . . mirabilem] (123.4). The poem does not mock miracles, since it depicts no truly miraculous events but, rather, only a series of pseudomiraculous

events that appear miraculous to the eyes of the provost and the others but that are devised for the goal of trickery.[90]

One-Ox himself attains a fairy-tale ending, partly through luck, mainly through his own ingenuity and work. He knows better than anyone else that no miracles have occurred. In addition to being a trickster who takes advantage of gullibility, One-Ox is a tale-teller, who purveys wonder tales that he presents so effectively as to persuade his listeners to accept them as reality. The tale is an object lesson in not mistaking fairy tales for reality.

With a vehemence that has been typical of realistic satire, *One-Ox* kills its version of the classic "goose that lays the golden egg"—that is, the pseudo-*Goldesel*, the donkey that is supposed to defecate golden dung but that turns out to be all too much a real-life ass in what it emits. The presence of it in *One-Ox* is a clear borrowing from fairy tale[91]—the animal that produces gold is a motif (*MI* B103.1.1) familiar from such classic fairy tales as *KHM* 36, "Tischlein deck dich" (Table-Be-Set) (ATU 563). *One-Ox's* mockery of credulity and stupidity comprehends contempt for belief in wonders.

The key in all the deceptions is an event that the trickster misrepresents as a wonder.[92] The skin that One-Ox claims to have sold at an extraordinarily high price is not enchanted, as is the hide in *The Donkey Tale* or in "Donkeyskin" ("Peau d'Âne," a verse fairy tale by Perrault [1694]). But One-Ox is able to dupe his opponents into believing that it and all other hides are invested with inexplicably marvelous worth in the market of the border town. Twice One-Ox is a theater director, putting together props and preparing stunts or rehearsing his fellow actors so as to create an illusion. His pieces of theater would be well suited to accompanying mime play, for which the prologue to the poem prepares us.

For the deception to succeed requires a two-sided equation (what other kind is there?), of which One-Ox's cunning is one side and his opponents' greedy gullibility the other. One-Ox's dupes respond by forgiving him his past misdeeds and by rewarding him, until they understand through their unsuccessful imitation of the event that they have once again been tricked—whereupon, incapable of remembering all their mistakes and learning from them, they renew the cycle. The three opponents choose to believe the unbelievable—that ox hides can be sold for vast sums, that a horn can resurrect dead women, that a mare can produce coins rather than excrement, and that herds of pigs dwell beneath the seas. Part of their avarice is a greed for wonder: this greed makes them susceptible again and again to perceiving One-Ox's deceptions as wonders (strophes 33, 123, 126). Once the men have slaughtered their cattle, they are "confirmed in stupidity" [Firmati per stultitiam] (47.1), and they have space only to go further "to madness" [ad insaniam] (47.2). The priest is "armed with madness" [armatus ex insania]

(99.1). Their only wealth is in foolishness, as they are "rich in idiocy" [Fatuitatis divites] (196.1). They outdo each other in *stultitia* (211.1). Rather than face reality, they try to live in a fairy-tale dreamworld ("inani pleni somnio," 49).

Even when deception is not involved, the poet is irreverent. *One-Ox* is unique among the stories like it in having treasure be found when the title character is responding to the call of nature:[93] the pot of treasure is made to become dangerously similar to a chamber pot. The "miracle" that makes One-Ox a marvel to behold is a kind of peristalsis of distention and emptying. The movements from full to empty and from empty to full are basic to human existence. Only One-Ox the trickster is able to master the cycle to profit and survive. Thanks to fortune, he receives money for feces, sells feces for money, and trades deadly emptiness for profit. After selling the hide of his dead ox, One-Ox fills his belly, mounts his mule, and sets out for home. Now swollen ("Distento ventre turgidus," 16.3), he stops to relieve himself by emptying the basin of his belly. As he reaches to break off grass to wipe his anus, he finds the treasure, and he places the money in his formerly empty purse—which then is made swollen ("Quos in flaccenti sacculo / Ponit mox facto turgido," 19.3–4). The movement has the spare symmetry of a law in physics: a full stomach empties as an empty purse fills. Plenitude has been conserved, but with a transformation: One-Ox begins and ends his homeward journey full, but with two types of fullness. He has lost one bloated bag but gained another, far richer one.

The equal but opposite of this process takes place in subsequent episodes. The reeve rushes to tell his companions about the incredible trade One-Ox made with the ox hide. The poet describes him as being "packed full of such great reports" [Fartus tantis rumoribus] (32.2). But the band of three simpletons returns home empty-handed, "with depleted purses / in empty carts" [Exhaustis in marsuppiis, / Otiosis in curriculis] (66.3–4). They turn over their money to One-Ox to purchase his mare, which excretes for them not money but ordure. The same opposition comes to the fore in the final scene, in which the three foes place One-Ox in an empty barrel with the intent to kill him. Before rolling the barrel into the sea, they leave it to refresh themselves. In the meantime One-Ox tricks the swineherd into taking his place. The swineherd enters the hollow vessel in his place ("Subulcus intrat concavum / vas," 189.1). The pattern here is empty barrel to full (with One-Ox inside), empty to full (with the swineherd inside). Only One-Ox attains lasting fullness. On returning from his supposed death, "foresighted, he bugles with a prolonged sound" [distente prudens bucinat] (199.1). He reminds his foes of how he duped them before (206–7).

By the end of *One-Ox,* the poet has delivered a QED or maybe two.

One is that if there is a marvel, it is not any of the supposed wonders that One-Ox peddles to his victims. Rather, it is One-Ox himself. At the beginning of the poem, he is anything but fortunate or wonderful: he is not a god, not a hero, not even just what nature made him—a man. But eventually he turns into what fortune makes him—a marvel. Proving that two negatives can make a positive, he is the anti-hero of an anti–wonder tale. In wonder tales, the norms and values of the public are upended by the extraordinary; in trickster tales, such as *One-Ox,* those norms and values are subverted rather than transcended.[94] The two forms of literature exist nonetheless interlocked with each other, like positrons and electrons in an atomic structure.

One way of viewing *One-Ox* is to regard it as having been far ahead of its time.[95] Another perspective is to see it as the only extant written form of a kind of story that had to have circulated widely orally. The attitude toward the marvelous presupposes that there were wonder tales toward which the educated struck a contemptuously or amusedly dismissive pose. But like the genre of "monks' jests" (*ioca monachorum,* which involve questions and answers that may seem initially to be as superficial as the board game Trivial Pursuit),[96] the wonder tales had a serious backdrop. Augustine had adumbrated a theory of miracles that had served well for more than half a millennium. According to him, the only miracle was resurrection.[97] He maintained that people fail to see the miraculous in the everyday world of nature, because familiarity breeds contempt rather than awe. Accordingly, in Augustine's estimation, God undertakes to show power in miracles, and such miracles are not really against nature but, rather, beyond or above it.[98]

Miracles were closely, often inextricably related to *mira, monstra, prodigia,* and *signa:*[99] miracles could become interwoven with exotic and inexplicable wonders. In ecclesiastical histories, the "normal miracles" (if that oxymoron may be allowed) were those of saints, but in secular histories and elsewhere, writers permitted themselves ever greater latitude. It may be no coincidence that Letaldus's poem about Within, one of the first great strides toward the literary use of wonder tales in Medieval Latin, appears in the one extant manuscript as a pendant to Bede's *Ecclesiastical History.* In the twelfth century, parallel worlds are established, with miracles of saints in one and prodigies or marvels of the natural world in another. The latter world encompasses Walter Map's *Courtiers' Trifles* and other such texts. But maybe the worlds were not always parallel. Maybe the planes sometimes warped and touched, as often happens in romance (both the genre and the emotional phenomenon). The Medieval Latin wonder tales of the twelfth century belong to these new contacts. Once again, the *Cambridge Songs* anticipate what was to become more fully developed and entrenched a century later. Two of the

comic texts (*ridicula*) in the collection—one about a false prophet and Arch-bishop Heriger of Mainz (app. 2E) and the other about an aspiring desert fa-ther named "Little John" (app. 2G)—belong to the genre that has been called "saints' jokes" (*ioca sanctorum*), in an allusion to the "monks' jests."[100] Such *ioca* are not attacks on miracles but, rather, wry appreciation of the in-congruities between the power of God and the inconsequentiality of human ambitions and pretensions. *One-Ox* fits into this same category.

THE *RUMOR* OF *ONE-OX:*
THE TALE BEFORE THE POEM

Many of the puzzles surrounding *One-Ox* can be understood once we accept that the earliest literary version of such a tale is not necessarily the earliest of all versions and that the oral reflexes may have circulated in the most diverse of milieus. In other words, the tale could have existed with a recognizably similar structure of motifs and array of characters in oral culture. This tale could then have been appropriated to very different ends by an artist who aimed to satisfy the aesthetics and values of a court audience or a religious audience. To be specific, the monk or cleric who composed *One-Ox* in Latin may have co-opted both the voice and the tale of a popular performer pre-senting a tale orally at a feast. Thus the "playful words" [verba jocularia] (2.4) of the *One-Ox* poet may have Latinized what had been originally the vernac-ular words of a decidedly nonmonastic and nonclerical jongleur.

If we seek a model for the kind of interaction that may have taken place, Guibert of Nogent's *Monodiae,* written around the year 1115, contains a pas-sage that provides a fascinating one. In this episode, a rebellious mob whose ringleader is a peasant named Theudegaud seeks out Bishop Gaudry, who has taken refuge from them.

> As the others were searching for Gaudry among the containers, Theudegaud halted in front of the barrel in which the bishop was hiding, smashed in the cover and twice asked: "Who is in there?" Shaken by the blows Gaudry was hardly able to move his frozen lips to answer: "A prisoner." Now the bishop had the habit of calling Theudegaud by the derisive name of Isengrin, on account of his wolfish profile—that is the name some people give to wolves. So this scoundrel called out to the bishop: "Might it not be my lord Isengrin hiding in there?"[101]

This anecdote hints that both clerics and commoners were well acquainted with the character Isengrin (or Ysengrimus, as he was sometimes designated

in Latin), the wolf who was an archenemy of the fox Reynard (Reinardus in Latin), even before the French form of the name, Renard, became so popular as to drive out the native word meaning "fox" (*goupil*).[102] (To find an equivalent of Reynard's name becoming the standard word meaning "fox" in French, we would need to imagine the names of the cartoon characters Mickey Mouse or Bugs Bunny entirely displacing the usual nouns for a mouse or a rabbit in English.) The longest Latin reflexes of the *Roman de Renart* (e.g., the *Ecbasis captivi* and the *Ysengrimus,* a twelfth-century epic often ascribed to Nivard of Ghent)[103] are connected with monasteries—but the place of origin of "The Priest in the Pit" (*Cambridge Songs* 35; app. 2F) is not immediately apparent. Later versions connected with vernacular authors (the earliest extant vernacular texts are Old French) seem to have been by clerics and to have been intended for noble audiences. But this interaction, which antedates all of both types of texts, presupposes that stories about Isengrin and Reynard circulated orally and formed a culture shared by both laypeople and literati.

A similar paradigm in U.S. culture would be embodied in Joel Chandler Harris's Uncle Remus stories. Over the past thirty years, Uncle Remus has been rejected as a kind of Uncle Tom because of his seeming subservience to his young master and his superficially benign harmlessness, qualities that would have made him attractive to the market of middle-class book buyers in the late nineteenth century but that, with changed social attitudes, have sent even the Walt Disney film (with both animation and live action) *Song of the South* (1946), which is based on Uncle Remus, into banishment with Helen Bannerman's *Little Black Sambo* (1899) and other such bestsellers of yore that became tainted with racism.[104] At the same time, Uncle Remus offers, in both his own person and his alter ego of Brer Rabbit, an example of considerable independence and a clever ability to survive. In other words, Uncle Remus not only represents the loyal slave or retainer who dotes on his young master but also embodies the frequently subversive life experience and indomitable survival skills of generations of slaves and is anything but an Uncle Tom. The stories purportedly related by Uncle Remus can have had one meaning or set of meanings for the oral storytellers from whom they were collected (not necessarily with whom they originated) and another for those who wrote them down, and the central characters in the tales of Uncle Remus, the heroes and antiheroes, may have been judged in one way by the "original" African American audiences of the oral tales and in another by the subsequent public of white readers.[105]

How does all this relate to *One-Ox*? One-Ox bears a family resemblance to Brer Rabbit in the stories of Joel Chandler Harris. He has the least power of any character with whom he interacts, but through cunning he manages

always to prevail. Even when he chooses his ostensible mode of death in strophe 163, he resembles his furry relative: for him, the barrel is "anywhere but the briar patch, anywhere but the briar patch."[106] The story of One-Ox, a desperately poor peasant at the beginning and a cash- and chattel-rich burgher at the end, could have meant different things in different tellings and to different audiences. The tale could be shot through with tensions between at least one earlier set of meanings and its new telling context or contexts. In the tale's oral form, One-Ox could have been a culture hero to a popular or peasant audience—to what could be considered subaltern classes. In Latin verse, his story could have been an amusement for highly literate courtiers, whether at a noble court, an ecclesiastic court (e.g., a bishop's court), or both. The values of the original audience that are infixed in the story could have been the object of merriment or even contempt for the new audience. Thus One-Ox would have been a predecessor of the later peasant wit Marcolf from *Salomon et Marcolfus* (Solomon and Marcolf), who is introduced to us as a peasant descended from peasants ("rusticus de rusticis"), in terms coincidentally very similar to those in which One-Ox is brought on stage in the exordium of *One-Ox*.

> 1a In fact, King Solomon, when he had noticed them, began to speak in this way, saying: "Who are you, and what is your lineage?" 1b Marcolf replied, "You tell us first your genealogy and that of your forefathers, and then I will indicate to you our lineage." 2a Solomon said, "I come from twelve generations of prophets . . . and I am King Solomon." 2b Marcolf replied, "And I come from twelve generations of boors: Rusticus begot Rustan; Rustan begot Rusticius; Rusticius begot Rusticellus; Rusticellus begot Tartar; Tartar begot Tartol; Tartol begot Farsi; Farsi begot Farsol; Farsol begot Marcuil; Marcuil begot Marcuart; Marcuart begot Marcol; Marcol begot Marcolf, and I am Marcolf the fool."[107]

One-Ox has the same sort of complexity: some may regard him as foolish (*stultus*), but in the poet's judgment he is an "artificer of cunning" [artificem versutiae] (118.3) who is characterized by "cleverness" [calliditas] (119.1). In fact, he has an almost Odyssean capacity to turn dangerous situations to his advantage, to survive, and sometimes even to win. The most famous epithet to characterize the Greek hero was *polytropos,* "having many devices or turns" (Homer *Odyssey* 10.330). One-Ox is "versutus" (69.1), "artifex versutie" (118.3), "vestitus tegnis" (131.1), and "versipellis" (134.1). So well versed in wiles is One-Ox that it would be tempting to connect this clan of "turning points" with the first word of the title *Versus de Unibove,* as referring not only

to "verses" of poetry but also to the "turn" One-Ox's life takes from poverty to riches, a kind of boustrophedon.

One-Ox may have started his existence as a buffoon figure, whose antics amused courtiers: even the most book-learned are relieved sometimes to see worldly wisdom prevail over learning, especially when the learning is not the deep erudition to which they aspire themselves but, rather, the veneer that is acquired by country folk with pretensions. Alternatively, One-Ox may have begun life as a trickster-hero in the fireside tales of peasants. Finally, it may be pointless to conceive of his origins in such polar terms, since, from the earliest times, One-Ox may have coexisted in the entertainments of both the poor and the privileged. When we encounter One-Ox for the first time in a document, he already has an ambiguous history. He is pinioned fascinatingly at the overlap of three seemingly discrete spaces: the village setting in which he performs his feats, the noble milieu in which his story is purportedly related viva voce, and the Latin verse and manuscript in which *One-Ox* is recorded.

HANS CHRISTIAN ANDERSEN AND EARLIER LITERARY VARIANTS OF THE ONE-OX TALE

Andersen crossed a bridge when he transferred a number of tales from folklore to literature, but we, the scholars, investigate either one or the other side of the bridge. We have not quite succeeded in describing the crossing itself.[108]

In "Big Claus and Little Claus" Hans Christian Andersen succeeded in writing one of the most popular of his stories without making any significant changes in the tradition as he had learned it.[109]

Quite emphatically, the Hans Christian Andersen tale of "Little Claus and Great Claus" seems, in its roll of characters, to be far removed from courts and courtiers. Although it is much more broadly known than *One-Ox,* not all readers carry its narrative etched in their hearts. Accordingly, I will here recapitulate its events summarily.

The tale features two chief characters, both named Claus, who live in the same village. The protagonist is a poor man called Little Claus, the antagonist a rich one known as (surprise!) Great Claus. Great Claus owns four horses, Little Claus one. By mutual agreement, Great Claus has the right to use Little Claus's horse six days of the week. In recompense, Little Claus has Great Claus's horse at his disposal on Sundays. On his sole day of possession, Little Claus infuriates Great Claus by lording it up so much (exclaim-

ing, "Gee up, all my horses!" as churchgoers pass by) that finally, to punish and silence him, Great Claus strikes dead Little Claus's only horse.

On his way to salvage what good he can from this terrible loss by selling the horse's hide, Little Claus is forced by a storm to seek shelter at a farm. When the farmer's wife refuses to allow him inside the farmhouse, he rests on a thatched roof over a haystack. From that vantage, he sees a deacon[110] ready to enjoy a lavish meal with the wife. Little Claus also sees how the wife hides both the deacon (in a chest) and the meal (in the oven) when her farmer-husband returns unexpectedly. The narrator reveals that the farmer loathes the deacon greatly and that the mere sight of the deacon suffices to send him flying into a rage. Through the hospitality of the farmer, Little Claus is finally invited within to dine on porridge that the wife grudgingly serves. Pretending that the squeaks emitted by pockets of air in the horse's hide that he sees at his feet are the words of a wizard, Little Claus draws the farmer's attention to the hidden food and drink. The farmer at this point asks if the wizard can make the Devil appear. Little Claus convinces him that the deacon in the chest is truly the Devil. Eventually Little Claus swaps the supposed wizard for a bushel of money. In return for a barrow, he also undertakes to rid the farmer of the chest and the Devil. Then, as a bribe from the deacon for not drowning him, he collects another bushel of money.

Back at home, Little Claus's improved circumstances become known to Great Claus when the former sends a boy to Great Claus to borrow a bushel measure for measuring his money. Great Claus smears the bottom of the measure with tar, so that three coins are stuck to it when it comes back to him. Little Claus convinces his fellow Claus that the money came from the sale of the horse's hide, which motivates Great Claus to slay and flay all four of his horses. At the market, predictably, he obtains from the shoemaker and tanners nothing of the fortune he awaited. Instead, they mock him and give him a beating.

Determined to avenge himself, Great Claus sets out to kill Little Claus. In the meantime Little Claus's grandmother has by chance died and been laid out in Little Claus's bed. As a result, Great Claus axes the already dead grandmother thinking that she is Little Claus. Little Claus transports the lifeless old woman as if she were still alive in his cart to an inn, where the innkeeper, furious at her unresponsiveness to him, tosses a glass full of mead in her face and causes the corpse to topple. Following a quick tussle, Little Claus receives another bushel of coins as hush money in return for a promise to remain silent about the apparent crime. Little Claus once again sends his boy to borrow Great Claus's bushel measure. After Little Claus assures him that his latest trove of money came from retailing the cadaver of his grandmother to an

apothecary, Great Claus takes an ax to his own grandmother but soon discovers that he will incur only punishment for his action.

Enraged, Great Claus takes a big sack and thrusts Little Claus into it with the aim of drowning him. En route to a river to dump him, Great Claus stops at a church. While he is inside, an old herdsman passing by hears Little Claus talking of being too young to go to heaven. The old herdsman, who would like nothing more than to reach heaven, takes his place in the sack. Great Claus throws the sack into the river. On the way home, Great Claus meets Little Claus as he herds his newly acquired cattle. Little Claus persuades him that the cattle came from a wonderful land of people at the bottom of the river. Great Claus has Little Claus put him in a sack and push it into the river. With that event the tale concludes.

As the preceding summary confirms, "Little Claus and Great Claus" is not identical in its every character or motif to *One-Ox,* but the two stories are remarkably similar for two tales that most definitely do not stand in a direct source-and-influence relationship and that are separated by some seven hundred years in their dates of composition. Both feature three tricks that involve the selling of an animal skin, deceit involving the death of a woman, and doomed-to-riches drowning. Both have stupid and credulous antagonists.

The differences between the two accounts tend to reveal the earlier version to be more logical and less inconsistent. They also suggest that Andersen may have sanitized the tale, perhaps because he suspected already that children would be an important part of his audience.[111] In any case, they reveal that the social milieus in which the authors operated were very different. In Andersen's tale, Little Claus is not introduced with the mixture of hauteur and awe that One-Ox elicits in the Latin poem. Instead, Little Claus is meek. Little Claus and Great Claus share the same occupation, but they are separated by their differing economic circumstances. One-Ox, although rustic and poor like the village potentates, stands apart from them by having no special authority; he is a mere farmer, whereas they hold secular and ecclesiastic offices. The struggle in Andersen takes place between rich and poor, whereas the prevailing distinction in *One-Ox* is more a matter of the powerful versus the powerless.

In each of the two stories, the killing of women forms an essential episode, but no wife killing or even mention of wives occurs in "Little Claus and Great Claus." The corresponding character is the grandmother. In *One-Ox* the episode at the market fair leads smoothly into the murder. One-Ox himself stages the scene, in which his antagonists are portrayed as the greatest of fools (*stultissimi*) who can be mislead easily by a trick (*dolo*). In contrast, One-Ox comes across as being a trickster par excellence. In "Little

Claus and Great Claus" the same scene occurs by accident and is considerably less gruesome: Little Claus's grandmother dies spontaneously, and the feature of the true bloodbath is unnecessary. His reactions to the death suggest that Little Claus has a very simple character, in both good and bad senses. The narrator reveals that the grandmother had never been nice to Little Claus and yet that he felt sad at her passing and placed her corpse in his bed in a doomed attempt to resuscitate her. Later developments introduce peculiar inconsistencies of a sort not found in *One-Ox*. For instance, the businessman twice refers to the dead old woman as if she had been Little Claus's mother rather than grandmother.

A comparison of the concluding episode of the barrel or sack also favors *One-Ox* as more authentic. In *One-Ox* the title character uses his wiles much more deliberately, showing greater cunning and ingenuity. The trickster-hero makes loftier promises and evidences a shrewder sense of character and a more pronounced ability to control his emotions. In "Little Claus and Great Claus" the episode seems to come about almost by accident. The deceit is softened: whereas in *One-Ox* the swineherd is an innocent passerby who succumbs to an appeal to his greed and ambition, in "Little Claus and Great Claus" the herdsman is an old man who actually wants to die.

"Little Claus and Great Claus" was published in 1835 as one of five tales that propelled Andersen to fame as a fairy tale author. In a preface that appeared in 1837, when these tales were reprinted with additional tales as *Fairy Tales Told for Children,* Hans Christian Andersen professed to have drawn two of the five tales ("Little Claus and Great Claus" and "The Tinderbox") from oral tradition.[112] He wrote:

> In my childhood I loved to listen to fairy tales and stories. Many of them are still very much alive in my memory. Certain of them seem to me to be Danish in origin for I have never heard them anywhere else. These I have told in my own way: where I thought it fitting, I have changed them and let imagination freshen the colors in the picture that had begun to fade. There are four such stories in this volume: THE TINDERBOX, LITTLE CLAUS AND BIG CLAUS, THE PRINCESS AND THE PEA, and THE TRAVELING COMPANION. In Anacreon's poem, as most people know, the fable THE NAUGHTY BOY is to be found.[113]

Of the more than 150 "fairy tales and stories" that Andersen published between 1835 and 1872, only seven are definitely drawn from Danish oral tradition. The three other members of this select group, in addition to the ones Andersen himself identified, are "The Swineherd," "All That Father Does Is Right," and "Simple Simon."[114] The Danish oral traditions connected with

"Little Claus and Great Claus" have been widely attested, but not before the mid-nineteenth century.[115]

Andersen's narrative style owes much to folktale,[116] but the overt reference in his preface to a Greek lyric poet of the sixth century BCE should tip us off that Andersen derived his stories from a number of sources, far from all of them oral. Some he created whole cloth; or rather, to mix metaphors, he "cooked" them. Others he took from oral sources,[117] some of which were indebted directly or indirectly to textual traditions. Andersen himself had had formal schooling, which means that he may have recast some tales from written sources. In addition, he had heard literature read by his father and folktales told by his mother.

In the case of "Little Claus and Great Claus," there are at least two direct channels through which the story could have entered Danish oral tradition through German texts that were well known in the decades before Andersen's literary activity began. Most important, it is interesting to note a close analogue that was incorporated as no. 61 in the second edition of the *KHM* by the Brothers Grimm.[118] The title of the Grimms' tale, "Das Bürle," means roughly "The Little Peasant" or "The Little Farmer," which hints that this version, like its protagonist, is also anything but courtly. The tale has at its center the comic main portion of *One-Ox,* but with adaptations to make it fit an unmedieval and bourgeois setting.[119] In the Grimms' version the farmer who has no cow at the beginning progresses to a level of comfort through his own cleverness; at the end he owns the whole city. The brothers also collected a variant of the same tale from Kassel in 1811, which happily survives, even though they passed over it in making their choices of tales to include in the *KHM.* It would be wonderful to know exactly how and when the Brothers Grimm became aware of the Latin *One-Ox* manuscript in Brussels, since undoubtedly they saw the similarities between it and the tales they had collected in the second decade of nineteenth century; but unfortunately no records survive to give us insight into this matter.

More or less simultaneously with *KHM* 61, Johann Gustav Gottlieb Büsching (1783–1829) published in German the tale of the farmer Kibitz ("Bauer Kibitz") in which a few traits differ from the Grimm version.[120] Büsching's version, first printed in 1812, was reprinted in 1820, and an English adaptation was published in 1823 (see app. 3F). Kibitz has his wife killed by the farmers and puts her then with a basket full of fruit on a railing, where a servant, to whom she gives no response when he wants to make a purchase from her for his master, topples her into the water. For this mishap Kibitz obtains the wagon that the servant drove, together with all its appurtenances.

Behind both the Grimms' "Little Peasant" and Andersen's "Little Claus

and Great Claus" stretched centuries in which the tale meandered back and forth between oral and written versions.[121] Long before evidence for any of these other versions stands *One-Ox*. Although *One-Ox* is by far the earliest attestation of the tale and may well offer the most logical version of it, the subsequent spread of the tale into vernacular languages is most unlikely to have taken place on the basis of a single Latin poem attested in one manuscript. This fact suggests that the poet was not the creator of the tale but, rather, the adapter of a tale that was already circulating orally—as the poet intimates, although not unambiguously. For want of earlier versions or even of variants chronologically close to *One-Ox*, it is hard to know which of the distinctive features in the poem are innovations the poet introduced and which are elements that typified the tale as it circulated in his time and region.

The next literary variant with something approaching a full array of motifs comparable to *One-Ox* is *The Story of the Peasant Campriano* (*Storia di Campriano contadino* [app. 3B]). The first printing of it was from 1518 at the latest, and three more followed before the printing of Straparola's version of the tale, featuring Father Scarpafico (Scarpacifico). Although *The Story of the Peasant Campriano* is sometimes ascribed to an author named Palantrini,[122] it is usually regarded as anonymous. In this tale, Campriano corresponds to One-Ox. Campriano sells merchants a donkey that supposedly produces gold, a rabbit that supposedly serves as a messenger, a kettle that supposedly boils by itself, and a trumpet that supposedly brings to life the dead. In its conclusion, the trickster-hero convinces a herdsman to take his place in a sack, with the promise that he will get to marry a noble maiden. The closing episode, which also appears toward the end of Giulio Cesare Croce's (1550–1609) *The Very Clever Tricks of Bertoldo* (*Le sottilissime astuzie di Bertoldo* [1605]), has been thought by some not to have belonged to the original tale of Campriano.[123] Earlier episodes in the tale became proverbial in Tuscany, in such phrases as "Campriano's pot" (*La pentola di Campriano*), used for either something momentous or a vessel that continues to boil when taken away from the fire; "Campriano's trumpet" (*La trombetta di Campriano*), used for a device or technique that can revive the dead or awake a person from deep sleep; and "Campriano's donkey" (*L'asino di Campriano*), used to designate an inexhaustible source of money.[124]

Following *The Story of the Peasant Campriano* is another Italian version, that of the sixteenth-century author Giovanfrancesco (Zoan Francesco) Straparola, published in his *Delightful Nights* (*Le piacevoli notti*) as the third story on the first night ("Father Scarpafico" [app. 3C]).[125] Straparola has been called "the first conscious cultivator of the folktale genre in Italy."[126] Athough this characterization may be arguable, he does include in one of

his tales most of the elements in *One-Ox*, and there can be no dreaming of a direct, text-to-text relationship between the two stories. Although his tale of Scarpafico omits the motif of the coin-defecating donkey, it otherwise contains the most important motifs found in *The Story of the Peasant Campriano*.[127] In place of the treasure found by accident while the protagonist is relieving himself, both the Italian variants have the sale of an animal that can supposedly serve as an errand boy. Both have in common with *One-Ox* the motifs of the musical instrument (not a trumpet in the Italian tales) that can resurrect the dead, the liberation from a container (in the Italian tales a sack) by a herdsman, and the deaths of the antagonists when they wish to fetch their own herds from the water. One of the most interesting discrepancies between the tale of Scarpafico and the story of Campriano is that the former is a priest, the latter a farmer.

Straparola's tale exercised a powerful influence on the subsequent tradition. Nine years after the publication of Straparola's *Delightful Nights* appeared Valentin Schumann's *Little Nighttime Book* (*Nachtbüchlein* [1559]), which contains, one after the other, two tales—nos. 5 and 6—that together tell most of the *One-Ox* story.[128] No. 5, entitled "A Tale of a Baker, Who Brings His Wife to Life with a Fiddle, and a Merchant" ("Ein hystori von einem becken, der sein Weib mit der geygen lebendig machen und einem kaufmann"), has only the motif of the wife painted in calf's blood and supposedly resurrected.[129] No. 6, with the title "A Tale of a Peasant Named Einhirn and His Peasants in the Same Village, until They All Drowned Themselves" ("Ein hystori von einem bawren mit namen Einhirn und seinen bawren im selben dorff, biss sie sich alle ertrenckten"), tells more of the story, but with a different set of motifs. Much like *One-Ox*, it ends with the moral of "those who dig a pit for other people and in the end fall in it themselves" [die ander leüten ein gruben graben unnd (sic) zu letst selber darein fallen].[130]

The version in Schumann's *Nighttime Book* is independent of *One-Ox*.[131] It has the dissimilar motifs of a worthless material being sold or swapped for gold, of an animal hide or bird being exchanged for the chest in which an adulterer is hidden, and of a dead mother being "killed" and of blood money being paid by the ostensible killer. The only motifs that it shares with *One-Ox*, albeit with substantial modifications, are the liberation of the trickster from the sack by changing places with a herdsman and the death of his antagonists, who drown themselves out of a desire to secure herds for themselves. One of the most important differences between Schumann's version and *One-Ox* is that the rich man kills the cow of the poor man. This is the same situation in other German versions also (and also in Hans Christian Andersen), but not in *One-Ox*. The killing makes the story more

logical, since it gives the poor man a motive for being vengeful toward the rich man.

Because Schumann's version is not indebted to *One-Ox,* folklorists in the twentieth century hypothesized that it emerged from a centuries-long oral tradition.[132] But the endeavor to qualify the transmission of such tales as either oral or literary may be inherently mistaken. Tales of this sort have passed back and forth repeatedly between oral and written forms. In this case it is interesting to find that a variant very similar to Schumann's survives in no. 15 of the *Novelle* of Giovanni Sercambi (1347–1424).[133] Sercambi's tale, entitled "De bono facto," relates how the donkey of Pincaruolo, a poor young peasant from the Milan area, collapses. Pincaruolo removes the donkey's hide, sells it in the city, grabs a raven that sits on the carcass, and wanders off with it. When he comes in the evening to a lonely house and knocks, the woman has him wait outside until her husband Bartolo returns home. Eventually Bartolo invites Pincaruolo to a meager dinner and points out a bed to him. But the man, after thinking about wonderful dishes that he had seen the woman stealthily preparing beforehand, pinches the raven until it crows loudly. When Bartolo questions why the raven crows, Pincaruolo responds that the bird was asking for the food the woman had hidden. What is the affiliation between Sercambi and Schumann? It cannot be literary, since Schumann was not a learned man and would not have had access to the much earlier Italian tale—but did the tale pass from Italy to Germany by oral transmission?[134]

The kind of complexity in the relationship between Sercambi and Schumann would only be heightened if we had better evidence, which for premodern literature most often comes in the guise of texts and occasionally in the representational arts. To return to "Little Claus and Great Claus," it may be significant that the related story by Straparola was translated into Danish by J. Chr. Riise (1818).[135] There is no way to be sure that this story did not influence Andersen, directly through his father's reading and indirectly through his mother's knowledge of an oral tradition that took from the written as freely as it gave to it.

After centuries of to-and-fro between oral and written versions of his story, One-Ox eventually became Little Claus, whose tale as written by Hans Christian Andersen maintains most of the same ambiguities between oral and written as well as between subordinate and privileged classes. What prospects the adventures of One-Ox/Little Claus will face in coming centuries it is hard to predict, but a tale that is known to have succeeded for the better part of a millennium among social classes as different as peasants, bourgeois, and courtiers will surely not disappear without a fight. In any case, the tale's continued survival attests that fairy tale is typified by a delicate

but durable relationship between stability and change and between oral and written.

THE CLERIC IN THE CHEST

More than any other scene in "Little Claus and Great Claus," the one with the chest has sparked the imaginations of artists,[136] as if they intuited that the motif of the hiding was not just a matter of the farmer's dislike for the deacon but, rather, an echo across the centuries of the stock situation in fabliaux in which a village priest is caught in flagrante delicto in illicit amorous activities with a village woman. The scene with the chest is absent from *One-Ox,* but an analogue to it is evident in the anecdote about Gaudry cited earlier in this chapter. Poking fun at parish priests was a commonplace already in Latin literature in the eleventh and twelfth centuries, as the whole of "The Priest in the Pit" (*Cambridge Songs* 35) and sections of the *Ysengrimus* confirm. The ATU folktale classification contains more than a dozen tales about parsons and sextons (ATU 1775–99). But such mockery was not appropriate in Andersen's context, where the church plays a more central role in the lives of characters and where village religiosity was taken more seriously. In many variants, the antagonists who are taking the trickster-hero to be drowned leave the sack unattended while they stop at an inn, but in Hans Christian Andersen's "Little Claus and Great Claus," Great Claus stops not for a drink but to hear a hymn or two in church.[137] In the rural Protestant milieu in Denmark in Andersen's day, the priest (*pastoren*) was held too much in awe to be imagined in the inappropriate situations that medieval comic tales routinely depicted.[138] But the deacon (*degn*) was the perfect figure on whom to load the mockery that could no longer be aimed at the priest. The deacon, who assisted in church, sang, and also taught in the village school, was a stock comic character in Danish folklore—a peasant himself, but with a pretense of learning, arrogant because of his ecclesiastic office, and held in cowed disdain by his fellow villagers. The archetype of this figure is Peer Degn, who gets the better of the title character (Rasmus Berg) in *Erasmus Montanus* (1722), one of the most successful comedies by Ludwig Holberg (1684–1754), who can be claimed by both Norway and Denmark as one of their own. It is consonant with such stereotypes about deacons that Andersen's Little Claus makes the deacon into the Devil.

The entire subplot about the deacon in the chest is not a component of *One-Ox.* Where and how it became part of the tale that Andersen relates is not just hard to say but indeed impossible to prove. Yet the similarity to fabliaux could suggest that a storyteller familiar with either oral or written

forms of short comic narratives—French fabliaux, Italian *novelle,* German *Schwänke,* Latin *facetiae,* Dutch *boerden* or *kluchten,* and the like—chose to attempt a narrative fusion.[139]

One of the earliest scholars who attempted to gather folktales from the Middle Ages into a large collection with chronological and geographical range described *Märchen* as "the toughest and longest living of all genres of folk poetry."[140] He also commented on the stunning durability of many stories: "It is astonishing how much in the present collection accords almost verbatim with pieces from modern collections, without there being a question of influence."[141] *One-Ox* is a case in point for this toughness and durability.

As even the patchwork of surviving literary versions attests, *One-Ox* was a favorite in many places and times. By a principle of attraction, all sorts of motifs from other stories were incorporated into different variants of it. This variability in no way undercuts the durability of the story, but it does create difficulties in determining the ur-form of the tale. The most recent folkloric analysis of *One-Ox* and related tales—an article probably less accessible and less well known than the longer and earlier studies—contends that the heart of the original story conjoins two motifs, that of a man lying shut in a chest who changes places with a shepherd and that of rich men who die by drowning when they enter the water in the hope of getting sheep from a world beneath the surface. The same examination identifies two other motifs as introductions to the heart of the story, namely, the motif that cowhides can be sold at a high price in the city and that a musical instrument can resurrect.[142] Whether or not these contentions convince both folklorists and literary scholars, they deserve serious consideration, and an accounting must be given to justify not using *One-Ox* as the basis for a historic-geographic study of the type of story it represents.

To establish the exact genealogy of *One-Ox* and its relatives is a quixotic goal, since there are more missing links than securely attested ancestors in this sort of family tree. It is more important to recognize, open-mindedly, that *One-Ox,* much like Apuleius's story of Cupid and Psyche long before it, offers ample evidence of a rich storytelling tradition that went largely undocumented. In one sense, the composer of *One-Ox* faced an enormous challenge. Because he did not have a genre of book folktale behind him, he had to improvise to create a genre of his own for his written version. This improvisation is one dimension of the "novelties" the poet mentions so early in the poem. In another sense, there can be no question that the poet

had behind him long traditions of both trickster tales and wonder tales. *One-Ox* contains ample indicators to uphold the view that the wonder tale (what would be popularly called the "fairy tale") already existed and indeed was so familiar as to be liable to parody in other types of folktale. *One-Ox* is not itself a wonder tale, but it plays deftly with basic elements of the wonder tale.

In the century that followed the composition of *One-Ox,* Latin authors grew ever bolder in their willingness to reach out for folk literature and to bring it within a Latin ambit—to draw on the oral and rework it as the written. Tricksters, such as Reynard the Fox and Marcolf, made their way into narratives both short and long, as authors tried to devise means of exploiting resources that had not been employed extensively in previous literature. Folktales, such as that of Amicus and Amelius, popped up in narrative poetry in Latin, in Old French epic poems (chansons de geste), and in Old French romances, as poets sought to find the most appropriate medium for them.

Around 1200, two or three Latin poets went so far as to make poems of wonder tales. These tales have an eerie familiarity about them, not so much because they were appropriated by the Brothers Grimm for inclusion in the *KHM* (although that is indeed the case) as because they bear powerful resemblances to other, better-known folktales. One of these tales, *The Donkey Tale,* could be called a male-oriented equivalent of "Beauty and the Beast," which is itself related to the Cupid and Psyche story. The other tale has as the second of its two main components an episode in which the central figure is stuck in a sack but frees himself by duping a foolishly ambitious wayfarer into taking his place.[143] This tale is the type known as "Two Presents for the King" (ATU 1689A). Its first expression is in a Latin poem known as *The Turnip Tale.* Just as One-Ox pretends to be a mediator to another world through magic, so does the man in the sack in *The Turnip Tale.* Not too many people would risk speculating that the poet of *The Turnip Tale* somehow secured a copy of *One-Ox,* which seems to have had only very limited circulation. Rather, both Latin texts are monuments to what has been lost: a large body of medieval oral literature that is extant only here and there in Latin literature and in early vernacular literatures.

The exchange of places in a sack and its often fatal consequences are widely attested in folk literature—for instance, as an independent tale in the tale type "The Clergyman in the Sack to Heaven" (ATU 1737) and as the conclusion for another trickster tale, "The Master Thief" (ATU 1525). Folktale survives by being recorded, which until around 1900 meant being recorded in writing. Fairy tale lives on most easily when collected for family reading or for children's literature. Although the formula for success was not

yet clear, Latin authors had the right instincts in believing that the material had a potential attraction to their audiences.

In the case of *One-Ox,* the poet was willing to venture that a noble banquet hall would listen with pleasure to an account of a wily peasant who could "make good" and have a fairy-tale ending at the cost of the local authorities. A little more than a century later, in the case of *The Turnip Tale,* a poet made the hero a knight so impoverished as to be reduced to turning the soil. In both instances the hero is a man who begins in abject poverty but has amassed greater wealth at the end of the story than is held by anyone in his community. Their trajectory is from rags to riches, not by the route of a wedding and marriage (which was among the very few means for social advancement available to young women in the Middle Ages or early modern period), but by luck and craft. As such, these heroes could give hope to an audience of young men—precisely the sort of audience to which many Latin texts were designed to appeal, since Latin existed not only by schooling but also for schooling, at a time when education was mostly a male preserve. The creator of *One-Ox* and the later poets may even have helped pave the way for the later reception of folktale and fairy tale by courtly audiences, since their transmission—even if limited—signifies that learned communities were willing to commit scarce resources to the preservation of oral literature and to devote energies to accommodating within Latin literature senses of wonder that were ever further removed from saintly miracles.

The Wonder of *The Turnip Tale* (ca. 1200)

Or can the Medieval Latin narration of the *Raparius* [*The Turnip Tale*] become in any stage of its ramification a fairy tale [*Märchen*], as which we should identify the tale [*Märlein*] of the turnip, following the wish of the Brothers Grimm?[1]

his chapter touches on not just a single past but, at a minimum, three different ones. In this triptych, the leftmost panel is lost medieval oral folk narrative, such as can be discerned behind the thick varnish of medieval textuality; the central frame contains the Latin verse adaptation of that oral narrative; and, last but not least, the rightmost panel is occupied by the eventual reformulation of the tale in the *KHM* of the Brothers Grimm. The investigation will rest on two different versions of a single tale that are separated by six hundred years. By exploring the relationships in form, content, and text between this tale as it appears in the *KHM* and the medieval poem on which it was based, I hope to delineate the Platonic, or rather Napoleonic, idea of fairy tale (*Märchen*) that Jacob and Wilhelm Grimm held. A concomitant aim will be to suggest through this one example that a number of other tales in the *KHM* share a medieval past.

THE BROTHERS GRIMM IN 1814

Jacob and Wilhelm Grimm came of age in the Romantic period. The main phase of Romanticism (designated in German as *Jüngere Romantik* or

Hochromantik, in English as high Romanticism) falls into the years of the Napoleonic Wars and overlaps with the beginning of the Restoration in 1815. It was centered on Heidelberg and Berlin. When working with tales, Jacob and Wilhelm were as attracted to medieval material as was their younger brother Ludwig when he sketched Gothic sculptures on German cathedrals in 1812, the very year in which the first volume of the fairy tales (*Märchen)* was published.[2] Indeed, in that same year, the two also published their edition of the early ninth-century Old High German *Lay of Hildebrand* (*Hildebrandslied*), a collaborative venture like the collection of fairy tales. Both of them already had acquired ample credentials as what would today be termed "medievalists."[3] In 1811 Jacob had produced individually a book on courtly love poetry, Wilhelm a volume of translations of heroic poetry.[4] The medieval past, seen through the very particular lenses of Romantic optics, lurks in the hinterground of the *KHM.*

The emergence of Romanticism is too complex a phenomenon to be reduced to the result of any formulaic progression of earlier developments. Nonetheless, the very term *Romanticism* acknowledges the strong antiquarian interest in such genres as the medieval romance, the medieval chanson de geste, and the ballad (which was thought to preserve medieval traditions). Similarly, it is not at all strained to identify as a contributing factor the craze for Celtic folklore and myth that goes by the name of Ossianism.

Coming to terms with the most direct legacy of the Middle Ages to the *KHM* requires paying close attention to whatever textual information we can retrieve. Although the image (and reality) of the castle endures and although cultural materialism can help to explain much, the fact remains undeniable that we gain fullest access to the Middle Ages through texts, a tenet with which the Brothers Grimm would have heartily agreed. Moreover, we need to bear in mind that the medieval past remains embedded in the very essence of certain tales even if the handling of them has been altered drastically, as happens in mass-media echoes of them that are far removed from both the Middle Ages and the Brothers Grimm.

As attractive as it would be to deal with a tale as deeply entrenched in popular culture as is "The Frog King, or Iron Heinrich" (*KHM* 1), I will instead set my sights on a lesser known but still appealing tale entitled "The Turnip" (*KHM* 146). Before introducing this vegetable narrative (and hoping that it does not induce vegetation in the reader), I will step back nearly two centuries, to Strasbourg in the early summer of the year 1814. In European history, the major figure who towered over this year (as over many others surrounding it) is Napoleon Bonaparte (1769–1821), whose activities (especially as emperor of the French from 1804 to 1815) tore apart the Continent and restitched it into an altogether new fabric. In this year, Napoleon rode forth

to do battle in France with the allied armies of Britain, Prussia, and Russia.[5] Little did he know how great a defeat or how rapid a decline in power lay ahead. At the end of March, he was convinced to yield the throne in favor of his son.[6] By the early summer, Napoleon was in the midst of his exile of less than a year on Elba, where he had been shipped after his defeat and abdication. Many will remember the famous palindrome "Able was I ere I saw Elba," ascribed erroneously by legend to Napoleon himself.[7] Eighteen fourteen was the year of Elba and Napoleonic disability. While Napoleon was sequestered on the island, the fate of the Continent was being renegotiated by the victors.

Wars are baneful events that destroy lives and endanger cultures, but they often also purvey incentives to intellectuals—among them philologists, folklorists, and others—to investigate and create national or supranational identities. The disruptions of the Napoleonic Wars were as directly responsible for bringing the Grimms into contact with many manuscripts (including Latin manuscripts) that they would not otherwise have seen as the Second World War was for isolating the erstwhile librarian Erich Auerbach in Turkey from the resources he had once taken for granted or for fostering the proclivity in Ernst Robert Curtius to surround himself in Bonn among medieval texts as Germany sank into the cruel madness of the Nazi era.

The redrawing of the maps involved movement toward the eventual creation of a German nation, a process that only very recently has been completed successfully. For centuries, there had been no single German nation but, instead, more than 300 principalities, which had their own dialects and folk traditions. Through publication of dictionaries, formulation of linguistic principles and historical grammars, compilation of mythological handbooks, and collection of fairy tales, the indefatigable Brothers Grimm played starring roles in providing their nascent fatherland with documentation about the languages and verbal traditions that in their view reflected a common spirit—a shared Germanness.[8]

Rather than speak generally of their life's work, I will here zero in on the narratives associated with the particular time and place I identified earlier, namely, Strasbourg in the summer of 1814. For several of the years in which Napoleon was most active, Jacob, the elder of the renowned Brothers Grimm, had been in the employ of the French, but in 1814 he returned to Hessian diplomatic service as a secretary. While en route to the Congress of Vienna, which had been convoked to reconfigure Europe, Jacob spent productive days rummaging in libraries in Strasbourg. By this date, Jacob and Wilhelm had already completed the first volume of their fairy tales, which was published in 1812. Although the brothers entitled their book *Kinder- und Hausmärchen* without specifying the Germanness of the tales (contrast

their later *German Legends* [*Deutsche Sagen*]), their sense of ethnic identity as Germans cannot be divorced from their work as folklore collectors.

A drawing made in 1817 by Ludwig shows his brother Jacob from behind as he toils over his dictionary, surrounded by German, Scandinavian, English, Dutch, and other dictionaries.[9] He would not have looked very different in the summer of 1814 when he consulted medieval manuscripts in Strasbourg. Two other sketches, also by Ludwig, capture the likeness of Wilhelm in the very year of 1814.[10] But we are not obliged to rely solely on visual representations for insights about Jacob's work habits and results. On 21 June 1814, he wrote from Strasbourg to his younger brother and collaborator Wilhelm to report on his activities.[11] This fascinating document gives us a glimpse of Jacob's irritation at the political views and behavior of the French, especially toward him as a German.[12] The letter reveals his increasing comfort and even joy upon entering Alsace (339), because of features he perceives as German in its architecture (high roofs, narrow windows, painted exteriors),[13] urban planning (curving streets, varying placement of houses on streets), diet (sauerkraut and white wine), and customs. Although Jacob does not resort to the use of the adjective "fairy-tale-like" (*märchenhaft*), it is not hard to see that he is enchanted also by the fairy-tale Germanness of the landscape, with its forests and ruined castles ("voll Wälder und Burgruinen," 339). Strasbourg itself fills him with nostalgic memories of living in Marburg with his brother Wilhelm (340). Jacob states bluntly (340) that the city looks German, with the French touches in its architecture being limited.

Jacob's general observations culminate in a paragraph that helps to make understandable why Jacob (and Wilhelm) would have been predisposed to regard texts he found in Strasbourg as being likely to preserve old German materials.

> In general, in view of all that I see and hear, Alsace and the people in it seem to me to be of a capable, fundamentally good German type that despite the long time has preserved itself here more vigorously and distinctively than in regions such as Baden, Württemberg, and so on, that is, according to their narrower, original component, without regard to anything better that they have appropriated for themselves. In all of this I feel clearly that in Germany the ancient and not yet extinct divisions by language, customs, and so forth in Swabia, Bavaria, Franconia, Saxony, Hesse, Thuringia, etc. ought to be reestablished. All else is worse, and it matters much less, and people make a mistake if they fail to recognize how much that is good today depends on those good old qualities. In this good matter the limited and poor

views of the Prussian as well as of the Austrian diplomats pose the greatest obstacle, and it is hardly possible now to accomplish it, but above all it should not be abandoned.[14]

Immediately after making the foregoing ethnographic and political declarations, Jacob proceeds to relate to Wilhelm the texts he lighted upon in manuscripts in Strasbourg. Among them were two fifteenth-century codices of Latin materials, one of which (Strasbourg, Bibliothèque Municipale [formerly Bibliothèque de la Ville], MS Johann. C. 105) included a Medieval Latin poem known as *The Donkey Tale* and the other of which (Strasbourg, Bibliothèque Municipale [formerly Bibliothèque de la Ville], MS Johann. C. 102) contained a poem that is today conventionally called *The Turnip Tale* (*Rapularius*; Jacob entitled it slightly differently, as *Raparius*).

As the saying goes, "Books have their destinies" [Habent sua fata libelli].[15] Both of these manuscripts, together with others that Jacob perused, had the fate of perishing in the fire that burned the library during the 1870 siege and bombardment of Strasbourg, during the Franco-Prussian War.[16] For the discovery and destruction of the manuscripts to have taken place in a region contested twice (actually, more often than twice) between the French and the Germans is not without relation to what the Brothers Grimms made of *The Donkey Tale* and *The Turnip Tale*. Many crises in nineteenth- and twentieth-century European history, especially the major wars, can be construed as physical expressions of political and intellectual debates over what constitutes Germanness and over how Germanness relates to the conception of a German nation. The Brothers Grimm saw Germanness as residing in language and in the culture associated with and concretized in that language.

In this case, each of the two Strasbourg manuscripts furnished the source materials for one of the so-called Grimms' fairy tales, since in 1815 Wilhelm's reworkings in German of the contents of these Latin poems in Jacob's transcriptions were incorporated in the second volume of the first edition of the *KHM*: what became "The Donkey" ("Das Eselein," originally no. 58 in vol. 2, but *KHM* 144 from 1819 on) is based on *The Donkey Tale* (*Asinarius*), "The Turnip" ("Die Rübe," originally no. 60 in vol. 2, but *KHM* 146 from 1819 on) on *The Turnip Tale* (*Rapularius*). *The Donkey Tale* will be examined in detail in chapter 6 of this book. As for "The Turnip," a statement in the notes by the Brothers Grimm—and, to be sure, most of the work on both the tales themselves and the notes was done by Wilhelm rather than Jacob—declares unhesitatingly that the Latin poem, despite making no claim to have been dictated from the oral performance of a storyteller, was a folktale (*Märchen*).

Even in regard to its external formulation it is an old fairy tale; to wit, it is translated from a Latin poem of the Middle Ages and in fact on the basis of the paper manuscript extant in Strasbourg, where it contains 392 lines in elegiac meter and is entitled *Raparius* . . . without doubt on the basis of an oral folk story.[17]

By the preceding statement's first phrase ("der äußern Form nach," in the German), the brothers did not denote what would today be considered genre or style but, rather, the essential narrative components. These elements—what, in the terminology of folkloristics, would encompass both ATU tale types and *MI* motifs—are what the brothers sought to isolate so as to bring to light the original folktale "form" from beneath the Latinate patina it had developed. Jacob and Wilhelm, if it is permissible to continue speaking of them on a first-name basis, clearly viewed the texts as having mediated, albeit in Latin verse, the tales of oral tellers whose native language would have been a German dialect and whose tales, despite their adaptation for a Latin-literate audience, still preserved popular values and qualities associated with the German *Volk*.

In the cases of both *KHM* 144 and 146, the Brothers Grimm relied entirely for their tales on the written sources that Jacob had unearthed in Strasbourg, and they made no secret of this reliance. They had no oral informants, but they evidenced no worry about needing any, since they were convinced beyond a doubt that oral sources lay behind *The Donkey Tale* and *The Turnip Tale*. If they penned drafts of "The Donkey" and "The Turnip" before the 1815 printing, those disappeared long ago. But Jacob's partial transcriptions from the destroyed medieval manuscripts survive in the Preussische Staatsbibliothek in Berlin, and the brothers included a long extract from *The Turnip Tale* in the notes to the tale.[18] Furthermore, other extant manuscripts of the medieval poem enable us to reconstruct with precision what the version Jacob read would have contained in the portions omitted from the published extracts. In working on these Medieval Latin narratives, Jacob showed the same painstaking respect for the medieval manuscripts as he and his brother had acquired in working for Friedrich Karl von Savigny (1779–1861), the great historian of law.

The role of Latin and literature written in Latin during the Romantic era is a many-branched tale that awaits its teller. Romanticism is associated rightly with a heightened interest in the native and folkish, and it is often equated with national literatures in the vernaculars. Yet literature in the common learned language, Latin, played a not inconsiderable role, mainly but not exclusively as a medium for international communication about native languages that were (and sometimes still are) hardly known except locally.

Thus we have the seeming paradox of Henrik Gabriel Porthan (1739–1804), whose dissertation on Finnish poetry (*De poësi Fennica* [1766–78]) was written in Latin, which was understood then as now by more non-Finns than Finnish would be. This one example exemplifies how entrenched Latin was as a learned language, but it was by no means imprisoned in the schools. The father of Johann Wolfgang Goethe (1749–1832), Johann Caspar Goethe (1710–82), kept his domestic accounts in Latin before shifting to German.[19]

But beyond the vague light that can be shed on Romanticism by delving into one unusual use of Latin, what good can be accomplished by comparing *The Donkey Tale* in Latin with "The Donkey" or *The Turnip Tale* with "The Turnip"? In 1815 Jacob Grimm composed and had printed a "circular" in which he urged that persons committed to collecting "folk poetry" show rigorous fidelity to their informants. To be specific, Jacob stipulated (immediately after listing the main genres of material to be gathered):

> It is important above all that these items be comprehended faithfully and truly, in the most accurate and detailed fashion, without make-up and addition, from the mouth of the narrators, where possible in and with their very own words.[20]

But did the Brothers Grimm, when they produced the *KHM,* fall short of the guiding principles espoused in the circular? They have been criticized harshly for having misrepresented the origins of their tales, for having overstated the Germanness of the tales, and for having understated their own contributions to the style and content of the tales.[21] The modifications made by the brothers have been studied by examining tales for which source materials used by them or, perhaps more accurately, early sketches drafted by them survive in a text that they sent on 25 October 1810 to Clemens Brentano (1778–1842), an author who was central in the Heidelberg group of Romantics.[22]

Brentano had collaborated with Ludwig Joachim (Achim) von Arnim (1781–1831) in publishing a three-volume collection of more than seven hundred German folk songs, entitled *The Boy's Wondrous Horn: Old German Songs* (*Des Knaben Wunderhorn: Alte deutsche Lieder* [1805–8]), and he had contemplated assembling a folktale compendium. In *The Boy's Wondrous Horn,* Brentano and von Arnim made many changes to suit their own tastes. Although more nationalistic than the cosmopolitan Johann Gottfried Herder (discussed in chap. 1 of the present book), they drew both wittingly and unwittingly on non-German materials. Indeed, the title piece is a translation of an old French lay. *The Boy's Wondrous Horn* was not very solid as scholarship, but it did serve to make known to the public a wide range of German folk songs.

After losing interest in carrying through his folktale project, Brentano misplaced or forgot the whereabouts of the 1810 manuscript the Brothers Grimm had sent him in Berlin. This gathering of tales, known as the Ölenberg Manuscript (after the monastery of Ölenberg where it was housed), surfaced again after a little more than a century.[23] Literary critic John M. Ellis compared the style and content of the twelve tales that were recorded in the Ölenberg Manuscript with the same tales as they were published in the first and six later editions of the *KHM*. Through his collation, he determined that the source material is doubled in length and recast entirely in style, plot, theme, character, and motivation.[24] Elements entailing violence, incest and sex, and magic are downplayed or expurgated. Ellis argued that when the brothers made changes in the other tales, they tried to polish peasant tellings to make them suitable for a bourgeois audience. Although Ellis is not responsible for what is quoted on his book cover, the back of the paperbound edition features the following quotation from *The Globe and Mail* (Toronto): "A damning exposé of generations of scholars who perpetuated the greatest fairy tale of them all: Jacob and Wilhelm Grimm, path-breaking collectors of the authentic German oral tradition." The influence of Ellis's arguments has hardly been confined to journalism. Indeed, among professional folklorists, the tales of the *KHM* have even been denounced as "fakelore," "to the extent that oral materials are rewritten, embellished and elaborated, and then presented as if they were pure, authentic oral tradition."[25]

If questions have been raised about the genuineness of the tales of the *KHM* as folktales, even greater questions have been posed about the utility of considering literary forms of fairy tales and other folktales alongside oral evidence. There has been a tendency for those studying fairy tales to be riven into camps over the issue of the oral and the written. Folklorists have focused on active bearers of tradition and have looked askance at written evidence, particularly when the information about the performance has been restricted. The rejection of the literary seems regrettable, since any of the *KHM* tales and their literary antecedents are, if not oral fairy tales, at least built on tales that often circulated orally. Much is to be learned about the provenance of folktales by looking closely at their correspondents in earlier literature.

Much sparring has gone on about the nature and extent of the changes that the Brothers Grimm made and about the openness or lack thereof that they displayed in acknowledging their tamperings. In all of the recent debate, no one, astonishingly, has scrutinized *KHM* 146. An opportunity has been missed to gauge exactly how the brothers operated as they drafted one of their fairy tales. Setting *The Turnip Tale* alongside "The Turnip" enables precise recognition of what they opted to include and exclude, to add, and

to modify. In effect, the juxtaposition holds the promise of laboratory-quality data for determining what the brothers thought a fairy tale should be and what adaptive techniques they deployed in shaping sources to achieve this ideal.[26] The relationship between *The Turnip Tale* and "The Turnip" also needs to be considered when calculating how much (or how little) Jacob, in contrast to Wilhelm, contributed to the second volume of the *KHM*. Although a handwritten annotation by Wilhelm gives Jacob ("von Jacob erzählte") acknowledgment for five fairy tales in the second volume of the *KHM*, it would seem justifiable to add at least partial credit for both "The Donkey" and "The Turnip" to the count.[27] Jacob was absent from Kassel on diplomatic service in France and Vienna for almost the entire year in which the second volume was being prepared, but as these two tales and the others indicate, he continued to contribute materials as he came upon them.

In the case of the two Latin-derived tales, the brothers had to effect almost the opposite of what they are alleged to have done when concocting written *Märchen* from stories they had heard: they had to take out the artifices of Latin rhetoric so as to restore what they regarded as the underlying nature, or rather the naturalness, of the tale. The recuperation of *The Turnip Tale* went far beyond the merely cosmetic or superficial to encompass full overhauls in both style and content. Rather than being a straightforward translation (as if translation is ever simple!) from Latin to German, it was a thoroughgoing generic reworking of a Latin poem into a German prose *Märchen*.[28] The decisions of the brothers about how to refashion the Latin poem tell us worlds about their preconceptions of what a wonder tale should be.[29]

MEDIEVAL LATIN TURNIP TALES

A few preliminary paragraphs of information are needed to lay out essential information about the Latin poem Jacob consulted.[30] *The Turnip Tale* survives in three versions. One text, amounting to 442 lines in elegiac distichs in the most recent edition, will here be designated *The Turnip Tale "frivola"* [1].[31] The *frivola* refers to the word that makes this version's incipit ("Fama fuisse duos testatur frivola fratres") distinct from the first line of the other version; the numeral 1 within brackets is a convenience, acknowledging older and now probably outmoded scholarship in which it was thought certain that *The Turnip Tale "frivola"* [1] was composed first. Another text, 388 lines in elegiac distichs, will be called here *The Turnip Tale "prodiga"* [2]. The adjective *prodiga* is the distinctive word in its incipit ("Fama fuisse duos testatur prodiga fratres"); the numeral 2 preserves the designation *The Turnip Tale II* that was used when it was believed that this version was posterior to

The Turnip Tale "frivola" [1]. It was a codex of *The Turnip Tale "prodiga"* [2] that Jacob consulted in Strasbourg.

The two versions are closely, even incestuously, related. Of the 442 verses in *The Turnip Tale "frivola"* [1], 45 are identical with verses in *The Turnip Tale "prodiga"* [2], while 40 are substantially the same.[32] The incest only increases in the third version, with the sigla γ: it is a full-blown hybrid, composed of three-quarters of material that is drawn from *The Turnip Tale "frivola"* [1] and of roughly one-quarter from *The Turnip Tale "prodiga"* [2]. For the present purposes, the hybrid is interesting mainly for establishing the text of *The Turnip Tale "frivola"* [1], since readings preserved in γ are sometimes preferable to those in the uncontaminated family of manuscripts itself.

As far as the time of composition is concerned, the Brothers Grimm were inclined to date *The Turnip Tale* as they knew it in the fourteenth century. But the text of at least *The Turnip Tale "frivola"* [1] had to have existed substantially before it was mentioned in 1280 as a standard school text. The consensus holds now that this recension was probably written around 1200, since the poem would had to have been composed at least a few decades prior to becoming a fixture in the scholastic curriculum.[33] For much of the twentieth century, it was held that *The Turnip Tale "prodiga"* [2] appreciably postdated *The Turnip Tale "frivola"* [1]. The main reason for this inference was the date of the manuscript witnesses: Karl Langosch (1903–92) knew of nine manuscripts for *The Turnip Tale* in its three forms, all of the fifteenth century except for one of *The Turnip Tale "frivola"* [1] of the thirteenth century. Conditioned by this evidence, Langosch dated the composition of *The Turnip Tale "frivola"* [1] well before 1280, while placing *The Turnip Tale "prodiga"* [2] in the fourteenth century. This picture changed dramatically when Paolo Gatti publicized that fragments from the second third of the thirteenth century survived with part of the text of *The Turnip Tale "prodiga"* [2].[34] This revelation made the issue of priority far more embroiled. Right now it is not known for certain which version was composed first; there are good reasons to conclude that *The Turnip Tale "prodiga"* [2] was written earlier, rather than later, than *The Turnip Tale "frivola"* [1].

As for the place of composition, it has been generally assumed that the author of at least *The Turnip Tale "frivola"* [1] came from southern Germany.[35] This assumption has rested mainly on the manuscript tradition (all extant witnesses are German), partly on the circumstance that the motif of the giant turnip is particularly well attested in Alsace. Also tying *The Turnip Tale "frivola"* [1] to the south of Germany is the fact that in 1280, Hugo of Trimberg, who lived in what is today northern Bavaria, cites it as one of a half-dozen school texts (used presumably in his region) that he singles out for particular praise. But the geographico-cultural origins of the poem may

need eventually to be reassessed, since the views on this topic held by both the Brothers Grimm (as we have seen) and the most influential twentieth-century editor of *The Turnip Tale,* Karl Langosch,[36] are likely to have been colored by the different but related nationalistic ideologies of the times in which they lived and worked.

In regard to authorship, all three versions are anonymous in the manuscripts. Although unlikely, it is conceivable that one and the same author created the two main recensions—*The Turnip Tale "frivola"* [1] and *The Turnip Tale "prodiga"* [2]—or even all three of them.[37] In this case, the poet would have accomplished the equivalent in Latin literature of what the author (possibly a pseudonym) William Langland (ca. 1325–ca. 1388) is supposed to have achieved in Middle English when he wrote three or more versions of *Piers Plowman.* Both principal texts of *The Turnip Tale,* by the mere fact that they are in Latin, had to have been composed by educated clerics rather than by illiterate peasants; but beyond that, nothing can be declared with certainty.

Alongside the mystery of the author's identity, another open question concerns the listenership or readership for which the poem was intended. Within the two versions of the poem itself, the most suggestive hint is the vocative "O brothers" [O fratres] in *The Turnip Tale "prodiga"* [2] (237). Yet the term *frater,* when applied beyond its strict use in reference to a full or uterine brother, had a wide range of significations. It was indeed used with specific reference to brethren in a religious sense (to monks, canons regular, friars, and other such orders), but it served equally as a general form of address to "an equal, especially fellow Christian."[38] Indeed, later on in *The Turnip Tale "prodiga"* [2] itself, the word is used twice (315 and 374) in contexts that could have a specific religious dimension, except that in the second instance it is shown soon to be a synonym for the very general *socius* (378). Although Medieval Latin was a predominantly male domain, there is not even justification for assuming that the plural refers exclusively to boys or men: the masculine plural could encompass both women and men.

An additional piece of evidence is that in his *Registrum multorum auctorum* (List of Many Authors) of 1280, Hugo of Trimberg classes *The Turnip Tale "frivola"* [1] (the incipit of which he quotes) among six texts commonly read in the schools.[39] Such scraps of information are not enough on which to build a solid case, but together with the demographics of literary production around 1200, they buttress the inference that *The Turnip Tale* emanated from the world of secular clerics, who both had access to vernacular literature (e.g., romances and fabliaux) and produced texts that were alternatives to it (e.g., Walter Map's *Courtiers' Trifles* [De nugis curialium], Petrus Alfonsi's *Scholar's Guide* [Disciplina clericalis], and Gervase of Tilbury's *Recreation for an Emperor* [Otia imperialia]).[40]

A secular cleric writing for a royal or noble court would have had strong motivation to cast the leading characters as brothers who were knights, not unrelated men who were a peasant and a courtier (as in the version recorded by Desiderius Erasmus [1466–1536]) or brothers who were soldiers (as in the Grimms' version). The development of the narrative underpins this same view. The author, toeing a careful line on social issues, does not present a rigid, unchanging nobility. In depicting the socioeconomic redemption of the poor brother, he reinforces the idea of innate nobility; in portraying the behavior of the wealthy brother, he implies that greed, envy, and other such moral failings can lead to a fall from nobility. Yet the closing section of the tale does assert the superiority of the nobility over the clergy.

One final aspect of *The Turnip Tale* that merits consideration in this preamble is genre. There are actually two parts to this examination, since we need to give attention to the genre of first the poem itself and then what it intimates about its source. As far as the genre of the poem itself is concerned, even though the identifiers *Rapularius* and *Raparius* give no generic information, two manuscripts of *Rapularius* γ[41] are entitled "A Certain Lovely Moralization against Envy" (*Quedam pulchra moralizatio contra invidiam*)[42] and "A Certain Lovely Moralization against Pride and Envy, in Verse" (*Quedam pulchra moralisatio metrice composita contra superbiam et invidiam*).[43] The third manuscript of the hybrid *Rapularius* concludes with the explicit statement "Here ends the story about a turnip" [Explicit historia de rapa]. Yet the value of the two titles and the explicit statement, already vague, diminishes with the realization that they are all attested only in fifteenth-century manuscripts, written more than two hundred years after *The Turnip Tale* was composed. For want of internal clues as to the genre of the poem, the most recent editor has classified it as an elegiac comedy by virtue of its similarity to other narratives from more or less the same time with similar types of narrative, comparable uses of dialogue and monologue, and Ovidian-influenced meter and style.[44] This categorization of *The Turnip Tale* has a faute de mieux ring to it, evident even in Gatti's closing statement on the matter: "At this point I would not feel myself ready to cast doubt on the affiliation of *The Turnip Tale* with this genre of compositions."[45]

The poet provides safer ground, although no more than a toehold, in the opening hexameter of *The Turnip Tale "frivola"* [1]: "A trifling story reports that there were two brothers" [Fama fuisse duos testatur frivola fratres].[46] In this line, he owns up to the fact that his source for the story was oral tradition (*fama*), but he at the same time gives voice to the stock disparagement of folktale, fairy tale, and related genres by tagging the story as *frivola* ("worthless," "silly," or "trivial"). This ambivalent term can be taken as meaning either "lightweight" (Gatti translates it as "di poco conto") or "lighthearted"[47]

(Langosch takes it as "lustig"). Emphasized through both its primary position and its alliteration, it is the closest to a generic indication offered within the poem itself.[48] The need to compensate for the supposed triviality may explain why the two copyists labeled the poem a *moralizatio,* when explicit moralization is only a relatively small part of the story.

TALL TALES OF TURNIPS

In all the medieval versions of *The Turnip Tale,* the poem comprises two major narrative units that must have been initially independent. Although the two stories could have been fused already in the oral or written source used by the tale's earliest poet, they could have been assembled first by the Latin poet.[49] In any case, it can be considered a given that the tale's earliest poet lengthened the story appreciably from its oral source or sources.

The first of the two main ingredients in *The Turnip Tale* is the tale of the gigantic turnip that has been designated AT and ATU 1689A, "Two Presents to the King," which is related to the tale type AT and ATU 1960D, "The Great Vegetable (cabbage, potato, etc.)." AT 1689A is summarized as follows:

> *Two Presents to the King:* the beet and the horse. Raparius. A farmer takes an extraordinary beet as present to the king and receives a large reward. His companion is eager for a reward and leads a handsome steed to the palace. The king rewards him with the beet [*MI* J2415.1].

This summary incorporates the title *Raparius,* by which *The Turnip Tale* has been alternatively known, but without issuing any guidance about what the word means (it is not even italicized) or where an edition bearing it can be found. Furthermore, the description that follows is not based entirely on either *The Turnip Tale* or the Grimms' fairy tale that derives from it, as can be seen by the identification of the invidious brother as "his companion" and of the oversized vegetable as a beet (English versions of the *KHM* translate the noun in question as "turnip"). Here as elsewhere in AT, the Latinity of the oldest surviving tale poses special problems. Aarne and Thompson like to classify versions of tales according to language and geography. Thus, in this entry, we encounter listings of Finnish, English, Italian (Tuscan), Hungarian, Greek, Indian, Spanish-American (Puerto Rican), and West Indian tales. Tales that come from border zones and that are written in languages not associated with modern national identities or ethnic groups fit awkwardly in such a taxonomy. This misfit has been remedied considerably in ATU, but the effects of the rebalancing have been slow to penetrate broader scholarship.

In *The Turnip Tale "frivola"* [1], the turnip is introduced immediately after the key human protagonist—and it is described in considerably more detail.

> For him there grew more enormous than the rest one little turnip, which can be called in the full sense of the word a turnip, so extensive in foliage and so large in body that no one at all has ever seen its equal before. Its very shadow sufficed for twelve men, so that beneath it the heat of the sun would not burn them. It was so enormous that by itself it would fill a cart and four oxen could scarcely draw the load.[50]

In effect, the turnip is the title character. I cannot claim to have grasped fully the psychology that would elucidate the obsession of some people with oversized vegetables, but it is an ancient one. The ancient Roman naturalist Pliny the Elder (23/24–79 CE), extolling the turnip for its ability to grow wondrously under even the most adverse conditions, cannot resist citing the weight of the biggest he claims to have seen: "It actually thrives on mist and frost and cold, growing to a marvellous size: I have seen turnips weighing over 40 pounds."[51] In North America the humble turnip lands even more seldom on the dinner table than does the pumpkin. In the United States no one waits at Thanksgiving for a slice of hot turnip pie, and the idea of a cartoon entitled *It's the Great Turnip, Charlie Brown* is preposterous.[52] But nonetheless the turnip continues to have its own avid fans, and turnip mania remains an abiding force in media today. Just as local papers have carried headlines about the magnitude of prizewinning pumpkins at agricultural fairs, the Web now features sites on behemoth turnips.[53]

Sometimes the description of a large turnip or other comparable vegetable forms is a tall tale (a form that in this case could more appropriately be designated a "wide tale"). Often such exaggeration is part of a competitive exchange of exaggerations, as can be attested in *MI:* "X1423.1. Lie: the great cabbage. (Usually matched by tale of great pot to put cabbage in.)." This entry in *MI* is only one in a long grocery list of outrageously big vegetables and such.

> X1424. The great mushroom; X1431. Lies about turnips; X1431.1. Lies about big turnips; X1411.1.1. Lie: large watermelon; X1411.2. Lies about large pumpkins.

Not entirely by the bye, turnips—particularly gargantuan turnips—have been strongly connected with Strasbourg. In the notes that the Brothers Grimm published in 1856, they referred to the German proverb "turnips to

Strasbourg" (*Rüben nach Strassburg*), which had a meaning comparable to the English "[carry] coals to Newcastle" or "owls to Athens" and which appeared in the preface by Bernhard Jobin (died 1593) to *Das Ehezüchtbüchlein* (1572) by the Strasbourg-born and -educated satirist Johann Fischart (1546–90).[54] Tall tales of outlandishly large Strasbourg turnips can be tracked in popular literature and folktales from the sixteenth century at least down to the end of the nineteenth. *New Tidings from the Whole World* ("Neuwen Zeytungen auß der gantzen Welt"), printed in 1597, a traveler tells the innkeeper: "In Strasbourg I saw standing on the field a turnip that grew so large, I could not go around it in three summer days on a swift horse."[55] A *Volksbuch* (book of folktales) about the boastful Urban Fettsack contains a virtually identical exaggeration.[56] A later folktale tells of a turnip so sizable that a steer and cow that eat their way into it become invisible, except for their tails, by the third day; another account refers to a turnip reputed to have been so massive that it took seven men to heave it onto a wagon.[57]

The extraordinarily large turnip has far from met its extinction even today in popular culture, especially children's literature. There is no call to dwell long on the idiosyncratic blend of urban legend, Elvis Presley lore, and turnip humor that shows up in a children's book entitled *Elvis the Turnip . . . and Me,* since the vegetable in question there is remarkable not for its magnitude but rather for its mellifluous vocalizing.[58] Yet it repays the effort to linger for a moment over a folktale of "The Great Vegetable" tale type that has proliferated in illustrated books for bedtime reading. The tale type (AT [modified and enlarged in ATU] 1960D) relates to *MI* Z49.9: "Pulling up the turnip. Final formula: The mouse holds onto the cat, the cat holds onto Mary, Mary holds onto Annie, Annie holds onto grandmother, grandmother holds onto grandfather, grandfather holds onto the turnip—they all pull and pull it out."[59] Entitled variously *The Turnip, The Gigantic Turnip, The Enormous Turnip,* and *The Great Big Enormous Turnip,* the story tells of an old man and woman who plant a turnip that grows so large they cannot extract it from the ground. They perform a protracted tug-of-war, in which they are joined by one after another of the animals on their farm. Their efforts are for naught, until finally they are assisted by the smallest of creatures—variously, a mouse, a cricket, and a beetle. With this additional help, the turnip finally explodes out of the ground.

As a workbook of German children's songs makes explicit, the tale of the turnip points up a readily identified moral: "Together we are stronger" [Gemeinsam sind wir stärker].[60] But the point of the story is not just to drive home a moral but to take pleasure in repetition with variety. This characteristic of repetition has caused tales of this type to be designated "cumulative stories" or "chain tales."[61] As the handling of the final scene in

illustrated children's books implies, this scene usually climaxes the illustrations—and I choose the word *climax* advisedly, since at least one representation captures the participants in a curious posture that is the visual equivalent of a sexual double entendre. Yet in most versions, the story ends altogether unsuggestively, with the old man and woman celebrating by cooking a big turnip dinner.[62]

The chief elements in "The Great Vegetable" that relate to the wonder tale told by the Brothers Grimm are the marvelous magnitude of the turnip, the peasant setting, and the use of the turnip as food (which is touched on *en passant* in the Grimms' tale and is put into effect in "The Great Vegetable"). The first two of these elements appear also in *KHM* 112, "The Threshing Flail from Heaven" ("Der Dreschflegel vom Himmel"). *KHM* 112 is hardly unique, since the big turnip, like the great cabbage, was for many centuries a beloved object in the humor of "lying tales" (*Lügenmärchen*) or "tall tales," which often dealt with objects of extraordinary size.[63]

What is the basic story line of "The Turnip" as the Brothers Grimm recount it? The tale falls into two parts. Only the first revolves around the turnip. There are two brothers. In a "classic" fairy tale situation, one is rich, the other poor.[64] Not unexpectedly, the equation suggested eventually in this part of the story is that the rich one is bad, the poor one good. The poor one sows a turnip that grows enormous, and he resolves to give it to the king. The king is overjoyed and rewards the poor man lavishly. The rich brother, upon hearing of his poorer relation's success, is envious. He resolves to present great wealth to the king, with the expectation of proportionately greater dividends than his brother had received. Such is not the case, because the king, unable to match the riches the rich brother has given him, finds a fairy-tale solution to the stock dilemma of figuring out what to give a man who has everything: he reciprocates with nothing other than the turnip.

At this point the story could draw to a close—and many versions of it do conclude here, leaving the audience with the symmetry of the turnip as a gift that brings riches in the beginning and the turnip as a gift in return for riches at the end. The two acts of giving, in absolute equilibrium, have opposite consequences for the brothers, but the economy of their world is shown to operate according to a zero-sum principle that is preserved: one brother is enriched, another impoverished, while the king's wealth is temporarily lessened before being returned to its starting point.[65]

After *The Turnip Tale,* the portion of the tale devoted to the turnip is next attested in Erasmus's *Colloquia,* in a colloquy entitled "The Fabulous Feast" ("Convivium fabulosum"), first printed in 1524.[66] The Brothers Grimm were of course acquainted with at least some of Erasmus's works (their library contained a copy of his *Letters to Friends* [*Epistolae familiares*]), but they seem

not to have known of the version of their tale transmitted in his *Colloquia*.[67] Although it is within reason that Erasmus encountered one or another text of *The Turnip Tale* directly, the likelier scenario is that he heard an oral rendering of the same story. It would be a mere parlor game to guess at how much this putative spoken version might have owed obliquely to *The Turnip Tale* and how much it might have relied on an independent oral tradition that evolved from the form of the story that preexisted *The Turnip Tale*. Caution is in order when dealing with a cultural tradition in which exchanges back and forth between the oral and the written have taken place as long and as complexly as they have in Western Europe.[68]

Another example of the complexity is the circumstance that at least two German schoolbooks of the late nineteenth century incorporate versions of the tale that are indebted ultimately to the Erasmian version and not to *The Turnip Tale* in any of its manifestations. Just as the question of the relationship between *The Turnip Tale* and the Erasmian version of the tale is involved, so (particularly because of these intervening versions) is that of the relationship between the versions of Erasmus and the Grimms. It is conceivable, though very speculative, that the Brothers Grimm had encountered the tale in schoolbook form when they were boys and, without remembering it consciously, were influenced by having been exposed to it in their childhood.[69] In any case, it is interesting to ponder how many retellings that derive directly or indirectly from the Erasmian version were printed in Latin, Italian, French, German, Spanish, and English.[70]

Whatever Erasmus's sources, his tale is noteworthy for both the similarities and differences it reveals when compared with the Latin poems and the *KHM* tale. For a start, his narrative is not a wonder tale but a humorous anecdote about a visit by an allegedly real peasant, named Conon, to a specific ruler, King Louis XI (1423–83), and a subsequent misbegotten attempt by a courtier to profit by emulating the peasant's generosity. One scholar has called the Erasmian tale "a historical anecdote imbued with fictional realism."[71] In keeping with the purported historicity, the Erasmian account rationalizes the turnip, making it merely first "unusually big" [insigniter magna][72] and later "half-shrivelled" [subaridam].[73]

One major difference between the anecdote about Conon and "The Turnip" is in the representation of women. In contrast to *KHM* 146, Erasmus's version, although it has the king consult with his counselors rather than with the queen, retains the highlighting of the peasant's wife as an adviser—a role found in *The Turnip Tale* "*frivola*" [1] but not in *The Turnip Tale* "*prodiga*" [2], the latter of which was the source for Jacob Grimm's transcription. Erasmus wrote:

Soon after Louis was restored and was already ruling in France, Conon's wife urged him to remind the king of their former hospitality—pay him a visit and take him some fine turnips as a gift. Conon baulked, saying it would be effort wasted, that princes don't remember such services. But his wife prevailed. Conon chose some of his best turnips and prepared for his journey. On the way, though, he himself found the food too tempting and gradually consumed all the turnips except one unusually big one.[74]

The salience of the wife could betray an indebtedness to *The Turnip Tale* "*frivola*" [1]. Alternatively, it could reflect an oral tradition in which the femaleness of some storytellers and/or audience members may have encouraged the encoding of roles favorable to women into the narrative.

The anecdote about Conon is unique in setting up as opponents not brothers (as in all versions of *The Turnip Tale* and in "The Turnip") but otherwise unrelated characters. This divergence raises a question: what was "original," the fraternal relationship in *The Turnip Tale* or the nonrelationship in Erasmus? Furthermore, Erasmus draws a stark contrast between the two antagonists in their social status: the turnip giver is a peasant ("a peasant named Conon, an honest, good-hearted fellow"),[75] and the eventual turnip receiver is a courtier. The courtier perceives his higher status as being grounds for better treatment by the king: "If he gave so large a reward for a turnip presented by a peasant, how much more lavishly will he pay for such a horse offered by a courtier!"[76] This pairing of unrelated peasant and courtier contrasts with the poor and rich knight-brothers in *The Turnip Tale* and the poor and rich soldier-brothers in the Brothers Grimm.

TURNIPS AND THE POOR

Although in differing ways, social issues lie at the root, so to speak, of all expressions of the turnip story. The turnip belongs to the same genus of the family *cruciferae* (the mustard family) as does the cabbage. There has long been confusion about how to classify the turnip.[77] Already in Roman times, a distinction was made between the *rapa,* which was large and round, and the *napus,* which was slender and pointed.[78] In the Linnaean system, *Brassica rapa* designates the common white turnip, *Brassica napus* or *Brassica napobrassica* the yellow turnip. The category of the yellow turnip encompasses the rutabaga, the swede (also known more fully as the Swedish turnip), and, confusingly, the rape (whence comes rapeseed oil), whose name is the English survival of the Latin *rapa.* The Scottish English word

neep, which derives from *napus,* is reserved for the swede. The French *navet* is another derivative of *napus,* a close relative to the obsolete English *navew* (*navew* as a synonym for the rape, *navew gentle* for the edible form). Although the body of the turnip is technically not a true root but, rather, the swollen base of the stem, the turnip is designated, loosely speaking, a root crop. Root vegetables are "plants whose underground parts in particular are edible." If root crops in general are associated with the poor, the turnip is a vegetable that for millennia epitomized poverty or at best mere subsistence.

The diet of peasants in the Middle Ages relied heavily on roots, such as beetroot, carrots, celeriac, salsify, radishes, and turnips.[79] Before the more nutritious potato was introduced into the European diet after its discovery in South America, the turnip was a staple for the poor because it grows well even in cool climates and because it keeps well. Pliny rates the turnip immediately after grain and beans in importance, because of its utility to both men and animals (birds as well as beasts consume it), and he reports that the turnip is third after wine and grain in its frequency of cultivation north of the Po River.[80] The turnip was grown in Germanic lands long before the Roman era.[81]

Fulfilling the adage that "familiarity breeds contempt," to this day the turnip is held in mixed regard popularly.[82] It embodies the poverty of farmers, both because growing it requires hard work and because eating it is associated with indigence.[83] Even when regarded favorably, the turnip has something comic about it, which helps to explain why a parodic and cartoon-filled magazine for culinary literature would be named *The Turnip.*[84] Even before the Middle Ages, the turnip was viewed ambivalently. On the one hand, it was presented as being healthful and even virtuously humble. Its healthfulness is mentioned by Horace (*Satires* 2.2.43–44), who describes how a glutted stomach will prefer little turnips (here the noun is the neuter *rapulum*) and the pickled root of the elecampane to richer and more expensive foods. It was central in the diet associated with the Roman Republic, before the Roman Empire enabled the importation of foods and especially luxury foods from elsewhere. An anecdote was told that when Manius Curius Dentatus (died 270 BCE)—war hero, consul, and censor—was approached by Samnites who sought to bribe him to defect, he ignored their offer of gold and instead continued what he had been doing, namely, roasting turnips over a fire.[85] Among vegetables, the turnip offers the sharpest contrast to precious gold.

On the other hand, the turnip was implicated already in the medieval period so much in the miseries of hardscrabble poverty that hell was purportedly sown with turnips: "The demon is dead, and hell is sown with turnips" [Mortuus est demon, et tartara sunt sata rapis].[86] Its worthlessness became proverbial: Old French has "not worth a turnip" [ne pas valoir un

naveau [navet]], Middle English "not worth a withered neep."[87] The reasons are not far to see—or taste, feel, hear, and smell. A heavy diet of turnips subjected its consumers first to the sharp bite of the turnip and then to their own bloated stomachs and flatulence.[88] In late medieval and early modern estimation, the turnip was not just a food to be restricted exclusively to the menu of the poor but a crop to be planted, harvested, and consumed only by the lowest of classes. Knights were to consume foods particular to their station, with meat and fish, wine, and white bread predominating, while the poor were to subsist on vegetables.[89]

According to the division of labors in the stock medieval view of society, neither clerics nor knights were supposed to engage in digging. The Arch-poet stated pithily, "I ought not to dig, because I am a scholar / born of knights proficient in warfare" [Fodere non debeo, quia sum scolaris / ortus ex militibus preliandi gnaris].[90] Neither group was meant to live on turnips. In the twelfth century it was still unusual when a knight chose to exchange the sword ("emblem of the knightly function") for the book, as Peter Abelard and others opted to do.[91] There was an even greater shock value in depicting a knight so desperately impecunious as to be reduced to scrabbling the soil for his subsistence—in other words, to become a peasant or serf. The shock is only intensified by matching the same déclassé knight with the turnip.

The turnip was a plant that required working in the soil, an activity that was proper to the peasant. A German proverb probably recorded in the early fourteenth century exclaimed, "Let the lowborn dig turnips!" [Den schwachen laßt rüben graben!].[92] Tradition held that peasants should not just grow turnips but also eat them. Those who were desperately poor were supposed to embrace the turnip virtuously rather than coveting the foods of other classes. A common Medieval Latin proverb stated: "Why do you seize another's property? Can't you feed yourself on turnips? / You often take wind, when you wish to feed yourself on turnips" [Cur aliena rapis? Nescis te pascere rapis? / Ventum sepe rapis, dum vis te pascere rapis].[93] To turn to an even clearer example, in a passage from a late fifteenth-century novella (probably composed in 1492), Giovanni Sabadino degli Arienti (ca. 1445–1510) has one character rebuke another:

> Next time leave alone the fruit of people like me and eat the fruit of the people like you, in other words: turnips, garlic, leeks, onions, and shallots with sorghum bread.[94]

The late sixteenth-century *Bertoldo* by Giulio Cesare Croce refers famously to the "turnips and beans" and chestnuts eaten by the title character, the

cunning peasant Bertoldo.[95] Bertoldo suffers grievously when fed the wrong sorts of food—kinds inappropriate to his social station.

> The doctors, not knowing his complexion, gave him remedies that would have been suitable for the gentlemen and knights of the court. He [Bertoldo], who knew his own nature, asked that they bring him a pot of fava beans with some onions and some turnips cooked in the ashes of the fire. He knew that with such food he would be cured.[96]

According to Bertoldo's epitaph and his deathbed aphorisms, he was eventually killed by his failure to remain within the circumscribed menu allowed him as a peasant.

> [H]e died painfully because he was not given any turnips and fava beans.
> He who is used to turnips must not eat meat pies.
> He who is used to a hoe must not take a spear in his hand.
> He who is used to the fields must not go and live at court.[97]

This same set of assumptions is operative in *The Turnip Tale "frivola"* [1], where the lineages of the plant and of the poor man are seen as being entangled (75–80). Because of his indigence, the man cannot afford to plant anything but turnip.

THE GREAT TURNIP AND THE WONDER OF THE WONDER TALE

One of the foremost paradoxes in both *The Turnip Tale* and "The Turnip" is that a turnip, emblematic of poverty, brings untold riches to its planter.[98] As a lowly root vegetable, it corresponded to the humblest entities in the medieval social hierarchy. Yet through its exaggerated size, it became a wonder that achieved the redemption of its grower.[99] Indeed, *The Turnip Tale* is a wonder tale that offers a coherent outlook on wonder.[100] It teaches that wonder may bring dividends but that it is not to be sought: the brother who attempts to barter his possessions for even greater wealth learns this lesson, as does the scholar who seeks to buy an easy route to knowledge of the wonders of nature.

If the early Middle Ages gravitated toward miracles, the later Middle Ages and early modernity were preoccupied in both fiction and reality with natural marvels and wonders. Wonder was the province of the cultural elite, who cultivated it for power, prestige, or praise of their divine creator.[101]

Probably within a decade or two of when the earliest form of *The Turnip Tale* was composed, Gervase of Tilbury wrote his *Recreation for an Emperor* (*Otia imperialia*) (ca. 1210) and dedicated it to Emperor Otto IV (1175/82–1218). The centerpiece of this miscellany is a long section on marvels, the introduction to which unfolds a philosophy of the wonderful.

> And since the appetite of the human mind is always keen to hear and lap up novelties, the oldest things will have to be presented as new, natural things as miraculous, and things familiar to us all as strange. For we reckon that things are adjudged novelties on four criteria: for their originality, or their recentness, or their rarity, or their strangeness. So, anything that is newly created gives pleasure by reason of the working of nature. Anything that has only just happened causes excitement, less if it happens often, more if it is rare. When anything strange is observed, we seize on it, partly because of the inversion of the natural order which surprises us, partly because of our ignorance of the cause, whose working is a mystery to us, and partly because of seeing our expectation cheated in unfamiliar circumstances of which we lack a proper understanding. From these causes arise two things, miracles and marvels, though they both result in wonderment.[102]

Partly because of its wondrousness, the turnip looks to have been a brilliant choice of topic for a verse wonder tale. Whereas most mirabilia were exotic rarities from outside Europe, the turnip was something home-grown.[103] Its ordinariness—it could be called the "wonder bread" of the Middle Ages—would have lent it a modest charisma or at least a recognition factor among humble folk when the tale was told orally. But it would have attracted also a contemporary clerical audience preoccupied with what all such peculiar footnotes to the book of nature meant.[104] Finally, the poem itself would have been seductive to kings and nobles, who not only collected real marvels as a display of their wealth, power, and culture but also patronized the literary expression of such marvels.[105]

An argument has been made to connect the spread of "wonder chambers" (*Wunderkammer*) in Europe around the middle of the sixteenth century with the production of fairy tales by Straparola.[106] According to this line of reasoning, the "wonder chambers" embody a yearning for novelty, variety, and exoticism, one of the driving forces that propelled court culture, as well as one of the principal forces to which Straparola responded in his writing. This argument may well hold, but it can be applied equally well to the Latin poem written three and a half centuries earlier.

The notion that an oversized vegetable would have had special value to a king already around 1200 is not preposterous. The *Wunderkammer* and wondrous objects that survive from the Middle Ages and early modernity do not include turnips, for the obvious reason that vegetables do not have shelf lives of centuries. What may come to mind first when one thinks of these wonder collections are monsters and exotic beasts. As an example of the former, take a so-called siren, evidently fabricated from the remains of various once-living creatures, now located in the Museo Civico in Modena.[107] For the latter, envisage a Halle an der Saale collection dating to the eighteenth century and surmounted by a crocodile suspended from the ceiling.[108] It is worth peering more closely into the display cases to inspect the assemblages of supersized pinecones, gigantic (and provocatively shaped) nuts, and other durable plant objects. Alongside other such things in cabinets of curiosities, particularly before the age of exploration opened access to more novel flora and fauna, it would be easy to imagine that a mega turnip once stood, until its inevitable dissolution set in.

To the kings and nobles, *The Turnip Tale,* in its extant forms, does not articulate support or sympathy for peasants so much as it brings home, with anxiety, that wealth and noble birth have become dissociated. The poet may well have reshaped the folktale as he received it, by, as one critic put it, altering "the identity of the hero in the folktale to establish a cultural polarity with his brother and to create the social anomaly of the knight behind the plow";[109] whereas the protagonist in Erasmus is a poor farmer, that in *The Turnip Tale* is a knight. The poem graphs a tension between, on the one hand, an old system in which hereditary nobility determined standing and, on the other, a newer system based on wealth. *The Turnip Tale* may give voice to the unease prompted by a new world in which knights of the lower nobility were sometimes genuinely impoverished and resentful toward peasants, clerics, and princes alike.[110] Having the clever brother who prevails be a nobleman fallen on hard times would have appealed to the minor nobility who engaged in culture (especially literature) during the Middle High German period. At the same time, the same lesser noblemen (*ministeriales*) would have understood the wealthier brother's sense of injustice at seeing the size of the rewards that the king gave to his peasant brother: their everyday life would have made them all too familiar with frustration at the undeserved good fortune of parvenus whose gains seemed to come at their own cost. If the poor knight raises one set of questions about the role of wealth as a determinant of social standing, the largesse of the king to a man who is a peasant in *officium,* if not in *titulus,* gets at the then-current controversy over excessive generosity by kings to peasants in preference to poor knights.

THE TALE OF THE GULLIBLE SCHOLAR

"The rich man is everywhere pleasing, the poor lies spurned everywhere"[111]—
this dictum brings me finally to the second component in *The Turnip Tale*
and "The Turnip," what could be called the tale of a stupid scholar. In terms
of tale types, it corresponds to the first act in the final episode of "fatal de-
ception" in AT 1535, "The Rich and the Poor Peasant (Unibos)" (now ATU
1535 "The Rich and the Poor Farmer [Unibos]"): "The trickster escapes from
a sack (chest) through exchange with a shepherd [K842]." Many other tales
relate this first half of the final episode by itself (AT 1737, "The Parson in the
Sack to Heaven"), while others incorporate it as the final episode in several
adventures (AT 1525A, "Theft of Dog, Horse, Sheet or Ring; IV. Places Ex-
changed in Sack"; AT 1539, "Cleverness and Gullibility"). A version of the
nearly universal motif in which one character tricks another into exchanging
places in a trap (*MIK* 842), this sort of role reversal enjoyed especially great
vitality in stories from the second half of the eleventh through the early thir-
teenth centuries, with one prominent appearance in the eleventh-century
Latin comic tale known as *Unibos* and another in the cycle of stories about
Reynard the Fox.[112] The *One-Ox* version of the story survives, though not by
direct influence, in *KHM* 61, "The Little Peasant" ("Das Bürle").

The version of this story in *The Turnip Tale* starts out by showing the
bad brother, now no longer wealthy, plotting against the good. Furious at
his brother's enrichment and his own impoverishment through the turnip,
the bad brother hires assassins to do away with his sibling. He persuades his
brother to accompany him to share a buried treasure, when in fact the as-
sassins lie in ambush. But before they can slay the good brother, they flee in
fright at the sound of an approaching rider. Before taking to their heels,
they hang the good brother in a sack in a tree. At this point, the good
brother, placed in a true cul de sac, shows intelligence, along with a change
for the worse in his character. Although it is fully justified for him to wish
to escape from the sack, he gains salvation by persuading the rider, a travel-
ing scholar, that spending time in the sack brings wisdom. Eventually he is
freed from the sack, forces the scholar to take his place in a contorted posi-
tion inside the sack, raises it aloft once again, and rides off on what had
been the scholar's horse.

One of many enigmas about *The Turnip Tale* concerns the source for the
motif of wisdom acquired through suspension atop a tree. This device is
loosely reminiscent of shamanism, since ritual ascent of trees played a role in
shamanic initiation rites throughout the world.[113] A particularly striking par-
allel to the idea that a person may acquire wisdom by hanging from a tree is
found in the Old Norse myth of Odin, as the Brothers Grimm themselves

were the first to remark.[114] The key source is one of the Eddic poems, the *Há-vamál* (The Speech of Hávi [= Óðinn]).[115] The portrayal of Odin's self-sac-rifice on the tree has long been connected with shamanism.[116]

Yet it is also curious that two of the manuscripts (admittedly, one of the fifteenth century and the other Jacob's copy of the lost late medieval Stras-bourg codex) insinuate a mention of Socrates into this situation.[117] Gatti views this reading as a deliberate insertion by a well-read reader or copyist who was familiar with Aristophanes' *The Clouds,* which includes in a satire of sophists a cameo of Socrates in a basket dangling in midair.[118] Although it is far likelier that a reader or copyist would have known Greek and been acquainted with *The Clouds* in the fifteenth century than earlier in the Middle Ages, the intriguing fact remains that the comedies of Aristophanes were available already in the early thirteenth century at the monastery of San Nicola di Casole, in the Greek-speaking Terra d'Otranto.[119] The manu-script was collected by Abbot Nicolas (Nectarius) of Casole, who died in 1235; eventually it wended its way to Venice.

The section in the Aristophanic comedy and the concluding episode in *The Turnip Tale* have suggestive overlaps. Both have as their main theme the satire of devotees of philosophy who are called sophists. Both have episodes in which a supposed scholar is suspended aloft and from there claims to gain special understanding of the heavens. Both culminate in disasters for the re-puted sages at the hands of unlearned, but far more practical, antagonists. In *The Clouds,* the greedy peasant Strepsiades, who has come to the sophists in search of a means for escaping his debts, sets their school on fire and throws in Socrates' face the words that the philosopher had used to boast of the wis-dom he was gaining from contemplating the skies from his basket. In *The Turnip Tale,* the knight ridicules the unfortunate scholar mercilessly as he leaves him dangling from the tree and rides off on his horse.

More mystifying than the source for the motif of arboreal insight in the concluding episode of *The Turnip Tale* is the volte-face in the characteri-zation of the brother who had been reduced to poverty. In his conduct to-ward the wayfaring scholar, he shows a spiteful side that seems inconsistent with the personality manifested in the earlier part of the tale. This incom-patibility between the two stories suggests that they were originally separate tales. In *KHM* 146, the story conveys the message that school learning will get its recipient only so far—that true wisdom does not come from the schools.[120] In the idiom of our own day, would-be savants would be well ad-vised to "bag" formal education altogether. This outlook accords well with the satire against schools and scholars that is widely attested in the twelfth and early thirteenth centuries. But the author's successful effort to broaden the social satire comes at the cost of the integrity of his chief character.

The two tales that together constitute *The Turnip Tale* seem not to be integrated effectively, especially since the personalities of the poor brothers in the two parts have nothing in common.[121] Yet other similarities remain. At the basis of both tales is the conflict between a poor and a rich brother, which is simultaneously a duel between good and evil. Both stories share a preoccupation with alterations in status. The first story foregrounds one man who is first lowered from nobility into peasantry and later reelevated and another who is brought down from nobility into poverty. The second presents one man who is cunning and high but who swaps places with another who is erudite and low. Additionally, the two stories are tied together through the theme of good fortune, which comes to those who do not strive to engineer their own success but who instead trust in God's providence and who can recognize true wonder for what it is.[122] In the first half of the poem, Fortune restores the hero to his proper social level by transforming a detail of peasant life into a marvelous instrument of her favor. But the fortune of the poor brother has far from ended once he has come to wealth, since his subsequent escape from death reconfirms him as a lucky devil. Furthermore, both parts manifest an unease over the developing money economy. The two antagonists were victims of their own covetousness, the one for wealth and the other for knowledge. The implication that wisdom can be bought seems as troubling to the author as the idea that lack of wealth can undermine a hierarchy predicated on nobility.

Finally, the two stories contradict the system of values attached in the late Middle Ages and early modernity to different types of plants.[123] According to the rules of vegetational hierarchy as they were understood in the later Middle Ages, plants were points on an ascending scale. At the low point were root crops, which belonged to the peasants. At the high point were fruit trees, which were appropriate to nobles. In between were herbaceous plants. *The Turnip Tale* plays with this equation, since it makes one of the lowliest root vegetables into something good (for one brother at least) while eventually ridiculing the assumption that being high necessarily makes one closer to God or intelligence. In the first part of *The Turnip Tale,* a lowly root vegetable brings prosperity, which runs counter to the conviction that the fruits of the earth were to be cultivated and eaten by the poor. In the second part, a misguided pedant becomes the unhappy fruit of a tree and thereby suffers both a blow to his pride and the loss of a possession that is a token of class, namely, the horse. Low food raises one to the heights, while high food is not even food for thought. Thus the tale told in *The Turnip Tale* would seem to have been designed to fit with specifically medieval schemas about plants, wonders, and also the social orders. It depicts a shifting that was taking place in the class system's tectonic plates in the greater twelfth century.

THE GRIMMS' REWORKING OF *THE TURNIP TALE*

What happens to *The Turnip Tale* in the hands of the Brothers Grimm? For a start, the turnip remains a turnip, but it goes through a composting process. Wilhelm begins the preface to the first edition (1812) of the *KHM* with a botanical metaphor to describe the organic life cycle of a *Märchen*.

> When a storm or some other mishap sent by heaven destroys an entire crop, it is reassuring to find that a small spot on a path lined by low hedges or bushes has been spared and that a few stalks remain standing. If the sun favors them with light, they continue to grow, alone and unobserved, and no scythe comes along to cut them prematurely for huge storage bins. But at the end of the summer, once they have ripened and become full, poor devout hands come to seek them out; ear upon ear, carefully bound and esteemed more highly than entire sheaves, they are carried home, and for the entire winter they provide nourishment, perhaps the only seed for the future. That is how it all seems to us when we review the riches of German poetry from olden times and discover that nothing of it has been kept alive, even the memory of it is lost—folk songs and these innocent household tales are all that remain. The places by the stove, the hearth in the kitchen, attic stairs, holidays still celebrated, meadows and forests in their solitude, and above all the untrammeled imagination have functioned as hedges preserving them and passing them on from one generation to the next . . .
>
> It is probably just the right time to collect these tales, since those who have been preserving them are becoming ever harder to find (to be sure, those who still know them know a great deal, because people may die, but the stories live on). The custom of telling tales is ever on the wane.[124]

According to Wilhelm's trope, a storm knocks down seeds of grain that happen to be sheltered beside a low hedge. As the weather improves, the seeds sprout and prosper. In late summer, human hands arrive, harvest the ears of grain, and bring them home as food and perhaps also as seed grain for the future. In the analogy Wilhelm draws, the seeds and grain plants are the tales, and the hedges are the places and conditions that foster their preservation.

 This lovely and intricate image accords well with the Romantic concept of art in general and poetry in particular as being expressions of nature. But, as I mentioned earlier, considerable controversy has raged over just how passive a role the disembodied human hands played in the production of the

KHM. The Brothers Grimm positioned themselves as collectors rather than as creators of the tales that are now known the world over: from the first edition, the title page of the collection has read *Kinder- und Hausmärchen, gesammelt durch die Brüder Grimm.* They claimed to have endeavored to keep the tales pure and to have refrained from padding or embellishing them.[125] This claim is expanded in the 1819 edition.

> As regards the method of our collecting, its main concerns were fidelity and truth. So far as the manner in which we collected is concerned, accuracy and truth were what counted for us above all. We did not add anything from our own resources, nor did we embellish any events and features of the story itself. Instead we tried to relate the content just as we had heard it; we hardly need emphasize that the phrasing and filling in of details were mainly our work, but we did try to preserve every particularity that we noticed so that in this respect the collection would reflect the diversity of nature.[126]

But did the brothers merely harvest the tales like so many plants and bundle them so that they could be printed in fascicles? Did they collect heirloom seeds without altering them, or did they engage in a little bioengineering? Despite their evident yearning to pass on pure folktales of the sort told by traditional oral storytellers, they recognized that they could only try their best.

In reworking *The Turnip Tale,* the brothers sought to present a version of the story that would sound as if it had been told by a nineteenth-century German peasant, not written by a Latin-using medieval cleric. As we have already seen, they maintained in their notes that the Latin poem was composed "without doubt on the basis of an oral folk story." To their way of thinking, their version of the tale was not so much a translation as a restoration of the presumptive original folktale from a poeticized, clericized, and Latinized form.

The style of *The Turnip Tale* had been esteemed as one of its strong points. In his *Registrum multorum auctorum,* Hugo of Trimberg characterizes *The Turnip Tale* as having more to offer stylistically than in content.[127] The Brothers Grimm aspired to a very different style. In their effort to regain the putative original contours of the tale, they reduced the scale starkly. Ellis calculated that the Grimms usually doubled in length the tales in the 1810 Ölenberg Manuscript that they incorporated into the first volume in the 1812 edition of *KHM,*[128] but in adapting *The Donkey Tale* and *The Turnip Tale* from the Latin, they followed a nearly opposite procedure by

cutting close to three-quarters of the manuscript versions. The economy of the Grimm version of *The Turnip Tale* is impressive. In the standard edition, the number of lines in *The Turnip Tale "prodiga"* [2] is 388. In contrast, the prose of the Grimms' version amounts to only eighty-eight lines in the most widely available, 1819 edition. This represents a reduction by more than three-quarters of the original. Roughly this proportion holds already in the openings of the two texts: the first fourteen lines of *The Turnip Tale "prodiga"* [2] are scaled down to four lines of prose in *KHM* 146.

The brothers sought to present the story as plainly and simply as they could, without digressions for either stylistic or moralistic purposes. They strove for economy by ridding the tale of details that could be regarded as extraneous or inconsequential, of repetitions, and of whole passages that they regarded as departures from the essence of the story. In the process, they shortened the Latin considerably and used more basic words.[129]

In what was obviously an effort to replace the formal rhetoric of the Latin school tradition with a technique more in keeping with their image of oral tale-telling, they shifted monologues and soliloquies into second-person address.[130] In a related procedure, the brothers shortened or deleted speeches, such as those of the peasant to the king (69–98, reduced to five lines of German) and of the queen to the king (185–96, deleted). The recruiting of the murderers by the rich brother sprawls over thirty-five lines in *The Turnip Tale "prodiga"* [2] (229–64) but is allotted only a single sentence in the Grimms' version. The Grimms' aspiration toward narrative thrift in *Märchen* excluded any embellishment that made description "thick."[131] Accordingly, to remove rhetorical embellishment, they rid the text of most such devices as personification (83–86, 209, 358), metaphor and simile (292, 297), anaphora (e.g., "qui . . . qui . . . quo sine . . . quo sine," 31–34), chiasmus (37, 66), asyndeton, paronomasia, alliteration, and synonymy. For the same reason, they removed the classical tags that are found now and then in the Medieval Latin poem. Because the Grimm brothers subscribed to different doctrines of decorum, both rhetorical and behavioral, than did poets in the Middle Ages, they excised every instance of the Latin *decet* (meaning "to accord with approved standards of taste or behavior") and associated words (e.g., 46, 98, 231).

Less often, the brothers (primarily Wilhelm) supplied new material to fit with their expectations of what a folktale that originated in medieval Germany would have sounded like when told by a traditional storyteller of their own day. Thus many of their additions are stylistic, in supplying turns of phrase that sounded either folksy or old-fashioned and biblical.[132] In *The Turnip Tale "prodiga"* [2], the formerly poor brother, when dangling from the tree after the murder attempt, assures the wayfaring student that the

sack is superior to any formal institution of learning: "you will know that only here are true schools."[133] In "The Turnip," this same assurance is expressed using a metaphor of the wind to express worthlessness or nothingness: "In comparison all the schools are but a wind." This proverbial (or pseudo-proverbial) turn of phrase is modeled on other uses of the word meaning "wind" in Middle High German, uses of which the brothers were well aware through their lexicographic work on their German dictionary (*Deutsches Wörterbuch*).[134] Their insertion of this proverb reflects their belief that the narrative of the poet who composed this Medieval Latin poem, like the narratives of the early nineteenth-century informants on whom the Grimms drew for other fairy tales, preserved centuries-old oral material.

In stripping down the poem, the brothers omitted features that helped to unify the story it told. In their labor (which was not so much translation as paraphrase), they lopped off much fat but also some flesh, in both style and content. In the Latin, extended speeches and scenes had helped to develop the characters and concerns of the chief actors. For instance, the Latin poem devoted much attention to the efforts of the knightly brother to obtain rich rewards from the king. The parallel visits to the court in the Latin poem conveyed disparities in the characters and behavior of the two brothers. These contrasts vanish in "The Turnip."

To achieve their goals, the Brothers Grimm had to drop or trim aspects of the story that appeared to them anachronistic or out of keeping with the folklife of their own time. Such angles include the emphasis of *The Turnip Tale* on feudal relations. The medieval version deals in its main action with the interactions of representatives of the three social classes as they were often conceived in the Middle Ages. It recounts the story of a knight who suffers the ignominious debasement of being reduced to performing manual labor and working the soil. While relating the tale of a knight who first ascends out of the peasantry and then outwits a cleric, *The Turnip Tale* assumes, but also maybe contests, acceptance of the natures and functions of the three main classes or estates that the Middle Ages understood as its social structure: the knights, who bore arms to protect society militarily; the clerks, who attended to the spiritual welfare of society; and the peasants, who tilled the soil to provide food.[135] Thus *The Turnip Tale* can be analyzed usefully within the medieval framework of the tripartite class system discussed by Georges Duby in *The Three Orders: Feudal Society Imagined* (1980).

The Latin poet, who seems obsessed with the permutations in social class that fortune can effect, states unambiguously his view when the lead character is reduced from being a knight to a peasant: "for shame!" [proch pudor!] (10). In a reading preserved only in Jacob Grimm's transcription of the perished Strasbourg manuscript,[136] the poor knight utters the same exclamation

(73, MS S) in the midst of a twenty-five-line lament (68–93) about his dimin-
ished status—about the antithesis between his past knighthood and his pres-
ent poverty and peasanthood. In the Grimms' tale, all of this is reduced to a
comparison with the brother. Whereas the medieval poem expresses a con-
trast in terms of noble and nonnoble, the Grimms place the accent instead on
the difference between rich and poor. When at court, the medieval protago-
nist laments his lost nobility and complains that the common people mistreat
him by not recognizing nobility (79–80), whereas the Grimms' hero merely
complains that no one respects him because he has no money. In the medieval
poem, the rich brother calls on his vassals (229–30), although they are not so
identified. He refers to himself as their king and father (240). In contrast, the
Grimms' villainous brother hired murderers.

To expunge all traces of the medieval social orders, the Brothers Grimm
turn the knight into a soldier and the cleric into a scholar. The word *soldier*
carries no undercurrent of nobility, *scholar* no implications of clerical status;
thus the brothers remove the friction between clergy and laity that was im-
manent in the words *miles* and *scolaris* in the Medieval Latin poem.[137] Jacob
and Wilhelm Grimm aimed to present their tales as common folk, such as
farmers, would have told them. They may have thought that peasant story-
tellers of their day or earlier days would not have been interested in stories
of noblemen who met adverse fortune but that such storytellers would have
had sympathy for people who suffered financial setbacks through no fault
of their own.

The Brothers Grimm had to make the story both respond to the differ-
ences they sensed between the Middle Ages and their own times and corre-
spond to their beliefs about the point of view of a folktale. At the same
time, they retained aspects (e.g., the emphasis on agriculture) that remained
pertinent to their conception of folktale—German folktale, in particular.
The feudal world was no longer relevant, but the supposed peasant teller of
the tale could still relate to the basics of a medieval agricultural economy.
Therefore they left the turnip, oxen, cart, and other details of peasant life,
and they kept the standards of wealth (land, animals, and gold) substan-
tially the same.

In the Latin poem, family relations are mentioned repeatedly. Two quo-
tations illustrate this point.

> A trifling story reports that there were two brothers whom one
> mother bore to one man. The rank of knighthood distinguished
> them both, of whom the one was rich and the other destitute. [5] The
> rich one held the rank, together with the name, of a knight; the other
> bore the sad burden of poverty. (*The Turnip Tale "frivola"* [1] 1–6)[138]

O my full brother, no one is left to me apart from you, whom love
joins to me in a brotherly bond. We are one flesh and nature does not
sunder us; one mother bore us to one man. Perhaps one soul resides
in two persons, [290] whom an indivisible love joins and unites. (*The
Turnip Tale "frivola"* [1] 287–90)[139]

The fact that one and the same mother bore the boys to one husband is
pointed out twice. But since the relationship between brotherhood and true
love held more importance in the twelfth century than in the nineteenth,[140]
all of the second passage is boiled down to the phrase "dear brother" ("lieber
Bruder") in the Grimms' tale. Interestingly, the preoccupation of the Latin
poem with brotherhood seems to reemerge independently in *The Turnip*
(1927) by Walter de la Mare (1873–1956), which begins: "Once upon a time
there were two brothers, or rather half-brothers, for they had had the same
father, but different mothers; and no two human beings could be more un-
like one another."[141]

As a result of altered conceptions about both society in general and fam-
ilies in particular, the Brothers Grimm modified in a major way the role of
women in "The Turnip" from what it had been in *The Turnip Tale*. *The
Turnip Tale "prodiga"* [2] was much closer to their biases than was *The
Turnip Tale "frivola"* [1]. In *The Turnip Tale "frivola"* [1], women serve such
a prominent and positive function as advisers as to suggest that female
tellers created the story or at least that the proportion of women in the au-
dience of the tale when it was performed orally was so high that tellers felt
obliged to portray female characters in a favorable light. Both the poor
knight, when he needs to decide what to do with the giant turnip, and the
king, when confronted with the abundance of gifts from the poor knight's
rich brother, turn to their wives for sage counsel (the rehearsal of the phrase
utile consilium in lines 52 and 228 brings home the parallel). Furthermore,
the wife of the poor brother greets him enthusiastically upon his return, in
a triumph he would not have enjoyed had it not been for her advice. The
plain implication is that it is good to have a wife and to seek her guidance.
Indeed, only the brother who is not identified as being married and who
does not seek advice suffers adverse consequences. This uxorious aspect of
the tale is partially preserved in Erasmus's version, in which the peasant's
wife advises her husband on how to proceed in taking advantage of the
good fortune of having an extraordinary turnip; as we will see, this common
feature signals that Erasmus relied on a source more closely related to *The
Turnip Tale "frivola"* [1] than to *The Turnip Tale "prodiga"* [2].

In *The Turnip Tale "prodiga"* [2], the prominence of women is reduced.
The poor brother's plan is presented as an internal dialogue, rather than as

a discussion with his wife. The reasoning about the turnip that she presented in *The Turnip Tale "frivola"* [1] is absent, as is her prediction that the king will enrich the farmer. Although the king is depicted as consulting his wife, the symmetry of having the poor knight initially seek the advice of his wife is lacking. Evidently believing that the women were not essential characters and maybe also that the idea of a woman giving advice was not appropriate to the fairy tale world, the Grimm brothers took the process a further step by omitting the queen. They noticed the presence of a woman in the episode with the king, regarded it as inessential, and deleted it. They stated simply that the king took the gifts and that he thought immediately of giving the large turnip.

It is possible that the omission of the queen is no more than one of many economies to scale down the narrative to the length the Brothers Grimm thought a *Märchen* should be. By this way of thinking, the excision of the queen is no more provocative than the disappearance of the female personifications Wisdom or Philosophy, who had been bit characters in *The Turnip Tale 2*. Alternatively, this alteration may give a glimpse of the brothers editing the text to fit with their own patriarchal view that men make the decisions and that women are not to be consulted in open communication.

The greatest of the many changes between *The Turnip Tale "prodiga"* [2] and "The Turnip" lies in the nature and scope of wonder itself. Both the Medieval Latin poems and the version in the *KHM* contain significant elements of wonder tales, but the sense of wonder differs starkly. All three are success stories, but the success is not financial. An observation made by Max Lüthi (1909–91), although not about this particular tale in the *KHM,* is nonetheless quite apt: "these are images for something more fundamental: man's deliverance from an unauthentic existence and his commencement of a true one."[142] The Grimms' *Märchen* have their own morality, which is not a Christian morality. In the Medieval Latin, God and Christianity are present in the background, perhaps not continuously but at least recurrently. The Brothers Grimm delete all discussion of divinities (not just pagan gods, but especially the Christian God) and all explicit moralizing (e.g., mentions of providence or harangues on the perils of avarice and envy).[143] Thus the Grimm brothers expurgate a long prayer by the farmer (31–40) not only because it is a digression but also because it offers a view of the world that conflicts with their own preconceptions about wonder tales.

The Latin poem emphasizes that, in at least the poor brother's opinion, the turnip comes about for a reason: "This did not happen without a reason" [Non accidit hoc sine causa] (*The Turnip Tale "prodiga"* [2] 23). This faith in providence even enters into the manuscript tradition. In a slip that is less Freudian than divinely inspired, Jacob Grimm transcribed the open-

ing line of the poem to read, "A prophetic story reports that there were two brothers" [Fama fuisse duos testatur provida fratres]. In a prayer in the medieval poem, the poor brother expresses the view that God creates nothing, not even an oversized turnip, without a purpose. In the Grimms tale, the turnip is not a miracle but just an unusually large turnip. The Grimms go out of their way to underscore this fact: in describing this aspect of the turnip, they actually add substantially to the wording of the Latin, with adjectives, phrases, and even a metaphor.[144] They play down the idea of supernatural marvels and miracles, so important in the twelfth and thirteenth century,[145] and focus instead simply on a natural wonder, namely, the extravagant size of the turnip, which accords with their conception of a wonder tale. In the process, they sacrifice much of the depth in the medieval poem, in which the turnip is more than merely a gigantic object of wonder but is actually a tool of providence that rewards the good and punishes the greedy and invidious. In fact, the Grimms' heighten the salience of fortune in the first story, which was more latent in the medieval poem; the good fortune of the poor brother is more aleatory.[146]

In friction with their accentuation of fortune in the first story, the Brothers Grimm make the formerly poor brother more active physically in securing freedom from the sack through his own agency in the second story. Whereas the bag seems already to be perforated from wear and tear in both *The Turnip Tale "frivola"* [1] and *The Turnip Tale "prodiga"* [2], the brother is shown working a hole into it on his own initiative in *KHM* 146. Through the aperture he has created for himself, he descries the wandering scholar who becomes the means of his liberation.

KHM 144 and 146 were not revised extensively in subsequent versions, as was the case with other tales (particularly from the first [1812] volume).[147] This fact may suggest that Wilhelm judged these two tales to have embodied from the outset the ideals of *Märchen,* at least in their style. Yet in the seventh edition of 1857, Wilhelm Grimm added a crucial concluding sentence that changes the story. In both the Latin poem and the *KHM,* the story is an ungainly portmanteau, striking listeners and readers today as a juxtaposition, rather than a successful fusion, of two very different stories. People in the Middle Ages may have been more comfortable with such forms, since they were exposed on a regular basis to the diptych of the Old and New Testaments, to say nothing of true diptychs in churches as well as other representations of the complementarity that the diptych embodies. Additionally, it is possible that the aesthetics of oral narrative accustomed audiences to such joinings of different stories into a single narrative with various "movements."[148] In any case, the wonder tale of the turnip gives way to the trickster story of the sack. Between the two stories, the character of

the poor brother undergoes an abrupt and startling transformation. In the Latin poem, the poor brother is described as lacking all guile (283). Even so, he shows an unexpectedly and decidedly vindictive bent toward the hapless scholar at the end, whose horse he steals and whom he leaves hanging in a torturous position. To lessen the abruptness of the ending and to avoid putting the farmer in a bad light, Wilhelm has the poor brother, the farmer, send an unidentified person to free the scholar after an hour in the sack: "With that, he mounted the scholar's horse, rode forth, but after an hour sent someone to let him down again" [Damit stieg er auf des Schülers Pferd, ritt fort, schickte aber nach einer Stunde jemand, der ihn wieder herablassen mußte].[149] This new ending fits with the Grimms' sense of right behavior and decency. They are second guessing the original on what its essential message was, believing it to have been kinder and gentler. In effect, the Grimms' version is less grim than the medieval version. They have the tale end not with a taunt but with an action they supplied of their own accord—a Disney-style happy ending.[150]

With the benefit of hindsight, it appears inevitable that the Brothers Grimm would have regarded *The Turnip Tale*—a Medieval Latin tale that tends to be classified today as an elegiac comedy—as a proto–fairy tale. As Jacob's letter to Wilhelm made clear, the political climate that enveloped him predisposed him to see Alsace in general and Strasbourg in particular as "of a capable, fundamentally good German type." The Brothers were ever on the prowl for materials from the Middle Ages that would expand and undergird their understanding of Germany's past. To find in Strasbourg a tale about a once-privileged young man who had fallen on hard times but who was saved by a supernatural gift of an enormous turnip would have been a dream come true. (Beyond the politics of their day, would they not have felt a personal impulse to identify themselves with their protagonist, since they were in the midst of raising themselves from the impoverishment into which their family had tumbled after the premature death of their father?) Their delight at this narrative trouvé would have only been enhanced by the realization that the turnip was a vegetable associated with Strasbourg (Germanic Strassburg) in both actuality and legend.

One Romantic view of the nation envisaged it as an organic entity. Jacob's report to Wilhelm attaches Germanness explicitly to white wine and sauerkraut. In "The Turnip," for which they are owed joint credit, the brothers may well have regarded the turnip itself as an emblem of Strasbourg's German ethnicity. Today Alsace is renowned for, among many other things, *choucroute garnie,* the main ingredient in which is sauerkraut. The turnip has slipped in standing.

The changes the Brothers Grimm wrought in the *Raparius* (as they called

it) to make it a *Märchen* fit with the preoccupations of their own times and circumstances, chief among which would have been the concerns with nature and nationalism that are defining traits of Romanticism. Their handling of the Medieval Latin poem that they took as their point of departure was in a sense opposite to that of the Ossianic material that was discussed in chapter 1 of the present study. Whereas James Macpherson presented his own eighteenth-century composition as a translation of a nonexistent original, the Grimm brothers interleaved their translations of medieval material among their nineteenth-century reworkings of supposedly oral folktales.

But the brothers were not perpetrating a deliberate fraud. As they re-created the fairy tale that they were sure lay behind the Medieval Latin poem, they sought to retain as much of the original tale's form as possible. After all, their Romanticism was deeply embedded in what they perceived as the Middle Ages. (The derivation of the very term *Romanticism* from medieval "romances" must not be forgotten.) The Grimms' process of change and retention should not catch us unawares, since the author of *The Turnip Tale* himself had appropriated a folktale and retooled it to suit his views on the social structures and tensions of his own period. Fairy tale is a kind of narrative protoplasm that may be shaped and reshaped to accommodate an infinite number of new needs, social and personal. Like most supposedly elementary life forms, like the heirloom seeds the Brothers Grimm made a metaphor for the folklore they collected, or like the turnip seeds sown by the poor man in both *The Turnip Tale* and "The Turnip," it has a wondrous capacity to survive and sustain, to mutate and yet to remain the same.

Neither the Brothers Grimm nor the poet of *The Turnip Tale* held professional degrees in folkloristics. None of them attempted to produce verbatim transcriptions of any single telling of the tales they recorded. Yet all of them have transmitted to us texts that provide priceless aid as we seek to recover the folklore of the past. To be sure, they interposed between us and the folklore preceding them a coating that complicates analysis; but at least in this case complication can be regarded as enrichment. Who would argue that we are not better off for the existence of the *Märchen* and its medieval predecessor, however great and frustrating are the interpretive challenges they pose?

The Reorientation of *The Donkey Tale* (ca. 1200)

The first European fairy tale?[1]

Even less a part of the oral tradition of Europe is the story of The Ass (Type 430). It is really a retelling by the brothers Grimm of a four-teenth century Latin poem, *Asinarius*. The prince who has been trans-formed to an ass plays a lyre and is entertained at the king's court. A princess disenchants him and becomes his wife.[2]

It is a lucky circumstance that a wonder tale passed on in oral trans-mission has also been preserved in the form of a courtly adaptation from the time around 1200.[3]

[T]here can be no doubt that here a popular tale was transformed just as tales transmitted five hundred years later at the court of Ver-sailles were developed into stylized "book tales" according to the un-derstanding of a fantastic, fairy-oriented Romanticism.[4]

Whoever says "fairy tale" thinks first of all of princes and princesses.[5]

INTRODUCING *THE DONKEY TALE*

n this chapter, I will focus on the medieval background of a story that goes by the title "Das Eselein" (which means "The Donkey" or "The Little Ass") in the famous fairy tale collection of the Brothers Grimm (app. 5C).[6] At the heart of the tale lies the motif of a man transformed into a donkey, which also appears in such famous ancient stories as Apuleius's *Metamorphoses,* or *The Golden*

Ass (from the second half of the second century CE), and "Lucius, or The Ass" (which is among the pseudoepigrapha of Lucian), neither of which was readily available in the Latin Middle Ages.[7] The similarities between the ancient stories and the Grimms' "The Donkey," though initially striking, are not extensive. In the Grimms' tale, the central figure is not a picaresque character whose metamorphosis occurs as the result of his own lust and curiosity (like the protagonist Lucius in both Apuleius and pseudo-Lucian) but a well-mannered prince with an improbable, unfortunate, and ultimately remediable birth defect: he is born an ass. He exits permanently from his animal form not when he eats roses, which brings about the resolution in the two ancient stories, but after marrying a princess, when his father-in-law snatches and burns the hide that the donkey prince doffs by night.

In looking at this tale, I have four objectives. The first is to explore the meanings that reside in the story in its earliest European version, a Medieval Latin poem entitled *Asinarius* (which is far less likely to translate into English as *The Donkey Man* than as *The Donkey [Book]* or *The Donkey Tale*).[8] To fulfill this aim, I will examine how what had been an orally transmitted tale could have been modified as it became a written Latin poem in the Middle Ages. This part of the study will suggest the suitability of the Latin poem as a male-oriented equivalent to the tale "Beauty and the Beast" (ATU 425C): in both tales, a man in beast form first becomes the bridegroom of a beautiful young woman and then attains human form, although the protagonist of "Beauty and the Beast" is the female character (the beauty), whereas that of *The Donkey Tale* is the male (the beast).

My second aim is to delve into an association that seems to have become encoded in the story as it wended its way westward. On the basis of internal evidence from *The Donkey Tale*—which, to reiterate its chief claim to fame, is the earliest European version of the tale—I will advance the hypotheses that this tale of a musically talented man in an animal's body could have held a special appeal and place in the repertoire of medieval entertainers and that the salience of music as a theme within it may hint that the story was carried into Europe by traveling mime players.

My third objective is to put forward the notion that the story reached Europe from somewhere in the East and, in at least one earlier guise, was not a fairy tale or folktale but a myth. In so doing, I revive and modify for application to this one particular story (which was not investigated by any of the scholars who are cataloged in the remainder of this paragraph)[9] the nineteenth-century Indianist or migrational theory of the German Sanskritist and philologist Theodor Benfey (1809–81), who contended that collections of very old Indian tales were the sources of most later oriental and many later occidental fairy tales—in other words, that most folktales originated among

the Buddhists and reached Europe at a comparatively late date.[10] Benfey's theory lost much of its early luster when it was rebutted by Joseph Bédier (1864–1938) in regard to Old French fabliaux, yet in the nineteenth century it won many adherents, such as Emmanuel Cosquin (1841–1919), Reinhold Köhler (1830–92), and Gaston Paris (1839–1903).[11]

The Indianist theory and what might be called the anti-Indianist reaction to it fit into a long-standing alternation in scholarship on European literature (ancient, medieval, and modern alike) between equally gross exaggeration and understatement of non-European influences.[12] The Orientalist theory advanced by the late Edward W. Said in his *Orientalism* (New York: Pantheon, 1978) to describe (and problematize) modern Western studies on the Muslim Orient, and the Afrocentric theory propounded by Martin Bernal in his *Black Athena: The Afroasiatic Roots of Classical Civilization* (New Brunswick, NJ: Rutgers University Press, 1987–) are only the comparatively most recent and headline-grabbing manifestations of trends that have been detectable for centuries in research on ancient romance, fairy tale, and other genres—trends toward, on the one hand, seeking out and acknowledging—even to excess—sources and analogues in the East and, on the other, denying categorically any such influences.[13] Rather than add one more voice to this competition, I propose not to venture a broad theory of origins or counterorigins but instead to limit myself to assessing a single small group of texts.

Finally, as my fourth goal, I wish to identify the changes that the Brothers Grimm wrought as they adapted the story for inclusion in their *KHM*. Specifically, I undertake to consider briefly the fate of the tale as the Grimm brothers reshaped the Medieval Latin version to suit the mores and values of their nineteenth-century German reading public.[14] The availability of *The Donkey Tale* provides us with a magnificent opportunity—almost a laboratory test case—to scrutinize just how the Brothers Grimm may have proceeded when reforming their raw materials and rough edges in the *Märchen* they eventually published. Here we have not only the allegedly authentic fairy tale that they created but also the very text that served as their source— what they judged to be a fairy tale tainted by the highly literary form in which it had been preserved.[15]

In honing my thoughts on the different versions of "The Donkey," I have found helpful the basic principles of "conduit theory" as it has been enunciated by Linda Dégh (1920–) and others.[16] According to conduit theory, the messages of folklore and folktales do not come into being spontaneously and do not travel randomly. Rather, messages are transmitted and received with the least interference when they pass among individuals who have similar personal situations, personalities, and personal characteristics.

When messages reach listeners who do not share the same environments and attributes, either they stop there and are not retransmitted, or else they are altered to conform to their new circumstances. Folktales represent inherent qualities of societies. If the social characteristics at stake change fundamentally, the folktales perish or change in response. If folktales are imported into a society from the outside world, they will survive only if adopted to be palatable and meaningful to the native audiences.

Another tool that has been beneficial to my thinking has been a concept of Vladimir Propp's that could be translated into English as "many-stagedness," "multistratification," or "polystadiality."[17] According to Propp, folklore experiences changes due not solely to economically induced social changes but also to religious changes, noneconomically induced social changes, and so forth. As folklore develops, it may retain and accumulate imprints of changes that it has undergone in earlier stages of its existence, which may extend over thousands of years. Propp sees the task of folkloristics as being to isolate and identify the various strata of works according to their components, beginning from the most ancient works and concluding with the most recent. According to him, the correlation of these strata with what is known about changes in the economic and social conditions permits the folklorist to determine the genesis and the cause of the changes, which include atrophications and new formations.

To facilitate the pursuit of one particular tale as it passes through at least three conduits over six hundred years or more and across thousands of miles, I offer three texts in the appendix (app. 5A–C). The first is my English translation of *The Donkey Tale,*[18] the second a translation by Franklin Edgerton (1885–1963) of the Sanskrit analogue,[19] and the third my translation of the Grimms' version of this tale. These texts can function as a convenient casebook for anyone with an interest in the destiny of this curious story.

The Grimms' version makes a good point of departure. Of the three versions, it is not only the shortest but also the closest to us culturally and chronologically. It can be summarized as follows: Once upon a time there were a king and queen who possessed everything they desired except children. Finally, God granted them a baby, but the infant boy looked like a young donkey rather than a human being. As he grew up, the donkey became very accomplished, especially at playing the lute. All went well until, one day, the donkey prince glimpsed his reflection in the water of a spring and went into shock; apparently a little imperceptive, he had not intuited before this moment that he was not a normal man. Thereafter, dismayed at his donkeydom, he left home and wandered the world with a friend until he reached the palace of an old king who had an exceedingly beautiful daughter.

Here he ingratiated himself so much through his music and manners that the king offered him the princess as his bride. On his wedding night the king had a servant observe the newlyweds. The servant saw that at night the bridegroom took off the donkey skin and became a handsome young prince but that in the morning he donned it once again and resumed his masquerade as a donkey. The king crept into their room on the following night, stole the donkey skin, and threw it into a fire. The prince and princess lived happily ever after.

A MALE-ORIENTED "BEAUTY AND THE BEAST"

At this time, we have no decisive means of dating the Medieval Latin version of "The Donkey," since it is anonymous and contains no internal references to datable events. Still, we have a *terminus ante quem:* it must have been composed before 1280, when the German author Hugo of Trimberg (ca. 1230–ca. 1313), master of the abbey school in Teuerstadt near Bamberg, notes it—in his Latin *Registrum multorum auctorum* (a concise literary history of classical Latin authors and Medieval Latin authors)—as a text commonly read in his day.[20] On prosodic and stylistic grounds, the poem, usually entitled *Asinarius,* has customarily been dated around 1200.[21]

The working assumption of most earlier scholars who have occupied themselves with *The Donkey Tale* has been that the poet participated somehow in the revival of German culture under the Hohenstaufen dynasty, which ruled Swabia from 1079 to 1268, Germany from 1138 to 1254, and Sicily from 1194 to 1266.[22] The inference has been that the poet of *The Donkey Tale* moved in court circles—a conclusion that could be underpinned by the poem's repeated evocations of kings and nobility, courtly entertainment, and courtly manners.[23] The donkey starts as the son of one king and finishes as the son-in-law of another. He gains entrance to the foreign court through his virtuosity as a lutanist and singer; he consolidates his acceptance in the court through his manners. Yet by adhering to such a mode of argument, we could conclude that almost any rags-to-riches fantasies about improvement of the heroine's or hero's fortune, whether fairy tales or even harlequin romances, were intended for noble readers, which obviously cannot be.

An even stronger case can be mounted—on both external and internal evidence—that the author of *The Donkey Tale* created the poem for a school milieu. External evidence comes from Hugo of Trimberg's inclusion of the poem in his *Registrum multorum auctorum* (which is, after all, not the shelf list of a royal library but a roll call of school favorites) among "books not disdained that are very often read in the schools" [libelli nec despecti / Qui leguntur sepius in scolis][24] and from the subsequent transmission of the

poem in manuscripts that were intended for scholastic, rather than courtly, use. The manuscripts in which *The Donkey Tale* is preserved contain familiar school texts, such as the *Distichs of Cato* (Berlin, Staatsbibliothek zu Berlin/Preussischer Kulturbesitz, MS Diez B. Sant. 4, Prague, Knihovna Metropolitní kapituly, MS 1482); the *Facetus* (Berlin, Staatsbibliothek zu Berlin/Preussischer Kulturbesitz, MS Diez B. Sant. 4); the *Physiologus* (The Naturalist) (Basel, Universitätsbibliothek, MS F.VII.8; [Vienna lost]); pseudo-Ovidiana, such as the *De vetula* (The Old Woman) (Berlin, Staatsbibliothek zu Berlin/Preussischer Kulturbesitz, MS Diez B. Sant. 4; Frankfurt am Main, Stadt- und Universitätsbibliothek, MS Barth. 62); and the *Speculum stultorum* (The Mirror of Fools) (Frankfurt am Main, Stadt- und Universitätsbibliothek, MS Barth. 62).[25] This very partial list of contents in manuscripts that contain *The Donkey Tale* reveals a tendency to group the poem with some texts that were designed to form the ethics or etiquette of students, others that explored the vicissitudes of love, and one that also featured a donkey as hero.

Since the value of such external evidence is curtailed by our realization that a work of literature not meant for school use may end up suffering that fate (one outstanding example from Latin poetry would be Virgil's *Aeneid*), it is fortunate that the contents of the poem itself offer many indications of its suitability for use among the adolescent males who constituted most of the audience in medieval classrooms. By writing in Latin, the poet of *The Donkey Tale* chose a language that was restricted by and large to men and boys. With scarcely any exceptions, boys learned Latin from men by studying texts written by other men. Not without reason, Walter Ong has presented the study of Latin in the Renaissance as being a puberty rite for adolescent males.[26]

At first blush, the idea that *The Donkey Tale* could have been pressed into service in the curriculum seems far-fetched. After all, the poem lacks any pretense of being edifying—as Hugo of Trimberg recognized in appraising it and *The Turnip Tale:* "Even if their contents are only moderately useful, they are still quite worthy poems" [Horum si materie sint utilitatis / Modice, sunt carmina tamen digna satis] (888–89).[27] But however devoid the poem may be of outright moralizing, it nonetheless explores themes that would have struck home in young boys as they perused it. It tells of a boy who comes to terms with physical transformations on the way to becoming a husband, of a boy who triumphs in a challenging transition en route to winning the full acceptance of the father figures in his life and to discovering his own identity (it is worth noting that he remains pointedly anonymous until the very end); and it affords tantalizing glimpses of the physical changes through which girls pass during the same stages of life.

Indeed, the masculine orientation of *The Donkey Tale* lent itself well to the poet's playful exaggeration of the powers and joys of sex. His descriptions of the princess's pubescent charms and the servant's voyeuristic mission interject into the poem the medieval equivalent of locker-room humor. The sequence of observations that precedes the donkey's entry into the hall of the Western king seems to suggest that the beast seeks to penetrate not only the court but also the man-hungry maiden who lies waiting on her bed (129–36).

> At that time the maiden had already completed her years of girlhood: [130] her private parts had already given forth fine hairs; the nipples of her breasts had already given signs that she can hardly sleep alone on her bed without a man.
>
> Coming here, the ass makes his way to the king's hall. He shouts out and knocks; and having spoken thus, he said: [135] "Let the door be opened wide so that a stranger may enter! A guest is at the door: open the door!"

The donkey is characterized as living in a mesmerized state, which is broken precisely when he is offered the prospect of sex with the king's daughter (255–57).

> "One option is still to be given you, son," said the king. "If you reject it, you will always be a little donkey. [255] Do you wish that our daughter should be given you between your arms, so that she may occupy herself with you in nighttime games?"

Finally, on his wedding night, the donkey prince is described for the first time as putting aside the donkey hide and becoming a new man ("Exposita veteri pelle novus fit homo," 310).

Heightening the sexuality of the atmosphere that envelops *The Donkey Tale* is the age-old interest that human beings have shown in the sexuality of asses—a preoccupation that might have appealed particularly to boys going through puberty. The ithyphallic endowment of donkeys has attracted remark often in art and literature, from before Apuleius's *Metamorphoses* (more commonly known as *The Golden Ass*) and pseudo-Lucian's "Lucius, or The Ass" (both of which refer to women consorting with donkeys in public performances) down to the twentieth century (when unions between prostitutes and donkeys were reportedly popular in a Mexican bordello).[28] Indeed, its large member is as distinctive a characteristic of the donkey as are its large ears and bray. In fact, when the ass-man in "Lucius, or The Ass" has regained human form, he is spurned by the woman who

had sought out his sexual favors when he was a donkey; she has him tossed out of her house because he no longer sports "the great token of the ass" [to mega tou onou sumbolon] he once bore, and she is most definitely not referring to his ears! On the same analogy, men who had a penis far beyond the average in size merited the nickname *Onos* (Donkey).[29]

Although manifesting a lubricious streak, the poet of *The Donkey Tale* is also deeply concerned with what could be called social values. To supplement themes that would have resonated well with young adolescents because of their heightened hormonal states, his poem also features themes that would have accorded with basic values inculcated in formal medieval education, which was restricted almost entirely to an elite of young men— male, literate (and Latinate), and clerical. *The Donkey Tale* assumes and reiterates systems of beliefs that medieval Christian education inculcated. From the outset, it emphasizes the importance of male lineage.[30] As we have seen, issues of genealogy, inheritance, legitimacy, and lineage are prominent in Medieval Latin versions of fairy tales and folktales: "The Wish-Goat" ("Wunschbock" [app. 2A]) deals with the division of an inheritance, "The Snow-Child" (app. 2C) with an illegitimate birth and its consequences, "Modus florum" (app. 2D) with the legitimacy of kingship, *The Turnip Tale* with the relationship between noble birth and wealth or poverty. These preoccupations, rather than originating among the clerks (many of whom were bound by vows not to become entangled in procreation), reflect the concerns of the lower nobility, which placed great importance on establishing lineage and which often rooted its legitimacy in folkloric culture, mythic stories, local legends, and the world of fairies.[31]

In *The Donkey Tale,* considerations about parentage fit within a broader context of paternal rule (patriarchy) as well as subordination of women because of their presumed biological inferiority (misogyny).[32] The story as constructed in *The Donkey Tale* imparts the closely intertwined messages that power and protection come through older men, that women are by nature inconstant creatures whose chief function is to produce sons as heirs, and that the ideal woman is one who obeys first her father and later her husband. Patrimony and matrimony go hand in hand.

At the beginning of the story, the queen bursts into a lament provoked by her infertility—and she grieves for her husband rather than for herself! All their joys of a highly active sex life, with which the poem begins (3, 8), are for naught because of her inability to have a baby. The queen likens herself to barren land and a punctured sack because she cannot make profitable use of her husband's seed by generating an heir, without which she finds everything else in her life meaningless. Not long after, her husband, the king, protects his newborn son against the queen when she orders the infant

to be drowned; his rationale is that the newborn, even though a divine force had imposed the form of a donkey upon him, had full patrilineal rights (36–38): "He will be on the throne as king of my realm, his head will bear his father's crown, and his father's entire glory is owed to him."[33] Consequently, he arranges for the son to have the rearing befitting the scion of a king. When the donkey prince quarrels with the harpist over his intended musical training, his heaviest threats are ones that conjure up the power of his father (78) and lineage (69). The donkey, upon discovering his asinine nature, worries that when his father has died, he will lose all status.

After forsaking his father's realm, the donkey wins special and unexplained support from the king in a foreign kingdom, who has no son of his own and becomes a surrogate father to him.[34] This new father is so concerned with the well-being of his male protégé that he does not hesitate to discuss the sexual charms of his own daughter with the young man (190–200). The daughter of this foreign king is portrayed as being susceptible to the sexual impulses that take hold of women as they mature sexually, but fortunately she knows enough to heed her father and agrees to the union with the ass purely out of filial obedience.[35]

The donkey's permanent restoration to human form occurs through the intervention of his father-in-law. The poem ends with the perpetuation of paternalism in a new generation, when the donkey has discovered his identity and has inherited his two patrimonies, the realms of both his real and his surrogate fathers. From a patriarchal point of view, the twin crises of the poem—fathers who lack sons as heirs—have been resolved in joyous simultaneity. As will be seen shortly, in all of these cases, *The Donkey Tale,* in consonance with the operations of medieval patriarchy and misogyny, diverges from its Eastern analogue in strengthening the stature of male characters and in weakening or darkening the portrayal of women. The emphatic misogyny of the poem makes likely that it was written for an all-male school setting rather than a mixed courtly audience.

The manners described in *The Donkey Tale* reinforce the hierarchies in the society depicted. Everyone has a place, everything a due order: king precedes queen, queen other nobles, nobles the commoners. When the donkey enters the castle and sings, he is greeted by laughter that descends the social ranks in an orderly progression: first the king, then the queen, and finally everyone else in the court. The ensuing meal is readied according to court protocol ("legitimo cursu," 168). When the donkey is to be seated, he must establish that he belongs not with the servants, not with the knights, but with the royal family itself. Through the dealings of the music master and the doorkeeper with the donkey prince and of the servant with the foreign king, the reader of *The Donkey Tale* gains a sense of how to negotiate with men in

positions of authority.[36] Indeed, the poem could be viewed as helping to instruct future courtiers in dealings with people in power. *The Donkey Tale* is not a book of manners on the order of the *Facetus,* but it is related to them. Whether or not the story of the donkey prince was written for the schools, its manuscript transmission indicates that it was certainly received into them; and yet the values it is designed to inculcate are meant for a world outside the school—a courtly world.[37]

The emphases on sexuality, patriarchy, misogyny, and manners that the poet of *The Donkey Tale* instilled in his poem take advantage of a potential present in the basic contours of the tale he recounts. As a representative of the tale type featuring an animal groom, *The Donkey Tale* would have appealed much more exclusively to boys than would have "Beauty and the Beast," which is indisputably the best-known representative of the genre.[38] The genius of the poet of *The Donkey Tale* lay in having sensed that his story would hold special meaning for young males.[39]

In this regard it bears noting that both Apuleius's tale of Cupid and Psyche (an episode within *The Golden Ass*), which is our earliest evidence for one vast complex of tales about animal grooms (ATU 425–49), and the fairy tale "Beauty and the Beast" by Madame Marie Leprince de Beaumont (1711–1780), the tale's most familiar version, have come down to us framed in tales in which older women relate their tales to younger women.[40] Their center of gravity lodges in the female characters and their perspectives.

In Apuleius, an old woman tells the tale of Cupid and Psyche to a young woman who has been kidnapped on her wedding day by a band of brigands.[41] The heart of the tale itself is the progress of the heroine: how she comes to wed her supernatural husband, how she interrupts her happy life through disobedience to him, and how she regains him.[42] Not surprisingly, the tale has been singled out for extensive psychological analysis because of its attention to the feminine.[43]

In the case of Madame Jeanne-Marie Leprince de Beaumont's version, the tale appears in a work entitled *Magasin des enfans, ou dialogues entre une sage gouvernante et plusieurs de ses élèves de la première distinction* (London: J. Haberkorn, 1756), published in English later as *The Young Misses Magazine, Containing Dialogues between a Governess and Several Young Ladies of Quality, Her Scholars* (London: C. Nourse, 1783).[44] Madame Leprince de Beaumont's book purports to record dialogues between a wise governess and her charges and opens with the author's defense of her stories as suitable for the intellectual and moral development of young ladies.[45] (Leprince de Beaumont was working as a governess in England at the time of publication.) She based her story "La belle et la bête" on a far longer tale ("Histoire de la bête") that formed part of a five-volume narrative entitled *The Young*

American Woman and Sea Tales (*La Jeune Amériquaine et les contes marins*), by Madame Gabrielle-Suzanne Barbot de Gallon de Villeneuve (1685–1755).[46] In both French versions, the figure of Beauty (Belle) becomes a cynosure far beyond what is found in *The Donkey Tale*. It is probably going too far to contend, as does one recent commentator, that "all the males in the tale—Beauty's father, brothers, and future husband—are assigned passive roles, all of them giving up Beauty, at one point or another, without asserting themselves beyond an ineffectual protest."[47] Beauty's father struggles to save the family, but due to ill luck and a mistake on his part, Beauty must rise to the challenge by sacrificing herself. Insofar as her role is active, it consists in the activity of self-sacrifice that seems to be urged on girls like her—presumably girls of the bourgeoisie, as Beauty is depicted as being and as Leprince de Beaumont's charges were.

The Donkey Tale belongs to a closely related body of narrative, except that its protagonist is not the young female but the young male and except that the story stops short without including any of the sections in "Beauty and the Beast" that allow for the fullest and most sympathetic treatment of the female character, the beauty. AT 425C (revamped radically in ATU 425C) breaks down "Beauty and the Beast" as follows:

> *The Search for the Lost Husband*
> I. The Monster as Husband
> (b) He is a man at night
> (c) A Girl promises herself as bride to the monster
> (d) or her father promises her
> II. Disenchantment of the Monster
> III. Loss of the Husband
> (c) Staying too long at home
> V. Recovery of Husband
> (b) Disenchants him by affectionate treatment[48]

Even a cursory look at *The Donkey Tale* confirms that it is essentially the first half of this story—the portion of the AT outline that focuses on men, especially the so-called monster. The poet of *The Donkey Tale* may also hint that he knew an alternative tradition closer to "Beauty and the Beast" or "The Frog Prince," in which the disenchantment of the beast results from romantic involvement with a woman;[49] but even if he was familiar with such traditions, the poet chose instead to credit the definitive disenchantment of his beast to a man: it is the king who cremates the donkey skin.

Both "Beauty and the Beast" and *The Donkey Tale* underscore the values of a woman's self-sacrifice and of a submissive knowledge of her place for the

men around her who seek to attain fulfillment; but whereas "Beauty and the Beast" implies a moral of a beastly man who is made handsome through the perseverance of a self-sacrificing young lady, *The Donkey Tale* shows a courtly beast whose physical defect is overcome partly through the sagacity of a well-disposed older man, partly through his own command of etiquette. Thanks to his social graces, the donkey, who starts the poem as a freak whose musical talents run against the laws of nature, ends up being a functional member, even a ruler, of his community. Through his mastery of music and manners, he wins acceptance and success in the stratosphere of society. His ability to serve his future wife at the table, to cut her bread and pour her drink, in short to do everything in as seemly a fashion as was feasible for an ass—all this knowledge of manners helps him to secure his bride and ultimately the full benefits of his humanity and nobility.

"BEASTY BOY" STORIES ABOUT ANIMAL SUITORS

The emphasis on etiquette separates *The Donkey Tale* not only from "Beauty and the Beast," which is directed toward young women, but also from stories (it is a temptation to call them "beasty boy" stories, but a more earnest designation would be "beast bridegroom" or "animal suitor" stories) in which the protagonist is apparently an animal but is born to parents of humbler social rank and has both talents and accoutrements befitting his lower status. After *The Donkey Tale,* the next main expression of such a story is Straparola's "King Pig" ("Il re porco" [app. 5D]) from 1550–53, which is related as the first story on the second night of his *Delightful Nights* (*Le piacevoli notti*).[50] This story has been subjected recently to two very different brands of analysis, first on the assumption that the sequence of events was Straparola's borrowing from *The Donkey Tale* itself and second that it was his own invention, rather than traditional.[51] The former interpretation rests on correspondences in vocabulary that are too vague and insubstantial to carry conviction.[52] According to the latter analysis, "King Pig" holds remarkable importance as the first rags-to-riches tale of its kind, the first of several such "rise tales" to be composed by Straparola in a genre he created himself.[53] As the argument is extended, Straparola's "King Pig" actually became *KHM* 108, "Hans My Hedgehog" ("Hans mein Igel"). Its direct influence on the Grimms' tale is in addition to its earlier influence, since it was adapted by Madame de Murat (Henriette-Julie de Castelnau, Comtesse de Murat [1670–1716]) in her "Roy Porc" and was related to "Le Prince Marcassin" by Madame d'Aulnoy (Marie Catherine Le Jumel de Barneville, baronne d'Aulnoy [ca. 1650–1705]) and to "Histoire de Pertharite et de Férandine" by Count Anthony Hamilton (ca. 1646–1720).[54] Wilhelm Grimm was definitely aware of Straparola's story before the

publication of the first edition of the *KHM,* since he refers to it in his 1811 *Alt-dänische Heldenlieder, Balladen und Märchen* (529); but the brothers credit their version of the story to Dorothea Viehmann (29 June 1813). Furthermore, "King Pig" is attested in later Italian sources, in both literature of a literary sort and texts based on oral literature. The later reputation of the story does not necessarily provide any firm proof of its origins: cases abound in which materials thought to be traditional turn out later to have been pseudo-traditional. More telling is that the later oral versions are in many cases stronger narratives, which may signal that they are following an oral tradition from which Straparola departed in creating his version of the story.[55]

The Danish story of "King Lindorm" (in Danish, "Kung Lindorm"), found in versions by Svend Grundtvig (1854) and Niels Levinsen (1958), and the German "Hans Wunderlich," told by Ulrich Jahn in his *Volksmärchen aus Pommern und Rügen* (1891), have both enjoyed modest fame. The former is interesting because the transmission that has been hypothesized for it could parallel that of *The Donkey Tale.* According to the hypothesis, "King Lindorm" originated ultimately in India in simple legends, out of which a two-part tale was formed in the Near East and transported by the seventeenth century to Scandinavia.[56] The proximity of the plot of "King Lindorm" to that of *The Donkey Tale* is immediately apparent from the summary of it in AT 433B.

> A childless queen bears a boy who stays in serpent form. When he grows up he demands a wife and his father finds a maiden who is willing. (In some versions, he devours the bride and only after several have tried does the bride survive.) She (or her father) disenchants him by bathing, or by burning his serpent skin while he is transformed.

Yet no cross-reference to the donkey story is provided. This defect has been alleviated in the references in ATU 433B, which offers a much more detailed and complex résumé of the "King Lindorm" tale type.

The best-known of the "beasty boy" stories is probably *KHM* 108, "Hans My Hedgehog."[57] In this story, a childless farmer expresses a desire to have offspring, even if the baby should be a mere hedgehog. Predictably, he duly becomes the parent of a bouncing baby hedgehog. Eventually the hedgehog, disliked by his father, leaves home, accompanied by a faithful rooster that serves as his mount and taking with him some recently acquired bagpipes. He goes to the forest, where he raises swine. From each of two kings who lose their way in the forest and who are drawn to his bagpipe music, Hans obtains, through a rash promise on their part, the right to take as his own whatever the kings first meet upon returning home; this is a motif (*MI*

S241) found most famously in the Bible account of Jephthah's daughter (Judges 11.29–40). In both cases, the hedgehog's prize turns out to be a daughter of the king, whom Hans is entitled to have as his wife. When eventually he comes to collect his side of the bargain, he is received badly by the daughter of the first king before being accepted by that of the second. After his animal hide has been incinerated, he turns into a wonderfully handsome young man. (The burning of the hide gives him a singed appearance, but he receives treatment for it.)

As even this superficial summary conveys, there are pronounced likenesses and equally distinct differences between "Hans My Hedgehog" and *The Donkey Tale.* To begin with the similarities, music is prominent in both tales. The hedgehog is distinguished by bagpipes and a rooster, the donkey by a lute and his trusty servant. In both stories, the animal groom starts out as a freak who defies the laws of nature by playing music; in both, he ends up becoming an accepted and even esteemed member of society. Both stories may be viewed very broadly as sketching a young man in the process of self-discovery.[58]

As for the dissimilarities between the two stories, the animal protagonist in the one is a hedgehog and in the other a donkey. In terms of social class at birth, the protagonist in the one comes of farmer or peasant stock, whereas that in the other is a prince.[59] In occupation, the one is a swineherd, the other a gentleman lutanist. Whereas the hero in "Hans My Hedgehog" remains outside palaces until the end, the hero in *The Donkey Tale* is born and bred in one royal court, embarks on a new life in another, and eventually holds sway over both of them. Thus Hans follows the rags-to-riches (or "hide-to-riches") trajectory that is standard in wonder tales, whereas the leading character of *The Donkey Tale* is less conventional.

The basic similarities between the two stories are obscured in the summaries of them in AT, and the differences are made more salient by the motifs that are isolated as being especially important or characteristic.

AT 430 *The Ass.*

The prince transformed to an ass. Plays a lyre and is entertained at king's court. Becomes husband of a princess who disenchants him. For analysis see AT 425 (I a, II b).

Motifs: *MI* C758.1. Monster born because of hasty (inconsiderate) wish of parents. *MI* D132.1.

Transformation: man to ass. *MI* D963. Man transformed to ass plays the lyre. *MI* B641.4. Marriage to person in ass form. *MI* D721.3 Disenchantment by destroying skin (covering).

AT 441 *Hans my Hedgehog.*
A childless woman gives birth to a hedgehog [*MI* C758.1, T554]. The king unwittingly promises the hedgehog his daughter when the latter shows him the way out of the forest [*MI* S226]. The hedgehog takes the bridge [*MI* B641.5]. His hedgehog's skin is burnt, and he changes into a handsome youth [*MI* D721.3]. For analysis see AT 425 (I a, d3; II b or c).

Among the parallels between the two stories that are lost, no mention is made of the hedgehog's musical endeavors or of the burning of the donkey's skin. Additionally, the Medieval Latin version of "The Donkey" is not listed in the brief catalog of versions of AT 430, whereas Straparola's "King Pig" is indexed as a literary treatment of AT 441. Most of these short comings have been resolved in the ATU handlings of these same two tale types, which improves the chances that the connections between the types will receive attention.

THE MUSICAL TALENT OF THE DONKEY AND
THE ROLE OF MIME PLAYERS

Besides differentiating between the social classes of the characters within *The Donkey Tale* and the social classes for which the poem was intended, we need to distinguish between the social classes of the anonymous Medieval Latin poet and the storytellers or entertainers who may have given the narrative of the donkey story the shape that it had when it reached him. If we assume that the tale was traditional and not his own invention, there is no justification for assuming that the poet of *The Donkey Tale* would have belonged to the same stratum of society or would have intended his poem for the same audience as those of the people who brought the tale to him. No one would hold that the poet of *The Donkey Tale*—who wrote an elegant Latin idiom for a literate male audience rather than performing in the vernacular for a mixed audience of women and men—was himself a mime player. No one would maintain that all stories that feature musicians prominently as characters were necessarily created and transmitted by a class of professional entertainers. Yet in the case of *The Donkey Tale,* circumstances render plausible the notion that mimes or minstrels participated in the transmission of the tale before it reached the Latin poet.

According to the Grimms' version of the tale, the donkey first studies with a minstrel (*Spielmann*) and later becomes a professional musician (*Musikant*) himself. Such mentions of professional entertainers come to the fore even more frequently and forcefully in the Medieval Latin version of the tale. For instance, the donkey's teacher and the donkey himself are identified repeatedly as mime players (*mimi*). We are told that the donkey prince ful-

fills many roles appropriate to a young man of his standing but "takes special delight in the art of harpists" [citharedorum mage delectatur in arte] (47).

Although neutral words to designate lute players are used repeatedly,[60] the poet makes evident that mime players and other professional entertainers had questionable standing in his society. One scene is especially revealing of these attitudes toward mime players—and incidentally it exemplifies the humor that permeates the Latin poem. When the donkey prince asks a celebrated musician to teach him to play the lute, the musician demurs (56–66):

> What are you asking of your servant, my little lord? O king, why do you seek what does not become you? Alas, alas! You are mistaken, you are deceived, you entertain empty hopes: you cannot learn this art at all, since [60] your fingers are enormous, my little lord. And if, by your leave, it should be permitted me to speak home truths, you are seeking, my little lord, what nature denies. Without a hand you cannot distinguish the strings of the lute, which (I think) will blow apart if you touch them with your foot. [65] According to its custom, an ass brays and never plays well; the wild sound of a sack-bearing ass as it sings is hee-haw.[61]

To preface the prince's irate reaction to this refusal, the narrator refers to the musician—who has until this point been designated respectfully as a *magister* (50, 52)—as a *mimus* (67). The prince takes the mime to task for his presumptuousness and reminds him of his lowly status by calling him a *leccator* and *scurra*, cognates to the Modern English words *lecher* and *scurrilous:* "What opinion do you, scoundrel [literally, "lecher"], have of me—what opinion, buffoon?" [Quid tibi, leccator, de me, quid scurra, videtur?] (73).[62]

Much later, the donkey, after having abdicated as prince and having begun to travel anonymously as a lute player, refers to himself as "an upstanding mime player" [mimus honestus] (142), and the doorkeeper describes him as "a most unusual mime player" [mimus rarissimus] (153). The need to mark the term *mimus* with adjectives meaning "upstanding" and "unusual" may well presuppose that the average mime player was not regarded as being particularly honest and was seen to be "common" in more than one sense of the word.[63] At the same time, the donkey's self-identification as a mime player vindicates, at least implicitly, the music master whose social class the prince earlier impugned.

The donkey prince and his music instructor are not the only characters in *The Donkey Tale* to be associated with mime players. The entertainment at the wedding feast of the donkey prince and his bride gives a fleeting glimpse of other such paid performers as they ply their trade.

> A great throng of mime players streams together like bees; each one, well-trained, toils over his craft. A female mime player, balanced with her feet upward and her head downward, walks and accords to her hands the function of her feet. (293–96)[64]

Though similarly realistic vignettes of mime playing can be located elsewhere in Medieval Latin poetry, the common features more probably derive from the shared experience of a reality in medieval life than from literary borrowing.[65] Mime players, with their varied repertoire of music and acrobatics, brought amusement that, because of the limited entertainment available in the Middle Ages, would have left a deep impression on medieval people of all social classes.

Why would the poet of *The Donkey Tale* have presented his donkey as a lute player? At first the decision seems eccentric, since behind the poet lay an ancient and well-entrenched tradition—perhaps of Eastern origin—that donkeys and lyres or lutes cannot mix.[66] The Roman fabulist Phaedrus (ca. 15 BCE–ca. 50 CE) is credited with a fable entitled "The Ass and the Lyre" ("Asinus ad lyram") in which an ass who finds a lyre cannot produce harmonious music because it has no knowledge of the art.[67] The fable ascribed to Phaedrus provides a narrative context for a saying that was already a cliché among Greek speakers: "Onos lyras" [The donkey [hears] the lyre [but does not understand it]].[68] Both the fable and the proverb signified a lack of artistic appreciation in the person at whom it was directed. Among the Romans, the proverb had been absorbed into Menippean satire already by Varro (116–27 BCE), only fragments of whose satire entitled *Onos lyras* survive.[69] The proverb retained its authority in the Middle Ages thanks to Boethius (ca. 480–524 CE), who included it in the *Consolation of Philosophy* (1.4); and eventually it infiltrated a number of modern European languages.[70] A particularly germane use preceding *The Donkey Tale* by only a few decades can be found in the Old French *Roman de Thèbes* (ca. 1150), a romance recasting of Statius's *Thebaid*. The anonymous twelfth-century author warns away the uncouth by reminding his audience, "Now those of every calling may go on their way / Unless they are clerks or knights, / For they can listen only / As the ass to the harper."[71] Why, if there was such a firmly established opposition between the ass and stringed instruments, would the poet of *The Donkey Tale* have made his ass precisely a lutanist?

Perhaps the very incongruity of the donkey and the musician—the one hugely heavy and maladroit in its extremities, the other light-fingered and graceful; the one cacophonous, the other melodious of voice—encouraged not only storytellers but also representational artists to cast the donkey as a musician. Such scenes are richly attested long before the lute playing of the

ass in either *The Donkey Tale* or the famous Grimms' fairy tale of the Bremer Stadtmusikanten ("The Bremen Town Musicians" [*KHM* 27])—from Sumerian art of the third millennium BCE through ancient Egyptian art to medieval stone capitals, choir seats, and miniatures.[72] In the earliest period, the ass appears as a harpist, but later he becomes a very versatile instrumentalist—now a psalterist, now a trumpeter, now a fiddler, and sometimes even a bagpiper.[73] In the Middle Ages the particular juxtaposition of a lyre instructor would have offered a droll contrast to the classical myth (often represented in art) according to which the centaur Chiron taught Achilles to play the lyre.[74] More generally, it would have called to mind comic illustrations of donkeys as teachers.[75]

The ludicrous incompatibility of the donkey and the musician may also have motivated popular performers in search of a laugh to associate themselves with donkeys. Here I postulate that there were storytellers who performed to music or who incorporated musical interludes into recitations and that such a story as "The Donkey" would have lent itself well to such delivery. In this connection, it is noteworthy that the author who wrote one version of the friendship story "Lantfrid and Cobbo" claims that his telling of the story, which begins with "Once upon a time," conforms faithfully to the version related by "companions of mime players": "Once upon a time there were two noblemen, as the tale and companions of mime players relate" [Quodam tempore fuerunt duo viri nobiles / sicut fabule testantur et scurrarum complices].[76] Adding to the enticement of this passage is the fact that narrative motifs in the story of Lantfrid and Cobbo may point to oriental origins.[77]

Traces of oral performance may remain within *The Donkey Tale* itself. For instance, it is hard not to detect a playful allusion to the bray of an ass when the music teacher laments—"Alas, alas!" [Heu heu!] (57)—that the prince is ill-equipped to learn the lute, especially since he resorts a few lines later to the unmistakable onomatopoeia of hee-haw ("hy ha," 66). Furthermore, *The Donkey Tale* includes at least three scenes that would have been suitable for miming: the self-recognition of the donkey prince as he catches sight of his reflection in the water (88–96); the rapping at doors in three separate instances (135, 328, 386); and the peeping from behind an arras to watch a sexual union between a woman and a donkey (305–6, 341–44).[78]

The story of the donkey prince and donkey musician would even have lent itself to performance by a mime player masked as a donkey. That such disguises existed in popular theater can be surmised from images in medieval manuscripts in which mimes are disguised as donkeys—not to mention evidence at either end of the Middle Ages, such as ancient vases with ass-headed men or the scene featuring the character Bottom in Shakespeare's *A Midsummer Night's Dream* (written ca. 1595–96). The last-mentioned

episode is particularly relevant to the notion that there was a symbiosis of mime and fairy tale, since it combines the fairy tale motif of partial human-to-animal metamorphosis with mime play. Such instances suggest that donkey mimes were the stock-in-trade of premodern performers who were the equivalents of vaudevillians.[79]

The Donkey Tale bears a resemblance to a number of vernacular texts roughly contemporary with it, in that its protagonist, although seemingly from the highest nobility, earns the ability and maybe even the right to advance not through his dexterity in handling a lance and performing on the battlefield but instead through such refinements as good table manners and musical skill. The wish fulfillment that the tale offers would seem especially relevant to those in the lower reaches of the knightly class—the *ministeriales,* from whose ranks came the entertainers known accordingly as minstrels. Such knights, perhaps not so desperately destitute as the poor brother in *The Turnip Tale* (Latin version) but still not financially comfortable, could have taken solace in the wish fulfillment of a tale that encouraged fantasizing about advancement on the basis of attainments they had already acquired—or were gaining as they studied Latin and all that came with it.

One illustrious and exactly contemporary comparandum that can be set alongside *The Donkey Tale* is Gottfried von Strassburg's *Tristan* (ca. 1200–1210).[80] More than any of the other Tristan romances, Gottfried's version, in Middle High German verse, emphasizes the protagonist's courtly talents—for instance, his fluency in multiple languages, including Latin; his command of courtly protocol, as exemplified most spectacularly in his knowledge of both the latest fashions in butchering game and the most current jargon to describe them; and, last but not least, his versatility as an instrumental soloist and vocalist.

Another text that warrants at least passing comparison with *The Donkey Tale* is the Middle High German *Salman und Morolf* (composed in the second half of the twelfth century), about Solomon and a character named Morolf (who is distantly related to Marcolf).[81] It is one of a handful of texts that were designated "minstrel epics" (*Spielmannsepen*) in the early nineteenth century, in the romantic belief that they were the creations of wandering and illiterate performers.[82] Over the past two centuries, scholars have gradually shifted their views of the poets and their audiences, often elevating the former and sometimes lowering the latter. Although much about these poems has been contested, it is clear that they are deeply engaged with oral traditions. *Salman und Morolf* is particularly indebted to oriental materials about King Salman (Solomon), the pagan princess Salme, and Salman's brother Morolf. The ultimate source of these materials in the Middle East is suggested by its setting in the Christian Kingdom of Jerusalem. Although

Salman's harp playing is a motif drawn from the Bible, Morolf's decision to disguise himself at one point as a minstrel may hint at the social status of the intermediaries who were responsible for transporting the basic ingredients of this complex narrative from Jerusalem (or via Byzantium) to Germany.

EASTERN ORIGINS

Krohn's major conclusion, that ancient India and medieval Europe were the most important centers for tale diffusion, is now mocked.[83]

The musical avocation of the donkey and, even more so, the mime elements in *The Donkey Tale* may relate to performance situations far removed from those feasible for a Latin poet. The many references in *The Donkey Tale* to the activities of mime players are especially arresting since the closest medieval analogue to the Medieval Latin poem is a Sanskrit prose text destitute of all such references. If the Sanskrit text can be demonstrated to record a tale that antedates *The Donkey Tale,* if the case can be made convincingly that the myth extant in the Sanskrit text could represent the ultimate source of *The Donkey Tale* or at least a stage closer to that source than *The Donkey Tale,* the question of why the theme of the mime players was added takes on a heightened urgency. In view of these other possibilities, we need to be alert not only to the unassailable fact of the Latin poem written down for readers or listeners somewhere in Western Europe but also to the unverifiable possibility of a traditional tale ferried from elsewhere by tellers of a different background from the Latin poet's and shaped by them to different purposes. To be blunt, I would propose that the mentions of mime players and other professional entertainers are present in the story of the donkey prince because they were the vectors of the tale to Europe from the East, and I would back this proposal not on the basis of vague resemblances between artistic representations of asinine musicians in Eastern and Western art but, rather, on the basis of impressive parallels between *The Donkey Tale* and a Sanskrit tale.[84]

If *The Donkey Tale* was indeed written for early thirteenth-century Hohenstaufen circles, the Sicilian connections of the dynasty raise provocative possibilities; Sicily would constitute a likely point of entry for the Eastern material that may well lie at the middle of *The Donkey Tale* narrative. Alternatively, the story could have percolated into Europe during the Crusades. Less plausibly, it could have wended its way along the Silk Road, independently of either Sicily or the Crusades.

Whatever oral or written versions in Persian or Arabic have perished, what still exists is a short Sanskrit tale known as "The Story of Vikramāditya's Birth" (app. 5B), which is found prefixed to at least three manuscripts of the

Jainistic recension of the *Vikramacarita* (sometimes also referred to as the *Sin-hâsanadvâtrinçikâ*), which is a frame tale of thirty-two stories about the adventures of King Vikramāditya, also known as Vikrama.[85] The collection begins when a much later king named Bhoja discovers a glorious throne that had belonged to Vikramāditya. Each of the thirty-two divine statuettes that supported the throne tells Bhoja a story about the amazing qualities of King Vikramāditya.

On stylistic grounds, "The Story of Vikramāditya's Birth" is generally acknowledged to be an accretion, probably attached to the *Vikramacarita* later than the thirteenth century.[86] The tale attracted the remark of several prominent nineteenth-century researchers, among them James George Frazer (1854–1941), who discusses it at one point in *The Golden Bough,* and Richard Burton (1821–90), who touches on the Sanskrit tale only very cursorily but does connect it with Apuleius.[87] Its relevance to "The Donkey" has been signaled at least three times over the past eighty years.[88]

In the section of the Sanskrit collection that is relevant to *The Donkey Tale,* a god who has the form of an ass (Gandharvasena, son of the great god Indra and father of Vikramāditya) demands the daughter (Madanarekha) of a king (Premasena) in marriage. He confesses that for failing to control his sexual impulses in a former life, he has been reborn as an ass—a beast that in Indian tradition, as in many others, embodies lustfulness.[89] He promises that if he is granted the daughter, the king will fare well; otherwise both the king and his subjects will suffer affliction. Eventually the god marries the princess, who discovers that her new husband can shed his ass-shaped body by night to become a handsome being. All goes according to this routine for many years, until the young woman's mother pays a visit, discovers the god's ability to remove his donkey skin, and casts it into the fire. At this peripeteia, the god announces that he will ascend to heaven and that his wife is pregnant with his son (Vikramāditya). While making a clean breast of everything, he also reveals that his wife's slave woman is carrying a son by him.

"The Story of Vikramāditya's Birth" shares with *The Donkey Tale* such remarkable similarities as the marriage of a noble man in ass form to a princess, the release of the ass-man by the burning of the donkey skin,[90] and the disclosure of the being's true name only at the conclusion of the story. Yet "The Story of Vikramāditya's Birth" differs from the Medieval Latin story in many major areas. A comparison of the first sentences in the two texts proves to be immediately instructive, almost a textbook case of the disparities between myth and fairy tales. The Sanskrit myth pinpoints the place ("In Gurjarī-land between the rivers Sābhravatī and Mahilā, there is a grove"), fixes the reign and thereby the time ("where Tāmraliptarṣi was king"), and identifies the principal characters by name ("He had a daughter

Yaçovatī, whose husband was a king named Premasena. While they lived in the enjoyment of worldly pleasures, a daughter Madanarekhā was born to them"). In contrast, *The Donkey Tale* is resolutely timeless, placeless, and anonymous ("Once upon a time there was a king of an unknown region and city, and, what is more, no tale tells the king's name" [1–2]).[91] The Medieval Latin poem sets out no geographical grid except to say that the donkey's bride lives at the westernmost frontiers of the earth, where Phoebus drives his exhausted steeds into the sea (121–22).

The generic discrepancies between the two stories are not confined to their exordiums. As in most fairy tales, the hero in *The Donkey Tale* acquires a protector or magic means—in this instance, the foreign king—to guarantee his success in subsequent tests.[92] In contradistinction, the donkey prince in the Indian myth, like a good mythic hero, operates autonomously—apart from the one, seemingly chance episode in which his mother-in-law kindles his hide. To their very last words, the two stories continue to diverge along generic lines, with the one remaining true to the norms of fairy tales and the other to those of myths. As Eleazar Meletinsky observes, *The Donkey Tale* draws to a close in the stock fashion of many classical fairy tales: "Marriage with a princess, and acquisition as well of half the kingdom, is the typical happy ending of these tales."[93] Indeed, *The Donkey Tale* concludes more optimistically and less problematically for the protagonist than do any of the other major representatives of the tale type featuring an animal groom. In such tales as those of Cupid and Psyche, Melusine, and the Swan Maiden, the character who has an animal disguise usually disappears with unfortunate consequences when spied by night, but here the spying leads swiftly to a happy resolution of the man/animal tension.[94] Largely because *The Donkey Tale* depicts such a stark and unambivalent improvement of its hero's circumstances, it qualified in medieval terminology as a comedy (*comedia*).[95] As is the case in many fairy tales, the hero in *The Donkey Tale* aspires ultimately to two goals: a happy marriage and a generous inheritance. In contrast, *comedia* is not a designation that anyone would dream of attaching to the Indian myth. It concludes on a less undilutedly joyous note (with the death of the princess as she gives birth), since its hero has set his sights on a truly mythic goal: restoration as a god to heaven.

In general, the Sanskrit myth contains many fewer inconsistencies and illogicalities in its narrative development. It is conceivable that the Sanskrit myth depends on the tale type evidenced in *The Donkey Tale* rather than vice versa. But it is easier to understand how a myth that migrated elsewhere would have given rise to illogicalities as its mythological context was lost than to understand how a very illogical folktale would have been appropriated and wondrously streamlined as a myth.

Just which features in *The Donkey Tale* and in the Sanskrit tale differ? The most efficient way of proceeding is simply to list and discuss them in the order of their occurrence in the stories.[96]

(1) Whereas the Sanskrit tale reveals that Gandharvasena has been made an ass on account of his lust, *The Donkey Tale* gives no clear reason why the queen should give birth to a donkey. The only explanation in *The Donkey Tale* for the childlessness of the donkey's parents is the vague implication that the fates have denied them children (20)—but why the fates should have been opposed to them a priori is never explained. Similarly, there are two veiled intimations that a god lay behind the misbirth (35, 95–96), but no details are given. Perhaps because the composer of *The Donkey Tale* was aware of the improbability of the birth, he presented it as a "matter to be marveled at" (*res miranda*) and took care to set the poem in a mythical context, with Jupiter, Juno-Lucina, and other members of the Roman pantheon. Probably unwittingly, by doing so he restored the story to the kind of mythological context in which it appears in its Sanskrit setting.[97]

(2) *The Donkey Tale* gives no information to account for the strange prescience of the donkey's father, who is ready to leave his realm to an animal; could he have known that his son would regain human form? The Sanskrit tale has no need to involve the donkey's father in its cast of characters, since the plight of its donkey results from his own conduct rather than from any problem on the part of his parents.

(3) The Sanskrit tale contains a scene in which first one slave boy and then another hear a disembodied voice and then finally the king himself, after questioning the veracity of his servants, goes to the river and hears, from behind a tree, as the voice threatens the king and his city unless the king wed his daughter to the voice. Although this episode does not enter into *The Donkey Tale,* the Medieval Latin poem does include a similar scene in which the king doubts the truthfulness of his servant, is bidden to go to the bridal chamber himself, and eavesdrops. Possibly the riverside encounter in the Sanskrit had to be suppressed because it explains the donkey form of the god on the basis of a metempsychosis unacceptable in medieval Christianity, but memory of the eavesdropping in it remained and surfaced in the bedroom spying.

(4) In the Sanskrit tale, Gandharvasena is well aware of the difference between his inner and outer nature. In the Medieval Latin poem, the prince seems inexplicably ignorant of having an animal appearance until he sees himself reflected in the waters of a river (87–106). This obtuseness is perplexing, since the minstrel seems to reveal long before this moment that the prince is a donkey with a hoof instead of a hand and with a bray instead of a singing voice (59–66).

(5) In the Sanskrit tale, the donkey apparently works for a potter, which is a suitably asinine employment. In the Latin tale, the ass subsists on what he earns by playing a musical instrument, the mechanics of which feat are left unexplained.

(6) In the Sanskrit story, the princess's father has strong and understandable motivations for accepting the donkey as his son-in-law. In the Latin story, we are left to wonder why the father in the other kingdom shows favor to the donkey prince—if not solely for his manners and musical abilities—and promises the hand of his daughter to him. In the Latin tale, the king makes one remark (253–54) to reveal his awareness that the donkey must wed his daughter if he is to regain human form. This observation and the narrator's comment that the donkey responded to the marriage proposal "as if awakening from a sleep" (257) suggest that marriage or close physical proximity to the girl will cause the disenchantment (as is the case in such stories as "The Frog King" and "Beauty and the Beast").

(7) In the Sanskrit tale, it is easier to appreciate the compulsions that drive the princess to marry the donkey. In the Medieval Latin tale, she acquiesces out of loyalty to her father, but his motivations are unclear.

(8) As has been mentioned already, in *The Donkey Tale,* it is baffling that the donkey does not know he is a donkey until after seeing his reflection. Obviously, early in the story, he does not take off his skin at night. Later in the story, the donkey's habit of taking off his hide every night and putting it on every morning is presented as a self-evident fact.[98] The explanation for this incongruity may be that the Medieval Latin poet was skittish (even within the bounds of a wonder tale) of granting the possibility of thoroughgoing man-to-animal transformation. Christian theology disallowed that men could be turned to donkeys or werewolves, since men who were turned to animals would lose their ability to save or damn themselves through their free will. But some theologians—such as Augustine, who dwelled with palpable anxiety on supposed transformations of men into asses—left open the possibility that in certain instances people resorting to diabolic powers could create the illusion of having achieved such metamorphoses.[99]

(9) In *The Donkey Tale,* the donkey's father-in-law seems to reveal that he has nurtured a secret hope of restoring the donkey permanently to human form.

(10) *The Donkey Tale* gives no reason for why the donkey prince should be momentarily distressed upon having his donkey skin taken away from him and incinerated.[100] In the Sanskrit myth, the destruction of the hide leads instantly to the apotheosis of the donkey. Perhaps the reaction of the donkey prince in *The Donkey Tale* reflects an awareness of other stories in which animal-to-man transformation is attended by physical suffering. For

example, in "Hans My Hedgehog," the burning of the animal hide causes Hans to become coal black in human form and to require healing.

(11) In the Sanskrit tale (as in "Hans My Hedgehog"), the mother-in-law takes the donkey skin and burns it. In *The Donkey Tale*, the father-in-law performs these deeds. The Sanskrit tale avoids the prurience of the scopophilia that is explicit in *The Donkey Tale* and suppressed but implicit in "The Donkey," since the queen acts as soon as the donkey skin has been shed rather than waiting in hiding until after the married couple's night of lovemaking. It is interesting (and perhaps not coincidental) that both *The Golden Ass*/"Lucius, or The Ass" (52) and *The Donkey Tale*/"The Donkey" contain scenes in which masters watch donkeys having sex with women after their servants have spied on the same activities.[101]

What are we to make of the complex resemblances and differences between the Medieval Latin and Sanskrit stories? The substantial intersections between the two stories seem to rule out polygenesis, the theory that they could have evolved without any even indirect give-and-take.[102] Alternatively, it is conceivable that a story with the illogicalities of *The Donkey Tale* could have originated somewhere between Europe and India and then migrated westward to become *The Donkey Tale* and eastward to become the *Vikramacarita*. The implausibility in this particular hypothesis of diffusionism is accepting the presupposition that anyone would have been inspired to mythologize and rationalize such a secular tale.[103]

More convincing is the converse hypothesis, namely, that the Sanskrit myth passed into regions where Hindu gods were not worshiped and where their functions in the story had to be suppressed or altered and that the carriers of the tale, the entertainers who had transported the story into their repertoires, grafted themselves and their art into the tales as a way of endowing it with a new raison d'être and a new internal consistency. It has been said that "a folktale is understandable to everyone, passes effortlessly across all linguistic borders, moves from one people to another, and remains alive for millennia . . . This happens because a folktale contains eternal and incorruptible values."[104] Much of this statement may hold true, but I reiterate my belief, not necessarily contradictory, that the unchanging values are only part of the picture. To some extent, fairy tale survives owing to its plasticity, because it is susceptible of having imposed on it many different interpretations.

Regardless of whoever ferried the tale into Europe, it is well worth resurrecting an old proposal that the tale made the transition to being a wonder tale partly because of its exoticism, that it became an object of wonderment (*res miranda*) precisely because of its alterity—that is, because it was foreign, not fully comprehensible, and somehow uncomfortable.[105] The in-

tensely Ovidianizing style of the poem could have suggested itself partly as a means of compensating for the otherwise strange, exotic, and unprecedented brand of story that the poet was recounting.[106] Aligning the metamorphoses and eroticism in *The Donkey Tale* with those in Ovid may have been an effort to Westernize the former and thereby to legitimate them. If so, the strategy succeeded, and the salience of the Ovidianizing in the medieval poem had its desired effect, since *The Donkey Tale* came to be grouped often in manuscripts with Ovidian and pseudo-Ovidian poetry.[107]

The acceptance of *The Donkey Tale* into the higher reaches of Medieval Latin belles lettres is all the more stunning when one considers the ambivalence about its fundamental orality or literacy that is attested in the sharply divided textual tradition of its first two lines (1–2). This ambivalence has led the two most recent editors to opposite choices. One favored the word *pagina*,[108] whereas the other opted for *fabula,* with its strong connotations of speech (deriving as it does from *for, fari*).[109]

> Rex erat ignote quondam regionis et urbis
> Sed nomen regis pagina nulla docet.

[Once upon a time there was a king of an unknown region and city,
and, what is more, no page tells the king's name.]

> Rex erat ignote quondam regionis et urbis
> Sed nomen regis fabula nulla docet.

[Once upon a time there was a king of an unknown region and city,
and, what is more, no tale tells the king's name.]

The destiny of this donkey story, caught between the written and the spoken as well as between the learned and the lewd, had not ended when it received elegant literary treatment around 1200. My final goal is to consider briefly the fate of the tale when the Grimm brothers appropriated the Latin version and reshaped it for their nineteenth-century German audience.

THE GRIMMS' REWORKING OF *THE DONKEY TALE*

As various scholars of the *KHM* have emphasized, the Brothers Grimm must not be regarded as folklore collectors of the sort late twentieth-century folklorists would care to encounter.[110] Rather than using tape recorders or even meticulous field notes to preserve verbatim the stories of illiterate storytellers

who had been untouched by outside influences, the brothers tampered to varying extents with stories that they sometimes drew from literate story-tellers who were well acquainted with written sources. The shortcomings of the Brothers Grimm as "folklorists" in our sense do not stop there, since in a few instances they even re-created (or, in Joel Chandler Harris's terminology, "cooked") ostensibly authentic fairy tales out of written tales.[111]

The Grimms' "The Donkey" is a spectacularly overt example of a fairy tale that the brothers generated from a written tale. In June 1814, Jacob Grimm happened on a Strasbourg manuscript that he transcribed in part and summarized in toto, long before its unfortunate destruction by fire in 1870, when Strasbourg was besieged during the Franco-Prussian War. Thereafter his brother took this Medieval Latin poem of 201 elegiac couplets and reworked it to match the conceptions he and Jacob held of what a proper German *Märchen* should be—what we would call a fairy tale.[112] The brothers incorporated this *remaniement* in 1815 as no. 58 in the second volume of the first edition of the *KHM*. According to the count followed in the 1857 edition, the tale is designated as no. 144.

From extant manuscripts, we can discern that *The Donkey Tale* found a readership in late medieval Germany, Italy, and France;[113] but whereas the language of *The Donkey Tale* would have restricted it mainly to privileged audiences of males, the tales of the Brothers Grimm were intended for bourgeois audiences of not only men but also women and children. Furthermore, the Grimms' fairy tales rested on a substantially different conception of storytelling. To the Brothers Grimm, the utility of the Latin poem lay in having preserved an oral *Märchen* that they sought to recover, like an authentic old house, from beneath the unwanted accretions and alterations of its later owners. Because of the values that they deemed appropriate for their readers and because of the narrative and stylistic qualities that they judged proper for fairy tales, the Grimms had to refashion *The Donkey Tale* substantially in creating their version.

In the case of most tales in the *KHM,* we do not have the luxury of comparing original field notes with the text that the brothers chose eventually to print. For this reason, we are privileged to have in *The Donkey Tale* and "The Donkey" a kind of control sample alongside a test specimen. Comparison between the two versions documents beyond any ambiguity the ideological shaping that Jacob and Wilhelm Grimm gave to their materials.

To begin with the changes in content made to *The Donkey Tale,* the Brothers Grimm expurgate altogether the eroticism that pervades the medieval poem. For example, in the Latin version, the introduction of the princess tells us (129–32):

At that time the maiden had already completed her years of girlhood; [130] her private parts had already given forth fine hairs; the nipples of her breasts had already given signs that she can hardly sleep alone on her bed without a man.[114]

Of this lusty anatomical appreciation, only the fact that the princess is "exceedingly beautiful" (wunderschöne)[115] is retained by the Brothers Grimm. Similarly, the Latin text boasts a later scene in which the king quizzes the donkey, "Little donkey, do you like our daughter?" (190), and the donkey replies with a drooling inventory of her most appetizing features (193–200):

Amazing! Why do you ask? O king, why do you labor to know? Why ought I not like her? [195] On the contrary, I like her, I like her, I like her very much . . . Certainly the man who does not like her at all is made of iron. Her fair face, suffused with rosiness, brings delight, as if I should contemplate lilies mixed with roses. And I like her hair; her ivory-white neck brings delight; [200] and I confess that I like her whole body.[116]

In comparison, the Grimms' version could not be tamer.

"Donkey, how do you like my daughter?" The donkey turned his head toward her, looked at her, nodded, and said, "Extraordinarily well. I have never seen a girl as beautiful as she is."[117]

Not long after this juncture in *The Donkey Tale,* the narrator alludes proleptically to the carnal pleasure that the girl will have of the donkey when he is her husband (220–22). The narrator of the Grimms' tales would allow himself no such coy rhetoric here or on the wedding night, where the Latin poet reveals slyly that the intercourse of the bride and groom would remain a secret between them and the marriage bed—and the servant peeping from behind the arras (318–20). Emblematic of the bowdlerization that the Grimms effected is that they place the servant in the room to ensure good behavior, whereas the author of *The Donkey Tale* presses him into service as an intermediary to achieve the king's frankly voyeuristic ambitions (303–6, 343–44).

How much of the eroticism that the Grimms removed from *The Donkey Tale* would have been present in the tellings of the story that preceded the Medieval Latin poet and that were not directly indebted to any written version? The question can be answered only speculatively. My speculation is

that the Medieval Latin poet picked up on a tone already current in oral tellings of the story and that he refined an aspect of the story that could have been handled with broader humor for audiences of a humbler sort.

The Grimm brothers tampered in no way with the nobility of the characters—both their version and *The Donkey Tale* rely on a stock of royalty in narrating their story—but they deleted features that would have seemed too highbrow to their audience. Thus, whereas the donkey prince in *The Donkey Tale* takes up music because he loves art, his counterpart in the Grimms' tale does so because he is merry and frolicsome. In the same scene, the Brothers Grimm eliminate the social tensions between the prince and the musician. Instead, they stress that the virtue of the donkey in persevering is rewarded by success: "No excuse helped: the donkey wanted and was determined to play the lute, was persistent and diligent, and in the end learned it as well as his instructor himself."[118] Their donkey is apparently imbued with a good Protestant work ethic!

Although "The Donkey" remains like a fairy tale in the idealized landscape in which its events take place, it does so without retaining many of the courtly preoccupations that pervade *The Donkey Tale*. The lute playing, table manners, and general etiquette of the donkey receive more cursory attention from the Brothers Grimm than they did from the Medieval Latin poet. Instead, they imprint on the tale a fairy-tale charm: if an anachronism may be forgiven, they make their donkey almost a Walt Disney character, by referring to him constantly with the diminutive "little donkey" (*Eselein*) and by insinuating the word *fein* (nice, fine, entirely) into several statements about him.[119]

As for changes in style, the Grimm brothers made only sparing additions. Two of the most striking take the form of proverbs that were not in the Latin and that are presumably intended to make the tale sound more genuinely homespun—and more authentically German. In the Latin poem, the childless queen utters a lament that is at once elegantly metaphoric and gruesomely explicit: "I am an unfortunate woman, most similar to a barren land that without hope of a harvest swallows the seeds that are cast" (5–16).[120] In the German of the *KHM,* this lament is shortened in a way that may well be meant to conjure up the language of the Bible: "I am like a field on which nothing grows" [Ich bin wie ein Acker, auf dem nichts wächst]. Later the brothers interpolate, on the basis of a turn of phrase attested already in Gottfried von Strassburg's *Tristan* (11222–23), an expression not found in any form in *The Donkey Tale*: "You look so sour, like a jar of vinegar" [Du schaust ja sauer, wie ein Essigkrug].[121]

More often than adding, the Brothers Grimm effected changes by stripping away. For instance, they deleted altogether the classical coloring of the

Latin poem (which was heavily Ovidian, enhancing the steamily erotic atmosphere). Gone are the deities of classical mythology, such as Jupiter, Lucina, Venus, Hercules, Hesperus, and Phoebus. Gone are the Latin poem's oaths by Jupiter (237) and the gods above (249), together with its prayers to the divinities (21).[122] Gone are the many turns of phrase that are drawn from or allude to classical poets, especially Ovid and Virgil but also Horace, Lucan, and Statius.[123] They also cut out stylistic embellishments, such as alliteration, wordplay, and rhetorical parallelism and antithesis.[124]

A consequence of their changes is to make the story faster-paced. Beyond amputating such overtly self-conscious narratorial devices of the Latin poem as direct interventions and foreshadowing (e.g., 219–22), they sliced away most of the dialogue in *The Donkey Tale* to make it more purely narrative. Thus, whereas the queen in the Medieval Latin requires eight hexameter lines (13–20) to bemoan her childlessness and apparent sterility, her counterpart in "The Donkey" declares simply, "I am like a field on which nothing grows"; and whereas in *The Donkey Tale* we are treated to a long conversation between the donkey prince and his music master when the prince first conceives the fancy of studying the lute, in "The Donkey" we are told only that the prince refused to be dissuaded.

Thanks to its many deletions, the Grimms' tale amounts to only roughly one-third the length of the Latin original. The reader emerges with the impression that the brothers detached the purely narrative couplets from *The Donkey Tale* and translated them into German. In the process, they made many small adjustments to bring their telling of the tale into accord with their preconceptions of a truly popular fairy tale style.[125] Perhaps inadvertently, but more probably out of a conviction that the *Volk* among whom such tales originated and circulated were fundamentally earnest people, the Brothers Grimm made the tale a much more serious one. With the straightforward language of their vernacular prose, they sidestep the absurd incongruity of a jackass who expresses himself in fluent elegiac couplets. With their excision of mythological references and classical quotations, they eschew the bathetic contrast between an overrefined rhetoric and allusivity, on the one hand, and sometimes slapstick events, on the other.

THE TAIL END OF *THE DONKEY TALE*

My topic in this chapter has been literally, but I hope not figuratively, asinine. Although folklorists often prefer not to grapple with the written evidence of the premodern period, much remains to be learned, both about the Middle Ages and about the nineteenth century, from close comparisons of medieval texts and their nineteenth-century postscripts. In this case, I

may have unearthed no incontestable facts; but I may have isolated tracks in the metamorphosis of an Indian myth (perhaps through an entertainment transmitted by mime players) into a medieval European tale for the entertainment and formation of privileged young men, which is ultimately transmuted, in its turn, into a nineteenth-century fairy tale in one of the "classic" collections. "The Donkey Tale," like "The Turnip Tale," provides insights into changes that occur as traditional stories pass from one culture into another over long stretches of time.

The Brothers Grimm were right in their instinct that the narrative related in *The Donkey Tale* deserves status as a fairy tale.[126] The first line of the story contains the word *quondam,* a marker in Latin that serves the same function as *once upon a time* in English or *es war einmal* in German. The account begins in vintage fairy tale fashion (Once upon a time there was a king of an unknown region and city [1]), by presenting a setting that is indeterminate both spatially and temporally and that appears to be tranquil but turns out to be marred by great tensions, in the form first of a lacking (a childless couple) and then of a flaw (the deformity of the child who is marvelously born to them).[127] *The Donkey Tale* introduces an unidentified king and queen of a nameless land who have everything their hearts desire except for a child. Like most other fairy tales, this one displays great narrative thrift. Just as it imposes on the audience almost no names, so it keeps to the bare minimum the number of characters it introduces; and it refrains from characterizing even these few characters. Without any fussing about the why and wherefore, the tale proceeds to introduce the wonder of a baby in asinine form born of human parents—and to compound it by relating that this donkey, despite the inconvenience of having hooves in place of hands, becomes adept in playing a musical instrument. In typical fairy tale fashion, *The Donkey Tale* is marked by the dynamic of having two realms, the one where the story and problem begin and the one where the problem is resolved and the story ends.[128] Above all, the dilemma at the center of the story is a wonder: a prince who must be freed from the animal form in which he has been magically enveloped. If both his affliction and its resolution are not a wonder tale, it is hard to know what should qualify as one.[129] In fact, the greatest wonder is that this tale has been so long denied status as a fairy tale.

Conclusion

Sadly Never After

The transcription of a folktale can seem, at first glance, a very simple thing that can be done by anyone, without requiring a special background. Is it possible then to speak of a historical development in the collection of folktales?[1]

ne simple but sophisticated definition holds that "[t]he fairy tale is a form of artistic narrative using marvellous motifs in addition to motifs referring to social reality in a way that influences the development of the plot."[2] Both *The Turnip Tale* and *The Donkey Tale* meet this definition, but they have two features that have impeded their acknowledgment as fairy tales. Although the definition makes no mention of style, the tales of the Brothers Grimm, their predecessors, and their successors have characteristics that relate to both oral traditional storytelling and literary narration. Because *The Turnip Tale* and *The Donkey Tale* are in Latin, which fulfilled the function of the father tongue in the diglossia of Western Europe in the Middle Ages, they give the impression automatically of being irrecuperably distant from the orality of popular culture.[3]

Beyond the question of style lies that of transmission. Because the two Latin poems are separate tales that circulated by themselves, they have not been hallowed as fairy tales. Had they been recorded in a vernacular language

(which would have facilitated recognition of their fairy tale style) and had they formed part of collections (which would have helped to certify their content as qualifying as a fairy tale), they would have been acknowledged as fairy tales long ago and universally. Instead, they have been trapped in a limbo, certified as fairy tales by none other than the Brothers Grimm, but either ignored or denied the same status by most literary historians and folklorists who study fairy tales.

In the first anthology that sought to assemble medieval *Märchen* as translated into a modern European language, the German folklorist Tegethoff referred to "the dark beginnings of European fairy tale telling."[4] Like Hansel and Gretel or Little Red Riding Hood before the happy outcomes of their respective tales, we may still be at risk in a murky forest, but I hope at least to have put down blazes to signal part of the path that leads out. One of the marks to help in pathfinding takes the form of the interpretations I have offered in the six preceding chapters, where I attempted to construct an argument about the development of wonder tales over more than two centuries. Another comes in the appendix that follows, where the reader will find gathered five clusters of material, all of them in Modern English translation. These mini-sourcebooks will allow independent analysis and interpretation of the tales, as well as at least preliminary testing of my arguments.

Before stepping back to allow the tales to speak for themselves (and they are often the most eloquent witnesses on their own behalf), I will draw together two of the most important implications that have emerged from the interpretations of the individual tales. One of these pertains to wonder and helps to show why it is justified to consider the last of these tales as fairy tales. The other relates to the history of tale collecting and explains why uncollected medieval folktales, even wonder tales, failed to achieve recognition as fairy tales, even after the Brothers Grimm drew on them directly and Hans Christian Andersen did so indirectly.

Between the late tenth and early thirteenth centuries, Latin authors bear witness to an increasing openness to the literary recording of tales in which wonder plays a central role.[5] Although initially they strove to coordinate these wonders with miracles of a religious sort, later they became receptive to the portrayal of the nonreligious wonder that distinguishes many fairy tales, especially the ones known as wonder tales. In accord with this progression, we find at the early end of the chronological spectrum the poem of Letaldus, with its fisherman protagonist and his unsettlingly Jonah-like and un-Jonah-like vicissitudes, and the lines by Egbert of Liège about the little girl spared by the wolves, in which baptism and God are given prominent places. In the middle we encounter *One-Ox,* the hero or antihero of which

employs credulity about miracles and wonders in order to foil his opponents. At the end come *The Turnip Tale* and *The Donkey Tale,* which are constructed on such purely wondrous motifs without any religious undercurrent (a supernaturally large turnip and a donkey-human hybrid, respectively) that the Brothers Grimm were entirely justified in having incorporated them into their *KHM.* Perhaps these texts give evidence of a trend toward the desacralization or secularization of wonder, from miracle to marvel or magic. At the same time, they suggest that wonder tales in literary form had not yet been quarantined to children, as would tend to happen after the Enlightenment. But it is prudent to be cautious in making generalizations about the relationship between the marvels of fairy tales, on the one hand, and "reason" and "classicism" as characteristics of seventeenth-century culture, on the other.[6]

The picture that the poems present could be given added depth by considering other types of texts, first Latin and later vernacular, into which wonder tales were fitted with particular frequency. Such consideration could result in other books much lengthier than this one. In Medieval Latin literature alone, four genres stand out for the great richness that they display in this regard.[7] The first and earliest of the four was the *modus* or *ridiculum,* which was collected on a few occasions in the eleventh century. Although probably the impulse to collect short folkloric fiction had had literary consequences earlier, the collections of *ridicula* in the so-called *Cambridge Songs* and of *modi* in a present-day Wolfenbüttel manuscript, in Paderborn in the Middle Ages, are the earliest extant evidence of it.

Such collections seem to have had their origins in the patronage and cultivation of the German courts, which is interesting since the next manifestations of the same impulse—the second genre of interest in the present discussion—are court-connected miscellanies that were produced in the second half of the twelfth century by Walter Map's *Courtiers' Trifles (De nugis curialium),*[8] Gervase of Tilbury's *Recreation for an Emperor (Otia imperialia),* and Petrus Alfonsi's *Scholar's Guide (Disciplina clericalis).* The very titles of the first two works indicate how much they depart from earlier medieval literature in advertising themselves ostensibly as leisure literature or trivial literature and as either lacking a real claim to serious moral value or at least combining education with a prominent dose of entertainment.[9] At the same time, these works may well mark movement toward a new outlook on story, one in which the free interpretability of tales became an overriding concern and in which elasticity in the interpretation of narratives became one of their main draws.[10]

Closely related to the miscellanies is historical writing, since history and story in the twelfth century saw many close unions in which folktales in

general and marvels in particular intrude themselves; the works of William of Malmesbury (ca. 1095–ca. 1142), William of Newburgh (ca. 1136–ca. 1198), and Saxo Grammaticus (ca. 1150–after 1200) are only three of many possible examples.[11] A culture in which the production of manuscripts required great investment of resources (in both the time of scribes and the cost of writing materials) could not have the equivalent of modern-day "junk reading," but the titles of Walter's and Gervase's works offer testimony of movement in that direction. Both of these forms indicate that in the latter half of the twelfth century, the princes of the church and state were cultivating interests in collecting marvels both real and written. Though it may be true that this coincidence of marvelous objects and texts was not yet on the scale that the sixteenth century would witness, a new aesthetic was taking shape.[12]

The third genre of importance to this discussion would be the frame tale (sometimes called a "cornice"), of which the earliest example, the *Dolopathos* by the Cistercian John of Alta Silva, is a reflex of the Seven Sages cycle that is packed with folktales.[13] John's text is thoroughly monastic—and especially Cistercian—in its obsession with silence and its powerful misogyny.[14] At the same time, it shares with courtly literature an attraction to the wonders of the East, particularly in their literary manifestation. This attraction gives it common ground with *The Donkey Tale*.

The fourth and final genre to consider here would be compendiums of exempla (illustrative stories) that were used to add entertainment to the edification of sermons. As preaching became more frequent, those responsible for delivering sermons sought out interesting stories to which they gave a moralizing or religious-philosophical interpretation.[15] Although such "illustrations" may seem banal in comparison with the many forms of narrative readily available today, to audiences of earlier times—who had both less free time and fewer resources for entertainment—the exempla must have been very exciting. It is even plausible to draw a comparison between the place exempla occupied among the entertainment options then available to the uneducated and the roles fairy tales have played among children as nursery tales for centuries.[16]

Our earliest extant records of systematic large-scale collections of exempla date to the thirteenth century. Their compilers are usually clerics, such as Jacques de Vitry (canon regular, died 1240), Caesarius of Heisterbach (Cistercian, ca. 1180–1240), Odo of Cheriton (ca. 1180–ca. 1246), Stephen of Bourbon (Dominican, died ca. 1261), and John Bromyard (Dominican, fourteenth century); but the stories contained in them are in large part of folkloristic origin.[17] More specifically, a high number of the tales appear to derive from Eastern sources. Jacques de Vitry, who had spent time and traveled widely in the

East, was responsible for the first collection of exempla, which is filled with Eastern folktales. Stephen of Bourbon resembles Jacques in his openness to including many tales of Eastern origin in his exempla collection.[18]

On the whole, these four genres of Latin materials antedated the burgeoning of short, usually comic novelistic forms that can be documented in Old French fabliaux, Middle High German *Schwänke,* Italian *novelle,* and other vernacular genres from the mid-thirteenth century on.[19] These short forms, which qualify as being novelistic not in the sense of a modern novel but, rather, in the sense of a medieval or early modern Italian *novella* (similar to a short story), contributed decisively to the formation and development of European literature.[20] They are associated with such major medieval authors as Boccaccio and Chaucer, as well as with the structure of the frame tale.[21]

A progression appears to have taken place in the recording and dissemination of folktales in writing. In the earliest period, folktales were reworked in a variety of forms on an experimental basis. The greatest success occurred in sequences that were brought together in small-scale collections determined by their similar melodies, poetic form, and content and intended to entertain courts. In the middle period, more complex folktales, especially wonder tales, were recorded at greater length in Latin *comedie* and exempla. Eventually these Latin forms were displaced by the vernacular successors of the *comedie,* such as fabliaux in French and *novelle* in Italian. Although these vernacular forms were deeply indebted to a variety of folktales, on the whole they shrank from the experimentation with wonder tale that had been a characteristic of the *ridicula,* some *comedie,* and various other genres of earlier years. But collectively all these various efforts over the centuries to find places in literature for the narratives present in the humblest forms of storytelling led eventually to the collections of Basile and Straparola. Which work or works to credit with being the beginning point or points of fairy tale may be less important than simply making the effort to view them all as points in a continuum of experimentation and development.

The collections of *ridicula* or *modi,* the courtly miscellanies, the frame tale, and the exempla repertories cover an extraordinary spread in terms of their authors, audiences, and patrons, with schools, courts, and congregations being involved in their production and transmission. Not all or even most of them pass muster as wonder tales, but stories with the content (if not the style) of wonder tales were one of their constituents. Why have they been examined so rarely in conjunction with the freestanding Latin poems examined in this book?

In most cases, the reason is their resemblance to *novelle.* They are novella-like in the seemingly earthy realism of their style, which is a far cry from the

magical simplicity that has come to be associated with fairy tales. In their content they differ from the vagueness of tales of "once upon a time." Rather than being presented in the indeterminate way that is characteristic of fairy tales, these tales have the specificity of naming names, citing times, and the like that is found in anecdotes, legends, and many *novelle*.

Another part of the explanation for the usual neglect of these assemblages in considerations of fairy tales is that the wonder tales that do appear within them are as isolated and intermittent as the ones that have been the focus of the last three chapters. In this book, I have argued that the isolated tales deserve equal consideration. I have implied that a new openness toward short fiction developed in Latin in the eleventh century and grew in the late twelfth and early thirteenth centuries. A further suggestion would be that the short forms in Latin from 1200 and earlier set the stage for the rise of short fiction in the vernaculars, which led eventually to the collections that have been identified as the earliest fairy tale collections. But this effort of mine to attribute fairy tale status to isolated tales runs counter to the tendency to assume that a tale that has not been previously subsumed into a canonical collection of fairy tales cannot pass muster as a fairy tale. Therein lies a story that helps considerably to explain why Medieval Latin fairy tales have failed to acquire the recognition to which they would seem to be entitled.

Fairy tales are known to many people around the world who have never laid eyes on books that have emblazoned on their covers or spines the names of Charles Perrault, Jacob and Wilhelm Grimm, or Hans Christian Andersen. Nonetheless, most of the fairy tales that have entered mass culture would not be there if they had not been canonized in the collected tales for children that are associated with these authors. To restate the matter, fairy tales have acquired their current niche in Western and even in world culture thanks to the imprimatur of having been subsumed in collections that are not at all anonymous or collective (as would be expected with folk literature) but that are instead attached indissolubly to particular writers. Although the constituents of these collections were not meant by their collectors to be regarded exclusively or even primarily as children's literature, the tales have remained a constant in the ever-changing koine of mass culture by dint of entering public consciousness regularly at the preschool level. Very few people, probably only the most motivated of children and the most dedicated of scholars, peruse entire fairy tale collections from cover to cover. On the contrary, many experience the tales individually, in board books dedicated to a single tale or in the feature-length cartoons that have been released over the decades by Walt Disney and his studio and that in most cases take single tales as their points of departure.

Taxonomists of literature, who may be called literary critics, literary historians, literary theologians, philologists, or any of various other names, have drawn all sorts of minute distinctions to designate fairy tales, wonder tales, and related types of literature. Despite these valiant efforts at precision, fairy tale ends up being understood as the kind of tale that is included in the classic fairy tale collections, such as the Grimms' or Hans Christian Andersen's, and especially in the wonder tales that are a chief constituent of these collections. One consequence of our experience of fairy tale collections, I would suggest, is that we have difficulty comprehending a period in which folktale collecting did not take place but in which the recording of folktales occurred at a very fast rate.

Often, what is not collected becomes lost or at least unappreciated. This principle holds true to an extent for the neglect that all of Medieval Latin literature has suffered in publishing over the past century. Classical Latin literature has been gathered into series, which, although not always as inexpensive as potential users might wish, are nonetheless affordable. Consider the rows of blue-backed Oxford Classical Texts or the serried red ranks of the Latin volumes in the Loeb Classical Library. Isidore of Seville is the latest entry chronologically in the former, the Venerable Bede in the latter. German publication series have been more inclusive of the medieval, so that there is a sprinkling of Medieval Latin and even Neo-Latin in the Biblioteca Teubneriana and in Reclam paperbacks. But by and large those who wish to consult Medieval Latin editions find themselves in a very expensive, separate, scattered, and all too separate world, where the places of continents and archipelagoes are taken by series that often bear impressively and maybe also forbiddingly Latin titles, such as Corpus Christianorum, Monumenta Germaniae Historica, Corpus Scriptorum Ecclesiasticorum Latinorum, Analecta Hymnica, Rolls Series, Oxford Medieval Texts, and dozens of other—sometimes distinguished, sometimes ephemeral—text series. For all that professional medievalists may grumble at the slipshod and predatory editorial practices of the notorious abbé Jacques-Paul Migne (1800–1875), he accomplished more than any other single figure in the nineteenth or twentieth century for putting medieval texts within reach of users.[22] The picture will change if and when the electronic databases into which the largest series are being converted become easily and affordably accessible—but that is not a guaranteed prospect at the present, since many of the most essential ones are presently available only at great expense.

What is happening with digitized texts offers a valuable lesson about the fates that texts have had in the past, for it confirms the elementary principle that where and how a text is collected affects who can and will access it. Nowhere is the last truism more relevant than in regard to fairy tales. Today

the status of fairy tale is accorded most readily to tales that are found within collections, especially of wonder tales, which are seen as being particularly suited for children. This tyranny of the collection has its correspondent in literary history, where fairy tale status has been denied to medieval poems because they were not bundled together in the Middle Ages in versions by single authors. Collecting involves multiples. As a result, there has been a tendency to seek out earlier dates for the beginning of fairy tale, but always by looking for the origin of the first collection, whether early nineteenth-century Germany, seventeenth-century France, sixteenth-century Italy, or fifteenth-century Italy. In the process, there has been a tendency to minimize the heterogeneity of the collections—to conceal the reality that they include much that is not fairy tale in the sense of wonder tale—and an even greater tendency to discount from consideration single or isolated fairy tales.

Both fairy tales and fairy tale scholarship have many paradoxes. One is that questions of which is the first fairy tale and which is the first fairy tale collection have often been conflated. The recording of fairy tales from popular sources took place in large quantities only in the Romantic era, when systematic collection and analysis of folktale reached new levels with the *KHM* of Jacob and Wilhelm Grimm. But in smaller numbers, fairy tales had been brought together in the works of Basile, Straparola, and Perrault, and, working backward, we can trace the gradual emergence into elevated literature that this branch of popular literature achieved earlier in the Middle Ages.[23]

What constitutes the corpus of fairy tales best known today is the result of a process in some ways arbitrary. Many tried-and-true stories are in the collections, but others are not. Although the Brothers Grimm and Hans Christian Andersen had a good sense for the authentic, their corpora could have included other stories. By adapting *The Turnip Tale* and *The Donkey Tale* to match with their model of *Märchen,* Jacob and Wilhelm demonstrated a willingness to incorporate into their collection stories that they believed had been circulating orally in the Middle Ages. In this willingness, the Brothers Grimm displayed the right instincts. Despite the anachronism and paradox, there is a healthy dose of truth in the view that Romanticism gave rise to the Middle Ages as we conceive of them. The Brothers Grimm were central figures in the creation of medieval literature as well as in the establishment of fairy tale as a ubiquitous component of modern Western culture. The two processes were intertwined. Jacob and Wilhelm Grimm did not have at their disposal the evidence to hypothesize (even if they had wanted to do so) a pattern of development in the handling of wonder tales during the Middle Ages. The editiones principes of *About a Certain Fisherman* by Letaldus, *The Richly Laden Ship* (*Fecunda ratis*) by Egbert of Liège,

and *One-Ox* were not published until 1849, 1889, and 1838, respectively. Yet these texts were located and edited as a consequence of the enthusiasm for Medieval Latin that the Brothers Grimm helped to foster.

In Western culture, it has become ever more difficult, ever more alien, to appreciate the functions that Latinity served in the Middle Ages. Not just the language of the Scriptures and liturgy, not just the vehicle for solemnifying treaties and contracts, not just the medium of scholastic disputations, Latin was also a channel for experimentation and entertainment. Not all Medieval Latin writers were adventurous or playful souls. But authors who opted to write in the learned language may sometimes have enjoyed greater latitude than those who chose the vernacular. Latin writers operated within the ambit of a language that required an education that formed its users not merely linguistically but also morally and culturally. Because Latin belonged to a special in-group, those who employed it were allowed to venture into areas that might have been riskier for vernacular writers. For this reason, it is not surprising that there were particularly creative poets whose false fictions and lies went so far as to embrace what we now call fairy tales. The tales themselves are wonder tales, and the tale of their development and discovery is a cause for wonder too.

Appendix

Man Swallowed by Fish (ATU 1889G)

A. The "Great Fish" in the Book of Jonah (Rheims-Douay)

Translation from the official Roman Catholic English Bible, published in 1609–10, which was based mainly on the official Latin Bible, the Vulgate. The English Vulgate is named after Rheims and Douay (often spelled "Douai"), because the translating (of the Hebrew Bible and the New Testament, respectively) was performed in these two cities in France by members of the English Catholic University. Although this version of the Bible has been overshadowed by the King James Version, it remains useful because of its fidelity to the Latin. Jonah's name is spelled "Jonas" throughout, and there are obsolete features in both language and orthography.

Chapter 1. *Jonas being sent to preach in Ninive, fleeth away by sea: a tempest riseth: of which he being found, by lot, to be the cause, is cast into the sea, which thereupon is calmed.*

1 Now the word of the Lord came to Jonas the son of Amathi, saying:

2 Arise, and go to Ninive the great city, and preach in it: for the wickedness thereof is come up before me.

3 And Jonas rose up to flee into Tharsis from the face of the Lord, and he went down to Joppe, and found a ship going to Tharsis: and he paid the fare thereof, and went down into it, to go with them to Tharsis from the face of the Lord.

4 But the Lord sent a great wind into the sea: and a great tempest was raised in the sea, and the ship was in danger to be broken.

5 And the mariners were afraid, and the men cried to their god: and they cast forth the wares that were in the ship, into the sea, to lighten it of them: and Jonas went down into the inner part of the ship, and fell into a deep sleep.

6 And the shipmaster came to him, and said to him: Why art thou fast asleep? Rise up, call upon thy God, if so be that God will think of us, that we may not perish.

7 And they said every one to his fellow: Come, and let us cast lots, that we may know why this evil is upon us. And they cast lots, and the lot fell upon Jonas.

8 And they said to him: Tell us for what cause this evil is upon us, what is thy business? of what country art thou? and whither goest thou? or of what people art thou?

9 And he said to them: I am a Hebrew, and I fear the Lord the God of heaven, who made both the sea and the dry land.

10 And the men were greatly afraid, and they said to him: Why hast thou done this? (for the men knew that he fled from the face of the Lord: because he had told them.)

11 And they said to him: What shall we do to thee, that the sea may be calm to us? for the sea flowed and swelled.

12 And he said to them: Take me up, and cast me into the sea, and the sea shall be calm to you: for I know that for my sake this great tempest is upon you.

13 And the men rowed hard to return to land, but they were not able: because the sea tossed and swelled upon them.

14 And they cried to the Lord, and said: We beseech thee, O Lord, let us not perish for this man's life, and lay not upon us innocent blood: for thou, O Lord, hast done as it pleased thee.

15 And they took Jonas, and cast him into the sea, and the sea ceased from raging.

16 And the men feared the Lord exceedingly, and sacrificed victims to the Lord, and made vows.

Chapter 2. *Jonas is swallowed up by a great fish: he prayeth with confidence in God: and the fish casteth him out on the dry land.*

¹ Now the Lord prepared a great fish to swallow up Jonas: and Jonas was in the belly of the fish three days and three nights.

² And Jonas prayed to the Lord his God out of the belly of the fish.

³ And he said: I cried out of my affliction to the Lord, and he heard me: I cried out of the belly of hell, and thou hast heard my voice.

⁴ And thou hast cast me forth into the deep in the heart of the sea, and a flood hath compassed me: all thy billows, and thy waves have passed over me.

⁵ And I said: I am cast away out of the sight of thy eyes: but yet I shall see thy holy temple again.

⁶ The waters compassed me about even to the soul: the deep hath closed me round about, the sea hath covered my head.

⁷ I went down to the lowest parts of the mountains: the bars of the earth have shut me up for ever: and thou wilt bring up my life from corruption, O Lord my God.

⁸ When my soul was in distress within me, I remembered the Lord: that my prayer may come to thee, unto thy holy temple.

⁹ They that are vain observe vanities, forsake their own mercy.

¹⁰ But I with the voice of praise will sacrifice to thee: I will pay whatsoever I have vowed for *my* salvation to the Lord.

¹¹ And the Lord spoke to the fish: and it vomited out Jonas upon the dry land.

B. Letaldus of Micy, *About a Certain Fisherman Whom a Whale Swallowed*

Translated from Letaldus of Micy, *De quodam piscatore quem ballena absorbuit*, ed. and trans. Ferruccio Bertini, *Letaldo di Micy, Within piscator*, Biblioteca del Medioevo latino (Florence: Giunti, 1995), 2–15.

If the notes of Pindar's lyre-string lay within my power and if the Thracian bard, Orpheus, were present, who overpowers everything with his voice, compels rivers to course upstream, and captivates with his lyre the woods everywhere eager for music, [5] even so I would not be able to produce the splendid song that I have in mind, that I try to strum out on awkward gut-strings.

An elder, commanding respect by his behavior and weighted down by age, whose words are radiant like copper-tinged gold, reported this event.

An island, lying in the northern regions of the ocean, [10] formerly called Albion and later Britannia, has brought forth races sturdy in temperament and rejoicing in arms. Gentle enough in its climate and abounding in choice things, now inhabited by the fairheaded settlers of the Angles, the island, which for a long time knew to gnash its teeth in its foreign tongue, sings—thanks to Pope Gregory—the pious hymns of Christ [15].

We sing a deed done in this place, a deed that we prepare to strum fittingly.

He was named Within, well known for the art of fishing, an investigator of the river, an investigator of the deep sea as well, whom neither fresh nor salty billows can deter [20] from carrying booty ashore from the swift waves. As Aurora leaves behind the golden bed of Tithonus, he seeks out the deeps, borne on his friendly coracle, and he takes steel and flint, and stores away tinder, so that if need be he might kindle faint flames; [25] and, trusting in his two-edged sword, he girds his thigh.

He prepares everything, nothing is missing for his trade: the nets are not wanting, the anchor that can hold still the wave-tossed deck on the sea occupies the crossbeams, and the coiled rigging covers the planking; a basket of bread is at hand and fresh water in a jug, [30] so that he would not be hindered by the briny salt of the sea and its crashing waves.

Thus Within entrusts himself alone to the open sea. He goes far from land: the mountains and woods drop out of sight. Thus cutting the salty channels, he exults amid the waves. Then, pondering in which area he should put the net, in which the hook, [35] he prepares to hold fast the raft with the tooth of the anchor, where the sea remained unmoved by the waves as a gentle zephyr blew.

A little later, from amid the surges an immense beast arises, like Scylla and like Charybdis in its maw and eyes, with snake-like teeth and with an ever gaping gullet, [40] a gullet that could tumble entire cities to the underworld.

Within, collecting the netting, strives to wrench out the curved anchorteeth and to head ashore on the calm winds; but with trembling hands and with a chest altogether gasping for air, he abandons the attempt and stays in the billowing waves. [45] Thereupon the wild beast, in rage, guides its gigantic maw toward his wretched head, and it shifts the coracle and Within into its greedy belly, just as a traveler, burning from the sun amid a hot spell, drinks from cool fountains the water he has found.

Within, sitting on the poop, is shut up in a dark cave. [50] There is no need for oars, nor to stretch the canvas before the winds, and the radiant constellations do not insist upon a sure course; and yet in the swelling waves he still follows a course.

Within, what thoughts do you have, in the belly of the beast? Your sweet

children hasten to the shore to see you, [55] and your wife, bereft of you, crosses barefoot the sacred threshold and entreats that you return under favorable sails.

Put by yourself in a life-and-death plight, take counsel by yourself, marshal your forces, show your mettle. No strength reveals itself so long as fortune favors the circumstances: [60] it is best in unfavorable situations to keep up courage.

Therefore Within, shut in the belly as if in a lightless prison, soon strikes steel and flint: a gleaming spark shoots out. Shining, it grows as the tinder is placed next to it, and it shows that it can stay alive amid the loud-sounding waves. [65] The doughty twin-edged sword that had girded his side is unsheathed, and he decides to chop into bits the creaking oars, and to tear the uppermost layer of the wicker framework from the raft, which is soon to burn.

As the fire catches hold of these pieces, it blazes enormously to the ceiling; the smoke, flying up high, seeks open air above, [70] but repelled downward by the thick back of the beast, it heads toward the mouth, eyes, ears, and gullet of the wicked enemy, and passes violently into open air.

Mount Etna, raging just like it, spews forth sulphurous fumes and batters the bright stars with the ashes it discharges; [75] in the same way this harpy seethes, incited by the swift fires, thrusting its jaws through the loudly sounding waves. There is nowhere where it may flee; it bears its enemy within itself. Now roaring, it stretches its vast limbs over the surface of the sea; now seeking the gloomy depths of the ocean, it rambles and sweeps the azure depths, [80] and unable to endure and insane, it builds a savage rage.

No less does the new guest shut within it make the torment mount. Now, when the flame has spread to the outer beams of his shelter, he leaps forth and tears at each side of the Fury with his sword. Stabbing and inflicting wounds everywhere, he cuts the entrails. [85] The sword cuts apart the intestines, traversing all the innermost parts, and strikes in its stomach, tears into the secluded places of its heart, and strives to create in its powerful ribs gashes, through which the avenging sea should burst with salty waves.

The high house groans at the stout blows he strikes, [90] and at once a twofold lamentation arises and slaps the surface of the sea. The food produces death; the bait devours the raging devourer; and the prey, the tables now turned, lays low the immense predator.

The guest, surfeited by the slaughter and tired in his heart, sits down amid the vaulted chamber of the vast structure, [95] prepares things fit for a banquet, and fixes still quivering organs on spits, restoring his stomach with its stomach and his body with its body.

So then, in this effort Within spends five days and, as the stars came and

went, four nights. Hope of survival was slim, but all the while the motivation of his efforts [100] remains intact, and he does not know how to spare the enemy. The fierce creature, rumbling, is rolled ashore by the waves; the sea lays it out bloodless on the tawny sands.

The port of the city Rochester receives this booty, the city where Within was born, where he learned to set a hook. [105] The astonished townsfolk sight the rich windfall. One man carries a twin-bladed sword that is greedy for booty, another carries a two-edged ax; they strive to ascend to the peak of the great mass with ladders and to carry home the extraordinary booty. They seek out the steep roof and, with their sturdy axes brought into action, [110] they redouble their blows and tire the shore with their shouts. Through many wounds they approach the inmost entrails, not knowing that their comrade is being held in the concealed cave.

When he senses that the cruel axes were close to hand and that he had been borne to the shore of the land he had longed for, [115] he addresses his comrades in the native language: "Alas, spare me, my townsmen! Spare me, wretch that I am," he said. "It is Within who is held in this belly!"

At these words, a tremor strikes their bones; the axes, set to trembling, fly out of their hands; faces turn white; and voices stick in their throats. They take headlong flight, the fleeing mob rushes [120] in a thick column, and each one vies to outrun the other. In no time at all this hubbub stirred up the aforementioned city; the people run up, women bearing the day's work of spinning, and youths and children fly, while bent old age, not mindful of its years, thinks to imitate the gait of men in their prime.

[125] As the bishop heard the sound, he quickly sought out the sacred threshold. At once he calls together the revered clergy according to their rank, summons with tranquil mouth the whole congregation of people, apprises them of the matter, and induces them all to prayer, so that the wicked bane that lay hidden should not harm the inviolate city [130] and so that the demon should not be able to prattle his vicious ravings. "Speaking false deceptions to cause the death of our people, it has brought something lamentable to our shore."[1]

At once he elects men distinguished by piety and orders them to bring forth the holy pledges and revered fluid,[2] [135] whereby the bane may be put to flight, the hostile power [of the Devil] grow weary and terrified by the holy tokens, take to the air above.

The nobles go forth, with a great crowd pressing around them, and the shores fill with throngs eager to look on. Shortly, once ladders have been set in place, they ascend the [140] ribs already eaten away to the bone and they pour holy water over everything.

They swear: "If you are hiding anywhere here, hostile power, confess your

name, business, and justification. You have no hope of hiding from the holy pledges we bear;[3] in the holy name [of God], announce openly what you are!"

[145] "I am Within," he said, "whom with ravening throat this choking Fury has seized and submerged in its pitiless gut. But act, O citizens, so that, led forth, I may earn the right to glimpse the light of day and to see my yearned-for homeland."

At these words, their courage returns, their terrified hearts rest easy, [150] and, vying, they rush to work and they tire out their cutting tools. The whole shore resounds, the air rages with frequent blows, and butchered chunks of the beast are strewn on the blood-absorbent sands.

The greatest share is given to the bishop; and they carry back an extraordinary windfall, those who carry the water and holy pledges; [155] the people divide up the wares of the pleasing booty, and no one returns empty-handed to the happy city.

Out of the whale Within comes forth filthy into the open air. Just as a turtledove which has been laid bare of its feathers in midwinter returns in early spring or as when youthful appearance, about to return, raises the morale of [160] eagles that are featherless after a long span of life (the limbs of these creatures are stripped as their covering falls off and a hateful cloud covers their keen sight for a long time; their weapons [their talons] fall from their feet, their throats are deprived of beaks, and no hope of prey encourages their tired spirits), [165] in the same way baldness, eating away, had scrubbed smooth the whole head of the Englishman, as he looks at the light restored from the sea. The burnt-off skin had left his nails protruding, and his eyelids in growing had brought in thick shadows; and the new light, as it returns, injures his eyes, [170] which had been made heavy beneath so long a night, and they no longer are adequate to see the pleasant shore, and a voice or touch alone (and not the gifts of sight) give away the identity of the neighbors who rush from the city.[4]

When Within was safe after such a while, he would not usually go back to his dear city with a comparable reception. [175] Returning from the sea, behold! Crowded about by mobs of people, as if a king, he gazes at the rejoicing troops. The bishop meets him; the clergy honors him with reverence. The noblemen form a palisade around him on one side, while on the other the common folk hem him in. Three times and four times they beg to hear the critical moments of [180] the novel event. They ask many things and they tire the man with much talk.

Then word swiftly reached the ears of his wife. She flies and, in her course, heads in a blaze toward the shore. His children leap forth from their home and the whole household brings forth its energies in an extended competition to cover ground.

[185] And then the shipwrecked man, like another Jonah, in the middle of

the city apprises the astonished people about the miracles of life restored. But his anxious wife had passed along the whole shore and was roaming around among the high prows of the ships that had been brought ashore. Just as a parti-colored swallow in flight courses through high halls, [190] cuts through the teeming air along lakes and around echoing swamps, and, as it follows the various bends and turns, collects captured food as fodder for her chirping nestlings;[5] in like manner this woman wanders among the prowed boats in the port, redoubling her cries for her husband, and the land bellows back in response. [195] The echo resounding from the mountains takes up the assaults (of sound), and the reverberating shore cries, "Within, Within!"

Hardly even as Within addresses the people in the lofty city is his wife able at length to recognize her newfound husband: his attractiveness, cast out, had taken away his familiar appearance, [200] and a new baldness had laid bare his dear forehead. In her husband when he came back only his voice survived as its familiar self. As it reached the astonished ears of his fearful wife, she is reminded of him, and, restored to her full faculties, she watered his bare head three and four times with tears.

[205] Then Within returns to his own hearth and his domestic quarters, distinguished by gifts and rich booty. Living happy days over a long, long period of time, he deservedly returned to the attractiveness of his former good looks.

Here ends [the story of Within].

C. Rudolph Erich Raspe, *Baron Munchausen: Narrative of His Marvellous Travels* (1785), Chapter 8

*R*eprinted from *The Surprising Adventures of Baron Munchausen,* introduction by Thomas Secombe, illustrated by William Strang and J. B. Clark (London: Lawrence and Bullen, 1895), 53–57.

Bathes in the Mediterranean—Meets an unexpected companion—Arrives unintentionally in the regions of heat and darkness, from which he is extricated by dancing a hornpipe—Frightens his deliverers, and returns on shore.

I was once in great danger of being lost in a most singular manner in the Mediterranean: I was bathing in that pleasant sea near Marseilles one summer's afternoon, when I discovered a very large fish, with his jaws quite extended, approaching me with the greatest velocity; there was no time to be lost, nor could I possibly avoid him. I immediately reduced myself to as small a size as possible, by closing my feet and placing my hands also near

my sides, in which position I passed directly between his jaws, and into his stomach, where I remained some time in total darkness, and comfortably warm, as you may imagine; at last it occurred to me, that by giving him pain he would be glad to get rid of me: as I had plenty of room, I played my pranks, such as tumbling, hop, step, and jump, &c., but nothing seemed to disturb him so much as the quick motion of my feet in attempting to dance a hornpipe; soon after I began he put me out by sudden fits and starts: I persevered; at last he roared horridly, and stood up almost perpendicularly in the water, with his head and shoulders exposed, by which he was discovered by the people on board an Italian trader, then sailing by, who harpooned him in a few minutes. As soon as he was brought on board I heard the crew consulting how they should cut him up, so as to preserve the greatest quantity of oil. As I understood Italian, I was in most dreadful apprehensions lest their weapons employed in this business should destroy me also; therefore I stood as near the center as possible, for there was room enough for a dozen men in this creature's stomach, and I naturally imagined they would begin with the extremities; however, my fears were soon dispersed, for they began by opening the bottom of the belly. As soon as I perceived a glimmering of light I called out lustily to be released from a situation in which I was now almost suffocated. It is impossible for me to do justice to the degree and kind of astonishment which sat upon every countenance at hearing a human voice issue from a fish, but more so at seeing a naked man walk upright out of his body, in short, gentlemen, I told them the whole story, as I have done you, whilst amazement struck them dumb.

After taking some refreshment, and jumping into the sea to cleanse myself, I swam to my clothes, which lay where I had left them on the shore. As near as I can calculate, I was near four hours and a half confined in the stomach of this animal.

D. *Hisperica famina* B, Lines 157–217, and Letaldus's Poem: Source and Influence, or Parallels?

The following juxtaposition does not include information about the many possible common sources in Virgil, Arator, and other earlier poets.

Hisperica famina B Ledaldus

[De *Gesta* Re] [16] Hac *gestum* canimus, quod cudere rite paramus.

Quidam olim furibund(us): draconei tumoris tirranus
 solito: regni non contentus solio

inormem: arcessiviti expeditionem
> [37] Fluctibus e mediis mox belua surgit *enormis*

[160] Tum arcessitis: *undique* copiis
> [178] hinc vallant proceres, artant hinc *undique* plebes

superbo: inflatus fastu
contractis: que *ad littora* alnis
> [20] quin praedam a rapidis *ad litora* devehat undis
> [101] Belua dira fremens *ad litora* volvitur undis

†inserere † classem parat;
Hinc robustis: bathmorum flexibus
[165] amplis: *lustrantes* prata *cuneis*
> [189] Versicolor velut, alta volans, per*lustrat* hirundo
> [176] stipatus quasi rex, *cuneos* speculatur ovantes

rostratas: ansportant cervicibus cimbas:
> [188] expositasque rates atque ardua *rostra* pererrat

Littorea: que calcantes *gressibus* arva
> [124] immemor aetatis, *gressus* meditatur heriles

fragoricantia: trudunt plantis marmorea;
Ac torsis: gigantum tumorem (tumore) inter *cerula* alnis
> [79] nunc, pelagi tenebrosa petens, vaga *cerula* verrit

[170] statutis: lecto tramitte tunsis
solida: consedunt remiges in *transtra;*
> [28] *transtra* tenet teretesque tegunt tabulata rudentes

Tensum: que lintrantiant *rudentibus carbasum*
> [50] non remis opus est, non *tendere carbasa* ventis
> [28] transtra tenet teretesque tegunt tabulata *rudentes*

tunc *frementibus* inter fulstra (flustra) *remis*
> [73] Sulphureos velut ille *fremens* vomit Ethna vapores
> [101] Belua dira *fremens* ad litora volvitur undis
> [50] non *remis* opus est, non tendere carbasa ventis
> [66] et placet argutos *remos* incidere frustis

vehitur in *altum* clasis;
> [22] linqueret, *alta* petit, carabo devectus amico

[175] Iam *validis:* navigantes per equorea (*equora*) tunsis
> [109] Ardua tecta petunt *validis*que securibus actis
> [78] Nunc vastos rugiens super *aequora* porrigit artus

tremulus: quasat *freta* nothus
 [33] Sic *freta* salsa secans mediis exultat in undis

astriferos: *salsus* imber spargit turbine in sulcos:
 [33] Sic freta *salsa* secans mediis exultat in undis
 [88] quis vindex pelagus *salsis* irrumperet undis

fluctivagis: que motibus
 [27] anchora, *fluctivagam* quae sistat in aequore puppim

discriminosa: †mactatur†(-antur) pupium latera:
[180] *Salsa:* populaba[t] in proras sentina:
 [33] Sic *freta* salsa secans mediis exultat in undis
 [88] quis vindex pelagus *salsis* irrumperet undis

Imis: *undarum* vallibus
 [88] quis vindex pelagus salsis irrumperet *undis*

trepidæ: decidebant carine
 [43] sed manibus *trepidis* et pectore prorsus anhelo
 [202] haec *trepidae* attonitas ut coniugis attigit aures

crebris: que fulgebat *ether scindellis.*
 [151] Litora cuncta sonant, *crebris* furit ictibus *aether*
 [62] mox calibem *silicem*que ferit: *scintilla* relucens

Tinsurus: que per*sonabat* in pontum clangor
 [151] Litora cuncta *sonant,* crebris furit ictibus aether

[185] offensos: que †formidabat† (-ant) naute scopulos;
 †Latebrosos *naufragia*† tenere putabant in punices (pumices) bracha;
 [185] *Naufragus* ast media, Ionas velut alter, in urbe

Hinc vitreas: *undisoni* gurgitis *verrentes* pupibus per spumas
 [30] ne maris *undisoni* sale comprimeretur acerbo
 [79] nunc, pelagi tenebrosa petens, vaga cerula *verrit*

trucibus: dehiscit *belua* facibus (*faucibus*)
 [130] neve *truces* daemon valeat garrire furores
 [80] impatiensque *truces* cumulat male sana furores
 [37] Fluctibus e mediis mox *belua* surgit enormis
 [76] aestuat, altisonas *fauces* exerta per undas

Horrendoque pavidam: sorbuit *hiatu* classem:
 [39] dentibus anguineis et gutture semper *hianti*

[190] *Vasta*que nauticeus: consedit †multa (in *alta*) coetus
 [78] Nunc *vastos* rugiens super aequora porrigit artus
 [22] linqueret, *alta* petit, carabo devectus amico

Dein ferres (ferreis) duriles: *cudentes* metallis *silices*

> [6] quod meditor, rudibus quod fibris *cudere* conor
> [16] Hac gestum canimus, quod *cudere* rite paramus
> [24] (his opus affuerit tenues ex*cudat* ut ignes)
> [23] et calibem *silicem*que gerit fungumque reponit
> [62] mox calibem *silicem*que ferit: scintilla relucens

Collecta: que aprici *fungiminis* nepta

> [23] et calibem silicemque gerit *fungum*que reponit

torridum: †aunt † (alunt) remiges †rotum † (rogum)

ac beluicina: carnace *molis* trucidant frameis *frusta;*

> [107] nituntur gradibus tantae fastigia *molis*
> [66] et placet argutos remos incidere *frustis*
> [152] caesaque *frusta* ferae bibulis sternuntur arenis

[195] tunc torrentibus: *viscera flamis*

> [84] *viscera*que inflictis fodiens secat undique plagis
> [82] Iamque, ubi *flamma* sui perfudit limina tecti

serpentibus: que per crementa arvinæ stillicidiis

roseo: que frementæ (*fremente*) *camino*

> [73] Sulphureos velut ille *fremens* vomit Ethna vapores
> [101] Belua dira *fremens* ad litora volvitur undis
> [75] haut secus eumenides rapidis haec acta *caminis*

lacessitis: adeo tolibus

digesta funereum: irruit *belua* vorotrum.

> [37] Fluctibus e mediis mox *belua* surgit enormis

[200] Iam periclitantes: fameo ardore remiges

delficino: construnt graticulam in utero;

et asato: carniferi ponderis refuculant precordia pastu

tum *tremula: undisonæ* tithis fulstr[a] (flustra)

> [95] Praeparat apta epulis veribusque *trementia* figit
> [30] ne maris *undisoni* sale comprimeretur acerbo

inormem: torquebant *ad litora beluam*

> [37] Fluctibus e mediis mox *belua* surgit *enormis*
> [20] quin praedam a rapidis *ad litora* devehat undis
> [101] *Belua* dira fremens *ad litora* volvitur undis

[205] spumantia delficinum: transvehant *cerula* gigantem;

> [79] nunc, pelagi tenebrosa petens, vaga *cerula* verrit

Littoreos: *inormi mole* pendebat inter scopulos.

> [37] Fluctibus e mediis mox belua surgit *enormis*
> [107] nituntur gradibus tantae fastigia *molis*

Hac humanis: incutiebat horrorem posteris.
Qui solitum (? insolitum): vasti gurgitis prospectabant in scropibus
 munstrum
irruentibus: *undique* cuntæ telluris accolis
 [178] hinc vallant proceres artant hinc *undique* plebes
 [140] conscendunt undasque pias per cuncta refundunt
 [151] Litora cuncta sonant, crebris furit ictibus aether

[210] *inorme:* intueri scropulum
 [37] Fluctibus e mediis mox belua surgit *enormis*

beluicinis: ambutare frameis pernas
ingentes: vehere cervicibus toles:
Ampla: ansportabant pondera
biternas: que trucidantes *securibus costas.*
 [109] Ardua tecta petunt validisque *securibus* actis
 [87] nititur et validis rimas infligere *costis*

[215] Improvisum *nuditatis* crito *teg[mine]* verticibus illico prospectant
 latrunculum
 [200] et nova calvities frontem nudarat amicam
 [161] illis deciduo spoliantur *tegmine* membra

Et hoc clariferum humana: enituit fabulamentum per genimina
edicta: que crevit inter soboles fama

TWO

Truths and Lies

A. "The Wish-Goat" ("Wunschbock")

Translated from "The Wish-Goat" (incipit "Tres iuuenes fratres, uno de patre creati"), in *Carmina sangallensia,* ed. Ernst Dümmler, MGH *Poetae Latini Aevi Carolini* 2 (Berlin: Weidmann, 1884), 474–75.

There were three young brothers, begotten by one father,
who was, as is reported, not very wealthy in property.
When he died, he left to his children one goat—
one single goat that the poor man could barely keep,

while he lived his wretched life. To be sure, he did not own 5
sheepfolds crowded with sheep and he had neither fat bulls
grazing on rush-filled fields nor randy kids
with the habit of running about through the green grass
with butting horns. All his hope lay in the single goat,
which was his whole joy—and a common source of food for them. 10
At the death of the father the sons take possession of this goat
and decide among themselves what should be done with it.
To be sure, each expected an equal share, since they were equal in birth,
and each demanded one of three parts for himself.
The eldest of the brothers, advising all of them, 15
said, "It is not worthwhile dividing such a goat,
which appears very handsome and very noble.
In the hope of preserving its offspring it is evidently more useful
if we agree that whichever of us
should prove more judicious in mind than the rest, 20
he would keep this goat safe and sound—and with reason intact."
Then all agreed upon what their brother had persuaded them,
and they enact a rule among themselves that whichever of them
should manage to wish for a goat larger than the rest
(so large that no larger one could be described by them), 25
he should at once have the goat as his share.
Then the first pronounces from his heart the following speech:
"O if only the Lord would give me now so great a goat
that, if throughout the whole world beneath the expanse of the sky
the valleys should be made level with the lofty mountains, 30
and of course heaps of salt should stand everywhere on top,
the flesh of one shoulder could not be salted by it
or even be touched by a mere sprinkling,
with the whole rest of the body surpassing this limb."
When this had been said, the second brother then responded: 35
"Present me, Christ, a goat with so large a body
that if a cord should be fastened together and join in a straight line
all the threads that have been spun since the beginning of time,
the smallest hoof of its foot could not be surrounded
even superficially, and the whole body would surpass it." 40
Then the smallest, sighing deeply, produces such words:
"O if now, God willing, I should have such a goat
that it would have so great a space between its two horns:
if . . . [letters missing or illegible in the manuscript] should fly from its
 nest at daybreak

[letters missing or illegible in the manuscript] and hope to return in
　　swift flight,　　　　　　　　　　　　　　　　　　　　　　　　45
it would lose its feathers in bitter . . . [letters missing or illegible in the
　　manuscript]
before it could attain the tip of the other horn."
They brought forth these words as they competed.
But whoever accounts himself wise,
let him decide which of them should be rightly considered the winner　50
and should keep the handsome goat as a lucky prize!

B. "Lantfrid and Cobbo" (*Carmina Cantabrigiensia* 6)

eprinted from *The Cambridge Songs (Carmina Cantabrigiensia)*, ed.
and trans. Jan M. Ziolkowski, Garland Library of Medieval Litera-
ture, vol. 66, ser. A (New York: Garland, 1994; repr., Tempe, AZ: Medieval
and Renaissance Texts and Studies, 1998), 22–27.

1a　Every sound of song comes about in one of three ways:
　　for either the sound consists in the harmony of strings
　　by strumming with the plectrum and hand,
　　since there are differences in tone according to
　　the various pitches of strings;
1b　or the blowing of wind instruments is rendered tuneful,
　　inasmuch as there are differences in the pipes,
　　and, making beautiful sounds as the bellows of the stomach work
　　and as the mouth is puffed out and blows,
　　they sound soothing to the soul;
2a　or in various ways the same sound is produced with the
　　melodious voice of many a throat by people, birds, and animals;
　　and thus sound is created by strumming, blowing, and singing.
2b　Let us celebrate in these modes the deeds of the dear ones
　　and friends, in whose honor this fine proem is inscribed
　　with the most noble title of Lantfrid and Cobbo.
3　Although one may read about many kinds of friendship,
　　there have been none so outstanding
　　as the friendship of these comrades,
　　who were so sharing
　　that neither of them
　　possessed anything solely his own,
　　neither treasure nor servants

nor any sort of furnishing;
whatever one of them wanted
would be granted by the other.
In character the two were coequal,
in no way ever in disagreement;
the two were as if one,
alike in all respects.

4 Long ago Cobbo, the first to speak,
said to his bosom friend, his brother,
"My service to the king here
has weighed upon me for a long time,
in that I, unmindful of my people,
have not gone
to visit brothers and kinsmen.
Therefore I shall return beyond the sea
whence I came here;
in coming to them there
I will do justice
to their affection."

5 "It makes me weary," said Lantfrid,
"of my own so dismal life
to pass my time without you here in these parts
that I will snatch up my wife and
go off with you, an exile with you
just as you have been with me for a long time,
repaying your love in kind."
And thus setting off,
they arrived at the seashore side by side.
Then Cobbo said to his comrade,
"I encourage you, brother, to go back;
let me return to see you.
Look, as life is your companion,
may you leave as brother to brother
one memento:

6 Surrender to me the wife
whom you have claimed
as yours alone,
so that I may freely enjoy her embrace."
Not hesitating one whit,
passing her hand to his, he said joyously,
"Enjoy her as it please you, brother,

so that it shall not be said that I seemed
to own anything separately."
When the ship was readied,
he takes her with him to sea.

7 Lantfrid, standing above the shore,
said, to the accompaniment of strings,
"Cobbo, brother, keep faith,
as you have done up to now,
for it is unseemly in pursuing a desire
to destroy the honor of a vow;
let a brother not become a dishonor to a brother."
And singing thus for a long time,
gazing after him,
no longer descrying him,
he dashed the psaltery on the cliff.

8 But Cobbo, not bearing
to see his brother crushed,
soon returns and soothes him:
"Here you have, my sweetest love,
what you gave, untouched
before the test of love.
Now there is nothing further to be tested;
I will abandon the journey I began."

C. "Modus Liebinc," or "The Song to the Liebo Tune" (*Carmina Cantabrigiensia* 14; ATU 1362 "The Snow-Child")

Reprinted from *Cambridge Songs,* ed. and trans. Ziolkowski, 62–69.

1a Listen,
all you people,
to an amusing story,
and hear how
a wife deceived a Swabian 5
and how he deceived her
in turn.

1b A humble Swabian,
a citizen of Constance

who was transporting rich freight
across the ocean in ships,
left 5
at home
an all too wanton wife.

2a Scarcely has he cleaved
the sea with gloomy oars
when look! suddenly
a storm arises
and the sea rages, 5
the winds battle with one another,
the billows surge,
and, after many seas,
the south wind deposits him,
a wanderer, 10
on a distant shore.

2b In the meantime
his wife is not idle at home;
mime players are there,
young men follow,
and, unmindful 5
of her exiled husband,
she receives them with joy.
Pregnant
on the very next night,
she bore an unrightful son 10
on the rightful day.

3a After two
years have passed,
the aforesaid exile
returns.
The unfaithful wife 5
runs to meet him,
dragging with her
a little boy.
After they have given kisses,
the husband says to her, 10
"Tell me from whom
you have this child,
or else you will suffer
the utmost."

3b But she,
 fearing her husband,
 applies deceit
 to everything.
 At last she says, "My— 5
 my husband,
 once,
 stricken with thirst
 in the Alps,
 I quenched my thirst with snow. 10
 So, pregnant from that,
 alas, I gave birth
 to this son
 in a ruinous childbirth."

4a Five years or more
 passed after this,
 and the wandering merchant
 repairs his oars,
 refits the shattered ship, 5
 fastens the sails,
 and takes
 the snow-child with him.

4b Once he has traversed the sea,
 he puts the child up for sale
 and, handing him over to a trader
 for hard cash,
 receives one hundred pounds; 5
 after selling
 the lad
 he returns a rich man.

5a And upon entering his home
 he says to his wife,
 "Give solace, dear wife,
 give solace:
 I lost your child, 5
 whom not even you yourself
 loved more
 than I.

5b A storm arose
 and a raging wind drove us,
 too tired to resist,

onto sandy shoals;
and the sun scorched us all 5
terribly,
and that child of yours
melted."

6 Thus the treacherous
Swabian tricked
the wife;
thus fraud overcame fraud:
for the child whom snow engendered 5
quite rightly melted
under the sun.

D. "Modus florum," or "The Song to the Flowers Tune" (*Carmina Cantabrigiensia* 15; ATU 852 "Lying Contest")

eprinted from *Cambridge Songs,* ed. and trans. Ziolkowski, 68–71.

1 The lying ballad that I sing,
I will give (highly recommended) to little boys,
so that they may bring great laughter
to listeners through lying little measures of song.

2a To a certain king was born
a noble and comely daughter,
whom he offered to suitors to be wooed
under terms of this sort:

2b "If anyone experienced in lying
should apply himself to deception
so well that he is called a deceiver
by the emperor's own mouth, that man may marry the daughter."

3a Having heard this, a Swabian
began without delay,
"When I went alone to hunt
with the weapons I had picked up,
among the wild animals a little hare met its death 5
after having been struck by my spear.
Soon, after gutting it,
I severed the head, ripping it off along with the hide.

3b And as I was lifting the severed head
with my hand,
a hundred measures of honey
spilled out from the wounded ear;
and when I touched the other ear, 5
it spilled out just as many measures of peas.
I bound them inside the skin and,
while carving the hare itself,
I grasped a royal charter hidden
at the very base of the tail: 10
4 It confirms that you are my servant."
"The charter lies," the king shouts, "and so do you!"
Thus, having deluded the king, by a deceitful trick
the Swabian became the king's son-in-law.

E. "The False Prophet and Archbishop Heriger of Mainz: Otherworldly Voyages to Hell and Heaven, This-Worldly Punishment" (*Carmina Cantabrigiensia* 24)

eprinted from *Cambridge Songs,* ed. and trans. Ziolkowski, 88–91.

1 Heriger, archbishop of the city Mainz,
saw a certain prophet
who said that he had been carried off to hell.
2 As he reported many details about it,
he added that all hell
was encircled everywhere by thick woods.
3 Laughing, Heriger responded to him,
"I don't want to send my swineherd there
with scrawny pigs to pasture!"
4 The false man said, "I was conveyed
to the temple of heaven and I saw Christ
happily sitting and eating.
5 John the Baptist was wine-steward
and presented goblets of the finest wine
to all the invited saints."
6 Heriger said, "Christ acted wisely
in appointing John the wine-steward,
since he never drank wine."

7 [lacuna of one strophe conjectured]
8 "You are proven a liar, when you say
 that Peter is the head cook there,
 since he is the doorkeeper of highest heaven.
9 In what esteem did the god of heaven
 hold you there? Where did you sit?
 I want you to tell what you ate."
10 The man responded, "In a corner;
 I stole a piece of lung from the cooks.
 I ate it and left."
11 Heriger ordered him to be bound with thongs
 to a stake and beaten with switches,
 rebuking him with a stern speech,
12 "If Christ should invite you
 to take food with him at his mealtime,
 take care: Thou shalt not steal!"

F. "The Priest in the Pit" (*Carmina Cantabrigiensia* 35)

Reprinted from *Cambridge Songs*, ed. and trans. Ziolkowski, 110–13.
Compare AT 31.

1 Let those who have play and facetious song in their hearts
 hearken to this amusing story. It is truth, not fiction.
2 A country priest, already in his declining years,
 was fond of sheep; for this is the custom among country folk.
3 Every expedient to this liking of his was available, except that
 a little forest, breeding ground of wolves, lay quite nearby.
4 Wolves diminish the number and, destroying the principle of kind,
 produce odd numbers from even and even from odd.
5 The priest, lamenting that his flock was being diminished, sought
 revenge through craft, because he had no faith in his strength.
6 He digs a very large ditch, places a little lamb within, and, so that
 it would not be visible to enemies, covers it over with branches.
7 Human beings have been granted no greater advantage than cunning.
 A wolf, prowling by night, falls in, taken captive by its hope of prey.
8 In the morning the priest runs up and rejoices to have triumphed thus.
 He threatens the eye of the wolf within by holding out a rod.
9 "Now," he said, "worst of beasts, I will pay back what is owed you:
 either this staff will be broken or that eye will burst."

10 Having said this, he attacked at once, but the deed failed to match the
words; for the wolf, preserving its eye, grips the staff in its teeth.

11 But that wretched old man, as it dragged him more firmly,
fell in when the bank gave way, and ended up the wolf's companion.

12 Here stands the wolf, there the priest; they fear, but unequally,
for, as I judge in good faith, the wolf stood in a safer position.

13 The priest mutters to himself and mouths the seven penitential
psalms, but repeats particularly often, "Have mercy on me, God."

14 "This bit of misfortune comes to me," he said, "through the prayers of
people, whose souls I have neglected, whose offerings I have eaten."

15 For the benefit of the deceased he chants, "I will be pleasing to the
lord," and for the prayers of the living he chants the whole psalter.

16 After the psalter was finished, the priest's fear
and the wolf's guile provide a common advantage.

17 For when the bowing priest was finishing the paternoster
and was crying to the lord, "But deliver us from evil,"

18 the wolf leaps upon his back and with a bound runs off scot-free;
and it used as a ladder the man by whose craft it had been caught.

19 At this the priest chants in great joy, "Praise ye the lord!"
and promised that from then on he would pray for the people.

20 Then he is looked for by neighbors and, when found, extricated;
but never afterward did he pray more devoutly or faithfully.

G. "Little John" (*Carmina Cantabrigiensia* 42)

Reprinted from *Cambridge Songs*, ed. and trans. Ziolkowski, 118–21.

1 In the deeds of the early fathers I read a certain amusing story,
fit nonetheless as an example, that I will tell you in rhythmic poem.

2 Abba John (small in stature, but not in virtues)
spoke thus to a taller companion who was with him in the wilderness:

3 "I wish to live as carefree as an angel,
not to need clothing or food that is produced by the toil of hands."

4 The taller replied, "I warn you not to be hasty, brother, in undertaking
what afterward it might be better for you not to have begun."

5 But the shorter said, "Who does not battle neither falls nor triumphs,"
and naked he goes into the inner wilderness.

6 For seven days he survives there, barely, by feeding on grasses;
and on the eighth hunger bids him return to his comrade.

7 The friend is sitting safe in the little cell, the door closed, for it is late,
 when the shorter calls out in a weak voice, "Brother, open up.
8 John, needing assistance, stands at the familiar doors.
 Let your mercy not spurn one who has been brought back by want."
9 From within the other responds, "John has become an angel
 and marvels at the poles of heaven. He cares no more for mortals."
10 John keeps watch outside and endures a bad night
 and carries out this involuntary penance.
11 At daybreak he is admitted and is rebuked with words enough;
 but intent upon crusts of bread he endures everything patiently.
12 Refreshed, he thanks the lord and his companion.
 Then he tries with weakened arms to move a hoe.
13 Punished by distress for undue fickleness,
 since he could not be an angel, he learned to be a good man.

THREE

One-Ox: The Rich and the Poor Farmer (ATU 1535)

A. *One-Ox* (*Unibos*)

Reprinted from Jan M. Ziolkowski, "A Medieval 'Little Claus and Big Claus': A Fabliau from Before Fabliaux?" in *The World and Its Rival: Essays on Literary Imagination in Honor of Per Nykrog,* ed. Kathryn Karczewska and Tom Conley, 1–37 (Amsterdam: Rodopi, 1999).

People's eyes are not satisfied 1
by seeing the realities of the world;
their ears are
fond of novelties.
At the table of a great prince 2
is told the account of One-Ox;
it is presented as a fabliau
in playful words.
Banquets come about through foods, 3
but literary compositions through words;
in a performance of characters
let us sing of One-Ox.

A son of ridiculous sons, 4
he is a peasant from peasant stock.
Nature made him a man
but fortune a *wunderkind.*
Through ill-fated commerce 5
the poor man bought oxen;
following the model of a farmer,
he toils to break the soil.
By a frightful turn of events 6
he never leads two oxen,
nor does he prick two at the same time with a goad,
nor does he put two under one yoke.
In vain he strives in his poverty 7
to conquer fortune;
owing to the harsh thread of the Fates
he loses oxen regularly.
When the rest have been skinned, 8
he becomes the follower of one ox.
He is mocked by the neighbors;
the wretch is called "One-Ox."
Harsh destiny snatches away the last 9
of the lowing oxen;
now the property of the wretch becomes even less
than the poverty of his nickname.
With his name rendered void, 10
with his cattle stall emptied,
he undertakes to sell the hide,
once the corpse has been laid bare.
Having taken the wrap of the ox, 11
he leaves the body at the crossroads;
he places it, the hope of his life,
on the saddle of his beast of burden.
He brings the hide[6] of the dead ox 12
to the market of a town across the border;
he does not dawdle en route
as he hastens to the fair.
And as he enters the market, 13
he puts the skin on sale,
which he thinks worth a great price,
just like a handsome cloak.
Tradesmen measure 14

the extent of the skin
in fixed measures of feet,
according to the practices of shoemakers.
No one helps One-Ox; 15
he alone holds the hide to be great;
he gives away the dirty tunic of the ox
for eight pennies.
After making the trade 16
he mounts his mare;
he is swollen, with distended belly,
as he turns his steps backward.
Having a presage of silver, 17
he enters a frondy grove
where,[7] as he purges the vessel of his belly,
he gets a money-filled reward.
As he strives to wipe his backside, 18
he hurries to tear off grass;
but in plucking grass he finds
that which greedy folk love.
Soon he stumbles upon three hidden 19
pint measures of coins,
which he places in a drooping little sack
that is soon made swollen.
With all his might the man swiftly places 20
upon the beast of burden
the riches found by chance;
he goes back to his ancestral home.[8]
Having returned he unbinds the sack. 21
The fool calls a child
whom he sends off for the most accurate
pint measure of the provost.
The boy seeks the measure, 22
the provost the cause of the business;
the boy, all too simple, reveals
the matter of the silver.
The provost grants the vessel, 23
giving it swiftly to the child;
he is astounded that One-Ox, the poorest,
has become the richest.
He goes behind the back of the boy 24
who is carrying the wheat scale;

he sees the silvery mass
as he inspects the smoky house.
Having seen the mountains of coins, 25
he says, clapping together his hands:
"The joy of this pauper
comes from theft, not trade.
There is not in the treasure horde of emperors 26
or in the coffer of bishops
so much value of silver
as this hovel conceals."
Irked, he [One-Ox] replies 27
to the most envious provost:
"This does not come from theft by night,
but from the trade of a skin.
Beyond the boundary of this realm 28
a regular market takes place;
when the tunic of an ox is turned over,
an abundance of silver smiles.
There is no marketing 29
like that of an ox hide;
if you want to take an example
from me, a poor man, follow it!"
After these words the officials— 30
the mayor of the village, provost,
and celebrated priest of the church—
come together in a public crossroads.
Astonished, the administrator 31
reports to his companions
the news of the recent deal,
the profit from a single hide.
Then, overjoyed, the provost, 32
packed full of such great reports,
heaves portentous sighs,
saying such words with pomp:
"I will tell you a miracle, 33
reveal a wonder,
disclose a most profitable
tip that must be kept secret.
If you wish to be rich 34
and fortunate, companions,
do the things that I am going to do;

consider now carefully the following:
Through the greatest deal 35
of deals, all unrewarding fortune
will depart
from our tabernacles.
There is a blessing, 36
which the power of God has sent, in trading
in the skins of calves,
in the hides of young heifers.
This poor One-Ox of ours 37
has many silver coins
that he measures not by counting
but in an ironclad pint measure.
He has had sudden good fortune 38
from the price of one hide,
which he sold recently
with a most favorable outcome.
There is no need for us 39
to plow any longer in rainstorms,
if you agree that in one day
a wealthy man can be made out of a pauper.
But let the business that I relate 40
be concealed for three days;
if the money changers should know,
they would never coin silver.
A demonstration of this business opportunity 41
has been given;
let us deliberate
about what we should have in mind."
Sighing at these words the priest 42
responds first, energetically,
full of new joy,
more than he can show:
"If the noble wife whom I married 43
could be changed into an ox,
in the good hope of such great profit
she would soon lose her little hide."
Soon the mayor of the village, as the third, 44
whose possessiveness has no bounds,
belched forth wonderful schemes
that he devised as a result of the tale:

"I swear by this staff, 45
by this body, and by this spirit
that my oxen will not chew the cud
at daybreak in the stable!"
They compete in turn 46
to join their right hands in the secret pact
that they should secretly brain their oxen
and flay them after slaying them.
Confirmed in stupidity, 47
they progress to madness;
they slaughter the oxen savagely
and flay them violently.
They hang the meats on beams; 48
they heap the hides in carts;
in the quiet of nighttime
they head to market, like renegades.
In their arrogance, 49
filled with an idle dream,
they place the wagons carrying the hides
at the edge of the market.
In silence they shoot looks 50
along the routes of the marketplace;
they expect to be accosted[9]
entreatingly by a crowd.
People come, people go; 51
no one pays attention out of concern;
there is not one who seeks eagerly
a deal involving a hide.
After a passage of time 52
the mayor, holding a goad,
shouts with hoarse throat,
"Who wishes to buy these skins?"
Shabby shoemakers come near 53
who have seven shillings
and who want together to buy
one designated hide.
A shoemaker says, "How much will I pay 54
for this ox hide?"
At once the mayor replies,
"Pay three pounds immediately!"
The shoemaker says, "Are you drunk?" 55

The mayor says, "Am I a fool?
I will not drop even a penny
from the three pounds."
Then the brush-bearing shoemaker says, 56
"Do you speak in jest?"
In reply the mayor, in a dream state,
shouts resolutely, "Three pounds!"
In the noisy market amazement 57
spreads at once among the populace;
people are there to look on,
with their merchandise left behind.
Aroused by anger the priest 58
says harshly to the mayor,
"Stupid, you don't know how to sell
what you are exhibiting here publicly!
By this stake I decree 59
that my hide is worth three pounds.
Undo your purse, shoemaker;
you have heard the sum fixed!"
"What rate of exchange 60
does the mind of this priest offer?"
the shoemaker replies, "There is not
a more foolish seller on earth!
Let these three, who think that the skins 61
of oxen are the greatest of riches,
tell here and now
from which region they come.
They inflate a hide worth ten pennies 62
to a great price:
go barefoot,
inhabitants of this kind of country!"
Each party exchanges reproaches 63
in turn; in response to the abuse
the assembly of shoemakers
increases, with angered minds.
They are led off by bailiffs, 64
presented to judges,
handed over to executioners,
punished according to the laws.
As bail they turn over 65
the collection of hides

that they put out in the market
on the advice of One-Ox.
They pay off their legal obligations, 66
they return to their own property
with depleted purses
in empty carts.
The three, stripped of money, 67
but armed with grief,
endeavor to kill
One-Ox at high noon.
Under the canopy of heaven 68
such things have never been heard
as One-Ox perpetrated
to calm the great fools.
The sly man renders them meek 69
when he sees the three of them angry;
through pretenses, wise words
answer mad ones.[10]
When, trembling, he thinks he will die, 70
he contrives an opportunity,[11]
painting on his wife the appearance of death,
stained[12] with swine's blood.
By cunning, the wife 71
of a cunning man lies stretched out in the hut,
as if she were truly dead,
slain by her husband's right hand.
The woman's body 72
appears to be a corpse foul with blood;
in the face of the crime, the cruel
men begin to calm down.
Those who had come to slay 73
compete to lament the murdered woman,
rebuking One-Ox
while weeping for his slaughtered spouse.
In unison they say fiercely, 74
"Alas, senseless fellow,
for what reason did you commit
the direst misdeeds?
Savage creator of confusion, 75
you led us wickedly astray;
as soon as we experienced the market,

we deliberated your death.
Most foolish of men, you have gained 76
a great loss on account of your wife:
it is not a minor sin
to have extinguished the life of one's wife."
One-Ox speaks without care, 77
leading the three men even more astray:
"The outrage I committed
with a sword can be healed.
If you make peace with me, 78
if you overcome the anger in your hearts,
you will soon see alive
the woman whom you perceive as killed."
"So be it, so be it," say cheerfully 79
the men, led astray together,
"We dispel from our breasts
the plagues of enmity."
When One-Ox hears his three opponents 80
speaking thus,
he runs to a wooden chest
and takes out a willow bugle.
He circles the cadaver of his wife 81
as the misguided witnesses watch;
he circles twice, sounds the bugle often,
and predicts the time of resurrection.
In the third circling, 82
as if by magic power,
just when he says the name of his wife,
he revives her from her repose.
Arising abruptly, the wife 83
stands present, disfigured in her appearance;
she is ordered by One-Ox
to cleanse herself of the blood.
Immediately, upon having her face washed 84
and being a little better clothed
she appears more attractive,
more beautiful with her countenance cleansed.
Misled by One-Ox, 85
they marvel at the beauty
of the revived woman;
astounded, they applaud her.[13]

They say with hushed voices: 86
"Never have we seen so beautiful
the form of this woman,
who has been resurrected on this day.
Before death she was ugly; 87
she has returned from death beautiful.
Blessed is the death that beautifies,
that embellishes the unsightly!
How blessed the sound of the bugle, 88
by which old women are rejuvenated!
On account of advanced years our wives
are becoming decrepit.
If divine grace should honor 89
us with this bugle,
we would slay our wives,
detestable as they are for their wrinkles.
Let us entreat One-Ox now[14] 90
to lend to us in turn
or to sell this bugle
that removes the taint of ugliness.
Let us try to buy the trumpet 91
so that we can kill our wives
and at one and the same time
make them adorned with beauty.
When the bugle resounds, 92
harsh death will be put to flight,
just as we have experienced in this woman
whom we saw lifeless.
With our wives brought back to life 93
we will celebrate second weddings;
let us offer money
so that he will sell us the bugle."
By offering a great gift, 94
they manage to buy the trumpet;
after buying the bugle,
they turn to madness.
The priest says to the other two: 95
"I pray, I beg solemnly
that I first may kill
the wife most dear to me.
Look, let the most pleasing bugle of life 96

be made available to me.
I will reduce the old age of Mrs. Priest
by cutting her throat.
After me he will be the second to take 97
the most beneficial bugle
who first will slay his wife
like a heifer."
They agree to the requests 98
of the priest, whom they love,
that he should slay, that he should cut
her throat, that he should revive her when slain.
Armed with madness, 99
the priest goes with the bugle;
holding fast her womanly hair,
he gives kisses to her as she is soon to die.
The priest shows the knife; 100
the woman says, laughing,
"What do you intend to do, dear?
Don't act harshly!"
The death-dealing priest says, 101
"I will slit your throat sweetly;
at the sound of the bugle
you will arise in a youthful body."
The woman cries only "Woe!" 102
She lies, struck down, dead.
The stupid head of the household
cries out: "Thank God!"
He sets the bugle to his mouth, 103
blows on it presumptuously;
as he circles three times the woman lying there,
he rebukes her with indecent words:
"O cunning pretender, 104
rise, deceitful she-ape,
just like a wanton she-ass,
raise your head on account of the bugle!"
Having heard these shouts, 105
the provost, out of his mind,
hastens to kill his woman,
putting his hope in the life-bringing bugle.
After the homicide 106
he comes to the priest, a widower now,

to lend him the bugle
to awake the provost's wife.
Having at last received the bugle 107
he quizzes the priest about his
wife, if from being a dead woman
she arose a fresh young thing.
To him as he quizzes is given the reply: 108
"She will not be seen by you
until she goes to the threshold of the church
with your wife."
The provost, a wife-killer, 109
bereft of his mind's senses,
carries to his own home
the bugle of beguilement.
Never did the priest bugle 110
higher or lower
with sad lowings of the trumpet
than did the idiotic provost.
Just as much as the hollowness of the trumpet 111
helps, so much does the blowing of it;
just as the priest's wife came back to life,
so the provost's wife was resurrected.
The mayor of the village is no lesser 112
in crime, albeit later:
he squanders the life of his spouse;
he bugles but he does not resurrect.
Three biers, three dead women 113
are presented to the church
in a mournful spectacle
when sad daybreak has arrived.
Thanks to the madness of their husbands 114
the corpses are buried;
three wives are laid away
to the accompaniment of lamenting dirges.
Departing from the burial mounds 115
the three, sighing deeply,
whisper to each other in turn:
"Let's kill One-Ox,
who took away our treasures 116
and betrayed us with his words,
when he said that old women

grow young at the lowing of the bugle.
Let the creator of such great damage 117
be destroyed by us:
Let bitter death assault
his ignoble brow!"
Stirred by passions of the mind, 118
they run immediately to arms,
ready to slay most harshly
the artificer of cunning.
The cunning of One-Ox, 119
filled with many stratagems,
overcame the hotheaded boasting
of the three men.
One-Ox, previously impoverished, 120
runs to his silver coins,
takes a mass of small change,
and deceives his armed enemies.
He drags the mare from the stable, 121
raises its tail more than is customary,
and endeavors to implant the change
in its natural opening.
The tether of the mare is fixed 122
in the middle of the hovel;
soon he lays out a white linen
cloth for the beast of burden.
The three opponents are present 123
at the doors of the hovel;
as they threaten One-Ox,
they see the marvelous state of affairs.
The three stand on the threshold of the house, 124
wanting to kill One-Ox,
but they are unable,
as they are astounded at the new deed.
Observing the silvery 125
activity of One-Ox,
who as he rubs the mare's flanks
induces a discharge of change,
they cry out, "What is this, One-Ox? 126
It gives rise in us to a state of marvel
that an animal gives birth openly
to silver coins for you!"

One-Ox replies cautiously, 127
"Do you see these silver coins?
The belly of this mare pours forth
change instead of base dung.
Every single night the mare 128
shoots out such money:
Ops, queen of money,
resides in the opening of the anus."
Upon seeing such things 129
and hearing these words,
the foes instantly cast away anger
and speak thus to One-Ox:
"If you wish to enjoy good fortune, 130
sell us this animal;
the three of us will put aside hate
if we buy this swollen animal."
One-Ox, clad in wiles, 131
says this to the three comrades:
"It is not easy to give away
this begetter of money.
Beneath the hide of the beast 132
lurks a coffer of joy;
this is not a worthless animal
that produces such great gifts."
"If your soul wants to rejoice 133
in your property,"
they say, "dearest one,
don't delay selling this!"
Soon crafty One-Ox 134
says to the three mindless men,
"I will sell the noble beast of burden,
but not for a small fee.
You have seen what it produced; 135
you know what it rained forth here;
if you wish to own the hiding-place
of coins, pay the price.
But to be well-disposed, 136
pay fifteen pounds!
In a short time it will pay back
many more pounds in place of dung."
When these three pay off fifteen 137

pounds to One-Ox,
they lead the mare by the reins,
guarding it greedily.
In haste the priest says, 138
"Hear me, as is fitting:
I wish to lead the animal
to the stable of my house;
I, who am the first in church, 139
should be the first to have custody,
at daybreak I will regain
the money that I have given.
Let the first night be the priest's, 140
let the second be the provost's,
let the third night be the mayor's,
according to the scales of equity."
"Let it be done," says the provost. 141
"So be it," says the mayor, third.
"This is our pact,
in meek forbearance."
The priest looks after the mare, 142
gives barley rapidly;
in the watches of the night
he lends his ears to the mare.
Yet when day has broken, 143
the priest drags the shared animal
from the manger
so that it may set down money.
That mare, thinking that it is being led off 144
to the plow (well known to it),
releases from under its tail, as it is wont to do,
the foulest droppings.
When the splattering of dung 145
is heard by the priest,
he thinks that change is issuing
from the belly of the brute animal.
The priest shouts, "Boys, 146
servants, leave!
I alone will regain
the money that I gave."
When the priest makes an examination 147
amid the stinking ordure,

he finds one coin of the lowest denomination
which he collects in haste.

The beast, when once it had been 148
 a filly six months old,
received a wound on a stump
at the threshold of its soft young anus.

There the tiny coin took hold 149
and remained hidden in the scar,
when the mare gave back the change
that One-Ox had inserted secretly.

That groove of the deep wound 150
profited the finder,
when, leaning over, he poked around
the money—made of barley.

There is a popular proverb 151
"There is not an evil that does not bring profit."
The injury of the wounded anus
gives joys to the priest.

Out of eagerness the provost 152
heads to the house of the priest
in the morning, seeking to obtain
the belcher of money.

"Hand over the beast, priest! 153
From one night
you will remain rich for all time
with a multitude of coins."

"I will surrender the mare, provost," 154
said the priest lukewarmly.
"You compel me today, somewhat
early, to give back the mare.

At the cockcrow of dawn 155
poorly cooked coins,
fresh and made of barley,
came forth from the belly."

The provost leads away the mare 156
with great display of might,
but nonetheless he acquires the same
as the priest, apart from the tiny coin.

On the third night the mayor 157
shuts up in his house the beast,
only to find at dawn

what was reeking in a corner.
The shared mare ate 158
the fodder of barley,
which created stench-bringing
dung in the hours of the nights.
What One-Ox is going to do 159
against his angry antagonists,
he ponders upon his little bed
with many a sigh.
After the murk of night 160
they come together in a whirlwind,
the three in an ironclad battle line,
approaching One-Ox.
The three men shout together, 161
"Come out, criminal con artist!
You will be slaughtered in the flesh,
slain cruelly."
He who is sought beneath the straw stalks 162
responds to his opponents,
"I am right here, your One-Ox;
I call you my lords.
If you wish to kill 163
the man whom you seek most harshly,
I will relate to you at once
how I wish to perish.
There are many manners of death; 164
all lead to one outcome.
To satisfy you,
I will elect at once a way of death.
Sweetest lords, you have never experienced, 165
and may you not experience,
what manner of death may be most bitter
or sad in the world.
Yet I will tell you peaceably 166
in what fashion you can
destroy me on this day
or tomorrow, in the future.
Bind me with ropes 167
or with twisted cords,
put me in a keg
and shut it when I have been put in it.

Let the barrel be bound fast 168
with bands by skilled coopers;
roll the barrel with my body
to the great sea.
Sink me with the barrel, 169
send me into the deep;
in this way destroy me,
thus may I perish, with myself passing judgment."
"Let it be done to you," the three say, 170
"Our minds desire this,
that you should perish by such a death,
that you should thus depart from us."
They bind with thongs One-Ox, 171
who is detested on earth,
and after the barrel is closed
he is set on the brink of the sea.
Thus enclosed One-Ox says, 172
leading the three men still more astray:
"I confess here today,
I have been shut up most justly.
I have been subjected 173
to the death penalty of a last judgment;
now lay aside hate,
because it is my final day.
Wretch that I am, I cannot raise my hands 174
in this prison;
alas, my arms hurt my loins
on account of the cursed bonds.
But by the parting gift of your pity—[15] 175
by the airhole in the barrel—
I am not producing a lie,
I am proclaiming an act of charity.[16]
There are twelve coins 176
in the bottom of my purse;
drink them, most pious men,
in honor of highest God!"
The charitable priest 177
says in worldly fashion,[17]
"So long as we drink sweetly,
sleep sweetly in the barrel!"
The three hasten to the cups, 178

to drink the last prayers;
they sit, talk too much,
drink the clearest wine.
There goes a swineherd 179
with his loud[18] piggish herds of grunters;
he passes by, crossing the way
with a quiver on his back.
When One-Ox hears the pigs 180
rub the bands of the barrel,
he cries out, "Ah, my opponents
are still not drunk!"
The swineherd shudders at the 181
unknown sound of One-Ox;
he touches the oaken vessel with his staff,
saying to the wretch enclosed within,
"For what crime have you been shut 182
in the keg, desperado?"
One-Ox replies readily,
"I do not want the greatest honors.
The citizens of this country 183
accost me daily,
wishing to appoint me
provost in charge.
Never will I[19] be provost 184
as long as I live;
for what I have is sufficient;
I reject the honors of the realm."
The greedy swineherd says, 185
"The greatest honor befits me;
I, provost in your stead,
will be made most wealthy.
By fate I have been impelled, 186
wretch, to touch your keg
with this staff of mine.
Strive to put me in the barrel!"
The swineherd knocks off the bands; 187
One-Ox is very happy;
the wooden vessel is opened;
an exchange of fortune occurs.
He is cast out, untied, 188
hastily sent off;

he who had lain beneath the bands
becomes free of hard bonds.
The swineherd enters the hollow 189
vessel, adjusting his own body
as if he felt it a bed
made of flowers.
Savagely One-Ox blocks up the vessel, 190
puts back the bands tightly,
and passes through roadless regions,
leading the very well-fattened pigs.
To the drinkers who have returned 191
from their drinking,
the swineherd dares to say,
as the three roll the barrel into the sea:
"I will become, yes, I will become provost 192
according to your wishes,
so that I, who have already been prevailed upon by you,
may not be tossed about by the waves of the sea."[20]
Full of wine, the provost 193
in indignation
says[21] to the simpleminded swineherd,
"These words are not sweet to me.
Strive to roll the barrel, 194
O comrades! Most surely
this most wicked One-Ox
becomes provost—of the waves."
The keg is submerged in the salty 195
sea and is dashed;
the swineherd, alas, is destroyed,
forgotten by everyone.
The three peers, rich in idiocy, 196
believe that they have
performed the very last rites
of One-Ox.
Yet on the third day after these events, 197
on a solemn holiday,
One-Ox returns to visit
his idiotic masters.[22]
He goes through the village crossroads, 198
holding in his right hand a staff,
leading before him

a host of pigs.
Foresighted, he bugles with a prolonged sound, 199
whistles in the manner of a swineherd,
calls together the red ones with the dark,
puts a fright into the ones causing harm with their teeth.
Those who had seen One-Ox 200
said that he was like the one
about whom the rumor had flown
that he had already died.
It is announced to the provost, 201
the mayor, and the priest,
that One-Ox who had been sunk in the sea
had come back to life.
Those three arise befuddled, 202
believing the rumor to be a nightmare,
shaking their benches
with their knees and hams.
They see the form of One-Ox, 203
leading a herd of pigs,
but they do not think that he exists;
they thought they had killed him.
They recognize One-Ox, 204
see him rich in swine,
ask who gave
or sold so many pigs.
He responds in miraculous fashion: 205
"The plunging into the sea:
by the plunge
I went to a most blessed realm.
Never would I have gone away from there 206
if I had not loved my wife,
whom you saw arise
at the sound of the true trumpet.
It was not the fault of the bugle 207
but of the person bugling most badly
if all your wives
now snore beneath the dust.
Alas, why did you not cast me 208
in my boyhood into the places
from which I return blessed
and come back wiser?

Out of hate you cast me 209
into a place of grace,
where there are herds of pigs
countable by no one."
In wonder 210
the provost says first,
"Highest hope of hams advises
us to try the seas.
Whoever will be more foolish than me 211
will be evident," he says, quite foolishly.[23]
They seek out the waves of the sea;
One-Ox goes behind them.
The tides of the sea resound; 212
they think that pigs are grunting;
they ask of One-Ox
where the paths to the pigs are.
But One-Ox in speaking 213
points toward the worst of dangers:
"Where the shore is steeper,
where the sea is deeper,
hasten there swiftly; 214
without fear sink yourselves!
There are bigger pigs in the water
than there are on dry land."
At the advice of One-Ox 215
the three consign themselves to the precipices
in fatal frenzy,
dying foolishly from the leap.
This tale shows 216
for ever and ever that
the sly counsels of an enemy
must not be believed.

B. *The Story of the Peasant Campriano*
(*Storia di Campriano contadino*)

Translated from the anonymous fifteenth-century Italian *Storia di Campriano contadino,* ed. Albino Zenatti (Bologna: Presso Gaetano Romagnoli, 1884), 3–29 (on the basis of a 1521 printing).

[1] To bring amusement to each and every listener, I wish to relate to you a tale [*novella*] in rhyme about the enterprise of a laborer, who had only a she-ass. If you listen to the teller, I believe that maybe it will seem attractive to you, and if the Holy Spirit aids me, I flatter myself that I will make you laugh by my singing.

[2] If it was true, it was a strange matter. I have put it into rhymes, because the topic of the peasant is an attractive one that people have sung. My discerning listener, he was from Gello. By name he was known as Campriano, and, as I have said, he had an ass and six daughters, his wife was pregnant, and his house had been shaken free of every asset.

[3] He said to himself, "What am I supposed to do? O cruel Fortune, I am just a pauper. I have six daughters here to marry off without having any asset under my roof, and I have a wife who is expecting a child, and I have nothing other than this donkey and five lire that my landlord wants. So how are my daughters to manage?

[4] Let it happen as it will. I have decided to see if I can make a gain. I intend to go to the market with my donkey; perhaps I can make some deal. The five lire that I have reserved for the innkeeper, I am going to stuff them into the body of the donkey." No sooner had he thought this than he did it: he stuffed them into the body of the donkey, up the anus.

[5] Then he placed himself behind that beast, which had all the money in its hole. So that Fortune would not give him trouble, he said to himself, "It brings sorrow upon the greedy!" and other modest words. Whoever needs to learn, let him learn from Campriano who took a risk and trusted fortune. Now you will hear what happened to him.

[6] So, going along the road, he came across some merchants of a town. He stopped to speak with them, and in talking said such words: "I have gone from home with this ass to sell it, if I can, this month; it has shit so much copper money and silver that it has become a nuisance to me!"

[7] The merchants mocked what Campriano was saying, and the one and the other laughed, wondering if he was out of his mind. In the meantime the ass was gathering the goods to set them on the ground and, without embarrassment and too much discomfort, it shit the coins that it had in its body.

[8] The merchants said to the peasant, "Pick up the coins that it produced!" Campriano replied to them, "O woe is me, wretch that I am, I am exhausted from picking up so much. I have my house and big vat full of it! I would like to sell the ass or to make a deal with it. My wife and daughters are so tired of it that no one wants it in the house anymore.

[9] The merchants then spoke in each other's ears, they wanted to buy it; and the two of them happily agreed to be willing to give whatever he re-

quested for it. Then they spoke to Campriano: "How much is this ass going to cost us?" Campriano said, "Fifty ducats, which are gained in three days of shitting."

[10] This seemed excessive to the merchants. They said to him, "Does it have any flaw?" "You will see it for yourselves: I will have it gallop, I will show you its mouth to your satisfaction. You will see that it is not blind or lame, that it is worth quite definitely more than a hundred ducats. If I did not have a house full of coins, I would not give it to you, even if you gave me Siena."

[11] "I don't want to drag out matters more in talking," said one of the merchants at this point. "Come on, we want to count out the money for you." And then in fact they gave him the money. When this one saw the counting, he said to himself, "Which of us is crazier?" He took the coins and left them in peace, and turned back toward his home.

[12] When he reached his wife, he said: "We need to use all our brains, otherwise we will suffer injury and shame. Here it is: I sold the donkey to some merchants by lying. I believe that soon they will return it, but if we want to get out of such danger, you be attentive to what I advise you.

[13] Tomorrow make sure to get up early, and kill a couple of good capons, and place them, one roasted and one boiled, in one pot, so that they may be comfortable.²⁴ And be diligent about it. When I knock, take care that the pot is cooked, because I want to give dinner to those dickheads. And when I am at the door, put it in the middle of the house, so that it seems as if it cooked in the shade on its own.

[14] I want to see if I could sell the pot too to these merchants. If not, may it be in good time! I will return to them all the money, and at least I will be rid of this worry. We will do our best, and bear the hardship together. Be clever, if you want us to trick them. Have them come, if they come, to the field."

[15] Now let us return to those two fatheaded fools of merchants, who have made their way home with the ass. Both the idiots reached home and right away they requested two white sheets; those simpletons swaddled the beast and then they went to bed with their wives until the break of the following day.

[16] The merchants, having arisen in the morning to see the activity of the donkey, carried a sack into the stall, thinking to fill it to their pleasure. It seemed that they had given it a laxative, so full in fact were the sheets. As they unwrapped it, they smelled the odor—think of what, discerning listener!

[17] One could see the green essences of the grass upon which it had grazed that evening, in some places a black substance mixed up with a hundred thousand disgusting colors. Having seen what there was to see, their

hearts were inflamed with anger and rage, and they said: "That rogue tricked us, but he will pay for the sin by death!

[18] I want us to go to his house to attack him and to put him to death at our own hands. Before we go out his door, we will make him give us our money. I know that he will never be able to trick us again, so let us leave now without other companions." They set off to find Campriano, to give him death by their own hands.

[19] Campriano went off to the field, with his spade, hoe, and large, two-pronged hoe. He had two rabbits, one of which he carried with him wrapped up in his hood and the other he left to remain at home; for he had thought out well the sham that he wished to pull, and he gears up well to screw the merchants again.

[20] The merchants saw him in the field, and at once they went in haste toward him, as it really seemed that they were steamed. They went off fast, like an arrow. Campriano said to himself, "If I get off safely from this business, I will keep my head down in the future!"[25] They reached him without giving a greeting; Campriano wanted to greet them all the same.

[21] "Good day!" he said, "What are you doing so early, with such rage and passion? Speak up! I am dying of fright! Don't keep such anger inside any longer!" One of the merchants said, "Rascal! You have tricked us, and you are still putting us on? Give us back the money that we gave you, and keep for yourself your shitty donkey!"

[22] "Do you have an irritation other than this one?" Campriano said then. "Don't worry! I will give you back your money right away here, but first I want you to dine with me." Then he woke up from his cloak the rabbit, and he said to them, "I want you to see! Go tell Lisa to kill two capons at once, and to prepare one boiled and the other roasted."

[23] "Go quickly," he said, "so that I don't have to give you a thrashing, and tell her that I have with me two merchants who are coming this morning to dine with me, that she should put out the decorations, and that she should set the table nicely, to honor everyone." And he let it go: the rabbit went off, never to be found again, into the woods.

[24] Once that rabbit had left, he said, "Come on! Let's go at once to dine." He grabbed the hoe and hood, and he said, "I can't wait to get home. I am falling apart from hunger—and then let's give back your money." Neither merchant was heard to speak, since they were waiting to see how it would turn out.

[25] They reached the house. He knocked on the door with the hoe that he had in his hand, and his wife, who was aware of the fact, took the pot right away from the brazier and carried it into the middle of the house, took

away the brazier right away very gently, and then said, "Who is it?" and opened the door. "Who the devil is it?" and showed an angry face.

[26] All three came into the living room together at once, and the pot was boiling in the middle. Campriano said to the woman, "Is it cooked? We're licking our chops." The woman said a word to the merchants. Meanwhile the rabbit came out from a bench. The merchants saw it and they said words of this sort to each other:

[27] "It is a good idea that we forgive the death sentence on this man and that the money we gave him be his—but that pot that is boiling so vigorously and that rabbit, he should sell them to us. We will not go out through these doors if he does not sell them to us—but let us tell him this after having eaten!" Campriano said, "Let us go dine, so that afterward I may give you your money!"

[28] They sat down there on the ground to take their seats at the table, for there was not another table there, may God help me. The table was a chest, if the word is not mistaken, without napkin or tablecloth, and for cups they had earthenware bowls; but even so each one hurls himself on the capons. They eat and drink, as peasants do, mouths full and both hands too!

[29] When they had devoured the chickens, one of the merchants said to Campriano, "What I am going to say, see to it that you don't get too stirred up about it." Campriano promised him what he wanted. "The pot there where you are boiling meat—you have to sell it to us, and we want that rabbit as a message boy." Look now if these were not full of madness!

[30] And Campriano, who hears such words, don't you think that his eye twinkled? With words that were not indeed coarse or slow, he responded in kind to their verbiage: "O honest and attractive merchant, you will not pay me even with a florin! For the pot I want thirty ducats, which it will save you in wood alone!

[31] I can tell you another of its capacities: it also makes for a great savings in salt. And that rabbit that you see up there has served me much as an errand boy: it belonged to my grandfather and great-grandfather. From heaven it certainly has a great boon, that it will (by my faith) never grow old; and for thirty ducats I will give it to you.

[32] Thirty plus thirty makes sixty: I would not reduce the price by a cent." To compensate them well for the ass, he boasts further of having had even greater gains from the pot and the rabbit. He swears and perjures by the Holy Cross, the peasant does, to make them believe him. They agreed to give sixty ducats: look, if these had a foolish idea or not!

[33] Then they took their leave with great festivity and playfulness; it seemed to them that they had gained much, since the pot boiled without

fire. They had great joy in their faces on that account. My discerning listener, wait a little for the joy then quickly to be taken from them! They reached home and reported to their wives the qualities of the rabbit and the pot.

[34] Now we return to Campriano in his distress, who waits for the pot to come back. Now he finds himself without recourse and believes that this swindle will fail. His wife, who hears him lamenting, said, "Don't worry about their return! Listen to what I have thought and then, if it suits you, let it be carried out.

[35] We have that rusty horn that has been hanging there so many months. If they come here, I want you to say first thing that it was I who committed the offense against them, and make your face unhappy and angry; make a show that it pains you and oppresses you. Wrap a bladder filled with blood around my neck, then pierce it, and I will play dead.

[36] You can revive me with that horn. Then it will actually seem that it is true. And as I hear that it is resounding, I will rise up full of zest, I will say that I have been in a tomb, and I will relate some tale of mine [novella]. And the desire will come to them then to buy this horn that makes the dead rise again."

[37] Sometimes it is good all the same to have wives, as they can give you some piece of advice. See this man, that he accepts anything just to get out of this great danger—and he takes what his wife says, without screaming or making a whisper. They put in order what they needed to do, and happily awaited the merchants.

[38] The tale [novella] returns to the merchants. In the morning when they sent meat to their wives, they did not indeed choose veal, lamb, poultry, or partridge, but beef, the story tells, just to put it to the test. Then they wait for the rabbit, to come back to their fields, to give them some refreshment.

[39] Wait, wait: the rabbit does not come, and there was appetite for eating. The torments of the merchants grew, because it seemed to them the dinner hour. Not knowing what was happening,[26] they resolve to return home. Their wives had sent the rabbit, but it had taken a rest elsewhere!

[40] "Has he then played a trick on us?" said one of them. "He has probably stuck it to us again." Yet they go off on the road, and they look for the rabbit, but it has forgotten. They say to themselves, "It seems late to me! Come on, let's go. We will have a large meal." Talking this way, they make their way home—but they will not eat meat!

[41] You know, in the countryside the doors stand open, so as not to have always to knock. The clever merchants went inside, wishing to eat that beef, but their thoughts will have to be abandoned. "It is not cooked!" they began to shout to their wives and they punched their hands, saying: "He has made fools of us!

[42] This scoundrel has stuck it to us! He has pulled one trick on us— and with this it makes two! Just wait: retaliation will be made for his trick, as I have set my mind on it. Let's go off to his house this very day, because I want to bash in his head with my hands." And so they went to Campriano's house, and with great anger began to say to him . . .

[43] "O you sorry trickster, boorish loafer, find for us our money right away, or else we will punish you for your sin. And so that you will learn not to play a trick again . . ." Campriano replied, "I never tricked anyone, and never people like you." The merchants replied to such palaver, "The ass, the pot, and the rabbit?

[44] You convinced us that it [the pot] has a special feature and that the rabbit has another. Just as the meat was when put in the pot, so it came out. And that rabbit, when it was let loose, took off in another direction. Now give us back our money without a word, if you do not want another type of heat than what comes from the sun!"

[45] Now the danger was apparent to Campriano, yet he began to say with his words, "Do not wonder that the rabbit had to go in a different direction. Why did you not teach him the way and the place where he was to come back to you? Now, that the meat was not cooked—maybe my wife made a swap.

[46] Wait for me a little, as I want to find out if my wife tricked you; if she did it, I will make you understand how much I am troubled by that! Lisa, come on down. If I get alongside you, I will make you come down this flight of stairs with this cudgel of mine that I have in hand. You know of what stuff Campriano is made!"

[47] "What the devil is going on? What the hell will it be then?" said the woman with knitted brows. "Is there anything else to do between us, if not to shout or to make some palaver! Now go on, be quick: tell me what you want, do not keep me any longer in upheaval!" "I wish misfortune upon you, wretched woman! What pot is it that you gave them?"

[48] "I will tell you the truth, my husband. The magic pot I broke while washing it. By my God, I heard nothing except the bursts. To escape the sound of the wicked cane, and so as not to pose obstacles to the oak rod, I gave them the one that they carried off; but I beg you to be merciful!"

[49] "Are these the honors that you do me? Lazy, roguish wretch! Woe is me, rest assured that you will rue this before this day is over." "Do what you will, you will not find it, even if you have beaten me well for it!" Campriano said, "You are still talking back?" He ran up behind her and pierced the bladder.

[50] The woman then threw herself to the ground and really acted as if she were dying. The merchants see her on the ground; they began to speak

to each other as follows: "See then that Campriano is not mistaken. But I would not like for it to have to be known that she died for our sake!" And each of them thus comforts Campriano:

[51] "We grieve over this incident and regret it. We would rather not have seen such things. How will these daughters of yours manage? God himself will have to look after them."²⁷ Campriano said, "Your words show that you value my well-being! If you wish, I will revive her: for your sake I will pardon her."

[52] "How will you revive her? Would you be then Christ or Saint Peter, who raised the dead?" "I am not Christ, nor St. Peter, but you will see something that will not in fact seem nasty or wicked, when you hear sounding the horn that is hanging there." Then he took it down. Each merchant was in a state of wonderment, and each asks advice of the other in words.

[53] "If he revives her with this horn, by all accounts I will take it to buy it. It has the power to extract the dead from the tomb?" Campriano said, "When the son of God comes for the resurrection, it resounds to bring happiness to one and dismay to another. Adam made it so by his own hand, and with it we raise anyone dead."

[54] One merchant said, "I would like to see it! Play it a little now!" And Campriano sounded it. The woman sprung erect from lying, showing them that she was reviving. After being somewhat delayed in silence, she began then to speak in such a way as to give them the impression of having been in hell below, as a damned soul.

[55] "I have seen in hell the Devil and Versiera, Satan's wife. They did to me as the worm does to the cabbage—they gnawed all my weary limbs so. I wished to flee, and I called Saint Paul, and all the same I went down below among serpents, toads, spiders, and lizards, so many that a thousand carts could not haul them away.

[56] When I heard the heavenly sound of this horn, the Devil let me go, and it seemed really that my soul put forth wings, with such rapidity it returned to rest in the mortal body. I will always bewail my sins: hell is more bitter than wormwood!" And having said this, she then fell into silence.

[57] Whereupon the merchants said to Campriano, "Listen, wait to hear what I will set forth for you now. We want from you this horn, on which I will gladly spend money. Ask how much you want and we will give it to you, because I wait eagerly to have it." "I will give it to you for fifty ducats, so that you may be restored by me."

[58] They seemed to have a good bargain for it: they couldn't wait to pay for it! They took the horn, and each one headed homeward, and they chatter with each other: "And when I arrive home, I thought I would want my-

self to put this horn to the test—to kill my wife, and you to kill yours, and then we can both revive them!"

[59] They make arrangements to give the final turn of the screw to their wives: wait to see the party! When they had reached their hovels, they began to shout and make a racket, and each one drew his knife and gave a stab to their wives upon the head. They bathe the whole house in blood, and they slaughter them like chickens on the ground.

[60] Then, when neither was breathing any longer, they wish to make a start toward reviving them; and they sounded the horn powerfully, as they believed for certain that they would arouse them. They sound and sound again, but neither of the women arises. They see that there is need to bury them. One of the merchants said, "For woe, what a disaster! This has been a double humiliation!

[61] We need to take a gamble in every way, if we do not want to lose our lives. But it behooves us to slay Campriano, and then we will swiftly depart from here." The other one says, "I have advice, so that our wish may be fulfilled: we will go to his house, we will take him, then we will put him inside a sack.

[62] Then we will go out walking by night to a great river (I know the way well); there is a high bridge there between two rocks, and we will throw him away in that river and in that way he will pay his dues, and he will be punished then for every wrong." Having thought it over, they went to find him, with a big sack in which they intended to put him.

[63] It was probably almost three hours after dark when they found Campriano, who had just gone outside his house. And they lay in ambush for him quite ably, ran up behind him in a great rage, and soon bound him in that sack. One of them placed it upon his shoulders to carry it down into that valley.

[64] Campriano was unable to talk; it seems that he has tasted the waters of Lethe, which cause the person who has drunk from them to forget. But in the end you will soon see that God will aid him as follows: he caused thirst to come upon the merchants, and the one began to say to the other, "It is a good idea to set this down a little while.

[65] Let us go slowly up that hill. There is a fountain of clear water there. We will drink as much as to slake our thirst. Now let us put him down on this plain." So there they set Campriano, since the effort is not bearable for them. So they left and go to the fountain, which was located halfway up the mountain.

[66] A shepherd, who was going toward Maremma, passed by where Campriano was. Campriano heard him and said, "Dear brother!" shouting out with great fear, "I don't want it," with a bitter lament, "because such a

jewel does not suit me well." The shepherd said, "Who is down here? What is it that you don't want?"

[67] "I will tell you, brother, the dastardly deed! Two merchants have come from Spain. They say that they have been inspired by God, the stars, and some saints that I should be given to the king's daughter as husband. I am not accustomed to such luxury. They want to take me by force to Spain. They are off drinking on the mountain."

[68] The shepherd said, "You are mad, for sure, to refuse such a position. If you wish that I should go there, I will make a deal: one day, without a delay, I will make you rich." Campriano said, "Release me at once." Whereupon he obeyed him in his proposal: the shepherd gave him his herd and ten gold florins and six copper ones.

[69] Then he had himself tied up in that sack, and Campriano tied him very well. He stayed quiet, like a hunting dog.[28] Meanwhile Campriano went off with the herd in such way that he appeared to be a Cacus.[29] Meanwhile the merchants returned. They set the sack on their shoulders, went off, and threw it into that valley.

[70] Then they took the route home because they wished to settle their affairs. Listen, pay attention to this verbiage of mine, as everything is resolved in this bit. At a mill they found Campriano, who is heading home with the herd. Seeing him in this way, they crossed themselves; they asked if he was Campriano.

[71] He turned with a joyous face and said, "Yes, don't you see me? You believed, surely, that you were doing me a great wrong, but you were as stupid as oxen. You threw me, wrapped up, down into that river. We do not have among us a country that is as beautiful as the one at the bottom; it truly seemed to me another world.

[72] I went down, and I entered into a beautiful garden. The vines are tied with sausages. There is a river, which is made of perfect wine. I drank from it bellyfuls. And cooked capons go about in that realm; there are mountains of grated cheese, and a woman who makes macaroni, and people eat them down there in great mouthfuls.

[73] And on the stake for the grapevine there is a cooked thrush, with an orange under its foot, and, if I remember, there is definitely there a crystal glass full of malmsey. The beds are fluffed up: I was stunned for a bit, to be completely truthful. White cakes with blood pudding, pies, and marzipan, and pine nut confections put together in unusual ways.

[74] And furthermore there are there many young women, who are always ready to play around, and you have probably never seen more beautiful ones. I know that they will astound you with their coiffure and with the

skirts that women wear in that country, with the kisses and courtesies they do you, such as not to leave them in a year.

[75] When you arrive, they wash your feet in a noble and precious earthenware vessel.[30] Then you stand up and take a seat at the table, and they set before you biscuits, turtledoves, and quails, and I want you to be sure that there you do not later pay the bill for it! Capons, partridges, big pigeons and crossbred ones—they are never late in serving them to you!

[76] I could not tell you then on the black days, [lean days] like Friday and Saturday morning: sturgeon as big as tapers are readied there in gelatin, and herb-spiced tortes are found along the paths, the vats are full of fresh eggs, and tench, pike, gray mullet, lamprey, and yet other cooked fish can be seen.

[77] I left and when coming out of the river I was given ten ducats, because they have the custom down there of giving them to people who have been thrown in the river. This group of animals with their fleeces and feathers, a hundred head of beasts, were given to me. I am taking them home and then I wish to return there to stay there eight more days to celebrate."

[78] The merchants imitated the Magi and, kneeling before Campriano, said: "If you could enable us to have such ease in that place, as you tell, which is so pleasant, we will take flight from the discomforts of mortal life to inhabit so serene a place. Come on, Campriano, throw us into the river, that we may have a taste of that beautiful light."

[79] "To do your pleasure, I will go back." With a cord he bound both of them (to shorten our song now) and tossed both of them into that river. Having resumed his journey, he returned home with his scepter, and celebrate with his children and wife, and never again suffered toothache.

[80] I departed after I saw that in this world we have need of good fortune, so that, even if Christ wishes to help you, you may emerge safe and free from every hard and intense undertaking. He who in making his rounds has seen himself in many deadly dangers, he really needs to have some star looking over him! Now the tale [*novella*] in your honor is finished.

C. Straparola, "Father Scarpafico"
(*Le piacevoli notti,* Night 1, Fable 3)

Translation adapted from Gianfrancesco [Giovanni Francesco] Straparola, *Le piacevoli notti,* trans. W. G. Waters in *The Facetious Nights of Straparola* (London: Privately Printed for Members of the Society of Bibliophiles, 1898), 1:61–78.

The Third Fable.

Father Scarpafico, having been once duped by three robbers, dupes them thrice in return and lives happily for the rest of his days.

The end of Signora Alteria's story, which she has set forth with so great skill, supplied me with a theme for my own, which perhaps may please you no less than hers, though on one point it will show a variance, inasmuch as she pictured to us Father Severino neatly entrapped by Cassandrino; while in the story I am about to tell you, Father Scarpafico threw the net no less adroitly over various scoundrels who were trying to get the better of him.

Near Imola, a city always plagued by factious quarrels and ultimately destroyed by them, there lived once upon a time a priest named Scarpafico, who served the village church of Postrema. He was well-to-do, but miserly and avaricious beyond measure, and he had for housekeeper a shrewd and clever woman named Nina, who was so frank and forward that she would never scruple to tell any man whatever might come into her mind. And because she was faithful and prudent in administering his affairs, he held her in high esteem.

Now when good Father Scarpafico was young, he was as jolly a priest as there was to be met in all the country round; but at this time age had made walking on foot irksome to him, and so the good Nina was always persuading him to buy a horse, in order that his days might not be shortened through too great fatigue. At last Scarpafico, overcome by the persuasions of his servant, went one day to the market, and having seen there a mule which appeared exactly to suit his need, bought it for seven golden florins.

It happened that there were at the market that day three merry fellows, the kind who would rather live on the goods of others than on their own earnings—as sometimes happens even in our own time—and, as soon as they saw the bargain struck, one said to the other, "Friends, I have a mind that the mule over there should belong to us." "But how can that be managed?" said the others. Then the first speaker replied, "We must post ourselves along the road he will take on his journey home, about a quarter of a mile apart one from another, and as he passes, each one must affirm positively that the mule he has bought is not a mule at all, but an ass, and if we are brazen enough in our declaration, the mule will be ours."

Accordingly they started from the market and stationed themselves separately on the road, as they had planned, and when Father Scarpafico approached the first of the thieves, the fellow, pretending to be on the road to the market, said, "God be with you, sir!" to which Scarpafico replied, "And welcome to you, my brother." "From where do you come, sir?" said the thief. "From the market," Scarpafico answered. "And what good bargains

have you picked up there?" asked the thief. "This mule," said Scarpafico. "Which mule?" exclaimed the robber. "Why, the mule I am riding," returned Scarpafico. "Are you speaking in sober truth, or do you mock me?" asked the thief, "because it seems to me to be an ass, and not a mule." "Indeed," Scarpafico answered, and without another word he went his way. Before he had ridden far he met the next robber, who greeted him, "Good day, sir, and where may you come from?" "From the market," answered Scarpafico. "And was there anything worth buying?" said the robber. "Yes," answered Scarpafico, "I bought this mule which you see." "What, sir!" said the robber, "Do you mean to say you bought that for a mule, and not for an ass? What rascals must be about, seeing you have been thus cheated!" "An ass, indeed," replied Scarpafico. "If anyone else should tell me this same tale, I will make him a present of the beast at once." Then going his way, he soon met the third thief, who said to him, "Good morrow, sir. You come perhaps from the market?" "I do," replied Scarpafico. "And what may you have bought there?" asked the robber. "I bought this mule which I am riding," said Scarpafico. "Mule!" said the fellow, "Do you really mean what you say? Surely you must be joking when you call that beast a mule, when it is really an ass." Scarpafico, when he heard this tale, said to the fellow, "Two other men I have met told me the same story, and I did not believe them, but now it appears certain that the beast is an ass," and having dismounted from the mule, he handed it over to the thief, who, having thanked the priest for it, went off to join his companions, leaving good Father Scarpafico to make his way home on foot.

As soon as he came to his house, he told Nina how he had bought a nag at the market, thinking it to be a mule, but that it had proved to be an ass; and how, having been told that he had mistaken one beast for the other by several people he had met on the road home, he had given the beast to the last of them. "Ah, you poor simpleton!" cried Nina. "Can you not see that they have played you a trick? I thought you were cleverer than this. In truth, they would not have fooled me thus." "Well, it is no use to grieve over it," said Scarpafico. "They may have played me a trick, but see if I do not play them two in return. Rest assured that these fellows, after having once fooled me, will not remain content with that, but will soon be weaving some new plot whereby they may plunder me afresh."

Not far from Father Scarpafico's house there lived a peasant, who had among his goats two which were so much alike that it was impossible to tell one from the other. These two goats the priest bought, and the next day ordered Nina to prepare a good dinner for himself and some friends he proposed to invite—some boiled veal, and roasted chicken and meat, and to make savory sauces to go with them, and a tart of the sort she was accustomed

to serve him with. Then he took one of the goats and tied it to a hedge in the garden, and having given it some fodder, he put a halter round the neck of the other and led it off to the market, where he was at once accosted by the three fine fellows of the last escapade.

"Welcome, good sir, and what may be your business here today? You are come, no doubt, to make another good purchase?" To which Scarpafico replied, "I have come to buy various provisions, for some friends are coming to dine with me; and if you will consent to join our feast it will please me greatly." The cunning rascals willingly accepted Scarpafico's invitation, and he, when he had bought everything he required, placed all his purchases on the back of the goat, and said to the beast, "Now go home and tell Nina to boil this veal, and to roast the chickens and the meat, and tell her, moreover, to make savory sauce with these spices, and a nice tart. Do you understand? Now go in peace." And with these words he drove off the goat with its load, which, being left to go where it wished, wandered away, and what happened to it, no one knows. Scarpafico and his companions and some other friends of his strolled about the marketplace until dinnertime, and then they all went to the priest's house, where the first thing they saw on entering the garden was the goat which Scarpafico had tied to the hedge, calmly digesting after its meal of greens. The three adventurers at once took it to be the goat that Father Scarpafico had dispatched home with his purchases, and they were extraordinarily amazed at it; and when they all had come in, the priest said to Nina, "Have you prepared everything as the goat told you?" and she, understanding his meaning, replied, "Yes, sir, in a few minutes the roasted loin and chickens and the boiled veal will be ready, and the sauce made with spices, and the tart likewise; all as the goat told me."

The three robbers, when they saw the roasted chickens, boiled veal, and tart set out, and heard what Nina said, were more astonished than ever, and at once began to cast about how they might gain possession of the goat by theft; but when the dinner had come to an end, and they found themselves as far as ever from carrying out their felonious purpose, they said to Scarpafico, "Sir, will you do us the favor to sell us that goat of yours?" But Scarpafico replied that he had no wish to part with it, for it was worth more money than the world held; but, after a little, he consented to oblige them, and to take in exchange for it fifty golden florins. "But," he added, "take warning, and blame me not afterwards if the goat does not obey you as it obeys me, for it doesn't know you or your ways."

But the three adventurers paid no heed to this speech of Scarpafico, and, without further talk, carried off the goat, rejoicing in their bargain. When they came to their homes, they said to their wives, "See that you prepare no food tomorrow except what we shall send home by the goat." On the mor-

row they went to the piazza, where they purchased chickens and various other foods, and they packed them on the goat's back, and directed it to go home, and to tell to their wives all they ordered. The goat, thus laden, when it was set at liberty, ran away into the country and was never seen again.

When dinnertime came, the three conspirators went home at once and demanded of their wives whether the goat had come back safely with the provisions, and whether they had duly cooked these according to the directions given. The women, amazed at what they heard, cried out, "What fools and numskulls you must be to suppose that a beast like that would do your bidding! You surely have been prettily duped. With your cheating other people every day, it was quite certain you would be caught yourselves at last."

As soon as the three robbers saw that Scarpafico had truly made fools of them, besides having emptied their pockets of fifty golden florins, they were hotly enraged against him, and, having grabbed weapons, they set forth to find him, swearing they would take his life. But the cunning priest, who fully expected that the robbers would seek vengeance upon him when they had discovered how he had tricked them, had taken counsel with Nina about what to do. "Nina," he said, "take this bladder, which you see is full, and wear it under your dress; then, when these robbers come, I will put all the blame on you, and in my rage will make believe to stab you; but I will thrust the knife in this bladder, and you must fall down as if you were dead. The rest you will leave to me."

Scarcely had Scarpafico finished speaking when the conspirators arrived, and at once headed for Scarpafico as if to kill him. "Wait, brothers!" he cried, "What you would blame me for is none of my doing, but instead the work of this servant of mine, most likely on account of some offense of which I know nothing." And, turning towards Nina, he struck his knife into the bladder, which he had previously filled with blood, and she immediately pretended to be dead and fell down, while the blood gushed in streams around her where she lay. Then the priest, looking upon his work, made great show of repentance, and bawled out loudly, "Oh, wretched man that I am! what have I done in thus foolishly slaying this woman who was the prop of my old age? How shall I manage to live without her?" But after a little he fetched a bagpipe, made according to a design of his own, and blew a tune upon it, until at last Nina jumped up safe and sound, as if recalled to life.

When the robbers saw what happened, they forgot their anger in their astonishment, and, after a little haggling, they purchased the bagpipe for two hundred florins, and went highly delighted to their homes. A day or two after, it happened that one of them had a quarrel with his wife, and, becoming enraged, stabbed her in the breast with his knife and killed her. The

husband at once took the bagpipe which had been bought from Scarpafico, and in the hope of reviving her blew into them as Scarpafico had done; but he spent his wind to no purpose, for the poor woman had truly passed from this life to the next. When the second thief saw what his comrade had done, he cried out, "What a fool you are! you have bungled the affair. Wait and see how I do it." And with these words he seized his own wife by the hair, and cut her throat with a razor. Then, taking the bagpipe, he blew with all his might, but with no better result than the first. The third fellow, who was standing by, not at all daunted by the failure of the others, treated his own wife in the same way to no better purpose; so the three were all alike wife-less. With hotter anger against Scarpafico than ever, they hurried to his house, resolved that this time they would pay no heed to his plausible tales, and seized him and thrust him into a sack, intending to drown him in a neighboring river. But as they bore him along something gave them an alarm, and they ran to hide themselves for a while, leaving Father Scarpafico in his sack by the wayside.

They had not been gone many minutes before a shepherd, driving his flock to pasture, went by; and, as he drew near, he heard a plaintive voice saying, "They want me to take her, but I will have none of her; for I am a priest, and have no concern with such matters." The shepherd stopped short, somewhat frightened, because he could not discover from where the voice came, which kept repeating the same words over and over again; but, having looked now here, now there, his eye at last fell on the sack in which Scarpafico was tied up. The shepherd opened the sack and let the priest come out, demanding why he had been tied up in this way, and what he meant by the words he kept uttering. In response Scarpafico declared that the lord of the town insisted on marrying him to one of his daughters, but that he himself had no stomach for the match, because, besides being a priest, he was too old to take a wife. The shepherd, who, like a simpleton, believed every word the cunning priest told him, at once cried out, "Good father, do you think the lord would bestow her upon me?" "I believe he would," said Scarpafico, "provided you get into this sack and let me tie you up." The silly shepherd at once crept in, and Scarpafico, having fastened the sack, got away from the place as quickly as he could, driving the poor shep-herd's flock before him.

When an hour or so had passed, the three thieves returned, and, without examining the sack, they bore it to the river and threw it in, thus sending the wretched shepherd to the fate they had destined for Father Scarpafico.

Then they took their way homewards, and, as they were conversing, they perceived a flock of sheep grazing nearby, and at once began to scheme how they might easiest carry off a couple of lambs. But when they drew

near, imagine their amazement at seeing Father Scarpafico, whom they believed to be lying at the bottom of the river, tending the flock as a shepherd. As soon as they had recovered from their amazement, they demanded of him how he had managed to get out of the river, and he answered at once: "Away with you! You have no more sense than so many jackasses. If you had thrown me a little farther into the stream, I would have come back with ten times as many sheep as you see here." When the robbers heard this, they cried out, "Ah! Father Scarpafico, will you at last do us a good turn? Will you put us into sacks and throw us into the river? Then, you see, we shall no longer have need to be scoundrels and rascals, and will live as honest shepherds." "Well," answered Scarpafico, "I will do that for you; indeed there is no favor in the world I would not grant you, on account of the love I have for you"; and, having got three good sacks of strong canvas, he tied the three thieves in them so firmly that there was no chance of their getting out, and threw them into the river. Thus they went to the place which was their due, and Scarpafico went back to Nina with good store of gold and cattle, and lived many years in happiness and prosperity.

Cateruzza's tale gave great pleasure to all the company, and won high praise, especially the part of it which dealt with Father Scarpafico's cunning scheme, by which, in exchange for the mule he gave away, he gained much money and a fine flock of sheep.

D. Brothers Grimm, "About the Tailor Who Became Rich Quickly" (BP 2:1–3)

This version of the tale was reportedly heard in German in Kassel from the Hassenpflugs on 18 April 1811.

Once upon a time a poor tailor, wanting to visit his brother, went in wintertime through the fields. While en route he found a frozen thrush. Saying to himself, "Anything bigger than a louse, the tailor takes to his house," he picked up the thrush and put it away in his clothing. As he came to his brother's house, he took a look first in the window to see if they were home; then he saw a fat priest sitting next to his sister-in-law at a table, on which there stood a roast and a bottle of wine. In the meantime there was a knocking at the door and the husband wanted to come in; then the tailor saw how the wife shut the priest quickly in a chest, put the roast in the oven, and stuck the wine in the bed.

After the husband had now entered, the tailor himself went into the

house and greeted his brother and sister-in-law; but he set himself down upon the chest where the priest was. The husband said, "Wife, I am hungry; don't you have anything to eat?" "No, I'm sorry, but today there's absolutely nothing in the house." But the tailor took out his frozen thrush; then his brother said, "My brother, what are you doing with the frozen thrush?" "Oho, it is worth a lot of money; it can prophesy." "Then go ahead and have it prophesy now!" The tailor held it to his ear and said, "The thrush says, there's a dish full of roast in the oven." The husband went there and found the roast: "What else does the thrush say?" "In the bed there's a bottle of wine." The husband found the wine, "Oho, I would like to have the thrush; come on and sell it to me!" "You can have it, if you give me the chest I am sitting on." The man wanted to do so right away, but the woman said, "No, that won't work; the chest is far too dear to me, I am not giving it away." But the man said: "Don't be so stupid! What good is such an old chest to you!" and gave his brother the chest in return for the bird.

The tailor took the chest on a wheelbarrow and pushed it out. While en route he said, "I'll take the chest and toss it in the water, I'll take the chest and toss it in the water." Finally the priest moved inside and said, "You know well what is in the chest. Let me out and I will give you fifty dollars." "All right, for that I will certainly do it," let him out, and went home with the money.

People wondered where he had gotten so much money, but he said, "I'll tell you; hides are worth so much that I slaughtered my old cow and was given so much cash for the hide." People in the village wanted also to profit from this situation, rushed home, cut off the necks of all their oxen, cows, and sheep, and took the hides into the city, where they got in return murderously little, because so many of them were offered for sale at once.

Then the farmers grew angry about their loss and threw dirt and other bad stuff at the tailor's door. But he put all of it into his chest, went with it to the city to an inn, and asked the innkeeper if he could watch for a while the chest, which contained great valuables; they would not be safe with him. The innkeeper said, "Quite gladly," and took the chest into his possession. Some time afterward the tailor came, asked to have the chest back, and opened it, to see if everything was still in it. But since it was now full of dirt, he raged horribly, scolded the innkeeper, and threatened to denounce him, so that the innkeeper, who feared a scene and worried about his reputation, gladly gave him a hundred dollars.

The farmers were angry again that everything they did to harm him turned out to the tailor's profit. They took the chest, put him forcibly inside it, set it on the water, and let it float away. The tailor stayed still and silent for a while, until he had floated away a short distance; then he cried out

very loudly, "No, I won't do that, I won't do that, even if the whole world wants it." A shepherd heard the shouting and asked, "What is it then that you don't wish to do?" "Oho, said the tailor, "there is a king who has a foolish notion and insists that the man who comes in this chest down the current shall marry his only daughter, a beauty—but I have already made up my mind and will not do it, even if the whole world wants it." "Listen now, would it not work if another were to put himself in the chest and obtain the king's daughter?" "O yes, that would work." "Then I will put myself inside in your place." Then the tailor got out and the shepherd got in; the tailor shut the chest again, and the shepherd soon sank. But the tailor took the whole of the shepherd's herd and guided it home.

But the farmers wondered how it came about that he returned and, what is more, had many sheep. The tailor said, "I sunk down, deep, deep, and there I found on the bottom the whole herd and took it with me from there." The farmers wanted them too to get sheep for themselves and went out together to the water. That day the sky was entirely blue with little white clouds, and they cried out: "We already see the lambs below on the bottom!" Then the mayor said, "I will go down first and look around, and if it is good, I will call you." As he now plunged in, it made a rushing noise in the water: Splash! Then they thought that he called to them "Come on!" and they all plunged in behind him. Then the whole village belonged to the tailor.

E. Brothers Grimm, "The Little Farmer" ("Das Bürle" [*KHM* 61])

There was a village where there were nothing but rich farmers and just one poor one, whom they called the little farmer. He did not even have a cow, much less money to buy one; and he and his wife would have very gladly had one.

One day he said to her, "Listen, I have a good idea. Our godfather is a carpenter, he shall make us a calf out of wood and shall paint it brown, so that it looks like any other. In time it will grow big and become a cow." This also appealed to his wife, and the godfather who was a carpenter built the calf and planed it into shape, painted it as was appropriate, and made it so that it had its head lowered, as if it were eating.

The next morning, when the cows were being driven out, the little farmer called over the herdsman and said, "Look, I have here a little calf, but it is still small and has to be carried still."

The herdsman said, "Fine," took it in his arm, carried it out into the

pasture, and put it on the grass. The little calf kept standing there steadily like a calf that is eating, and the herdsman said, "It will soon be running on its own. Look at how it is eating already!"

In the evening, when he wanted to drive the herd back home, he said to the calf, "If you can stand there and eat yourself full, then you can also walk on your own four legs; I have no desire to carry you home again in my arms." But the little farmer stood in front of his door and waited for his little calf; when the cowherd now drove the cattle through the village and the little calf was missing, he asked about it. The herdsman answered, "It is still standing out there as ever, eating: it did not want to stop and to come along." Little Farmer said: "Oh, I must have my livestock back!"

Then they went together back to the meadow, but someone had stolen the calf, and it was gone. The herdsman said, "It has probably run off." But the little farmer said, "I don't think so!" and he brought the herdsman before the mayor, who condemned the herdsman for his negligence to give the little farmer a cow in place of the escaped calf. Now the little farmer and his wife had the long hoped-for cow; they rejoiced from the bottoms of their hearts, but they had no fodder and could not give anything to it, and so it soon had to be slaughtered. They salted the meat, and the little farmer went to the city and intended to sell the hide there, so as to buy a new little calf with the proceeds.

On the way he came to a mill, where a raven with broken wings was sitting. Out of pity he took it and wrapped it in the hide. But because the weather turned very bad and it stormed with wind and rain, he could go no further, stopped at the mill, and asked for shelter. The miller's wife was home alone and said to the little farmer, "Lie down there on the straw," and gave him bread and cheese. The little farmer ate and lay down, with the hide next to him, and the wife thought, "He is tired and asleep."

In the meantime the village priest came; the miller's wife received him well and said, "My husband is out, so we will ply ourselves with food." Little Farmer perked his ears, and when he heard about plying, he grew angry that he had to make do with bread and cheese.

Then the wife brought over and served up items of four sorts: roast, salad, cake, and wine. When they now sat down and wanted to eat, there was a knocking outside. The wife said, "Oh, God, that is my husband!" Quickly she stuck the roast in the tile oven, the wine under the pillow, the salad on the bed, the cake under the bed, and the village priest in the cupboard in the entrance hall. Then she opened the front door for her husband and said, "Praise be to God that you are back here! It is storming as if the world were coming to an end." The miller saw the little farmer lying on the hay and asked, "What is that fellow doing there?"

"Ah," said the wife, "the poor rascal came in the storm and rain and asked for shelter, so I gave him bread and cheese and pointed out the hay to him." The man said, "I have nothing against that, but put together something for me to eat right away." The wife said, "But I have nothing except bread and cheese."

"I will be content with anything," answered the husband, "with bread and cheese, as far as I am concerned"; he looked at the little farmer and called out, "Come on and eat again with me." Little Farmer did not make him say that twice; he got up and ate with him. Then the miller saw lying on the ground the hide where the raven was, and asked, "What do you have there?" The little farmer answered, "I have a fortune teller in there."

"Can he tell my fortune too?" said the miller. "Why not?" answered the little farmer. "But he tells only four things, and the fifth he keeps to himself." The miller was curious and said, "Have him tell my fortune, will you?" Then Little Farmer pushed the raven on the head, so that it cawed and made a "krrr krrr" sound. The miller said, "What did he say?" Little Farmer answered, "First, he said that there is wine under the pillow."

"By dickens!" shouted the miller, who went over and found the wine. "Go on now," said the miller. The little farmer caused the raven to caw again and said, "Second, he said that there was a roast in the tile oven."

"That would be a sight to behold!" shouted the miller, who went over and found the roast. Little Farmer had the raven tell his fortune once again and said, "Third, he said that there is salad on the bed."

"That would be a sight to behold!" shouted the miller, who went over and found the salad. Finally the little farmer pushed the raven once again (so that it growled), and said, "Fourth, he said that there was a cake under the bed."

"That would be a sight to behold!" shouted the miller, who went over and found the cake.

Now the two of them took a seat together at the table, but the miller's wife grew anxious for her life, laid down in bed, and took all the keys with her. The miller would have gladly known the fifth prediction, but Little Farmer said, "First we want to eat the four other things in peace, since the fifth is something bad." So they ate, and afterward they negotiated over how much the miller would give for the fifth prediction, until they reached an agreement on three hundred talers.[31] Then the little farmer pressed the raven once again on the head, so that he cawed loudly.

The miller asked, "What did he say?"

The little farmer answered, "He said that out there in the cupboard in the corridor is the Devil."

The miller said, "The Devil must get out of there," and opened wide the

front door, but his wife had to turn over the key, and Little Farmer un-
locked the cupboard. Then the village priest ran out as best he could, and
the miller said, "I have seen the black fellow with my own eyes: the predic-
tion was correct!"

Little Farmer, however, made off with the three hundred talers at dawn
on the following morning.

Back at home, the little farmer gradually revealed his wealth, he built a
pretty house, and the farmers said, "The little farmer has certainly been
where golden snow falls and people carry home money in shovels." Then
Little Farmer was summoned before the mayor to say from where his wealth
came. He answered, "I sold my cowhide in the city for three hundred
talers." When the farmers heard that, they wanted also to enjoy the great
advantage, ran home, slew all their cows, and stripped the hides, so as to sell
them in the city with great profit. The mayor said, "But my maid must go
first." When she came to the merchant in the city, he gave her nothing more
than three talers for a hide; and when the others came, he gave them not
even so much, and said, "What am I supposed to do with all the skins?"

Now the farmers grew angry that they had been duped, wanted to take
revenge on Little Farmer, and filed a complaint against him for fraud with
the mayor. The innocent little farmer was sentenced unanimously to death
and was to be rolled into the water in a barrel shot through with holes.

Little Farmer was led out and a cleric was brought who was to read him
the last rites. All the others had to remove themselves, and as the little
farmer looked at the cleric, he recognized him as the village priest who had
been with the miller's wife.

He said to him, "I freed you from the cupboard, you free me from the
barrel."

Just then there came by with a herd of sheep the shepherd, about whom
the little farmer knew that for a long time he had wanted to become mayor.
So he cried out with all his might, "No, I will not do it! And even if the
whole world wanted to have it, no, I will not do it!" The shepherd, who
heard this, came along and asked, "What do you have in mind? What will
you not do?"

Little Farmer said, "They want to make me mayor, if I put myself in the
barrel, but I will not do it."

The shepherd said, "If it takes no more than that to become mayor, I
would put myself right away in the barrel."

Little Farmer said, "If you are willing to put yourself in, then you will
be mayor." The shepherd was satisfied with this, put himself inside, and the
little farmer banged the lid onto; then he took the herd of the shepherd for
himself and drove it on.

Meanwhile the village priest went to the congregation and said that the last rites had been read. Then they came and rolled the barrel down to the water. When the barrel began to roll, the shepherd called out, "I will indeed gladly become mayor." They believed nothing but that the little farmer was crying out in this way, and they said, "We share that opinion too, but first you have to look around down under," and rolled the barrel into the water. Then the farmers went home, and when they came into the village, the little farmer came there too, drove a herd of sheep calmly in, and was quite satisfied. Then the farmers were astounded and said, "Little Farmer, from where have you come? Are you coming from the water?"

"Of course," answered the little farmer, "I sank deep, deep, until finally I came to the bottom; I kicked out the bottom of the barrel and crawled out; there were beautiful meadows, on which grazed many lambs, a herd of which I brought with me."

The farmers said, "Are there still more there?"

"Oh, yes," said the little farmer, "more than you could use." Then the farmers agreed that they also wanted to get sheep for themselves, each one a herd; but the mayor said, "I go first." So they went together to the water, and just then there were in the blue sky little woolly clouds that people call "little lambs," which were reflected in the water; and so the farmers shouted, "We already see the sheep on the bottom below."

The mayor pushed forward and said, "Now I will go down first and look around; if things are good, I will call you." When he jumped in, it made a plopping sound in the water. They believed nothing but that he was calling "Come!" to them, and the whole lot plunged into the water in haste after him. Then the village died out, and Little Farmer, as the sole heir, became a rich man.

F. "Kibitz"

eprinted (with modifications) from *Popular Tales and Romances of the Northern Nations* (London: Printed for W. Simpkin and R. Marshall, 1823), 2:305–16. The three volumes of *Popular Tales* contain translations of German tales by such authors as Johann Karl August Musäus and Ludwig Tieck. Although no information is provided in the anonymous English translation of this particular item, the tale of the farmer Kibitz is adapted from Johann Gustav Gottlieb Büsching, *Volks-Sagen, Märchen und Legenden* (1812), 296. Büsching's tales were collected orally in the Uckermark, a region in Brandenburg in Germany (northeast of Berlin, toward Poland).

There was once a poor peasant named Kibitz, who, though but little favored by fortune, enjoyed nevertheless more contentment and satisfaction than many of his more prosperous neighbors; his chief maxim was to make the best that he could of everything; and, if affairs proceeded untowardly, to hope that they might take a turn for the better, without vexing himself unnecessarily. One day, as he was ploughing his little field with his two oxen, he thought that he heard someone call him and, looking round, perceived that it was a bird, which repeated his name several times, it being the kibitz or pewit, whose cry resembles the sound of its own name. The simple clown, conceiving that the bird was mocking him, felt provoked, despite his usual good nature, and took up a heavy stone to fling at it; the bird, however, flew away in a very leisurely way, while the stone unluckily fell upon one of his oxen and killed it on the spot. This was a terrible misfortune for Kibitz; yet there was no means of restoring the dead animal to life, so thinking that its yoke-fellow would be of little service by itself, he, without more ado, killed the other also. Then he flayed them both and carried the hides to a tanner, in order to make some trifling profit in return for the heavy loss he had sustained.

When he arrived at the tanner's, finding that no one seemed very anxious to answer his knocking, he peeped in through a casement and perceived that the good man's wife was cramming a lover into a chest, in order to conceal him from her unwelcome visitor. Master Kibitz was not altogether so displeased at this scene as the tanner himself would have been, for he shrewdly thought that he might turn it to his own advantage. In a little while the woman opened the door, and hearing his errand, informed him that her husband was absent, and that she could not transact the business on which he had come. Kibitz said that she need not refuse him, for though she had no money, yet he would be contented with that old lumber chest that stood in one corner, and it would be an excellent bargain for her. To this proposal the woman demurred, as may well be supposed; Kibitz insisted upon having it, saying that it was the best bargain she could possibly make, while she as resolutely refused to comply; for it is in vain to offer the most advantageous bargains in the world, if people are so blind to their own interests as to refuse them. In short, they quarreled so loud and so long about the matter that the tanner himself returned, in the midst of the dispute, and so settled it by insisting upon his wife's complying with their customer's whim by letting him have the old worm-eaten chest. [The tanner was] heartily glad to obtain the two hides so cheaply and at the same time considered Kibitz to be a very great blockhead. The latter, therefore, obtained his wish, in spite of the good wife's exclamations and opposition, and, hoisting his prize into a cart that he had brought with him, drove off

towards his home. He had not proceeded far, however, before the inhabitant of the chest, who conceived himself not to be included in the purchase, took care to let him know that he was carrying away more than he had any right to and to entreat him therefore to let him out. This, however, was a proposal to which Kibitz was but little disposed to accede. Instead, he set about proving formally, according to the best logic of which he was master, that in purchasing the chest, he had also purchased him. The lover found himself driven to extremity and thought it hopeless, encased as he was, and with very little breath to waste upon words, to think of refuting an adversary who could give his lungs full play. Therefore he surrendered fully at Kibitz's discretion and was permitted to march out, on giving up all his valuables and money. As it so happened, the money was a very considerable sum, sufficient to purchase several pairs of oxen, instead of those which the countryman had lost.

Kibitz now returned home quite rich, and his neighbors, upon being informed of the excellent bargain he had made by his hides, killed their oxen also and took their skins to the same tanner. But instead of obtaining as much as they expected, they were informed that Kibitz had gotten only an old chest, hardly worth a single hide. At this they supposed that they had been maliciously imposed upon by him, in order that they might be induced to kill their cattle, and they determined to put so envious a fellow to death. Fortunately our good Kibitz received some information of their designs. For a long time he was puzzled in contriving some stratagem by which to defeat their murderous intent, and, at length conceiving that his poor wife would be quite inconsolable at being left a widow, he generously resolved to spare her this excessive affliction. He told her, therefore, that he had a mind by way of frolic to let her wear the breeches for once in her life; and accordingly ordered her to dress in his clothes and to go and work in the garden. Like an obedient spouse, accustomed to humor all her lord's whims, however extravagant they might be, the poor woman complied. The wicked neighbors shortly after came, and finding her digging in the garden, they fell upon her, put her to death, and then immediately fled, satisfied that they had revenged themselves on Kibitz.

Our friend Kibitz, in the meanwhile, was too overjoyed at the singular success of his stratagem to have much time to bewail his wife. On the contrary, he thought that she might even yet prove of some service to him; he therefore took her, and having dressed her in her ordinary attire, put a basket of flowers in her hand and seated her by the roadside as if she were offering nosegays for sale. Presently a stately equipage passed by and the lady who was in the carriage, being smitten with the beauty of the flowers, ordered one of her lackeys to enquire the price. This he did several times, but receiving no

answer, and therefore supposing that she was asleep, he shook her somewhat rudely in order to wake her. Instantly she fell down into a deep ditch, Kibitz having taken care to place her in a precarious situation, and he, being on the watch, now rushed out upon the fellow, exclaimed that he had killed his wife, and protested that he would accuse all of them of murder. The lady, alarmed at the accident and the unpleasant circumstances in which she might be involved, offered, by way of pacifying him, to give all the money she had about her and also a fine horse, upon which a groom was mounted. Kibitz protested that he had lost the best wife in the world; that even so he was far from bearing malice, seeing that the lady was heartily sorry for what had happened; and that he would therefore comply with her request, out of pure good nature. So filling his pockets and mounting on his steed, Kibitz set off home, well pleased with his own prudence and ingenuity.

As he passed through the village, everyone looked out to see who it should be was mounted on so fine a horse, but how great was their astonishment at perceiving that it was actually Kibitz, whom they thought they had killed. But though at first somewhat alarmed, conceiving it to be his spirit, on finding that it was really himself, they determined to get rid of him at all events; and in order to do so the more effectively, they seized hold of him and shut him up in a large cask, in which they resolved to throw him into the sea. All now seemed to be over with poor Kibitz; his good fortune appeared quite at an end. Chance and good luck, however, often effect escapes that prudence cannot contrive. The stars had decreed that Kibitz should be prosperous.

It so chanced that in their way to the sea they passed by an ale-house, and considering that Kibitz could hardly run away while imprisoned in the cask, they left it standing in the road, while they went in to refresh themselves with a draft. No sooner did Kibitz find himself alone than he began to consider how he might best take advantage of those few precious moments in order to regain his freedom. At almost the very same instant he heard a flock of sheep pass by, upon which he began to cry out, "I will not be chosen mayor. I am determined not to be a mayor." The shepherd, astonished at his exclamation, went up to the cask and questioned him as to the cause of his being there. "Friend," replied Kibitz, "according to an ancient and singular custom of our town, whoever is chosen mayor, is borne in procession by the inhabitants of our town, in this cask. I am appointed to this honor, but I am by no means ambitious of it."—"How!" exclaimed the shepherd with astonishment. "Are you in earnest when you say that you do not wish for the honor? I would then that it were some other person's good luck to be chosen mayor." "Well then, my honest fellow, just let me out of this cask and take my place as quickly as you please." This was no sooner said than done, and

Kibitz, upon being extricated himself, enclosed the ambitious fool in his new shell, in which he was to be hatched into a mayor. Then, thinking that the poor sheep would be at a loss for want of a master, or if left there might fall into worse hands than his own, he determined at once to drive them home.

On returning from the tavern, the boors began to roll the cask on again, in spite of the cries of the unfortunate shepherd, and, at length, plunged it fully into the water.

Satisfied that they had now got forever rid of Kibitz, they were returning in a very leisurely way to the village, but how extreme was their surprise, on suddenly meeting him, not only quite safe and sound, but driving a fine flock of sheep.

"Is it possible, Kibitz, that it is you?" exclaimed they all together, concealing their vexation as well as they could.

"Yes, it is so, my kind and worthy neighbors. I perceive your astonishment; you are doubtless much surprised to see these sheep, but I will explain the whole business. You noticed the white foaming spray when you plunged me into the water? Now you must understand that there is a little enchantment in the case, for—thanks to the violence with which you soused me—the cask broke, and as I caught at the foam, it turned to sheep, and very fine sheep they are. Many thanks, therefore, to you. To prove to you my gratitude, I would advise you, one and all, to enrich yourselves in the same manner."

No sooner had they heard this than each determined immediately to make the experiment, after having before them such a convincing proof of its success. Away, therefore, they scampered back to the water. The foremost jumped in at once, the others directly after him; but although they made foam and froth enough with their plunging about, no sheep appeared. On the contrary, they buffeted each other about in the water at such a rate that they were all drowned. Thus did Kibitz safely rid himself of all his envious neighbors at once and thereby render himself master of the whole village.

G. Hans Christian Andersen, "Little Claus and Great Claus"

eprinted from Hans Christian Andersen, *Stories for the Household,* trans. H. W. Dulcken (London: George Routledge and Sons; New York: E. P. Dutton, 1888), 24–33.

There lived two men in one village, and they had the same name—each was called Claus; but one had four horses, and the other only a single horse. To

distinguish them from each other, folks called him who had four horses Great Claus, and the one who had only a single horse Little Claus. Now we shall hear what happened to each of them, for this is a true story.

The whole week through Little Claus was obliged to plough for Great Claus, and to lend him his one horse; then Great Claus helped him out with all his four, but only once a week, and that on a holiday. Hurrah! how Little Claus smacked his whip over all five horses, for they were as good as his own on that one day. The sun shone gaily, and all the bells in the steeples were ringing; the people were all dressed in their best, and were going to church, with their hymn-books under their arms, to hear the clergyman preach, and they saw Little Claus ploughing with five horses; but he was so merry that he smacked his whip again and again, and cried, "Gee up, all my five!"

"You must not talk so," said Great Claus, "for only the one horse is yours."

But when no one was passing Little Claus forgot that he was not to say this, and he cried, "Gee up, all my horses!"

"Now, I must beg of you to let that alone," cried Great Claus, "for if you say it again, I shall hit your horse on the head, so that it will fall down dead, and then it will be all over with him."

"I will certainly not say it anymore," said Little Claus.

But when people came by soon afterwards, and nodded "good day" to him, he became very glad, and thought it looked very well, after all, that he had five horses to plough his field; and so he smacked his whip again, and cried, "Gee up, all my horses!"

"I'll 'gee up' your horses!" said Great Claus. And he took the hatchet and hit the only horse of Little Claus on the head, so that it fell down, and was dead immediately.

"Oh, now I haven't any horse at all!" said Little Claus, and began to cry.

Then he flayed the horse, and let the hide dry in the wind, and put it in a sack and hung it over his shoulder, and went to the town to sell his horse's skin.

He had a very long way to go, and was obliged to pass through a great dark wood, and the weather became dreadfully bad. He went quite astray, and before he got into the right way again it was evening, and it was too far to get home again or even to the town before nightfall. Close by the road stood a large farm-house. The shutters were closed outside the windows, but the light could still be seen shining out over them.

"I may be able to get leave to stop here through the night," thought Little Claus; and he went and knocked. The farmer's wife opened the door; but when she heard what he wanted she told him to go away, declaring that her husband was not at home, and she would not receive strangers. "Then I

shall have to lie outside," said Little Claus. And the farmer's wife shut the door in his face.

Close by stood a great haystack, and between this and the farm-house was a little outhouse thatched with straw. "Up there I can lie," said Little Claus, when he looked up at the roof. "That is a capital bed. I suppose the stork won't fly down and bite me in the legs." For a living stork was standing on the roof, where he had his nest.

Now little Claus climbed up to the roof of the shed, where he lay, and turned round to settle himself comfortably. As he did so, he discovered that the wooden shutters did not cover the windows at the top, and he could look straight into the room. There was a great table, with the cloth laid, and wine and roast meat and a glorious fish upon it. The farmer's wife and the clerk were seated at table, and nobody besides. She was filling his glass, and he was digging his fork into the fish, for that was his favorite dish.

"If one could only get some too!" thought Little Claus, as he stretched out his head towards the window. Heavens! what a glorious cake he saw standing there! Yes, certainly, that was a feast.

Now he heard some one riding along the high road. It was the woman's husband, who was coming home. He was a good man enough, but he had the strange peculiarity that he could never bear to see a clerk. If a clerk appeared before his eyes he became quite wild. And that was the reason why the clerk had gone to the wife to wish her good day, because he knew that her husband was not at home; and the good woman therefore put the best fare she had before him. But when they heard the man coming they were frightened, and the woman begged the clerk to creep into a great empty chest which stood there; and he did so, for he knew the husband could not bear the sight of a clerk. The woman quickly hid all the excellent meat and wine in her baking-oven; for if the man had seen that, he would have been certain to ask what it meant.

"Ah, yes!" sighed Little Claus, up in his shed, when he saw all the good fare put away. "Is there any one up there?" asked the farmer; and he looked up at Little Claus. "Who are you lying there? Better come with me into the room." And Little Claus told him how he had lost his way, and asked leave to stay there for the night. "Yes, certainly," said the peasant, "but first we must have something to live on."

The woman received them both in a very friendly way, spread the cloth on a long table, and gave them a great dish of porridge. The farmer was hungry, and ate with a good appetite; but Little Claus could not help thinking of the capital roast meat, fish, and cake, which he knew were in the oven. Under the table, at his feet, he had laid the sack with the horse's hide in it; for we know that he had come out to sell it in the town. He could not

relish the porridge, so he trod upon the sack, and the dry skin inside crackled quite loudly.

"Why, what have you in your sack?" asked the farmer.

"Oh, that's a magician," answered Little Claus. "He says we are not to eat porridge, for he has conjured the oven full of roast meat, fish, and cake."

"Wonderful!" cried the farmer; and he opened the oven in a hurry, and found all the dainty provisions which his wife had hidden there, but which, as he thought, the wizard had conjured forth. The woman dared not say anything, but put the things at once on the table; and so they both ate of the meat, the fish, and the cake. Now Little Claus again trod on his sack, and made the hide creak.

"What does he say now?" said the farmer.

"He says," replied Claus, "that he has conjured three bottles of wine for us, too, and that they are standing there in the corner behind the oven."

Now the woman was obliged to bring out the wine which she had hidden, and the farmer drank it and became very merry. He would have been very glad to see such a conjuror as Little Claus had there in the sack.

"Can he conjure the demon forth?" asked the farmer. "I should like to see him, for now I am merry."

"Oh, yes," said Little Claus; "my conjuror can do anything that I ask of him. Can you not?" he added, and trod on the hide, so that it crackled. "He says 'Yes.' But the demon is very ugly to look at: we had better not see him."

"Oh, I'm not at all afraid. Pray, what will he look like?"

"Why, he'll look the very image of a clerk."

"Ha!" said the farmer, "that is ugly! You must know, I can't bear the sight of a clerk. But it doesn't matter now, for I know that he's a demon, so I shall easily stand it. Now I have courage, but he must not come too near me."

"Now I will ask my conjuror," said Little Claus; and he trod on the sack and held his ear down.

"What does he say?"

"He says you may go and open the chest that stands in the corner, and you will see the demon crouching in it; but you must hold the lid so that he doesn't slip out."

"Will you help me to hold him?" asked the farmer. And he went to the chest where the wife had hidden the real clerk, who sat in there and was very much afraid. The farmer opened the lid a little way and peeped in underneath it.

"Hu!" he cried, and sprang backward. "Yes, now I've seen him, and he looked exactly like our clerk. Oh, that was dreadful!"

Upon this they must drink. So they sat and drank until late into the night.

"You must sell me that conjuror," said the farmer. "Ask as much as you like for him: I'll give you a whole bushel of money directly."

"No, that I can't do," said Little Claus: "only think how much use I can make of this conjuror."

"Oh, I should so much like to have him!" cried the farmer; and he went on begging. "Well," said Little Claus, at last, "as you have been so kind as to give me shelter for the night, I will let it be so. You shall have the conjuror for a bushel of money; but I must have the bushel heaped up."

"That you shall have," replied the farmer. "But you must take the chest yonder away with you. I will not keep it in my house an hour. One cannot know, perhaps he may be there still." Little Claus gave the farmer his sack with the dry hide in it, and got in exchange a whole bushel of money, and that heaped up. The farmer also gave him a big truck, on which to carry off his money and chest.

"Farewell!" said Little Claus; and he went off with his money and the big chest, in which the clerk was still sitting.

On the other side of the wood was a great deep river. The water rushed along so rapidly that one could scarcely swim against the stream. A fine new bridge had been built over it. Little Claus stopped on the center of the bridge, and said quite loud, so that the clerk could hear it, "Ho, what shall I do with this stupid chest? It's as heavy as if stones were in it. I shall only get tired if I drag it any farther, so I'll throw it into the river: if it swims home to me, well and good; and if it does not, it will be no great matter."

And he took the chest with one hand, and lifted it up a little, as if he intended to throw it into the river.

"No! let be!" cried the clerk from within the chest; "let me out first!"

"Hu!" exclaimed Little Claus, pretending to be frightened, "he's in there still! I must make haste and throw him into the river, that he may be drowned."

"Oh, no, no!" screamed the clerk. "I'll give you a whole bushel-full of money if you'll let me go."

"Why, that's another thing!" said Little Claus; and he opened the chest.

The clerk crept quickly out, pushed the empty chest into the water, and went to his house, where Little Claus received a whole bushel-full of money. He had already received one from the farmer, and so now he had his truck loaded with money.

"See, I've been well paid for the horse," he said to himself when he had got home to his own room, and was emptying all the money into a heap in the middle of the floor. "That will vex Great Claus when he hears how rich I have grown through my one horse; but I won't tell him about it outright."

So he sent a boy to Great Claus to ask for a bushel measure.

"What can he want with it?" thought Great Claus. And he smeared some tar underneath the measure, so that some part of whatever was measured should stick to it. And thus it happened; for when he received the measure back, there were three new eight-shilling pieces adhering to it.

"What's this?" cried Great Claus; and he ran off at once to Little Claus. "Where did you get all that money from?"

"Oh, that's for my horse's skin. I sold it yesterday evening."

"That's really being well paid," said Great Claus. And he ran home in a hurry, took an axe, and killed all his four horses; then he flayed them, and carried off their skins to the town.

"Hides! hides! who'll buy any hides?" he cried through the streets.

All the shoemakers and tanners came running, and asked how much he wanted for them.

"A bushel of money for each!" said Great Claus.

"Are you mad?" said they. "Do you think we have money by the bushel?"

"Hides! hides!" he cried again; and to all who asked him what the hides would cost he replied, "A bushel of money."

"He wants to make fools of us," they all exclaimed. And the shoemakers took their straps, and the tanners their aprons, and they began to beat Great Claus.

"Hides! hides!" they called after him, jeeringly. "Yes, we'll tan your hide for you till the red broth runs down. Out of the town with him!" And Great Claus made the best haste he could, for he had never yet been thrashed as he was thrashed now.

"Well," said he when he got home. "Little Claus shall pay for this. I'll kill him for it."

Now, at Little Claus's the old grandmother had died. She had been very harsh and unkind to him, but yet he was very sorry, and took the dead woman and laid her in his warm bed, to see if she would not come to life again. There he intended she should remain all through the night, and he himself would sit in the corner and sleep on a chair, as he had often done before. As he sat there, in the night the door opened, and Great Claus came in with his axe. He knew where Little Claus's bed stood; and, going straight up to it, he hit the old grandmother on the head, thinking she was Little Claus.

"Do you see," said he, "you shall not make a fool of me again." And then he went home.

"That's a bad fellow, that man," said Little Claus. "He wanted to kill me. It was a good thing for my old grandmother that she was dead already. He would have taken her life."

And he dressed his grandmother in her Sunday clothes, borrowed a

horse of his neighbor, harnessed it to a car, and put the old lady on the back seat, so that she could not fall out when he drove. And so they trundled through the wood. When the sun rose they were in front of an inn; there Little Claus pulled up, and went in to have some refreshment.

The host had very, very much money; he was also a very good man, but exceedingly hot, as if he had pepper and tobacco in him.

"Good morning," said he to Little Claus. "You've put on your Sunday clothes early today."

"Yes," answered Little Claus. "I'm going to town with my old grand-mother: she's sitting there on the car without. I can't bring her into the room; will you give her a glass of mead? But you must speak very loud, for she can't hear well."

"Yes, that I'll do," said the host. And he poured out a great glass of mead, and went out with it to the dead grandmother, who had been placed up-right in the carriage.

"Here's a glass of mead from your son," said the host. But the dead woman replied not a word, but sat quite still.

"Don't you hear?" cried the host, as loud as he could, "here is a glass of mead from your son!"

Once more he called out the same thing, but as she persisted in not hear-ing him, he became angry at last, and threw the glass in her face, so that the mead ran down over her nose, and she tumbled backwards into the car, for she had only been put upright, and not bound fast.

"Hallo!" cried Little Claus, running out at the door, and seizing the host by the breast, "you've killed my grandmother now! See, there's a big hole in her forehead."

"Oh, here's a misfortune!" cried the host, wringing his hands. "That all comes of my hot temper. Dear Little Claus, I'll give you a bushel of money, and have your grandmother buried as if she were my own; only keep quiet, or I shall have my head cut off, and that would be so very disagreeable!"

So Little Claus again received a whole bushel of money, and the host buried the old grandmother as if she had been his own. And when Little Claus came home with all his money, he at once sent his boy to Great Claus to ask to borrow a bushel measure.

"What's that?" said Great Claus. "Have I not killed him? I must go my-self and see to this." And so he went over himself with the bushel to Little Claus.

"Now, where did you get all that money from?" he asked; and he opened his eyes wide when he saw all that had been brought together.

"You killed my grandmother, and not me," replied Little Claus, "and I've been and sold her, and got a whole bushel of money for her."

"That's really being well paid," said Great Claus; and he hastened home, took an axe, and killed his own grandmother directly. Then he put her on a carriage, and drove off to the town with her, to where the apothecary lived, and asked him if he would buy a dead person.

"Who is it, and where did you get him from?" asked the apothecary.

"It's my grandmother," answered Great Claus. "I've killed her to get a bushel of money for her."

"Heaven save us!" cried the apothecary, "you're raving! Don't say such things, or you may lose your head." And he told him earnestly what a bad deed this was that he had done, and what a bad man he was, and that he must be punished. And Great Claus was so frightened that he jumped out of the surgery straight into his carriage, and whipped the horses, and drove home. But the apothecary and all the people thought him mad, and so they let him drive whither he would.

"You shall pay for this!" said Great Claus, when he was out upon the high road: "yes, you shall pay me for this, Little Claus!" And directly he got home he took the biggest sack he could find, and went over to Little Claus, and said, "Now, you've tricked me again! First I killed my horses, and then my old grandmother! That's all your fault; but you shall never trick me any more." And he seized Little Claus round the body, and thrust him into the sack, and took him upon his back, and called out to him, "Now I shall go off with you and drown you."

It was a long way that he had to travel before he came to the river, and Little Claus was not too light to carry. The road led him close to a church: the organ was playing, and the people were singing so beautifully! Then Great Claus put down his sack, with Little Claus in it, close to the church door, and thought it would be a very good thing to go in and hear a psalm before he went farther; for Little Claus could not get out, and all the people were in church; and so he went in.

"Ah, yes! yes!" sighed Little Claus in the sack. And he turned and twisted, but he found it impossible to loosen the cord. Then there came by an old drover with snow-white hair, and a great staff in his hand: he was driving a whole herd of cows and oxen before him, and they stumbled against the sack in which Little Claus was confined, so that it was overthrown.

"Oh, dear!" sighed Little Claus, "I'm so young yet, and am to go to heaven directly!"

"And I, poor fellow," said the drover, "am so old already, and can't get there yet!"

"Open the sack," cried Little Claus; "creep into it instead of me, and you will get to heaven directly."

"With all my heart," replied the drover; and he untied the sack, out of which Little Claus crept forth immediately.

"But will you look after the cattle?" said the old man; and he crept into the sack at once, whereupon Little Claus tied it up, and went his way with all the cows and oxen.

Soon afterwards Great Claus came out of the church. He took the sack on his shoulders again, although it seemed to him as if the sack had become lighter; for the old drover was only half as heavy as Little Claus.

"How light he is to carry now! Yes, that is because I have heard a psalm."

So he went to the river, which was deep and broad, threw the sack with the old drover in it into the water, and called after him, thinking that it was little Claus, "You lie there! Now you shan't trick me any more!"

Then he went home; but when he came to a place where there was a cross road, he met little Claus driving all his beasts.

"What's this?" cried Great Claus. "Have I not drowned you?"

"Yes," replied Little Claus, "you threw me into the river less than half an hour ago."

"But wherever did you get all those fine beasts from?" asked Great Claus.

"These beasts are sea-cattle," replied Little Claus. "I'll tell you the whole story, and thank you for drowning me, for now I'm at the top of the tree. I am really rich! How frightened I was when I lay huddled in the sack, and the wind whistled about my ears when you threw me down from the bridge into the cold water! I sank to the bottom immediately; but I did not knock myself, for the most splendid soft grass grows down there. Upon that I fell; and immediately the sack was opened, and the loveliest maiden, with snow-white garments and a green wreath upon her wet hair, took me by the hand, and said, 'Are you come, Little Claus? Here you have some cattle to begin with. A mile farther along the road there is a whole herd more, which I will give to you.' And now I saw that the river formed a great highway for the people of the sea. Down in its bed they walked and drove directly from the sea, and straight into the land, to where the river ends. There it was so beautifully full of flowers and of the freshest grass; the fishes, which swam in the water, shot past my ears, just as here the birds in the air. What pretty people there were there, and what fine cattle pasturing on mounds and in ditches!"

"But why did you come up again to us directly?" asked Great Claus. "I should not have done that, if it is so beautiful down there."

"Why," replied Little Claus, "in that I just acted with good policy. You heard me tell you that the sea-maiden said, 'A mile farther along the road'— and by the road she meant the river, for she can't go anywhere else—'there is a whole herd of cattle for you.' But I know what bends the stream makes— sometimes this way, sometimes that; there's a long way to go round: no, the

thing can be managed in a shorter way by coming here to the land, and driving across the fields towards the river again. In this manner I save myself almost half a mile, and get all the quicker to my sea-cattle!"

"Oh, you are a fortunate man!" said Great Claus. "Do you think I should get some sea-cattle too if I went down to the bottom of the river?"

"Yes, I think so," replied Little Claus. "But I cannot carry you in the sack as far as the river; you are too heavy for me! But if you will go there, and creep into the sack yourself, I will throw you in with a great deal of pleasure."

"Thanks!" said Great Claus; "but if I don't get any sea-cattle when I am down there, I shall beat you, you may be sure!"

"Oh, no; don't be so fierce!"

And so they went together to the river. When the beasts, which were thirsty, saw the stream, they ran as fast as they could to get at the water.

"See how they hurry!" cried Little Claus. "They are longing to get back to the bottom."

"Yes, but help me first!" said Great Claus, "Or else you shall be beaten."

And so he crept into the great sack, which had been laid across the back of one of the oxen.

"Put a stone in, for I'm afraid otherwise I shall not sink," said Great Claus.

"That can be done," replied Little Claus; and he put a big stone into the sack, tied the rope tightly, and pushed against it. Plump! There lay Great Claus in the river, and sank at once to the bottom.

"I'm afraid he won't find the cattle!" said Little Claus; and then he drove homeward with what he had.

H. List of Folk-Literature Motifs in *One-Ox*

MI Classification	Description
B103	Treasure-producing animals
D457.13	Transformation: animal dung to other object
D563	Transformation by encircling object thrice
D1221	Magic trumpet
D1222	Magic horn (musical)
D1223.1	Magic flute
D1224	Magic pipe (musical)
D1454.5	Treasure from excrements
D1791	Magic power by circumambulation

D1865	Beautification by death and resuscitation
E55.3	Resuscitation by blowing trumpet
F111	Journey to earthly paradise
F701	Land of plenty. *Yields everything to heart's desire.*
F725	Submarine world
F931	Extraordinary occurrence connected with sea
J216	Choice of deaths
J1115.6	Clever peasant
J2300	Gullible fools
J2401	Fatal imitation
J2411.1	Imitation of magic rejuvenation unsuccessful
K110	Sale of pseudo-magic objects
K111.1	Alleged gold-dropping animal sold
K113	Pseudo-magic resuscitating object sold. *Dupe kills his wife (mother) and is unable to resuscitate her.*
K135	Pseudo-magic animals sold
K527	Escape by substituting another person in place of the intended victim
K714.2	Victim tricked into entering box
K842	Dupe persuaded to take person's place in a sack: killed. *The bag is to be thrown into the sea. The trickster keeps shouting that he does not want to go to heaven (or marry the princess); the dupe gladly substitutes for him.*
K890	Dupe tricked into killing himself
K890.1	Poor man deceives rich man, plays tricks on him, causes his death
K891	Dupe tricked into jumping to his death
K 894.3	Dupes are persuaded to be thrown over a precipice[32]
K941	Trickster's false report of high prices causes dupe to destroy his property
K941.1	Cows killed for their hides when large price is reported by trickster
K944	Deceptive agreement to kill wives (children). *Trickster shams the murder; dupe kills his.*
K1051	Diving for sheep. *Dupe persuaded that sheep have been lost in river.*
K1816.6	Disguise as herdsman (shepherd, swineherd, etc.)
K1860	Deception by feigned death (sleep)
L143	Poor man surpasses rich
L144	Ignorant surpasses learned man

N534	Treasure discovered by accident
N534.6	Treasure found by man when he obeys call of nature
N630	Accidental acquisition of treasure or money
P412.2	Swineherd
Q467.1	Casting into water in sack (barrel) as punishment
X1503	Schlaraffenland. (Land of Cockaygne.) *Land in which impossible things happen.*

FOUR
The Turnip Tale: Two Presents for the King (ATU 1689A)

A. *The Turnip Tale* [1] (*Rapularius "frivola"*)

Reprinted from Jan M. Ziolkowski, "The *Rapularius* and 'The Turnip' in *Grimms' Fairy Tales:* A Comparative Study with Translations," *Journal of Medieval Latin* 13 (2003): 61–126, at 105–14.

The two most useful editions of *The Turnip Tale "frivola"* [1] are by Karl Langosch (*Asinarius und Rapularius,* Sammlung mittellateinischer Texte 10 [Heidelberg: Carl Winter, 1929], 56–73 [text] and 74–79 [notes]) and Paolo Gatti (*Rapularius I,* in *Commedie latine del XII e XIII secolo,* vol. 5, Pubblicazioni dell'Istituto di filologia classica e medievale 95 [Genoa: Istituto di Filologia classica e medievale, 1986], 35–79 [text and notes]). When I have opted not to follow the edition by Gatti or when Langosch's edition diverges significantly from Gatti's, I have provided concise details in the notes. Gatti (32–34) has a separate list of all differences between his text and Langosch's.

A trifling story reports that there were two brothers whom one mother bore to one man. The rank of knighthood distinguished them both, of whom the one was rich and the other destitute. [5] The rich one held the rank, together with the name, of a knight; the other bore the sad burden of poverty. Yet so that he could not be accounted altogether a beggar, woe! he began to learn an unfamiliar work. Therefore he breaks apart the soil more gently with a drag-hoe, now with a plow;[33] [10] now with a mattock he clears the root-filled pieces of land. He entrusts to the wide-open furrows unproductive oats, inasmuch as he had but a small supply of wheat, and he sows also

the seed of which the little turnip is the fruit; from it a boundless harvest bears fruit.

[15] For him there grew more enormous than the rest one little turnip, which can be called in the full sense of the word a turnip, so extensive in foliage and so large in body, that no one has ever seen its full equal before. Its very shadow sufficed for twelve men, [20] so that beneath it the heat of the sun would not burn them. It was so enormous that by itself it would fill a cart and four oxen could scarcely draw the load.

Thereupon the poor man, having seen the fruit of such great mass, is astounded and begins to say to himself as follows: [25] "O all-powerful God, creator of heaven and earth, by whom was created the first man and every man since, who adorn the heavens with the sun, moon, and stars, who paint the ground with buds of many sorts, and who make the sea inhabitable for sundry fishes: [30] all of creation obeys your will. Without your bidding a tree does not put forth a leaf, without you neither the land nor the ground produces fruits—and without you this marvelous turnip, which exceeds the standard and violates the norm, did not grow. [35] I pray that this fruit be a cause of well-being for me, that it be the end of poverty and the giver of wealth. If God ordains that nothing on earth be without cause, the ground did not produce this fruit in vain. Until now, alas, lord, I have been exhausted by a poverty [40] that ruins me and makes me fall from nobility. Great God, I know that you can release me from such fetters, if only you so will."

Therefore he consults his wife as to what should be done about such a monstrosity. At once his wife says to this, [45] "If this turnip should be sold, it will bring a low price; if eaten in your stomach, it will do even less good. It is advantageous for this rarest of turnips to be given to the king, for rare gifts ought to be given to the king. [50] Perhaps you will be enriched with many an honor by the king, who fittingly gives great gifts in return for small ones."

"This seems good, this I will obviously do," said the man to his wife. "Your counsel and proposal are useful."

Accordingly, he soon puts together and sets in order an appropriate cart, and to the cart he hitches up four oxen. [55] Creaking under so great a weight, the axle groans, and he goes swiftly to take rare gifts to the king. Well then, proceeding thus for three days, the good man reaches the royal stronghold—lo and behold!—on the fourth. He asks to be presented to the king, has his request granted, and enters [60], as is natural for a person who intended to give a great gift. For in fact, the court of kings—like all courts— has ordained for itself this, namely, that everyone who has brought nothing should stand outside before the gates. Yet the ordinance of laws does not deny entrance to that person who approaches the king's thresholds with gifts.

[65] Therefore this man is conveyed into the hall of his king. Standing in the presence of the king he says respectfully, "My lord, accept a certain marvelous gift, which I judge is rightly to be given to the king alone."

At once, having observed so absurd a specimen of produce, [70] the king says, "Heavens, what kind of freak can this be? I ask you, good man: tell from where this marvelous turnip, from where such a turnip came to be yours? To be sure, I know that I have frequently seen many marvels, but never has any human being seen any such thing. [75] This turnip is perhaps not a daughter of the earth; rather, I think that this fell from heaven. As I see, this will be a source and origin of well-being for you, and I think that it is a token of good omen. Come now, say honestly: who are your kinsmen, [80] what is your homeland, what is your native soil?"

When these last words had been spoken by the king, that man responded: "I was born in the dominion of your empire. My parentage is noble and well born; my father was a knight and I myself once was a knight. [85] At hand is a knight as a witness of my twofold nobility; my two parents produced him as my full brother and, although he is puffed up with much wealth and pomp, nevertheless he hardly denies that he is my brother. Your majesty holds this man among his foremost friends; [90] scarcely anyone in the realm is richer than he is. But my unremitting poverty so ruins me that among acquaintances there is no honor for me. Alas, I am distressed daily by such great torments that living is not a small punishment for me. [95] How great a torment, lord, do you think that my brother's glory is for me, since a life of need lays me prostrate before my own kinsman? Look how proud he is, whom nature had created as my equal; but being poor and a peasant oppresses me. Woe! I know by experience how true the saying is: [100] 'the rich man is everywhere pleasing, the poor man everywhere lies low.' See how my brother pleases the king and pleases the city. Alas for me, every territory despises me as a wretch. Since both wealth and material resources were abandoning me, I laid down my sword and the game of soldiering. [105] And now in place of a sword this hand uses a mattock, so that by my toil I may dig my own fields. I, who once was accustomed to frighten all enemies, now poke the backsides of oxen with goads. I, who once was eager to handle the business of war, [110] now as a poor man sow my own fields by hand.³⁴ Thus I lead a wretched life in the manner of a peasant. From it comes my food, from it clothing, and from it, lord, the present turnip that you behold, of a sort that no human being has ever seen or will see. [115] And because great things befit great men, I wished to bring these to you, greatest prince, in return for a great gift."

Replying to him, the king says, "What you offer, friend, is pleasing. You should know that you have earned the king's friendship. Look, good man:

I will pay you back with a worthy exchange [120] and I will give great rewards³⁵ for your merits. You will be enriched so much by the emperor's hand that you will seem completely equal to your brother."

At once the king orders his private caskets to be opened, which a great heap of wealth had swollen. [125] Therefore the king, then burdening the man with property of many different kinds, packs him with a great weight of treasures. To the treasures he adds horses (and the horses are not without caparisons), and he adds a herd of cattle and wool-producing sheep. Why should I list each and every one of the goods the king gave the man? [130] Let it suffice to say that he gave the man many things. The man, loaded up with differing property of various types, arranges to approach his own home as a rich man. Therefore, bidding farewell and rendering thanks to the king, he directs his route to his home with everything loaded up.

[135] Now look! As he returns, his wife runs to meet him and, plying him with one sweet kiss after another, said "Hello!" "Tell me," she said also, "if you accomplished anything, or what this long delay has bestowed upon you. Tell, come on and tell, what sort of reward you acquired!"

Whereupon he [140] points out each and every good that he had obtained. "See," he said, "a favoring fortune has now smiled upon me and the generous hand of the king has conferred these things upon me. Now look! Notice how many goods I reap from a worthless seed! See how many goods the great turnip has given me! [145] O wife, rejoice! The entire bounty is at your disposal. From now on you will not be at all poor or destitute. Prosperity and great affluence will be ours, for we will not suffer the burden of poverty. Therefore joys will now dissolve our sorrows. [150] Let joys take their place, for all hardship is absent."

Then he orders neighbors and friends to be summoned, so that he may relate his successes to one and all. Behold, a large assembly of people close to him is gathered and a great abundance of food is served to them. [155] And when he sees them joyful and drunk, he begins thus to tell of his own successes: "Listen, I beg you, acquaintances; mark my words! I will make known to you my good fortune. For all of you know how great a poverty reduced me; [160] but I have been saved from it by God's goodness. It happened that a rare turnip grew in my garden; this same turnip grew large beyond measure. I gave this to the king in return for a great gift; in return for it he gave me these riches."

[165] At the same time as the man was saying these things, the knight whom we said was the man's full brother was present among the friends. He began actually to waste away with a pernicious envy when he saw the gains of his brother increasing, and having marveled at the sudden honor of his brother, [170] he thinks himself to be nothing in respect to him. In fact,

every envious man claims this quality as his own, that he thinks the gains of another harm him. Envious man, tell: why are you tormented by the honoring of a brother? If a poor man is made rich, you do not lose your possessions on account of this, do you? [175] Envious man, believe me: his fortune takes nothing away from you. It befits you rather to be happy for this reason. His good fortune is not a cause of ruin for you, and a brother's gains do not amount to losses for you. Having given these brief reminders about the sickness of envy, [180] let us now regain the course of the story itself.

Therefore, when the guests had been stuffed with food and wine, and each person returns full and happy to his home, then too the brother of the man returns to his house, taking with him the dreadful venom of envy, [185] thirsting for gold although covered by much gold, in the same way as Tantalus looks for water amid the waters. Then, so that he may hunt and increase wealth with wealth, (watch now!) he says, weaving a new net of slyness, "If this brother of mine, whom such great poverty oppressed, [190] received such great wealth in return for a base commodity, I will win the king's favor with quite precious gifts, which the king will restore to me one hundredfold."

At once he deprives himself of his own silver and gold, doubtless so that he might present his king with them. [195] He takes precious necklaces of gems (long-closed strongboxes had been laboring with a bundle of these gems), and he folds up clothes woven with ornate design, with which it is fitting to adorn the limbs of a king. To all these things he adds horses covered with fine trappings, [200] whose manes are encircled with tawny metal—gold. The knight, burdened with such splendors and others like them, sets off and is conveyed all the way to the king's gates.[36] And when he had greeted the king in the manner in which he was supposed to, the knight says, pointing out each and every gift, [205] "Accept, my lord, what your knight offers you; I beg you not to despise them, revered king. Few indeed are these things and hardly befitting a king. When I am rich, then I will give better things."

Faced with these sights the king says, "Accept my thanks! [210] By Hercules, I admit that such great gifts please me. Beneath the poles of heaven no one is believed to exist who has given so many precious things to his king."

The king is also reported to have consulted his queen as to what he could bestow upon so great a benefactor. [215] Thereupon she, abounding in the logic of royal wisdom, rendered these words of response to her husband: "Renowned king, this man is filled up with too much wealth and cannot at all need a gift from you; and he disdains your silver and likewise your gold. [220] If you give gems, they will be like hail. If you give clothes, if you give gifts appropriate for noblemen in wartime, he will despise them

all and account them to be nothing. Yet so that the man not despise all royal gifts, it remains that the enormous turnip be given him. [225] He, who despises everything else, will not despise it. On the contrary, it will supply the equivalent of a rare gift."

The wife spoke these words. To her the king responds and states: "Your counsel and proposal are useful."

Without delay, at the king's bidding the turnip is brought out [230] and it becomes the emperor's gift to the man. "Look here!" said the king, "I present you with a rare gift. Nothing rarer than it can be mine or anyone's. Just recently in fact a certain poor man gave it to me; to him this bountiful hand gave many goods."

[235] That wretch accepts the gift, clearly unacceptable because what he accepted was a worthless turnip.

Thus it is fitting, O brothers, that a greedy man should be tripped up, whom a large heap of wealth cannot fill completely. For if the whole world should be given to a greedy person, [240] nevertheless that unfortunate believes that he has nothing. Thus the aforesaid person, whom wealth made destitute, is bereft of his own possessions, seeing that he thirsts for those of others. As the fool hunts for profit, he loses his own property and—see!— he who had given great gifts received a worthless vegetable. [245] Thus the madman is deceived through his own ploy; as he wishes to be enriched, he loses even what he has. Is not a person who puts a fountain into the sea mad? He takes waters from the fountain that he may enrich the sea with waters. Hardly otherwise this knight, so that he may enrich the king with a gift, [250] does not fear to strip himself of his own goods.

And now he returns home, represses his bitter anger,[37] and grieves at having given such great gifts to the king for nothing. Gnashing his teeth as a result, he mutters with silent mouth in this way:[38] "See how I suffer these losses through the trickery of my brother! [255] He is raised aloft; I—woe!— am pressed down. Therefore he will not go unpunished, by my head!" he said.

Therefore he calls together his people, whom he knew to be trustworthy, and raging more than a lion he began to say as follows: "You certainly know how great my glory was previously. [260] It was common to me as well as to you. Now, by the cunning of a certain scoundrel, all of this same glory has tumbled headlong. All the resources by which I was elevated have been taken away. Alas, I now bear the heavy yoke of poverty! [265] Alas, I have fallen wretchedly! Yet it is your task to remember that in my fall you have likewise fallen. Now if you have any pulse of loyalty in you or any respect for loyalty, may vengeance strike against my enemy through you so [270] that you may give him the repayment he has earned."

They say, "He who is your enemy is ours as well; and whatever you bid, we will do it to him."

When they had said these words, he is heartened by the voices of his men and, as if out of his mind, says such things besides: [275] "Not far away is a valley planted with trees in groves; it was never fit for any crops. I beg you, enter this valley with arms manfully taken up—but let no one at all except you know the reason! Until I come, do not go off anywhere; [280] after picking up my enemy I will follow you quickly." He said this; they obey and go ahead of him as he follows. They come into the valley and occupy the sites as bidden.

The brother approaches his brother, the former filled with bile, the latter lacking it, and, falsely using sweet words, says: [285] "O my full brother, no one is left to me apart from you, whom love joins to me in a brotherly bond. We are one flesh and nature does not sunder us; one mother bore us to one man. Perhaps one soul resides in two persons, [290] whom an indivisible love joins and unites. I have a secret that I do not wish to reveal to anyone, and yet I do not wish it to be hidden from my brother. There is nearby and not far removed from the city a dense valley, overgrown by tree branches, lacking in crops. [295] This is filled up with so great a mass of treasure that it would profit you and suffice for me. This I will share with you in brotherly love. No, that is wrong: as God is my witness, the larger share will be yours. Now come along, put an end to delays, leave off stalling, arise! [300] Let us be on our way while no one is the wiser!"

The man is ensnared by these feigned blandishments, for he does not know that treacheries lie within his brother's words. Therefore he gives assent at once to his brother and adviser; he arises and goes off without any suspicion of evil. [305] The brother goes with his brother and comes upon the aforementioned place in which armed men lay hidden. The men leap out like dogs and, handling the just man unspeakably, even prepare to put him to death. As his own dogs once seized Actaeon, [310] so that man falls prey to his own townsmen. Now with all their efforts they strive to bind the man and now endeavor to cut the throat of their prey. But Fortune aids and safeguards her protégé, and halts the horrific course of this crime.

[315] In the meantime it happened that a certain scholar was hastening, who was about to go alone through this valley. He came, sitting on a horse, sounding out his songs with his voice; as travelers do, he was shortening his route in this way. As he raises his voice, at once a responsive echo returns his voice [320] and this sound is heard from afar. But when the same voice struck the ears of the henchmen, to them comes only fear of being betrayed. And because it was not allowed to carry out this criminal act, in panic they put their hope in flight alone. [325] Yet so that this man should not escape,

he is put in a sack and is bound—still alive—on a tree branch. He dangles, the henchmen flee, and in addition the instigator of the crime does not linger but instead flees.

Look now, the scholar arrives, wishing to rest beneath the shade [330] of the tree, on the branch of which the man dangled. And because this very sack had holes in its side, that dangling man sees the youth through the holes. Presently, when he sees the tonsure of the head, look now! he knows that it is a scholar's and says, crying out, "Hello there, whoever you are!"

[335] But when this voice came down to the ears of the scholar, exceeding fright and dread took hold of him. Then, arising in astonishment, he surveys the nearby places with his eyes, wishing to know from whose mouth that voice resounds. And since he stood for a long time in astonishment and saw no one, [340] he figures that he is being deceived by the craft of a demon. For this reason he thinks to depart quickly from the place. Fear forbids him to stay, but shame prevents him from going. Though unwilling, he stays as shame overcomes fright and, speaking these words, he cries out to the person greeting him, [345] "Whoever you are or wherever you are, from whom this voice reechoes, I would like gladly to know, if I could."

Once again the man dangling speaks from the sack: "You should fear nothing, young man. Put aside this fear! Raise your troubled head, if you wish to look upon the person speaking. [350] I am in happy possession of the sky; I spurn the ground. I sit in a sack and wisdom sits here with me; dangling here, I have learned many things in a short time. By heavens, scholars seek out schools far and wide; you should know that true schools are only here. [355] And so that you should know what the present sack has conferred upon me, I will relate to you at least a few of many things. Here philosophy taught me many arts, so that the entire mechanism of the heavens should be known to me. Here I learned to recognize the signs of the stars, [360] so that I should know from them whatever the future holds. Here I confess that I learned the natures of wild beasts; here the nature of every bird is revealed to me. I add that I learned to differentiate the powers of herbs, so that I might figure out well which are good and which evil. [365] Here I learned the powers of trees and stones, and I learned what advantage resides in them. And I learned to investigate the depth of the swelling sea. This sack has bestowed all this upon me. You have heard what is the nature of this sack, [370] which grants such great boons to its possessor. Certainly this sack is worthier than precious purple, better and more useful than a king's robe.[39] Certainly I know from experience that scholars are raving mad who seek out and tour many schools. [375] Certain men make the rounds of Paris or other cities, spend much, and profit little. Here I passed a brief moment without expense and learned whatever was necessary to know. If even a brief hour of studying

here should be granted you, [380] you will learn what advantage this place holds."

The naive youth, overly credulous in this nonsense, begs that he be able to have a place in the sack. The man dangling said, "Far be it, for you will not thus delude me. Not so has a man come into the sack, my friend."

[385] In reply the youth bursts out into this statement: "Unless I am deceived, I will be the guest of this sack. Now I know in how much power the sack abounds, in the inner fold of which philosophy rests. Now you are learned enough, now you are so erudite that there can be [390] no one more erudite than you in the world. Whoever you are in the sack, I entreat you: take pity on me in my wretchedness, that I may make a brief stay in the sack. If perhaps the words of my prayers do not sway you, the love of a gift will succeed in doing so, I hope. [395] And if you are not willing to be swayed without prompting, I will take care to pay out whatever you wish to have for love of a reward."[40]

Then, as if unwilling, he showed himself from the sack; dangling, he repays him once more with these words: "You strive in vain; affluence is not of such great worth to me[41] [400] that this sack could be sold at your price. Do you hope that I wish to abandon this school? Far be it! You are deceived; your hope will be like the wind. I prefer to die, friend, rather than to lose these delights. If I should be bad to myself, to whom can I be good? [405] You are not hoping that I will sell you the delights of the sack, are you? Far be it! In such fashion no person has come into this sack. It will not befall me to put on sale this sack, in the inner fold of which philosophy rests. Yet because you are aflame with a great love of learning, [410] I grant it to you free of charge for a brief time. And when you have drunk enough from the font of wisdom, then return to me the delights of my sack! Swiftly climb the bough and cut the cord, so that you may be put in possession of your desire!"

[415] Having heard this, the unfortunate happily obeys the man dangling there so that he may be able to enjoy the advantage of the sack. The one emerges but the other makes haste to step in and demands that he be hauled up. The first one refuses, saying: "Wait a little! The rule of the sack does not so prescribe; [420] in this manner, friend, a person has not come into the sack."

And pushing down toward the ground his head and turning up his heels, he says, "This is the law of the sack; in such a way you will be inside."[42]

Saying this, he suspended the sack in the air above and bound it on a knotty branch. [425] Then he stood and began to insult the scholar as follows and spoke with the voice of a mocker: "Look! What you wished, what you sought, what you loved: now you have been made the possessor of your desire. Now I think you have begun to be a most erudite sage, [430] so that in

the whole world there is no one like you. O you all too blessed and outstanding master, whom philosophy cherishes in her lap. I know for certain from experience how great the delight you now feel, whom the fortunate cloisters of such a sack hold. [435] Now philosophize! State what you have learned here, and insofar as you are able, philosophize now! Enjoy your lot, which you sought wholeheartedly, and enjoy your lot, which God has granted! Now it remains for me—by your leave—to regain my home; [440] now I do not care to come into my sack."[43] Having said these words, he mounts the horse of the man hanging and goes off. Shouting out he said, "Great sage, farewell!"

B. *The Turnip Tale* [2] (*Rapularius "prodiga"*)

eprinted from Jan M. Ziolkowski, "The *Rapularius* and 'The Turnip' in *Grimms' Fairy Tales:* A Comparative Study with Translations," *Journal of Medieval Latin* 13 (2003): 61–126, at 115–24.

The two most useful editions of *The Turnip Tale "prodiga"* [2] are by Karl Langosch (*Asinarius und Rapularius,* 86–102 [text], 103–6 [notes]) and Gatti (*Rapularius II,* in *Commedie latine del XII e XIII secolo,* vol. 6, Pubblicazioni del D.Ar.Fi.Cl.Et., n.s., 176 [Genoa: Dipartimento di Archeologia, Filologia classica e loro Tradizioni, 1998], 331–78 [text and notes]). When I have opted not to follow the edition by Gatti or when Langosch's edition diverges significantly from Gatti's, I have provided concise details in the notes.

An extravagant story reports that there were two brothers whom one mother bore to one man. The rank of knighthood distinguished them both, of whom the one was rich and the other destitute. [5] The rich one held the rank, together with the name, of a knight; but the other lived destitute, with a poor income.[44] Therefore, because his property had been taken away, the latter ceased to be a knight and chose to be a wretched peasant. Accordingly, he bids farewell to Mars and serves as knight no longer, [10] but rather—for shame!—devotes himself to Ceres. To dispel for himself[45] the expenses of a wretched life, he strikes the ground with a hoe as a countryman does. And thus he sows the seed of which the little turnip is the fruit; and he takes the yield of its seed.[46]

[15] For him there grew more enormous than the rest one little turnip, which can be called in the full sense of the word a turnip, and it was so large that he had not seen its like before—nor is anyone believed to have seen the like. It was so enormous that by itself it would fill a cart [20] and two oxen would hardly draw such a weight.

Having seen this, the peasant is stirred as if by a portent and is astounded at the novelty of the unusual thing. And while in astonishment, he said: "This did not happen without a reason." And yet he does not have foreknowledge of the good fortune. [25] As he marvels over the end to which this omen is leading, he conjectures that it is a token of good luck. And because the mind of human beings is not prescient of the future, hope and fear arise together in him at once. But since the unclear omen gave cause to hope to the fearful man, [30] he repeats to himself these words with a mouth that is indeed cautious: "O all-powerful God, who alone created all things, who can know where every single thing is headed, without whom no tree is believed to drop leaves and without whom what is high and mighty could not be brought down low to ruin, [35] I ask you, highest God, who govern all created things, do not deprive me of your accustomed goodness. Take away whatever can hinder; bestow what I wish, so that this rare fruit may be for me a harbinger of good! Until now I have been suffering a wretched life here; [40] therefore I entreat you, God: change my lot from now on!"

When the man had spoken these words, he considers what seems necessary to do and says these things to himself, with no one present: "If this turnip is sold, it will bring a low price; but if eaten in my stomach, it will do even less good. [45] Therefore I will give this so exceptional thing to the king, for indeed an exceptional thing suits the king." As the poor man ponders these things within himself, he says: "I can think of nothing more useful; this suits me and I will do this."

Therefore he hurries and prepares swiftly an appropriate cart [50] and orders this great burden to be placed upon it; and hitching up two oxen he hastens to the hall to offer rare gifts to his king: "Receive, my lord, the small gifts of this poor man, which I think should be given to no one rather than you! [55] Even if you judge them not very precious, you will not deny that they are rare, and in my opinion rare things are rightly given to the king."

At once, having inspected the weight of so great a fruit, the king said, "Heavens, what kind of freak can this be? Certainly I recall that I have seen many marvels, [60] but never has a person seen such a thing—nor have I. Tell, I ask, tell from where this fruit has come, from where this so very exceptional spectacle has come to you. I believe that this fruit will become a cause of well-being for you, and I think that it is a mark of good fortune. [65] Tell, come now, tell who you are, what your lineage is and what rank you hold and what your work is!"

The man, encouraged by the king's words that flowed so sweetly, spoke immediately a response of such a sort: "I have been made a poor man, not born of a poor father; [70] I was born, lord, of a knightly father. My

brother, whom you know well, remains rich still; he denies that I am his full brother. Woe! I know from experience how true the adage is: 'The rich man is everywhere pleasing, the poor man everywhere lies low.' [75] Indeed my brother himself pleases you and pleases the city, and a not at all small retinue announces him. Alas, I lie buried beneath the dregs of poverty, and I lack the title of nobility. For the common people rate wealth as being of more worth than nobility; [80] for this reason 'the poor man everywhere lies low.' When nature blessed me in my mother's lap, then I was a knight with the name not yet void. When Fortune promised me prosperity, I prospered in material goods no less than in uprightness. [85] But when Fortune showed herself a cruel stepmother to me, she cast down all wealth. From then on, as if made useless for knighthood, I began to be scorned for my peasant status. Ah, who is poorer than a poor knight? [90] No one can know what a moneyless knight suffers. For that reason, king, I do not serve you as a knight now that my material goods have been taken away, but I am compelled instead to avail myself of peasanthood. Now I cleave my fields with a plow⁴⁷ and now I rend them with a hoe, and this toil produces money, although scant. [95] From it came to me the ever so great mass of the present fruit, the likes of which no person has seen or will see. But because great things befit great people, it befits me, greatest of kings, to bring it to you in place of a great gift."

When that man said those things in the hearing of the king, [100] the good king in like manner caresses the man with soothing words : "Yet I do accept this gift as dear and rare, so that I may give thanks and return the favor. For the rest, you will neither be poor nor needy nor lacking anything, for a great abundance of things will be given to you. [105] Put aside apprehension, take hope, and be more resolute; for your affairs are now being handled well, in accord with good fortune. Believe me, you will be enriched by me with such great things that you will well be considered equal to your full brother."

At once a mass of precious metal is brought out [110] and, at the king's command, is given to the aforesaid man. Not content with that, he commands that assorted goods be given, and the words of the commander have an effect. A great holding of fields is added and, together with a flock of bleating sheep,⁴⁸ oxen of each sex are given. [115] Just as a stream in need floods with drops of rain, so a heap of wealth amasses suddenly for the man. So that he would not be ungrateful, the man lies prone and adores the king; then, bidding farewell, he goes off happily to his own property. And he brings forth such sweet gifts to his wife [120] that she herself should be the witness of so great a boon.

"O wife!" he says, "Rejoice with me, because the best of harvests is ready

at hand for us in return for a worthless seed!" He orders neighbors and friends to be summoned, and himself relates the story of the matter to everyone. [125] And afterward he orders a generous banquet to be prepared for everyone; he creates festive bowls with food as well as drink.

Dining among the friends there was also present the knight, whom we said above was the man's brother. And, seeing his brother (who until this point had been poorer than he) [130] so much enriched and enjoying delights, he saw and envied, inferring that he was suffering a loss, as he saw the gains of his brother increasing.

In fact, every envious man claims this quality as his own, that he thinks the gains of another are his losses. [135] And here is to be added this fact also, that he spoke only as the truth who first said, "A greedy man always feels need." Listen closely to this, whoever you are who are considered greedy, whoever you are who come voluntarily under the yoke of greed. Against you are hurled the barbs of our criticism; [140] perhaps they will cause a wound that will bring health. Do tell: for whom do you guard the treasures that you amass, in which you place—alas, rashly—hope and faith? Do you perchance keep these for a thief or perhaps for a tyrant, so that a thief or a violent hand may seize them? [145] You are a shameful idolater, devote your time to images of Satan, and, showing contempt to God, cultivate money shamefully. What does wealth buried in the ground or shut in a coffer do for you? I reckon that it will be of no profit. Therefore be content, rich man, with what you have got and profit from it [150] so long as you are able to profit yourself; and restrain the biting tooth of your envy, and do not think the gains of a brother to be losses of your own. If a needy man becomes rich, what do you lose by this, envious wretch? Nothing, unless you wish to be envious for no reason. [155] If a needy man is made rich, you are tormented without reason, greedy man: your brother reaps profits and you lose nothing thereby.

Leaving behind these matters, let us return to our topic and again approach the route that we began! That one, seeing the unexpected prosperity of his brother [160] and that things turn out well for him in accord with his wishes, grieves that he is, so to speak, depleted and, as it were, deprived of possessions; he began to regard as nothing the wealth he possessed. Therefore, plotting, he lays his snares for his brother, so that he may hunt down wealth through his cunning. [165] Pondering and pondering again many things in his heart, he chews over such words to himself with his mouth clapped shut: "Because he has received many goods in return for a cheap harvest, I will give many things and receive even more rewards."

Soon therefore he gathers a mass of valuable money, [170] in such a fashion that it amounts to the wealth of the king and city. To horses with trap-

pings he adds caparisons woven with gold, and he assembles every manner of every adornment. The new fowler of riches uses snares of this kind, but the desired booty will not fulfill his wishes. [175] He rises, goes away, carries off with him all of the goods, and gives precious gifts to his king.

The king, having accepted the gift of this rich man, said: "O man, truly generous in heart and hand, ancient times do not know one out of many thousands of forefathers [180] who gave such great things to his king."

The king, not knowing what to give back or what to repay, is reported to have consulted his queen. After she reflects well upon this, she brings forth these words at once and replies to her husband: [185] "O king, this man is all too affluent and filled up with wealth, and I know that he does not need your gift. If you give gold or clothes, he will spurn each of them; if gems, the gems will be like hail. Indeed he does not accept horses for himself, not knightly arms: [190] this man overflows amply with all of these. For the sea never needs floods of rain, because it always overflows amply with its own waters. If you give anything, he will turn nauseous to the extent that in satiety he will spurn all manner of food.[49] [195] But so that you not seem to have given nothing to a generous giver, it is appropriate that the great turnip be given him." These words of the queen as she admonished pleased the ears of the king no little bit, and the king said, "So it will be done!"

To the man when he has been summoned the king says, "O richest of men, [200] I thank you greatly, for your gifts please me. Yet I am uncertain what I should repay as a reward, out of what I should give back to you and return the favor. But instead of a payment I give you a great gift—not I nor anyone can have anything rarer than it.[50] [205] For a certain poor man recently gave me this; then this hand of mine conferred worthy rewards." Immediately the apparatus of a cart presents the turnip, and it becomes an imperial gift to the man. See with what craft of Fortune this man is deceived: [210] as he hunts wealth, he loses the very thing he has, and he falls headlong into the ditch of poverty that, although unwittingly, he dug for himself.

That man, seeing that commensurate things are not given and that worthy things are not repaid, at once grieves to have given such great things to the king. [215] And, extremely distraught, he mutters these words to himself as follows: "What should I undertake, wretch that I am? What should I do, what should I try? Who will take compassion on me in my beggary and need, I who seem to have despoiled myself by my own hand?[51] A fearful thief did not carry off my things, nor did a violent robber; [220] I myself was the worst thief and robber to myself."

From then on he fires darts of envy against his brother, as if *he* were guilty in the disastrous business. "These are your schemings, brother," he says, "and I suffer such things on account of your false fraud and trickery."

[225] And as if pierced by his brother with a bleeding wound, he says, "By this head I swear that you will not get away unpunished!"

And so returning home, stirred by wicked furies he rages with his heart and hand to injure his brother. And he summoned his men who he knew were faithful [230] and whose faith past experiences had proven,[52] and he harangues them, addressing them in such a discourse: "It is now fitting, O comrades, for you to be mindful of me.[53] For you know who I am, from what parentage I arose, and in what a great whirlpool of wealth I have been submerged. [235] Now, having been deceived by the cunning of an impostor I complain that I am nothing, bereft of everything. I ask, may the damage to me be shared by you, in suffering together a wrong, in fact, not in committing one. The very same damage that has befallen me—who have always been a king and father to you—has been done to you. [240] Therefore let your faith be demonstrated by the performance of a deed, and also let true love give evidence of itself."

Weeping was a hindrance as he was about to speak more, for numerous tears wet his cheeks. [245] Those present take compassion upon him as he is so afflicted, and the grief of one becomes a common ill. Therefore, wishing to know why the man weeps, they say to him: "For what cause, good man, for what cause does this grief come to you? Tell and it will be our care to bestow care; [250] share the burden you bear and it will be light."

When these words have been said, the poor man checks the font of tears and responds: "If you wish to bring aid to me, as I seek, promise—of course—that you are ready to do whatever I bid!" [255] They promise and at length, with the trustiness of his men providing the means, anger and rage assail the man more gently. Then he says, "Go, search out a place in the neighboring valley that is verdant, cloaked in much foliage of bushes! May you find a place for sitting there until I come there. [260] After picking up my enemy I will follow you very quickly. Let him perish at your hands, with his vitals pierced through by a sword, or let the man be slain by a noose in the manner of a thief!" "He who is your enemy," they say, "is just as much ours. You hand over the man now—he will pay for his impious deeds!"

[265] At once they arm themselves, approach the inmost parts of the grove, and inspect places suited for evil endeavors. The brother approaches his brother,[54] greets him even with pretended peaceableness, and offers up sweet words filled with deceits, as if a doctor should give honey seasoned with poison, [270] in which there will be for the unwitting a lethal potion. Heavens, why do you rave, scoundrel, deceitful with whispering? Why do you trick a brother with your feigned love? He is a scorpion, who feigns love for a person to a person, and pretended good faith is like a hidden dagger. [275] Thus the base brother, a hunter and fowler of his brother, lays snares

for him with these sweet words: "O good brother," he says, "apart from whom no one is alive whom I may so call according to natural relation! You who are the sole hope of my life and the staff of my old age, [280] believe me: everything which is mine is yours. We are one flesh and nature does not sunder us; one mother bore us to one husband. Dearest brother, I will reveal to you a secret matter, which no one is to learn from you. [285] Do not betray what I am going to tell you alone; make it, please, that I speak these words to trustworthy ears! A mass of precious metal has been shown to me, of which—if you wish—a great portion awaits you. Therefore come along briskly and let delay not tempt you. [290] Indeed, as the gods above are my witness, the larger share will be yours."

Ensnared by these words, the man of great ingenuousness heads toward the snare unknowingly like a bird. He turns aside to the place, which is to say, the place of ambush, in which armed men lay hidden. [295] The butchers are present, run together like barking dogs, lay brutal arms upon their prey. As his own dogs once seized Actaeon,[55] so this man falls prey to his own townsmen.

In the meantime the voice of a person singing sweetly resounds nearby [300] and a hoof striking the ground gives sound repeatedly. For a certain young and boisterous scholar comes, singing a tune sweetly as a traveler does. Without delay, the captive is cast headlong into a sack; the man is bound upon the bough of a lofty tree. [305] Quickly they flee and leave behind the man hanging; and thus those guilty of this unspeakable business hid.[56]

Distraught at these deeds, he hangs; and look! the scholar on horseback passes by and the man dangling hears him. And because a very large section of the sack had become perforated [310] as time and toil had worn it down, as he looked out he therefore saw the same man, and the sign and rank of office did not escape his notice.[57] Then, carefree (as it were), he greets him with a happy voice and says, as if enduring nothing painful, "Greetings, my brother, dearest of people, greetings! You are present here, as I hope, with good fortune favoring." That man raises his head and turns around his stunned eyes; he is uncertain whose voice it is and from where it is sounding. As he hesitates over whether to flee or stay put [320]—for fear prompts him to go but shame forbids him to go—resolve firms his wavering mind in such a way: he said, "Let your voice resound again, whoever you are who are here."[58]

In response a voice is again heard from the sack: "If you doubt what I am,[59] look up, raise your head! [325] I sit in a sack and Wisdom sits here with me. Through studies here I have learned many things in a short time. By heavens, scholars seek out schools far and wide; you will know that only here are true schools. If it should be possible to settle here even for a short

hour, [330] philosophy will give me everything in full. And when I emerge, I think that there will be no person among people on earth wiser than I am. Shut up within my mind, the circuit of an entire year is hidden, so too the entire framework of the heavenly poles. [335] By the power of reason I comprehend the two chief lights, nor do the lesser stars escape my senses, and on the contrary the twelve signs of the zodiac cannot be hidden from me: I understand what capacities each and every sign has; I know what inhabits the sea, land, and air. [340] I am pleased to have learned this in this place. Here I learned all: what the entire globe contains, this sack of mine contains here in its entirety. This noble sack is worth more than precious purple, from the recesses of which flows such great grace. [345] If you should enter it once, the experience would grant knowledge of how much advantage this sack holds."

That unfortunate scholar, overly credulous in this nonsense, begs that he be able to have a place in the sack. Then, as if he were coming forth unwillingly from the sack, [350] the other said, "Not so does a person come into this sack. But if I should deserve to gain a suiting reward, I would permit you to settle here for a brief time. But, I ask you, wait until this hour passes by; a small portion of learning still remains." [355] That man, desirous of the thing, does not endure a modest hour. He says, "The present time and hour are squandered for no reason.[60] Come on: put an end to delay, if you wish to make good what is desired! For divine wisdom burns my heart.[61] See, I learn through experience outside what sweetness this sack has within, [360] from which so good an odor comes forth to me." The man dangling replies to him entreating in such fashion:[62] "Brother, you compel me to relinquish a great boon. And so that I may satisfy you, let me down from above and you will be granted possession of your desire."

[365] That one does not delay; he releases the sack and the man—so great in the end was the longing to be hanging. Do you not see the man engineering his own losses for himself, as he prepares his own snare voluntarily for himself? Energetically the young man descends into the open sack [370] and demands that he be drawn up—"and without delay." "Wait a little while," he says, "for not so does the befitting procedure demand and not thus does a person come into the sack." Therefore he presses down the man's head and turns up his heels. "Brother, a person comes into the sack in this way," he says. [375] Very swiftly he suspended the wretch up in the air. "Thus is the custom of the sack; in such a way you will be inside," he says. Again taunting the one hanging, he says thus: "See then, how a person has come into the sack, comrade?[63] Now I think you have begun to be a most erudite sage; [380] your experiences teach you, if I am not mistaken. Therefore sit down, until you are made wiser; for truly you are now proven

to be foolish." Having said these words, he mounts the horse and abandons that place; and he who came on foot goes home on horseback. Unharmed, happy, and peaceful in unbroken tranquillity he passes his life in the favor of good fortune. He flourishes in riches and takes pride in prosperity, until hostile death takes away everything at once.

C. Brothers Grimm, "The Turnip" ("Die Rübe" [*KHM* 146])

Reprinted from Jan M. Ziolkowski, "The *Rapularius* and 'The Turnip' in *Grimms' Fairy Tales:* A Comparative Study with Translations," *Journal of Medieval Latin* 13 (2003): 61–126, at 124–26.

Except in the paragraph divisions, my translation follows the text of the 1819 edition of the *KHM.* Differences—other than the merely orthographic—between the 1819 and the 1857 edition are mentioned in the notes. The paragraph divisions are those of the 1857 edition (2:256–59), since the 1819 edition (2:489–92) prints the text continuously.

Once upon a time there were two brothers, both of whom served as soldiers, and[64] one was rich, the other poor. Then the poor one wanted to help himself out of his poverty, doffed his soldier's coat,[65] and became a farmer. So he dug and hoed his little plot of land and sowed turnip seed. The seed took, and there grew in that place a turnip that became big and thick and perceptibly stouter, and it would not stop growing at all, so that it could be called a princess of all turnips, for never had such a one been seen—and never will such a one be seen again. In the end it was so big that by itself it filled an entire wagon, and two oxen were needed to draw it, and the farmer did not know what he should do with it, and whether it was his fortune or his misfortune.

Finally he thought, "If you sell it, what of any amount will you get for it, and if you intend to eat it yourself, then the little turnips could provide the same service; the best is if you bring it to the king and with it do him honor."[66] So he loaded it on the wagon, hitched two oxen, brought it to the court, and gave it to the king. "Hey!"[67] said the king, "What kind of a rare thing is this? Much that is wonderful has come before my eyes, but never before such a monster; from what kind of seed is it possible that it has grown? Or does it turn out like this for you only because you were born lucky?"

"Oh, no," said the farmer, "I was not born lucky, I am a poor soldier who could not feed himself any longer and therefore hung his soldier's coat on a nail and worked the soil.[68] I still have a brother who is rich and is also

well known to you, Lord King, but I, because I have nothing, am forgotten by the whole world." Then the king felt compassion for him and said, "You shall be raised up from your poverty and so endowed with gifts from me that you will well become the equal of your rich brother." Then he bestowed upon him a mass of gold, fields, meadows, and herds, and made him filthy rich, so that the riches of the other brother could not be compared at all with his.

When the other heard what his brother had acquired with a single turnip, he envied him and pondered backwards and forwards how he could direct towards himself as well such good fortune. He wanted however to do things much more cleverly; he took gold and horses and brought them to the king, and did not think anything else, except that the king would give him a much greater gift in return; since his brother had obtained so much for a turnip, what all would it not yield him for such beautiful things? The king took the gift and said he knew of nothing to give him in return that was rarer or better than the big turnip. Therefore the rich one had to put his brother's turnip on a wagon and have it taken home.

At home he did not know on whom he should vent his rage and anger, until evil thoughts came to him and he resolved to kill his brother. He hired killers who were obliged to place themselves in an ambush, and then he went to his brother and said, "Dear brother, I know a hidden treasure; we will dig it up and divide it up with each other." The other also found the plan appealing and went along unsuspecting; but when they came out, the killers rushed upon him, tied him, and intended to hang him from a tree. Just as they were about to do this, loud singing and a hoofbeat resounded from the distance, so that fear hit them in the gut and they stuck their captive head over heels into the sack, hoisted him up on a branch, and let him hang.[69] However, he worked on it until he had a hole in the sack through which he could stick his head. At that point they took flight.

But the person who came along the way from there[70] was nothing but a wandering scholar, a young fellow who rode on the road through the forest, happily singing his song. As the one above noticed now that someone was going by beneath him, he called, "Greetings to you—good timing!" The scholar looked all around, did not know where the voice was sounding, and finally said, "Who is calling me?" Then the answer came from the treetop, "Raise your eyes, I am sitting up here in the sack of wisdom; in a short time I have learned great things. In comparison all the schools are but a wind. In a little while I will have finished learning, I will get out and be wiser than all men. I understand the constellations and the zodiac, the blowing of the winds and the sand in the sea,[71] healing of sickness, powers of herbs, birds, and stones. If you were in it once, you would feel what splendor flows out of it."[72]

The scholar, as he heard all that, was astonished and said, "Blessed be the hour in which I found you![73] Couldn't I come into the sack even a little while?" The one above answered, as if he did it grudgingly: "For pay and kind words I will let you in it for a little while, but you must however wait an hour yet; there is a bit remaining that I must learn first."

When the scholar had waited a little, the time became too long for him, and he asked that he might nevertheless be let in—his thirst for wisdom was indeed too great. The one above then pretended as if he were finally giving in and said, "So that I can come out from the house of wisdom, you must let down the sack by the rope; in that way you shall enter." So the scholar let him down, untied the sack, and freed him. Then he himself cried out, "Now pull me up quickly, right away!" and wanted to step standing upright into the sack. "Stop!" said the other, "That is not how it is done." He grabbed him by the head, stuck him facing backwards into the sack, tied it, and pulled the devotee of wisdom up the tree by the rope and dangled him in the air.[74] "How do things stand, my dear fellow? See, already you feel that wisdom is coming to you, and you are getting good experience. So sit nice and quiet, until you become wiser."

With that, he mounted the scholar's horse and rode forth.[75]

FIVE

The Donkey Tale: The Ass (ATU 430)

A. *The Donkey Tale* (*Asinarius*)

eprinted from Jan M. Ziolkowski, "The Beast and the Beauty: The Reorientation of 'The Donkey,' From the Middle Ages to the Brothers Grimm," *Journal of Medieval Latin* 5 (1995): 53–94, at 82–90. I follow Simond Rizzardi, ed. and trans. *Asinarius,* in *Commedie latine del XII e XIII secolo,* 4:137–251, Università di Genova, Facoltà di lettere, Pubblicazioni dell'Istituto di filologia classica e medievale 79 (Genoa: Istituto di filologia classica e medievale, 1983).

Once upon a time there was a king of an unknown region and city, and, what is more, no tale tells the king's name. This king had acquired for himself as consort of his realm and companion of his bedchamber a woman who was his peer in nobility. [5] Although the high majesty of an empire

blessed them, and an ample mass of wealth ennobled them, all the same Lucina was hostile to them and had denied offspring; for they practiced the games of Venus to no effect. Hence grief and moans afflicted both of them, for the reason that [10] they had no heir for their realm. In the end the queen, taking pity upon her unfortunate husband, said repeatedly in such a speech or one like it: "What are we doing? We are accomplishing nothing. It has become dreary now to live and it is tiresome to have been intent so often on nighttime games. [15] I am an unfortunate woman, most similar to a barren land that without hope of a harvest swallows the seeds that are cast. Rightly do I compare myself to a punctured sack, which spews out elsewhere what it receives with open mouth. Alas, what does nobility avail, what does wealth, what does the glory of the realm, [20] if the fates deny me an heir?"

Therefore, entreating the faithful gods with uninterrupted prayers, she asks by night and day that she be made a mother. What she seeks, she obtains and she becomes a mother—but of a little donkey, for her offspring was a beautiful little donkey! [25] O what a delivery, when a woman gives birth to a little donkey! O what a marvelous, yet rather miserable, thing! Having seen this newborn, the mother, who had earlier applauded that she had conceived, now grieves at having given birth. Therefore, rather than to be the mother of a little donkey, she prefers not to be a mother [30] and orders that he be given as food to fishes.

But the king, having learned of the mother's wicked directive, said, "Far be it! This monster should not die." He said, "The son of a queen should not die. On the contrary, I order that this son of mine should live. [35] Whichever of the gods it was who gave him as heir, he will be on the throne as king of my realm, his head will bear his father's crown, and his father's entire glory is owed to him."

Then, at his father's bidding, he is reared in extreme honor, [40] inasmuch as he was the noble scion of the king. He progresses and grows, he raises his ears aloft; now he began to be a youth of good character. Now he is called, and is, "the little lord" in his father's realm; now every courtier fears him with due respect. [45] Now he travels around the towns, now he goes around the cities of the realm, now he takes delight in pastimes and games, but he takes special delight in the art of lute players and, if fortune should be favorable, he desires to learn it. Therefore he approaches with a retinue a man whom he knew to be skilled, [50] who was a renowned maestro in the art. He went to him in this way and employed words of such a sort: "Be my teacher," he said, "O lute player! Cause your little lord to know the art as you do, so that he may be no less able than you in your art." [55] He spoke words of this kind.

To his words the lute player responded: "What do you ask of your subject, my little lord? O king, why do you seek what does not become you? Alas, alas! You are mistaken, you are deceived, you entertain idle hopes: you cannot learn this art at all, since [60] your fingers are enormous, my little lord. And if, by your leave, it be permitted me to speak home truths, you seek, little lord, what nature denies. Without a hand you cannot distinguish the strings of the lute, which (I think) will blow apart if you touch them with a foot. [65] According to its custom, an ass brays and never plays well; the wild sound of a sack-bearing ass as it sings is hee-haw."

The mime player said this; the little donkey growls and goes to pieces, scarcely controlling the turmoil of his heart. "Is the lineage of my blood not lofty?" he said, [70] "Do you not know that I am your king and lord? From where, scoundrel, does the presumptuousness of so great a statement come to you, that you should not fear to speak so harshly to me? What opinion do you, scoundrel, have of me—what opinion, buffoon? Do you deny perhaps that I am the beloved son of the emperor?"

[75] The other said, "I do not deny it nor will I deny it, little lord; on the contrary, I believe and know that you are my lord."

"Then obey my commands promptly," he said, "if you wish to dwell within my father's realm."

To these words the servant replied, "Lord, calm the fury of your mind! [80] Look, I willingly obey your commands."

Accordingly, the lute player sounds out sweet melodies on the lute, and in response the quick-learning donkey harmonizes with equal skill. Indeed, in a brief time he progressed so much in the art that he became better taught than his teacher. [85] Now in the style of a mime player he sings with a very tuneful mouth, now he makes a sweet melody with a clumsy thumb. And when on a certain day he skirted a river while strolling, the water betrayed to him his disfigured features. As he considers his head and the ears on his head, he said, [90] "Amazing! I wonder greatly what this form means!"

Surveying with his eyes, he considers his legs and feet, and his whole body displeases him. Gnashing his teeth because of this, he is stirred by a wicked fit of anger. With a blasphemous mouth he hisses to himself such words: [95] "Whichever of the gods it was who assembled me and gave existence to me hardly deserved a cent. Surely I, a little donkey, will not take possession of the crown of the realm? I will not be able to be called king *and* little donkey, will I? Far be it that a crown should surmount this donkey's forehead. [100] A golden rod does not befit this hand, I admit. Therefore let not a golden seal hang from my neck, nor let pure purple cover a donkey's bristles. Alas, when my father has died I will be deprived of the honor

of kingship and in addition I will be compelled to suffer many annoyances. [105] It is better therefore that I should depart while my father is alive than that a violent hand[76] should expel me afterward."

Therefore out of all the servants, he approaches one whose faith experience had proven more than once, and he reveals to him what he had in mind [110], and he commands him to accompany him on his way. That servant agreed, giving assent to his little lord, and, taking an oath, declares that he will give aid. Then the ass, putting his musical instruments upon the servant, undertakes the journey by night, a quadruped together with a biped.

[115] And they come to the shore of a nearby sea and behold! a ship is near. The fee for crossing is duly given; the sailor gives it back to the youth: "To have guided so great a king—so great a glory will suffice for me, lord!"[77] The sails are raised; the surface of the deep sea is furrowed and the skiff flies with the favor of the winds.

And he began to wander far and wide upon the vast sea; [120] and he seeks a place of refuge in the world. At length it pleases him to visit the outermost frontiers of the world, where Phoebus immerses in the sea his tired steeds.

In that very place a certain king, distinguished in nobility of virtues, distinguished in ancestors, had raised the capital of his realm. [125] As rumor reports, he had only a single daughter; apart from her he had no other heir. If fortune should favor, if the fates should allow, the father had ordained that she be the heir of his realm.

At that time the maiden had already completed her years of girlhood: [130] her private parts had already given forth fine hairs; the nipples of her breasts had already given signs that she can hardly sleep alone on her bed without a man.

Coming here, the ass makes his way to the king's hall. He shouts out and knocks; and having spoken thus, he said: [135] "Let the door be opened wide so that a stranger may enter! A guest is at the door: open the door!"

Having heard the racket of the little donkey knocking, the doorkeeper asks, "Why are you shouting? You, who are you? From where do you come? Why do you beat so importunately at the king's front door? [140] Why do you strike the door panels with such great presumptuousness?"

Responding, the ass said, "Open swiftly! At the door, without any doubt, an upstanding mime player stands near." When he had uttered this response, he began to strum the lute with his foot and sings in harmony a sweet melody with wide-open mouth.

[145] As the doorkeeper perceives with his ear the sweet harmony, he leaps out to see who this may be and what he is doing, and seeing the shape of a clumsy and unsightly little donkey, he is astounded that this creature can

play so competently. The man does not delay at all: he enters the privy chambers of the king, [150] wishing to reveal the marvels he has seen. Then he said, "Look here, glorious king, I know something hitherto unknown that I will convey to you if you want to know. A most unusual mime player stands outside before the gates"—he said—"As I believe, no other will be more unusual than he is. [155] This unusual mime player, O king, is a foul little donkey who makes music with the lute and makes music with his mouth at the same time. He requests entrance. If the king bids, he may come inside."

And the king in response said, "Let him come inside!"

Then the mime player, striking the strings with the thumb of a donkey, [160] steps inside, fingering new melodies. Having gazed at him, the king relaxes his restraints upon laughter, and the measure of such great laughter becomes measureless. For her part the queen, laughing as her husband laughs, could not say anything because laughter prevents. [165] Every class of young people and old guffaws, and the entire court resounds with equal laughter. While all thus take joy that the little donkey plays, in the meantime the day comes to a close as the sun hurries on. According to proper etiquette, a dinner fit for a king is prepared; [170] the entourage, ready to be seated, streams into the castle. The king and queen are placed in the seating for royalty; the daughter takes a seat alongside the mother.

Next the men who are adorned by the mantle of knighthood take their places; then servants sit down in a lower place. [175] Then one of the court dignitaries approached and ordered the donkey to take a seat with the servants.

"Far be it!" said the little donkey. "I am not the table companion of retainers! The rank of servant does not suit me well—I am not a common donkey nor am I a stable donkey—[180] rather, I am guided by a refined nobility."[78]

"Do you wish," said the attendant, "to be joined with the knights?"

"Far be it!" said the little donkey. "This placement does not please me either. Until now the king's own table has elevated me without constraint as its companion and has afforded generous banquets."

[185] "What do you wish me to do for you?" replied the steward to the little donkey.

"That I be assigned to the king's table!" said the little donkey.

Learning this, the king said, "Let the little donkey draw near!"

At once, when called by the king's voice, he comes close. To him the king, smiling jestingly with a calm expression, [190] said, "Little donkey, do you like our daughter?"

Straightway the donkey, raising his head, directs his gaze towards the little lady and speaks thus, "Amazing! Why do you ask? O king, why do you

labor to know? Why ought I not like her? [195] On the contrary, I like her, I like her, I like her very much." He said, "Certainly the man who does not like her at all is made of iron. Her fair face, suffused with rosiness, brings delight, as if I should contemplate lilies mixed with roses. And I like her hair; her ivory-white neck brings delight; [200] and I confess that I like her whole body."

The king said, "Do you wish to be the tablemate of this girl?"

Responding to this the exiled little donkey said: "I like this idea, I say. My heart of a poor little donkey urges this. This seat and this placement suit me. [205] If I dine together with the little lady, I will be content with this; this will be a sufficient claim to honor for me."

"Seeing that you like her," said the king, "be the girl's tablemate; and I command that one and the same food feed the two of you."

"O king, rightly do I thank you," said the little donkey, [210] "because such great grace comes to me owing to you." And mounting a step, he takes possession of a seat up high, and the little lady seats him as her tablemate. While dining the little donkey serves her well, breaking the bread into pieces and cutting the cakes. [215] Raising goblets and drinking bowls, he himself offers to her when she wishes to drink, and he holds up the table-cloth as the little lady drinks. Why should I recall every single fact? I should touch upon all of them succinctly in one statement: insofar as he is an ass, he does everything competently. Therefore her tablemate pleased the girl to no little extent [220] but, unless I am mistaken, he is going to please her even more. In sitting together he pleases; in lying together he will please more, when she has wedded him as her beloved husband.

Moreover the decorous behavior of the little donkey delights the king, since this creature was more obliging than a donkey. [225] The knights too extol him in praise-filled reports and the whole large city pronounces him praiseworthy.

And when the exile had made a sojourn there for some time, he thinks he wishes to return to his homeland and home. Therefore bursting sadly into the king's privy chambers, [230] he began with downcast head to speak in such fashion: "A person's native soil is accustomed to be sweeter than exile; and I admit that what pleases everyone pleases me. If an occasion to speak without offense may be granted me, look, king: on the verge of departure I bid you farewell."

[235] To him the king says, "No partings remain, and I will not allow us to be sundered except by the fate of death. I call Jupiter as witness that no freedom to leave remains and no occasion to do so is given you. Are you not content, my son, with the honor from us? [240] Are you not content to be my son? Tell, son, what is the problem? Why are you sad? From where does

this stream of grief well up? Tell me, I ask! Here you will not be a guest nor will you now be considered an exile; you ought not to be less than any citizen. [245] Or, son, do you thirst for a heap of coins—whatever type you will? By Hercules, I will measure these out beyond measure for you. You are not in quest of clothes or horses or other such things, are you, which a pleasure-seeking man thirsts for and seeks? Indeed I call to witness the gods and the other divine powers of the countryside: [250] if it so pleases you, I will even halve with you my realm."

The donkey is not at all swayed by these promises; he spurns everything for love of his native soil. "One option is still to be given you, son," said the king. "If you reject it, you will always be a little donkey.[79] [255] Do you wish that our daughter should be given you between your arms, so that she may occupy herself with you in nighttime games?"

Then, as if awakening from a sleep, the little donkey shouts out: "This arrangement alone pleases me, I admit this. For me she will be the end of sorrow and anxiety, [260] the gateway to happiness, the door to well-being. If you should confirm your words with deeds, O greatest of kings, then I will be able to say that I am greater than Jupiter. Let Jupiter take possession of his Juno in heaven; the maiden daughter of the king suffices for me on earth. [265] May those things that are yours be yours, O king, may you keep everything for yourself; let the maiden be given me. I seek nothing apart from her. I will be content with just this maiden alone, and I do not complain of my exile, venerable king. Let her be my homeland, honor, glory of my realm, [270] and let her be also an already sufficient mass of riches for me."

"You will have the lover I have pledged you," said the king, "only deign to be my son-in-law." Consequently his royal majesty summons his daughter. She appears and comes near; and her father and king asks, [275] "Daughter of the king, do you wish to wed a young man? If you wish, then wed this man, daughter!"

The maiden, her face suffused with a blush as was her habit, turns her eyes toward the ground at this statement of her father. And saying nothing, she reflects by herself for a brief time [280] what she ought to respond to her father. At last bursting out and loosening the restraints on her mouth she said, "It is appropriate that a father's bidding be done. Not my will but that of my father should be pondered.[80] My father, I am totally dependent upon your wish. [285] If you wish, I am the wife of the man to whom you have betrothed me. May you be his father-in-law; may he be your son-in-law."

Thereupon the king, rejoicing, said to the ass: "Have the girl, so that you may be her husband and she your betrothed."

The ass accepts the girl with the father consenting; [290] and the king and father fixed a day of celebration. Then the city is decorated and shines

bright with such great honor that the very same city is clearly more pleasing
than the heavens. Like bees, a great throng of mime players streams to-
gether; each one, well-trained, toils over his craft. [295] A female mime
player, balanced with her feet upward and her head downward, walks and
accords to her hands the function of her feet. Afterward the commoners are
invited and are assigned seating to eat; and so the whole day becomes a
bearer of happiness. And when the evening star was granting to them in
their fullness the hour of sleep [300] when a woman and a man rightly are
free for lovemaking, then the fearless little donkey enters the maiden's bed-
chamber so that he may caress the tender breast of his bride. Therefore he
enters the bedchamber of the beloved maiden, in which two lights have been
placed at the king's bidding. [305] So that he may see what this little donkey
and this little lady do, a servant is present, having been placed by night be-
hind a wall hanging. When everyone has stepped outside, when no one is
thought to be present, the house door is barred and bolted. Immediately the
bridegroom puts aside the donkey garb; [310] when his old hide has been
laid away, he becomes a new man. The maiden, seeing the noble body of a
handsome man whose appearance previously had been repulsive, having
marveled before long at the unbelievable charm of her spouse, rushed head-
long into the bond of lovemaking.[81] [315] Then at once the two embrace
their necks with their arms and join their mouths to mouths. Immediately
he leaps into bed and the girl follows. What follows they know—and the
bed itself knows. (Nor do I think that the man hiding could have failed to
notice [320] which games and what sorts of games were conducted there by
night!) For a time he tempers the heat of amorous desire, and she fulfills the
offices of a wife for her husband. And as soon as rosy dawn returns once
darkness has been dispelled, he leaps up from the lap of his bride. [325]
Then he is again clothed in the donkey garb and becomes a little donkey
just as he had been before.

In the morning the father, coming and knocking at the door, said,
"Hello! Daughter, your father is at the door. Open the door!"

Quickly releasing the bars and greeting her father, she said to him, [330]
"O welcome, my father! Rightly do I give you countless thanks, because
through your arrangements I wed a dear husband."

"Is this husband dear to you?" asked her father.

Then with a joyous expression she spoke thus to her father: [335] "In the
whole world there is no one dearer to me than he is, and I cherish my hus-
band truly with my whole heart."

Yet she does not reveal what is the actual character of her husband and
what manner of man lies hidden beneath the hideous hide. As soon as there
had been a brief lapse of time, leaving his daughter and son-in-law [340] the

king arises after bidding farewell and goes off outside. The zealous servant who had rested there by night behind the curtain follows the steps of the king; the king had commanded him to be a night watchman so that he could spy on what he and she did. [345] Accordingly, as he was about to relate what he had heard and seen, he trickles into the ears of his king these words: "O invincible king, renowned king, noble king, deign to hear the words of your servant. Last night a quite extraordinary event was seen by me [350] as I rested behind the curtain. When this son-in-law of yours believed that he was alone in the nighttime with only his wife, at once he is stripped bare of his usual donkey's hide and he is granted the appearance of an emperor. [355] Why should I repeat, lord, what he or she did? You should know that they devoted themselves the whole night through to lovemaking. And when the husband bid farewell to his bride and to lovemaking, once again he is cloaked in his former hide. Now come on, my lord, if you wish to know what I am indicating, [360] see, you can confirm it on the coming night. Therefore on this night enter very secretly the bridal chamber, in which your daughter and son-in-law will rest. And as soon as you have found in that same place the donkey's hide, stealthily take it away from your son-in-law and toss it in the fire. [365] And when raging fire has consumed the base covering, he will remain a man right until the day of death."

The king said, "Let it so be done! What you urge I will put to the test by night; perhaps this night will grant me what I have hoped."

Accordingly the king enters the bridal chamber at the time of dark night [370] and look! his daughter and son-in-law lie abed. And because it is usual for sleep to creep up after lovemaking, they both were held fast by deep sleep. Gently approaching and drawing near the marriage-bed, the king perceives a handsome man reclining. [375] A little later he removes the skin of the donkey's hide and escapes with his son-in-law hardly noticing, and he orders a furnace to be set ablaze with much kindling, in which at the king's bidding the skin becomes ashes. The king, wishing also to know what that man would do, [380] remains awake the whole night before the door. Therefore the son-in-law arises in the morning satisfied with sleep, wishing to be covered with the donkey skin just as before. Not finding it and goaded by a great grief, he began to be anxious only about flight, [385] and he goes outside, but outside the king blocks his way and says: "Where are you rushing, son? What are you suffering? What do you have? Certainly this intention will be altogether in vain and your route will be completely hindered. I do not wish that you should object because the donkey skin has been taken away [390], since you are an attractive and well-groomed man. So long as I am alive, I now share my realm with you. After my death, have it all by yourself alone."

To him the son-in-law said, "I will do so and I will remain with you, and I pray that things begun well may produce a good outcome."

[395] Therefore the state is divided in two: one part of the realm is offered to the son-in-law; one part remains for the old man. After this division had so been made, not even a full circuit of a year has passed when the king, having served out his time, dies from the sword of death. And then Neoptolomus is created the sole ruler of the realm;[82] [400] for alone he claims the entire realm for himself. Moreover the same man takes as his share his father's honor, and thus as king rules two realms of two kings.

B. "The Story of Vikramāditya's Birth"

Reprinted from Franklin Edgerton, ed. and trans., *Vikrama's Adventures, or The Thirty-Two Tales of the Throne: A Collection of Stories about King Vikrama, as Told by the Thirty-Two Statuettes That Supported His Throne*, 2 vols., Harvard Oriental Series 26–27 (Cambridge, MA: Harvard University Press, 1926), 1:263–66 (English translation), 2:241–44 (Sanskrit text).

Translated by Franklin Edgerton. The only changes made in reproducing Edgerton's translation have been the alteration of a few anomalous spellings (e.g., *askt, astonisht, curst, establisht, perisht, reacht, rejoist, tho, thru*).

In Gurjarī-land between the rivers Sābhravatī and Mahilā, there is a grove, where Tāmraliptarṣi was king. He had a daughter Yaçovatī, whose husband was a king named Premasena. While they lived in the enjoyment of worldly pleasures, a daughter Madanarekhā was born to them; and she grew day by day like a digit of the moon. Moreover he had two young (slave-)boys, one of whom was named Devaçarman, and the other Hariçarman. Devaçarman went every day to the river to do the king's washing. There some god or other, his form unseen, said to Devaçarman with a human voice: "How now! Let that King Premasena marry his daughter to me, or else it will not go well with the king and the city." Thus every day there was (heard) a voice on high, without natural cause [literally, "unstruck"]. And he reflected in his heart: "Well! No one appears in visible presence; what can be the cause (of the voice)?" So in his amazement he told the tale before the king. The king said to him: "You are saying what is not true." Said he: "Sire, I will not go today, send some one else to do the washing." So the king sent Hariçarman. He also went thither, and did the washing, and in the same manner heard the voice of the (god) who had been there before. And Hariçarman too was astonished at heart; and he too came back and told the king.

When the king heard this he was filled with amazement. They both said: "There is a voice without natural cause (heard) there." Again a boy went forth to do the washing; and the king went by himself, in concealment. The king, going behind a tree, heard that voice in the very same way. There arose doubtful wonder in the king's mind: "What is this, a god, or a vyantara [a certain kind of divine being]?" Thereupon, returning to his house, he summoned his ministers and housepriests and other people and asked them: "Look now, what shall we do? Such is the voice that is heard at the river. Some one says: 'Let King Premasena give me his own daughter, and marry her to me, that things may go well (with him); otherwise a deformity will afflict him.' It is not known who this is." Thereupon the ministers and housepriests said: "O king, how can she be given to an unknown person? Ask him and find out the facts." So the king again went to the river and the same personage spoke in the very same way. Then the king asked: "Are you a god, gandharva, or demon [kimnara], or a man?" Thereupon he appeared (and said): "O king, in former time I was warder to Indra. I was lustful after women who did not belong to me, and could not leave them alone. Though Indra repeatedly forbade me, even then I could not leave them alone. After this I was cursed by Indra, and have been born as an ass [a type of lechery in India] in a potter's house here in your majesty's city, and roam about on the bank of the river. So I ask you for your daughter. If you give her, it will be well with you; but if not, a deformity will afflict the people of the city and yourself." The king said: "If you are a god, I will give my daughter to you who have the form of an ass?" He said: "Give her!"

After this, simply to prevent such a calamity, the king, fearing for his city, gave him his daughter. Again the king said: "O god, if you have divine power, make a rampart of copper about the city, and a palace, having the thirty-two superior marks, to dwell in." So in the fourth watch of the night the god did all just as he asked. In the morning all the people awoke, and seeing the copper rampart were filled with amazement. No one could unfasten the lock with which the main gate was provided, and all the people were at a loss. So it was reported to the king; and the king came to the main gate, and in astonishment called to mind the god. Hereupon he appeared and said: "O king, let the potter, at whose house I am, be summoned, that he may open it with a mere touch of his hand." Then the king summoned all the potters, but they fled in all directions. The potters thought: "Perhaps the king is going to kill us at the main highway." Thereupon the king sent a summons only to the potter at whose dwelling asses were kept. He also remained in hiding in his house, but was hauled out by the king's officers by main force and brought to the place, and at the command of the king he opened the highway. The people of the city and the king rejoiced.

At this time the girl Madanarekhā heard that the king in fear had given her to an ass, to save his people and his dependents in the city. Then she thought: "Well, even if my heart breaks, this has happened as was fated; such is my karma." So the king with great pomp married his daughter to him, who had the form of an ass. And Madanarekhā herself went and remained sunk in meditation in the palace constructed by the god. But the god put off his ass-shaped body, and put on one of glorious appearance, and indulged with Madanarekhā in daily enjoyment of sensual joys, along with pārijāta and mandāra [coral-tree] flowers and fragrant garlands. He abode with her now on Mount Meru, now by the fair lake of Mānasa, now in the city of the yakṣas, gandharvas, and demons, seeing and listening to charming dancing and music, and enjoying all manner of delights. She also was filled with supreme joy. And her throng of female attendants remained at her side, and spoke with no one. So a number of years passed by. Her mother wondered: "How is my daughter getting along with the ass?" So the mother went to the palatial home of her daughter. Then the god came into the harem, having laid aside his ass's skin according to his usual custom, and having put on a brilliant form. And seeing his form the queen reflected in her heart: "Ah, my daughter is virtuous and blessed, since she has obtained such a husband. Happy am I who have borne such a daughter; through her I have obtained merit." And on further reflection she thought: "I will throw his (ass's) skin into the fireplace; since his form is such, it shall remain so in the future." Thus reflecting she cast the skin into the fire. Next she beheld Gandharvasena [named here for the first time!] before her. But when he failed to see the skin, he said to his wife: "My dear, I am going to heaven; my curse is at an end, its limit has been reached." And she said: "How shall I get along? If it were not for the preservation of your unborn child in my womb, I should go with you. What shall I do?" The god said: "Remain here in peaceful meditation; protect the child, and when he is born give him the name Vikramāditya. In the womb of your slave-woman there is also a child by me; to him the name Bhartṛhari shall be given." Thus having obtained release, the god went to heaven.

The queen told the king about it. And thereupon the king asked a certain soothsayer: "What shall be born to my daughter?" He said: "A son shall be born, and he shall become king." Hearing this there arose alarm in the king's heart: "Ha, my daughter's son is to be king!" So the king sent officers to watch over her unborn child, and they kept guard. Madanarekhā thought: "Why are these men set to watch over my unborn child?" At this time a woman flower-gatherer came in, and she said to her: "Bring it about that my unborn child may be saved and protected." She agreed. And on the morning of the second day she brought a knife, and Madanarekhā cut open

her womb with this knife and gave her the child, but she herself perished. Then she took that child, together with the other child Bhartṛhari, and went to a village near the city of Ujjayinī, and carefully guarded them there. And he [Vikramāditya] grew up day by day with Bhartṛhari. And after this it was reported to the king: "A flower-woman has taken your daughter's child and has gone." So the king lost both of them; he had neither his daughter nor her son. And the king gave to the city the name of Stambhāvatī, and this name became established.

C. Brothers Grimm, "The Donkey" ("Das Eselein" [*KHM* 144]), 7th ed., 1857, 2:252–55; 2nd ed., 1819, 2:486:89.

eprinted from Jan M. Ziolkowski, "The Beast and the Beauty: The Re-orientation of 'The Donkey,' From the Middle Ages to the Brothers Grimm," *Journal of Medieval Latin* 5 (1995): 53–94, at 92–94. Translation made on the basis of Brothers Grimm, "The Donkey" ("Das Eselein" [*KHM* 144]), 2nd ed., 1819, 2:486–89, with reference to the 7th ed., 1857, 2:252–55.

Once there lived a king and a queen who were rich and had all that they wanted for themselves—but no children. She grieved about this day and night, and said: "I am like a field on which nothing grows." Finally God fulfilled her wishes, and yet when the child entered this world, he did not look like a human child but rather was a young donkey. When the mother beheld this, she began to moan and shriek more than ever that she would rather have had no child at all than a donkey, and she said that they should toss it into the water so that the fish could eat it. But the king said: "No. God has given him; he shall be my son and heir, sit on the royal throne after my death, and wear the royal crown." So the donkey was raised, grew up, and his ears grew really nice and tall and straight. In other respects he was of a happy nature, gamboled, played, and took special pleasure in music, so that he went to a famous minstrel and said: "Teach me your craft, so that I can play the lute as well as you." "Ah, my dear little lord," answered the minstrel, "that will be very difficult for you; your fingers are surely not made for that, and are really too big. I am worried that the strings will not be able to take it." But no excuse helped: the donkey wanted and was determined to play the lute, was persistent and diligent, and in the end learned it as well as his instructor himself.

Once, pensive, he went for a stroll and came to a spring. When he looked in and saw in the water (which was as clear as a mirror) his donkey's

shape, he became so distressed about it that he went off into the world and took with him only one trusty companion. They went here and there; at length they came to a realm where an old king ruled who had only a single but wonderfully beautiful daughter. The donkey said: "We intend to stay here," knocked on the gate, and called out: "There is a guest out here. Open up so that he can enter." When the gate was not opened, he sat down, took his lute, and sounded it with his feet in the loveliest fashion. Then the porter opened his eyes very wide, ran to the king, and said: "Out there, in front of the gate, is sitting a donkey, who is playing the lute in a very lovely way." "Okay, then let the musician come in to me," said the king. But when a donkey walked in, everyone began to laugh about the lutanist. Now the donkey was supposed to be seated and to eat down low among the servants, but he became resistant and said: "I am no common stable donkey, I am very noble." Then they said: "If you are that, then take a seat with the knights." "No," he said, "I wish to sit with the king." The king laughed and said in good humor: "All right, it shall be as you demand, donkey; come here to me." Then he asked: "Donkey, how do you like my daughter?" The donkey turned his head toward her, looked at her, nodded, and said: "Extraordinarily well; I have never seen a girl as beautiful." "All right, then you shall indeed take a seat near her," the king said. "That suits me just fine," said the donkey, and sat down at her side and ate and knew how to behave in a very fine and polished way. When the noble little beast had remained a good amount of time at the king's court, he thought, "What is all this accomplishing? You must return home," let his head hang sadly, went before the king, and asked to take leave. But the king was not at all pleased and said: "Donkey, what is on your mind? You look so sour, like a jar of vinegar. I will give you what you demand—do you want gold?" "No," said the donkey and shook his head. "Do you want valuables and jewelry?" "No." "Do you want half of my realm?" "Oh no!" Then the king said: "If only I knew what could make you satisfied . . . do you want my beautiful daughter as wife?" "Oh yes," said the donkey and was once again entirely happy and cheery, since that was exactly what he had wanted for himself. So a large and sumptuous wedding was held. In the evening, when the bride and groom were conducted to their bedroom, the king wanted to know whether the donkey would behave himself really nicely with courtesy and good manners, and he ordered a servant to hide himself there. When the two were then within, the groom bolted the doors, looked around, and once he believed that they were entirely alone, he then cast off his donkey skin all at once and stood there as a handsome, royal youth, who said: "You see who I am and that I have been worthy of you." Then the bride was overjoyed, kissed him, and loved him with all her heart. But when morning came, he

leapt up, donned his animal skin again, and no one would have thought what a man was hidden within it. Soon the old king came along too. He called out, "Hey, is the donkey already wide-awake? Are you really very sad," he said to his daughter, "that you have obtained no ordinary man as husband?" "Oh no, dear father, I love him so as if he were the most handsome of all, and I will keep him my whole life long." The king marveled, but the servant, who had hidden himself, came and revealed everything to him. The king said: "That is not at all true!" "Then you keep watch during the coming night; you will see it with your own eyes. And you know what, Lord King: take the hide away from him and cast it into the fire. In that way he must indeed show himself in his proper form." "Your advice is good," said the king, and in the evening, as they slept, he slipped in, and as he came to the bed, he saw in the moonlight a superb youth resting there, and the skin lay stripped off on the ground. Then he took it away, and he had a mighty fire kindled outside and had the hide thrown in, and he remained there himself until it had been burnt to ashes. But because he wanted to see what the one who had been divested would do, he stayed awake through the night and spied. When the youth had slept his fill, he got up at the first gleam of morning and wished to don the donkey hide, but it was not to be found. Then he was alarmed and spoke, full of grief and worry: "Now I must see to it that I escape." As he walked out, the king stood there and said: "Hey! My son, where are you going in such a hurry? What do you have in mind? Stay here; you are so handsome a man, you should not again go away from me; I now give you half of my realm, and after my death you will obtain the whole of it." The youth said: "So to a good beginning I wish likewise to have a good ending. I will stay with you." Then the old man gave him half of the realm, and when the former died after a year, the latter had the whole, and after the death of his father another whole kingdom besides, and he lived rich and happy.

D. Straparola, "King Pig" (*Le piacevoli notti,* Night 2, Fable 1)

*T*ranslation adapted from Gianfrancesco [Giovanni Francesco] Straparola, *Le piacevoli notti,* trans. W. G. Waters, 1:133–52.

Fair ladies, if man were to spend a thousand years in rendering thanks to his Creator for having made him in the form of a human and not of a brute beast, he could not speak gratitude enough. This reflection calls to mind the story of one who was born as a pig, but afterwards became a

handsome youth. Nevertheless, to his dying day he was known to the people over whom he ruled as King Pig.

You must know, dear ladies, that Galeotto, King of Anglia, was a man highly blessed in worldly riches, and in his wife Ersilia, the daughter of Matthias, King of Hungary, a princess who, in virtue and beauty, outshone all the other ladies of the time. And Galeotto was a wise king, ruling his land so that no man could hear a complaint against him. Though they had been several years married they had no child; for this reason both of them felt much grief. While Ersilia was walking one day in her garden, she felt suddenly weary, and noticing nearby a spot covered with fresh green turf, she went up to it and sat down on it, and, overcome with weariness and soothed by the sweet singing of the birds in the green foliage, she fell asleep.

And it chanced that while she slept, there passed by three fairies who held mankind somewhat in scorn, and these, when they beheld the sleeping queen, halted, and gazing upon her beauty, took counsel together how they might protect her, and cast a spell upon her. When they were agreed, the first cried out, "I will that no man shall be able to harm her, and that, the next time she lie with her husband, she may be with child and bear a son who shall not have his equal in all the world for beauty." Then said the second, "I will that no one shall ever have power to offend her, and that the prince who shall be born of her shall be gifted with every virtue under the sun." And the third said, "And I will that she shall be the wisest among women, but that the son whom she shall conceive shall be born in a pig's skin, with a pig's ways and manners, and in this state he shall be constrained to remain till he shall have three times taken a woman to wife."

As soon as the three fairies had flown away, Ersilia awoke, and at once arose and went back to the palace, taking with her the flowers she had plucked. Not many days had passed before she knew herself to be pregnant, and when the time of her delivery was come, she gave birth to a son with limbs like those of a pig and not of a human being. When tidings of this prodigy came to the ears of the king and queen, they lamented sorely concerning it, and the king, bearing in mind how good and wise his queen was, often felt moved to put this offspring of hers to death and cast it into the sea, in order that she might be spared the shame of having given birth to him. But when he debated in his mind and considered that this son, whatever he might be, was of his own blood, he put aside the cruel plan that he had been considering, and, seized with pity and grief, he made up his mind that the son should be brought up and nurtured like a rational being and not as a brute beast. The child, therefore, was nursed with the greatest care, was often brought to the queen, and put his little snout and his little paws in his mother's lap, and she, moved by natural affection, caressed him by

stroking his bristly back with her hand and by embracing and kissing him as if he had been of human form. Then he would wag his tail and give other signs to show that he was conscious of his mother's affection.

The piglet, when he grew older, began to talk like a human being, and to wander around in the city, but whenever he came near to any mud or dirt he would always wallow in it, after the manner of pigs, and return all covered with filth. Then, when he approached the king and queen, he would rub his sides against their lovely garments; defiling them with all manner of dirt, but because he was indeed their own son, they put up with it all.

One day he came home covered with mud and filth, as was his habit, and lay down on his mother's rich robe, and said in a grunting tone, "Mother, I wish to get married." When the queen heard this, she replied, "Do not talk so foolishly. What maid would ever take you for a husband, and think you that any noble or knight would give his daughter to one so dirty and foul-smelling as you?" But he kept on grunting that he must have a wife of one sort or another. The queen, not knowing how to manage him in this matter, asked the king what they should do in their trouble: "Our son wishes to marry, but where shall we find anyone who will take him as a husband?" Every day the pig would come back to his mother with the same demand: "I must have a wife, and I will never leave you in peace until you secure for me a certain maiden I have seen today, who pleases me greatly."

It happened that this maiden was a daughter of a poor woman who had three daughters, each one of them being very lovely. When the queen heard this, she had brought before her the poor woman and her eldest daughter, and said, "Good mother, you are poor and burdened with children. If you agree to what I say to you, you will be rich. I have this son who is, as you see, in form a pig, and I would like to marry him to your eldest daughter. Do not consider him, but think of the king and of me, and remember that your daughter will inherit this whole kingdom when the king and I are dead."

When the young girl listened to the words of the queen, she was greatly disturbed in her mind and blushed red for shame, and then said that on no account would she listen to the queen's proposition; but the poor mother entreated her so pressingly that at last she yielded. When the pig came home one day, all covered with dirt as usual, his mother said to him, "My son, we have found for you the wife you desire." And then she caused to be brought in the bride, who by this time had been dressed in sumptuous royal attire, and presented her to the pig prince. When he saw how lovely and desirable she was, he was filled with joy, and, all foul and dirty as he was, jumped round about her, trying by his pawing and nuzzling to show some sign of his affection. But she, when she found he was soiling her beautiful dress,

thrust him aside; at which the pig said to her, "Why do you push me in this way? Have I not had these garments made for you myself?" Then she answered disdainfully, "No, neither you nor any other of the whole kingdom of hogs has done this thing." And when the time for going to bed was come, the young girl said to herself, "What am I to do with this foul beast? This very night, while he lies in his first sleep, I will kill him." The pig prince, who was not far off, heard these words, but said nothing, and when the two retired to their chamber he got into the bed, stinking and dirty as he was, and defiled the sumptuous bed with his filthy paws and snout. He lay down by his spouse, who was not long in falling to sleep, and then he struck her with his sharp hoofs and drove them into her breast so that he killed her.

The next morning the queen went to visit her daughter-in-law, and to her great grief found that the pig had killed her; and when he came back from wandering about the city, he said, in reply to the queen's bitter reproaches, that he had only done to his wife as she had intended to do to him, and then he departed in an ill humor. Not many days had passed before the pig prince again began to ask the queen to allow him to marry one of the other sisters, and because the queen at first would not listen to his request, he persisted in his purpose, and threatened to ruin everything in the place if he could not have her as wife. The queen, when she heard this, went to the king and told him everything, and he made answer that perhaps it would be wiser to kill their ill-fated offspring before he committed some fatal misdeed in the city. But the queen felt all the tenderness of a mother towards him, and loved him very dearly in spite of his bestial form, and could not endure the thought of being parted from him; so she summoned once more to the palace the poor woman, together with her second daughter, and had a long conversation with her, begging her the while to give her daughter in marriage. At last the girl agreed to take the pig prince for a husband; but her fate was no happier than her sister's, for the bridegroom killed her, as he had killed his other bride, and then fled quickly from the palace.

When he came back, dirty as usual and smelling so foul that no one could approach him, the king and queen reprimanded him severely for the outrage he had committed; but again he cried out boldly that if he had not killed her, she would have killed him. As it had happened before, the pig in a very short time began to pester his mother again to let him have to wife the youngest sister, who was much more beautiful than either of the others; and when this request of his was refused steadily, he became more insistent than ever, and in the end began to threaten the queen's life in violent and bloodthirsty words, unless he should have given to him the young girl for his wife. The queen, when she heard this shameful and unnatural speech, was almost brokenhearted and on the verge of going out of her mind; but, put-

ting all other considerations aside, she called for the poor woman and her third daughter, who was named Meldina, and addressed her as follows: "Meldina, my child, I should be greatly pleased if you would take the pig prince for a husband; pay no regard to him, but to his father and to me; then, if you will be prudent and put up with him patiently, you may be the happiest woman in the world." To this speech Meldina answered, with a grateful smile upon her face, that she was quite content to do as the queen asked her, and thanked her humbly for deigning to choose her as a daughter-in-law; for, seeing that she herself had nothing in the world, it was indeed great good fortune that she, a poor girl, should become the daughter-in-law of a powerful king. The queen, when she heard this modest and amiable reply, could not keep back her tears for the happiness she felt; but she feared all the time that the same fate might be in store for Meldina as her sisters.

When the new bride had been dressed in rich attire and covered with jewels, and was awaiting the bridegroom, the pig prince came in, filthier and muddier than ever; but she spread out her rich gown and asked him to lie down by her side. Whereupon the queen ordered her to thrust him away, but to this she would not consent, and spoke to the queen as follows: "There are three wise sayings, gracious lady, which I remember having heard. The first is that it is folly to waste time in searching for that which cannot be found. The second is that we should believe nothing we may hear, except those things which bear the marks of sense and reason. The third is that once you have gained possession of some rare and precious treasure, appreciate it well and keep a firm hold upon it."

When the maiden had finished speaking, the pig prince, who had been wide awake and had heard all that she had said, got up, kissed her with his tongue on the face, neck, bosom, and shoulder, and she was not slow in returning his caresses, so that he was fired with a warm love for her. As soon as the time for retiring for the night had come, the bride went to bed and awaited her unseemly spouse, and, as soon as he came, she raised the coverlet and asked him to lie near her and to put his head upon the pillow, and she covered him carefully with the bedclothes and drew the curtains so that he might feel no cold. When morning had come, the pig got up and went out to forage, as was his habit, and very soon after the queen went to the bride's chamber, expecting to find that she had met with the same fate as her sisters; but when she saw her lying in the bed, all defiled with mud as it was, and looking pleased and contented, she thanked God for this favor, that her son had at last found a spouse according to his liking.

One day, soon after this, when the pig prince was chatting pleasantly with his wife, he said to her: "Meldina, my beloved wife, if I could be completely certain that you could keep a secret, I would now tell you one of

mine; something I have kept hidden for many years. I know that you are very prudent and wise, and that you love me truly; so I wish to let you share my secret." "You may safely tell it to me, if you will," said Meldina, "for I promise never to reveal it to anyone without your consent." At this, since he was now sure of his wife's discretion and fidelity, he at once shook off from his body the foul and dirty skin of the pig, and stood revealed as a handsome and well-shaped young man, and all that night rested closely folded in the arms of his beloved wife. But he enjoined her solemnly to keep silence about this wonder she had seen, for the time had not yet come for him to be freed entirely from this misery. So when he left the bed, he donned the dirty pig's hide once more. I leave you to imagine for yourselves how great was the joy of Meldina when she discovered that, instead of a pig, she had gained a handsome and gallant young prince for a husband. Not long after this she turned out to be pregnant, and when the time of her delivery came she gave birth to a handsome and well-formed boy. The joy of the king and queen was unbounded, especially when they found that the newborn child had the form of a human being and not that of a beast.

But the burden of the strange and weighty secret which her husband had confided to her pressed heavily upon Meldina, and one day she went to her mother-in-law and said: "Gracious queen, when first I married your son I believed I was married to a beast, but now I find that you have given me to be my husband the most handsome, the worthiest, and the most gallant young man ever born into the world. For know that when he comes into my bedroom to lie by my side, he casts off his dirty hide and leaves it on the ground, and is changed into a graceful, handsome youth. No one could believe this marvel unless they saw it with their own eyes." When the queen heard these words, she concluded that her daughter-in-law must be joking with her, but Meldina still insisted that what she said was true. And when the queen demanded to know how she might witness with her own eyes the truth of this thing, Meldina replied: "Come to my chamber tonight, just after we have fallen asleep; the door will be open, and you will find that what I tell you is the truth."

That same night, when the appointed time had come, and everyone had gone to bed, the queen had some torches lit and went, accompanied by the king, to her son's bedroom, and when she had entered, she saw the pig's skin lying on the floor in the corner of the room, and having gone to the bedside, found in it a handsome young man in whose arms Meldina was lying. And when they saw this, the delight of the king and queen was very great, and the king ordered that before anyone left the room, the pig's hide should be torn to shreds. So great was their joy over the recovery of their son that they almost died of it.

And King Galeotto, when he saw that he had such a fine son, and a grandchild too, laid aside his diadem and his royal robes, and abdicated in favor of his son, whom he had crowned with the greatest pomp, and who was ever afterwards known as King Pig. Thus, to the great contentment of all the people, the young king began his reign, and he lived long and happily with Meldina his beloved wife.

When Isabella's story was finished, the whole company broke into laughter at the notion of the pig prince, all dirty and muddy as he was, kissing his beloved spouse and lying by her side.

E. Brothers Grimm, "Hans My Hedgehog" ("Hans Mein Igel" [*KHM* 108])

Once upon a time there was a farmer who had ample money and property, but however rich he was, something was still lacking in his happiness: he had no children with his wife. Often, when he went to town with the other farmers, they mocked him and asked why he had no children. So finally he grew angry, and when he came home, he said, "I want to have a child, even if it should be a hedgehog."

Then his wife had a child that was a hedgehog in its upper part and a boy in its lower, and when she saw the child, she was horrified and said, "Do you see? You cursed us." Then the husband said, "That doesn't matter now, the boy must be christened, but we will not be able to get a godfather for him." The wife said, "Also, we will not be able to christen him anything but Hans My Hedgehog." When he was christened, the parish priest said, "Because of his quills he cannot go into a regular bed." So a little straw was set up behind the stove, and Hans My Hedgehog was laid on it. He could not suckle at his mother's breast, since he would have pricked her with his quills. So he lay there behind the stove for eight years, and his father was tired of him and thought, "If he would only die!"; but he did not die. Instead, he remained lying there.

Now it happened that there was a market in town, and the farmer wanted to go there. So he asked his wife what he should bring back with him for her. She said, "A little meat and a couple of rolls, what we need for the household." Then he asked the maid, who wanted a pair of slippers and of stockings embroidered along the sides. Finally he said also, "Hans My Hedgehog, what would you like to have then?"

"Father dear," he said, "please bring me back bagpipes." When the farmer came back home, he gave his wife what he had bought for her—meat and rolls. Then he gave the maid the slippers and the stockings embroidered

along the sides. Finally he went behind the stove and gave Hans My Hedgehog the bagpipes. And when Hans My Hedgehog had the bagpipes, he said, "Father dear, please go to the smith and have my rooster shod for me; then I will ride off and never again come back." Then the father was happy that he would be rid of him, and he had the rooster shod for him, and when it was ready, Hans My Hedgehog took a seat on it and rode off. He took pigs and donkeys as well, which he wanted to tend outside in the forest.

Once in the forest the rooster had to fly with him onto a high tree. He sat there and tended the donkeys and pigs, and sat many long years, until the herd was quite large, and his father knew nothing about him. And while he sat on the tree, he blew his bagpipes and made music, which was very beautiful.

Once a king came riding along who had lost his way and who heard the music. So he wondered about it and sent his servant to look around where the music was coming from. He looked around, but saw nothing except a little animal sitting up on the tree that was like a rooster on which a hedgehog was sitting, and it was making the music. Then the king said to the servant that he should ask why he sat there, and if he knew where the way led to his kingdom. Then Hans My Hedgehog came down from the tree and said that he would show the way, if the king would promise in writing to give him whatever met him first at the royal court as soon as he got home. Then the king thought, "I can easily do that, Hans My Hedgehog does not understand it anyway, and I can write what I want." So the king took pen and ink and wrote down something, and when it was done, Hans My Hedgehog showed him the way, and he got happily home.

But his daughter, when she saw him from afar, was so overjoyed that she ran to meet him and kissed him. Then he thought of Hans My Hedgehog and told her what had happened to him and that he had had to promise in writing what first met him at home, and that the animal had sat on a rooster as if on a horse and had made beautiful music; but he had written that Hans My Hedgehog should not have it, since Hans My Hedgehog could not read it anyway. The princess was happy about this and said that that was good, since she would never have gone along anyway. But Hans My Hedgehog tended the donkeys and pigs, was always cheery, sat on the tree, and blew on his bagpipes.

Now it happened that another king came passing by with his servants and footmen, and had lost his way and did not know how to get home again, because the forest was so large. Then, likewise, he heard the beautiful music from afar and told his footman that he should just look to see what that might be. Then the footman went beneath the tree and saw the rooster sitting and Hans My Hedgehog upon it above. The footman asked him

what he had in mind to do up there. "I tend my donkeys and pigs; but what is your desire?" The footman said that they had lost their way and could not get back again to the kingdom, [and asked] if he would not show them the way. Then Hans My Hedgehog came down with the rooster from the tree and said to the old king that he would show him the way, if he would give to him as his own what met him first at home in front of his royal palace. The king said "Yes" and signed his name to Hans My Hedgehog that he should have this. Once that had happened, he rode out upon the rooster and showed him the way, and the king reached his kingdom again happily. When he came to the court, there was great joy about it.

Now he had an only daughter who was very beautiful who ran out to meet him, threw her arms around his neck and kissed him, and rejoiced that her old father had come back. She also asked him where in the world he had been so long. So he told her that he had lost his way and had almost not come back home, but as he had traveled through a great forest, a creature, half like a hedgehog, half like a man, riding on a rooster, had sat upon a high tree and made beautiful music; this creature had helped him out and pointed out the way, but he had promised him in return what first came to meet him at the royal court, and that was her, and that now made him very sorry. But then she promised him that, for love of her old father, she would gladly go with him, when he came.

In the meantime Hans My Hedgehog tended his pigs, and the pigs gave birth to pigs in turn, and they became so many that the whole forest was full of them. Then Hans My Hedgehog wanted to live in the forest no longer and had his father told that they should clear out all the sties in the village, since he was coming with such a great herd that everyone who wanted to slaughter could slaughter as he wanted. Then his father was troubled when he heard that, since he thought that Hans My Hedgehog had died long ago. But Hans My Hedgehog took a seat upon his rooster, drove the pigs before him into the village, and had them slaughtered. Wow, there was then a butchering and a hacking that could be heard two hours away. Afterward Hans My Hedgehog said, "Father dear, have my rooster shod once again by the smith; then I will ride out and not come back so long as I live." Then the father had the rooster shod and was happy that Hans My Hedgehog would not come back.

Hans My Hedgehog rode out to the first kingdom, where the king had ordered that if anyone came riding on a rooster and had bagpipes with him, then they should all shoot at him, hit him, and stab him so that he could not come into the palace. When Hans My Hedgehog came riding there, they pressed at him with bayonettes, but he spurred the rooster, flew up over the gate before the king's window, set himself down there, and called

to him that he should give him what he had promised or else he would take his life and his daughter's.

Then the king gave his daughter a good talking-to: she should go out to him, so that she might save his life and her own. Then she dressed herself in white, and her father gave her a carriage with six horses and magnificent attendants, money, and property. She took a seat and Hans My Hedgehog sat with his rooster and bagpipes next to her, then they took their leave and drove away, and the king thought that he would not manage to see her again. But it happened otherwise than he thought, for when they were a bit of the way out of town, then Hans My Hedgehog took off her beautiful clothes and stuck her with his hedgehog's skin until she was all bloody, and said, "That is the reward for your falseness. Go off, I do not want you!" and with that he chased her home, and she was disgraced as long as she lived.

But Hans My Hedgehog rode further on his rooster and with his bag-pipes to the second kingdom, where he had also shown the king the way. He however had ordered that if a creature like Hans My Hedgehog were to come, they should present arms, give him free passage, shout out "Long life!", and bring him to the royal palace. When the king's daughter saw him now, she was horrified, because he looked very much too odd; but she thought that it could not be otherwise, since she had promised her father. Then Hans My Hedgehog was welcomed by her and was wedded with her, and he had to go with her to the royal table, and she took a seat at his side, and they ate and drank.

When evening fell, so that they wanted to go to sleep, then she was very afraid of his quills; but he said that she should not be afraid, no harm would befall her, and he said to the old king that he should command four men who should keep watch before the bedroom door and make a great fire, and when he entered the bedroom and wanted to lie down in bed, he would slip out of his hedgehog skin and would leave it lying by the bed; then the men should pounce quickly and toss it into the fire, and also remain by it until it had been consumed by the fire.

When the clock now struck eleven, then he went into the bedroom, stripped off the hedgehog skin, and left it lying by the bed; then the men came and took it rapidly and threw it into the fire; and when the fire had consumed it, then he was released and lay in bed there, just like a man in shape, but he was coal black, as if burned. The king sent for his doctor, who rubbed him with good ointments and anointed him; so he became white and was a handsome young lord. When the king's daughter saw that, she was happy, and on the following morning they arose with joy, ate and drank, and the marriage was then duly celebrated, and Hans My Hedgehog obtained the kingdom of the old king.

When several years had gone by, he went with his spouse to his father and said that he was his son; but the father said that he had no son, he had had only one, but he had been born like a hedgehog with quills and had gone forth into the world. Then he made himself known, and the old father rejoiced and went with him into his kingdom.

My tale is done,
Goes on the run,
Brings Gussie fun![83]

Notes

INTRODUCTION

1. Claudio Guillén, *The Challenge of Comparative Literature,* trans. Cola Franzen (Cambridge, MA: Harvard University Press, 1993), 3. For a recent sketch of how comparative literature has evolved, see Jan M. Ziolkowski, "Always Beyond Compare: The Past, Present, and Future of Comparative Literature," *Journal X: A Journal in Culture and Criticism* 8 (2004): 115–35.

2. See the essays collected in Jan M. Ziolkowski, ed., *On Philology* (University Park, PA: Penn State Press, 1990), and see the précis of subsequent developments in Jan M. Ziolkowski, "Metaphilology," *Journal of English and Germanic Philology* 104 (2005): 239–72.

3. The *New York Times* carried an article entitled "America Yawns at Foreign Fiction" by Stephen Kinzer on 26 July 2003 (late edition-final, section B, p. 7, column 1), on how few foreign-language books are translated annually into English.

4. A key enunciation of views in favor of a "world literature" was Erich Auerbach, "Philology and *Weltliteratur,*" trans. Maire Said and Edward Said, *Centennial Review* 13 (1969), originally published as "Philologie der Weltliteratur," in *Weltliteratur: Festgabe für Fritz Strich zum 70. Geburtstag,* ed. Walter Muschg and Emil Staiger (Bern: Francke Verlag, 1952), 39–50. How broadly the world was defined by those who spoke of "world literature" is another question.

5. See Vladimir IAkovlevich Propp, *La fiaba russa: Lezioni inedite,* ed. and trans. Franca Crestani (Turin: Giulio Einaudi editore, 1990), 111. For a dazzling exploration of the wisdom that has often been associated with women storytellers and with female figures within fairy tales, see Marina Warner, *From the Beast to the Blonde: On Fairy Tales and Their Tellers* (New York: Farrar, Straus, and Giroux, 1994).

6. In making the second part of this assertion, I am influenced by Otto Rank (1884–1939). See his *The Myth of the Birth of the Hero, and Other Writings,* ed. Philip Freund (New York: Knopf, 1932).

7. These tales have slipped between the cracks and have not been covered even in such valuable books as James M. McGlathery's edited volume *The Brothers Grimm and Folktale* (Urbana and Chicago: University of Illinois Press, 1988).

8. For the fullest coverage of such issues at present, see Rudolf Schenda, *Von Mund zu Ohr: Bausteine einer Kulturgeschichte volkstümlichen Erzählens in Europa* (Göttingen: Vandenhoeck und Ruprecht, 1993). No comparable work focused on premodern times has yet been produced. I took a very small and tentative step toward a study of one of these groups in my "Old Wives' Tales: Classicism and Anticlassicism from Apuleius to Chaucer," *Journal of Medieval Latin* 12 (2002): 90–113.

9. The term *classic fairy tales* has been applied to fairy tales at least four times in titles or subtitles of highly influential anthologies: compare, first, Iona Opie and Peter Opie, *The Classic Fairy Tales* (Oxford and New York: Oxford University Press, 1974); later, Jack Zipes, trans., *Beauties, Beasts, and Enchantment: Classic French Fairy Tales* (New York: Meridian, 1991); and, most recently, Maria Tatar, ed., *The Classic Fairy Tales* (New York and London: W. W. Norton, 1999), and Maria Tatar, ed., *The Annotated Classic Fairy Tales* (New York and London: W. W. Norton, 2002).

10. Croce made very apparent his resistance to what he considered arbitrary theories, "those of Indian origins or of primitive or savage origins insofar as reflecting the customs of distant times, or of mythological-naturalistic origins" [quelle dell'origine indiana o dell'origine primitiva o selvaggia in quanto riflesso del costume di età remote, o della origine mitologico-naturalistica] (Benedetto Croce, introduction to *Il pentamerone, ossia la fiaba delle fiabe,* by Giambattista Basile [Bari: Gius. Laterza e Figli, 1925], 1:XXXI).

11. Croce (introduction to *Il pentamerone,* 1:XXXII) observed, "So too the question of the origins of folktales is to be changed from now on into the history of each one of them, which is then, at each of its stages, that of creation anew" [Anche la questione dell'origine delle fiabe è da convertire ormai nella storia di ciascuna di esse, che è poi, a ogni suo passo, quella di una creazione a nuovo].

12. If such a basic principle requires scholarly support, I invoke Satu Apo, "The Two Worlds of the Finnish Fairytale: Observations on the Folk and Literary Fairytale Tradition of the 19th Century," *Arv: Scandinavian Yearbook of Folklore* 44 (1988): 47: "Every magic tale narrator was guided by his own particular and general culture in constructing his narrative world. In other words, he was tied to his own time, sex, social class and peer group."

13. The phrase "die Entzauberung der Welt," which Weber coined, appears in his *Wirtschaft und Gesellschaft* (Tübingen: J. C. B. Mohr, 1922).

14. *German Popular Stories translated from the Kinder und Haus Marchen* [sic], *collected by M. M. Grimm, from oral tradition,* trans. Edgar Taylor, illustrated by George Cruikshank, 2 vols., vol. 1 (London: C. Baldwyn, Newgate Street, 1823), and vol. 2 (London: James Robins; Dublin: Joseph Robins Junr., 1826).

15. The strongest and most influential of recent voices against eclecticism and for a single method of interpreting fairy tales was Bengt Holbek (1933–92), who elaborated his ideas in lucid and copious detail in *Interpretation of Fairy Tales: Danish Folklore in a European Perspective,* FFC 239 (Helsinki: Suomalainen Tiedeakatemia, Academia scientiarum fennica, 1998).

16. Stith Thompson, *The Folktale* (New York: Holt, Rinehart, and Winston, 1946; repr., Berkeley and Los Angeles: University of California Press, 1977), 396.

17. On von der Leyen's shifts in approach, see Propp, *La fiaba russa*, 156. For a concise treatment of von der Leyen's life's work, see Kurt Schier, "Leyen, Friedrich von der," in *EM* 8:1005–11. In view of von der Leyen's longevity, his willingness to consider new methods seems to me more admirable than faulty.

18. See Aron Aikovlevich Gurevich, *Lezioni romane: Antropologia e cultura medievale,* ed. Clara Castelli, Piccola Biblioteca Einaudi 549 (Turin: Giulio Einaudi editore, 1991), 73.

19. Jan M. Ziolkowski, "What Is Philology? Introduction," *Comparative Literature Studies* 27 (1990): 1–12, reprinted in Ziolkowski, *On Philology,* 1–12.

20. See Benedetto Croce, review of *Le radici storiche dei racconti di fate,* by V. J. Propp, *Quaderni della "Critica"* 15 (1949): 102–5.

21. Croce (review of *Le radici storiche,* 104) argued, "if we wish to think rigorously, their origin, or their author, lies in each one who tells or retells a folktale with a new emphasis and thus creates it on his or her own behalf" [a voler pensare con rigore, la loro origine, ossia il loro autore, è in ciascuno che narri o rinarri una fiaba con accento nuovo e la crei così per suo conto].

22. Propp, *La fiaba russa,* 226.

CHAPTER ONE

1. Linda Dégh, *Narratives in Society: A Performer-Centered Study of Narration,* FFC 255 (Helsinki: Suomalainen Tiedeakatemia, Academia scientiarum fennica, 1995), 264–65. The German word *Märchen* corresponds to both *fairy tale* and *folktale* in English.

2. In *Märchen des Mittelalters* (Berlin: H. Stubenrauch, 1925), xxii, Albert Wesselski claims, "Obviously not all the stories contained in the following pages are *Märchen* in the strict sense of the word—about that we are entirely clear—although no one has yet found a thoroughly satisfactory characterization of it; here reference to the example of the Brothers Grimm is relevant, in following whom no one can be subject to reproach."

3. For information on studies of the influence that the Brothers Grimm exercised on the collection of folktales among ethnic and national groups outside Germany, see Siegfried Neumann, "The Brothers Grimm as Collectors and Editors of German Folktales," in *The Great Fairy Tale Tradition: From Straparola and Basile to the Brothers Grimm,* ed. Jack Zipes (New York and London: W. W. Norton, 2001), 969–80.

4. On Bolte, see Hannjost Lixfeld, "Bolte, Johannes," in *EM* 2:603–5. On Polívka, see Viera Gašparíková, "Polívka, Jiří," in *EM* 10:1145–50.

5. Holbek, *Interpretation of Fairy Tales,* 251.

6. In my opinion, Propp (*La fiaba russa,* 20) overstates the necessity of orality, when he says, "È un racconto trasmesso di generazione in generazione soltanto per mezzo della narrazione orale" [It is a tale transmitted from generation to generation, solely by means of oral narration].

7. Christine Goldberg ("Folktale," in *Folklore* 1:356) references "[a] traditional narrative; more narrowly, a traditional fictional story in prose."

8. See Christine Goldberg, "Folktale," in *Encyclopedia of Folklore and Literature,* ed. Mary Ellen Brown and Bruce A. Rosenberg (Santa Barbara, CA: ABC-CLIO, 1998), 219.

9. This is the definition assumed by Bolte and Polívka, who canonized what had been set in place far earlier.

10. Sven Liljeblad, *Die Tobiasgeschichte und andere Märchen mit toten Helfern* (Lund: P. Lindstedts Univ.-Bokhandel, 1927), 10.

11. Jack Zipes, *Breaking the Magic Spell: Radical Theories of Folk and Fairy Tales* (Austin: University of Texas Press, 1979; repr., New York: Routledge, 1992), 20.

12. Of these categories, the last has been most amply treated in scholarship. To cite only a few studies from the past two decades, see Volker Klotz, *Das europäische Kunstmärchen: Fünfundzwanzig Kapitel seiner Geschichte von der Renaissance bis zur Moderne* (Munich: Deutscher Taschenbuch Verlag, 1987); Mathias Mayer and Jens Tismar, *Kunstmärchen*, 3rd ed., Sammlung Metzler 155 (Stuttgart and Weimar: J. B. Metzler, 1997); Paul-Wolfgang Wührl, *Das deutsche Kunstmärchen: Geschichte, Botschaft und Erzählstrukturen* (Heidelberg: Wuelle und Meyer, 1984). For a more concise but still thorough examination, see Manfred Grätz, "Kunstmärchen," in *EM* 8: 612–22. On *Buchmärchen*, see Hermann Bausinger, "Buchmärchen," in *EM* 2:974–77.

13. For a dense listing that draws no distinction between prose and verse or between Latin and vernacular, see Wolfgang Maaz, "Märchen und Märchenmotive im MA," in *LdM* 6:224–26.

14. The term *wonder tale* seems finally to have secured a lasting place in English-language folktale and fairy tale scholarship owing to the influence of Vladimir IAkovlevich Propp, who provides a lengthy section on this form in his *Theory and History of Folklore*, trans. Ariadna Y. Martin and Richard P. Martin, ed. Anatoly Liberman, Theory and History of Folklore 5 (Minneapolis: University of Minnesota Press, 1984), 65–123. Attempts have been made to anthologize Medieval Latin materials relating to folktale and fairy tale and to bring them to popular attention, particularly in German translation. The fullest such publication is Ernst Tegethoff's *Märchen, Schwänke und Fabeln,* Bücher des Mittelalters (Munich: F. Bruckmann, 1925), 1–41. The much more recent collection by Hans-Jörg Uther, *Märchen vor Grimm* (Munich: Diederichs, 1990), not only contains less but also comprises paraphrases rather than clearly indicated and organized translations. For Medieval Latinists, the most convenient compendium remains Karl Langosch's *Waltharius-Ruodlieb-Märchenepen: Lateinische Epik des Mittelalters mit deutschen Versen* (Darmstadt: Wissenschaftliche Buchgesellschaft, 1956), which includes the full texts of *One-Ox* (251–305), *The Turnip Tale* (307–31), and *The Donkey Tale* (333–57).

15. In the notes to the enlarged 1819 edition, the brothers acknowledged explicitly that *KHM* 144, "The Little Donkey" ("Das Eselein"), was based directly on *The Donkey Tale* and *KHM* 146, "The Turnip" ("Die Rübe"), on *The Turnip Tale.*

16. For an efficient overview of early theories, see Antti Aarne, "Ursprung der Märchen," in *Leitfaden der vergleichenden Märchenforschung* FFC 13 (Hamina: Suomalaisen Tiedeakatemia Kustantema, 1913): 1–22, reprinted in *Wege der Märchenforschung,* ed. Felix Karlinger, Wege der Forschung 255 (Darmstadt: Wissenschaftliche Buchgesellschaft, 1973), 42–60.

17. Jacob Grimm made pronouncements on fairy tale in his preface to the German translation of Basile's *Pentamerone,* in his volumes on Germanic mythology, and in articles. See Jacob Grimm, "Vorrede," in Giambattista Basile, *Der Pentamerone, oder, Das Märchen aller Märchen,* trans. Felix Liebrecht, 2 vols. (Breslau: J. Max, 1846), 1:V–XXIV; reprinted in Jacob Grimm, *Kleinere Schriften,* ed. Karl Müllenhoff and Eduard Ippel (Berlin: Dümmler, 1864–90), 8, part 1:191–201.

18. In the preface to *KHM,* 1st ed. (Berlin: Realschulbuchhandlung, 1815), 2:vii,

they state: "in these folktales resides pure, urGerman myth . . ." ("in diesen Volks-märchen liegt lauter urdeutscher Mythus . . .").

19. See Georg von Simson, "Benfey, Theodor," in *EM* 2:102–9.

20. For example, the German Reinhold Adalbert Johannes Köhler (1830–92) and the Englishman William Alexander Clouston (1843–96) emphasized the indebtedness of Western Europe to oriental story books. The Frenchman Emmanuel Cosquin (1841–1919) took an extremist Indianist position by arguing that all European folktales derived from Indian prototypes. *EM* contains entries on all three of these scholars (under their last names).

21. See Marie-Louis Tenèze, "Bédier, Joseph," in *EM* 2:21–25.

22. On Tylor, see *F&W* 1137. Entries on both Lang and Frazer are also included in *F&W*, but for fuller information on them, see Venetia Newall, "Lang, Andrew," in *EM* 8:766–70; Gertrud Werber, "Frazer, James George," in *EM* 5:220–27. For further information, see Richard M. Dorson, *The British Folklorists: A History* (Chicago: University of Chicago Press, 1968).

23. The classic exposition is Antti Aarne's *Leitfaden der vergleichenden Märchen-forschung*, FFC 13 (Hamina: Suomalaisen Tiedeakatemia Kustantama, 1913). For basic orientation, see Leea Virtanen, "Historic-Geographic Method," in *Folklore* 1:442–48.

24. Two volumes are exemplary of this trend: nothing on the Finnish school or the historic-geographic method is included in either Michael Groden and Martin Kreiswirth's *The Johns Hopkins Guide to Literary Theory and Criticism* (Baltimore and London: Johns Hopkins University Press, 1994) or Irena R. Makaryk's *Encyclopedia of Contemporary Literary Theory: Approaches, Scholars, Terms* (Toronto, Buffalo, and London: University of Toronto Press, 1993). Although the latter contains the delimiting term *contemporary* in its title, it includes twentieth-century scholars as distant as Wilhelm Dilthey (1833–1911), Sørem Aabye Kierkegaard (1813–55), and Ferdinand de Saussure (1857–1913). Among folklorists, it features Vladimir Propp.

25. Propp, *La fiaba russa*, 152–53.

26. Propp, *La fiaba russa*, 220.

27. Vladimir IAkovlevich Propp, *Le radici storiche dei racconti di fate*, 2nd ed. (Turin: Boringhieri, 1985), 31.

28. See Satu Apo, *The Narrative World of Finnish Fairy Tales*, FFC 112, no. 256 (Helsinki: Suomalainen Tiedeakatemia, Academia scientiarum fennica, 1995), 143.

29. The illustration is by P. Grot Johann in Jacob Grimm and Wilhelm Grimm, *Kinder- und Hausmärchen: Säkular-Ausgabe*, illustrated by P. Grot Johann and R. Leinweber (Stuttgart: Deutsche Verlags-Anstalt, 1912). It has been reproduced in Lutz Röhrich, *Wage es, den Frosch zu küssen: Das Grimmsche Märchen Nummer Eins in seinen Wandlungen* (Cologne: Eugen Diederichs Verlag, 1987), 12.

30. For two excellent examples, see Wolfgang Mieder, "Modern Anglo-American Variants of the Frog Prince (AT 440)," *New York Folklore* 6 (1980): 121–22. The second of the examples is a *Playboy* cartoon. In it, the castle stands in the background on the left, while the foreground is occupied by a naked recumbent princess and a frog who is pulling on a pair of trousers; the caption reads, "I lied!" The same cartoon is reproduced (from Mieder's article) in Röhrich, *Wage es,* 137.

31. For a quick sketch, see Patrick J. Geary, *The Myth of Nations: The Medieval Origins of Europe* (Princeton, NJ: Princeton University Press, 2002), 26–29.

32. See especially Jacob Grimm, *Reinhart Fuchs* (Berlin: Georg Reimer, 1834); Jacob

Grimm and Johann Andreas Schmeller, *Lateinische Gedichte des X. und XI. Jahrhunderts* [Latin Poems of the Tenth and Eleventh Century] (Göttingen: Dieterischsche Buchhandlung, 1838; repr. Amsterdam: Rodopi, 1967).

33. Jacob and Wilhelm Grimm, *Deutsche Sagen,* ed. Hans-Jörg Uther (Munich: Eugen Diederichs Verlag, 1993), 3:346–64, nos. 388, 390–96, 398–408, 410. *Deutsche Sagen* was originally published in 2 vols. (Berlin: Verlag der Realbuchhandlung, 1816–18). The text is available in translation in Donald Ward, trans. and ed., *The German Legends of the Brothers Grimm,* 2 vols. (Philadelphia: Institute for the Study of Human Issues, 1981).

34. Jack Zipes, ed., *The Great Fairy Tale Tradition: From Straparola and Basile to the Brothers Grimm* (New York and London: W. W. Norton, 2001).

35. Jack Zipes, *Spells of Enchantment: The Wondrous Fairy Tales of Western Culture* (New York: Penguin, 1991).

36. Martin Hallett and Barbara Karasek, eds., *Folk and Fairy Tales,* 2nd ed. (Peterborough, Ontario: Broadview, 1996).

37. See Propp, *La fiaba russa,* 114.

38. See Donald Haase, "Yours, Mine, or Ours? Perrault, the Brothers Grimm, and the Ownership of Fairy Tales," *Marvels and Tales: Journal of Fairy-Tale Studies* 7 (1993): 383–402.

39. From the many publications on the Brothers Grimm and philology, I will single out Lothar Bluhm's *Die Brüder Grimm und der Beginn der Deutschen Philologie: Eine Studie zu Kommunikation und Wissenschaftsbildung im frühen 19. Jahrhundert,* Spolia Berolinensia: Berliner Beiträge zur Geistes- und Kulturgeschichte des Mittelalters und der Neuzeit 11 (Hildesheim and Zurich: Weidmann, 1997).

40. See Pertti Anttonen, "Philological Approach," in *Folklore* 2:641–47.

41. Propp (*La fiaba russa,* 44) compares the AT system to Linnaean taxonomy or chemical symbols.

42. For a few efforts to answer this question, see the essays in Charlotte Oberfeld, ed., *Wie alt sind unsere Märchen?* (Regensburg: Erich Röth, 1990).

43. Goldberg, "Folktale," in *Folklore* 1:363.

44. See Propp, *La fiaba russa,* 171–72.

45. For information on the development of folkloristics in the Romantic era, see Giuseppe Cocchiara, *The History of Folklore in Europe,* trans. John N. McDaniel (Philadelphia: Institute for the Study of Human Issues, 1981). Romanticism receives only oblique attention in the essays devoted to Medieval Latin studies in *La filologia medievale e umanistica greca e latina nel secolo XX: Atti del Congresso internazionale; Roma, Consiglio Nazionale delle Ricerche, Università "La Sapienza," 11–15 dicembre 1989,* 2 vols., Testi e studi bizantino-neoellenici 7 (Rome: Università di Roma "La Sapienza," 1993). On the often chilly and distrustful relations between folklore studies and literary criticism, see Bruce A. Rosenberg, *Folklore and Literature: Rival Siblings* (Knoxville: University of Tennessee Press, 1991).

46. Specifically in regard to the Brothers Grimm, see Christa Kamenetsky, *The Brothers Grimm and Their Critics: Folktales and the Quest for Meaning* (Athens: Ohio University Press, 1992), 292–96; for a somewhat broader discussion, see Jack Zipes, *The Brothers Grimm: From Enchanted Forest to the Modern World* (New York and London: Routledge, 1988), 75–95.

47. The range of such scholars would include the Brothers Grimm, Albert Wesselski, and Vladimir Propp.

48. Gustav Gröber, *Übersicht über die lateinische Litteratur von der Mitte des VI. Jahrhunderts bis zur Mitte des XIV. Jahrhunderts,* vol. 2, part 1, of *Grundriß der romanischen Philologie,* II. Band. 1 Abteilung (Strasbourg: Karl J. Trübner, 1902; repr., Munich: Wilhelm Fink, [1974]).

49. Tegethoff, *Märchen, Schwänke und Fabeln,* 2: "Denn nicht ein Land und ein Volk hat die Märchen geschaffen, sondern jede Nation trug ihr Scherflein zum Märchenschatz der Weltliteratur bei."

50. On the datability and dating of folktale, see Heda Jason and Aharon Kempinski, "How Old Are Folktales?" *Fabula* 24 (1983): 1–27; Dietz-Rüdiger Moser, "Alterbestimmung des Märchens," in *EM* 1:407–19.

51. See Randal S. Allison, "Ur-form," in *Folklore* 2:823–24.

52. BP 4:95. The most recent and convenient repository of information on the Egyptian tale is Susan Tower Hollis, *The Ancient Egyptian "Tale of Two Brothers": The Oldest Fairy Tale in the World* (Norman and London: University of Oklahoma Press, 1990).

53. See Peter Burke, *Popular Culture in Early Modern Europe* (New York: New York University Press, 1978), 21.

54. See Hoxie Neale Fairchild, *The Noble Savage: A Study in Romantic Naturalism* (New York: Columbia University Press, 1928), 441–97.

55. See Propp, *La fiaba russa,* 370.

56. The standard edition of Egbert of Liège's *The Richly Laden Ship* remains Ernst Voigt's (*Fecunda ratis* [Halle an der Salle: Max Niemeyer, 1889]). "The Wish-Goat" (with the incipit "Tres iuuenes fratres, uno de patre creati") appears in *Carmina sangallensia,* ed. Ernst Dümmler, MGH Poetae Latini Aevi Carolini 2 (Berlin: Weidmann, 1884), 474–75. The most recent edition of the *Cambridge Songs* (*Carmina cantabrigiensia*), with English translation and extensive commentary, is my own, Garland Library of Medieval Literature, vol. 66, ser. A (New York: Garland, 1994; repr., Tempe, AZ: Medieval and Renaissance Texts and Studies, 1998). The newest edition of *One-Ox* (*Unibos*) is Ferruccio Bertini and Francesco Mosetti Casaretto's *La Beffa di Unibos,* Gli Orsatti: Testi dell'Altro Medioevo 9 (Alessandria: Edizioni dell'Orso, 2000). Editions and Italian translations of *The Donkey Tale* and the two versions of *The Turnip Tale* are in *Commedie latine del XII e XIII secolo:* vol. 4, Università di Genova, Facoltà di lettere, Pubblicazioni del Istituto di filologia classica e medievale 79 (Genoa: Istituto di filologia classica e medievale, 1983), 194–251 (*Asinarius,* ed. and trans. Simona Rizzardi); vol. 5, Pubblicazioni del Istituto di filologia classica e medievale 95 (Genoa: Istituto di filologia classica e medievale, 1986), 36–79 (*Rapularius I,* ed. and trans. Paolo Gatti); and vol. 6, Pubblicazioni del D.Ar.Fi.Cl.Et., n.s., 176 (Genoa: Dipartimento di Archeologia, Filologia classica e loro Tradizioni, 1998), 332–73 (*Rapularius II,* ed. and trans. Paolo Gatti).

57. Albert Wesselski (*Versuch einer Theorie des Märchens,* Prager Deutsche Studien 45 [Reichenberg i. B.: F. Kraus, 1931], 196) saw *Märchen* as a distinct genre that began with Straparola, Basile, or Perrault. The case that Straparola founded the European fairy tale tradition has been advanced most thoroughly by Ruth B. Bottigheimer in *Fairy Godfather: Straparola, Venice, and the European Fairy Tale Tradition* (Philadelphia: University of Pennsylvania Press, 2002). For a concise presentation of her arguments and a sweeping contextualization of their implications, see her "The Ultimate Fairy Tale: Oral Transmission in a Literate World," in *A Companion to the Fairy Tale,* ed. Hilda Ellis Davidson and Anna Chaudhri (Cambridge: D. S. Brewer, 2003), 57–70. For the view that Basile

originated the genre, see Nancy L. Canepa, *From Court to Forest: Giambattista Basile's "Lo cunto de li cunti" and the Birth of the Literary Fairy Tale* (Detroit: Wayne State University Press, 1999), where Canepa refers to Basile's book as the "first integral collection of literary fairy tales to appear in Western Europe" (11). In her earlier collective volume *Out of the Woods: The Origins of the Literary Fairy Tale in Italy and France* (Detroit: Wayne State University Press, 1997), she makes the not-incompatible assertion that "[t]he literary fairy tale first appeared in Europe in Italy in the sixteenth century" (10).

58. Jacques Berlioz, Claude Bremond, and Catherine Velay-Vallantin, trans., *Formes médiévales du conte merveilleux* (Paris: Éditions Stock, 1989). This volume contains both the poem by Egbert of Liège (133–39) and *The Donkey Tale* (211–26).

59. Lutz Röhrich, ed., *Erzählungen des späten Mittelalters und ihr Weiterleben in Literatur und Volksdichtung bis zur Gegenwart: Sagen, Märchen, Exempel und Schwänke,* 2 vols. (Bern and Munich: Francke Verlag, 1962–67).

60. See William A. Wilson, "Herder, Folklore, and Romantic Nationalism," *Journal of Popular Culture* 6 (1973): 824; Günter Arnold, "Herders Projekt einer Märchensammlung," *Jahrbuch für Volkskunde und Kulturgeschichte* 27 (1984): 99–106.

61. Herder edited the collection *Von deutscher Art und Kunst: Einige Fliegende Blätter* (Hamburg: Bey Bode, 1773), the first essay in which was his own "Auszug aus einem Briefwechsel über Ossian und die Lieder alter Völker"—a panegyric not only of Ossian but of all folk song and folk poetry.

62. Johann Gottfried Herder, *Volkslieder,* 1st ed. (Leipzig: Weygand, 1778–79), retitled in 2nd ed. as *Stimmen der Völker in Liedern,* ed. Johannes von Müller [1752–1809] (1807). See William A. Wilson, "Herder," 828–29, for more details.

63. William A. Wilson, "Richard M. Dorson as Romantic-Nationalist," *Journal of Folklore Research* 26 (1989): 41–42.

64. Propp, *La fiaba russa,* 4.

65. See Jan M. Ziolkowski, "Cultural Diglossia and the Nature of Medieval Latin Literature," in *The Ballad and Oral Literature,* ed. Joseph Harris, Harvard English Studies 16 (Cambridge, MA: Harvard University Press, 1991), 193–213; Jan M. Ziolkowski, "Towards a History of Medieval Latin Literature," in *Medieval Latin: An Introduction and Bibliographical Guide,* ed. F. A. C. Mantello and A. G. Rigg (Washington, DC: Catholic University of America Press, 1996), 506–7.

66. See Wolf Aly, "Märchen," in *Paulys Real-Encyclopädie der classischen Altertumswissenschaft,* ed. Georg Wissowa, vol. 14 (Stuttgart: J. B. Metzler, 1930): 254.

67. The locus classicus is Rhys Carpenter's *Folk Tale, Fiction, and Saga in the Homeric Epics* (Berkeley and Los Angeles: University of California Press, 1962).

68. On the response to Ernst Robert Curtius's *European Literature and the Latin Middle Ages,* trans. Willard R. Trask, Bollingen Series 36 (Princeton, NJ: Princeton University Press, 1990), see Jan M. Ziolkowski, "Ernst Robert Curtius (1886–1956) and Medieval Latin Studies," *Journal of Medieval Latin* 7 (1997): 147–67.

69. For the distinction between official or hegemonic and subaltern cultures, I rely on Alberto M. Cirese, *Cultura egemonica e culture subalterne: Rassegna degli studi sul mondo popolare tradizionale,* 2nd ed. (Palermo: Palumbo editore, 1973).

70. For a stimulating introduction with a rich bibliography, see Alexander Scobie, *Apuleius and Folklore: Toward a History of ML3045, AaTh567, 449A* (London: Folklore Society, 1983).

71. For examples, see Graham Anderson, *Fairytale in the Ancient World* (London

and New York: Routledge, 2000); William Hansen, *Ariadne's Thread: A Guide to International Tales Found in Classical Literature* (Ithaca, NY, and London: Cornell University Press, 2002).

72. See Gurevich, *Lezioni romane,* 27.

73. Walter J. Ong, *Orality and Literacy: The Technologizing of the Word* (London and New York: Methuen, 1982), 3.

74. See Elizabeth Wanning Harries, *Twice Upon a Time: Women Writers and the History of the Fairy Tale* (Princeton, NJ: Princeton University Press, 2001), 46–72, which greatly extends her earlier "Simulating Oralities: French Fairy Tales of the 1690s," *College Literature* 23 (1996): 100–115.

75. See Bonnie D. Irwin, "What's in a Frame? The Medieval Textualization of Traditional Storytelling," *Oral Tradition* 10 (1995): 27–53, especially 33 and 37.

76. See Jacques Le Goff, "Clerical Culture and Folklore Traditions in Merovingian Civilization," in *Time, Work, and Culture in the Middle Ages,* trans. Arthur Goldhammer (Chicago: University of Chicago Press, 1980), 153–58.

77. See Propp, *La fiaba russa,* 375.

78. The locus classicus is Herbert Grundmann's "Litteratus-illitteratus: Der Wandel einer Bildungsnorm vom Altertum zum Mittelalter," *Archiv für Kulturgeschichte* 40 (1958): 1–65, reprinted in *Ausgewählte Aufsätze,* vol. 3 (Stuttgart: Hiersemann, 1978), 1–66.

79. The expression *homo narrans* was coined by Kurt Ranke: see Hans-Jörg Uther, "Ranke, Kurt," in *EM* 11:211.

80. Carl Lindahl, John McNamara, and John Lindow, eds., *Medieval Folklore: An Encyclopedia of Myths, Legends, Tales, Beliefs, and Customs,* 2 vols. (Santa Barbara, CA: ABC-CLIO, 2000), reprinted in abridged ed. in 1 vol. as *Medieval Folklore: A Guide to Myths, Legends, Tales, Beliefs, and Customs* (New York: Oxford University Press, 2002).

81. Nancy Canepa, "Italy," in *The Oxford Companion to Fairy Tales,* ed. Jack Zipes (Oxford: Oxford University Press, 2000), 252.

82. See William M. Clements, "Oikotype/Oicotype," in *Folklore* 2:604–5.

83. Carl Wilhelm von Sydow, *Selected Papers on Folklore* (Copenhagen: Rosenkilde and Bagger, 1948), 11–12, 44–45; Burke, *Popular Culture,* 51–52.

84. See Burke, *Popular Culture,* 55.

85. Compare Propp, *Le radici storiche,* 52: "Il folclore è un fenomeno internazionale."

86. See Propp, *La fiaba russa,* 4.

87. Compare the phrases "composition in delivery" and the alternative "recomposition in performance" (corresponding to the German *Komposition bei Vortrag*) which are appraised by Albert Bates Lord in *Epic Singers and Oral Tradition* (Ithaca, NY: Cornell University Press, 1991), 76–77. For a short introduction to *reportationes,* see M. B. Parkes, "Tachygraphy in the Middle Ages: Writing Techniques Employed for *Reportationes* of Lectures and Sermons," in *Grafia e interpunzione del latino nel medioevo: Seminario internazionale, Roma, 27–29 settembre, 1984,* ed. Alfonso Maierù (Rome: Edizioni dell'Ateneo, 1987), 15–29, reprinted in M. B. Parkes, *Scribes, Scripts, and Readers: Studies in the Communication, Presentation, and Dissemination of Medieval Texts* (London and Rio Grande, OH: Hambledon, 1991), 19–33.

88. The distinction between *Verschriftung* and *Verschriftlichung* is discussed by Monika Fludernik in *Towards a "Natural" Narratology* (London: Routledge, 1996), 392 n. 13. Fludernik draws on the work of Wulf Österreicher.

89. In *Principles for Oral Narrative Research,* trans. Kirsten Wolf and Jody Jensen (Bloomington and Indianapolis: Indiana University Press, 1992), 9–10, Axel Olrik (1864–1917) notes, "the difference between oral production and oral transmission, on the one hand, and written production and written transmission, on the other, is profoundly significant, partly because the ability of literary works to enter oral tradition is surprisingly poor, and partly because their whole structure and external form will reveal their particular origin."

90. Much of this explosion in research has occurred ultimately in response to the work of Ong in *Orality and Literacy.*

91. The phrase was used, among other places, in publications by the United States Commission on Preservation and Access.

92. *Carmina cantabrigiensia* 14, "The Snow-Child," in *Cambridge Songs,* ed. and trans. Ziolkowski, 62–69, 209–15 (notes and commentary). Extensive materials on the "The Snow-Child" (ATU 1362; *MI* J1532.1) are printed by Röhrich in *Erzählungen des späten Mittelalters,* 1:204–21.

93. "The Trial of Joseph and Mary," so-called N-Town cycle, lines 273–80, in *Ludus Coventriae, or The Plaie Called Corpus Christi: Cotton MS. Vespasian D. VIII,* ed. K. S. Block, Early English Text Society, extra ser., 120 (London: Oxford University Press, 1922), 132.

94. *Carmina cantabrigiensia* 15, in *Cambridge Songs,* ed. and trans. Ziolkowski, 68–71, 217–21 (notes and commentary). Compare ATU 852 "Lying Contest" (formerly AT 852 "The Hero Forces the Princess to Say 'That Is a Lie'") (*MI* H342.1, H507.2).

95. Gervase of Tilbury, *Otia imperialia,* ed. and trans. S. E. Banks and J. W. Binns (Oxford: Clarendon, 2002); Walter Map, *De nugis curialium,* ed. and trans. M. R. James, rev. C. N. L. Brooke and R. A. B. Mynors (Oxford: Clarendon, 1983); Petrus Alfonsi, *Disciplina clericalis,* ed. Alfons Hilka and Werner Söderhjelm, vol. 1, Acta Societatis Scientiarum Fennicae 38, no. 4 (Helsinki: Druckerei der Finnischen Litteraturgesellschaft, 1911).

96. The closely related manuscript is Wolfenbüttel, Herzog August Bibliothek, MS 3610, codex Augustanus 8° 56.16 (eleventh century).

97. See Jan M. Ziolkowski, introduction to *Obscenity: Social Control and Artistic Creation in the European Middle Ages,* ed. Jan M. Ziolkowski (Leiden: E. J. Brill, 1998), 3–18.

98. The term *fakelore* originated with Richard M. Dorson in "Folklore and Fake Lore," *American Mercury* 70 (1950): 335–43. He reused the term as a title in both an article and a book: "Fakelore," *Zeitschrift für Volkskunde* 65 (1969): 60; *Folklore and Fakelore: Essays toward a Discipline of Folk Studies* (Cambridge, MA: Harvard University Press, 1976). For a consideration of the Grimms' *Kinder- und Hausmärchen* in this context, see Alan Dundes, *Folklore Matters* (Knoxville: University of Tennessee Press, 1989), 44–45. For recent overviews of the topic, see Ronald L. Baker, "Fakelore," in *Encyclopedia of Folklore and Literature,* ed. Mary Ellen Brown and Bruce A. Rosenberg (Santa Barbara, CA: ABC-CLIO, 1998), 203–5; Regina Bendix, "Fakelore," in *Folklore* 1:275–77.

99. See Jean-Claude Schmitt, *Medioevo "superstizioso,"* Universale Laterza 743 (Bari: Editori Laterza, 1992), 125.

100. On the Grimms, see Siegfried Neumann, "The Brothers Grimm as Collectors and Editors."

101. For a preliminary attempt to come to terms with the folk narratives in the

Dolopathos, see Jan M. Ziolkowski, "Vergil as Shahrazad: How an Eastern Frame Tale Was Authorized in the West," in *Studies for Dante: Essays in Honor of Dante Della Terza,* ed. Franco Fido, Rena A. Syska-Lamparska, and Pamela D. Stewart (Florence: Edizioni Cadmo, 1998), 25–36.

102. André Jolles, *Einfache Formen: Legende/Sage/Mythe/Rätsel/Spruch/Kasus/Memo-rabile/Märchen/Witz* (Halle an der Salle: Max Niemeyer, 1930). For bibliography on translations, see Walther Thys, *Andre Jolles (1874–1946): Gebildeter Vagant; Brieven en documenten bijeengebracht, ingeleid en toegelicht door Walter Thys* (Amsterdam: Amsterdam University Press; Leipzig: Leipziger Universitätsverlag, 2000), 1040–43.

103. Jolles wrote the introduction (VII–LXXXVII) to Wesselski's translation in Giovanni di Boccaccio, *Das Dekameron* (Leipzig: Insel-Verlag,1921).

104. Lutz Röhrich, *Folktales and Reality,* trans. Peter Tokofsky (Bloomington and Indianapolis: Indiana University Press, 1991), 9–56; Linda Dégh, *Legend and Belief: Di-alectics of a Folklore Genre* (Bloomington and Indianapolis: Indiana University Press, 2001), 79–97.

105. Bottigheimer (*Fairy Godfather,* 7) announces that the term *fairy tale* is con-fused by overlapping with various other terms. Accordingly, she speaks of "stories, tales, and plots" rather than fairy tales.

106. The standard study of the *conte de fées* was once Mary Elizabeth Storer's *Un Episode littéraire de la fin du XVIIe siècle: La mode des contes de fées (1685–1700),* Bib-liothèque de la Revue de littérature comparée 48 (Paris: Champion, 1928; repr., Geneva: Slatkine, 1972). Now it is best to consult Jacques Barchilon's *Le Conte mer-veilleux français de 1690 à 1790* (Paris: Honoré Champion, 1975) and Raymonde Robert's *Le Conte de fées littéraire en France de la fin du XVIIe à la fin du XVIIIe siècle* (Nancy: Presses universitaires de Nancy, 1982; repr., Paris: Honoré Champion, 2002).

107. On the history of the term *Märchen,* see Maren Clausen-Stolzenburg, *Märchen und die mittelalterliche Tradition,* Beiträge zur neueren Literaturgeschichte, 3rd ser., 138 (Heidelberg: Carl Winter, 1995), 3–93.

108. Dedication to Bishop Adalbold of Utrecht (ca. 970–1026), in Egbert of Liège, *Fecunda ratis* (The Richly Laden Ship), ed. Voigt, 1. The text is quoted and discussed in chapter 3 of the present study.

109. Egbert of Liège, *De puella a lupellis servata,* in *Fecunda ratis* (The Richly Laden Ship) 2.472–85, ed. Voigt, 232–33. The poem is translated in its entirety and discussed in chapter 3 of the present study.

110. Letaldus of Micy, *De quodam piscatore quem ballena absorbuit,* 185–86, in *Letaldo di Micy, Within piscator,* ed. and trans. Ferruccio Bertini, Biblioteca del Medioevo latino (Florence: Giunti, 1995), 12: "Naufragus ast media, Ionas velut alter, in urbe / edocet at-tonitos reducis miracula vitae." The tale is translated in its entirety in app. 1B in the pres-ent study.

111. *The Donkey Tale* 26, ed. and trans. Rizzardi, *Asinarius,* 196: "O res miranda, plus miseranda tamen!"

112. *The Donkey Tale* 151, ed. and trans. Rizzardi, *Asinarius,* 214: "Tunc ait: 'Ecce, novi quiddam, rex inclite, novi.'"

113. *The Turnip Tale "frivola"* [1] 24, ed. and trans. Gatti, *Rapularius I,* 38: *Obstupet;* 33 and 71, ed. and trans. Gatti, *Rapularius I,* 40, 42: *rapula prodigiosa;* 67, ed. and trans. Gatti, *Rapularius I,* 42: *quoddam mirabile munus.*

114. *One-Ox,* strophes 1–3, in *La Beffa di Unibos,* ed. Bertini and Mosetti Casaretto, 52: "[1] Rebus conspectis sæculi / non satiantur oculi; / *aures* sunt in hominibus / amicæ *novitatibus.* / [2] *Ad mensam magni principis* / est *rumor* Unius Bovis, / præsentatur ut *fabula* / per *verba iocularia.* [3] Fiunt cibis convivia, / sed *verbis exercitia;* / *in personarum drammate* / Uno *cantemus* de Bove." For a complete English translation, see app. 3A in the present study. Subsequent cites given parenthetically in text refer to this translation, by strophe and, where necessary, line numbers.

115. See Propp, *La fiaba russa,* 290.

116. Canepa (*From Court to Forest,* 11) calls *Märchen* "fairy tales (or folktales)," and Anttonen ("Philological Approach," 642) also points out the equivalence, when referring to "folktales—or fairy tales, as they have also been called."

117. See Burke, *Popular Culture,* 18–19.

118. See Burke, *Popular Culture,* 3.

119. William Thoms's definition of the term *folklore,* which he had just invented in 1846, is reprinted in Alan Dundes, ed., *The Study of Folklore* (Englewood Cliffs, NJ: Prentice-Hall, 1965), 4–5.

120. The source of the phrase "Das Volk dichtet" is at this point unknown, although it has been ascribed often to Wilhelm and sometimes to Jacob Grimm. Information on it can be found in Helen Child Sargent and George Lyman Kittredge, eds., *English and Scottish Popular Ballads* (Boston: Houghton Mifflin, 1904), xviii n. 1.

121. See Burke, *Popular Culture,* 21 (Burke refers to Patrice Coirault, *Recherches sur notre ancienne chanson populaire traditionelle,* 5th ed. [Vannes: Imprimerie Lafolye frères, 1933]); George Boas, *Vox Populi: Essays in the History of an Idea* (Baltimore: Johns Hopkins University Press, 1969), 112–42. For a sophisticated defense of the idea of collective creation, see Roman Jakobson and Petr Bogatyrev, "Die Folklore als eine besondere Form des Schaffens," in *Selected Writings,* ed. Roman Jakobson, vol. 4 (The Hague and Paris: Mouton, 1966), translated by Manfred Jacobson as "Folklore as a Special Form of Creativity," in *The Prague School: Selected Writings, 1929–1946,* ed. Peter Steiner, 32–46 (Austin: University of Texas Press, 1982).

122. See Burke, *Popular Culture,* 29–30.

123. See Burke, *Popular Culture,* 29.

124. Carlo Ginzburg suggests hypothesizing not one generic "cultura popolare" but, rather, a culture of "classi popolari": see Piero Camporesi, *Rustici e buffoni: Cultura popolare e cultura d'élite fra Medioevo ed età moderna,* Saggi brevi 23 (Turin: Giulio Einaudi editore, 1991), 9.

125. See Paul Freedman, "Sainteté et sauvagerie: Deux images du paysan au moyen age," *Annales* 47 (1992): 553.

126. On the history of the term *Gattung Grimm,* see Dégh, *Narratives in Society,* 122.

127. Ruth B. Bottigheimer, "Fairy Tales, Folk Narrative Research, and History," *Social History* 14 (1989): 356.

128. Albert Wesselski, *Versuch einer Theorie des Märchens,* Prager Deutsche Studien 45 (Reichenberg i. B.: F. Kraus, 1931). In many ways, Wesselski's truest and most persuasive follower has been Ruth Bottigheimer.

129. The standard edition of John of Alta Silva remains *Dolopathos sive De rege et septem sapientibus,* ed. Alfons Hilka, Sammlung mittellateinischer Texte 5 (Heidelberg: Carl Winter, 1913). For basic information on the *status quaestionis* about folktale mate-

rials in the *Dolopathos*, see Ziolkowski, "Vergil as Shahrazad." For guidance about the *Gesta Romanorum, EM* should be consulted. The standard editions are Hermann Oesterley's (Berlin: Weidmann, 1872) and Wilhelm Dick's *Die Gesta Romanorum: Nach der Innsbrucker Handschrift vom Jahre 1342 und vier Münchener Handschriften* (Erlangen and Leipzig: A. Deichert and G. Böhme, 1890).

130. For a study and an English translation, see Jan M. Ziolkowski, "The Spirit of Play in the Poetry of St. Gall," in *Sangallensia in Washington: The Arts and Letters in Medieval and Baroque St. Gall Viewed from the Late Twentieth Century*, ed. James C. King (New York: Peter Lang, 1994), 143–69.

131. See J. M. Clark, *The Abbey of St. Gall as a Centre of Literature and Art* (Cambridge: Cambridge University Press, 1926), 230, 237.

132. Thompson, *The Folktale*, 215. For attestations of the motif of "so and so many axe-handles" in both texts and oral literature, see Daniel Hoffman, *Paul Bunyan: Last of the Frontier Demigods* (Philadelphia: University of Pennsylvania Press for Temple University Publications, 1952; repr., East Lansing: Michigan State University Press, 1999), 5, 9, 55, 75. On the intertwining of oral and textual versions of such material—the interaction between "tall tales" and "tall literature"—see Carolyn S. Brown, *The Tall Tale in American Folklore and Literature* (Knoxville: University of Tennessee Press, 1987), 1–2, 5–7, 11–12.

133. Schenda (*Von Mund zu Ohr*, 74) points out that intersections of trade routes are favorable places for the production of folklore.

134. The most accessible harvest of passages containing the ancient and medieval terminology remains BP 5:41–56.

135. Tegethoff, *Märchen, Schwänke und Fabeln*, xiv: "Zwischen Fabel, Schwank, Märchen, Sage, und Legende reinlich zu scheiden ist nicht möglich."

136. Cicero, *De inventione* 1.19.27, in *De inventione, De optimo genere oratorum, Topica*, ed. and trans. H. M. Hubbell, Loeb Classical Library 386 (Cambridge, MA: Harvard University Press, 1949), 54–55: "*Fabula* is the term applied to a narrative in which the events are not true and have no verisimilitude, for example: 'Huge winged dragons yoked to a car'" [Fabula est in qua nec verae nec veri similes res continentur, cuiusmodi est: 'Angues ingentes alites, iuncti iugo'"].

137. A dense jungle of books and articles has grown around the tale of Cupid and Psyche. For an orientation, see Hansen, *Ariadne's Thread*, 106–14.

138. Apuleius, *Metamorphoses* 4.27–4.28, ed. and trans. J. Arthur Hanson, 2 vols., Loeb Classical Library 44, 453 (Cambridge, MA: Harvard University Press, 1989), 1:234–37: "'But right now I shall divert you with a pretty story and an old wife's tale.' And she began. 'Once upon a time in a certain city there lived a king and queen. They had three daughters of remarkable beauty. Yet the older two, although of very pleasing appearance, could still, it was thought, be worthily celebrated with mortal praise. But the youngest girl's beauty was so dazzling and glorious that it could not be described nor even adequately praised for the sheer poverty of human speech" ["Sed ego te narrationibus lepidis anilibusque fabulis protinus avocabo." Et incipit: "Erant in quadam civitate rex et regina. Hi tres numero filias forma conspicuas habuere. Sed maiores quidem natu, quamvis gratissima specie, idonee tamen celebrari posse laudibus humanis credebantur. At vero puellae iunioris tam praecipua, tam praeclara pulchritudo nec exprimi ac ne sufficienter quidem laudari sermonis humani penuria poterat"]. For a broad collection of information about *fabula anilis*, see Ziolkowski, "Old Wives' Tales."

139. For the Latin text, see Giovanni Boccaccio, *Genealogie* 14.9, ed. Vincenzo Romano, 2 vols. (Bari: Gius. Laterza e Figli, 1951), 2:708, lines 26–31; for the corresponding English, see Charles G. Osgood, trans., *Boccaccio on Poetry: Being the Preface and the Fourteenth and Fifteenth Books of Boccaccio's "Genealogia Deorum Gentilium"* (Princeton, NJ: Princeton University Press, 1930), 50–51: "Fiction has, in some cases, sufficed to lift the oppressive weight of adversity and furnish consolation, as appears in Lucius Apuleius; he tells how the highborn maiden Charis, while bewailing her unhappy condition as captive among thieves, was in some degree restored through hearing from an old woman the charming story of Psyche" [Fabulis laborantibus sub pondere adversantis fortune non nunquam solamen impensum est, quod apud Lucium Apuleium cernitur. Quem penes Carithes, generosa virgo infortunio suo apud predones captiva, captivitatem suam deplorans, ab anicula fabule Psycis lepiditate paululum refocillata est].

140. See Lorenz Diefenbach, *Glossarium latino-germanicum mediae et infimae aetatis* (Frankfurt am Main: J. Baer, 1857; repr., Darmstadt: Wissenschaftliche Buchgesellschaft, 1997), 221: "Fabula, ffagula."

141. See Christine Goldberg, "The Historic-Geographic Method: Past and Future," *Journal of Folklore Research* 21 (1984): 1–18.

142. The founding fathers of the Finnish school were Julius Krohn (1835–88), Kaarle Krohn, and Antti Aarne. For a descriptive bibliography of articles and books that provide a history of historical-geographical approaches, see David S. Azzolina, *Tale Type- and Motif-Indexes: An Annotated Bibliography* (New York and London: Garland, 1987), xxii n. 2.

143. Wesselski, *Märchen des Mittelalters,* xi.

144. See BP 4:166; Propp, *La fiaba russa,* 171, quoting Tronskii.

145. See F. Jesi, "Sul mito e la fiaba," in *"Tutto è fiaba": Atti del Convegno internazionale di studio sulla Fiaba,* ed. G. Cusatelli et al. (Milan: Emme Edizioni, 1980), 43–53. On Andrew Lang, see Newall, "Lang, Andrew"; on Saintyves, see Marianne Mesnil, "Saintyves, Pierre," in *EM* 11:1050–53.

146. See preface to Propp, *La fiaba russa,* xxxiii.

147. For an examination of the concept *gesunkenes Kulturgut* in relation to the work of one individual scholar, see Reinhard Schmook, *Gesunkenes Kulturgut, primitive Gemeinschaft: Der Germanist Hans Naumann (1886–1951) in seiner Bedeutung für die Volkskunde,* Beiträge zur Volkskunde und Kulturanalyse 7 (Vienna: Helmut-P.-Fielhauer-Freundeskreis, 1993). For a consideration of the term specifically in reference to folklore, see Hermann Bausinger, "Folklore und gesunkenes Kulturgut," in *Formen der "Volkspoesie,"* 2nd ed. (Berlin: E. Schmidt Verlag, 1980), 41–55.

148. Johann Gottfried Herder, *Ideen zur Philosophie der Geschichte der Menschheit,* 4 vols. (Riga and Leipzig: Bey Johann Friedrich Hartknoch, 1784–91), part 3, discussed by Burke (*Popular Culture,* 8) and quoted by W. Thoms (reprinted in Dundes, *The Study of Folklore,* 4–5).

149. See Hasan El-Shamy, "Gesunkenes Kulturgut," in *Folklore* 1:419–22.

150. Ed. and trans. Rizzardi, *Asinarius,* 194, apparatus to line 2 (*pagina nulla*).

151. Ed. and trans. Rizzardi, *Asinarius,* 194, text and apparatus to line 2 (*fabula nulla*).

152. *The Turnip Tale "frivola"* [1] 1, ed. and trans. Gatti, *Rapularius I,* 36; *The Turnip Tale "prodiga"* [2] 1, ed. and trans. Gatti, *Rapularius II,* 332.

153. Alexksandr Isaakovich Nikiforov, *K voprosu o zadachakh i metodakh nauchnogo sobiraniia* (Leningrad: G.R.G.O., 1928).

154. Bengt Holbek, "Hans Christian Andersen's Use of Folktales," *Merveilles et contes* 4 (1990): 222; Holbek, *Interpretation of Fairy Tales.* Holbek indicated that there is a marked difference between tales told by men and those told by women, in that men very consistently preferred tales with male protagonists.

155. See Ziolkowski, "Old Wives' Tales."

156. Ruth B. Bottigheimer, "Straparola's *Piacevoli notti:* Rags-to-Riches Fairy Tales as Urban Creations," *Marvels and Tales: Journal of Fairy-Tale Studies* 8 (1994): 281–95.

157. In particular, see Warner, *From the Beast to the Blonde.*

<div align="center">CHAPTER TWO</div>

1. Ann Lawson Lucas (in Zipes, *Oxford Companion to Fairy Tales*) calls Collodi's work "a fairy tale" (193) and "an authentic scion of the fairy-tale tradition" (385). Because of the incessant recurrence in it of folktale motifs, Ulf Diederichs includes it in his *Who's who im Märchen* (Munich: Deutscher Taschenbuch Verlag, 1995), 246.

2. Carlo Collodi, *Pinocchio: Story of a Puppet,* trans. Nancy Canepa (South Royalton, VT: Steerforth Italia, 2002), 71.

3. Collodi, *Pinocchio,* 3.

4. The hagiographic works definitely ascribed to Letaldus are the *Liber miraculorum sancti Maximini abbatis Miciacensis,* written after 982 (*PL* 137.795B–824B; *BHL* 5820); the *Delatio corporis sancti Juniani in synodum Karoffensem,* written after the Council of Charroux, in 989 (*PL* 137.823C–826B; *BHL* 4565); the *Vita et miracula sancti Martini Vertavensis,* probably written for the monastery of Saint-Jouin-sur-Marne or Saint-Jouin-de-Marnes between 994 and 1004 (*BHL* 5667–68); and the *Vita sancti Juliani Cenomannensis,* composed for the church of Le Mans after 996 (*PL* 137.781B–796A; *BHL* 4544). Additionally, Thomas Head (following Krusch and Poncelet) has argued for Letaldus's authorship of the *Vita et miracula sancti Eusicii,* written for the monastery of Selles-sur-Cher, probably between 1002 and 1004 (*BHL* 2754, 2756): see Thomas Head, "Letaldus of Micy and the Hagiographic Traditions of Selles-sur-Cher," *Analecta Bollandiana* 107 (1989): 393–414. On the hagiography, see Giuseppe Cremascoli, "Das hagiographische Werk des Letald von Micy," *Mittellateinisches Jahrbuch* 24–25 (1989–90): 87–93; Thomas Head, *Hagiography and the Cult of the Saints: The Diocese of Orléans, 800–1200,* Cambridge Studies in Medieval Life and Thought, 4th ser., 14 (Cambridge: Cambridge University Press, 1990): 211–27; Thomas Head, "Letaldus of Micy and the Hagiographic Traditions of the Abbey of Nouaillé: The Context of the *Delatio corporis S. Juniani,*" *Analecta Bollandiana* 115 (1997): 253–67. Head has translated the *Delatio* in Thomas Head and Richard Landes, eds., *The Peace of God: Social Violence and Religious Response in France around the Year 1000* (Ithaca, NY: Cornell University Press, 1992), 328–29.

5. The incipit is "Si mihi Pindareae praestarent organa cordae"; the two manuscripts are the destroyed florilegium of Saint-Gatien, written in the final quarter of the twelfth century (Tours, Bibliothèque Municipale, MS 890, fols. 45r–48v), and the extant early twelfth-century Paris manuscript (Paris, Bibliothèque Nationale, MS lat. 5230A, fols. 156v–158v), originally from Saint-Florent.

6. The poem, of which the editio princeps was published in the nineteenth century, was edited a half-dozen times in the twentieth century, in the following editions: Barthélemy Hauréau, "Versus Lethaldi monachi de quodam piscatore quem ballena

absorbuit," *Bulletin du Comité historique des monuments écrits de l'histoire de France* I (1849): 178–83; André Wilmart, "Le poème héroïque de Létald sur Within le pêcheur," *Studi medievali,* n.s., 9 (1936): 188–203; Jean-Paul Bonnes, "Un lettré du Xe siècle: Introduction au poème de Létald," *Revue Mabillon* 33 (1943): 23–47; Virgilio Paladini and Maria De Marco, eds., in *L'Epica post-Carolingia* (Bari: 1966), 39a–55a (with introductory notes on 23–29); Paul Pascal, "The Poem of Letaldus: A New Edition," in *Hrotsvit of Gandersheim: "Rara avis in Saxonia?"* ed. Katharina M. Wilson, Medieval and Renaissance Monograph Series 7 (Ann Arbor: Published for M.A.R.C./Medieval and Renaissance Collegium, 1987), 211–28; Bertini, *Letaldo di Micy, Within piscator;* Letaldus of Micy, *De quodam piscatore quem ballena absorbuit: Il pescatore Within,* ed. and trans. Feliciana L. Pennisi, Libellus I (Reggio Calabria: Giuseppe Pontari Editore, 1997). I follow the edition by Bertini, but I have consulted all the others except for that of Paladini and De Marco. Bonnes ("Un lettré du Xe siècle," 32–33) proposed that Letaldus was also the author of the *Versus de eversione monasterii Glomnensis.* This proposal was dismissed by Cora E. Lutz ("Letaldus, a Wit of the Tenth Century," *Viator* I [1970]: 99 n. 13) but has been accepted by Head (*Hagiography and the Cult,* 218); Head (218 n. 82) also regards Letaldus as the author of a short liturgical poem.

7. These allusions are discussed in Lutz, "Letaldus," 104.

8. The poem is called a "fantasy" and regarded as comic by Bonnes ("Un lettré du Xe siècle," 34 n. 1) and Lutz ("Letaldus," 97–107).

9. See Jan M. Ziolkowski, "Folklore and Learned Lore in Letaldus's Whale Poem," *Viator* 15 (1984): 107–18. On the problem of oral and learned tradition, see Bruce A. Rosenberg, "Oral Literature in the Middle Ages," in *Oral Traditional Literature: A Festschrift for Albert Bates Lord,* ed. John Miles Foley (Columbus, OH: Slavic, 1981), 440–50.

10. See Michael Lapidge, "Aldhelm's Latin Poetry and Old English Verse," *Comparative Literature* 31 (1979): 209–31.

11. See Peter Dronke and Ursula Dronke, *Barbara et antiquissima carmina* (Barcelona: Universidad Autónoma de Barcelona, 1977); Jürgen Beyer, *Schwank und Moral: Untersuchungen zum altfranzösischen Fabliau und verwandten Formen,* Studia Romanica 16 (Heidelberg: Carl Winter, 1969), 73–79; Helena M. Gamer, "The Ruodlieb and Tradition," *Arv: Tidskrift för Nordisk Folkminnesforskning* 11 (1955): 65–103.

12. Another tenth-century poem in which leonine rhymes may signify folkloric associations of the story is Hrotsvit of Gandersheim's fabliau-like saint's life *Gongolfus:* see Hrotsvit of Gandersheim, *Opera omnia,* ed. Walter Berschin (Munich and Leipzig: K. G. Saur, 2001), 42–62.

13. On the origins of leonine rhymes and the term *versus leonini,* see Paul Klopsch, *Einführung in die mittellateinische Verslehre* (Darmstadt: Wissenschaftliche Buchgesellschaft, 1972), 45–48 (with reference to Erdmann's article on the subject). See Carl Erdmann, "Leonitas. Zur mittelalterlichen Lehre von Kursus, Rhythmus und Reim," in *Corona quernea. Festgabe Karl Strecker zum 80. Geburtstage dargebracht* MGH Schriften des Reichsinstituts für ältere deutsche Geschichtskunde 6 (Leipzig: K. W. Hiersemann, 1941, 15–28).

14. See Gustav Henningsen, "The Art of Perpendicular Lying: Concerning a Commercial Collecting of Norwegian Sailors' Tall Tales," trans. Warren E. Roberts, *Journal of the Folklore Institute* 2 (1965): 202–4.

15. Henningsen, "The Art of Perpendicular Lying," 213.

16. For the Old English preposition, consult Joseph Bosworth and T. Northcote Toller, *An Anglo-Saxon Dictionary* (Oxford: Clarendon, 1898), s.v.

17. As evidence that *Within* is a *nom parlant* and not a common Christian name, it is not found in Ernst Förstemann's *Altdeutsches Namenbuch,* ed. Hermann Jellinghaus, 2nd ed., 2 vols (vol. 2 in 2 parts) (Bonn: P. Hanstein, 1900–1916), or in William George Searle's *Onomasticon Anglo-Saxonicum* (Cambridge: Cambridge University Press, 1897). For the interpretation of lines 115 and 145, I am indebted to Pascal, "The Poem of Letaldus," 227, commentary ad loc. Both Pascal's implicit points about *Within/wiþinnan* and my own explicit ones were taken up by Ferruccio Bertini in "La letteratura epica," in *Il secolo di ferro: Mito e realtà del secolo X, 19–25 Aprile 1990,* vol. 2 Settimane di studio del Centro italiano di Studi sull'alto medioevo 38 (Spoleto: Centro italiano di Studi sull'alto medioevo, 1991), 739.

18. For the argument that the elder was Within himself, see Pascal, "The Poem of Letaldus," 212; Bertini, *Letaldo di Micy, Within piscator,* 22, with commentary on 17.

19. The most thorough study of the significance—especially the economic significance—of whales in early medieval Britain is Vicki Ellen Szabo, "The Use of Whales in Early Medieval Britain," *Haskins Society Journal* 9 (1997): 137–57.

20. For the fullest digest of evidence, see W. M. A. De Smet, "Evidence of Whaling in the North Sea and English Channel during the Middle Ages," in *Mammals in the Seas: Report,* by the Food and Agriculture Organization of the United Nations, Working Party on Marine Mammals, FAO Fisheries Series 5, vol. 3 (Rome: Food and Agriculture Organization of the United Nations, 1981), 301–9.

21. See Janet Bately, ed., *The Old English Orosius,* Early English Text Society Supplementary Series 6 (London: Oxford University Press, 1980), 14–15; Niels Lund, ed., *Two Voyagers at the Court of King Alfred: The Ventures of Ohthere and Wulfstan, together with the Description of Northern Europe from the Old English Orosius,* trans. Christine E. Fell (York, UK: William Sessions, 1984), 19–20.

22. Ælfric, *The Colloquy of Ælfric,* ed. G. N. Garmonsway (London: Methuen, 1939), 29–30.

23. Rodulfus Glaber, *Historiarum libri quinque* 2.2.2, ed. and trans. John France (Oxford: Clarendon, 1989), 50–55. Compare "bestia inmense magnitudinis" in the anonymous *Navigatio sancti Brendani,* chap. 16.3, ed. Carl Selmer, Publications in Medieval Studies 16 (South Bend: University of Notre Dame Press, 1958; repr., Kill Lange, Blackrock County, Dublin: Four Courts, 1989).

24. In contrast to Lucien Musset ("Raoul Glaber et la baleine: Les sources d'un racontar du XIe siècle," *Revue du Moyen Age latin* 4 [1948]: 167–72), France (in Glaber, *Historiarum libri quinque,* 51–53 n. 5) dismisses the notion that Raoul drew on an otherwise unattested tradition for his account of Brendan's adventure.

25. For an interpretation of the runic verse inscription on the casket, see R. I. Page, *An Introduction to English Runes* (London: Methuen, 1973), 174–82. For the *Canons,* see Ludwig Bieler, ed., *The Irish Penitentials,* Scriptores latini Hiberniae 5 (Dublin: Dublin Institute for Advanced Studies, 1975), 176–77. For a survey of Scandinavian laws about whaling procedures and rights, see O. Lindquist, "Whaling by Peasant Fishermen in Norway, Orkney, Shetland, the Faeroe Islands, Iceland, and Norse Greenland: Medieval and Early Modern Whaling Methods and Inshore Legal Régimes," in *Whaling and History: Perspectives on the Evolution of the Industry,* ed. B. Basberg, J. E. Ringstad, and E. Wexelsen (Sandefjord: Sandefjord Museum, 1995), 17–54.

26. On the use of bones, see Ian Riddler, "Worked Whale Vertebrae," *Archaeologia Cantiana* 118 (1998): 205–15. On the acquisition and use of whales as food, see J. Lestoc-quoy, "Baleine et ravitaillement au Moyen Age," *Revue du Nord* 30 (1948): 39–43.

27. See Szabo, "The Use of Whales."

28. See George Philip Krapp and Elliott Van Kirk Dobbie, eds., *The Exeter Book,* Anglo-Saxon Poetic Records 3 (New York: Columbia University Press, 1936), 171–74.

29. See D. M. Dunlop, "The British Isles according to Medieval Arabic Authors," *Islamic Quarterly* 4 (1957):11–28; Bernard Lewis, *The Muslim Discovery of Europe* (New York: W. W. Norton, 1982), 144–45. For these references I am indebted to Szabo, "The Use of Whales." Dunlop ("The British Isles," 19–20) provides a translation of an ex-traordinary passage from the Spanish geographer al-ʿUdhrī, from a text written ca. 1058 but quoted by a later author ca. 1283, describing whaling near Ireland. Dunlop points out how a Romance derivative of the Latin *balaena* influenced the formation of the Arabic word for whale in this passage; he also suggests that the Germanic element for whale passed into Arabic in another word for the creature. Lewis quotes in English translation from the account of whale hunting given by Ibrāhīm ibn Yaʿqūb in the mid-tenth century.

30. Quoted from Dunlop, "The British Isles," 22.

31. Michael Crichton, *Eaters of the Dead: The Manuscript of Ibn Fadlan Relating His Experiences with the Northmen in A.D. 922* (New York: Knopf, 1976). The 1999 cine-matic adaptation of the novel, directed by John McTiernan and available on VHS, was entitled *The Thirteenth Warrior* (Touchstone Pictures, 1999).

32. See Pierre Riché, "La Renaissance intellectuelle du Xe siècle en Occident," *Cahiers d'histoire* (Lyon) 21 (1976): 28–29; Jean Vezin, "Leofnoth: Un scribe anglais à Saint-Benoît-sur-Loire," *Codices manuscripti* 3 (1977): 109–20.

33. Rodulfus Tortarius, *Epistula 9,* in *Rodulfi Tortarii Carmina,* ed. Marbury B. Ogle and Dorothy M. Schullian, Papers and Monographs of the American Academy in Rome 8 (Rome: American Academy in Rome, 1933), 328–29.

34. See C. Brunel, "Walmannus, waumannus," *Bulletin Du Cange: Archivum La-tinitatis Medii Aevi* 1 (1927): 31–32.

35. Brunel did not investigate the corresponding forms in older Germanic languages, although he pointed out the existence of the Modern English word *whaleman.* The word *hwælmann* does not appear in the most recent Web-based version of Antonette di Paolo Healey's *Dictionary of Old English: Old English Corpus* (Ann Arbor: University of Michi-gan, Humanities Text Initiative, 1998), available at http://nrs.harvard.edu/urn-3:hul .eresource:oldenglc (accessed 1 March 2006). *Hvalmaðr* is not listed in Richard Cleasby and Gudbrand Vigfusson's *An Icelandic-English Dictionary,* rev. William A. Craigie, 2nd ed. (Oxford: Clarendon, 1957).

36. *MI* F911.4–F921.

37. The main motifs within the story are *MI* F911.4, "Fish (or water monster) swal-lows a man"; F912.1, "Victim kills swallower from within by burning"; F912.2, "Victim kills swallower from within by cutting"; F913, "Victims rescued from swallower's body"; A535, "Culture hero swallowed and recovered from animal"; and F922, "Swallowed per-son bereft of clothing."

38. On the nature myth and sun god, see Leo Frobenius, *Weltanschauung der Naturvölker,* Beiträge zur Volks- und Völkerkunde 6 (Weimar: Verlag von Emil Felber, 1898), 186–91; Leo Frobenius, *Das Zeitalter des Sonnengottes* (Berlin: George Reimer,

1904), 59–220, 421; Ludwig Radermacher, "Walfischmythen," *Archiv für Religionswissenschaft* 9 (1906): 248–52; Ludwig Radermacher, *Mythos und Sage bei den Griechen* (Darmstadt: Wissenschaftliche Buchgesellschaft, 1968), 29–35; Hans Schmidt, *Jona: Eine Untersuchung zur vergleichenden Religionsgeschichte,* Forschungen zur Religion und Literatur des Alten und Neuen Testaments 9 (Göttingen: Vandenhoeck und Ruprecht, 1907); Edward Burnett Tylor, *Primitive Culture: Researches into the Development of Mythology, Philosophy, Religion, Language, Art, and Custom,* vol. 1, 7th ed. (New York: Brentano's, 1924), 339. Frobenius (*Das Zeitalter,* 421) presents a schematic representation of what he calls "the whale myth"; he places the stages mentioned above in a progression from west to east—in other words, from the setting to the rising of the sun. For early objections against solar and lunar interpretations, see Wilhelm Wundt, *Völkerpsychologie: Eine Untersuchung der Entwicklungsgesetze von Sprache, Mythus und Sitte,* vol. 5, part 2, 2nd ed. (Leipzig: Alfred Kröner, 1914), 289–92, 296–97.

39. See Wilmart, "Le poème héroïque," 190.

40. See Alfred Jeremias, *Das alte Testament im Lichte des alten Orients,* 4th ed. (Leipzig: J. C. Hinrichs'sche Buchhandlung, 1930), 726.

41. On the rite of initiation, see William Simpson, *The Jonah Legend: A Suggestion of Interpretation* (London: Grant Richards, 1899; repr., Detroit: Grand River, 1971), 11–12.

42. See Ferruccio Bertini, "Il 'Within piscator' di Letaldo di Micy," *Mittellateinisches Jahrbuch* 24–25 (1989–90): 39–48; Armando Bisanti, "Within il calvo," *Studi medievali,* 3rd ser., 40 (1999): 843–56. Bisanti convincingly places the baldness of Within within the ambit of purification, renewal, and nearness to God.

43. On this interpretation, see Joseph Campbell, *The Hero with a Thousand Faces,* 2nd ed., Bollingen Series 17 (Princeton, NJ: Princeton University Press, 1968), 247–48 (but cf. 90–95, 207–9).

44. Otto Rank, *Art and Artist: Creative Urge and Personality Development,* trans. C. F. Atkinson (New York: Tudor, 1932), 214–15. For this reference and the characterization of it, I am beholden to John Carey, "The Obscurantists and the Sea-Monster: Reflections on the *Hisperica famina,*" *Peritia* 17–18 (2003–4): 54.

45. Walther Suchier, ed., *Das mittellateinische Gespräch Adrian und Epictitus nebst verwandten Texten (Joca Monachorum)* (Tübingen: Max Niemeyer, 1955), 123 (text J, no. 10): "Ubi est sol in nocte?—In ventre coeti qui dicitur Leviathan." Various other medieval question-and-answer lists grapple with the puzzle of where the sun goes at night, with the closest other parallel being the Old English *Adrian and Ritheus* 6: see James E. Cross and Thomas D. Hill, *The "Prose Solomon and Saturn" and "Adrian and Ritheus,"* McMaster Old English Studies and Texts 1 (Toronto: University of Toronto Press, 1982), 35, with commentary on 131–34.

46. See the works cited in n. 36, particularly Frobenius, *Das Zeitalter.* Carey ("The Obscurantists and the Sea-Monster," 54) summarizes a few of the closest parallels in North American native sources as well as in island cultures of the Pacific Ocean.

47. See *F&W* 876 ("polygenesis") and 313 ("diffusion theory").

48. Bertini (*Letaldo di Micy, Within piscator,* XIV) groups me with earlier scholars who underestimated the presence in Western European literature of folktales of men swallowed by whales. This characterization is baffling, since the texts that he proceeds to cite are all ones identified in my 1984 article "Folklore and Learned Lore in Letaldus's Whale Poem," 110–12.

49. See Hans Schmidt, *Jona: Eine Untersuchung,* 3–12; Ludwig Preller, *Griechische*

Mythologie, vol. 2, *Die griechische Heldensage,* rev. Carl Robert, 4th ed. (Berlin: Weidmann, 1920), part 1, 549–54; Otto Weinreich, "Antiphanes und Münchhausen: Das antike Lügenmärlein von den gefrornen Worten und sein Fortleben im Abendland," *Akademie der Wissenschaften in Wien, Philosophisch-historische Klasse, Sitzungsberichte* 220. Band, 4. Abhandlung (Vienna and Leipzig: Hölder-Pichler-Tempsky, 1942), 17–21; Albin Lesky, "Herakles und das Ketos," in *Österreichische Akademie der Wissenschaften, Philosophisch-historische Klasse, Anzeiger (1967)* (Graz, Vienna, and Cologne: Hermann Böhlaus Nachfolger, 1967), 1–6.

50. Felix Jacoby, ed. *Die Fragmente der griechischen Historiker,* vol. 1, 2nd ed. (Leiden: E. J. Brill, 1957), 114 (4 F 26B). The fragment is preserved in a scholium on the *Iliad.*

51. Pseudo-Lycophron *Alexandra* 31–38, 470–78, ed. Lorenzo Mascialino, Bibliotheca scriptorum graecorum et romanorum teubneriana (Leipzig: B. G. Teubner, 1964), 3, 22–23. In a speech in the first passage, Alexandra describes how Herakles entered the monster to save Hesione. She speaks of Herakles "who, having been conceived in a threefold night, was once swallowed by Triton's sharp-toothed dog, but stayed alive, even though boiled in the heat of the belly as if in a flameless cauldron; he struck at its entrails and lost his hair." The second passage retells the same episode, but without mention of the heat, cutting, or hair loss.

52. Sextus Empiricus *Adversus mathematicos* 1.255, ed. Hermann Mutschmann, rev. Jürgen Mau and Karel Janácek, Bibliotheca teubneriana 3 (Leipzig: B. G. Teubner, 1954), 63, discussed fleetingly in H. I. Marrou, *A History of Education in Antiquity,* trans. George Lamb (Madison: University of Wisconsin Press, 1982), 168.

53. Eduard Scheer, ed., *Lycophronis Alexandra,* 2 vols. (Berlin: Weidmann, 1881–1908), 2:28–29.

54. The fullest and clearest exposition of the information in this paragraph is in Marcel Simon, *Hercule et le Christianisme* (Paris: Belles Lettres, 1955), 174–75. On Christian mockery of the word *trihesperos* in the patristic period, see Yves-Marie Duval, *Le livre de Jonas dans la littérature chrétienne grecque et latine: Sources et influence du Commentaire sur Jonas de saint Jérôme* (Paris: Études augustiniennes, 1973), 1:16 n. 17.

55. Cyril of Alexandria *Commentarius in Jonam prophetam* 2, in *PG* 71:616; Theophylaktos *In Ionam* 2.1, in *PG* 126:932C. The absence of any reference to Jonah losing hair is noted by John B. Friedman in "Bald Jonah and the Exegesis of 4 Kings 2.23," *Traditio* 44 (1988): 131 (citing Marc-René Jung, *Hercule dans la littérature française du XVI siècle: De l'Hercule courtois à l'Hercule baroque* [Geneva: Droz, 1966], 108–10), and also by Carey, "The Obscurantists and the Sea-Monster," 52. For additional information, see Duval, *Le livre de Jonas,* 1:15 n. 12, 29–30 n. 84.

56. The classic—but now very dated—work on Perseus is Edwin Sidney Hartland's *The Legend of Perseus: A Study of Tradition in Story, Custom, and Belief,* 3 vols., Grimm Library 2, 3, 5 (London: D. Nutt, 1894–96).

57. Aristophanes *Clouds* 555–56, in *Aristophanes,* ed. and trans. Jeffrey Henderson, vol. 2, Loeb Classical Library 488 (Cambridge, MA: Harvard University Press, 1998), 84–85.

58. On the localization of the myth, see Flavius Josephus *Jewish War* 3.420, ed. and trans. H. St. J. Thackeray, 3 vols., Loeb Classical Library 203, 210, 487 (Cambridge, MA: Harvard University Press, 1997), 2:122–23; Strabo [born ca. 64 BCE, died after 21 CE] *Geography* 16.2.28, ed. and trans. Horace Leonard Jones, 8 vols., Loeb Classical Li-

brary 49–50, 182, 196, 211, 223, 241, 267 (Cambridge, MA: Harvard University Press, 1960–70), 7:274–77. K. M. Coleman ("Manilius' Monster," *Hermes* 111 [1983]: 226–32) refers to these two passages. Others are listed in Jeremias, *Das alte Testament,* 726 n. 2.

59. Flavius Josephus *Jewish War* 3.420, ed. and trans. Thackeray, 2:122–23. Compare Pliny the Elder *Naturalis historia* 5.14.69, in *Natural History,* ed. and trans. H. Rackham, W. H. S. Jones, and D. E. Eichholz, 10 vols., Loeb Classical Library 330, 352–53, 370–71, 392–94, 418–19 (Cambridge, MA: Harvard University Press, 1949–62), 2:272–73.

60. Pausanias *Description of Greece* 4.35, ed. and trans. W. H. S. Jones, 5 vols., Loeb Classical Library 93, 188, 272, 297–98 (Cambridge, MA: Harvard University Press, 1918–35), 2:364–73.

61. Pliny the Elder *Naturalis historia* 9.4.11, ed. and trans. Rackham, Jones, and Eichholz, 3:170–71.

62. For both the French and English versions, see John Mandeville, *Mandeville's Travels,* ed. and trans. Malcolm Letts, 2 vols., Hakluyt Society, 2nd ser., 101–2 (London: Hakluyt Society, 1953), vol. 1, chap. 4.

63. The key passage is Jerome *Commentarius in Ionam prophetam* 2.1a, in *Jérôme, Commentaire sur Jonas,* ed. and trans. Yves-Marie Duval, Sources chrétiennes 323 (Paris: Les Éditions du Cerf, 1985), 180, lines 118–21. For concise discussions and selections of pertinent bibliography, see John Day, *God's Conflict with the Dragon and the Sea: Echoes of a Canaanite Myth in the Old Testament* (Cambridge: Cambridge University Press, 1985), 111; Duval, *Le livre de Jonas,* 1:13–16.

64. Rome, Vatican Museums, ARV 437, 116. For discussion, see Radermacher, *Mythos und Sage,* 204–5, 362 nn. 506–8; Carey, "The Obscurantists and the Sea-Monster," 54–55. For a reproduction, see John Boardman, *The History of Greek Vases: Potters, Painters, and Pictures* (London: Thames and Hudson, 2001), 91 and plate 24.

65. Lucian, *A True History,* in *Lucian,* vol. 1, ed. and trans. A. M. Harmon, Loeb Classical Library 14 (New York: Putnam, 1913), 284–305.

66. For a concise account of his life, see Theula Gehrmann, "Hieronymus v. Münchhausen und der Werdegang des Buches: Wie der Freiherr von Münchhausen zum Lügenbaron gemacht wurde," in *Münchhausen: Ein amoralisches Kinderbuch; Untersuchung zu einem Bestseller,* by Bernhard Wiebel, Arbeitsbericht 17 (Zurich: Schweizerisches Jugendbuch-Institut, 1996), 5–8.

67. The exhaustive account of these stories and their subsequent reception is Werner R. Schweizer's *Münchhausen und Münchhausiaden: Werden und Schicksale einer deutsch-englischen Burleske* (Bern and Munich: Francke Verlag, 1969).

68. Rudolph Erich Raspe, *The Surprising Adventures of Baron Munchausen,* with an introduction by Thomas Secombe, illustrated by William Strang and J. B. Clark (London: Lawrence and Bullen, 1985), 54.

69. *Hisperica famina* 157–217, ed. F. J. H. Jenkinson (Cambridge: Cambridge University Press, 1908), 28–30, discussed and translated by Carey in "The Obscurantists and the Sea-Monster," 40–60. The pertinence of this material to the poem of Letaldus was first pointed out viva voce by Michael Herren at a conference in Heidelberg in 1988 and then eventually incorporated into Bertini's *Letaldo di Micy, Within piscator,* XVII–XIX. This was the only parallel to the Within poem mentioned by Bertini that eluded me in my 1984 article "Folklore and Learned Lore in Letaldus's Whale Poem."

70. Carey ("The Obscurantists and the Sea-Monster," 49) proposes emending a word so that the text indicates that the sailors have lost the hair on their heads.

71. Bertini (*Letaldo di Micy, Within piscator,* XVII–XIX) italicizes all the words in the *Hisperica famina* passage that in his opinion coincide with words in the Within poem (see app. 1D in the present study). Although none of these instances convinces me (or Carey: see "The Obscurantists and the Sea-Monster," 52–53 n. 59) that the later poet was acquainted with the B-text, the source-and-influence argument has been accepted provisionally by Bisanti ("Within il calvo," 846) and Pennisi (Letaldus, *De quodam piscatore,* 12–13).

72. See Bertini, *Letaldo di Micy, Within piscator,* XVII; Pennisi, Letaldus, *De quodam piscatore,* 77, respectively.

73. *Duanaire Finn: The Book of the Lays of Fionn,* ed. and trans. Eoin MacNeill and Gerard Murphy, 3 parts, Irish Texts Society 7, 28, 43 (London: D. Nutt, 1908–53), part 2, 234–39 (poem 60, the fullest version), and part 3, 140–41 (references to various oral versions); Nicholas O'Kearney, ed., *Feis tighe Chónain: The Festivities at the House of Conan of Ceann-Sleibhe, in the County of Clare,* Transactions of the Ossianic Society for the Year 1854 (Dublin: John O'Daly, 1855), 2:65–70. Closely related is the account of the swallowing of Fionn and Bran by a monster, in which Fionn emerges having lost his clothes and Bran his hair and hide: see George Henderson, "The Fionn Saga," *Celtic Review* 2 (1905–6): 150–51. Other stories similar to that of Within are found in early Irish: see Tom Peete Cross, *Motif-Index of Early Irish Literature,* Indiana University Publications Folklore Series 7 (Bloomington: Indiana University Press, 1952), F910, "Extraordinary Swallowings."

74. Contrast the information on dates in *Duanaire Finn* (part 3, cxvi–cxvii and 139) with the information Carey synthesizes in "The Obscurantists and the Sea-Monster" (50 n. 43).

75. Although Bertini (*Letaldo di Micy, Within piscator,* XIX) ascribed to me the view that this episode in the Fionn cycle depended on Letaldus's poem, my contention remains now quite different, as it was already then: that both accounts follow similar patterns because both are indebted to similar and related oral traditions.

76. For example, W. G. Wood-Martin (*Traces of the Elder Faiths of Ireland, a Folklore Sketch: A Handbook of Irish Pre-Christian Traditions,* 2 vols. [London: Longmans, Green, 1902], 1:268–69) relates as "a tale recounted by the peasantry" a story in which Conan is swallowed by a serpent, out of which he cuts his way with his dagger.

77. Oesterley, *Gesta Romanorum,* 655–57.

78. Traces of such interaction are unfortunately not assessed in Robert Hood Bowers, *The Legend of Jonah* (The Hague: Martinus Nijhoff, 1971).

79. Jerome comments on Matthew 12.40 at *Commentarius in Ionam prophetam* 2.1a, ed. and trans. Duval, 220, lines 9–14: "In the Hebrew, however, we read 'great fish,' for what the translators of the Septuagint and the Lord in the Gospel call a whale [*cetus*], making clear the same thing more concisely. For in the Hebrew is said 'dag gadol,' which is translated as 'great fish.' There is no doubt that it means whale [*cetus*]" [In hebraico autem PISCEM GRANDEM legimus pro quo LXX interpretes et Dominus in Euangelio *cetum* uocant, rem ipsam breuius explicantes. In hebraico enim dicitur "dag gadol" quod interpretatur PISCEM GRANDEM. Haud dubium quin *cetum* significet]. On the Christian emphasis on the whale, see Fernand Cabrol and Henri Leclercq, *Dictionnaire d'archéologie chrétienne et de liturgie,* vol. 7 (Paris: Letouzey et Ané, 1927), 2572–2631, especially 2572–73.

80. On the Devil, see Gregory the Great *Moralia in Iob* 8.23.39, ed. Marc Adriaen,

Corpus Christianorum Series Latina 143–143A–143B (Turnhout: Brepols, 1979–85), 143:410, line 8–411, line 31. On hell, compare Zeno of Verona *Tractatus* 2.17, "De Jona propheta," in *PL* 11.448C–449A: "We have no doubt that the whale is hell; just as Jonah was in the belly of the whale three days and three nights and upon being vomited out betook himself to the city of Nineveh, so too the Lord, the day after being resurrected from hell, betook himself to the city of Jerusalem before going to heaven" [Cetum esse non dubitantur infernum: sicut enim Jonas tribus diebus et tribus noctibus fuit in ventre ceti, evomitusque Ninives se intulit civitati; ita Dominus postridie ab inferno resurgens, se civitati Jerusalem intulit ante quam coelo]; Isidore of Seville *Etymologiae* 12.6.7–8, ed. W. M. Lindsay, vol. 2 (Oxford: Clarendon, 1911): "a whale of such type received Jonah, the belly of which was of such great size that it attained the likeness of hell, with the prophet saying (Jonah 2.3): 'He heard me out of the belly of hell'" [qualis cetus excepit Ionam cuius alvus tantae magnitudinis fuit ut instar obtineret inferni, dicente Propheta (2.3): 'Exaudivit me de ventre inferni']; the Middle English *Patience,* lines 275 and 306, ed. J. J. Andersen (Manchester: Manchester University Press, 1969). Many more examples are found in the commentaries listed in n. 88 in the present chapter. The fullest study of the Christian exegetic tradition on Jonah is Duval's *Le Livre de Jonas.*

81. For illustrations, see Hans Schmidt, *Jona: Eine Untersuchung* , 180–82; Uwe Steffen, *Das Mysterium von Tod und Auferstehung: Formen und Wandlungen des Jona-Motives* (Göttingen: Vandenhoeck und Ruprecht, 1963), plate 16. The image of the whale's mouth as the mouth of hell may even figure in the late tenth-century Old English poem "Whale": see Gary D. Schmidt, *The Iconography of the Mouth of Hell: Eighth-Century Britain to the Fifteenth Century* (Selinsgrove, PA: Susquehanna University Press, 1995), 62.

82. On the whale in antiquity, see Hugo Rahner, *Symbole der Kirche: Die Ekklesiologie* (Salzburg: Müller, 1964), 291 and n. 133. On the genesis and propagation of the *Physiologus* account, see Cornelia Catlin Coulter, "The 'Great Fish' in Ancient and Medieval Story," *Transactions of the American Philological Association* 57 (1926): 32–50; Florence McCulloch, *Mediaeval Latin and French Bestiaries,* University of North Carolina Studies in Romance Languages and Literatures 33 (Chapel Hill: University of North Carolina Press, 1960), 91–92; J. Runeberg, "Le conte de l'Ile-poisson," *Mémoires de la Société néo-philologique à Helsingfors* 3 (1902): 345–95; Alexander Scheiber, "Motivgeschichte des Gedichts von Ady An den grossen Walfisch," *Fabula* 12 (1971): 229–38. For a systematic categorization of whale lore, see Rudolf Schenda, "Walfisch-Lore und Walfisch-Literatur," in *IV. International Congress for Folk-Narrative Research in Athens (1.9–6.9 1964),* ed. Georgios A. Megas, Laographia 22 (Athens, 1965), 431–48.

83. *Aspidochelone* is glossed tentatively as "(?) giant turtle" in R. E. Latham and D. R. Howlett, eds., *Dictionary of Medieval Latin from British Sources* (London: Oxford University Press, 1975–), fascicule 1:138. But the passage cited equates the beast with the *cetus* and identifies it as the beast that swallowed Jonah.

84. For examples of this motif from throughout the world, see *MI* J1761.1, "Whale thought to be island. Sailors light a fire on his back." Compare *MI* F730, "Extraordinary islands. R245. Whale-boat. A man is carried across the water on a whale (fish). (He usually deceives the whale as to the nearness of the land or as to hearing thunder. As a consequence the whale runs into the shore or is killed by lightning)."

85. To appreciate the number of classical allusions in the poem, see Wilmart, "Le poème héroïque," 200; Bonnes, "Un lettré du Xe siècle," 37–45.

86. Glaber *Historiarum libri quinque* 2.2.2, ed. and trans. France, 50–55.

87. See Werner Timm, "Der gestrandete Wal, eine motivkundliche Studie," *Staatliche Museen zu Berlin, Forschungen und Berichte* 3–4 (1961): 76–93, especially 82.

88. See Jerome *Commentarius in Ionam prophetam*, ed. and trans. Duval, 160–317; Haimo of Auxerre [died 855] *In Jonam prophetam*, in *PL* 117.127C–142D; Rupert of Deutz [1075–1129/1130] *In Jonam prophetam*, in *Commentarium in duodecim prophetas minores libri XXXI*, in *PL* 168.399C–440B. For medieval manuscripts and incunabula in which the swallowing and regurgitation of Jonah are juxtaposed to Christ's deposition and resurrection, see Steffen, *Das Mysterium*, 129 (figs. 18–19); Leonard Harrison Matthews, ed., *The Whale* (New York: Simon and Schuster, 1969), 265.

89. See Propp, *Le radici storiche*, 89.

90. On Christ as bait, see Gregory the Great *Homiliarum in Evangelia libri duo*, book 2, *Homilia* 25.7–8, in *PL* 76.1194C–1195A; Gregory the Great *Moralia in Iob* 33.7.14, ed. Adriaen, 143B:1684–85. Further references are provided in Werner von Koppenfels, *Esca et Hamus: Beitrag zu einer historischen Liebesmetaphorik*, Bayerische Akademie der Wissenschaften, philosophisch-historische Klasse, Sitzungsberichte (Munich: Verlag der Bayerischen Akademie der Wissenschaften, 1973), part 3, 39–43.

91. For an extended consideration of this image, see Johannes Zellinger, "Der geköderte Leviathan im Hortus deliciarum der Herrad von Landsperg," *Historisches Jahrbuch* 45 (1925): 161–77.

92. Ekkehard IV of St. Gall, "VII. Grabschrift für die Recluse Rachilda," 1–2 = Saint Gall 5.7 (no. 64), ed. Karl Strecker, in *MGH Poetae Latini Medii Aevi*, vol. 5, no. 2 (Berlin: Weidmannsche Verlagsbuchhandlung, 1939), 549. See also Audradus of Sens [Audradus Modicus] *De fonte vitae* (composed ca. 850) 1.310, ed. Francesco Stella, Il Nuovo Melograno 5 (Florence: Casa Editrice Le Lettere, 1991), 112, who argues that death and the serpent could not have endured the appearance of the Lord and would have taken flight at once had not the nearby power of Christ "and the majesty of God taken Leviathan with a hook / and [had not] the son of man slain death by dying" [Maiestasque dei leuiathan prenderet hamo / Et natus hominis mortem moriendo necaret].

93. Johannes Bolte and Georg Polívka (BP 4:107 n. 4) see the protagonists of the fairy tale and the biblical book as undergoing closely comparable experiences ("wenigstens entfernt").

94. This point is made by Elias Bickerman in *Four Strange Books of the Bible: Jonah/Daniel/Koheleth/Esther* (New York: Schocken, 1967), 11–12.

95. Ambrose John Wilson, "The Sign of the Prophet Jonah and Its Modern Confirmations," *Princeton Theological Review* 25 (1927): 630–42 (631–34 on the type of jaw, tongue, and gullet; 634–35 on the heat, gastric juices, and air quality; 635–38 on purportedly real swallowings and regurgitations of men).

96. This and the subsequent quotations are taken from Francis Fox [1844–1927], *Sixty-Three Years of Engineering, Scientific, and Social Work* (London: John Murray, 1924), 299–300. Substantial portions of them appear more accessibly, with slight typographical differences, in Ambrose John Wilson, "Sign of the Prophet Jonah," 636. See Carey, "The Obscurantists and the Sea-Monster," 53, for a translation of another, very detailed account (ultimately recorded in a Riga newspaper of 1896) of a fisherman in the Baltic who, together with his boat, was swallowed by a gigantic beast and forced the beast to spit him out by kindling a fire, cutting slices of meat and blubber from within, and roasting them.

97. See Edward Davis, "A Whale of a Tale: Fundamentalist Fish Stories," *Perspectives on Science and Christian Faith* 43 (1991): 224–37. Carey ("The Obscurantist and the Sea-Monster," 55) provides an additional reference on a version of the story in which Bartley is alleged to have "lost all the hair on his body."

98. Wilson, "Sign of the Prophet Jonah," 638.

99. "Wer wollte es nicht für ein Märlein halten, wenn es nicht in der Schrift stünde?"

100. See Johannes Wendland, *Miracles and Christianity,* trans. H. R. Mackintosh (New York: Hodder and Stoughton, 1911), 52–66; A. Michel, "Miracle," in *Dictionnaire de théologie catholique,* ed. Alfred Vacant and E. Mangenot, vol. 10, part 2 (Paris: Letouzey et Ané, 1927), 1803.

101. See Ernst Keller and Marie-Luise Keller, *Miracles in Dispute. A Continuing Debate,* trans. Margaret Kohl (Philadelphia: Fortress, 1969), 20–28; Benedicta Ward, *Miracles and the Medieval Mind: Theory, Record, and Event, 1000–1215,* 2nd ed. (Philadelphia: University of Pennsylvania Press, 1987), 3–4.

102. Jerome *Commentarius in Ionam prophetam* 2.7b, ed. and trans. Duval, 248, lines 302–5:

"Super Iona autem ita intellegi potest quod qui in uentre ceti iuxta naturam corporum corrumpi debuerat et in cibos bestiae proficere ac per uenas artusque diffundi, sospes et integer manserit."

103. Acta Pauli, Letter to the Corinthians, 3.29–30, in *Apocrypha, New Testament,* ed. Wilhelm Schneemelcher, trans. R. McL. Wilson, 2nd ed., 2 vols. (Louisville, KY: Westminster/John Knox, 1991–92), 2:256. This passage was cited already by Hans Schmidt in *Jona: Eine Untersuchung,* 95 n. 1.

104. A memorable depiction of Jonah bald after his adventure is a sculpture in the Bamberg cathedral (from around the year 1230): see Steffen, *Das Mysterium,* plate 8. The fullest discussion and set of plates are in Friedman, "Bald Jonah." The fullest consideration of the motif as it appears in Letaldus is now Bisanti's "Within il calvo," which was written without knowledge of Friedman's study.

105. See Hans Schmidt, *Jona: Eine Untersuchung,* 94–96 (including Figs. Abb. 16–17); Steffen, *Das Mysterium,* 127, Figs. 16–17; Matthews, *The Whale,* 17; Jeremias, *Das alte Testament,* fig. 292; Carl-Otto Nordström, "Some Jewish Legends in Byzantine Art," *Byzantion* 252–57 (1955–57): plates 8–9; plate 9 is Byzantine. Many more illustrations of the bald Jonah and the naked Jonah are to be found under the heading "Jonah: Cast Up" in the Index of Christian Art at Princeton University.

106. To my knowledge, there is no exhaustive treatment of Jonah in late antique art. The study by Otto Mitius—*Jonas in der altchristlichen Kunst* (Freiburg: C. A. Wagner, 1897), 35–36—is dated and incomplete. For further information, see Marion Lawrence's "Ships, Monsters, and Jonah," *American Journal of Archaeology* 66 (1962): 289–96.

107. A common point of entry into this tradition is through Louis Ginzburg's magnificent old reference work *The Legends of the Jews,* trans. Henrietta Szold, 7 vols. (Philadelphia: Jewish Publication Society of America, 1937–38), at 4:252, "The intense heat in the belly of the fish had consumed his garments, and made his hair fall out," and 6:351, "As to the falling out of the hair, see Ibn Ezra on Jonah 4.6." Unfortunately, Ginzburg's reference to Ibn Ezra is incorrect (the latter refers to the tenderness of skin that the stay inside the whale caused Jonah, but not to loss of clothing and hair). This slip misled both Carey ("The Obscurantists and the Sea-Monster," 51 n. 50) and Friedman ("Bald

Jonah," 129–30), the latter of whom concluded that the medieval Jewish tradition of the bald Jonah was later and more restricted than is actually the case. More exploration is required. Duval (*Le livre de Jonas,* 1:70) concluded, "une histoire de l'exégèse juive du *Livre de Jonas . . .* reste à écrire."

108. *Yalqut Shim'oni* (Salonika, 1527), 129b.

109. From Dei Rossi MS 563, printed in Chaim M. Horovitz, *Agudat agadot: O, Kovets midrashim ketanim* (Berlin: Bi-defus Ts. H. Ittskovski, 1881), 34. This part of the text can be found in German translation in *Aus Israels Lehrhallen,* trans. August Wünsche (Leipzig: E. Pfeiffer, 1907–8; repr., Hildesheim: Georg Olms, 1967), 2:50 ("Midrasch Jona"). I am grateful to my former colleague Professor James L. Kugel for finding and translating these passages for me. He further suggested that the motif of the heat inside the fish's belly may come from Jonah 2.6 ("The waters surrounded me unto death . . . "). The Targum of Jonathan renders this phrase into Aramaic as "aıpuni maya, ad mota," with the verb meaning "surrounded" thus being rendered here by a verb generally used to mean "to cause to congeal (by heat)." See *The Targum of the Minor Prophets,* trans. Kevin Cathcart and Robert P. Gordon (Wilmington, DE: M. Glazier, 1989), 107.

110. See Nordström, "Some Jewish Legends," 503–7 (on Jonah in particular); Carl-Otto Nordström, "Rabbinic Features in Byzantine and Catalan Art," *Cahiers archéologiques* 15 (1965): 179–205. For both these references, I am indebted to Friedman, "Bald Jonah," 129 n. 15. For further consideration, see Duval, *Le livre de Jonas,* 1:29–30.

111. *Speculum sacerdotale,* chap. 21, ed. Edward H. Weatherly, Early English Text Society, o.s., 200 (London: Humphrey Milford, Oxford University Press, 1936), 57, lines 27–28: "for the hete of the fisshe all the heeres of his hede were loste and gone of." Friedman ("Bald Jonah," 131) cites this passage but, because of its restricted circulation, says no more than that it was uninfluential.

112. John the Deacon [Johannes Hymmonides] *Cena Cypriani* 2.166 ("Jesus was drinking raisin-wine [*passum* puns on the Latin word for the Passion], bald Jonah Marsian wine" [Passumbibebat Iesus, Ionas caluus Marsicum]), 2.235 ("Bald Jonah was naked and shipwrecked at sea" [Ionas caluus nudus erat naufragus in maria]), ed. Karl Strecker, *MGH Poetae* 4, no. 2 (1923): 886, 891.

113. *De jejunio,* in *PG* 62:735, discussed in Duval, *Le livre de Jonas,* 2:468–70.

114. Archpoet *Die Gedichte des Archipoeta* 2.56, ed. Heinrich Watenphul and Heinrich Krefeld (Heidelberg: Carl Winter, 1958), 55.

115. The text is most readily accessible in Karl Young's *The Drama of the Medieval Church,* 2 vols. (Oxford: Clarendon, 1933), 2:160–61.

116. Lucian *A True History* 1.3, ed. and trans. Harmon, 250–51; Juvenal *Satire* 15.13–26, in *Juvenal and Persius,* ed. and trans. G. G. Ramsay, Loeb Classical Library 91 (Cambridge, MA: Harvard University Press, 1940), 288–91. For other instances of such criticism, see E. Courtney, *A Commentary on the Satires of Juvenal* (London: Athlone, 1980), 596 (comment on *Satire* 15.16).

117. Compare the beginnings of the *Vita sancti Juliani* and the *Liber miraculorum sancti Maximini. Vita sancti Juliani,* in *PL* 137.785B–785D. *Liber Miraculorum sancti Maximini,* in *PL* 137.797B–798C.

118. Compare the story that Letaldus relates in the *Liber miraculorum sancti Maximini* of Abbot Heiriricus, who requests and receives three fresh pears in the dead of winter. In defense of this anecdote, Letaldus remarks, "Being acquainted with this through the truthful account of elders, I could in no way allow it to be buried in silence" [Quod

ego veridica seniorum relatione cognoscens nequaquam silentio passus sum abscondi] (*PL* 137.804A).

119. Letaldus's lines 9–13 paraphrase in verse the prose of Bede's *Ecclesiastical History of the English People* 1.1, ed. and trans. Bertram Colgrave and R. A. B. Mynors, 2nd ed. (Oxford: Clarendon, 1991).

120. A copy of the original at the closest is in Paris, Bibliothèque Nationale, MS lat. 5230A, fols. 45r–48v: see Wilmart, "Le poème héroïque," 191. On the position of Letaldus's poem in the manuscript, see Bonnes, "Un lettré du Xe siècle," 34. By good fortune, a meticulous description of this manuscript was produced just a few years before its destruction: see André Wilmart, "Le florilège de Saint-Gatien: Contribution à l'étude des poèmes d'Hildebert et de Marbode," *Revue Bénédictine* 48 (1936): 3–40, 147–81, 235–58.

121. See Barthélemy Hauréau, *Histoire littéraire du Maine,* 2nd ed., 10 vols. (Paris: Dumoulin, 1870–77), 7:191, 196; Bonnes, "Un lettré du Xe siècle," 29–30; Jean Leclercq, *The Love of Learning and the Desire for God: A Study of Monastic Culture,* trans. Catharine Misrahi, 3rd ed. (New York: Fordham University Press, 1982), 160, 164.

122. Unless otherwise specified, subsequent references to Letaldus's saints' lives are to columns in *PL* 137.

123. For the second source cited, see the edition of Bruno Krusch: *Miracula Martini abbatis Vertavensis,* ed. Bruno Krusch, *Passiones vitaeque sanctorum aevi Merovingici et antiquiorum aliquot,* MGH Scriptores rerum Merovingicarum 3 (1896), 567–75.

124. For the source cited, see the edition of Philippe Labbé in *Nouae bibliothecae manuscript [torum] librorum,* 2 vols. (Paris: Apud Sebastianum Cramoisy, 1657), 2:463. The attribution of this text to Letaldus was argued by Head in "Letaldus of Micy and the Hagiographic Traditions of Selles-sur-Cher."

125. See 728B, cited in Cremascoli, "Das hagiographische Werk," 88.

126. *Liber miraculorum sancti Maximini,* in *PL* 137.818C: "hoc quod dicturi sumus miraculum." Compare 813C: "quod dico miraculum."

127. See Cremascoli, "Das hagiographische Werk."

128. See 786C, discussed in Cremascoli, "Das hagiographische Werk," 91.

129. On the motif, see the studies cited in n. 84, and see the anonymous *Navigatio sancti Brendani,* ed. Giovanni Orlandi, vol. 1, Testi e documenti per lo studio dell'antichità 38 (Milan: Istituto editoriale cisalpino, 1968), 43–56. A different section of the *Navigatio* has been analyzed as being based on an underlying pattern very close to that of the Jonah story: see Teresa Carp, "The Three Late-Coming Monks: Tradition and Invention in the *Navigatio Sancti Brendani,*" *Medievalia et Humanistica* 12 (1983): 127–42.

130. On the patristic scheme, see Rahner, *Symbole der Kirche,* 239–564.

131. On the vogue, see Head and Landes, *Peace of God,* 52–53.

132. *PL* 137.804A: "Quia etsi sunt rari nunc miracula facientes, multi tamen in sancta sunt Ecclesia, qui vitae merito operatoribus miraculorum dispares non sunt." Compare *PL* 137.784.

133. See Jerome *Commentarius in Ionam prophetam* 2.1a, ed. and trans. Duval, 224, lines 56–59; Augustine *Sex quaestiones contra paganos expositae, liber unus* (*epistola* 102), *quaestio sexta,* "De Jona propheta," in *Epistolae, Secunda classis,* in *PL* 33.382–86. The effort to prove the reality of the miracle continues to our own day: see Martin Ralph De Haan, *Jonah, Fact or Fiction?* (Grand Rapids, MI: Zondervan, 1957).

134. Under no circumstances have I ever understood Letaldus's poem merely or

even mainly as "a hagiographic text," pace Bertini (*Letaldo di Micy, Within piscator,* XIV).

135. For an instance in which fishermen from Flanders successfully invoked a saint to bring a raging whale under control, see Hariulf of Oldenburg [1105–43], *Vita Arnulfi Suessionensis,* ed. O. Holder-Egger, MGH Scriptores 15, no. 2 (Hanover: Impensis bibliopolii Hahniani, 1888), 901.

136. The tale is construed as an initiation myth by Bertini, especially in his edition of the poem by Letaldus.

137. Abbo of Fleury *Epistola* 11, in *Epistolae,* in *PL* 139.438A: "singularis scientia." Abbo's loyalty is evident in his *Apologeticus,* where he defends Letaldus against mistreatment by Bishop Arnulf of Orléans: see *PL* 139.469A. At the same time, *Epistula* 11 makes no secret of Abbo's distress at Letaldus's personal conduct in strife within the abbey of Micy. The letter pointedly praises Letaldus for his knowledge (*scientia*), while implying that he is rather short on wisdom (*sapientia*).

138. See Mario Petrini, *La fiaba di magia nella letteratura italiana* (Udine: Del Bianco, 1983), 25.

CHAPTER THREE

This chapter expands substantially on an article published in *Speculum* 67 (1992): 549–75. The text of the article, submitted early in 1991, was presented as a formal lecture in a number of venues in 1991. Only in 1993 did I become aware of Jacques Berlioz's "Un Petit Chaperon rouge médiéval? 'La petite fille épargnée par les loups' dans la *Fecunda ratis* d'Egbert de Liège (début du XIe siècle)," *Merveilles et contes* 5 (1991): 246–63. This article by Berlioz was itself based on two earlier pieces that had not been indicated in the standard bibliographies of Medieval Latin scholarship. In particular, Berlioz's translation and commentary were available already (unbeknownst to me) in Berlioz, Bremond, and Velay-Vallantin's *Formes médiévales du conte merveilleux,* 133–39. Berlioz's 1991 article was subsequently translated into English as "A Medieval 'Little Red Riding Hood'? 'The Little Girl Spared by the Wolves' in the *Fecunda ratis* of Egbert of Liège (Early 11th Century)," trans. Leslie Abend Callahan and Francesca Canadé Sautman, *Medieval Folklore* 3 (1994): 39–66. In 1992 appeared Günter Lontzen's "Das Gedicht 'De puella a lupellis servata' von Egbert von Lüttich: Eine Parabel zum Thema der Taufe," *Merveilles et contes* 6 (1992): 20–44. For want of any special mental acumen, I cannot invoke the principle of "great minds think alike" for the unusual conjunction of interest in one short poem, but it is at least interesting to note that medievalists sometimes reach similar conclusions. Although I have not attempted to signal all points of overlap or discordance between Berlioz's or Lontzen's arguments and my own, I have noted every instance in which my expansions in this chapter have been influenced by their publications.

1. Opie and Opie, *Classic Fairy Tales,* 93.

2. Wolfgang Maaz, "Märchen und Märchenmotive im MA," in *LdM* 6:224–25: "Ob Egbert von Lüttich eine Frühform des Rotkäppchen-Märchens (AaTh 333) tradiert, ist umstritten."

3. Alan Dundes, "Interpreting 'Little Red Riding Hood' Psychoanalytically," in *Little Red Riding Hood: A Casebook,* ed. Alan Dundes (Madison: University of Wisconsin Press, 1989), 192.

4. Diederichs, *Who's who im Märchen,* 276–77.

5. For a recent probing of meanings, both explicit and implicit, in different versions of the story from the late seventeenth century down to the present day, see Catherine Orenstein, *Little Red Riding Hood Uncloaked: Sex, Morality, and the Evolution of a Fairy Tale* (New York: Basic, 2002). An excellent, vast digest and analysis of material is available in Sandra Beckett's *Recycling Red Riding Hood,* Children's Literature and Culture 23 (New York: Routledge, 2001).

6. Emma Emily Kiefer, *Albert Wesselski and Recent Folktale Theories,* Indiana University Publications: Folklore Series 3 (Bloomington: Indiana University, 1947), 9 (quoting Reidar Thoralf Christiansen, who in turn was quoting Arthur Bonus).

7. For a brief history with reference to the Brothers Grimm, see Rolf Hagen, "Perraults Märchen und die Brüder Grimm," *Zeitschrift für deutsche Philologie* 74 (1955): 392–93.

8. For a detailed account of the conflict between literary and anthropological folklorists in the United States, see Rosemary Lévy Zumwalt, *American Folklore Scholarship: A Dialogue of Dissent* (Bloomington and Indianapolis: Indiana University Press, 1988). For a consideration of the divisions between literary and folklore studies that gives considerable attention to the Middle Ages, see Bruce A. Rosenberg, *Folklore and Literature.*

9. The quotation is drawn from Zipes, *Breaking the Magic Spell,* 21.

10. The classic exposition of the Finnish school methods is Kaarle Krohn, *Folklore Methodology Formulated by Julius Krohn and Expanded by Nordic Researchers,* trans. Roger L. Welsch, Publications of the American Folklore Society: Bibliographical and Special Series 21 (Austin: University of Texas Press, 1971). For a concise biography of Thompson's education and intellectual development, see Zumwalt, *American Folklore Scholarship,* 55–60. For his advocacy of balance in attention to the written and the oral, see Thompson, *The Folktale,* 442.

11. Kiefer, *Recent Folktale Theories,* 80 (she contrasts the Finnish school and von Sydow with Wesselski and De Vries).

12. Kiefer, *Recent Folktale Theories,* 18.

13. Kiefer, *Recent Folktale Theories,* 45.

14. Zipes, *Breaking the Magic Spell,* ix.

15. Zipes, *Breaking the Magic Spell,* 2.

16. Zipes, *Breaking the Magic Spell,* 23.

17. Zipes elsewhere recognizes the Middle Ages as an important transitional phase between the oral and the written in the narrative genre of the literary fairy tale (Zipes, *Great Fairy Tale Tradition,* 851–52).

18. See Linda Dégh, "What Did the Grimm Brothers Give to and Take from the Folk," in McGlathery, *The Brothers Grimm and Folktale,* 71; Carl Wilhelm von Sydow, "Folktale Studies and Philology: Some Points of View," in Dundes, *The Study of Folklore,* 219–42.

19. Dundes, *Little Red Riding Hood: A Casebook,* ix (my italics).

20. Dundes, *Little Red Riding Hood: A Casebook,* 196.

21. Dundes, *Little Red Riding Hood: A Casebook,* 197.

22. Nancy A. Mavrogenes and Joan S. Cummins, "What Ever Happened to Little Red Riding Hood? A Study of a Nursery Tale," *Horn Book* 55 (1979): 345.

23. Dundes, *Little Red Riding Hood: A Casebook,* 3. Most would accept the view that the French writer adapted a preexistent tale that was current in French oral tradition, although some would contend that he fabricated the Little Red Riding Hood tale entirely:

see Carole Hanks and D. T. Hanks, Jr., "Perrault's 'Little Red Riding Hood': Victim of the Revisers," *Children's Literature* 7 (1978): 77 n. 2.

24. If one accepts that the repertoire of stories among middle-class storytellers derived from centuries of lower-class storytellers, the fact that the Grimms' informants were middle-class and literate becomes less problematic. See Grimm and Grimm, *Kinder- und Hausmärchen: Ausgabe letzter Hand mit den Originalanmerkungen der Brüder Grimm,* ed. Heinz Rölleke, 3 vols. (Stuttgart: Philipp Reclam, 1980), 3:602. This acceptance has been challenged by John M. Ellis in *One Fairy Story Too Many: The Brothers Grimm and Their Tales* (Chicago: University of Chicago Press, 1983), 107–8; defended by Donald Ward in "New Misconceptions about Old Folktales: The Brothers Grimm," in McGlathery, *The Brothers Grimm and Folktale,* 91–100; and restated by Heinz Rölleke in "New Results of Research on *Grimms' Fairy Tales,*" in McGlathery, *The Brothers Grimm and Folktale,* 106. The fullest consideration of such questions is in Kamenetsky, *The Brothers Grimm and Their Critics.*

25. Lutz Mackensen, "Märchen," in *Handbuch der deutschen Volkskunde,* ed. Wilhelm Peßler, (Potsdam: Akademische Verlagsgesellschaft, 1934), 2:320: "Das Verhältnis von Literatur und Volksmärchen ist kein einseitiges Abhängigkeitsverhältnis." Compare Kiefer, *Recent Folktale Theories,* 18: "They keep reminding themselves, too, that an oral tale may be a literary variant returned to the folk mouth."

26. See, most recently, Bruce A. Rosenberg, *Folklore and Literature.*

27. This was much the position taken by Anderson: see Kiefer, *Recent Folktale Theories,* 33, 62.

28. The approach recommended here differs little from that enunciated by Lawrence W. Levine in "How to Interpret American Folklore Historically," in *Handbook of American Folklore,* ed. Richard M. Dorson (Bloomington: Indiana University Press, 1983), 338–44.

29. Dundes, *Little Red Riding Hood: A Casebook,* 13. Dundes looks like an adherent of the Finnish school in the early part of the century. Compare Kiefer, *Recent Folktale Theories,* 62: "Anderson accuses Wesselski of not having exhausted even the well-known and now available Asiatic material, and of having completely ignored the oral transmission from Asia."

30. See Hanks and Hanks, "Perrault's 'Little Red Riding Hood,'" 76–77 n. 2, for doubt that an oral text collected as recently as 1885 could possibly be considered the ancestor of Perrault's seventeenth-century tale. The 1885 version, recorded in Nièvre, is titled "Conte de la mère grande" in Paul Delarue's *Le Conte populaire français: Catalogue raisonné des versions de France et des pays de langue française d'outre-mer; Canada, Louisiane, îlots français des États-Unis, Antilles françaises, Haïti, Ile Maurice, La Réunion,* vol. 1 (Paris: Érasme, 1957), 373–74.

31. Dundes, *Little Red Riding Hood: A Casebook,* 202. For the best bases now available for comparison of the East Asian materials with Perrault's tale, see Günter Lontzen, "The Earliest Version of the Chinese 'Little Red Riding Hood,'" *Merveilles et contes* 7 (1993): 513–15; Huang Chih-Chün, "The Tale of the Tiger-Woman," translated into German from Chinese by Annette Specht and into English by Günter Lontzen and Jacques Barchilon, *Merveilles et contes* 7 (1993): 516–23.

32. Jack Zipes (*The Trials and Tribulations of Little Red Riding Hood: Versions of the Tale in Sociocultural Context* [South Hadley, MA: Bergin and Garvey, 1983], 2) takes similar issue with Dundes's emphasis on the Asian versions of the tale.

33. Dundes, *Little Red Riding Hood: A Casebook,* xi.

34. Marc Soriano, *Les Contes de Perrault: Culture savante et traditions populaires* (Paris: Gallimard, 1968), 148: "Cette fois, aucune hésitation possible: le texte que nous étudions vient en droite ligne de la littérature orale. Il n'a jamais affleuré avant 1697 au niveau de la littérature écrite."

35. Jeanne Morgan, *Perrault's Morals for Moderns,* American University Series II Romance Languages and Literatures 28 (New York: Peter Lang, 1985), 103.

36. See Dundes, *Little Red Riding Hood: A Casebook,* 3; Zipes, *Trials and Tribulations,* 6.

37. Egbert of Liège, *Fecunda ratis* (The Richly Laden Ship), ed. Voigt, 268.

38. BP 1:236, 4:128.

39. Even in French scholarship, the Latin poem did not receive notice between Jacques Berlioz in 1991 and Paul Delarue's "Les contes merveilleux de Perrault et la tradition populaire: I. Le petit chaperon rouge," *Bulletin folklorique d'Île-de-France* 13 (1951): 227. One exception is Bruno Bettelheim's *The Uses of Enchantment: The Meaning and Importance of Fairy Tales* (New York: Vintage, 1989), 168n; Bettelheim first recapitulates the myth of Chronos and the story by Egbert in succession and then offers a summary that assembles the two stories, as if they were unquestionably two parts of a whole.

40. The glosses are not all authorial: see Egbert of Liège, *Fecunda ratis* (The Richly Laden Ship), ed. Voigt, vii–viii.

41. On these three works and the school syllabus, see Günter Glauche, *Schullektüre im Mittelalter: Entstehung und Wandlungen des Lektürekanons bis 1200 nach den Quellen dargestellt,* Münchener Beiträge zur Mediävistik und Renaissance-Forschung 5 (Munich: Arbeo-Gesellschaft, 1970).

42. Elaine Golden Robison, "Egbert of Liège," in *Dictionary of the Middle Ages,* ed. Joseph R. Strayer, 13 vols. (New York: Charles Scribner's Sons, 1982–89), 4:399.

43. The proverbs have received fullest treatment in Samuel Singer, *Sprichwörter des Mittelalters,* 3 vols. (Bern: Herbert Lang, 1944–47), 1:65–142.

44. Sigebert of Gembloux *Catalogus de viris illustribus,* paragraph 147, lines 947–50, ed. Robert Witte, Lateinische Sprache und Literatur des Mittelalters 1 (Bern: Herbert Lang; Frankfurt am Main: Peter Lang, 1974), 93: "metrico stilo de enigmatibus rusticanis." Because *aenigma* is nearly synonymous with *prouerbium* and *parabola,* the title as a whole is roughly equivalent to the later *Li Proverbes au Vilain,* on which, see Eckhard Rattunde, *Li Proverbes au Vilain: Untersuchungen zur romanischen Spruchdichtung des Mittelalters,* Studia Romanica 11 (Heidelberg: Carl Winter, 1966).

45. Egbert of Liège, *Fecunda ratis* (The Richly Laden Ship), ed. Voigt, 1: "In communi enim sermone multi sepe multa loquuntur, et plurimis ad usum necessariis exemplis illa uulgi sententia profertur; quod quidem hausi, mecum id reputans, quod in his plurima uersarentur utilia, et si aliquatenus retineri possent perspicua, quę, quoniam nusquam scripta fuissent, quo magis memori pectore seruarentur, indiligentes propterea facerent auditores. Unde ego, quę comminisci per horas interdiu noctuque potui, singulis ea uersiculis, sepe duobus, interdum tribus, uti in ordine scriptos uidebis, mandans, pręterea nouis atque uulgaribus fabellis aliquot diuinisque paucis interserens, in duobus tantum coaceruaui libellis." The translation in text is mine.

46. Paulus Beudel, *Qua ratione Graeci liberos docuerint, papyris, ostracis, tabulis in Aegypto inventis illustratur* (Monasterii Guestfalorum: E typographia Aschendorffiana,

1911), 34–37, 51–56; August Hausrath, "Das Problem der äsopischen Fabel," *Neue Jahrbücher für das klassische Altertum* 1 (1898): 312–14.

47. Quintilian *Institutio oratoria* 1.9.2–3, ed. M. Winterbottom, Oxford Classical Texts (Oxford: Clarendon, 1970), 1:58, lines 1–9: "Igitur Aesopi fabellas, quae fabulis nutricularum proxime succedunt, narrare sermone puro et nihil se supra modum extollente, deinde eandem gracilitatem stilo exigere condiscant: uersus primo soluere, mox mutatis uerbis interpretari, tum paraphrasi audacius uertere, qua et breuiare quaedam et exornare saluo modo poetae sensu permittitur. Quod opus, etiam consummatis professoribus difficile, qui commode tractauerit cuicumque discendo sufficiet." The translation in text is mine.

48. Egbert of Liège, *Fecunda ratis* (The Richly Laden Ship) 2.472–85, ed. Voigt, 232–33. (For a facsimile of the manuscript, see Lontzen, "Das Gedicht," 23.) I have changed Voigt's punctuation in four places, by replacing a full stop with a semicolon at the end of line 475 and a comma with a full stop at the end of line 476, by deleting a semicolon at the end of line 477, and by adding a comma in line 478. Berlioz changes the comma at the end of line 476 to a semicolon.

49. The translation is mine. In just two of many small differences between our translations, Berlioz translates the title as "The Little Girl Spared by the Wolf Cubs" and line 3 as "Someone held a little girl over the baptismal fonts." My translation concurs in these regards with that of Lontzen in "Das Gedicht," 24 (for discussion, see 29–30).

50. Lontzen ("Das Gedicht," 24–25) construes this line to mean that the girl, after being baptized on the vigil of Pentecost, turned five years old at daybreak of the actual holiday.

51. Lontzen ("Das Gedicht," 21–22, 30) points out pertinently that *mulcere* here means specifically "to caress with the tongue," that is, "to lick," as a fawning dog would do a familiar or beloved face. He cites Virgil *Aeneid* 8.634, where the infinitive is used to describe the actions of the she-wolf toward Romulus and Remus. Other examples can be found in the poetry of Paulinus of Nola, one of them in a description of the behavior of the lions toward the prophet Daniel in their den: see *TLL* 8:1562.35–38.

52. On Egbert's style, see Franz Brunhölzl and F. J. Worstbrock, "Egbert von Lüttich," in *VL²* 2:362; Maurice Hélin, *A History of Medieval Latin Literature,* trans. Jean Chapman Snow, 2nd ed. (New York: William Salloch, 1949), 61–62.

53. See Burke, *Popular Culture,* 281.

54. At the risk of nitpicking, it is worth observing that Egbert does not claim to have heard the story from peasants, pace Wesselski (*Versuch einer Theorie des Märchens,* 20). Rather, Egbert asserts that both he and peasants know the story.

55. Zipes, *Breaking the Magic Spell,* 8.

56. Wolfgang Mieder, "Survival Forms of 'Little Red Riding Hood' in Modern Society," *International Folklore Review* 2 (1982): 36.

57. Dundes, *Little Red Riding Hood: A Casebook,* 208.

58. Michel Foucault, *The History of Sexuality,* trans. Robert Hurley (New York: Pantheon, 1978), 104 (quoted in Zipes, *Trials and Tribulations,* 16; 2nd ed., p. 34); Erich Fromm, *The Forgotten Language: An Introduction to the Understanding of Dreams, Fairy Tales, and Myths* (New York: Rinehart, 1951), 240.

59. Here I have incorporated a quotation from Berlioz's "A Medieval 'Little Red Riding Hood'?" 51.

60. Hans Robert Jauss, *Untersuchungen zur mittelalterlichen Tierdichtung,* Beihefte

zur Zeitschrift für romanische Philologie 100 (Tübingen: Max Niemeyer, 1959), 67: "Das Wunderbare im mittelalterlichen Märchen vom 'Röttkäppchen' ist noch ganz an das Übernatürliche der christlichen Legende gebunden." Compare p. 68: "Die Suche nach der 'einfachen Märchenforme' eines einheimischen 'Tiermärchens' führte zu der christlichen Legende. Inwieweit dieses Ergebnis für die Frage nach dem Wesen des mittelalterlichen Volksmärchens überhaupt kennzeichnend ist, kann hier nicht entschieden werden" [The search for the "simple folktale forms" of an indigenous "beast tale" led to Christian legend. To what extent this outcome is at all indicative for the essence of medieval folktale cannot be determined here].

61. See Susan Ann Keefe, "Baptism," in Strayer, *Dictionary of the Middle Ages,* 2:85.

62. Marianne Rumpf, *Rottkäppchen: Eine vergleichende Märchenuntersuchung,* Artes populares: Studia ethnographica et folkloristica 17 (Frankfurt am Main: Peter Lang, 1989), 46–58.

63. Rumpf, *Rotkäppchen,* 66–67: "Die Geschichte in der Fecunda ratis des Egbert von Lüttich, eine Urform des Rotkäppchen?"

64. Rumpf was followed by Hans Ritz, in *Die Geschichte vom Rotkäppchen: Ursprünge, Analysen, Parodien eines Märchens,* 1st ed. (Emstal: Muriverlag, 1981), 139–40. Ritz's book is now in a revised and expanded twelfth edition (Göttingen: Muriverlag, 1997), in which the passage in Egbert is discussed in greater detail (209–11).

65. Wesselski (*Versuch einer Theorie des Märchens,* 19) points out that in both Egbert's poem and the story of Wolfdietrich, God intervenes to calm the wolves and protect the child. For information on *Wolfdietrich,* see Winder McConnell, "Medieval German Heroic Epic," in *A Companion to Middle High German Literature to the 14th Century,* ed. Francis G. Gentry (Leiden: E. J. Brill, 2002), 200–204. For an edition, see Arthur Amelung and Oskar Jänicke, ed. *Ortnit und Die Wolfdietriche,* 2 vols., Deutsches Heldenbuch 3–4 (Berlin: Weidmann, 1871–73; repr., Zurich: Weidmann, 1968), 2:79–301.

66. A convenient—albeit very dated—account of both Wolfdietrich and Cormac remains Sophus Bugge, *The Home of the Eddic Poems, with Especial Reference to the Helgi-Lays,* trans. William Henry Schofield, 2nd ed. (London: D. Nutt, 1899), 67–96.

67. A locus classicus is the *Vita sancti Albei archiepiscopi de Imlech* [Life of Saint Ailbe, Archbishop of Imlech] 1, in *Vitae sanctorum Hiberniae,* ed. Charles Plummer (Oxford: Clarendon, 1910), 1:46: "Through the inspiration of the Holy Ghost, those servants did not kill the boy, but they placed him under a certain rock and left him there; his name is worshiped there even today. Under that rock a wild she-wolf dwelled, which loved the saintly boy exceedingly, and like a tender mother nurtured him with gentleness among her own whelps. One day, when that wild beast had gone roaming in search of food in the woods, a certain man, named Lochhan, son of Lugir, sighting the boy under that rock among the whelps, pulled him out and carried him home with him. As soon as the wild beast returned and saw that the boy was missing, she followed him swiftly with great exertion. As Lochhan approached his home, the beast held his cloak, and did not release him until she saw the boy. Then Lochhan said to the beast: 'Go in peace; this boy will no longer be among wolves but will remain with me.' Then that beast, crying and howling, returned sadly to its cave." See also *Vita sancti Barri episcopi Corcagie* 1, in Plummer, *Vitae sanctorum Hiberniae,* 1:65.

68. Rumpf, *Rotkäppchen,* 66–67. For an overview of different qualities that have been associated with red from ancient times through the present, see Marianne Oesterreicher-Mollino, *Herder Lexikon Symbole,* 6th ed. (Freiburg: Herder, 1978), 135.

69. Virgil, *Georgics* 3.372, in Vergil, *Opera,* ed. R. A. B. Mynors (Oxford: Claren-don, 1969), 76: "puniceaeue agitant pauidos formidine pennae" [they [do not] hunt beasts frightened by the "scare" of the crimson feather]; *Aeneid* 12.750, in *Opera,* ed. Mynors, 416: "ceruum aut puniceae saeptum formidine pennae" [[as when a hunting dog has caught] a stag hedged about by the "scare" of the crimson feather].

70. See Robert M. Zingg's "Feral Man and Cases of Extreme Isolation of Individ-uals," in J. A. L. Singh and Robert M. Zingg, *Wolf-Children and Feral Man,* Contribu-tions of the University of Denver 4 (New York: Harper, 1942), 177.

71. See Lucien Malson, *Wolf Children* (London: NLB, 1972), 39.

72. Arnold Gesell, *Wolf Child and Human Child: Being a Narrative Interpretation of the Life History of Kamala, the Wolf Girl* (New York: Harper, 1941). Wesselski (*Versuch einer Theorie des Märchens,* 19) mentioned modern wolf children in connection with Eg-bert's poem.

73. See Mariarosaria Pugliarello, *Le origini della favolistica classica* (Brescia: Paideia, 1973).

74. Contrast Lontzen, "Das Gedicht," 28–29.

75. See Ginzburg, *Legends of the Jews,* 4:348, 6:435 nn. 12–13.

76. Xenophon of Ephesus *An Ephesian Tale of Anthia and Habrocomes* 4.6. For a translation, by Graham Anderson, see *Collected Ancient Greek Novels,* ed. B. P. Reardon (Berkeley: University of California Press, 1989), 158.

77. Aulus Gellius *Noctes Atticae* [The Attic Nights] 5.14.5–30, ed. and trans. John C. Rolfe, 3 vols., Loeb Classical Library 195, 200, 212 (Cambridge, MA: Harvard Uni-versity Press, 1927), 1:422–27. Stories that follow this pattern are classed as AT 156, "Thorn Removed from Lion's Paw (Androcles and the Lion)."

78. This last example is provided by Lontzen in "Das Gedicht," 30–31.

79. For references, see Dorothy Ann Bray, *A List of Motifs in the Lives of the Early Irish Saints,* FFC 252 (Helsinki: Suomalainen Tiedeakatemia, Academia scientiarum fennica, 1992), 90, "*Sign of sanctity:* Animal licks feet of saint" and "Monster licks feet of saint."

80. The most famous publication to result from these struggles is Vladimir IAkov-levich Propp's *Morphology of the Folktale,* trans. Laurence Scott, rev. Louis A. Wagner, 2nd ed., Publications of the American Folklore Society, Bibliographical and Special Se-ries 9, Indiana University Research Center in Anthropology, Folklore, and Linguistics 10 (Austin and London: University of Texas Press, 1968).

81. All except for two of the titles, which appear only in the second book, were written by one hand: see Egbert of Liège, *Fecunda ratis* (The Richly Laden Ship), ed. Voigt, vi.

82. This observation was made by Wesselski (*Versuch einer Theorie des Märchens,* 19). The word *cappa* is late Latin: see *TLL* 3:354.23–36. It was employed in Medieval Latin to designate various sorts of clothing, among which were the linen fabrics used to cover infants at baptism: see Otto Prinz et al., eds., *Mittellateinisches Wörterbuch bis zum ausgehenden 13. Jahrhundert* (Munich: C. H. Beck, 1960–), 2:238, lines 35–40.

83. See pseudo-Alcuin *De divinis officiis,* chap. 38, in *PL* 101.1238BC; Albert Blaise, *Le Vocabulaire latin des principaux thèmes liturgiques* (Turnhout: Brepols, 1966), 107.

84. The first to conclude that the tunic was really a hooded cape was Rudolf Koegel, in *Geschichte der deutschen Litteratur bis zum Ausgange des Mittelalters* (Stras-bourg: Karl J. Trübner, 1897), 1/2: 273. The only recent scholar even to mention the pos-sible significance of these lines—albeit with considerable skepticism—has been Ritz

(*Die Geschichte vom Rotkäppchen,* 139–40). Berlioz ("A Medieval 'Little Red Riding Hood'?" 51–52) also determines that "we must reject Koehel's [*sic*] 1897 hypothesis," which he understands to mean that the girl's garment must have been a bonnet. In my interpretation, the garment is indeed a tunic, but one with a hood (pace Berlioz, "A Medieval 'Little Red Riding Hood'?" 52 n. 20).

85. Only later in the Middle Ages did the hood develop strong associations with hypocrisy and adultery: no evidence earlier than the *Roman de la Rose* is identified in Sarah Stanbury Smith's "'Game in myn hood': The Traditions of a Comic Proverb," *Studies in Iconography* 9 (1983): 1–12.

86. Joseph H. Lynch, *Godparents and Kinship in Early Medieval Europe* (Princeton, NJ: Princeton University Press, 1986), 302.

87. Amalar of Metz *Epistula Amalarii ad Carolum imperatorem de scrutinio et baptismo* 45, in *Amalarii episcopi opera liturgica omnia,* ed. Johann Michael Hanssens, vol. 1, Studi e testi 138 (Vatican City: Biblioteca apostolica Vaticana, 1948), 247, lines 9–16: "DE TEGUMENTO CAPITIS. Et hoc de veteri testamento adsumptum est. Sic enim scriptum est in Exodo: *Filios quoque illius,* quin Aaron, *applicabis, et indues tunicis lineis, cingesque balteo, Aaron scilicet et liberos eius, et inpones eis mitras.* Iam percepta gratia sacri baptismatis, non se confidat viribus suis, sed semper deprecetur, ut protectus sit Domini et caelesti auxilio. Protectionem Domini praeclaram volumus intellegere per linteum quo caput tegitur." The translation in text is mine, with quotation of the English of *The Holy Bible: Douay-Rheims Version* (Baltimore, MD: John Murphy, 1899).

88. See Valerie I. J. Flint, *The Rise of Magic in Early Medieval Europe* (Princeton, NJ: Princeton University Press, 1991), 187–88, 190.

89. See Amalar of Metz *Epistula de scrutinio et baptismo* 44, ed. Hanssens, 247.

90. See Soriano, *Les Contes de Perrault,* 13.

91. See Linda Dégh, "Grimm's 'Household Tales' and the Place in the Household: The Social Relevance of a Controversial Classic," *Western Folklore* 38 (1979): 102; Mieder, "Survival Forms of 'Little Red Riding Hood,'" 35.

92. See Paul Saintyves [Émile Nourry], *Les contes de Perrault et les récits parallèles* (Paris: Émile Nourry, 1923), 215–29. For references to other solar explanations, see Zipes, *Trials and Tribulations,* 59 n. 1.

93. For concise exposition of such interpretations, see Diederichs, *Who's who im Märchen,* 279.

94. Zipes, *Trials and Tribulations,* 1.

95. Delarue, "Les contes merveilleux de Perrault," 251: "Tel le taureau qui fonce sur la cape rouge que lui présente le toréador et s'acharne sur une enveloppe vide, les folkloristes se sont précipités sur cette coiffure rouge que leur offrait la version de Perrault."

96. Paul Delarue, "The Story of Grandmother," in Dundes, *Little Red Riding Hood: A Casebook,* 18. Delarue's view has been accepted almost universally by folklorists (and others): see Dundes, *Little Red Riding Hood: A Casebook,* 14; Soriano, *Les Contes de Perrault,* 160, 178; Yvonne Verdier, "Little Red Riding Hood in Oral Tradition," *Marvels and Tales: Journal of Fairy-Tale Studies* 11 (1997): 101–23, originally published as "Le Petit Chaperon rouge dans la tradition orale," *Le Débat* 3 (1980): 36; Zipes, *Trials and Tribulations,* 6.

97. Zipes, *Trials and Tribulations,* 9.

98. Guðbrandr Vigfusson and C. R. Unger, eds., *Flateyjarbók: En samling af norske konge-sagaer med inskudte mindre fortællinger,* 3 vols. (Christiania: P. T. Malling, 1860–68),

1:288–99; Edwin Gardiner, ed., *Fornar smásögur úr Noregskonunga sögum* (Reykjavik: Leiftur, 1949), 50–64; Ólafur Halldórsson, ed., *Ólafs saga Tryggvasonar en mesta,* Editiones Arnamagnæanæ, ser. A (Copenhagen: Munksgaard, 1958), 1:313–33, 349–51. On this short story, see Joseph Harris, "Folktale and Thattr: The Case of *Rognvald and Raud,*" *Folklore Forum* 13 (1980): 158–98. Harris generously made available to me a typescript translation of "The Tale of Rognvald and Raud."

99. This point was made by Harris, "Folktale and Thattr," 171: "The abandoned child is often identified by his rescuer as royal through S334 Tokens of royalty (nobility) left with exposed child."

100. *Lay Le Freine* 143–44, in *Middle English Verse Romances,* ed. Donald B. Sands (New York: Holt, Rinehart, and Winston, 1966), 238: "whoso hir founde schuld have in mende / That it [the child] were comen of riche kende." Although this lay shares a few features with "Little Red Riding Hood," it differs in at least two major ways: Freine acquires her name not from the cloth but from the ash tree in which she was found, and Freine is christened not before but only after her abandonment. The Middle English poem is based on Marie de France's *Fresne,* the only *lai* in her collection to take its title from the name of the heroine: see *Fresne* 121–34, in *Les lais de Marie de France,* ed. Jean Rychner, Classiques Français du Moyen Age 93 (Paris: Honoré Champion, 1973), 48. The motif was borrowed from Marie by Renaut or Jean Renart for *Galeran de Bretagne,* ed. Lucien Foulet, Classiques Français du Moyen Age 37 (Paris: Honoré Champion, 1925).

101. Delarue, "Les contes merveilleux de Perrault," 227: "S'il est aussi question d'une fillette et d'un loup dans cette histoire, qui est présentée comme le récit d'un événement réel qu'auraient rapporté des paysans, il est difficile d'y voir une version ou la forme première de notre conte. Sans doute, la robe de la fillette est-elle rouge, comme la coiffure de l'héroïne dans la version de Perrault. Mais le 'chaperon rouge' n'est qu'un trait accessoire, particulier à cette version, non un trait général du conte."

102. Rumpf, *Rotkäppchen,* 67: "Es erscheint mir gewagt, nur aus der Tatsache, daß in der einen Geschichte aus dem 12. Jahrhundert [*sic*] eine rote Tunica als Patengeschenk an ein kleines Mädchen eine Rolle spielt, auf Zusammenhänge mit dem Rotkäppchenmärchen zur schließen."

103. Wesselski, *Versuch einer Theorie des Märchens,* 20: "In den Märchen ist also von der Geschichte—Zwischenglieder haben ja wohl bestanden—außer dem Wolf nichts übrig geblieben als die Erinnerung an die rote Cappa, der eine Zug, der weder in der Geschichte noch in den Märchen eine motivische Bedeutung hat, gleichwohl aber die Namen Chaperon rouge und Rotkäppchen rechfertigt."

104. Verdier, "Little Red Riding Hood in Oral Tradition," 103; see also Rumpf, *Rotkäppchen,* 67: "Woher Perrault den Namen Rotkäppchen hat, konnte bisher nicht festgestellt werden" [Where Perrault got the name Little Red Riding Hood has not been determined until now].

105. See Verdier, "Little Red Riding Hood in Oral Tradition," 102–3. The motif of the pins and needles is examined by Bernadette Bricout in "Les deux chemins du Petit Chaperon Rouge," in *Frontières du conte,* ed. François Marotin (Paris: Editions du Centre national de la recherche scientifique, 1982), 47–54.

106. See Kiefer, *Recent Folktale Theories,* 53–55. It would be worthwhile to investigate how overtly the insistence on stability was expressed as an attempt to put folktale studies on a footing with other "sciences"—to enable the establishment of folktale stemmatas comparable to textual stemmata in philology.

107. See Dan Ben-Amos, "Transmission," in *Folklore* 2:807–11.

108. Quoted in Kiefer, *Recent Folktale Theories,* 15.

109. Wesselski, *Versuch einer Theorie des Märchens,* 153–57.

110. Dundes, *Little Red Riding Hood: A Casebook,* 193.

111. See Joachim Knuf, *Unsere Welt der Farben. Symbole zwischen Natur und Kultur* (Cologne: Dumont, 1988), 48–83 (especially 81–83, "Das Warnsignal am Anfang aller Kultur"). In *Warum die Liebe rot ist: Farbsymbolik im Wandel der Jahrtausende* (Düsseldorf and Vienna: Econ, 1981), 79 ("Das Problem der sexuellen Drohung"), Rudolf Gross notes, "So sind die 'Neidfleckerln,' die überall dort angewendet werden, wo man um Mensch und Tier bangt, rot: auf den Kleidern der Kinder, am Brautwagen, am Pferdegeschirr" [So the "envy spots," which are employed everywhere where one is anxious about man and animal, are red—on children's clothes, on the bridal carriage, on horses' harnesses].

112. Johann Wolfgang von Goethe, *Die Wahlverwandtschaften* (Tübingen: Cotta, 1809), part 2, chap. 2.

113. Bolte and Polívka (BP 1:234) declare that the conclusion of "Rotkäppchen" derives from AT 123; Dundes (*Little Red Riding Hood: A Casebook,* 202–3) assumes that "AT 123 and AT 333 are probably cognates, possibly subtypes of the same general tale type"; and Zipes (*Trials and Tribulations,* 15) states that "the Grimms borrowed a motif from the folk tale *The Wolf and the Seven Kids.*"

114. For two exemplary studies of such lost literature, see R. M. Wilson, *The Lost Literature of Medieval England,* 2nd ed. (London: Methuen, 1970); Alan Deyermond, *La literatura perdida de la Edad Media castellana,* vol. 1 (Salamanca: Ediciones Universidad de Salamanca, 1995).

115. It warrants mention that Egbert does not necessarily imply the girl to have been five when she was baptized (pace Lontzen in "Das Gedicht," 28). On the contrary, the presence of the past participle *facta* seems to suggest that an indeterminate length of time has passed between the baptism and the (mis)adventure with the wolf—and any length of time more than a few hours would have to be years. Complicating an evaluation of the participle is the circumstance that the words "facta puellae" (*puellae,* not the nominative *puella*) appear twice as a line ending in Ovid, at *Ars amatoria* 2.187, ed. E. J. Kenney, Oxford Classical Texts (Oxford: Clarendon, 1961), 149, and at *Remedia amoris* 299, ed. Kenney, 216. Although a specific allusion to Ovid would be out of keeping with Egbert's general style, it could be argued that he intended to draw a contrast between his altogether presexual little heroine and the more active women of Ovidian love poetry. It is likelier that the occurrence of this pairing in Ovid encouraged Egbert to use it as a sort of metrical formula, with the *facta* being almost a nonce word.

116. On the white chrismal robe of the newly baptized, see Rabanus Maurus *De clericorum institutione* 1.29, in *PL* 107.313C; Edward C. Whitaker, trans., *Documents of the Baptismal Liturgy,* rev. Maxwell E. Johnson, 3rd ed., Alcuin Club Collections 79 (London: SPCK, 2003), 261 (*Missale Gothicum*), 273 (*Bobbio Missal*), 282 (*Stowe Missal*), 301 *Sarum Rite;* Lynch, *Godparents and Kinship,* 103, 109, 293, 302, 304.

117. On the restriction of baptism to Easter and Pentecost, see John D. C. Fisher, *Christian Initiation: Baptism in the Medieval West; A Study in the Disintegration of the Primitive Rite of Initiation,* Alcuin Club Collections 47 (London: SPCK, 1965), 52, 58; Lynch, *Godparents and Kinship,* 295–96.

118. On the representation of the tongues in medieval art, see H. Zwetsloot, "De

Iconographie van Pinksteren," *Het Gildeboek* 34 (1952): 37–39; "De Iconographie van Pinksteren (II): Het uitgangspunt der stralen of tongen," *Het Gildeboek* 34 (1952): 68–73.

119. Raymond Deloy Jameson, "Whitsunday," in *F&W* 1175.

120. See St. Germanus of Paris, *The Second Letter,* in Whitaker, *Baptismal Liturgy,* 263–65.

121. See Pope Innocent III [Lothar of Segni] *Mysteriorum evangelicae legis et sacramenti eucharistiae libri sex* 1.65, "De quatuor coloribus principalibus, quibus secundum proprietatibus dierum vestes sunt distinguendae," in *PL* 217.799–802, especially 801AB; William Durandus *Rationale divinorum officiorum* 3.18.4, ed. Stefano Della Torre and Massimo Marinelli, trans. Gian Franco Freguglia, Monumenta studia instrumenta liturgica 14 (Vatican City: Libreria Editrice Vaticana, 2001), 258–59; Heide Nixdorff and Heidi Müller, *Weisse Westen, rote Roben: Von den Farbordnungen des Mittelalters zum individuellen Farbgeschmack* (Berlin: Staatliche Museen Preussischer Kulturbesitz, Museum für Völkerkunde und Museum für Deutsche Volkskunde, 1983), 45–53 ("Liturgische Farben," especially 45–46).

122. Contrast Lontzen, "Das Gedicht," 28.

123. Paul Delarue's version of a French oral version is available conveniently in English translation in Dundes, *Little Red Riding Hood: A Casebook,* 15–16. From the introductory information, it is easier to determine when and where Delarue printed the French than who is supposed to have recounted it when.

124. Soriano, *Les Contes de Perrault,* 442.

125. Fisher (*Christian Initiation*) explains that after baptism, a presbyter anointed the candidates' heads with chrism (17); that in the early history of baptism, the unction was not seen to be related to the giving of the Holy Spirit (18–19); but that later it was believed to convey the gift of the Holy Spirit (38, 45, 53–54, 56, 63–65).

126. Guillaume de Lorris, *Le Roman de la Rose* 2149–52, ed. Félix Lecoy, vol. 1, Les Classiques Français du Moyen Age 92 (Paris: Honoré Champion, 1970), 66–67; *Romance of the Rose,* trans. Charles Dahlberg (Princeton, NJ: Princeton University Press, 1971), 60: "A chaplet of flowers that costs little, or of roses at Pentecost—everyone can have these, since great wealth is not required for them."

127. Charles Perrault, *Perrault's Complete Fairy Tales,* trans. A. E. Johnson et al. (New York: Dodd, Mead, 1961), 71.

128. *KHM* 1:156–60, at 156 (7th ed.) (my translation).

129. See Lynch, *Godparents and Kinship,* 285–86, 305–32.

130. See Lynch, *Godparents and Kinship,* 51.

131. See Michel Pastoureau, *Couleurs, images, symboles: Etudes d'histoire et d'anthropologie* (Paris: Le Léopard d'Or, 1989), 20, 22 ("L'héritage antique: blanc, rouge, noir").

132. See Nixdorff and Müller, *Weisse Westen, rote Roben,* 137–40 ("Rosa und Hellblau in der Säuglingskleidung"). Lontzen, who makes a number of fine philological observations about words in Egbert's poem, seems to me to offer an extremely strained interpretation of the word *rubicundo* ("Das Gedicht," 36–41), by the end of which he claims that the adjective here refers to cheap, undyed wool.

133. See Lontzen, "Das Gedicht," 25.

134. See Lynch, *Godparents and Kinship,* 49.

135. Here I extend an observation made concerning proverbs in Gaston Paris, review of *Egberts von Lüttich Fecunda Ratis,* ed. Ernst Voigt, *Journal des savants,* 1890, 562 n. 1.

136. Bettelheim, *Uses of Enchantment,* 166–83.

137. See Rumpf, *Rotkäppchen*, 99–103 (on the meaning of the tale as a *Warnerzählung*). On the rise of such stories for children, see Gottfried Henssen, "Deutsche Schreckmärchen und ihre europäischen Anverwandten," *Zeitschrift für Volkskunde* 51 (1953): 84–97; Marianne Rumpf, "Ursprung und Entstehung von Warn- und Schreckmärchen," FFC 160 (1955): 3–16.

138. See Soriano, *Les Contes de Perrault*, 340.

139. See Soriano, *Les Contes de Perrault*, 150.

140. Charles Perrault, "Le Petit Chaperon rouge," trans. Maria Tatar, in Tatar, *Annotated Classic Fairy Tales*, 373.

141. Zipes (*Trials and Tribulations*, 1) argues, "But whatever her reputations and destiny, she has always been used as a warning to children, particularly girls, a symbol and embodiment of what might happen if they are disobedient and careless."

142. See Soriano, *Les Contes de Perrault*, 151. For an attempt to establish a typology of forest symbolism in medieval literature, see Paolo Golinelli, "Tra realtà e metafora: Il bosco nell'immaginario letterario medievale," in *Il bosco nel Medioevo*, ed. Bruno Andreolli and Massimo Montanari, Biblioteca di Storia Agraria Medievale 4 (Bologna: Clueb, 1988), 97–123. The notion of the woods as a magic realm in which miracles occur seems more relevant to the Grimms' version than to either Egbert's or Perrault's: see Hedwig von Beit, *Symbolik des Märchens: Versuch einer Deutung*, 2nd ed., 3 vols. (Bern: Francke Verlag, 1952–57), 1:46–47.

143. See Barry Holstun Lopez, *Of Wolves and Men* (New York: Scribner, 1978), 209–10.

144. Max Lüthi (*Once upon a Time: On the Nature of Fairy Tales*, trans. Lee Chadeayne and Paul Gottwald [Bloomington: Indiana University Press, 1976], 63) classifies Little Red Riding Hood as "one of a group of children's fairy tales, so called because children are the principal characters in them," and he adds: "A child has a natural right to be protected and cared for. It is said of Little Red Riding Hood that everyone who saw her liked her, and that grandmother 'simply couldn't think of anything else she might give the child'" ("simply couldn't think . . ." is a quotation from the Grimms' "Little Red Cap" story).

145. *TLL* 8:1691.10–12, "mus II. translate. A. de hominibus. 2. pro blandimento," cites Martial 11.29.3; *Novum Glossarium* "M" 990, lines 26–29, "1. mus. B) terme d'affection," provides two citations—both from Egbert. Although Lontzen ("Das Gedicht," 35) does not make reference to either of these dictionaries, he was the first to make this point about the usage of the Latin noun and to draw a parallel to the affectionate use in German of the expression "mein Mäuschen."

146. The poem is conveniently available with the Greek text and facing English translation in *Hesiod, The Homeric Hymns and Homerica*, ed. and trans. Hugh G. Evelyn-White, Loeb Classical Library 57 (Cambridge, MA: Harvard University Press, 1977), 542–63; Athena's speech is at lines 177–96 (pp. 554–55).

147. Callimachus *Victoria Berenices, Aetia III*, proemium, 259.9–33, ed. Peter J. Parsons and Hugh Lloyd-Jones, in *Supplementum Hellenisticum*, ed. Hugh Lloyd-Jones, Peter J. Parsons, H.-G. Nesselrath, and J. U. Powell, Texte und Kommentare 11 (Berlin and New York: Walter de Gruyter, 1983), 100–117. In my interpretation of the scene, I have been guided by Patricia A. Rosenmeyer's "The Unexpected Guests: Patterns of *Xenia* in Callimachus' 'Victoria Berenices' and Petronius' *Satyricon*," *Classical Quarterly* 41 (1991): 403–13, especially 410–11.

148. The theme of God's mercy to helpless females is sustained in *De lamentis uidue̜*, the seven-line selection with which Egbert follows this one in his *Puppis* (*Fecunda ratis* [Richly Laden Ship] 2.486–92, ed. Voigt, 233).

149. For a tabulation of the settings used in different versions of the Little Red Riding Hood tale, see Rumpf, *Rotkäppchen*, 59–60.

150. Von Sydow ("Folktale Studies," 233) points out the dangers of this hypothesis.

151. See Verdier, "Little Red Riding Hood in Oral Tradition," 105–8.

152. Kiefer, *Recent Folktale Theories*, 75.

153. See Kiefer, *Recent Folktale Theories*, 59: here I coincide with Krohn's statements in his review of Wesselski.

154. Quoted in Kiefer, *Recent Folktale Theories*, 62.

155. Von Sydow, "Folktale Studies," 241.

156. It is important not to fall into the trap of believing that similarities between two written versions, especially when one had as limited a textual transmission as is the case with Egbert's poem, indicate that there had to have been a direct source-and-influence connection between the two. Two recent interpretations that connect the eleventh-century poem with the eighteenth-century legend "The Beast of Gévaudan" ("La Bête de Gévaudan") contain many observations about Egbert's poem with which I concur, but the assertion that "someone (a clergyman? a publisher?) knew Egbert de Liège's story, appropriated it for himself, and distributed it while reconstructing it" strikes me as highly improbable. See Catherine Velay-Vallantin, "Little Red Riding Hood as Fairy Tale, *Fait-divers*, and Children's Literature: The Invention of a Traditional Heritage," in Canepa, *Out of the Woods*, 319. Contrast Catherine Velay-Vallantin, "From 'Little Red Riding Hood' to the 'Beast of Gévaudan': The Tale in the Long Term Continuum," in *Telling Tales: Medieval Narratives and the Folk Tradition*, ed. Francesca Canadé Sautman, Diana Conchado, and Giuseppe Carlo Di Scipio (New York: St. Martin's, 1998), 277, where the argument is made that the eighteenth-century accounts "attest to the circulation and exploitation of an oral narrative close to the eleventh-century one."

157. See Rumpf, *Rotkäppchen*, 67.

158. Ancient discussions of poetry had a commonplace that poets lied. This view was repeated often in the Middle Ages, but at the same time many Medieval Latin poets claimed that their compositions were unvarnished truth. See Ludwig Gompf, "Figmenta poetarum," in *Literatur und Sprache im europäischen Mittelalter: Festschrift für Karl Langosch zum 70. Geburtstag*, ed. Alf Önnerfors, Johannes Rathofer, and Fritz Wagner (Darmstadt: Wissenschaftliche Buchgesellschaft, 1973), 53–62.

CHAPTER FOUR

1. Thompson, *The Folktale*, 165.

2. For two of the more recently printed English translations, see Hans Christian Andersen, *Eighty Fairy Tales*, trans. R. P. Keigwin (New York: Pantheon, 1982), 17–26; *Fairy Tales: A Selection*, trans. L. W. Kingsland (Oxford: Oxford University Press, 1984), 11–27.

3. See Friedrich von der Leyen, "Märchen und Spielmannsdichtung," *Germanisch-romanische Monatsschrift* 10 (1922): 129.

4. R. Desmed, review of *Het lied van boer eenos*, by Andries Welkenhuysen, *Scrip-*

torium 32 (1978): 138: "Un des chefs-d'oeuvre de la littérature populaire, en latin, du moyen âge."

5. On the dating in the third quarter of the eleventh century, see Andries Welkenhuysen, *Het lied van boer eenos (uersus de uniboue): Kluchtig versverhaal uit de elfde eeuw (inleiding, facsimile-weergave, teksteditie, metrische vertaling, bijlage ter verantwoording en duiding)* 2 vols. [text volume and "Bijlage" with commentary] (Louvain: Acco, 1975), viii; on the dating in the first half of the century, see Thomas Klein, "'Versus de Uniboue': Neuedition mit kritischem Kommentar," *Studi medievali*, 3rd ser., 32 (1991): 843–86; on the dating in the final quarter of the century, see Benedikt Konrad Vollmann, "Unibos," in *VL*² 10:82.

6. See Welkenhuysen, *Het lied van boer eenos*, bijlage, 7.

7. For the editio princeps, see Jacob Grimm and Johann Andreas Schmeller, *Lateinische Gedichte des X. und XI. Jahrhunderts* (Göttingen: Dieterische Buchhandlung, 1838; repr., Amsterdam: Rodopi, 1967), 354–80, with notes on 380–83. In citations of the Latin, I follow the most recent edition, Bertini and Mosetti Casaretto's *La Beffa di Unibos*. But I also pay close attention to the preceding two editions by Welkenhuysen and Klein. The edition and translation by Karl Langosch (*Waltharius-Ruodlieb-Märchenepen*, 251–305), which are well known among German scholars and are often the most readily accessible form of the text, follow the text of Paul van de Woestijne, *De Klucht van boer Eenos naar een latijnsch gedicht uit de 11e eeuw: Versus de Unibove* (Antwerp: N. V. Standaard-Boekhandel, 1944). The English translations are my own, although I have consulted the version offered by Marc Wolterbeek in *Comic Tales of the Middle Ages: An Anthology and Commentary*, Contributions to the Study of World Literature 39 (New York: Greenwood, 1991). Both Welkenhuysen (especially in his very full commentary) and Wolterbeek (in several pages of close examination) represent indispensable contributions to *One-Ox* scholarship.

8. For examples, see *One-Ox* 1.1, "Rebús conspectis saeculi"; 5.2, "bovés emit pauper homo."

9. Welkenhuysen, *Het lied van boer eenos*, IX, and commentary volume 20.

10. On his knowledge of the Bible, see Gabriella La Placa, "I Versus de Unibove, un poema dell'XI secolo tra letteratura e folklore," *Sandalion* 8–9 (1985–86): 285–306. On his knowledge of Bible commentaries, see David A. Wells, "Die biblischen Wörter im 'Unibos': Ein Beitrag zum Verständnis des Antiklerikalismus im Frühmittelalter," in *Kleinere Erzählformen im Mittelalter: Paderborner Colloquium 1987*, ed. Klaus Grubmüller, L. Peter Johnson, and Hans-Hugo Steinhoff (Paderborn: Schöningh, 1988), 83–88.

11. Welkenhuysen, *Het lied van boer eenos*, text volume, XI–XII thought of a monk.

12. On slightly later images of the priest, see Daron Burrows, *The Stereotype of the Priest in the Old French "Fabliaux": Anticlerical Satire and Lay Identity* (Frankfurt am Main: Peter Lang, 2005).

13. Josef Müller, *Das Märchen vom Unibos*, Deutsche Arbeite der Universität Köln 7 (Jena: Eugen Diederichs Verlag, 1934), 101: "Jedes Märchen muß von der Forschung als Ganzes betrachtet und analytische Methode mit synthetischer Betrachtung verbunden werden, um zu einem befriedigenden Ergebnis zu gelangen."

14. Ferruccio Bertini examines strophes 2–3 for generic information: see "Il contadino medievale, ovvero il profilo del diavolo (Una nuova interpretazione dei *Versus de unibove*)," *Maia* 47 (1995): 325–41, at 331, reprinted in *Interpreti medievali di Fedro*, Nuovo Medioevo 57 (Naples: Liguori, 1998), 111–28. Following Gustav Ehrismann

(*Geschichte der deutschen Literatur bis zum Ausgang des Mittelalters,* 2nd ed., 2 vols. in 4 [Munich: C. H. Beck, 1932], part 1 [1932], 374) and Joachim Suchomski (*"Delectatio" und "Utilitas": Ein Beitrag zum Verständnis mittelalterlicher komischer Literatur* [Bern: Francke Verlag, 1975], 108), Bertini views these strophes as dramatic representation that foresees musical accompaniment.

15. Propp, *La fiaba russa,* 368.

16. K. C. Peeters, "De oudste West-Europese sprookjetekst: Unibos-problemen," *Volkskunde* 71 (1970): 8–24.

17. See Desmed, review of *Het lied van boer eenos,* 138, on popular literature; E. Schröder, "Zum Text des Unibos," *Zeitschrift für deutsches Altertum und deutsche Literatur* 68 (1931): 152, on "die älteste der mittelalterlichen Märchenquellen."

18. Wesselski, *Versuch einer Theorie des Märchens,* 187: "The comic tale [*Schwank*] about *One-Ox,* to which *KHM* 61 in the final literary instance goes back, we will even less call a fairy tale [*Märchen*]. Like the comic tale [*Schwank*] of the 'Snow Child,' which is told for us first in 'Modus Liebinc,' both are *Märlein,* which apply motifs connected with folly [*Wahnmotive*] only so as to mock them."

19. For the main studies of the European variants, see BP 2:1–18; Müller, *Das Märchen vom Unibos;* Maurits de Meyer, *Vlaamsche sprookjesthema's in het licht der Romaansche en Germaansche Kultuurstroomingen,* Koninklijke Vlaamsche Academie voor Taal- en Letterkunde, 6th ser., 63 (Leuven: De Vlaamsche Drukkerij, 1942); Toshio Ozawa, "Das Märchen von Unibos," *Doitsu Bungaku* 46 (1971): 35–43 (in Japanese, with German summary on 43).

20. Friedrich von der Leyen ("Zur Entstehung des Märchens," *Archiv für das Studium der neueren Sprachen und Literaturen* 116 [1906]: 288) responded to Benfey by saying that *One-Ox* had been part of Western literature in part for millennia. Emmanuel Cosquin (*Contes populaires de Lorraine,* 2 vols. [Paris: F. Vieweg, 1886; repr., Marseille: Lafitte, 1978], 1:108–9) sees the origin of this story as lying in India.

21. Thompson, *The Folktale,* 165.

22. See Müller, *Das Märchen vom Unibos,* 100.

23. Uther, *ATU,* 2:267–69.

24. See Peeters, "Unibos-problemen," 20.

25. See de Meyer, *Vlaamsche sprookjesthema's,* 163; La Placa, "I Versus de Unibove," 289 n. 14.

26. See Peeters, "Unibos-problemen," 22.

27. Thompson, *The Folktale,* 167.

28. Thompson, *The Folktale,* 166.

29. See de Meyer, *Vlaamsche sprookjesthema's,* 141.

30. Peeters ("Unibos-problemen," 24) points out the shortcomings of the geographic-historic method in analyzing this tale.

31. Müller, *Das Märchen vom Unibos,* 119. A more precise application of the geographical method appears in de Meyer, *Vlaamsche sprookjesthema's,* 133–63. For the most influential applications of the method to *Unibos,* see AT, pp. 440–41 (no. 1535), and Thompson, *The Folktale,* 165–70.

32. Karl Langosch ("Unibos," in *VL*¹ 4:634, 5:1103) divides the poem into four parts. Ehrismann (*Geschichte der deutschen Literatur,* part 1, 374) divides it into five. My division fuses their two schemata, in that it presents the fourth section as comprising two

subsections. I group them under a single heading, since otherwise the fourth section would be exceptional in not showing the peasant getting the better of his usual three opponents.

33. The instrument is a horn rather than a flute, pace Müller (*Das Märchen vom Unibos,* 75) and in agreement with Bertini ("Contadino," 334). In classical Latin, both *bucina* and *tuba* refer to forms of trumpet: see *Oxford Latin Dictionary,* s.vv. *bucina* ("a curved trumpet or horn"), *tuba* ("a trumpet with a straight tube"). On the trumpet in folktales, see *MI* K113, E55.3; "Trumpet," in *F&W* 1126–29.

34. See Lutz Röhrich, *Das große Lexikon der sprichwörtlichen Redensarten,* 2nd ed., 3 vols. (Freiburg, Basel, and Vienna: Herder, 1990–92), 1:530.

35. A fascinating enumeration of parallels to this episode is provided in Victor Chauvin's *Bibliographie des ouvrages arabes ou relatifs aux arabes publiés dans l'Europe chrétienne de 1810 à 1885,* 12 vols. (Liège: H. Vaillant-Carmanne, 1892–1922), 5:247 n. 1.

36. Paul Radin (*The Trickster: A Study in American Indian Mythology* [New York: Schocken, 1972], xxiii) writes: "Trickster is at one and the same time creator and destroyer, giver and negator, he who dupes others and who is always duped himself. He wills nothing consciously. At all times he is constrained to behave as he does from impulses over which he has no control. He knows neither good nor evil yet he is responsible for both. He possesses no values, moral or social, is at the mercy of his passions and appetites, yet through his actions all values come into being."

37. See Francesco Mosetti Casaretto, "Il tempo curvo del contadino: Per una lettura qohèletica dei 'Versus de unibove,'" *Studia monastica* 42 (2000): 73, on *One-Ox* 75.2, 77.2, 79.2, 85.1, 172.2.

38. For an English translation of the anonymous life of Aesop, see Lloyd W. Daly, *Aesop without Morals: The Famous Fables and a Life of Aesop* (New York and London: Thomas Yoseloff, 1961), 29–90. For editions of the works of the remaining three authors mentioned in text, see Douin de Lavesne, *Trubert, fabliau du XIIIe siècle,* ed. Guy Raynaud de Lage, Textes littéraires français 210 (Geneva: Droz, 1974); Der Stricker, *Pfaffe Amis,* ed. K. Kamihara, 2nd ed., Göppinger Arbeiten zur Germanistik 233 (Göppingen: Kümmerle Verlag, 1990); Giulio Cesare Croce, *Le astuzie di Bertoldo e le semplicità di Bertoldino,* ed. Piero Camporesi (Milan: Garzanti, 1993). *Trubert* was first mentioned in connection with *One-Ox* by Jürgen Beyer (*Schwank und Moral,* 75). Beyer (73–79) evaluates in detail the similarities and differences between *One-Ox* and vernacular genres of later times, such as fabliaux and novellas. For a comparison between Der Stricker's work and *One-Ox,* see Volker Honemann, "Unibos und Amis," in *Kleinere Erzählformen im Mittelalter: Paderborner Colloquium 1987,* ed. Klaus Grubmüller, L. Peter Johnson, and Hans-Hugo Steinhoff (Paderborn: Schöningh, 1988), 67–82. On One-Ox and Eulenspiegel, see Müller, *Das Märchen vom Unibos,* 123–24. On links between Bertoldo, Marcolf, Unibos, and Campriano, see Ernesto Lamma, ed., *El dyalogo di Salomon e Marcolpho* (Bologna: Gaetano Romagnoli, 1885), XLVI–XLVII. For a comparison between Aesop and Marcolf, see Jan M. Ziolkowski, "The Deeds and Words of Aesop and Marcolf," in *Scripturus vitam Lateinische Biographie von der Antike bis in die Gegenwart: Festsgabe für Walter Berschin zum 65. Geburtstag,* ed. Dorothea Walz (Heidelberg: Mattes Verlag, 2002), 105–23. On the roles that such tales played in the early modern period, see Burke, *Popular Culture,* 156, 218.

39. See Langosch, "Unibos," 634 ("Schwanknovelle").

40. See Radin, *Trickster,* 152.

41. Mikhail Mikhailovich Bakhtin, *Rabelais and His World,* trans. Hélène Iswolsky (Cambridge, MA: MIT Press, 1968; repr., Bloomington: Indiana University Press, 1985).

42. See Freedman, "Sainteté et sauvagerie."

43. See Léopold Genicot and P. Tombeur, eds., *Index Scriptorum operumque latino-belgicorum medii aevi: Nouveau répertoire des oeuvres médiolatines belges,* part 2, *XIe siècle,* ed. P. Fransen and H. Maraite (Brussels: Académie royale de Belgique, 1976), 22–23.

44. De Meyer (*Vlaamsche sprookjesthema's,* 161), admitting that *One-Ox* shared motifs with fabliaux, discounted the importance on the grounds that the motifs either developed independently or appeared in a different connection.

45. See Beyer, *Schwank und Moral,* 75.

46. See La Placa, "I Versus de Unibove," 287 n. 8.

47. Per Nykrog, *Les Fabliaux,* 2nd ed., Publications romanes et françaises 123 (Geneva: Droz, 1973).

48. *Carmina Cantabrigiensia* 14, in *Cambridge Songs,* ed. and trans. Ziolkowski, 62–69. See app. 2C in the present study.

49. See Röhrich, *Das große Lexikon,* 3:1707–8.

50. Burke, *Popular Culture,* 28.

51. See Honemann, "Unibos und Amis," 72–73.

52. The *prepositus* or *aeconomus* corresponds to the German *Vogt* or *Probst* or to the French *prévôt,* the *ville maior* to *Meier* or *Dorfschulze.* See B. Schmeidler, "Ein bisher nicht verwertetes Zeugnis zur Verfassungs- und Wirtschaftsgeschichte des 11. Jahrhunderts," *Historische Vierteljahrschrift* 20 (1920–21): 129–38; Arno Borst, *Lebensformen im Mittelalter* (Frankfurt am Main: Ullstein, 1979), 98–99; Karl-S. Kramer, "Bauer," in *EM* 1:1327–38.

53. This subsuming of individuals by their work is emphasized at the beginning and end of Jill Mann's *Chaucer and Medieval Estates Satires: The Literature of Social Classes and the "General Prologue" to the "Canterbury Tales"* (Cambridge: Cambridge University Press, 1973), xi, 202.

54. See Müller, *Das Märchen vom Unibos,* 121, on Montel.

55. The sixty-seven-minute film *Der kleine und der große Klaus* (Little Claus and Great Claus) was produced by Fernsehen der DDR and directed by Celino Bleiweiß. It was first broadcast on television on 25 December 1971. For further details, see Eberhard Berger and Joachim Giera, *77 Märchenfilme: Ein Filmführer für jung und alt* (Berlin: Henschel Verlag, 1990), 65–68.

56. In *Religious Poverty and the Profit Economy in Medieval Europe* (Ithaca: Cornell University Press, 1978), Lester K. Little makes no mention of *One-Ox,* but his book is very useful in providing a backdrop to our text. The first scholar to glean information about economic history from *One-Ox* was Schmeidler ("Ein bisher nicht verwertetes Zeugnis," 129–38).

57. See Apo, *Narrative World,* 222–24.

58. Sigmund Freud and D. E. Oppenheim, *Dreams in Folklore,* trans. A. M. O. Richards, ed. James Strachey (New York: International Universities Press, 1958), 36 (English translation), 69–111 (German text).

59. Freud and Oppenheim, *Dreams in Folklore,* 37.

60. See Röhrich, *Das große Lexikon,* 1:528–30, "Geld" (especially 529, figs. 2–3, "Geld scheißen").

61. See Little, *Religious Poverty.*

62. On greed and lust in the story, see Suchomski, *"Delectatio" und "Utilitas,"* 109.

63. See Suchomski, *"Delectatio" und "Utilitas,"* 109.

64. The connection has been handled with great insightfulness and delicacy by Nykrog (*Les Fabliaux,* 5, 9–10, 100–103, 248–52).

65. "Sed Unibos periculum [213] / Dicens designat pessimum: / 'Vbi litus est altius, / Vbi mare profundius, / Illuc festini currite, [214] / Sine metu uos mergite! / Maiores porci sunt aquis, / Quam sint in terris aridis.' / Vnibouis consiliis [215] / Tres dant se precipitiis / Sub capitali frenesi / Per saltum stulte mortui. / Inimici consilia [216] / Non sunt credenda subdola: / Ostendit ista fabula / Per seculorum secula."

66. See Honemann, "Unibos und Amis," 80, 82.

67. See Vollmann, "Unibos," 83.

68. Sese Honemann, "Unibos und Amis," 79.

69. See Mosetti Casaretto, "Il tempo curvo," 71–74; Honemann, "Unibos und Amis," 78–79.

70. See Honemann, "Unibos und Amis," 74.

71. Contrast the interpretation advanced by Bertini and Mosetti Casaretto in their edition of the poem.

72. C. Stephen Jaeger, *The Origins of Courtliness: Civilizing Trends and the Formation of Courtly Ideals, 939–1210* (Philadelphia: University of Pennsylvania Press, 1985).

73. Gerald A. Bond, *The Loving Subject: Desire, Eloquence, and Power in Romanesque France* (Philadelphia: University of Pennsylvania Press, 1995).

74. Nykrog, *Les Fabliaux,* 264.

75. The poet's education shows in his use of biblical words, such as *corbanan* and *musac,* as well as in his knowledge of Greek and other exotic words, such as *amphibalus* and *squibula.* Further information about his social class may be forthcoming in the scorn he manifests for the "shabby shoemakers" [sordidi sutores] (53.1). For the idea that the poet had to have been a cleric or clerically educated, see Langosch, "Unibos," 636.

76. Bertini ("Contadino," 331) pays close attention to the generic code words in strophes 2–3.

77. See Suchomski, *"Delectatio" und "Utilitas,"* 107.

78. See Langosch, "Unibos," 636, followed by La Placa, "I Versus de Unibove," 290.

79. The standard edition (with a facing German translation) of the *Cena Cypriani* is now Christine Modesto's *Studien zur "Cena Cypriani" und zu deren Rezeption,* Classica Monacensia 3 (Tübingen: Gunter Narr Verlag, 1992), 14–35. On the *Cena Cypriani* and its various later reworkings, see Martha Bayless, *Parody in the Middle Ages: The Latin Tradition* (Ann Arbor: University of Michigan Press, 1996), 19–56. The standard edition of the *Ecbasis* is Karl Strecker's *Ecbasis cuiusdam captivi per tropologiam,* MGH Scriptores rerum Germanicarum in usum scholarum separatim editi 69 (Hanover: Impensis Bibliopolii Hahniani, 1935). For information and analysis, see Jan M. Ziolkowski, *Talking Animals: Medieval Latin Beast Poetry* (Philadelphia: University of Pennsylvania Press, 1993), 153–97.

80. Schröder ("Zum Text des Unibos," 152) was probably the first to point out in regard to 3.3–4 "die stark mimische Vortragsart derartiger Schwänke" [the strongly mimetic delivery style of such farces].

81. See Langosch, "Unibos," 638.

82. See F. Lecoy, "La Farce de *Cauteleux, Barat et le Vilain*," in *Mélanges de langue et de littérature du moyen âge et de la Renaissance offerts à Jean Frappier*, vol. 2, Publications romanes et françaises 112 (Geneva: Droz, 1970), 598.

83. Wesselski, *Versuch einer Theorie des Märchens*, 187.

84. Leyen ("Märchen und Spielmannsdichtung," 131–32) avers that the main theme of *One-Ox* and other texts is the mocking of belief in miracles: "Die Verhöhnung des Wunderglaubens ist auch die leitende Idee der anderen aus dem 10. Jahrhundert überlieferten Spielmannsmärchen" [The mockery of belief in miracles is also the main idea of other minstrel tales handed down from the tenth century].

85. See La Placa, "I Versus de Unibove," 294.

86. Wesselski (*Versuch einer Theorie des Märchens*, 90) wrote, "Der Unterschied zwischen der Sage, die sich auf Wahnmotive stützt, und dem Märchen, das einen reinen Wunderglauben heischt, ist also für das Kind . . . nicht vorhanden" [The difference between the legend, which is based on motifs of delusion, and the folktale, which demands sheer belief in marvel, is then not present for a child].

87. See Müller, *Das Märchen vom Unibos*, 103–4.

88. See Müller, *Das Märchen vom Unibos*, 93.

89. Müller (*Das Märchen vom Unibos*, 102–4) believes that the mockery of belief in wonder comes from late antiquity.

90. See La Placa, "I Versus de Unibove," 293–94.

91. See Müller, *Das Märchen vom Unibos*, 54; Aarne, "Die Zaubergaben," *Journal de la société finno-ougrienne* 27 (1909): 1–96, at 33–96.

92. Thompson (*The Folktale*, 166) observes: "The next cheat, the unsuccessful imitation, we have met before in stories of magic or the miraculous. Here, however, there is no magic, but only a pretense of it."

93. See Müller, *Das Märchen vom Unibos*, 68, 71, 117.

94. Honemann ("Unibos und Amis," 79) notes, "Was der Autor des 'Unibos' uns vor Augen führt, ist eine Welt, die sich vor dem Normen- and Wertehorizont des Publikums als eine verkehrte abhebt" [What the author of *One-Ox* brings before our eyes is a world, which stands out as being a mistaken one against the audience's horizon of norms and values].

95. See Franz Brunhölzl, *Histoire de la littérature latine du moyen âge*, trans. Henri Rochais, 2 vols. (vol. 2 in 2 parts) (Turnhout: Brepols, 1991–2000), 2: 265.

96. For texts, see Suchier, *Das mittellateinische Gespräch Adrian*.

97. See Benedicta Ward, *Miracles*, 3.

98. See Benedicta Ward, *Miracles*, 4–5.

99. See Benedicta Ward, *Miracles*, 4, 201, 205–7.

100. See Benedicta Ward, *Miracles*, 211–13.

101. Guibert of Nogent *Monodiae* 3.8, ed. Edmond-René Labande, Les Classiques de l'histoire de France au Moyen Age 34 (Paris: Belles Lettres, 1981), translated by Paul J. Archambault as *A Monk's Confession: The Memoirs of Guibert of Nogent* (University Park: Pennsylvania State University Press, 1996), 156.

102. See Ziolkowski, *Talking Animals*, 208–10.

103. Nivardus, *Ysengrimus*, ed and tran. Jill Mann, Mittellateinische Studien und Texte 12 (Leiden: E. J. Brill, 1987).

104. On the controversy over a newly illustrated reprinting of *Little Black Sambo*,

see Louise Kennedy, "New Storybook Reopens Old Wounds," *Boston Globe,* 14 December 2003.

105. Burke (*Popular Culture,* 149) writes: "What were the fundamental attitudes and values of the craftsmen and peasants of early modern Europe? . . . The approach adopted in this chapter depends on the assumption that a culture's heroes, villains and fools form a system, that they reveal the standards of that culture by surpassing them, threatening them and falling short of them respectively."

106. The story to which I allude is "Brer Rabbit and the Tar Baby," which can be found in Joel Chandler Harris, *The Tar-Baby and Other Rhymes of Uncle Remus* (New York: D. Appleton, 1904), 1–16.

107. The translation is my own, following the Latin text in *Salomon et Marcolfus,* ed. Walter Benary, Sammlung mittellateinischer Texte 8 (Heidelberg: Carl Winter, 1914), 3–4. The comparison between One-Ox and Marcolf was first suggested by Honemann ("Unibos und Amis," 79).

108. Holbek, "Hans Christian Andersen's Use," 231.

109. Thompson, *The Folktale,* 165.

110. The term *degn* could alternatively be translated "parish-clerk" or "parson," but its ultimate descent from the Latin *diaconus* is obvious.

111. Contrast Karin Pulmer, "Vom Märchenglück zum Bürgeridyll: Zu H. C. Andersens Volksmärchenbearbeitungen," *Skandinavistik: Zeitschrift für Sprache, Literatur und Kultur der nordischen Länder* 10 (1980): 110, who sees Andersen as having retained the morality of folktales without much change.

112. See Holbek, "Hans Christian Andersen's Use," 220, 224; Pulmer, "Vom Märchenglück zum Bürgeridyll," 105. Pulmer counted three of four tales in the first collection as coming from folktales and saw the character of the tales as changing after Andersen specified that they were for children ("for Børn"). The label "fortalte for Børn" (told for children) formed part of the title of the first six booklets of fairy tales that Andersen published between 1835 and 1842, in two collections of three booklets each: *Eventyr, fortalte for Børn,* 6 parts in 2 vols (Copenhagen: C. A. Reitzel, 1835–42).

113. Hans Christian Andersen, *The Complete Fairy Tales and Stories,* trans. Erik Christian Haugaard (New York: Doubleday, 1974), 1069–70.

114. See Holbek, "Hans Christian Andersen's Use," 220–32. Holbek (224) notes that "The Princess and the Pea" was also possibly taken from oral tradition.

115. See Else Marie Kofod, *De vilde svaner og andre folkeeventyr: Sidestykker til syv af H. C. Andersens eventyr,* Foreningen Danmarks Folkeminders Skrifter 86 (Copenhagen: Foreningen Danmarks Folkeminder, 1989), which deals passim, especially at 42–45, with "Lille Claus og Store Claus."

116. See Ingvild Alnæs, "H. C. Andersen og folkeeventyrene," *Anderseniana,* 3rd ser., 2 (1974–77): 97–119, especially 113–14.

117. Alnæs ("H. C. Andersen og folkeeventyrene," 97, 119) counts seven, while Georg Christensen ("H. C. Andersen og de danske folkeeventyr," *Danske studier* [1906]: 103) put the number at six.

118. See *EM* 1:1330; BP 2:1–18, 4:130.

119. See Borst, *Lebensformen im Mittelalter,* 99.

120. Johann Gustav Gottlieb Büsching, "Kibitz," in *Volks-Sagen, Märchen und Legenden* (Leipzig: C. H. Reclam, 1812; repr., Hildesheim: Olms, 1969; 2nd printing, Leipzig:

C. H. Reclam, 1820), 296. Other versions with the name Kibitz or one like it are listed in BP 2:5–6. The most readily accessible oral version along these lines is "The Peasant Pewit" in Kurt Ranke's edited volume *Folktales of Germany*, trans. Lotte Baumann (Chicago: University of Chicago Press, 1966), 134–36, no. 51.

121. For folkloristic studies of the written versions, see BP 2:1–18; Müller, *Das Märchen vom Unibos;* de Meyer, *Vlaamsche sprookjesthema's*, 133–63; Peeters, "Unibos-problemen," 14–15. For lists of materials from the medieval and early modern periods, see Clausen-Stolzenburg, *Märchen,* 81 n. 173; Walter Keller and Lisa Rüdiger, trans., *Italienische Märchen* (Düsseldorf and Cologne: Eugen Diederichs Verlag, 1959), 379–80 n. 10.

122. Müller (*Das Märchen vom Unibos,* 33–35) credits the story of Campriano to one Pallantrini.

123. See Carlo Lapucci, ed., *Fiabe toscane* (Milan: Arnoldo Mondadori, 1984), 132–33. A Sicilian specimen of the story is translated in Thomas Frederick Crane, *Italian Popular Tales,* ed. Jack Zipes (Santa Barbara, CA: ABC-CLIO, 2001), 244–47, with many parallels listed at 305 n. 22.

124. See Lapucci, *Fiabe toscane,* 132.

125. For the Italian text, see Gianfrancesco Straparola, *Le piacevoli notti,* ed. Donato Pirovano (Rome: Salerno Editrice, 2000).

126. Giovanni Crocioni, *Le tradizioni popolari nella letteratura italiana,* ed. Giuseppe Anceschi (Florence: Leo S. Olschki, 1970), 171: "primo consapevole cultore del genere fiabesco in Italia." See also Giancarlo Mazzacurati, *All'ombra di Dioneo: Tipologie e percorsi della novella da Boccaccio a Bandello,* ed. Matteo Palumbo, Biblioteca di cultura 211, Serie Teoria e analisi dei testi letterari 2 (Scandicci [Florence]: La Nuova Italia, 1996), 151–89.

127. Müller (*Das Märchen vom Unibos,* 35) contends incorrectly that the story of Campriano also is lacking this motif.

128. The retelling by Jakob Ayrer (end of the sixteenth century)—"Der Beck, der sein Weib wider lebendig geiget hat," in *Ayrers Dramen,* ed. Adelbert von Keller, Bibliothek des litterarischen Vereins in Stuttgart 79 (1865): 2809–28—is completely dependent on Schumann's tale no. 5. The eighteenth-century Ruckard (1736) gives an almost verbatim recounting of Schumann's tale no. 6. Jokosus (Erfurt, 1794) contains the anecdote "Rutschki oder die Bürger zu Quarkenquatsch," which likewise depends on tale no. 6. For information on these tales, see Müller, *Das Märchen vom Unibos,* 36–38.

129. BP 2:9.

130. Valentin Schumann, *Nachtbüchlein,* ed. Johannes Bolte, Bibliothek des Literarischen Vereins in Stuttgart 197 (Tübingen: Literarischer Verein in Stuttgart, 1893), 28.

131. See the summary in BP 2:9.

132. See Müller, *Das Märchen vom Unibos,* 36–37.

133. Giovanni Sercambi, *Novelle,* ed. Giovanni Sinicropi, 2 vols., Filologia: Testi e studi 5 (Florence: Casa Editrice Le Lettere, 1995), 1:195–210.

134. Both these questions were raised by de Meyer, *Vlaamsche sprookjesthema's,* 149–50.

135. See Flemming Hovmann, "Kommentar," in H. C. Andersen, *Eventyr,* ed. Erik Dal, Erling Nielsen, Flemming Hovmann, 7 vols. (Copenhagen: C. A. Reitzels Forlag, 1963–90), 7:23.

136. The illustrations used most commonly are those of Vilhelm Pedersen, which

depict Little Claus after Great Claus has felled his horse, Little Claus showing the farmer the inside of the chest, and Little Claus after pushing the sack containing Great Claus into the river. These illustrations are found conveniently in Andersen's *Eighty Fairy Tales,* 17, 21, 26. For a helpful assemblage of other illustrations—depicting Little Claus boasting of his horses, Little Claus dining with the farmer, Little Claus showing the farmer the inside of the chest, Little Claus watching as the innkeeper hurls the glass of beer at the grandmother, Great Claus with Little Claus in the sack, and the whole series of sackings—see Heinz Wegehaupt, *Hundert Illustrationen aus anderthalb Jahrhunderten zu Märchen von Hans Christian Andersen* (Hanau: Verlag Dausien, 1990), 74, 77, 79, 83, 87, 89. For illustrations of Little Claus in his glory with all the horses, Little Claus showing the farmer the inside of the chest, and Great Claus as he decides to enter the sack so that Little Claus can toss him into the river, see Hans Christian Andersen, *Ausgewählte Märchen,* translated into German by Julius Reuscher (Leipzig: Ambr. Abel, 1883), 24, 28, 36.

137. See Müller, *Das Märchen vom Unibos,* 87.

138. On the parish priest in medieval literature, see Burrows, *The Stereotype of the Priest.* Compare Apo, *Narrative World,* 215.

139. Desmed (review of *Het lied van boer eenos,* 138) compares *One-Ox* aptly with fabliaux, *boerden,* and *kluchten.*

140. Tegethoff, *Märchen, Schwänke und Fabeln,* XIV: "die zäheste und langlebigste von allen Gattungen der Volksdichtung."

141. Tegethoff, *Märchen, Schwänke und Fabeln,* XIV: "Es ist verblüffend, wie vieles in der vorliegenden Sammlung fast wörtlich mit Stücken aus modernen Sammlungen übereinstimmt, ohne daß an eine Einwirkung der Literatur zu denken wäre."

142. Ozawa, "Das Märchen von Unibos," 43.

143. See Müller, *Das Märchen vom Unibos,* 91–92, 95.

CHAPTER FIVE

1. Wesselski, *Versuch einer Theorie des Märchens,* 93: "Oder kann die mittellateinische Erzählung des Raparius in irgendeinem Stadium der Verästelung ein Märchen werden, als das das wir das Märlein von der Rübe nach dem Wunsche der Brüder Grimm ansprechen sollten?"

2. See Ingrid Koszinowski and Vera Leuschner, *Ludwig Emil Grimm: Zeichnungen und Gemälde,* 2 vols., Quellen zur Brüder Grimm-Forschung 3, nos. 1–2 (Marburg: Dr. Wolfram Hitzeroth Verlag, 1990), 2:94, figs. L 23 (Gothic sculpture on a console under a baldachin in the cathedral at Regensburg), L 25 (Gothic figure on the cathedral at Bamberg).

3. For a quick and helpful guide to the place of the Brothers Grimm in medieval studies, see Maria Dobozy, "The Brothers Grimm: Jacob Ludwig Carl (1785–1863); Wilhelm Carl (1786–1859)," in *Medieval Scholarship: Biographical Studies on the Formation of a Discipline,* ed. Helen Damico and Joseph B. Zavadil, vol. 2, Garland Reference Library of the Humanities 2071 (New York: Garland, 1998), 93–108.

4. Jacob Grimm, *Über den altdeutschen Meistergesang* (Göttingen: Dieterich, 1811); Wilhelm Grimm, *Altdänische Heldenlieder, Balladen und Märchen* (Heidelberg: Mohr und Zimmer, 1811), translated as *Old Danish Ballads* (London: Hope, 1856).

5. For a depiction of the scene, see the oil painting on wood (1864) by Ernest

Meissonier (1815–91) in the Musée d'Orsay in Paris, reproduced in Meinrad Maria Grewenig, *Napoleon: Feldherr, Kaiser, Mensch* (Ostfildern-Ruit: Hatje, 1998), 49.

6. For a depiction of Napoleon at Fontainebleau a few days before abdicating, see the oil on canvas (1845) by Paul Delaroche (1797–1856) in the Museum der bildenden Künste in Leipzig, reproduced in Grewenig, *Napoleon,* 51.

7. Although the legend is certainly wrong, the actual authorship of this nineteenth-century palindrome remains unknown. No further details on the origin or early transmission of the palindrome are provided in the entry in Michael Donner's *S. Wordrow's Palindrome Encyclopedia: I Love Me,* vol. 1 (Chapel Hill: Algonquin, 1996), 8. O. V. Michaelsen (*Words at Play: Quips, Quirks, and Oddities* [New York: Sterling, 1997], 124) attributes the first appearance in print to Charles Bombaugh in *Gleanings from the Harvest Fields of Literature, Science, and Art,* 3rd ed. (Baltimore: T. N. Kurtz, 1867).

8. See Rainer Rosenberg, *Literaturwissenschaftliche Germanistik: Zur Geschichte ihrer Probleme und Begriffe* (Berlin: Akademie Verlag, 1989), 202–11; Rainer Rosenberg, *Zehn Kapitel zur Geschichte der Germanistik: Literaturgeschichtsschreibung* (Berlin: Akademie Verlag, 1981), 41–51; Ulrich Wyss, *Die wilde Philologie: Jacob Grimm und der Historismus* (Munich: C. H. Beck, 1979).

9. Koszinowski and Leuschner, *Ludwig Emil Grimm,* 2:273, fig. K 31.

10. Koszinowski and Leuschner, *Ludwig Emil Grimm,* 1:54 and 60, figs. P 84 and P 96.

11. Hermann Grimm and Gustav Hinrichs, eds., *Briefwechsel zwischen Jacob und Wilhelm Grimm aus der Jugendzeit,* rev. Wilhelm Schoof, 2nd ed. (Weimar: Hermann Böhlaus Nachfolger, 1963), 338–42. Subsequent parenthetic references in text will be to this edition.

12. When he believes he has been treated rudely by a librarian in Metz, he comments, "I experienced this discourtesy from a Frenchman" [diese Unhöflichkeit weiß ich mir an einem Franzosen] (338). On the coach from Nancy to Strasbourg, he is unhappy with his fellow travelers: "Nothing but common Frenchmen, incessantly ready for talking politics in their manner and for rude statements against Germans . . . This is the heart and soul of many, countless cafés and inns in all France" [lauter gemeine Franzosen, unaufhörlich bereit zu politisieren nach ihrer Art und zu Grobheiten gegen Deutsche . . . Dies ist die Seele aller unzähligen Cafés und Gasthäuser in ganz Frankreich] (339).

13. It is revealing to compare Jacob Grimm's perspective upon arriving in Strasbourg with that of Johann Wolfgang von Goethe, who, upon arriving there as a twenty-one-year-old in 1772, wrote his essay "On German Architecture" ("Von deutscher Baukunst," published in 1773 in Herder's *Von deutscher Art und Kunst*), to praise the German splendor of the Gothic cathedral.

14. "Überhaupt nach allem, was ich sehe und höre, scheint mir der Elsaß und das Volk darin von tüchtigem, kerngutem deutschem Schlag, der sich hier der langen Zeit ungeachtet kräftiger und eigentümlicher erhalten hat, als in Ländern wie Baden, Württemberg etc., d. h. ihrem engeren eigentlichen Bestandteil nach, ohne Rücksicht auf das Bessere, was sie zu sich gerissen haben. Ich fühle bei diesem allem deutlich, daß in Deutschland die uralten in Sprache, Sitte und anderem noch jetzt nicht erloschenen Abteilungen in Schwaben, Bayern, Franken, Sachsen, Hessen, Thüringen usw. wiederhergestellt werden sollten. Alles andere ist schlechter, und es hängt viel weniger daran, und man irrt, wenn man verkennt, wieviel gutes Jetziges an jenem Alten hängt. In

dieser guten Sache stehen beschränkte und schlechte Ansichten der preußischen wie der österreichischen Staatsmänner am meisten im Weg, und schwerlich ist sie jetzt durchzusetzen, vor allem aber nicht aufzugeben" (341).

15. This oft-quoted phrase is today the major—and maybe the sole—claim to fame of the African grammarian Terentianus Maurus (late second or early third century CE). (The Terentianean meter, named after him, is a topic of discussion only among Latin metrologists, not a numerous group.) The wording appears in one of his three didactic poems, *De syllabis* 1286, in *Grammatici latini*, ed. Heinrich Keil (Leipzig: B. G. Teubner, 1874; repr., Hildesheim and New York: Georg Olms Verlag, 1981), 6:363.

16. On the destruction of the library, see Alfred Marchand, *Le siège de Strasbourg, 1870: La Bibliothèque, la Cathédrale* (Paris: Librairie de J. Cherbuliez, 1871).

17. Jacob Grimm and Wilhelm Grimm, *Kinder- und Hausmärchen gesammelt durch die Brüder Grimm,* 7th ed., vol. 3 (Göttingen: Verlag der Dieterich'schen Buchhandlung, 1857), 229. The Grimms' volume of notes was reproduced, with additional notes, in the three-volume reedition by Heinz Rölleke, *Kinder- und Hausmärchen: Ausgabe letzter Hand mit den Originalanmerkungen der Brüder Grimm* (Stuttgart: Philipp Reclam, 1980), with the old pagination retained but with new numbering also added: "Schon der äußern Form nach ein altes Märchen, es ist nämlich übersetzt aus einem lateinischen Gedicht des Mittelalters und zwar nach der in Straßburg vorhandenen Papierhandschrift (MS. Johann. C. 102 aus dem 15. Jahrhundert), worin es 392 Zeilen in elegischem Versmaß enthält und Raparius überschrieben ist . . . ohne Zweifel nach mündlicher Volkssage" (241).

18. Grimm and Grimm, *Kinder- und Hausmärchen,* 7th ed., 3:230–31 (ed. Rölleke, 242–43). The extract corresponds to lines 313–46 in the most recent edition of the Latin text (with Italian translation) by Paolo Gatti, *Rapularius II,* in *Commedie latine del XII e XIII secolo,* vol. 6, Pubblicazioni del D.Ar.Fi.Cl.Et., n.s., 176 (Genoa: Dipartimento di Archeologia, Filologia classica e loro Tradizioni, 1998), 364–69. For information on lines that may or may not have been included in the Strasbourg manuscript, see the note to the composite edition of the three versions in BP 3:170–87. Jacob Grimm's transcription is found in Berlin, Preussische Staatsbibliothek, MS Germ. quart. 923, which covers lines 1–94, 97–98, and 291–388 in the edition by Gatti (who identifies the lost Strasbourg manuscript as having had the shelfmark "Johann C. 105"). For a very cursory listing of MS Germ. quart. 923, see Hermann Degering, *Kurzes Verzeichnis der germanischen Handschriften der Preussischen Staatsbibliothek,* vol. 2, *Die Handschriften in Quartformat* (Leipzig: Hiersemann, 1926; repr., Graz: Akademische Druck- und Verlaganstalt, 1970), 158.

19. Johann Caspar Goethe, *Rationum sumptuarium, sive rerum oeconomicarum fere omnium liber,* ed. Helmut Holtzhauer and Irmgard Möller, 2 vols. (Leipzig: Edition Leipzig, 1973).

20. Jacob Grimm, *Circular wegen Aufsammlung der Volkspoesie, Wien 1815: Facsimile,* ed. Ludwig Denecke (Kassel: Brüder Grimm-Museum, 1968), 3 (first side of the circular): "Es ist vor allem daran gelegen, daß diese Gegenstände getreu und wahr, ohne Schminke und Zuthat, aus dem Munde der Erzählenden, wo thunlich in und mit deren selbsteigenen Worten, auf das genaueste und umständlichste aufgefaßt werden."

21. In the past quarter century, the most outspoken criticism of the brothers was voiced by Ellis in *One Fairy Story Too Many.*

22. On the manuscript that the brothers sent to Brentano, see Kamenetsky, *The Brothers Grimm and Their Critics,* 39–41.

23. For the text, see Heinz Rölleke, ed., *Die älteste Märchensammlung der Brüder Grimm: Synopse der handschriftlichen Urfassung von 1810 und der Erstdrucke von 1812,* Texte: Bibliotheca Bodmeriana 1 (Cologny-Geneva: Fondation Martin Bodmer, 1975).

24. Ellis, *One Fairy Story Too Many,* 70.

25. Alan Dundes, "Nationalistic Inferiority Complexes and the Fabrication of Fakelore: A Reconsideration of Ossian, the *Kinder- und Hausmärchen,* the *Kalevala,* and Paul Bunyan," *Journal of Folklore Research* 22 (1985): 9.

26. The most extensive comparison to date has been that in Hermann Hamann's *Die literarischen Vorlagen der Kinder- und Hausmärchen und ihre Bearbeitung durch die Brüder Grimm,* Palaestra: Untersuchungen und Texte aus der deutschen und englischen Philologie 47 (Berlin: Mayer und Müller, 1906), 48–51.

27. See BP 4:448.

28. On the genre of the Latin texts (with reference to fabliau and *Märe*), see Stephen L. Wailes, "Fortuna and Social Anomaly: Principles of Mediaeval Humour in *Rapularius* and *Asinarius,*" *Seminar* 9 (1973): 88.

29. Thus comparison also helps to show just how versatile the tale could be, taking one form when elaborated by an author versed in the medieval verbal arts and in the genres of satire, *comedia,* and fabliau, another form when directed toward the middle class in nineteenth-century Germany.

30. In the manuscript Jacob consulted, the poem was entitled *Raparius.* Nowadays, it is conventionally entitled *Rapularius,* a form that is attested in manuscripts of both main versions and used as the poem's title by Hugo of Trimberg. For essential facts on the title and its possible interpretations, see Gatti, *Rapularius I,* 16 n. 10, 37. The word *rapularius* could denote a person who deals with turnips (e.g., a grower or seller of turnips)—but it could also be a substantive to designate a "turnip [book]" (*rapularius [liber]*). The Grimms entitled their version of the tale "The Turnip" tout court. If *Rapularius* signified the protagonist, this shift in title would move the reader's focus from the person to the object. Such a shift would be appropriate for a wonder tale, with its indeterminate setting and wonderful objects.

31. For the proposal to label one version *frivola* and the other *prodiga,* credit is due to Bernhard Bischoff, as reported by Gatti in *Rapularius II,* 324–25.

32. See Gatti, *Rapularius II,* 322 n. 10.

33. See Karl Langosch, ed., *Asinarius und Rapularius,* Sammlung mittellateinischer Texte 10 (Heidelberg: Carl Winter, 1929), VI.

34. Gatti, *Rapularius I,* 20–23.

35. See Birgit Gansweidt, "Rapularius," in *LdM* 7:445; F. J. Worstbrock, "Rapularius," in *VL²* 7:1000.

36. See Karl Langosch, *Asinarius und Rapularius,* VI; "Rapularius," in *VL¹* 5:929.

37. Gatti avers that the two versions are by the same author: see Paolo Gatti, "Elementi favolistici nell'*Asinarius* e nel *Rapularius,*" in *La Favolistica latina in distici elegiaci: Atti del convegno internazionale, Assisi, 26–28 ottobre 1990,* ed. Giuseppe Catanzaro and Francesco Santucci, Centro studi poesia latina in distici elegiaci 2 (Assisi: Accademia Properziana del Subasio, 1991), 157; *Rapularius I,* 21.

38. Compare Latham and Howlett, *Dictionary of Medieval Latin,* fascicule 4:1003, *frater* 4–10; J. F. Niermeyer and C. van de Kieft, *Mediae Latinitatis Lexicon Minus,* rev. J. W. J. Burgers, 2nd ed., 2 vols. ([Darmstadt]: Wissenschaftliche Buchgesellschaft, 2002), 1:592, *frater* 1–2.

39. Hugo of Trimberg *Registrum multorum auctorum* 716–19, in *Das "Registrum multorum auctorum" des Hugo von Trimberg: Untersuchungen und kommentierte Textausgabe,* ed. Karl Langosch, Germanische Studien 235 (Berlin: Verlag Dr. Emil Ebering, 1942), 191: "There are so many other works, not to be belittled, / which are read quite often in the schools and are choice" [Sunt quam plures alii libelli nec despecti, / Qui leguntur sepius in scolis et sunt lecti: / Pirrus, Asinarius Milesque Ruralis, / Simul Rapularius, Femidolus, Jocalis]. These lines were quoted previously by Langosch in *Asinarius und Rapularius,* iv; by Gatti in *Rapularius I,* 16; and by Wailes in "Fortuna and Social Anomaly," 96.

40. In "Fortuna and Social Anomaly," Wailes, expanding an earlier observation that both *The Turnip Tale* and *The Donkey Tale* "appeal to a sense of social dignity" and were "apparently written for courtly audiences" (87), comments rightly: "The humanism of courtly society around 1200 owed much to secular clerics, whose education and tastes have not yet received appropriate attention in the study of courtly literature. It would be mistaken to say that *The Turnip Tale* and *The Donkey Tale,* because they are Latin, were unknown to the early authors and audiences of humorous narrative in French and German, for we now believe that this narrative developed in cultivated society" (96).

41. Gatti, *Rapularius II,* 6.332.

42. Gatti, *Rapularius I,* 5.20.

43. Gatti, *Rapularius II,* 6.325.

44. See Gatti, *Rapularius I,* 14–16.

45. Gatti, *Rapularius I,* 16: "Non mi sentirei a questo punto di sollevare dubbi sull'appartenenza anche del *Rapularius* a questo genere di componimenti."

46. Gatti, *Rapularius I,* 5.36.

47. Gatti, *Rapularius I,* 5.37.

48. Although the similarity in phraseology is interesting, it is difficult to wrest additional clarity from Prudentius *Psychomachia* 231 ("nimirum vacuae credentur frivola famae"), in *Prudentius,* ed. and trans. H. J. Thomson, 2 vols., Loeb Classical Library 387 and 398 (Cambridge, MA: Harvard University Press, 1949–53), 1:294–95.

49. Langosch ("Rapularius," 928–29) believes that the Medieval Latin poet was the one who joined the two stories. Worstbrock ("Rapularius," 1001) leaves open the possibility that the two stories had been fused already in the medieval poet's unknown source.

50. *The Turnip Tale* "*frivola*" [1] 15–22, ed. and trans. Gatti, *Rapularius I,* 38: "Rapula crevit ei reliquis enormior una, / Que dici pleno nomine rapa potest, / Tam dilatata foliis, tam corpore grandis, / Ut nemo penitus viderit ante parem. / Ipsius umbra viris duodenis sufficiebat, / Ne sub ea solis ureret estus eos. / Tam fuit enormis, ut carrum sola repleret / Vixque boves traherent quatuor illud honus." The translation in text is my own: see app. 4A in the present study.

51. Pliny the Elder *Naturalis historia* 18.34.128, ed. and trans. Rackham, Jones, and Eichholz, 5:270–71: "nebula et pruinis ac frigore ultro aluntur, amplitudine mirabili: vidi XL libras excedentia."

52. *It's the Great Pumpkin, Charlie Brown,* directed by Bill Melendez, was an animation released in 1966.

53. For example, for full bibliography on nineteenth-century champion turnips from Oregon and Washington, see Kathy Mendelson, "Giant Vegetables: Weigh-Off Winners from Way Back When," *Pacific Northwest Garden History,* http://www.halcyon.com/tmend/giants.htm (accessed 13 August 2005).

54. For the German proverb, see Grimm and Grimm, *Kinder- und Hausmärchen,* 7th ed., 3:229 (ed. Rölleke, 241); Johann Fischart, *Das Philosophisch Eezuchtbüchlin,* in *Johann Fischarts Werke: Eine Auswahl,* ed. Adolf Hauffen, vol. 3, Deutsche National-Litteratur 18, no. 3 (Stuttgart: Union Deutsche Verlagsgesellschaft, 1894), 123 ("Ruben gen Straßburg"). For the English proverbs (both of which are attested in English from the sixteenth century at the latest), see Paul Harvey, *The Oxford Dictionary of English Proverbs,* 2nd ed. (Oxford: Clarendon, 1952), 80, 482.

55. Quoted in BP 3:187: "Bei Straßburg hab ich gsehn / Ein ruben auf dem felde stehn, / Die ist gewachsen also groß, / Daß ich mit einem schnellen ros / In treien summertagen lang / Nicht hab können tun ein umbgang."

56. Also quoted in BP 3:187, following the Grimms.

57. For these examples, see BP 3:188.

58. Dan Greenburg, *Elvis the Turnip . . . and Me,* illustrated by Jack E. Davis, Zack Files 14 (New York: Grosset and Dunlop, 1998).

59. In *MI* Z49.9, Stith Thompson lists a Lithuanian and a Russian source.

60. Christiane Knauf and Fredrik Vahle, *Die Rübe: Kinderliederarbeitsheft (ab 6 J.),* Kleine Rote Reihe 18 (Dortmund: Weltkreis-Verlags-GmbH, 1974), table of contents and 62–66.

61. On AT 1960 in this context, see Propp, *La fiaba russa,* 339. For the distinction between cumulative stories and chain tales, see the entries on them in *F&W* 207–8, 269.

62. See Kathy Parkinson, *The Enormous Turnip* (Morton Grove, IL: Albert Whitman, 1986), for a retelling with an unwittingly peculiar positioning of the old man beneath the turnip. For other versions, see Debby Slier, *The Enormous Turnip,* illustrated by Thomas Sperling, Domino Readers (New York: Star Bright, 1998); Aleksei Tolstoy, *The Great Big Enormous Turnip,* illustrated by Helen Oxenbury (New York: Franklin Watts, 1968); Aleksei Tolstoy, *The Gigantic Turnip,* illustrated by Niamh Sharkey (New York: Barefoot, 1999); Janina Domanska, *The Turnip* (New York: MacMillan, 1969); Harriet Ziefert, *The Turnip,* illustrated by Laura Rader (New York: Puffin, 1996).

63. See BP 3:187; Pirkko-Liisa Rausmaa, "Größe: Die ungewöhnliche G.," in *EM* 6:239–49, especially 243–44.

64. See Hans-Walter Nörtersheuser, "Arm und reich," in *EM* 1:789–94.

65. Regrettably, this tale is not among those treated in the early study of gifts in folktale and legend by Max Lüthi, *Die Gabe im Märchen und in der Sage: Ein Beitrag zur Wesenerfassung und Wesensscheidung der beiden Formen* (Bern: Buchdruckerei Büchler, 1943). For an overview of the most common roles of gifts in folktale and especially wonder tales, see Werner Wunderlich, "Gabe," in *EM* 5:625–37, especially 630–32.

66. References to the Latin text ("Convivium fabulosum" 184–217) follow *Opera Omnia Desiderii Erasmi Roterodami,* 1st ser., vol. 3, *Colloquia,* ed. L.-E. Halkin, F. Bierlaire, and R. Hoven (Amsterdam: North-Holland, 1972), 438–49, at 443–44; references to the English translation follow "The Fabulous Feast," in *Collected Works of Erasmus,* vol. 39, *Colloquies,* translated and annotated by Craig R. Thompson (Toronto: University of Toronto Press, 1997), 579, line 7–580, line 7 (with introduction on 571–72).

67. The contents of their library as it has been reconstructed today can be found in an annotated list in Ludwig Denecke and Irmgard Teitge's *Die Bibliothek der Brüder Grimm: Annotiertes Verzeichnis des festgestellten Bestandes,* ed. Friedhilde Krause (Stuttgart: S. Hirzel Verlag, 1989); Erasmus's *Epistolae* is item no. 956 on p. 113.

68. See Wesselski's *Märchen des Mittelalters* and *Versuch einer Theorie des Märchens.*

69. One of the schoolbooks is by Johan Georg Sulzer (1720–79): *Zum Gebrauch der letzten Classe des Königl. Joachimsthalischen Gymnasium,* part 1 of *Vorübungen zur Erweckung der Aufmerksamkeit und des Nachdenkens,* rev. Johann Heinrich Ludwig Meierotto [1742–1800], 3rd. ed.(Berlin: Friedrich Nicolai, 1780), 98–99. In part 4 of *Vorübungen zur Erweckung,* the source is indicated as "Anecdoten der Könige von Frankreich" (37), which refers in one way or another to Erasmus. The other schoolbook is by Valentin Karl Veillodter (1769–1828): *Lieder, Erzählungen und Fabeln für Kinder zur Uibung im Lesen und Deklamiren* (Nuremberg: Bauer und Mann, 1797), 221–22. For detailed descriptions of these schoolbooks, see Ingrid Tomkowiak, *Lesebuchgeschichten: Erzählstoffe in Schullesebüchern 1770–1920* (Berlin and New York: Walter de Gruyter, 1993), 25–29, 43–44.

70. For bibliography, see Albert Wesselski, ed., *Die Schwänke und Schnurren des Pfarrers Arlotto,* 2 vols. (Berlin: Alexander Duncker Verlag, 1910), 1:226; BP 3:189–92.

71. Marcel Bataillon, "Érasme conteur: Folklore et invention narrative," in *Mélanges de langue et de littérature médiévales offerts à Pierre Le Gentil Professeur à la Sorbonne par ses collègues, ses élèves et ses amis* (Paris: S.E.D.E.S., 1973), 91: "anecdote historique teintée de réalisme romanesque."

72. Erasmus, *Opera omnia,* 3.444, line 196.

73. Erasmus, *Opera omnia,* 3.444, line 216.

74. Erasmus, "The Fabulous Feast," 579, lines 14–21; Erasmus, "Convivium fabulosum," 444, lines 190–96: "Mox vbi Lodouicus restitutus iam rerum potiretur apud Gallos, submonuit Cononem vxor, vt regem veteris hospitii commonefaceret, adiret illum, et rapas aliquot insignes illi dono adferret. Tergiuersatus est Conon se lusurum operam, principes enim non meminisse talium officiorum. Sed vicit vxor, deligit Conon rapas aliquot insignes, accingitur itineri. Verum ipse per viam captus illecebra cibi, paulatim deuorauit omnes, vna duntaxat excepta insigniter magna."

75. Erasmus, "The Fabulous Feast," 579, lines 10–11; Erasmus, "Convivium fabulosum," 443, line 188: "cum Conone quodam homine rustico, sed animi simplicis ac synceri."

76. Erasmus, "The Fabulous Feast," 579, lines 35–37; Erasmus, "Convivium fabulosum," 444, lines 207–9: "Sic sic pensauit rapam donatam a rustico, quanto munificentius pensaturus est equum talem, oblatum ab aulico?"

77. See Alan Davidson, *The Oxford Companion to Food* (Oxford: Oxford University Press, 1999), 813.

78. Lucius Junius Moderatus Columella *On Agriculture* 2.10.22–24, ed. and trans. Harrison Boyd Ash, Loeb Classical Library 361 (Cambridge, MA: Harvard University Press, 1941), 170–73.

79. See Maguelonne Toussaint-Samat, *A History of Food,* trans. Anthea Bell (Cambridge, MA, and Oxford: Blackwell Reference, 1992), 63.

80. Pliny the Elder *Naturalis Historia* 18.34.126–8, ed. and trans. Rackham, Jones, and Eichholz, 5:268–21.

81. See Johannes Hoops, "Rübe," in *Reallexikon der Germanischen Altertumskunde,* ed. Johannes Hoops (Strasbourg: Karl J. Trübner, 1918–19), 4:1–2.

82. See Röhrich, *Das große Lexikon,* 2:1258.

83. On the hard work that is required, see Columella *On Agriculture* 2.10.23–24, ed. and trans. Harrison Boyd Ash, 170–71.

84. *Die Rübe: Magazin für kulinarische Literatur,* ed. Vincent Klink and Stephan Opitz (Zurich: Haffmans Verlag, 1988–).

85. The anecdote of the turnips is widely attested in both Greek and Latin: see Plutarch, "Sayings of Romans," in *Moralia,* vol. 3, ed. and trans. Frank Cole Babbitt (Cambridge, MA: Harvard University Press, 1931), 154–55; Megacles, ed. Karl Otfried Müller, in *Fragmenta Historicorum Graecorum,* ed. Karl Otfried Müller, Theodor Müller, and Charles Victor Langlois, 5 vols. (Paris: Firmin Didot, 1848–78; repr., Frankfurt am Main: Minerva, 1975), 4:443; Athenaeus *Deipnosophistae* 10.419, ed. and trans. Charles Burton Gulick, 7 vols., Loeb Classical Library 204, 208, 224, 235, 274, 327, 345 (Cambridge, MA: Harvard University Press, 1961), 4:396–97; Pliny the Elder *Naturalis Historia* 19.26.87, ed. and trans. Rackham, Jones, and Eichholz, 5:476–77; [pseudo-Sextus Aurelius Victor] *De viris illustribus* 33.7, ed. Franciscus Pichlmayr, in *Sexti Aurelii Victoris Liber de Caesaribus, praecedunt Origo gentis romanae et Liber de viris illustribus urbis Romae* (Stuttgart and Leipzig: B. G. Teubner, 1911; repr., 1993), 44, lines 25–27; Lucius Ampelius (third or fourth century CE) *Liber memorialis* 18.8, ed. and trans. Marie-Pierre Arnaud-Lindet (Paris: Belles Lettres, 1993), 29. Seneca the Younger (*Dialogorum Liber XII,* "Ad Helviam matrem De Consolatione," in *L. Annaei Senecae Dialogorum libri duodecim,* ed. L. D. Reynolds, Oxford Classical Texts [Oxford: Clarendon, 1977], 304, line 9) refers simply to "uilissimum cibum," without specifying that the food is turnips; and Valerius Maximus (*Memorable Doings and Sayings* 4.3.5, ed. and trans. D. R. Shackleton Bailey, 2 vols., Loeb Classical Library 492–93 [Cambridge, MA: Harvard University Press, 2000], 1:370–71) is similarly reticent, simply because the nature of the fare is obvious from the rustic setting.

86. Hans Walther, *Proverbia sententiaeque latinitatis medii aevi: Lateinische Sprichwörter und Sentenzen des Mittelalters in alphabetischer Anordnung,* Carmina medii aevi posterioris latina, part 2, vols. 1–6 (Göttingen: Vandenhoeck und Ruprecht, 1963–69), 2:950, no. 15273.

87. James Woodrow Hassell, Jr., *Middle French Proverbs, Sentences, and Proverbial Phrases,* Subsidia Mediaevalia (Toronto: Pontifical Institute of Mediaeval Studies, 1982), 174, N 8; Bartlett Jere Whiting, *Proverbs, Sentences, and Proverbial Phrases from English Writings Mainly before 1500* (Cambridge, MA: Harvard University Press, Belknap, 1968), 427, N 73. The figurative meaning of the turnip as "object of little value" follows immediately the definitions "turnip, swede" in the listing for *navet* in Alan Hindley, Frederick W. Langley, and Brian J. Levy, *Old French-English Dictionary* (Cambridge: Cambridge University Press, 2000), 441.

88. On the bite of turnips, see Egbert of Liège *Fecunda ratis* (The Richly Laden Ship) 1.180, ed. Voigt, 43 (= Walther, *Proverbia,* 3:828, no. 21521): "Piscis, auis licet ossa habeat: bona rapula nullum" [Although the fish and the bird have bones, the good turnip has none]. As Singer (*Sprichwörter des Mittelalters,* 1:137) explains, fish and fowl have something bony instead of teeth, but the turnip does not have it—and yet it still bites. On the bloating, see Walther, *Proverbia,* 4:112, no. 23661: "To the turnips you tear with your tooth, bloating is accompaniment" [Quas tu dente rapis, comes est inflatio rapis]. On the flatulence, see Walther, *Proverbia,* 4:519, no. 26237a: "The turnip is a good root, it gives its eater three gifts: / It cleanses the face, it soothes the stomach, it farts well" [Radix rapa bona est, comedenti dat tria dona: / Visum clarificat, ventrem mollit, bene bombit]; no. 33023: "You often take wind, if you wish to live on turnips" [Ventum sepe rapis, si tu vis vivere rapis].

89. In general, see Allen J. Grieco, "The Social Politics of Pre-Linnaean Botanical Classification," *I Tatti Studies: Essays in the Renaissance* 4 (1991): 131: "the mere mention

of certain vegetables classifies the eater once and for all"; "vegetable diets and poverty were felt to be intimately linked to each other beyond questions of economic necessity." I am grateful to Allen Grieco for having suggested to me the relevance of food history to a fuller understanding of *The Turnip Tale*. With specific reference to *The Turnip Tale*, see Wailes, "Fortuna and Social Anomaly," 90: "Readers of chivalric literature know the expressive force of meals set before the nobility—fish, fresh game, white bread, wine— and appreciate the wretchedness of existence where one must grow turnips for one's own table. By its nature the *rapula* identifies one of the social poles of the composition."

90. Archpoet *Poems* 4.18.1–2. See two editions: *Die Gedichte des Archipoeta,* ed. Heinrich Watenphul and Heinrich Krefeld (Heidelberg: Carl Winter, 1958), 59, with commentary and parallels on 108–9; *Die Gedichte des Archipoeta,* ed. and trans. Heinrich Krefeld, Schriften und Quellen der alten Welt 41 (Berlin: Akademie Verlag, 1992), 54–55, with commentary on 99. The earlier edition has fuller commentary.

91. See Georges Duby, *The Three Orders: Feudal Society Imagined,* trans. Arthur Goldhammer (Chicago: University of Chicago Press, 1980), 298.

92. For this proverb, see Heinrich von Neustadt *Apollonius von Tyrland* 342, in *"Apollonius von Tyrland" nach der Gothaer Handschrift, "Gottes Zukunft" und "Visio Philiberti" nach der Heidelberger Handschrift,* ed. Samuel Singer, Deutsche Texte des Mittelalters 7 (Berlin: Weidmann, 1906), 8. See also Jacob Grimm and Wilhelm Grimm, *Deutsches Wörterbuch,* 16 vols. (Leipzig: S. Hirzel Verlag, 1854–1971), 8:1332.

93. Walther (*Proverbia,* 1:563, no. 4662) lists six sources, with variants.

94. Giovanni Sabadino degli Arienti, *Novelle Porretane,* ed. Bruno Basile (Rome: Salerno Editrice, 1981), N332, novella 38 [22] = Grieco, "Pre-Linnaean Botanical Classification," 134–35: "un'altra volta lassa stare le fructe de li mei pari e mangia delle tue che sono le rape, gli agli, porri, cepolle e le scalogne col pan di sorgo."

95. Giulio Cesare Croce, *Le astuzie di Bertoldo.* See Piero Camporesi, *The Magic Harvest: Food, Folklore, and Society,* trans. Joan Krakover Hall (Cambridge, MA: Polity, 1993), 12: "Turnips, stewed or cooked in the ashes . . . were used in the 'Lombard' part of Emilia for making soup (the Lombards were called 'turnip-eaters'). Together with cabbage and leeks (cultivated since the Neolithic age), turnips were the most common vegetable for the minestra."

96. Giulio Cesare Croce, *Le astuzie di Bertoldo,* 148 = Grieco, "Pre-Linnaean Botanical Classification," 133: "I medici non conoscendo la sua complessione, gli facevano i rimedi che si fanno alli gentiluomini e cavalieri di corte; ma esso, che conosceva la sua natura, teneva domandato a quelli che gli portasero una pentola di fagiuoli con la cipolla dentro e delle rape cotte sotto la cenere, perché sapeva lui che con tal cibi saria guarito."

97. Giulio Cesare Croce, *Le astuzie di Bertoldo,* 149 = Grieco, "Pre-Linnaean Botanical Classification," 133: "morì con aspri duoli / Per non poter mangiar rape e fagiuoli. / Chi è uso alle rape non vada ai pasticci. / Chi è uso alla zappa non pigli la lancia. / Chi è uso al campo non vada alla corte."

98. Wailes ("Fortuna and Social Anomaly," 90) observes: "The conspicuous anomaly in this tale is, of course, the turnip . . . In its fabulous size it proves to be the instrument of Fortuna."

99. Compare Lorraine Daston and Katharine Park, *Wonders and the Order of Nature, 1150–1750* (New York: Zone, 1998), 68 (*The Turnip Tale* is not among the texts considered): "In the eyes of high and late medieval beholders, there was a hierarchy of natural

objects that corresponded to and, in some ways, naturalized the hierarchy of persons: the vegetable kingdom, for example, ascended from lowly tubers and root vegetables, associated with peasants, to rare and exotic fruits. More than anything else, wonders were nature's noblest creations, and they enveloped those around them with an aura of nobility and might. For these reasons marvels had strong courtly associations, though the cultural purposes served by these associations shifted with the gradual transformation of the European elites."

100. In the late Middle Ages, wonder had a number of milieus, among them the prince's court and the philosopher's study (see Daston and Park, *Wonders and the Order of Nature*, 15). In Latin, *admiratio* was used to describe the emotion, and *mirabilia*, *miracula*, and *ammiranda* were used to describe the objects (see Daston and Park, *Wonders and the Order of Nature*, 16).

101. See Daston and Park, *Wonders and the Order of Nature*, 18–19.

102. Gervase of Tilbury *Otia imperialia* 3, pref., 558–59: "Et quoniam humane mentis auiditas ad audiendas ac hauriendas nouitates semper accuitur, antiquissima commutari necesse erit in noua, naturalia in mirabilia, apud plerosque usitata in inaudita. Censemus enim noua quadruplici ratione iudicari: aut creatione, aut euentu, aut raritate, aut inauditu. Que ergo noua creantur delectant ex nature motu. Que nuper eueniunt, si frequentia minus, si rara plus habent admirationis. Que inaudita percipiuntur amplectimur, tum ex mutatione cursus naturalis quam admiramur, tum ex ignorancia cause cuius ratio nobis est imperscrutabilis, tum ex assuetudine nostra quam in aliis uariari sine cognitione iudicii iusti cernimus. Ex hiis, duo proueniunt: miracula et mirabilia, cum utrorumque finis sit admiratio." This passage is translated (with two short ellipses and only slight differences) and discussed stimulatingly in Daston and Park's *Wonders and the Order of Nature*, 22–23.

103. Daston and Park (*Wonders and the Order of Nature*, 67) note that "the value of such mirabilia sprang in part from their scarcity in the European market."

104. Daston and Park (*Wonders and the Order of Nature*) mention "the awestruck veneration owed to the omnipotent Christian God" (74) and observe, "It was well known that God had proclaimed his might in the book of nature as well as in scripture, and encyclopedic and clerical writers followed Augustine in especially praising the wonders of nature as testimony to the wonderfulness of their omnipotent creator" (76).

105. See Daston and Park, *Wonders and the Order of Nature*, 102.

106. See Mazzacurati, *All'ombra di Dioneo*, 146–47; Bottigheimer, *Fairy Godfather*, 37.

107. Adalgisa Lugli, *Wunderkammer* (Turin: Umberto Allemandi, 1997), no. 155.

108. Thomas J. Müller-Bahlke, *Die Wunderkammer: Die Kunst- und Naturalienkammer der Franckeschen Stiftungen zu Halle (Saale)* (Halle an der Saale: Verlag der Franckeschen Stiftungen, 1998), passim, especially 41, 49–52. For a late sixteenth-century woodcut of a very similar collection, see Ferrante Imperato, *Dell'historia naturale* (Naples: Costantino Vitale, 1599), frontispiece illustration (J. Paul Getty Research Institute for the History of Art and the Humanities, 84-B30646).

109. Wailes, "Fortuna and Social Anomaly," 91.

110. On the plight in which many knights found themselves at the close of the twelfth century, see Duby, *The Three Orders*, 324.

111. *The Turnip Tale "frivola"* [1] 99–100 = *The Turnip Tale "prodiga"* [2] 73–74: "Proh dolor! Experior quam sit sententia vera: / 'Dives ubique placet, pauper ubique iacet.'"

112. Bolte and Polívka (BP 3:192) pointed out that the second part of *The Turnip Tale* story corresponds to the barrel episode at the end of *Unibos.* On the corresponding adventures of Reynard the Fox, see Léopold Sudre, *Les Sources du Roman du Renart* (Paris: Université de Paris, 1892; Paris: E. Bouillon, 1893; repr., Geneva: Slatkine, 1974), 226–36; Lucien Foulet, *Le roman de Renard,* Bibliothèque de l'Ecole des Hautes Etudes, Sciences historiques et philologiques 211 (Paris: Honoré Champion, 1914), 289–322. In a review that appeared in 1818, Wilhelm Grimm indicated that a similar motif appeared in the second story of the first night in Straparola's *Le piacevoli notti:* see Wilhelm Grimm, *Kleinere Schriften von Wilhelm Grimm,* ed. Gustav Hinrichs, 4 vols. (Berlin: F. Dümmler, 1881–87; repr., Hildesheim: Olms-Weidmann, 1992), 2:223.

113. The classic study is Mircea Eliade, *Shamanism: Archaic Techniques of Ecstasy,* trans. Willard R. Trask, Bollingen Series 76 (Princeton, NJ: Princeton University Press, 1964); among the various passages that deal with the functions and meanings of trees in shamanic rituals, see especially 123–27.

114. Grimm and Grimm, *Kinder- und Hausmärchen,* 7th ed., 3:230 (ed. Rölleke, p. 242). The note was first included in the third volume of the second edition. The weight that the Brothers Grimm placed on the Odin myth is maintained in BP 3:192–93 and in Gatti, *Rapularius II,* 367, 369.

115. *Hávamál,* strophes 138, 141, 144, ed. and trans. David A. H. Evans, Text Series 7 (London: Viking Society for Northern Research, 1986).

116. The first major step in this direction was a booklet by Rolf Pipping, *Oden i galgen,* Studier i nordisk filologi 18, no. 2, Skrifter utgivna av Svenska literatursällskape i Finland 197 (Helsinki: Mercator tryckeri, 1928).

117. *The Turnip Tale "prodiga"* [2] 313: "Tunc quasi Socraticus hunc leta voce salutat." See Gatti, *Rapularius I,* 364–65.

118. Gatti, *Rapularius II,* 365. For the original scene, see Aristophanes *Clouds* 218–39, ed. and trans. Henderson, 36–41. Plato refers to this scene in *Socrates' Defense (Apology)* 19c, trans. Hugh Tredennick, in *The Collected Dialogues of Plato,* ed. Edith Hamilton and Huntington Ciarns, Bollingen Series 71 (Princeton, NJ: Princeton University Press, 1963), 5.

119. The source for all this information is Walter Berschin, *Greek Letters and the Latin Middle Ages, from Jerome to Nicholas of Cusa,* trans. Jerold C. Frakes, 2nd ed. (Washington, DC: Catholic University of America Press, 1988), 245–47 (text), 344 (notes).

120. See Stephen C. Ferruolo, *The Origins of the University: The Schools of Paris and Their Critics, 1100–1215* (Stanford: Stanford University Press, 1985), 93–130.

121. With clear but cautious understatement, Worstbrock ("Rapularius," 1001) observes, "Eine tiefergreifende erzählerische Integration der Teile unterblieb."

122. Wailes ("Fortuna and Social Anomaly," 95) notes, "In each story the social anomaly is a fusion of aristocratic essence with boorish attribute; in each, the restorative work of Fortuna depends on the essentially boorish made aristocratic."

123. See Grieco, "Pre-Linnaean Botanical Classification," especially 131, 146.

124. Preface to Jacob Grimm and Wilhelm Grimm, *Kinder- und Hausmärchen gesammelt durch die Brüder Grimm,* 1st ed., vol. 1 (Berlin: Realschulbuchhandlung, 1812), in Wilhelm Grimm, *Kleinere Schriften von Wilhelm Grimm,* 1:320–28, trans. Maria Tatar in *The Hard Facts of the Grimms' Fairy Tales* (Princeton, NJ: Princeton University Press, 1987), 204–5. Tatar (211–22) also translates the preface to the second volume of

the first edition (1814) and the preface to the second edition (1819). Hans Ulrich Gumbrecht and Jeffrey T. Schnapp translated the preface to the 1819 edition into English (without knowledge of Tatar's translation) in R. Howard Bloch and Stephen G. Nichols, eds., *Medievalism and the Modernist Temper* (Baltimore and London: Johns Hopkins University Press, 1996), 475–88 (notes on 488–92).

125. "Kein Umstand ist hinzugedichtet oder verschönert und abgeändert worden." The assertion appears in Jacob Grimm and Wilhelm Grimm, *Kinder- und Hausmärchen gesammelt durch die Brüder Grimm,* 1st ed., 1:XVIII.

126. Preface to Jacob Grimm and Wilhelm Grimm, *Kinder- und Hausmärchen gesammelt durch die Brüder Grimm,* 2nd ed. (Berlin: G. Reimer, 1819–22), in Wilhelm Grimm, *Kleinere Schriften von Wilhelm Grimm,* 1:328 (trans. Tatar, *Hard Facts,* 220; compare Bloch and Nichols, *Medievalism,* 486): "Wir haben nämlich aus eigenen Mitteln nicht hinzugesetzt, keinen Umstand und Zug der Sage selbst verschönert, sondern ihren Inhalt so wiedergegeben, wie wir ihn empfangen; daß der Ausdruck großentheils von uns herrührt, verstehet sich von selbst, doch habe wir jede Eigenthümlichtkeit, die wir bemerkten, zu erhalten gesucht."

127. Hugo of Trimberg *Registrum multorum auctorum* 720–21, ed. Langosch, 191: "Horum si materie sint utilitatis / Modice, sunt carmine tamen digna satis."

128. Ellis, *One Fairy Story Too Many,* 50.

129. See Hamann, *Die literarischen Vorlagen,* 49.

130. Hamann (*Die literarischen Vorlagen,* 50) observes, "Im Gegensatz zur lat. Vorlage ist der Monolog in der 2. Person ausgedrückt."

131. The term *thick description* was made famous in a chapter by Clifford Geertz entitled, "Thick Description: Toward an Interpretive Theory of Culture," which appeared in his *The Interpretation of the Cultures* (New York: Basic Books, 1973), 3–30.

132. In the first category, Hamann (*Die literarischen Vorlagen,* 49–50) singles out "er zog den Soldatenrock aus und ward ein Bauer"; "er wuchs da eine Rübe gross und stark, dass sie eine Fürstin aller Rüben heissen konnte"; "hing den Soldatenrock an den Nagel und baute das Land"; "dass ihnen der Schrecken in den Leib fuhr und sie Hals über Kopf ihren Gefangennen in den Sack steckten"; "ich habe grosse Dinge gelernt, dagegen sind alle Schulen ein Wind"; "Er machte ihn steinreich"; "sitze also fein ruhig"; and "ich wollt dich wohl hineinlasslen für Lohn und gute Worte." In the second, Hamann (50) gives as examples "'Wer ruft mir?'"; "'Um ein weniges, so werde ich ausgelernt haben'"; and "'Erhebe deine Augen.'"

133. *The Turnip Tale "prodiga"* [2] 328, ed. and trans. Gatti, *Rapularius II,* 366, "Hic tantum veras noveris esse scolas," corresponds exactly to the transcription by Jacob Grimm.

134. Grimm and Grimm, *Deutsches Wörterbuch,* 14, no. 2:255–57. This interrelationship was pointed out by Lothar Bluhm and Heinz Rölleke in *"Redensarten des Volks, auf die ich immer horche": Märchen-Sprichwort-Redensart; Zur volkspoetischen Ausgestaltung der "Kinder- und Hausmärchen" durch die Brüder Grimm,* 2nd ed. (Stuttgart and Leipzig: S. Hirzel Verlag, 1997), 140. By a curious coincidence, the formerly poor brother uses the metaphor of the wind as nothingness or worthlessness in negotiating over the sack with the wandering scholar in *The Turnip Tale "frivola"* [1] 402; but there is no evidence that the Brothers Grimm knew this version of the poem.

135. See Wailes, "Fortuna and Social Anomaly," 91–92.

136. On the manuscript, see Gatti, *Rapularius II,* 6.331.

137. I discount the possibility that the brothers thought of the two nouns solely in terms of their meanings in classical Latin: the Grimms were too experienced with post-classical Latin and too careful as philologists to have been misled in this way.

138. "Fama fuisse duos testatur frivola fratres / Quos uni mater edidit una viro. / Militie titulus hos insignaverat ambos, / Ex quibus unus erat dives et alter inops. / Militis officium cum nomine dives habebat, / Alter egestatis triste ferebat honus."

139. "O germane, michi preter te nemo superstes / Quem michi fraterno federe iungat amor. / Nos sumus una caro nec nos natura bipartit: / Nos uni mater edidit una viro. / Forsan inest anima personis una duabus / Quas individuus iungit et unit amor."

140. The most relevant manifestation of this relationship in twelfth-century literature appears in stories of Amicus and Amelius (Amys and Amelis), which describe two men who are not brothers by blood but who are twinned by date of birth, appearance, and attachment to each other. For a summary of the main branches in this tradition and for bibliography, see W. Verbaal, "Amys and Amelis," in *A Dictionary of Medieval Heroes,* ed. Willem P. Gerritsen and Anthony G. van Melle, trans. Tanis Guest (Woodbridge, UK: Boydell, 1998), 24–26.

141. Walter de la Mare, "The Turnip," in Walter de la Mare, *Told Again: Traditional Tales* (Oxford: B. Blackwell, 1927).

142. Lüthi, *Once upon a Time,* 138.

143. See Hamann, *Die literarischen Vorlagen,* 49.

144. The German reads: "Der Same ging auf und es wuchs da eine Rübe, die ward groß und stark, und zusehends dicker, und wollte gar nicht aufhören zu wachsen, so daß sie eine Fürstin aller Rüben heißen konnte" (Grimm and Grimm, *Kinder- und Hausmärchen,* 2nd ed., ed. Rölleke, 2:490). Hamann (*Die literarischen Vorlagen,* 50) points out the dilation but offers only a partially correct explanation: "Um der kindlichen Phantasie das Wachstum der ungeheuere Rübe recht anschaulich zur machen, häuft Grimm synonyme Begriffe."

145. Over the past quarter century and more, the literature on the marvelous in medieval literature and culture has become vast. For a sampling of approaches, see Lucienne Carasso-Bulow, *The Merveilleux in Chrétien de Troyes' Romances* (Geneva: Droz, 1976); C. Lecouteux, "Introduction à l'étude du merveilleux médiéval," *Etudes germaniques* 36 (1981): 2763–90; Jacques Le Goff, *The Medieval Imagination,* trans. Arthur Goldhammer (Chicago: University of Chicago Press, 1988); Francis Dubost, *Aspects fantastiques de la littérature narrative médiévale, XIIème–XIIIème siècles: L'autre, l'ailleurs, l'autrefois,* 2 vols., Nouvelle bibliothèque du Moyen Age 15 (Paris: Honoré Champion, 1991); Gérard Chandes, ed., *Le merveilleux et la magie dans la littérature: Actes du colloque de Caen, 31 août–2 septembre 1989* (Amsterdam: Rodopi, 1992).

146. In *Grimms' Bad Girls and Bold Boys: The Moral and Social Vision of the Tales* (New Haven and London: Yale University Press, 1987), 133, Ruth B. Bottigheimer comments in reference to *KHM* 146, "Serendipitous acquisition of wealth looms large in the fairy tale world, even when a logical inner dynamic guides the course of events."

147. The fullest study of the revisions remains Ernest Tonnelat's *Les contes des frères Grimm: Étude sur la composition et le style du recueil des "Kinder- und Hausmärchen"* (Paris: Armand Colin, 1912). A fascinating tracing of expurgations and other modifications from one edition to another is presented by Tatar in *Hard Facts.* For a detailed listing of other studies, see James M. McGlathery, *Fairy Tale Romance: The Grimms, Basile,*

and Perrault (Urbana: University of Illinois Press, 1991), 20 n. 22. For a translation of *KHM* 146, consult app. 4C in the present study.

148. I take this terminology from Propp, *La fiaba russa,* 217.

149. 7th ed., 1857, 2. 259.

150. This softening of *KHM* 146 is consonant with Wilhelm's tendency to excise the rough edges of life, such as sexuality and violence, from the collection: on this expurgation, see Tatar, *Hard Facts.*

CHAPTER SIX

1. Wesselski, *Versuch einer Theorie des Märchens,* 194 (heading): "Das erste europäische Märchen?"

2. Thompson, *The Folktale,* 100.

3. Walter Scherf, *Lexikon der Zaubermärchen,* Kroners Taschenausgabe 472 (Stuttgart: Kroner, 1982), 113 = *Das Märchenlexikon,* 2 vols. (Munich: C. H. Beck, 1995), 1:285: "Es ist ein Glücksfall, daß ein in mündlicher Überlieferung weitergegebenes Zaubermärchen auch in der Gestalt einer höfischen Anverwandlung aus der Zeit um 1200 erhalten geblieben ist."

4. Scherf, *Das Märchenlexikon,* 1:284: "kein Zweifel, daß hier ein volkstümliches Märchen ebenso umgewandelt wurde wie 500 Jahre später am Hof von Versailles überlieferte Erzählungen zu hochstilisierten Buchmärchen im Sinne einer phantastischen Feenromantik ausgestaltet wurden."

5. Max Lüthi, as quoted by Diederichs in *Who's who im Märchen,* 249: "Wer Märchen sagt, der denkt zuallererst an Prinz und Prinzessin."

6. The tale is *KHM* 58 in the 1815 edition; *KHM* 144 in the 1857 edition; and AT 430, "The Ass."

7. The basic starting point for study of the motif is *MI* D132.1, "Transformation man to ass." For the most convenient editions and translations for English speakers, see Apuleius, *Metamorphoses,* and pseudo-Lucian, "Lucius, or The Ass," in *Lucian,* vol. 8, ed. and trans. M. D. Macleod, Loeb Classical Library 432 (Cambridge, MA: Harvard University Press, 1967), 47–145. On the relationship between Apuleius's novel and "Lucius, or The Ass," see Helmut van Thiel, *Der Eselroman,* 2 vols., Zetemata: Monographien zur klassischen Altertumswissenschaft 54, nos. 1–2 (Munich: C. H. Beck, 1971–72). For the most thorough and provocative attempt to situate the ass tale of Apuleius within the context of folkore, see Alexander Scobie, *Apuleius Metamorphoses (Asinus Aureus) I: A Commentary,* Beiträge zur Klassischen Philologie 54 (Meisenheim am Glan: Verlag Anton Hain, 1975), 26–46.

8. The title is attested in most of the manuscripts: see Langosch, *Asinarius und Rapularius,* III. A noun of this form existed in classical Latin, denoting a "donkey man" in the sense of "donkey driver" (see the *Oxford Latin Dictionary,* ed. P. G. Glare [Oxford: Clarendon Press, 1968–82], s.v. *asinarius*). Yet the title could be explained as being on the analogy of other *anonyma* (anonymous works) such as the *Luparius,* where the adjectival ending does not seem to denote "a dealer in" (see the *Oxford Latin Dictionary,* s.v. *-arius*).

9. Nor did the tale merit so much as a mention in Otto Spies's *Orientalische Stoffe in den Kinder- und Hausmärchen der Brüder Grimm,* Beiträge zur Sprach- und Kulturgeschichte des Orients 6 (Walldorf: H. Vorndran, 1952).

10. See Simson, "Benfey, Theodor." Benfey's views achieved their broadest influence thanks to his *Pantschatantra: Fünf Bücher indischer Fabeln, Märchen und Erzählungen; Aus dem Sanskrit übersetzt mit Einleitung und Anmerkungen versehen,* 2 vols. (Leipzig: F. A. Brockhaus, 1859). For discussion of the comparable attempt to find the origins of Greek and Roman romances in Sanskrit literature, see Scobie, *Apuleius Metamorphoses,* 34.

11. The key anti-Indianist text is Joseph Bédier's *Les fabliaux: Études de littérature populaire et d'histoire littéraire du moyen âge* (Paris: Honoré Champion, 1893). For a concise discussion of Bédier's contribution to folkloristics, see Tenèze, "Bédier, Joseph."

12. Most relevant passages from the early nineteenth century or earlier are assembled in BP 4:90–91 (no. 190), 291.

13. If a balance has been struck, it has been in the study of medieval Spanish literature; see María Jesús Lacarra, *Cuentística medieval en España: Los orígenes* (Zaragoza: Departamento de literatura española, Universidad de Zaragoza, 1979): María Jesús Lacarra, *Cuentos de la edad media* (Madrid: Editorial Castalia "Odres nuevos," 1986), 9–85; Rameline E. Marsan, *Itinéraire espagnol du conte médiéval, VIIIe–XVe siècles,* Témoins de l'Espagne: Série historique 4 (Paris: Klincksieck, 1974), 120–36.

14. To the best of my knowledge, the one close comparison of the two pieces is in Hamann's *Die literarischen Vorlagen,* 45–48.

15. The only other closely comparable test case is offered by *KHM* 146, "The Turnip," also (as examined closely in chap. 5 of the present study) an adaptation of the Latin *Rapularius* (which is sometimes conjectured to have been the work of the same Medieval Latin poet who wrote *The Donkey Tale*): see Karl Langosch, "Asinarius," in *VL*[1] 1:509.

16. For succinct expositions of conduit theory and the major bibliographic references, see Linda Dégh, "Conduit-Theorie," in *EM* 3:124–26; "Conduit Theory/ Multiconduit Theory," in *Folklore* 1:142–44.

17. See Propp, *La fiaba russa,* 166. The term used in the Russian edition (Propp, *Russkaia skazka* [Leningrad: Izdatelstvo Leningradskogo universiteta, 1984], 162) is *polystadial'nost'yu.*

18. I follow the most recent edition, Rizzardi's *Asinarius,* but with attention to the older edition by Karl Langosch (*Asinarius und Rapularius,* 15–45).

19. Franklin Edgerton, ed. and trans., *Vikrama's Adventures, or The Thirty-Two Tales of the Throne: A Collection of Stories about King Vikrama, as Told by the Thirty-Two Statuettes That Supported His Throne,* 2 vols., Harvard Oriental Series 26–27 (Cambridge, MA: Harvard University Press, 1926), 1:263–66 (English translation), 2:241–44 (Sanskrit text).

20. Hugo of Trimberg *Registrum multorum auctorum* 718, 721de, ed. Langosch, 191.

21. The prosodic and stylistic features that have been cited in favor of this dating are predilection for alliteration and avoidance of rhyme, hiatus, and elision. See Langosch, *Asinarius und Rapularius,* IV, 14.

22. Langosch (*Asinarius und Rapularius,* VI, 13–14) holds for a provenance in southern Germany. Johannes Bolte (BP 3:154) inclined to northern France or the southern Low Countries, but Langosch ("Asinarius," 509) pointed out that Bolte had no factual basis for this inclination.

23. See Langosch, *Asinarius und Rapularius,* VI; Langosch, "Asinarius," 509; Fritz Wagner, "Asinarius," in *EM* 1:865–67. In discussing "The Donkey," Walter A. Berendsohn emphasizes its courtliness, which he sees as concomitant with its literariness: see

Grundformen volkstümlicher Erzählerkunst in den Kinder- und Hausmärchen der Brüder Grimm (Hamburg: Verlag W. Gente, 1921), 63 ("20 Stücke der Sammlung sind jedenfalls literarische Liebesgeschichten und deutlich vom volkstümlichen Liebesmärchen zu unterscheiden"), 71 ("Volkstümlich getönt, ist die Erzählung doch nach Gehalt und Gestalt deutlich vom Volksmärchen zu unterscheiden als heitere höfische Dichtung").

24. Hugo of Trimberg *Registrum multorum auctorum* 716–17, ed. Langosch, 191. These words of the *Registrum* were cited by Langosch in *Asinarius und Rapularius,* IV.

25. In one manuscript, both *The Donkey Tale* and the *Speculum Stultorum* are entitled *The Donkey Tale:* see Langosch, *Asinarius und Rapularius,* III.

26. Walter J. Ong, "Latin Language Study as a Renaissance Puberty Rite," *Studies in Philology* 56 (1959): 103–24, reprinted in *Rhetoric, Romance, and Technology: Studies in the Interaction of Expression and Culture* (Ithaca, NY: Cornell University Press, 1971), 113–41.

27. Cited in Langosch, *Asinarius und Rapularius,* VII.

28. See Martin Vogel, *Onos lyras: Der Esel mit der Leier,* 2 vols., Orpheus-Schriftenreihe zu Grundfragen der Musik 13–14 (Düsseldorf: Verlag der Gesellschaft zur Förderung der systematischen Musikwissenschaft, 1973), 1:201–2, 303–6 (303 on the bordello in Tijuana); Scobie, *Apuleius Metamorphoses,* 31 n. 18 (on lamps representing women copulating with asses).

29. Pseudo-Lucian, 142 (Greek), 143 (English). See Scobie, *Apuleius Metamorphoses,* 31, on *Commodus Antoninus* 10.9, published in *Historia Augusta,* ed. and trans. David Magie, 3 vols., Loeb Classical Library 139–40, 363 (Cambridge, MA: Harvard University Press, 1921–32), 1:290–91. Additionally, it is possible that the word recorded as *monobiles* at *Antoninus Elagabalus* 8.7 (*Historia Augusta,* 2:124–25) conceals *onobeli.* This hypothetical word, formed of the Greek elements for donkey and weapon, would refer to men who had penises comparable to those of asses: "quasi asinino telo insignes." See J. N. Adams, *The Latin Sexual Vocabulary* (Baltimore: Johns Hopkins University Press, 1982), 21.

30. Here, I am influenced generally by arguments advanced in R. Howard Bloch, *Etymologies and Genealogies: A Literary Anthropology of the French Middle Ages* (Chicago: University of Chicago Press, 1983).

31. See Schmitt, *Medioevo,* 107.

32. Contrast Rizzardi in *Asinarius,* 153: "Un vero e proprio atteggiamento misogino, nell'*Asinarius,* non è invece né dichiarato né evidente" [A true and proper misogynous attitude is neither declared nor evident in the *Asinarius*]. On patriarchalism in the closely related tale of "Hans mein Igel," see Ingrid Riedel, *Hans mein Igel: Wie ein abgelehntes Kind sein Glück findet,* Weisheit im Märchen (Zurich: Kreuz Verlag, 1984), 7.

33. "In solio regni rex erit ille mei / Portabitque caput eius diadema paternum / Et debetur ei gloria tota patris."

34. At the crisis, when the donkey seeks permission to leave the western kingdom, the king addresses him repeatedly as "my son" (239–41, 245).

35. In *The Donkey Tale* 282–86, the daughter follows entirely patriarchal reasoning to reach her decision about the proposed marriage. Her words echo the words of Jesus at Gethsemane as recorded at Matthew 26.39 and 26.42 (this is pointed out by Rizzardi in *Asinarius,* 153 n. 62).

36. On the due order of the court (called *legitimus cursus* in line 168), see lines 161–66, 171–86. On the dealings of servants with men in authority, see, for example, lines

55–80, 359–66. Rizzardi (*Asinarius,* 154–55) comments briefly on the descriptions of servants.

37. Rizzardi (*Asinarius,* 157) proposes that "The Donkey" be interpreted as a satire on the courtly world.

38. See K. Weinhold, "Über das Märchen vom Eselmenschen," *Sitzungsberichte der Königlich Preussischen Akademie der Wissenschaften zu Berlin* 29 (plenary session of June 15, 1893): 6.

39. In advocating this gender specificity, I am not pressing the sort of interpretation advanced by Bettelheim in *Uses of Enchantment,* 277–310 ("The Animal-Groom Cycle of Fairy Tales").

40. "Cupid and Psyche" is AT 425A, while "Beauty and the Beast" is AT 425C.

41. Apuleius *Metamorphoses* 4.24–6.25, ed. and trans. Hanson, 1:228–355.

42. Amid the vast scholarship on the tale type represented by "Cupid and Psyche," two particularly full and helpful studies are Ernst Tegethoff's *Studien zum Märchentypus von Amor und Psyche,* Rheinische Beiträge und Hülfsbücher zur germanischen Philologie und Volkskunde 4 (Bonn and Leipzig: Kurt Schroeder, 1922), and Jan-Öjvind Swahn's *The Tale of Cupid and Psyche (Aarne-Thompson 425 & 428)* (Lund: CWK Gleerup, 1955). For a thumbnail overview, see Thompson, *The Folktale,* 97–102.

43. See Erich Neumann, *Amor and Psyche: The Psychic Development of the Feminine; A Commentary on the Tale by Apuleius,* trans. Ralph Manheim, Bollingen Series 54 (New York: Pantheon, 1956).

44. The translation of Leprince de Beaumont is reprinted in Betsy Hearne's *Beauty and the Beast: Visions and Revisions of an Old Tale* (Chicago: University of Chicago Press, 1989), 190–203. The English is also included in Opie and Opie's *Classic Fairy Tales* (139–50), Tatar's *Annotated Classic Fairy Tales* (58–78) and *The Classic Fairy Tales* (32–42), and Zipes's *Beauties, Beasts, and Enchantment* (233–45). For context, see Jack Zipes, "The Origins of the Fairy Tale for Children, or How Script Was Used to Tame the Beast in Us," in *Children and Their Books: A Celebration of the Work of Iona and Peter Opie,* ed. Gillian Avery and Julia Briggs (Oxford: Clarendon, 1989), 119–34.

45. See Hearne, *Beauty and the Beast,* 17.

46. For a translation of the version by Villeneuve, see Zipes, *Beauties, Beasts, and Enchantment,* 151–229.

47. Hearne, *Beauty and the Beast,* 16.

48. From Hearne, *Beauty and the Beast,* 9–10.

49. The king's remark in *The Donkey Tale,* 253–54, presumes that the donkey prince must marry the princess before becoming human.

50. The text has been translated previously by Tatar (*The Classic Fairy Tales,* 42–47) and Zipes (*Great Fairy Tale Tradition,* 51–56; *Spells of Enchantment,* 32–38).

51. See Bottigheimer, *Fairy Godfather,* 18–20 (for a paraphrase), 40–41 (for analysis).

52. See Simona Rizzardi, "Le *Piacevoli notti* di Giovan Francesco Straparola e le 'commedie elegiache' latine medievali," in *Moving in Measure: Essays in Honour of Brian Moloney,* ed. Judith Bryce and Doug Thompson (Hull: Hull University Press, 1989), 71–73.

53. Bottigheimer (*Fairy Godfather,* 90) calls it "his first newly composed rise tale."

54. See Bottigheimer, *Fairy Godfather,* 129–30. For translations of Aulnoy and Murat, see Zipes, *Great Fairy Tale Tradition,* 57–81 and 82–95, respectively. For "Histoire de Pertharite et de Férandine," see *Contes d'Hamilton publiés avec une notice de M. de Lescure,* vol. 1, *Le Bélier* (Paris: Librairie des Bibliophiles, 1873), 79–133.

55. See Lapucci, *Fiabe toscane*, 102–4.

56. Anna Birgitta Waldemarson-Rooth, "Kung Lindorm, en orientalisk saga i Danske-Skånsk Sagotradition," *Folkkultur*, 1942, 176–245. The first part of the tale corresponds to Benfey, *Pantschatantra: Fünf Bücher*, 2:144–46 ("Nachtrag zum ersten Buch: Achte Erzählung").

57. Included in the 1812 edition of *KHM* as no. 108, the tale is AT 441. "The Donkey" and "Hans My Hedgehog" were juxtaposed in passing by Weinhold ("Über das Märchen vom Eselmenschen," 7). The Grimms' tale was adapted for television as the pilot episode for the series *Jim Henson's "The Storyteller"* (NBC, 1987). The director of the series, Jim Henson (1936–90), is best known as the creator of the Muppets. Like the other eight episodes in the *Storyteller* series, "Hans My Hedgehog" was written by Anthony Minghella. An adaptation of the text was printed in Anthony Minghella, *Jim Henson's "The Storyteller"* (New York: Knopf, 1991), 23–42. The episode won a 1986–87 Emmy Award for "Outstanding Children's Program (Prime Time)."

58. See Scherf, *Lexikon der Zaubermärchen*, 198, cited by Ines Köhler in "Hans mein Igel," in *EM* 6:498.

59. See Köhler, "Hans mein Igel," 496–97.

60. See *citharedus* in line 47; *citharista* in lines 52 ("'Esto magister' ait 'o citharista, meus!'"), 55, and 81.

61. "Quid petis a servo, mi domicelle, tuo? / O rex, quid queris quod non tibi competit? Heu heu! / Erras, deciperis, irrita vota geris: / Discere nequaquam potes hanc artem quoniam sunt / Enormes digiti, mi domicelle tui. / Et si pace tua liceat michi vera fateri, / Quod natura negat, hoc, domicelle, petis. / Non potes absque manu cithare distinguere cordas, / Que, puto, dissilient si pede tangis eas. / More suo rudit asinus, numquam bene ludit: / Sacciferi vox est seva canentis hy ha."

62. See *TLL* 7/2:1079.80–84 ("lecator"); Charles du Fresne Du Cange, D. P. Charpentier, and G. A. Louis Heschel, *Glossarium mediae et infimae latinitatis*, 7 vols. (Paris: Firmin Didot, 1840–50), 4:52 ("lecator, leccator"), 6:139 ("scurra, scurro"). A good general essay on the social standing of such entertainers remains J. D. A. Ogilvy's "*Mimi, Scurrae, Histriones:* Entertainers of the Early Middle Ages," *Speculum* 38 (1963): 603–19.

63. Hereafter, the donkey prince is several times designated, both by people within the poem and by the narrator himself, as a mime player: the doorman refers to the donkey as "mimus rarissimus" in line 153 and as "rarus mimus" in line 155, and the narrator labels him as "mimus" in line 159.

64. "Confluit instar apum mimorum magna caterva / Desudat quisque doctus in arte sua. / Mima pedes sursum suspensa caputque deorsum / Ambulat et manui dat pedis officium."

65. Rizzardi (*Asinarius*, 164) contends that the poet of *The Donkey Tale* was inspired by the *Ruodlieb*.

66. An exhaustive and well-illustrated treatment of the tradition occurs in Vogel's *Onos lyras*, especially 1:361–64. The most accessible English study that explores the origin, history, and diffusion of the proverb is Helen Adolf's "The Ass and the Harp," *Speculum* 25 (1950): 49–57.

67. See "Perotti's Appendix," no. 14, in *Babrius and Phaedrus*, ed. and trans. B. E. Perry, Loeb Classical Library 436 (Cambridge, MA: Harvard University Press, 1965), 390–91. This motif is *MI* J512.4, "Ass tries in vain to play lyre."

68. For an extensive listing of the occurrences in classical literature and a few indications of postclassical adaptations, see August Otto, *Die Sprichwörter und sprichwörtlichen Redensarten der Römer* (Leipzig: B. G. Teubner, 1890), 41 (no. 184: *asinus, asellus* 5); Reinhard Häussler, ed., *Nachträge zu A. Otto Sprichwörter und sprichwörtlichen Redensarten der Römer* (Hildesheim: Olms, 1968), VIII n. 1, 70, 136. For a more digestible presentation of some evidence, see K. Freeman, "Vincent, or the Donkey," *Greece and Rome* 14 (1945): 35.

69. Franciscus Bücheler, ed., *Petronii Saturae et Liber priapeorum*, 4th ed. (Berlin: Weidmann, 1904), fragments 348–69.

70. For a concise but richly multilingual catalog of appearances of the proverb in ancient and medieval European languages, see *Thesaurus Proverbiorum Medii Aevi: Lexikon der Sprichwörter des romanisch-germanischen Mittelalters*, 13 vols. with an additional index vol. (Berlin and New York: Walter de Gruyter, 1995–2002), 3:65–66, "Esel" 6.2. For information on appearances of the proverb in Middle English, see Whiting, *Proverbs, Sentences, and Proverbial Phrases*, 16 (no. A227); in Middle French, Hassell, *Middle French Proverbs*, 39 (no. A137); and in Middle and Modern High German, Röhrich, *Das große Lexikon*, 1:394–95. For citations of medieval and early modern versions in Latin hexameters, see Walther, *Proverbia*, and Paul Gerhard Schmidt, *Proverbia sententiaeque latinitatis medii aevi: Lateinische Sprichwörter und Sentenzen des Mittelalters in alphabetischer Anordnung*, Carmina medii aevi posterioris latina, part 2, vols. 7–9 (Göttingen: Vandenhoeck und Ruprecht, 1982–86), 4:336 (no. 25138), 7:221 (no. 34949), 9:342 (no. 39854a10); Langosch, *Asinarius und Rapularius*, 39. For a variety of related proverbs in early modern Czech and Polish, see BP 3:166 n. 4.

71. *Roman de Thèbes* 13–16, in *Le Roman de Thèbes, Publié d'après tous les manuscrits*, ed. Léopold Constans, 2 vols., Société des Anciens Textes Français (Paris: Firmin Didot, 1890), 1:2: "Or s'en voisent de tot mestier, / Se ne sont clerc e chevalier, / Car aussi pueent escouter / Come li asnes al harper." I quote the English of *Le Roman de Thèbes*, trans. John Smartt Coley, Garland Library of Medieval Literature 44 (New York: Garland, 1986), 2. Compare lines 13–16 in *Le Roman de Thèbes*, ed. Guy Raynaud de Lage, 2 vols., Les classiques français du moyen âge 94, 96 (Paris: Honoré Champion, 1967–68), 1:1: "Or s'en tesent de cest mestier, / se ne sont clerc ou chevalier, / car ausi pueent escouter / conme li asnes a harper."

72. For information on representations in art, see Rolf Wilhelm Brednich, "Esel als Lautenspieler," in *EM* 4:426–28, especially nn. 11–13.

73. See Vogel, *Onos lyras*, 1:350–70 (plates 118–46).

74. See, for example, the wall painting (ca. 75 CE) from the Basilica of Herculaneum, which is now located in Naples: Museo Nazionale, Inv. No. 9109 (reproduced as plate 1 in Vogel, *Onos lyras*, 1:14).

75. See Vogel, *Onos lyras*, 1:25–26, 300–303; Ziolkowski, *Talking Animals*, 137–39, 146–47.

76. "Lantfrid and Cobbo" 3.2, in *Die Cambridger Lieder: Carmina Cantabrigiensia*, ed. Karl Strecker, MGH Scriptores rerum Germanicarum in usum scholarum separatim editi 40 (Berlin: Weidmann, 1926), 18, line 8. For a Latin text of this version with facing English translation, see Wolterbeek, *Comic Tales of the Middle Ages*, 140–43.

77. See Benedikt K. Vollmann, "Lantfrid und Cobbo," in *VL*² 5:610–11. For the other version of "Lantfrid and Cobbo," see app. 2B in the present study.

78. Compare pseudo-Lucian "Lucius, or The Ass" 52, ed. and trans. Macleod,

136–37, where the master of the ass-man peeps through a crack in a door so that he can watch a woman who has paid to sleep with the donkey.

79. A man masked as an ass is clearly visible in a miniature by Jehan de Grise (died 1344) in Oxford, Bodleian MS 264 (*Li romans d'Alixandre*), reproduced as the frontispiece to E. K. Chambers's *The Mediaeval Stage*, 2 vols. (Oxford: Oxford University Press, 1903), vol. 2. Chambers (1:72 n. 8) also cites a brief passage that refers to mime players who imitated the braying of an ass as a form of entertainment. For a reproduction of an ancient vase that depicts a boisterous scene that includes a man masked as an ass, see the frontispiece to Hermann Reich's *Der Mann mit dem Eselskopf: Ein Mimodrama vom klassischen Altertum verfolgt bis auf Shakespeares Sommernachtstraum,* Separat-Abdruck aus dem Jahrbuch der Deutschen Shakespeare-Gesellschaft 40 (Weimar: R. Wagner Sohn, 1904). It is possible that a fragment of an Atellan farce by Lucius Pomponius (active ca. 100–85 BCE), entitled either *Asina* or *Asinus,* and an ass figure in Sophron's *Angelus* (fifth century BCE) constitute further evidence: see Scobie, *Apuleius Metamorphoses,* 28.

80. Gottfried von Strassburg, *Tristan,* ed. [according to the text of Friedrich Ranke] and trans. Rüdiger Krohn, 3 vols. (Stuttgart: Philipp Reclam, 1974).

81. For clear information on *Salman und Morolf,* see Michael Curschmann, "Salman und Morolf," in *VL*² 8:515–23.

82. The most recent concise introduction is Maria Dobozy's "Spielmannsepen," in *Medieval Germany: An Encyclopedia,* ed. John M. Jeep (New York and London: Garland, 2001), 728–30.

83. Goldberg, "The Historic-Geographic Method," 1.

84. See Brednich, "Esel als Lautenspieler," 428.

85. There is also a much less closely related tale of an animal suitor, known as "The Enchanted Son of the Brahmin," in the Sanskrit *Panchatantra.* See "Der verzauberte Brahmanensohn," in *Pantschatantra: Fünf Bücher indischer Fabeln, Märchen, und Erzählungen,* trans. Theodor Benfey, 2 vols. (Leipzig: F. A. Brockhaus, 1859), 1:142–44 (app. 7).

86. See Edgerton, *Vikrama's Adventures,* 1:liii; Scobie, "Eselmensch," in *EM* 4:450.

87. James George Frazer, "The Dying God," part 3 of *The Golden Bough: A Study in Magic and Religion,* 3rd ed. (New York: MacMillan, 1935), 4:124–33; Richard Burton, *Vikram and the Vampire: Tales of Hindu Devilry* (London: Longmans, Green, 1893), xv. In addition to the references that Frazer (125 n. 1) provides, see Albrecht Weber, "Ueber die Siṅhâsanadvâtriṅçkâ," *Indische Studien: Beiträge für die Kunde des indischen Alterthums* 15 (1878): 255 nn. 1–2. The first to remark on Burton in this connection was Scobie (*Apuleius Metamorphoses,* 35).

88. See Edgerton, *Vikrama's Adventures,* 1:263; Scobie, *Apuleius Metamorphoses,* 26–46; Gatti, "Elementi favolistici," 153.

89. See Albrecht Weber, "Ueber den Zusammenhang indischer Fabeln mit griechischen," *Indische Studien: Beiträge für die Kunde des indischen Alterthums* 3 (1855): 337. It is interesting that transformation into an ass is frequently a punishment for lasciviousness on the part of men: for instance, such is the case in Apuleius's *The Golden Ass* (where Lucius is transformed as a result of his twin failings of lust and curiosity) and in a tale summarized by Chauvin in *Bibliographie des ouvrages arabes* (2:183, no. 23).

90. On the burning of the skin, see *MI* D721.3, "Disenchantment by destroying skin (covering)."

91. Elizabeth Kutzer ("Das indische Märchen," in *BP* 4:288 lines 1–2) makes this

very point (without referring to *The Donkey Tale* or *Vikramacarita*) about the presence of precise details and the absence of an "Es war einmal" quality to Indian narrative.

92. See Eleazar Meletinsky, "Problem of the Historical Morphology of the Folktale," in *Soviet Structural Folkloristics,* ed. Pierre Miranda, vol. 1 (The Hague and Paris: Mouton, 1974), 57.

93. Meletinsky, "Problem of the Historical Morphology," 55; Eleazar Meletinsky, "Marriage: Its Function and Position in the Structure of Folktales," in Miranda, *Soviet Structural Folkloristics,* 1:61–72, especially 67.

94. For quick orientation toward Melusine (*MI* C31.1.2), see "Melusine," in *F&W* 705; Catherine Rager, *Dictionnaire des fées et du peuple invisible dans l'occident païen* (Turnhout: Brepols, 2003), 636–40. For a lengthy study of the Melusine stories on Proppian lines, see Laurence Harf-Lancner, *Les fées au Moyen Age: Morgane et Mélusine; La naissance des fées* (Geneva: Slatkine, 1984). On the Swan Maiden (*MI* D361.1), see Alfred Métraux, "Swan Maiden," in *F&W* 1091–92.

95. On the genre classification of the poem, see Rizzardi, *Asinarius,* 150–57.

96. Rizzardi (*Asinarius,* 147) enumerates several unresolved puzzles in the narrative development of *The Donkey Tale,* but without using them to argue anything about the relative priority of *The Donkey Tale* and the Sanskrit tale.

97. See Wesselski, *Versuch einer Theorie des Märchens,* 194.

98. Compare *KHM* 88 and 108. See Walter Anderson, "Eine Märchenparallele zu Antonius Diogenes," *Philologus* 66 (1907): 606.

99. The relevant section in Augustine is *De civitate Dei* 18.18, ed. B. Dombart and A. Kalb, 5th ed. (Stuttgart: B. G. Teubner, 1981), 2:277–80. Most scholarship on the problem of man-animal metamorphosis has been concerned with Augustine's views on werewolves rather than on donkey-men. For discussion, see Laurence Harf-Lancner, ed., *Métamorphose et bestiaire fantastique au Moyen Age,* Collection de l'École Normale Supérieure de Jeunes Filles 28 (Paris: École Normale Supérieure de Jeunes Filles, 1985); Laurence Harf-Lancner, "La métamorphose illusoire: Des théories chrétiennes de la métamorphose aux images médiévales du loup-garou," *Annales* 40 (1985): 208–26; Dennis Kratz, "*Fictus lupus:* The Werewolf in Christian Thought," *Classical Folio* 30 (1976): 57–79; Charlotte Otten, *A Lycanthropy Reader: Werewolves in Western Culture* (Syracuse, NY: Syracuse University Press, 1986).

100. See BP 3:166. On the burning of the hide as one of the most important motifs in the story, see Weinhold, "Über das Märchen vom Eselmenschen," 9.

101. *The Donkey Tale* is not considered in A. C. Spearing's *The Medieval Poet as Voyeur: Looking and Listening in Medieval Love-Narratives* (Cambridge: Cambridge University Press, 1993).

102. On polygenesis, see *F&W* 876.

103. For a short statement on diffusionism, see MacEdward Leach, "Diffusion Theory," in *F&W* 313.

104. Propp, *La fiaba russa,* 7: "Una fiaba . . . la capiscono proprio tutti. Essa oltrepassa senza fatica ogni confine linguistico, passa da un popolo all'altro e si mantiene viva per millenni . . . Questo avviene perché la fiaba contiene valori eterni, incorruttibili."

105. See Wesselski, *Versuch einer Theorie des Märchens,* 194–95.

106. See Wesselski, *Versuch einer Theorie des Märchens,* 194. For a long list of allusions to Ovid, see Rizzardi, *Asinarius,* 166–67.

107. See Langosch, *Asinarius und Rapularius,* V.

108. *The Donkey Tale* 2, ed. and trans. Langosch, *Asinarius und Rapularius,* 15. *Pagina* is also the word used by Hugo of Trimberg in *Registrum multorum auctorum* 891def (ed. Langosch, 191).

109. *The Donkey Tale* 2, ed. and trans. Rizzardi, *Asinarius,* 194. On the etymology of *fabula,* see Ziolkowski, *Talking Animals,* 16–17.

110. For the most detailed English exposition of the case against them, see Ellis, *One Fairy Story Too Many.* Ellis's book includes consideration of many specific tales in the *KHM,* although significantly not "The Donkey" or "The Turnip."

111. Harris claimed that as the "compiler merely" of his own tales he wrote "without embellishment and without exaggeration" and that "not one of them is cooked, and not one of them nor any part of one is an invention of mine": see Duncan MacDougald, Jr., review of *The Complete Tales of Uncle Remus,* by Joel Chandler Harris, in *Journal of American Folklore* 70 (1957), 188–90, at 189–90.

112. The manuscript that perished was Johann. C 105. A partial transcription by Jacob Grimm now resides in the Staatsbibliothek Preussischer Kulturbesitz, Berolinensis MS Germ. quart. 923: see Rizzardi, *Asinarius,* 178. For the letters that pertain to *The Donkey Tale* and *Rapularius,* see Grimm and Hinrichs, *Briefwechsel zwischen Jacob und Wilhelm Grimm aus der Jugendzeit,* 338–42, letter from Jacob to Wilhelm, 21 June 1814. Strasbourg, Bibliothèque Municipale (formerly Bibliothèque de la Ville), MS.

113. See Langosch, "Asinarius," 510.

114. "Virgo puellares tunc iam compleverat annos, / Iam dederant teneros membra pudenda pilos. / Ubera mammarum dederant iam signa, quod ipsa / Vix queat absque viro sola cubare thoro."

115. *KHM,* 7th ed., 2:253.

116. "Pape, quid inquiris? O rex, quid nosse laboras? / Cur non deberet ista placere michi? / Immo placet, placet illa michi, multum placet," inquit / "Ferreus est certe cui placet illa nichil. / Candida delectat facies permixta rubore, / Ac si contempler lilia mixta rosis. / Cesariesque placet; delectat eburnea cervix / Et corpus fateor omne placere michi."

117. *KHM,* 7th ed., 2:253–54: "Eselein, wie gefällt dir meine Tochter?" Das Eselein drehte den Kopf nach ihr, schaute sie an, nickte und sprach: "Aus der Massen wohl, sie ist so schön, wie ich noch keine gesehen habe."

118. *KHM,* 7th ed., 2:253: Es half keine Ausrede, das Eselein wollte und mußte die Laute schlagen, war beharrlich und fleißig und lernte es am Ende so gut als sein Meister selber.

119. See Hamann, *Die literarischen Vorlagen,* 48. In app. 5c in the present study these diminutives have been translated simply as "donkey," since etymologically the English word may itself be a diminutive of the adjective *dun* (see *Oxford English Dictionary,* s.v.).

120. *KHM,* 7th ed., 2:252: "Ich bin wie ein Acker, auf dem nichts wächst."

121. On both expressions, see Bluhm and Rölleke, *"Redensarten des Volks, auf die ich immer horche,"* 139.

122. See Hamann, *Die literarischen Vorlagen,* 45–46.

123. See Rizzardi, *Asinarius,* 166–68.

124. See Hamann, *Die literarischen Vorlagen,* 45–46.

125. See Hamann, *Die literarischen Vorlagen,* 47.

126. A short but convincing attempt to highlight the fairy tale qualities of the poem was made in a study to which I gained access only after publication of my initial study of "The Donkey" in 1995: Gatti, "Elementi favolistici," 149–54.

127. Propp (*La fiaba russa*, 195–96) analyzes Russian folktales that conform very closely in their general pattern to *The Donkey Tale*.

128. The structural feature of two realms is discussed by Propp in *La fiaba russa*, 202. Another Medieval Latin text deeply indebted to folkloric sources in which two realms are juxtaposed is *Ruodlieb*, but it could be qualified as a proto-romance with fairy tale features, not as a fairy tale. For an edition with translation, see C. W. Grocock, ed. and trans., *The Ruodlieb* (Chicago: Bolchazy-Carducci, 1985). The standard edition is Benedikt Konrad Vollmann's *Ruodlieb* (Wiesbaden: Dr. Ludwig Reichert Verlag, 1985).

129. Wesselski (*Versuch einer Theorie des Märchens*, 194) posits that *Märchen* demands *das Wunderbare*, but he fails to see it here.

CONCLUSION

1. Propp, *La fiaba russa*, 55: "La trascrizione di una fiaba può sembrare, a prima vista, una cosa molto facile che può essere fatta da chiunque, senza richiedere una preparazione particolare. È possibile allora parlare di uno specifico sviluppo storico della raccolta di fiabe?"

2. Wesselski, *Versuch einer Theorie des Märchens*, 104, as quoted by Satu Apo in *Narrative World*, 16: "Das Märchen ist eine Kunstform der Erzählung, die neben Gemeinschaftsmotiven auch in einer die Entwicklung der Handlung bestimmenden Weise Wundermotive verwendet."

3. Ziolkowski, "Cultural Diglossia," 193–213.

4. Tegethoff, *Märchen, Schwänke und Fabeln*, XIV: "der dunklen Anfänge europäischen Märchenerzählens."

5. The only scholar who has recently pinpointed the Middle Ages as the period in which the oral wonder tale and literary fairy tale traditions first took shape is Jack Zipes: see his excellent essay "Cross-Cultural Connections and the Contamination of the Classical Fairy Tale," in *Great Fairy Tale Tradition*, 845–69, especially 847, 851.

6. See Lewis Seifert, "The Marvelous in Context: The Place of the *Contes de Fées* in Late Seventeenth-Century France," in Zipes, *Great Fairy Tale Tradition*, 902–33.

7. Although Medieval Latin has romance-like texts, the very word for the genre points to its connection with the vernacular (in this case, Romance) languages. The prevalence of folktale patterns in romance has been much discussed. For a thorough but concise survey, see D. H. Green, *The Beginnings of Medieval Romance: Fact and Fiction, 1150–1220*, Cambridge Studies in Medieval Literature 47 (Cambridge: Cambridge University Press, 2002), 113–23. Similar observations could be made about *lais*, associated particularly with Marie de France.

8. For an interesting attempt to investigate folkloric constituents in *De nugis curialium*, see Albert Vàrvaro, *Apparizioni fantastiche: Tradizioni folcloriche e letteratura nel medioevo; Walter Map* (Bologna: Il Mulino, 1994).

9. See Michael Rothmann, "Mirabilia vero dicimus, quae nostrae cognitioni non subiacent, etiam cum sint naturalia: 'Wundergeschichten' zwischen Wissen und Unterhaltung; der 'Liber de mirabilibus mundi' ('Otia Imperialia') des Gervasius von Tilbury," in *Mirakel im Mittelalter: Konzeptionen, Erscheinungsformen, Deutungen*, ed.

Martin Heinzelmann, Klaus Herbers, and Dieter R. Bauer, Beiträge zur Hagiographie 3 (Stuttgart: Franz Steiner Verlag, 2002), 399–432.

10. See G. T. Shepherd, "The Emancipation of Story in the Twelfth Century," in *Medieval Narrative: A Symposium*, ed. Hans Bekker-Nielsen (Odense: Odense University Press, 1979), 44–57.

11. On marvels in the works of William of Malmesbury and William of Newburgh, see Monika Otter, *Inventiones: Fiction and Referentiality in Twelfth-Century English Historical Writing* (Chapel Hill and London: University of North Carolina Press, 1996), 102–8. On Saxo, see Axel Olrik, "Märchen in Saxo Grammaticus," *Zeitschrift für Volkskunde* 2 (1892): 117–23, 252–58, 367–74.

12. See Mazzacurati, *All'ombra di Dioneo*, 146–47.

13. On frame tales, see Stephen Belcher, "Framed Tales in the Oral Tradition: An Exploration," *Fabula* 36 (1994): 1–19; Irwin, "What's in a Frame?" 27–53.

14. See Ziolkowski, "Vergil as Shahrazad," 25–36.

15. For an overview of recent work on exempla, see Jacques Berlioz and Marie Anne Polo de Beaulieu, eds., *Les "Exempla" médiévaux: Nouvelles perspectives*, Nouvelle bibliothèque du Moyen Age 47 (Paris: Honoré Champion, 1998). At present, the best access to folklore motifs in exempla is through Frederic C. Tubach's *Index Exemplorum: A Handbook of Medieval Religious Tales*, FFC 204 (Helsinki: Suomalainen Tiedeakatemia, Academia scientiarum fennica, 1981). This index lists exempla without subsuming them under categories drawn from AT or *MI*.

16. Albert Wesselski (*Mönchslatein: Erzählungen aus geistlichen Schriften des XIII. Jahrhunderts* [Leipzig: Wilhelm Heims, 1909], XIII) observes, "bei der ungebildeten Menge, die, soweit sie nicht in Städten oder größern Flecken heimisch war, vielleicht nie vorher hatte predigen hören, mußte die schlichte Erzählung einen Erfolg haben, wie noch heute das Märchen bei den Kindern."

17. This holds equally true for Eastern European materials: see Propp, *La fiaba russa*, 56.

18. See Wesselski, *Mönchslatein*, XXVIII.

19. See Röhrich, *Erzählungen des späten Mittelalters*, 1:5.

20. See Propp, *La fiaba russa*, 8.

21. See Robert J. Clements and Joseph Gibaldi, *Anatomy of the Novella: The European Tale Collection from Boccaccio and Chaucer to Cervantes* (New York: New York University Press, 1977).

22. See R. Howard Bloch, *God's Plagiarist, Being an Account of the Fabulous Industry and Irregular Commerce of the Abbé Migne* (Chicago: University of Chicago Press, 1994).

23. See Tegethoff, *Märchen, Schwänke und Fabeln*, XIII.

APPENDIX

1. Bertini construes *dicens* as referring to the priest.

2. The reference is to eucharistic wafers and holy water.

3. Or "by the sacred pledges we bear."

4. Bertini construes lines 171–72 differently: "[his eyes] are no longer able to see . . . the relatives who meet him, running from the city. Only a voice, or just the contact of

a hand, furnish elements, not sight" [essi non sono in grado di scorgere . . . i congiunti, che gli si fanno incontro correndo dalla città. Solo la voce, o il contatto della mano gli forniscono elementi, non la vista].

5. This simile is modeled elaborately on Virgil *Aeneid* 12.473–77. Because Virgil employs *alta* to modify *atria,* I have taken the adjective and noun together here. In Virgil's simile, the verb *sonat* describes the swallow. Here, it belongs with *stagna,* as is confirmed by the verbs *remugit, resonans,* and *reboantia* in lines 194–96: just as the lakes and swamps resonate to the calls of the swallow, so do the earth, mountains, and shore to the cries of Within's wife. Since the wife, who prompted the comparison, was just described as being *anxia,* it makes no sense to qualify the bird as being happy: *laeta,* although often used to characterize soil in its sense of "fertile, abounding," would here refer to insect-filled air, since the goal of the swallow is to gather food for its young. Contrast, on all these points, Bertini, *Letaldo di Micy, Within piscator,* 13 (translation), 30 (commentary on line 190).

6. The manuscript reads *pestem.* Klein's paleographic arguments for preferring Grimm's emendation *pellem* to van Woestijne's *vestem* convince me, although Bertini and Mosetti Casaretto opt for the latter.

7. It would be possible to translate the manuscript *qui* as adverbial, meaning "whereby." I accept Klein's emendation to *quo.*

8. Although it has no effect on the translation, I accept Klein's emendation of *paternas* to *paternos.* The emendation assumes that *paternas* is a scribal error, rather than an indication that the poet understood *lares* to be feminine rather than masculine.

9. My translation accepts Klein's emendation of *interpretari* to *interpellari.*

10. Or "madness [and] prudence / make answer, through pretenses."

11. Klein emends *occasionem* to *occisionem,* in which case the reading would be "feigns a slaying."

12. Bertini and Mosetti Casaretto, like Welkenhuysen, print the manuscript reading of *tinctam,* whereas Klein, following Grimm, emends to *tincta,* in which case the reading would be "painting the appearance of death on his wife, / staining her with swine's blood."

13. In translating I follow Welkenhuysen. Bertini and Mosetti Casaretto construe *stupentes illam plaudere* as "sorpresi che ella stia esultando."

14. The verse is lacking a word. In accepting Haupt's conjecture *iam,* I follow Welkenhuysen, Klein, and Bertini and Mosetti Casaretto. Van de Woestijne's *hunc* was accepted by Langosch.

15. I follow Welkenhuysen. Contrast Bertini and Mosetti Casaretto's "per ottenere la vostra indulgenza."

16. The noun *caritas* may look forward already to the reference to drink in strophe 176, line 3, since it had special senses of "an offering of wine" and "a draft of love" (*Minnetrunk*): see Prinz et al., *Mittellateinisches Wörterbuch,* "C," 287, lines 38–69.

17. *Temporaliter* is also attested as meaning "happily," which would fit well here. See Niermeyer and van de Kieft, *Mediae Latinitatis Lexicon Minus,* 2:1327.

18. I follow Welkenhuysen and Bertini and Mosetti Casaretto, as opposed to Klein, who accepts Grimm's emendation of *sonoris* to *sonore.*

19. I accept Klein's emendation of *ergo* to *ego,* which was also followed by Bertini and Mosetti Casaretto.

20. Alternatively, the final two lines of strophe 192 could be understood as a separate sentence: "let me not be tossed about by the waves of the sea, I who have already been prevailed upon by you."

21. The manuscript reads *dixit,* which is printed by all editors except Welkenhuysen, Klein, and Bertini and Mosetti Casaretto.

22. Bertini puts forth tentatively the idea of emending *magistros* to *ministros.*

23. There may be textual problems in these two lines, which have elicited almost as many different interpretations as there have been editors and translators. If left unmended, the lines could have as their irony the contrast between, on the one hand, the provost's assertion that either of his comrades who fails to follow him will prove himself to be a fool and, on the other, the narrator's point-blank statement that the provost is himself a fool for proposing to hurl himself into the sea.

24. If the reading *dotta* is retained without the emendation to <p>otta, the translation would be "at one and the same time" rather than "and place them . . . in one pot." Not emending means that there is no antecedent for the feminine pronoun in "fa che la sia cotta."

25. Or "I will be dodging quite a blow!"

26. Meaning "from where the rabbit is coming."

27. That is, by providing them dowries.

28. The equivalent in colloquial English would be "as quiet as a mouse."

29. In Roman myth, Cacus was a monster who lived on a hill at Rome. He is most famous for having stolen cattle from Hercules, who discovered them in the monster's cave and killed Cacus.

30. If the noun *cotto* does not denote earthenware, it could mean "concoction."

31. Talers were silver coins that were a unit of currency in some German regions from the late Middle Ages until the nineteenth century. The term is related to the English word *dollar.*

32. This motif is drawn from D. P. Rotunda, *Motif-Index of the Italian Novella in Prose* (Bloomington: Indiana University Press, 1942), 94.

33. Langosch reads *rastro . . . aratri,* rather than *rastro . . . aratro.*

34. Or "sow the fields with my own hand."

35. My translation here follows Langosch, who accepts the reading in two manuscripts of *premia . . . magna,* instead of the *premia . . . digna* ("worthy rewards") preferred by Gatti. Langosch's choice seems to me to accord better with *The Turnip "prodiga"* [2] 97–98.

36. Langosch accepts the reading of *domum* as the final word in the line: thus the reading would be "to the king's house."

37. My translation follows Gatti, who accepts the conjecture of *amarum continet iram* by W. B. Sedgwick ("Coniecturae in poetas aliquot medii aevi," *Bulletin Du Cange: Archivum Latinitatis Medii Aevi* 5 [1929–30], 222). Langosch's *amarum condolet omen* ("grieves at the bitter omen") follows instead two manuscripts.

38. Gatti accepts the manuscript reading (supported by Sedgwick) of *tacito sic murmurat ore,* whereas Langosch conjectures *cauto sic murmurat ore* ("he mutters with wary mouth in this way").

39. Langosch reads *scola,* in which case the reading would be "this sack is worthier than the precious purple of kings, better and more useful than school."

40. Or "And, if not of your own accord, may you be swayed by love of a reward; I will take care to pay out whatever you wish to have."

41. Or, following Langosch, "you do not have resources of such value."

42. Or, following Langosch, "Pushing down the man's head . . . 'in such a way it will be inside.'"

43. Langosch, accepting different readings, printed not *Iam non in saccum curo venire meum* (Gatti) but *Ammodo non saccum quero videre meum* ("from now on I will not seek to see my sack").

44. To me, the reading in the Philadelphia fragments (hereafter MS P; see Gatti, *Rapularius II*, 374)—unique but far earlier than other manuscripts of *Rapularius "prodiga"* [2]—is preferable: "but the other lived, a destitute pauper, in lamentation."

45. Here again, the reading in MS P seems to me superior: "to provide [*procuret* instead of *protelet*] for himself."

46. Langosch reads *inde* instead of *ipse,* in which case the reading would be "and then he takes" or "and he takes from it."

47. Supplying the word *mea* between *aratro* and *rura* (as Sedgwick conjectured and Gatti accepted) solves the metrical problem in the Latin.

48. Gatti's text has the typographical error *cum rege balantum,* instead of *cum grege balantum.*

49. Or "If you give anything, he will turn very nauseous, as a man who is glutted spurns all manner of food."

50. Gatti, against the manuscripts and earlier editors, opens this sentence with *En* instead of *Sed.*

51. The manuscripts and all editions prior to that of Gatti have *video,* in which case the reading would be "I who see that I despoiled myself by my own hand." Gatti follows a conjecture of *videor* that was made by Karl Strecker and supported by Otto Schumann but rejected by Langosch.

52. Gatti notes the awkward polysyndeton of *-que* in lines 229 and 231. Could *Alloquiturque viros* conceal *Alloquitur quirites*? The phrase *arma quiritum* appeared in line 189. It is mentioned in line 294 that these are "armati . . . viri."

53. Gatti, in contrast to the other editors, prefers *Non decet* over *Nunc decet* and thus prefers the reading "it is not the case, O friends, that you remember me."

54. Gatti prints the typographical error *fratrem adit fratrem* for *frater adit fratrem.*

55. Gatti prefers *rapuere,* found in γ, over the *nocuere* of most other manuscripts, which Langosch printed and in which case the reading would be "As his own dogs once harmed Actaeon."

56. *Infandeque rei sic latuere rei* is the text Gatti prints, with the first word being a conjecture based on MS P. Langosch printed the unmetrical *In fraudeque rei sic latuere rei,* in which case the reading would be "and thus in the deceit of this business those guilty hid."

57. Gatti prints *Nec latuit nomen auspiciique gradus* (which he translates as "e gli fu chiaro chi fosse e che grado avesse"). I conjecture *omen* and prefer *officiique* of γ (which Oesterley and Bolte accepted). The line implies that the man in the sack, looking down, perceived the tonsure of the wayfarer beneath him and understood him to be a cleric.

58. My translation follows Langosch and all other editors. Following a suggestion by Sedgwick, Gatti punctuates with quotation marks after, rather than before, *item.* This

other punctuation causes *item* to be left untranslated and sacrifices the correspondence between *item* in this line and *rursus* in the next.

59. Alternatively, Gatti prefers the *ubi* of γ (thus "If you doubt *where* I am . . .") over the *quid* of other manuscripts and earlier editors.

60. Gatti prints *"Gratis," ait, "presens tempus et hora perit!"* Alternatively (per Langosch and most of the manuscripts), the line ends *preit,* in which case the reading would be "The present time and hour pass by for no reason."

61. Gatti prefers the *diva* of γ over the *dura* ("hard wisdom") of most other manuscripts and Langosch.

62. Gatti's text reads *Taliter oranti respondet pendulus ille.* Rejecting the reading of γ, Langosch and another editor print *intranti* as the second word, in which case the reading would be "in such fashion to him as he enters."

63. Gatti translates very differently: "Ehi, amico, come si sta nel sacco?"

64. The German *und* ("and") was omitted in 1857.

65. "To doff a soldier's coat" is a metonymy for "to leave the army."

66. The quotation marks appear in the 1857 edition but not in the 1819 edition.

67. The 1857 edition omits the exclamation *Ei* and begins immediately with the question "What kind of a rare thing . . . ?"

68. The 1857 edition makes the wording here more analytic and less paratactic.

69. In the 1857 edition, the text drops one phrase and is rearranged slightly, so that the translation would read "hoisted him up on a branch and took flight. However, he worked on it . . ."

70. The 1857 edition shifts "from there" from the second clause of the German to the third.

71. The 1857 edition changes "constellations" to "stars" and drops the "and" between "the winds and the sand."

72. Rather than simply "out of it," a reading based on the 1857 edition would be "out of the sack of wisdom."

73. The 1819 edition stops short: *wo ich dich gefunden.* The 1857 has the additional auxiliary verb: *wo ich dich gefunden habe.*

74. In the 1857 edition, the text presents three small changes, all evidently with a view to clarifying the events in the story. Rather than *rücklings* ("facing backwards"), Wilhelm writes *umgekehrt;* rather than using words meaning "and dangled," he specifies with words meaning "then dangled." Finally, he introduces the brother's final speech with words meaning "and spoke."

75. The conclusion of the 1857 edition may be translated as "With that, he mounted the scholar's horse, rode forth, but after an hour sent someone to let him down again."

76. "Violent band" is an equally plausible translation.

77. This couplet, stricken by Langosch, was restored by Rizzardi. Following the manuscripts and earlier editions (by Mone and Bolte), she placed the two lines after line 118. I have placed them after line 116. *Refert* could also mean "gives back an answer, replies."

78. Rizzardi's translation is "semmai appartengo all'aristocrazia cittadina." Langosch's is "Was vielmehr mich umfangen hat, das ist die Vornehmheit der Stadt."

79. The phrase *semper asellus eris* alludes to the last line of Avian's fifth fable, about the ass in the lion's skin: the farmer who has stripped the ass of the stolen skin chides him by saying, "To me you will always be a donkey as before."

80. Langosch (*Asinarius und Rapularius,* 43) accepts the reading *Non mea, sed patris fiat liberta voluntas* and translates it "Nicht soll mein Wille jetzt geschehn, vielmehr solls nach dem Vater gehn!" Rizzardi marks one word as a crux in the text, which she prints as *Non mea sed patris fiat †liberata† voluntas* and translates as "Venga eseguita non la mia volontà, ma quella di mio padre." I propose that the correct reading is *librata.*

81. Literally, "Venus's knot."

82. Langosch (*Asinarius und Rapularius,* 45) proposes that *Neoptolomus* may here metonymically mean "son."

83. For information on the concluding formulation, see Bluhm and Rölleke, *"Redensarten des Volks, auf die ich immer horche,"* 123.

Bibliography

Aarne, Antti. *Leitfaden der vergleichenden Märchenforschung.* FFC 13. Hamina: Suoma-
laisen Tiedeakatemia Kustantama, 1913.

————. "Die Zaubergaben." *Journal de la société finno-ougrienne* 27 (1909): 1–96.

————. "Ursprung der Märchen." In Aarne, *Leitfaden,* 1–22. Reprinted in *Wege der
Märchenforschung,* ed. Felix Karlinger, Wege der Forschung 255 (Darmstadt: Wis-
senschaftliche Buchgesellschaft, 1973), 42–60.

Abbo of Fleury. *Epistolae.* In *PL* 139.419–61.

Adams, J. N. *The Latin Sexual Vocabulary.* Baltimore: Johns Hopkins University Press,
1982.

Adolf, Helen. "The Ass and the Harp." *Speculum* 25 (1950): 49–57.

Ælfric. *The Colloquy of Ælfric.* Ed. G. N. Garmonsway. London: Methuen, 1939.

Allison, Randal S. "Ur-form." In *Folklore* 2:823–24.

Alnæs, Ingvild. "H. C. Andersen og folkeeventyrene." *Anderseniana,* 3rd ser., 2 (1974–
77): 97–119.

Aly, Wolf. "Märchen." In *Paulys Real-Encyclopädie der classischen Altertumswissenschaft,*
ed. Georg Wissowa, 14:254–81. Stuttgart: J. B. Metzler, 1930.

Amalar of Metz. *Epistula Amalarii ad Carolum imperatorem de scrutinio et baptismo.* In
Amalarii episcopi opera liturgica omnia, ed. Johann Michael Hanssens, 1:236–51.
Studi e testi 138. Vatican City: Biblioteca apostolica Vaticana, 1948.

Amelung, Arthur, and Oskar Jänicke, eds. *Ortnit und Die Wolfdietriche.* 2 vols. Deutsches
Heldenbuch 3–4. Berlin: Weidmann, 1871–73. Repr., Zurich: Weidmann, 1968.

Ampelius, Lucius. *Liber memorialis.* Ed. and trans. Marie-Pierre Arnaud-Lindet. Paris:
Belles Lettres, 1993.

Andersen, Hans Christian. *Ausgewählte Märchen.* Translated into German by Julius
Reuscher. Leipzig: Ambr. Abel, 1883.

————. *The Complete Fairy Tales and Stories.* Trans. Erik Christian Haugaard. New
York: Doubleday, 1974.

———. *Eighty Fairy Tales.* Trans. R. P. Keigwin. New York: Pantheon, 1982.

———. *Eventyr.* Ed. Erik Dal, Erling Nielsen, and Flemming Hovmann. 7 vols. Copenhagen: C. A. Reitzels Forlag, 1963–90.

———. *Fairy Tales: A Selection.* Trans. L. W. Kingsland. Oxford: Oxford University Press, 1984.

———. *Stories for the Household.* Trans. H. W. Dulcken. London: George Routledge and Sons; New York: E. P. Dutton, 1888.

Anderson, Graham. *Fairytale in the Ancient World.* London and New York: Routledge, 2000.

Anderson, Walter. "Eine Märchenparallele zu Antonius Diogenes." *Philologus* 66 (1907): 606–8.

Anttonen, Pertti. "Philological Approach." In *Folklore* 2:641–47.

Apo, Satu. *The Narrative World of Finnish Fairy Tales.* FFC 112, no. 256. Helsinki: Suomalainen Tiedeakatemia, Academia scientiarum fennica, 1995.

———. "The Two Worlds of the Finnish Fairytale: Observations on the Folk and Literary Fairytale Tradition of the 19th Century." *Arv: Scandinavian Yearbook of Folklore* 44 (1988): 27–48.

Apocrypha, New Testament. Ed. Wilhelm Schneemelcher. Trans. R. McL. Wilson. 2nd ed. 2 vols. Louisville, KY: Westminster/John Knox, 1991–92.

Apuleius. *Metamorphoses.* Ed. and trans. J. Arthur Hanson. 2 vols. Loeb Classical Library 44, 453. Cambridge, MA: Harvard University Press, 1989.

Archpoet. *Die Gedichte des Archipoeta.* Ed. Heinrich Watenphul and Heinrich Krefeld. Heidelberg: Carl Winter, 1958.

———. *Die Gedichte des Archipoeta.* Ed. and trans. Heinrich Krefeld. Schriften und Quellen der alten Welt 41. Berlin: Akademie Verlag, 1992.

Aristophanes. *Clouds.* In *Aristophanes,* ed. and trans. Jeffrey Henderson, 2:1–211. Loeb Classical Library 488. Cambridge, MA: Harvard University Press, 1998.

Arnold, Günter. "Herders Projekt einer Märchensammlung." *Jahrbuch für Volkskunde und Kulturgeschichte* 27 (1984): 99–106.

Athenaeus. *Deipnosophistae.* Ed. and trans. Charles Burton Gulick. 7 vols. Loeb Classical Library 204, 208, 224, 235, 274, 327, 345. Cambridge, MA: Harvard University Press, 1961.

Audradus of Sens. *De fonte vitae.* Ed. Francesco Stella. Il Nuovo Melograno 5. Florence: Casa Editrice Le Lettere, 1991.

Auerbach, Erich. "Philology and *Weltliteratur.*" Trans. Maire Said and Edward Said. *Centennial Review* 13 (1969). Originally published as "Philologie der Weltliteratur," in *Weltliteratur: Festgabe für Fritz Strich zum 70. Geburtstag,* ed. Walter Muschg and Emil Staiger (Bern: Francke Verlag, 1952), 39–50.

Augustine. *De civitate Dei.* Ed. B. Dombart and A. Kalb. 5th ed. 2 vols. Stuttgart: B. G. Teubner, 1981.

———. *Sex quaestiones contra paganos expositae, liber unus (-epistola 102).* In *Epistolae, Secunda classis,* in *PL* 33.370–86.

Ayrer, Jakob. "Der Beck, der sein Weib wider lebendig geiget hat." In *Ayrers Dramen,* ed. Adelbert von Keller, Bibliothek des Litterarischen Vereins in Stuttgart 79, 2809–28. Stuttgart: Gedruckt auf Kosten des Litterarischen Vereins, 1865.

Azzolina, David S. *Tale Type- and Motif-Indexes: An Annotated Bibliography.* New York and London: Garland, 1987.

Baker, Ronald L. "Fakelore." In *Encyclopedia of Folklore and Literature,* ed. Mary Ellen Brown and Bruce A. Rosenberg, 203–5. Santa Barbara, CA: ABC-CLIO, 1998.

Bakhtin, Mikhail Mikhailovich. *Rabelais and His World.* Trans. Hélène Iswolsky. Cambridge, MA: MIT Press, 1968. Repr., Bloomington: Indiana University Press, 1985.

Barchilon, Jacques. *Le Conte merveilleux français de 1690 à 1790.* Paris: Honoré Champion, 1975.

Basile, Giambattista. *Il pentamerone, ossia la fiaba delle fiabe.* Trans. Benedetto Croce. 2 vols. Bari: Gius. Laterza e Figli, 1925.

———. *The Pentamerone.* Trans. N. M. Penzer. 2 vols. New York: E. P. Dutton, 1932.

Bataillon, Marcel. "Érasme conteur: Folklore et invention narrative." In *Mélanges de langue et de littérature médiévales offerts à Pierre Le Gentil, Professeur à la Sorbonne, par ses collègues, ses élèves et ses amis,* 85–104. Paris: S.E.D.E.S., 1973.

Bately, Janet, ed. *The Old English Orosius.* Early English Text Society Supplementary Series 6. London: Oxford University Press, 1980.

Battle of the Mice and Frogs (Batrachomyomachia). In *Hesiod, The Homeric Hymns and Homerica,* ed. and trans. Hugh G. Evelyn-White, 542–63. Loeb Classical Library 57. Cambridge, MA: Harvard University Press, 1977.

Bausinger, Hermann. "Buchmärchen." In *EM* 2:974–77.

———. "Folklore und gesunkenes Kulturgut." In *Formen der "Volkspoesie,"* 2nd ed., 41–55. Berlin: E. Schmidt Verlag, 1980.

Bayless, Martha. *Parody in the Middle Ages: The Latin Tradition.* Ann Arbor: University of Michigan Press, 1996.

Beckett, Sandra. *Recycling Red Riding Hood.* Children's Literature and Culture 23. New York: Routledge, 2001.

Bede. *Ecclesiastical History of the English People.* Ed. and trans. Bertram Colgrave and R. A. B. Mynors. 2nd ed. Oxford: Clarendon, 1991.

Bédier, Joseph. *Les fabliaux: Études de littérature populaire et d'histoire littéraire du moyen âge.* Paris: Honoré Champion, 1893.

Beit, Hedwig von. *Symbolik des Märchens: Versuch einer Deutung.* 2nd ed. 3 vols. Bern: Francke Verlag, 1952–57.

Belcher, Stephen. "Framed Tales in the Oral Tradition: An Exploration." *Fabula* 36 (1994): 1–19.

Ben-Amos, Dan. "Transmission." In *Folklore* 2:807–11.

Bendix, Regina. "Fakelore." In *Folklore* 1:275–77.

Benfey, Theodor, trans. *Pantschatantra: Fünf Bücher indischer Fabeln, Märchen und Erzählungen; Aus dem Sanskrit übersetzt mit Einleitung und Anmerkungen versehen.* 2 vols. Leipzig: F. A. Brockhaus, 1859.

Berendsohn, Walter A. *Grundformen volkstümlicher Erzählerkunst in den Kinder- und Hausmärchen der Brüder Grimm.* Hamburg: Verlag W. Gente, 1921.

Berger, Eberhard, and Joachim Giera. *77 Märchenfilme: Ein Filmführer für jung und alt.* Berlin: Henschel Verlag, 1990.

Berlioz, Jacques. "A Medieval 'Little Red Riding Hood'? 'The Little Girl Spared by the Wolves' in the *Fecunda ratis* of Egbert of Liège (Early 11th Century)." Trans. Leslie Abend Callahan and Francesca Canadé Sautman. *Medieval Folklore* 3 (1994): 39–66.

———. "Un Petit Chaperon rouge médiéval? 'La petite fille épargnée par les loups' dans la *Fecunda ratis* d'Egbert de Liège (début du XIe siècle)." *Merveilles et contes* 5 (1991): 246–63.

Berlioz, Jacques, and Marie Anne Polo de Beaulieu, eds. *Les "Exempla" médiévaux: Nouvelles perspectives.* Nouvelle bibliothèque du Moyen Age 47. Paris: Honoré Champion, 1998.

Berlioz, Jacques, Claude Bremond, and Catherine Velay-Vallantin, trans. *Formes médiévales du conte merveilleux.* Paris: Éditions Stock, 1989.

Berschin, Walter. *Greek Letters and the Latin Middle Ages, from Jerome to Nicholas of Cusa.* Trans. Jerold C. Frakes. 2nd ed. Washington, DC: Catholic University of America Press, 1988.

Bertini, Ferruccio. "Il contadino medievale, ovvero il profilo del diavolo (Una nuova interpretazione dei *Versus de unibove*)." *Maia* 47 (1995): 325–41. Reprinted in *Interpreti medievali di Fedro,* Nuovo Medioevo 57 (Naples: Liguori, 1998), 111–28.

———. "Il 'Within piscator' di Letaldo di Micy." *Mittellateinisches Jahrbuch* 24–25 (1989–90): 39–48.

———. "La letteratura epica." In *Il secolo di ferro: Mito e realtà del secolo X, 19–25 Aprile 1990,* 2:723–54. Settimane di studio del Centro italiano di Studi sull'alto medioevo 38. Spoleto: Centro italiano di Studi sull'alto medioevo, 1991.

———, ed. and trans. *Letaldo di Micy, Within piscator.* Biblioteca del Medioevo latino. Florence: Giunti, 1995.

Bertini, Ferruccio, and Francesco Mosetti Casaretto, eds. and trans. *La Beffa di Unibos.* Gli Orsatti: Testi dell'Altro Medioevo 9. Alessandria: Edizioni dell'Orso, 2000.

Bettelheim, Bruno. *The Uses of Enchantment: The Meaning and Importance of Fairy Tales.* New York: Vintage, 1989.

Beudel, Paulus. *Qua ratione Graeci liberos docuerint, papyris, ostracis, tabulis in Aegypto inventis illustratur.* Monasterii Guestfalorum: E typographia Aschendorffiana, 1911.

Beyer, Jürgen. *Schwank und Moral: Untersuchungen zum altfranzösischen Fabliau und verwandten Formen.* Studia Romanica 16. Heidelberg: Carl Winter, 1969.

Bickerman, Elias. *Four Strange Books of the Bible: Jonah/Daniel/Koheleth/Esther.* New York: Schocken, 1967.

Bieler, Ludwig, ed. *The Irish Penitentials.* Scriptores latini Hiberniae 5. Dublin: Dublin Institute for Advanced Studies, 1975.

Bisanti, Armando. "Within il calvo." *Studi medievali,* 3rd ser., 40 (1999): 843–56.

Blaise, Albert. *Le Vocabulaire latin des principaux thèmes liturgiques.* Turnhout: Brepols, 1966.

Bloch, R. Howard. *Etymologies and Genealogies: A Literary Anthropology of the French Middle Ages.* Chicago: University of Chicago Press, 1983.

———. *God's Plagiarist, Being an Account of the Fabulous Industry and Irregular Commerce of the Abbé Migne.* Chicago: University of Chicago Press, 1994.

Bloch, R. Howard, and Stephen G. Nichols, eds. *Medievalism and the Modernist Temper.* Trans. Hans Ulrich Gumbrecht and Jeffrey T. Schnapp. Baltimore and London: Johns Hopkins University Press, 1996.

Bluhm, Lothar. *Die Brüder Grimm und der Beginn der Deutschen Philologie: Eine Studie zu Kommunikation und Wissenschaftsbildung im frühen 19. Jahrhundert.* Spolia Berolinensia: Berliner Beiträge zur Geistes- und Kulturgeschichte des Mittelalters und der Neuzeit 11. Hildesheim and Zurich: Weidmann, 1997.

Bluhm, Lothar, and Heinz Rölleke. *"Redensarten des Volks, auf die ich immer horche": Märchen-Sprichwort-Redensart; Zur volkspoetischen Ausgestaltung der "Kinder- und*

Hausmärchen" durch die Brüder Grimm. 2nd ed. Stuttgart and Leipzig: S. Hirzel Verlag, 1997.

Boardman, John. *The History of Greek Vases: Potters, Painters, and Pictures.* London: Thames and Hudson, 2001.

Boas, George. *Vox Populi: Essays in the History of an Idea.* Baltimore: Johns Hopkins University Press, 1969.

Boccaccio, Giovanni. *Das Dekameron.* Trans. Albert Wesselski. Leipzig: Insel-Verlag, 1921.

———. *Genealogi.* Ed. Vincenzo Romano. 2 vols. Bari: Gius. Laterza e Figli, 1951.

Bombaugh, Charles. *Gleanings from the Harvest Fields of Literature, Science, and Art.* 3rd ed. Baltimore: T. N. Kurtz, 1867.

Bond, Gerald A. *The Loving Subject: Desire, Eloquence, and Power in Romanesque France.* Philadelphia: University of Pennsylvania Press, 1995.

Bonnes, Jean-Paul. "Un lettré du Xe siècle: Introduction au poème de Létald." *Revue Mabillon* 33 (1943): 23–47.

Borst, Arno. *Lebensformen im Mittelalter.* Frankfurt am Main: Ullstein, 1979.

Bosworth, Joseph, and T. Northcote Toller. *An Anglo-Saxon Dictionary.* Oxford: Clarendon, 1898.

Bottigheimer, Ruth B. *Fairy Godfather: Straparola, Venice, and the European Fairy Tale Tradition.* Philadelphia: University of Pennsylvania Press, 2002.

———. "Fairy Tales, Folk Narrative Research, and History." *Social History* 14 (1989): 343–57.

———. *Grimms' Bad Girls and Bold Boys: The Moral and Social Vision of the Tales.* New Haven and London: Yale University Press, 1987.

———. "Straparola's *Piacevoli notti:* Rags-to-Riches Fairy Tales as Urban Creations." *Marvels and Tales: Journal of Fairy-Tale Studies* 8 (1994): 281–95.

———. "The Ultimate Fairy Tale: Oral Transmission in a Literate World." In *A Companion to the Fairy Tale,* ed. Hilda Ellis Davidson and Anna Chaudhri, 57–70. Cambridge: D. S. Brewer, 2003.

Bowers, Robert Hood. *The Legend of Jonah.* The Hague: Martinus Nijhoff, 1971.

Bray, Dorothy Ann. *A List of Motifs in the Lives of the Early Irish Saints.* FFC 252. Helsinki: Suomalainen Tiedeakatemia, Academia scientiarum fennica, 1992.

Brednich, Rolf Wilhelm. "Esel als Lautenspieler." In *EM* 4:426–28.

Bricout, Bernadette. "Les deux chemins du Petit Chaperon Rouge." In *Frontières du conte,* ed. François Marotin, 47–54. Paris: Editions du Centre national de la recherche scientifique, 1982.

Brown, Carolyn S. *The Tall Tale in American Folklore and Literature.* Knoxville: University of Tennessee Press, 1987.

Brunel, C. "Walmannus, waumannus." *Bulletin Du Cange: Archivum Latinitatis Medii Aevi* 1 (1927): 31–32.

Brunhölzl, Franz. *Histoire de la littérature latine du moyen âge.* Trans. Henri Rochais. 2 vols. (vol. 2 in 2 parts). Turnhout: Brepols, 1991–2000.

Brunhölzl, Franz, and F. J. Worstbrock. "Egbert von Lüttich." In *VL²* 2:361–63.

Bücheler, Franciscus, ed. *Petronii Saturae et Liber priapeorum.* 4th ed. Berlin: Weidmann, 1904.

Bugge, Sophus. *The Home of the Eddic Poems, with Especial Reference to the Helgi-Lays.* Trans. William Henry Schofield. 2nd ed. London: D. Nutt, 1899.

Burke, Peter. *Popular Culture in Early Modern Europe*. New York: New York University Press, 1978.

Burrows, Daron. *The Stereotype of the Priest in the Old French "Fabliaux": Anticlerical Satire and Lay Identity*. Frankfurt am Main: Peter Lang, 2005.

Burton, Richard. *Vikram and the Vampire: Tales of Hindu Devilry*. London: Longmans, Green, 1893.

Büsching, Johann Gustav Gottlieb. "Kibitz." In *Popular Tales and Romances of the Northern Nations*, 2:305–16. London: Printed for W. Simpkin and R. Marshall, 1823.

———. "Kibitz." In *Volks-Sagen, Märchen und Legenden*, 296. Leipzig: C. H. Reclam, 1812. Repr., Hildesheim: Olms, 1969. 2nd printing, Leipzig: C. H. Reclam, 1820.

Cabrol, Fernand, and Henri Leclercq. *Dictionnaire d'archéologie chrétienne et de liturgie*. Vol. 7. Paris: Letouzey et Ané, 1927.

Callimachus. *Victoria Berenices. Aetia III*. Ed. Peter J. Parsons and Hugh Lloyd-Jones. In *Supplementum Hellenisticum*, ed. Hugh Lloyd-Jones, Peter J. Parsons, H.-G. Nesselrath, and J. U. Powell, 100–117. Texte und Kommentare 11. Berlin and New York: Walter de Gruyter, 1983.

The Cambridge Songs (Carmina Cantabrigiensia). Ed. and trans. Jan M. Ziolkowski. Garland Library of Medieval Literature, vol. 66, ser. A. New York: Garland, 1994. Repr., Tempe, AZ: Medieval and Renaissance Texts and Studies, 1998.

Campbell, Joseph. *The Hero with a Thousand Faces*. 2nd ed. Bollingen Series 17. Princeton, NJ: Princeton University Press, 1968.

Camporesi, Piero. *The Magic Harvest: Food, Folklore, and Society*. Trans. Joan Krakover Hall. Cambridge, MA: Polity, 1993.

———. *Rustici e buffoni: Cultura popolare e cultura d'élite fra Medioevo ed età moderna*. Saggi brevi 23. Turin: Giulio Einaudi editore, 1991.

Canepa, Nancy L. *From Court to Forest: Giambattista Basile's "Lo cunto de li cunti" and the Birth of the Literary Fairy Tale*. Detroit: Wayne State University Press, 1999.

———. "Italy." In Zipes, *Oxford Companion to Fairy Tales*, 252–65.

———, ed. *Out of the Woods: The Origins of the Literary Fairy Tale in Italy and France*. Detroit: Wayne State University Press, 1997.

Carasso-Bulow, Lucienne. *The Merveilleux in Chrétien de Troyes' Romances*. Geneva: Droz, 1976.

Carey, John. "The Obscurantists and the Sea-Monster: Reflections on the *Hisperica famina*." *Peritia* 17–18 (2003–4): 40–60.

Carp, Teresa. "The Three Late-Coming Monks: Tradition and Invention in the *Navigatio Sancti Brendani*." *Medievalia et Humanistica* 12 (1983): 127–42.

Carpenter, Rhys. *Folk Tale, Fiction, and Saga in the Homeric Epics*. Berkeley and Los Angeles: University of California Press, 1962.

Chambers, E. K. *The Mediaeval Stage*. 2 vols. Oxford: Oxford University Press, 1903.

Chandes, Gérard, ed. *Le merveilleux et la magie dans la littérature: Actes du colloque de Caen, 31 août–2 septembre 1989*. Amsterdam: Rodopi, 1992.

Chauvin, Victor. *Bibliographie des ouvrages arabes ou relatifs aux arabes publiés dans l'Europe chrétienne de 1810 à 1885*. 12 vols. Liège: H. Vaillant-Carmanne, 1892–1922.

Chih-Chün, Huang. "The Tale of the Tiger-Woman." Translated into German from Chinese by Annette Specht and into English by Günter Lontzen and Jacques Barchilon. *Merveilles et contes* 7 (1993): 516–23.

Christensen, Georg. "H. C. Andersen og de danske folkeeventyr." *Danske studier* (1906): 103–12.

Cicero. *De inventione, De optimo genere oratorum, Topica.* Ed. and trans. H. M. Hubbell. Loeb Classical Library 386. Cambridge, MA: Harvard University Press, 1949.

Cirese, Alberto M. *Cultura egemonica e culture subalterne: Rassegna degli studi sul mondo popolare tradizionale.* 2nd ed. Palermo: Palumbo editore, 1973.

Clark, J. M. *The Abbey of St. Gall as a Centre of Literature and Art.* Cambridge: Cambridge University Press, 1926.

Clausen-Stolzenburg, Maren. *Märchen und die mittelalterliche Tradition.* Beiträge zur neueren Literaturgeschichte, 3rd ser., 138. Heidelberg: Carl Winter, 1995.

Cleasby, Richard, and Gudbrand Vigfusson, eds. *An Icelandic-English Dictionary.* Rev. William A. Craigie. 2nd ed. Oxford: Clarendon, 1957.

Clements, Robert J., and Joseph Gibaldi. *Anatomy of the Novella: The European Tale Collection from Boccaccio and Chaucer to Cervantes.* New York: New York University Press, 1977.

Clements, William M. "Oikotype/Oicotype." In *Folklore* 2:604–5.

Cocchiara, Giuseppe. *The History of Folklore in Europe.* Trans. John N. McDaniel. Philadelphia: Institute for the Study of Human Issues, 1981.

Coirault, Patrice. *Recherches sur notre ancienne chanson populaire traditionelle.* 5th ed. Vannes: Imprimerie Lafolye frères, 1933.

Coleman, K. M. "Manilius' Monster." *Hermes* 111 (1983): 226–32.

Collodi, Carlo. *Pinocchio: Story of a Puppet.* Trans. Nancy Canepa. South Royalton, VT: Steerforth Italia, 2002.

Columella, Lucius Junius Moderatus. *On Agriculture.* Vol. 1. Ed. and trans. Harrison Boyd Ash. Loeb Classical Library 361. Cambridge, MA: Harvard University Press, 1941.

Cosquin, Emmanuel. *Contes populaires de Lorraine.* 2 vols. Paris: F. Vieweg, 1886. Repr., Marseille: Lafitte, 1978.

Coulter, Cornelia Catlin. "The 'Great Fish' in Ancient and Medieval Story." *Transactions of the American Philological Association* 57 (1926): 32–50.

Courtney, E. *A Commentary on the Satires of Juvenal.* London: Athlone, 1980.

Crane, Thomas Frederick. *Italian Popular Tales.* Ed. Jack Zipes. Santa Barbara, CA: ABC-CLIO, 2001.

Cremascoli, Giuseppe. "Das hagiographische Werk des Letald von Micy." *Mittellateinisches Jahrbuch* 24–25 (1989–90): 87–93.

Crichton, Michael. *Eaters of the Dead: The Manuscript of Ibn Fadlan Relating His Experiences with the Northmen in A.D. 922.* New York: Knopf, 1976.

Croce, Benedetto. Introduction to *Il pentamerone, ossia la fiaba delle fiabe,* by Giambattista Basile. 2 vols. Bari: Gius. Laterza e Figli, 1925.

———. Review of *Le radici storiche dei racconti di fate,* by V. J. Propp. *Quaderni della "Critica"* 15 (1949): 102–5.

Croce, Giulio Cesare. *Le astuzie di Bertoldo e le semplicità di Bertoldino.* Ed. Piero Camporesi. Milan: Garzanti, 1993.

Crocioni, Giovanni. *Le tradizioni popolari nella letteratura italiana.* Ed. Giuseppe Anceschi. Florence: Leo S. Olschki, 1970.

Cross, James E., and Thomas D. Hill. *The "Prose Solomon and Saturn" and "Adrian and*

Ritheus." McMaster Old English Studies and Texts 1. Toronto: University of Toronto Press, 1982.

Cross, Tom Peete. *Motif-Index of Early Irish Literature.* Indiana University Publications Folklore Series 7. Bloomington: Indiana University Press, 1952.

Curschmann, Michael. "Salman und Morolf." In *VL²* 8:515–23.

Curtius, Ernst Robert. *European Literature and the Latin Middle Ages.* Trans. Willard R. Trask. Bollingen Series 36. Princeton, NJ: Princeton University Press, 1990.

Cyril of Alexandria. *Commentarius in Jonam prophetam.* In *PG* 71:597–638.

Daly, Lloyd W. *Aesop without Morals: The Famous Fables and a Life of Aesop.* New York and London: Thomas Yoseloff, 1961.

Daston, Lorraine, and Katharine Park. *Wonders and the Order of Nature, 1150–1750.* New York: Zone, 1998.

Davidson, Alan. *The Oxford Companion to Food.* Oxford: Oxford University Press, 1999.

Davis, Edward. "A Whale of a Tale: Fundamentalist Fish Stories." *Perspectives on Science and Christian Faith* 43 (1991): 224–37.

Day, John. *God's Conflict with the Dragon and the Sea: Echoes of a Canaanite Myth in the Old Testament.* Cambridge: Cambridge University Press, 1985.

Degering, Hermann. *Kurzes Verzeichnis der germanischen Handschriften der Preussischen Staatsbibliothek.* 3 vols. Mitteilungen aus der Preussischen Staatsbibliothek 7–9. Leipzig: Hiersemann, 1925–1932. Repr., Graz: Akademische Druck- und Verlaganstalt, 1970.

Dégh, Linda. "Conduit-Theorie." In *EM* 3:124–26.

———. "Conduit Theory/Multiconduit Theory." In *Folklore* 1:142–44.

———. "Grimm's 'Household Tales' and the Place in the Household: The Social Relevance of a Controversial Classic." *Western Folklore* 38 (1979): 83–103.

———. *Legend and Belief: Dialectics of a Folklore Genre.* Bloomington and Indianapolis: Indiana University Press, 2001.

———. *Narratives in Society: A Performer-Centered Study of Narration.* FFC 255. Helsinki: Suomalainen Tiedeakatemia, Academia scientiarum fennica, 1995.

———. "What Did the Grimm Brothers Give to and Take from the Folk?" In McGlathery, *The Brothers Grimm and Folktale,* 66–90.

De Haan, Martin Ralph. *Jonah, Fact or Fiction?* Grand Rapids, MI: Zondervan, 1957.

De la Mare, Walter. *Told Again: Traditional Tales.* Oxford: B. Blackwell, 1927.

Delarue, Paul. *Le Conte populaire français: Catalogue raisonné des versions de France et des pays de langue française d'outre-mer; Canada, Louisiane, îlots français des États-Unis, Antilles françaises, Haïti, Ile Maurice, La Réunion.* Vol. 1. Paris: Érasme, 1957.

———. "Les contes merveilleux de Perrault et la tradition populaire: I. Le petit chaperon rouge." *Bulletin folklorique d'Île-de-France* 13 (1951): 221–28.

Denecke, Ludwig, and Irmgard Teitge. *Die Bibliothek der Brüder Grimm: Annotiertes Verzeichnis des festgestellten Bestandes.* Ed. Friedhilde Krause. Stuttgart: S. Hirzel Verlag, 1989.

Desmed, R. Review of *Het lied van boer eenos,* by Andries Welkenhuysen. *Scriptorium* 32 (1978): 137–38.

De Smet, W. M. A. "Evidence of Whaling in the North Sea and English Channel during the Middle Ages." In *Mammals in the Seas: Report,* by the Food and Agriculture Organization of the United Nations, Working Party on Marine Mammals, 301–9.

Durandus, William. *Rationale divinorum officiorum, Liber I et III.* Ed. Stefano Della Torre and Massimo Marinelli. Trans. Gian Franco Freguglia. Monumenta studia instrumenta liturgica 14. Vatican City: Libreria Editrice Vaticana, 2001.

Duval, Yves-Marie. *Le livre de Jonas dans la littérature chrétienne grecque et latine: Sources et influence du Commentaire sur Jonas de saint Jérôme.* 2 vols. Paris: Études augustiniennes, 1973.

Edgerton, Franklin, ed. and trans. *Vikrama's Adventures, or The Thirty-Two Tales of the Throne: A Collection of Stories about King Vikrama, as Told by the Thirty-Two Statuettes that Supported His Throne.* 2 vols. Harvard Oriental Series 26–27. Cambridge, MA: Harvard University Press, 1926.

Egbert of Liège. *Fecunda ratis* (The Richly Laden Ship). Ed. Ernst Voigt. Halle an der Saale: Max Niemeyer, 1889.

Ehrismann, Gustav. *Geschichte der deutschen Literatur bis zum Ausgang des Mittelalters.* 2nd ed. 2 vols. in 4. Munich: C. H. Beck, 1932.

Ekkehard IV of St. Gall. "VII. Grabschrift für die Recluse Rachild," 1–2 = Saint Gall 5.7 (no. 64). Ed. Karl Strecker, in *MGH Poetae Latini Medii Aevi,* vol. 5, no. 2:549. Berlin: Weidmannsche Verlagsbuchhandlung, 1939.

Eliade, Mircea. *Shamanism: Archaic Techniques of Ecstasy.* Trans. Willard R. Trask. Bollingen Series 76. Princeton, NJ: Princeton University Press, 1964.

Ellis, John M. *One Fairy Story Too Many: The Brothers Grimm and Their Tales.* Chicago: University of Chicago Press, 1983.

Erasmus, Desiderius. "Convivium fabulosum." In *Opera Omnia Desiderii Erasmi Roterodami,* 1st ser., vol. 3, *Colloquia,* ed. L.-E. Halkin, F. Bierlaire, and R. Hoven, 438–49. Amsterdam: North-Holland, 1972.

———. "The Fabulous Feast." In *Collected Works of Erasmus,* vol. 39, *Colloquies,* translated and annotated by Craig R. Thompson, 571–89. Toronto: University of Toronto Press, 1997.

Erdmann, Carl. "Leonitas. Zur mittelalterlichen Lehre von Kursus, Rhythmus und Reim." In *Corona quernea. Festgabe Karl Strecker zum 80. Geburtstage dargebracht.* MGH Schriften des Reichsinstituts für ältere deutsche Geschichtskunde 6, 15–28. Leipzig: K. W. Hiersemann, 1941.

Fairchild, Hoxie Neale. *The Noble Savage: A Study in Romantic Naturalism.* New York: Columbia University Press, 1928.

Ferruolo, Stephen C. *The Origins of the University: The Schools of Paris and Their Critics, 1100–1215.* Stanford: Stanford University Press, 1985.

La Filologia medievale e umanistica greca e latina nel secolo XX: Atti del Congresso internazionale; Roma, Consiglio Nazionale delle Ricerche, Università "La Sapienza," 11–15 dicembre 1989. 2 vols. Testi e studi bizantino-neoellenici 7. Rome: Università di Roma "La Sapienza," 1993.

Fischart, Johann. *Das Philosophisch Eezuchtbüchlin.* In *Johann Fischarts Werke: Eine Auswahl,* ed. Adolf Hauffen, 3:115–332. Deutsche National-Litteratur 18, no. 3. Stuttgart: Union Deutsche Verlagsgesellschaft, 1894.

Fisher, John D. C. *Christian Initiation: Baptism in the Medieval West; A Study in the Disintegration of the Primitive Rite of Initiation.* Alcuin Club Collections 47. London: SPCK, 1965.

Flint, Valerie I. J. *The Rise of Magic in Early Medieval Europe.* Princeton, NJ: Princeton University Press, 1991.

FAO Fisheries Series 5, vol. 3. Rome: Food and Agriculture Organization of United Nations, 1981.

Deyermond, Alan. *La literatura perdida de la Edad Media castellana.* Vol. 1. Salaman Ediciones Universidad de Salamanca, 1995.

Dick, Wilhelm, ed. *Die Gesta Romanorum: Nach der Innsbrucker Handschrift vom Ja 1342 und vier Münchener Handschriften.* Erlangen and Leipzig: A. Deichert and Böhme, 1890.

Diederichs, Ulf. *Who's who im Märchen.* Munich: Deutscher Taschenbuch Verlag, 19

Diefenbach, Lorenz. *Glossarium latino-germanicum mediae et infimae aetatis.* Frankf am Main: J. Baer, 1857. Repr., Darmstadt: Wissenschaftliche Buchgesellschaft, 19(

Dobozy, Maria. "The Brothers Grimm: Jacob Ludwig Carl (1785–1863); Wilhelm C (1786–1859)." In *Medieval Scholarship: Biographical Studies on the Formation of a D cipline,* ed. Helen Damico and Joseph B. Zavadil, 2:93–108. Garland Reference 1 brary of the Humanities 2071. New York: Garland, 1998.

———. "Spielmannsepen." In *Medieval Germany: An Encyclopedia,* ed. John M. Jee 728–30. New York and London: Garland, 2001.

Domanska, Janina. *The Turnip.* New York: MacMillan, 1969.

Donner, Michael. *S. Wordrow's Palindrome Encyclopedia: I Love Me.* Vol. 1. Chapel Hi Algonquin, 1996.

Dorson, Richard M. *The British Folklorists: A History.* Chicago: University of Chicag Press, 1968.

———. "Fakelore." *Zeitschrift für Volkskunde* 65 (1969): 60.

———. "Folklore and Fake Lore." *American Mercury* 70 (1950): 335–43.

———. *Folklore and Fakelore: Essays toward a Discipline of Folk Studies.* Cambridg MA: Harvard University Press, 1976.

———, ed. *Handbook of American Folklore.* Bloomington: Indiana University Pres 1983.

Dronke, Peter, and Ursula Dronke. *Barbara et antiquissima carmina.* Barcelona: Univei sidad Autónoma de Barcelona, 1977.

Duanaire Finn: The Book of the Lays of Fionn. Ed. and trans. Eoin MacNeill and Gerar Murphy. 3 parts. Irish Texts Society 7, 28, 43. London: D. Nutt, 1908–53.

Dubost, Francis. *Aspects fantastiques de la littérature narrative médiévale, XIIème–XII Ième siècles: L'autre, l'ailleurs, l'autrefois.* 2 vols. Nouvelle bibliothèque du Moyei Age 15. Paris: Honoré Champion, 1991.

Duby, Georges. *The Three Orders: Feudal Society Imagined.* Trans. Arthur Goldhammei Chicago: University of Chicago Press, 1980.

Du Cange, Charles du Fresne, D. P. Charpentier, and G. A. Louis Heschel. *Glossariur mediae et infimae latinitatis.* 7 vols. Paris: Firmin Didot, 1840–50.

Dundes, Alan. *Folklore Matters.* Knoxville: University of Tennessee Press, 1989.

———, ed. *Little Red Riding Hood: A Casebook.* Madison: University of Wisconsii Press, 1989.

———. "Nationalistic Inferiority Complexes and the Fabrication of Fakelore: A Re consideration of Ossian, the *Kinder- und Hausmärchen,* the *Kalevala,* and Paul Bun yan." *Journal of Folklore Research* 22 (1985): 5–18.

———, ed. *The Study of Folklore.* Englewood Cliffs, NJ: Prentice-Hall, 1965.

Dunlop, D. M. "The British Isles according to Medieval Arabic Authors." *Islamic Quar terly* 4 (1957): 11–28.

Fludernik, Monika. *Towards a "Natural" Narratology.* London: Routledge, 1996.

Förstemann, Ernst. *Altdeutsches Namenbuch.* Ed. Hermann Jellinghaus. 2nd ed. 2 vols. (vol. 2 in 2 parts). Bonn: P. Hanstein, 1900–1916.

Foucault, Michel. *The History of Sexuality.* Trans. Robert Hurley. New York: Pantheon, 1978.

Foulet, Lucien. *Le Roman de Renard.* Bibliothèque de l'Ecole des Hautes Etudes, Sciences historiques et philologiques 211. Paris: Honoré Champion, 1914.

Fox, Francis. *Sixty-Three Years of Engineering, Scientific, and Social Work.* London: John Murray, 1924.

Frazer, James George. *The Golden Bough: A Study in Magic and Religion.* 3rd ed. 12 vols. New York: MacMillan, 1935.

Freedman, Paul. "Sainteté et sauvagerie: Deux images du paysan au moyen age." *Annales* 47 (1992): 539–60.

Freeman, K. "Vincent, or the Donkey." *Greece and Rome* 14 (1945): 33–41.

Freud, Sigmund, and D. E. Oppenheim. *Dreams in Folklore.* Trans. A. M. O. Richards. Ed. James Strachey. New York: International Universities Press, 1958.

Friedman, John B. "Bald Jonah and the Exegesis of 4 Kings 2.23." *Traditio* 44 (1988): 125–44.

Frobenius, Leo. *Weltanschauung der Naturvölker.* Beiträge zur Volks- und Völkerkunde 6. Weimar: Verlag von Emil Felber, 1898.

———. *Das Zeitalter des Sonnengottes.* Berlin: Georg Reimer, 1904.

Fromm, Erich. *The Forgotten Language: An Introduction to the Understanding of Dreams, Fairy Tales, and Myths.* New York: Rinehart, 1951.

Gamer, Helena M. "The Ruodlieb and Tradition." *Arv: Tidskrift för Nordisk Folkminnesforskning* 11 (1955): 65–103.

Gansweidt, Birgit. "Rapularius." In *LdM* 7:445.

Gardiner, Edwin., ed. *Fornar smásögur úr Noregskonunga sögum.* Reykjavík: Leiftur, 1949.

Gašparíková, Viera. "Polívka, Jiří." In *EM* 10:1145–50.

Gatti, Paolo. "Elementi favolistici nell'*Asinarius* e nel *Rapularius.*" In *La Favolistica latina in distici elegiaci: Atti del convegno internazionale, Assisi, 26–28 ottobre 1990,* ed. Giuseppe Catanzaro and Francesco Santucci, 149–60. Centro studi poesia latina in distici elegiaci 2. Assisi: Accademia Properziana del Subasio, 1991.

———, ed. and trans. *Rapularius I.* In *Commedie latine del XII e XIII secolo,* 5:5–79. Pubblicazioni dell'Istituto di filologia classica e medievale 95. Genoa: Istituto di filologia classica e medievale, 1986.

———, ed. and trans. *Rapularius II.* In *Commedie latine del XII e XIII secolo,* 6:319–78. Pubblicazioni del D.Ar.Fi.Cl.Et., n.s., 176. Genoa: Dipartimento di Archeologia, Filologia classica e loro Tradizioni, 1998.

Geary, Patrick J. *The Myth of Nations: The Medieval Origins of Europe.* Princeton, NJ: Princeton University Press, 2002.

Gehrmann, Theula. "Hieronymus v. Münchhausen und der Werdegang des Buches: Wie der Freiherr von Münchhausen zum Lügenbaron gemacht wurde." In *Münchhausen: Ein amoralisches Kinderbuch; Untersuchung zu einem Bestseller,* by Bernhard Wiebel, 5–8. Arbeitsbericht 17. Zurich: Schweizerisches Jugendbuch-Institute, 1996.

Gellius, Aulus. *Noctes Atticae* [The Attic Nights]. Ed. and trans. John C. Rolfe. 3 vols. Loeb Classical Library 195, 200, 212. Cambridge, MA: Harvard University Press, 1927.

Genicot, Léopold, and P. Tombeur, eds. *Index Scriptorum operumque latino-belgicorum medii aevi: Nouveau répertoire des oeuvres médiolatines belges.* Parts 1–3, in 4 vols. Brussels: Académie royale de Belgique, 1973–.

Gervase of Tilbury. *Otia imperialia.* Ed. and trans. S. E. Banks and J. W. Binns. Oxford: Clarendon, 2002.

Gesell, Arnold. *Wolf Child and Human Child: Being a Narrative Interpretation of the Life History of Kamala, the Wolf Girl.* New York: Harper, 1941.

Ginzburg, Louis. *The Legends of the Jews.* Trans. Henrietta Szold. 7 vols. Philadelphia: Jewish Publication Society of America, 1937–38.

Glauche, Günter. *Schullektüre im Mittelalter: Entstehung und Wandlungen des Lektürekanons bis 1200 nach den Quellen dargestellt.* Münchener Beiträge zur Mediävistik und Renaissance-Forschung 5. Munich: Arbeo-Gesellschaft, 1970.

Goethe, Johann Caspar. *Rationum sumptuarium, sive rerum oeconomicarum fere omnium liber.* Ed. Helmut Holtzhauer and Irmgard Möller. 2 vols. Leipzig: Edition Leipzig, 1973.

Goethe, Johann Wolfgang von. *Die Wahlverwandtschaften.* Tübingen: Cotta. 1809.

Goff, Jacques Le. "Clerical Culture and Folklore Traditions in Merovingian Civilization." In *Time, Work, and Culture in the Middle Ages,* trans. Arthur Goldhammer, 153–58. Chicago: University of Chicago Press, 1980.

———. *The Medieval Imagination.* Trans. Arthur Goldhammer. Chicago: University of Chicago Press, 1988.

Goldberg, Christine. "Folktale." In *Encyclopedia of Folklore and Literature,* ed. Mary Ellen Brown and Bruce A. Rosenberg, 219–20. Santa Barbara, CA: ABC-CLIO, 1998.

———. "Folktale." In *Folklore* 1:356–66.

———. "The Historic-Geographic Method: Past and Future." *Journal of Folklore Research* 21 (1984): 1–18.

Golinelli, Paolo. "Tra realtà e metafora: Il bosco nell'immaginario letterario medievale." In *Il bosco nel Medioevo,* ed. Bruno Andreolli and Massimo Montanari, 97–123. Biblioteca di Storia Agraria Medievale 4. Bologna: Clueb, 1988.

Gottfried von Strassburg. *Tristan.* Ed. and trans. Rüdiger Krohn. 3 vols. Stuttgart: Philipp Reclam, 1974.

Grätz, Manfred. "Kunstmärchen." In *EM* 8:612–22.

Green, D. H. *The Beginnings of Medieval Romance: Fact and Fiction, 1150–1220.* Cambridge Studies in Medieval Literature 47. Cambridge: Cambridge University Press, 2002.

Greenburg, Dan. *Elvis the Turnip . . . and Me.* Illustrated by Jack E. Davis. Zack Files 14. New York: Grosset and Dunlop, 1998.

Gregory the Great. *Homiliarum in Evangelia libri duo.* In *PL* 76.1075–1312.

———. *Moralia in Iob.* Ed. Marc Adriaen. Corpus Christianorum Series Latina 143–143A–143B. Turnhout: Brepols, 1979–85.

Grewenig, Meinrad Maria. *Napoleon: Feldherr, Kaiser, Mensch.* Ostfildern-Ruit: Hatje, 1998.

Grieco, Allen J. "The Social Politics of Pre-Linnaean Botanical Classification." *I Tatti Studies: Essays in the Renaissance* 4 (1991): 131–49.

Grimm, Hermann, and Gustav Hinrichs, eds. *Briefwechsel zwischen Jacob und Wilhelm Grimm aus der Jugendzeit.* Rev. Wilhelm Schoof. 2nd ed. Weimar: Hermann Böhlaus Nachfolger, 1963.

Grimm, Jacob. *Circular wegen Aufsammlung der Volkspoesie, Wien 1815: Facsimile.* Ed. Ludwig Denecke. Kassel: Brüder Grimm-Museum, 1968.

———. *German Popular Stories Translated from the Kinder und Haus Marchen [sic], Collected by M. M. Grimm, from Oral Tradition.* Trans. Edgar Taylor. Illustrated by George Cruikshank. 2 vols. Vol. 1, London: C. Baldwyn, Newgate Street, 1823. Vol. 2, London: James Robins; Dublin: Joseph Robins Junr., 1826.

———. Preface to Giambattista Basile, *Der Pentamerone, oder, Das Märchen aller Märchen.* Trans. Felix Liebrecht. 2 vols. Breslau: J. Max, 1846. 1:V–XXIV. Reprinted in *Kleinere Schriften.* Ed. Karl Müllenhoff and Eduard Ippel. Berlin: Dümmler, 1864–90. Reprinted: Forschungsausgabe. Ed. Ludwig Erich Schmitt. Part 1, vols. 1–8: Die Werke Jacob Grimms, Kleinere Schriften. Hildesheim: Olms-Weidmann, 1985–.

———. *Reinhart Fuchs.* Berlin: Georg Reimer, 1834.

———. *Über den altdeutschen Meistergesang.* Göttingen: Dieterich, 1811.

Grimm, Jacob, and Wilhelm Grimm. *Deutsche Sagen.* Ed. Hans-Jörg Uther. 3 vols. Munich: Eugen Diederichs Verlag, 1993. Originally published in 2 vols. (Berlin: Verlag der Realbuchhandlung, 1816–18.)

———. *Deutsches Wörterbuch.* 16 vols. Leipzig: S. Hirzel Verlag, 1854–1971.

———. *Kinder- und Hausmärchen gesammelt durch die Brüder Grimm.* 1st ed. 2 vols. Berlin: Realschulbuchhandlung, 1812–15.

———. *Kinder- und Hausmärchen gesammelt durch die Brüder Grimm.* 2nd ed. 3 vols. Berlin: G. Reimer, 1819–22. Repr. ed. Heinz Rölleke. Cologne: Diederichs, 1982.

———. *Kinder- und Hausmärchen gesammelt durch die Brüder Grimm.* 7th ed. 3 vols. Göttingen: Verlag der Dieterich'schen Buchhandlung, 1857. Reprinted as *Kinder- und Hausmärchen: Ausgabe letzter Hand mit den Originalanmerkungen der Brüder Grimm.* Ed. Heinze Rölleke. 3 vols. Stuttgart: Philipp Reclam, 1980.

———. *Kinder- und Hausmärchen: Säkular-Ausgabe.* Illustrated by P. Grot Johann and R. Leinweber. Stuttgart: Deutsche Verlags-Anstalt, 1912.

Grimm, Jacob, and Johann Andreas Schmeller. *Lateinische Gedichte des X. und XI. Jahrhunderts.* Göttingen: Dieterischsche Buchhandlung, 1838. Repr., Amsterdam: Rodopi, 1967.

Grimm, Wilhelm. *Altdänische Heldenlieder, Balladen und Märchen.* Heidelberg: Mohr und Zimmer, 1811. Translated as *Old Danish Ballads* (London: Hope, 1856).

———. *Kleinere Schriften von Wilhelm Grimm.* Ed. Gustav Hinrichs. 4 vols. Berlin: F. Dümmler, 1881–87. Repr., Hildesheim: Olms-Weidmann, 1992.

Gröber, Gustav. *Übersicht über die lateinische Litteratur von der Mitte des VI. Jahrhunderts bis zur Mitte des XIV. Jahrhunderts.* Vol. 2, part 1, of *Grundriß der romanischen Philologie,* II. Band. 1 Abteilung. Strasbourg: Karl J. Trübner, 1902. Repr., Munich: Wilhelm Fink, [1974].

Grocock, C. W., ed. and trans. *The Ruodlieb.* Chicago: Bolchazy-Carducci, 1985.

Groden, Michael, and Martin Kreiswirth, eds. *The Johns Hopkins Guide to Literary Theory and Criticism.* Baltimore and London: Johns Hopkins University Press, 1994.

Gross, Rudolf. *Warum die Liebe rot ist: Farbsymbolik im Wandel der Jahrtausende.* Düsseldorf and Vienna: Econ, 1981.

Grundmann, Herbert. "Litteratus-illitteratus: Der Wandel einer Bildungsnorm vom Altertum zum Mittelalter." *Archiv für Kulturgeschichte* 40 (1958): 1–65. Reprinted in *Ausgewählte Aufsätze,* vol. 3 (Stuttgart: Hiersemann, 1978), 1–66.

Guibert of Nogent. *Monodiae.* Ed. Edmond-René Labande. Les Classiques de l'histoire de France au Moyen Age 34. Paris: Belles Lettres, 1981. Translated by Paul J. Archambault as *A Monk's Confession: The Memoirs of Guibert of Nogent* (University Park: Pennsylvania State University Press, 1996).

Guillaume de Lorris and Jean de Meun. *Le Roman de la Rose.* 3 vols. Ed. Félix Lecoy. Les Classiques Français du Moyen Age 92, 95, 98. Paris: Honoré Champion, 1970.

———. *Romance of the Rose.* Trans. Charles Dahlberg. Princeton, NJ: Princeton University Press, 1971.

Guillén, Claudio. *The Challenge of Comparative Literature.* Trans. Cola Franzen. Cambridge, MA: Harvard University Press, 1993.

Gurevich, Aron Aikovlevich. *Lezioni romane: Antropologia e cultura medievale.* Ed. Clara Castelli. Piccola Biblioteca Einaudi 549. Turin: Giulio Einaudi editore, 1991.

Haase, Donald. "Yours, Mine, or Ours? Perrault, the Brothers Grimm, and the Ownership of Fairy Tales." *Marvels and Tales: Journal of Fairy-Tale Studies* 7 (1993): 383–402.

Haimo of Auxerre. *In Jonam prophetam.* In *PL,* 117.127C–42D.

Hagen, Rolf. "Perraults Märchen und die Brüder Grimm." *Zeitschrift für deutsche Philologie* 74 (1955): 392–410.

Halldórsson, Ólafur, ed. *Ólafs saga Tryggvasonar en mesta.* Editiones Arnamagnæanæ, ser. A, 3 vols. Copenhagen: Munksgaard, 1958–2000.

Hallett, Martin, and Barbara Karasek, eds. *Folk and Fairy Tales.* 2nd ed. Peterborough, Ontario: Broadview, 1996.

Hamann, Hermann. *Die literarischen Vorlagen der Kinder- und Hausmärchen und ihre Bearbeitung durch die Brüder Grimm.* Palaestra: Untersuchungen und Texte aus der deutschen und englischen Philologie 47. Berlin: Mayer und Müller, 1906.

Hamilton, Anthony. "Historie de Pertharite et de Férandine." In *Contes d'Hamilton publiés avec une notice de M. de Lescure,* vol. 1, *Le Bélier,* 79–133. Paris: Librairie des Bibliophiles, 1873.

Hanks, Carole, and D. T. Hanks, Jr. "Perrault's 'Little Red Riding Hood': Victim of the Revisers." *Children's Literature* 7 (1978): 68–77.

Hansen, William. *Ariadne's Thread: A Guide to International Tales Found in Classical Literature.* Ithaca, NY, and London: Cornell University Press, 2002.

"Hans My Hedgehog." Episode of *Jim Henson's "The Storyteller."* Directed by Jim Henson. Written by Anthony Minghella. NBC, 1987.

Harf-Lancner, Laurence. *Les fées au Moyen Age: Morgane et Mélusine; La naissance des fées.* Geneva: Slatkine, 1984.

———, ed. *Métamorphose et bestiaire fantastique au Moyen Age.* Collection de l'École Normale Supérieure de Jeunes Filles 28. Paris: École Normale Supérieure de Jeunes Filles, 1985.

———. "La métamorphose illusoire: Des théories chrétiennes de la métamorphose aux images médiévales du loup-garou." *Annales* 40 (1985): 208–26.

Hariulf of Oldenburg. *Vita Arnulfi Suessionensis.* Ed. O. Holder-Egger. MGH Scriptores 15, no. 2. Hanover: Impensis bibliopolii Hahniani, 1888.

Harries, Elizabeth Wanning. "Simulating Oralities: French Fairy Tales of the 1690s." *College Literature* 23 (1996): 100–115.

———. *Twice Upon a Time: Women Writers and the History of the Fairy Tale.* Princeton, NJ: Princeton University Press, 2001.

Harris, Joel Chandler. "Brer Rabbit and the Tar Baby." In *The Tar-Baby and Other Rhymes of Uncle Remus*. New York: D. Appleton, 1904.

Harris, Joseph. "Folktale and Thattr: The Case of *Rognvald and Raud*." *Folklore Forum* 13 (1980): 158–98.

Hartland, Edwin Sidney. *The Legend of Perseus: A Study of Tradition in Story, Custom, and Belief*. 3 vols. Grimm Library 2, 3, 5. London: D. Nutt, 1894–96.

Harvey, Paul. *The Oxford Dictionary of English Proverbs*. 2nd ed. Oxford: Clarendon, 1952.

Hassell, James Woodrow, Jr. *Middle French Proverbs, Sentences, and Proverbial Phrases*. Subsidia Mediaevalia 12. Toronto: Pontifical Institute of Mediaeval Studies, 1982.

Hauréau, Barthélemy. *Histoire littéraire du Maine*. 2nd ed. 10 vols. Paris: Dumoulin, 1870–77.

———. "Versus Lethaldi monachi de quodam piscatore quem ballena absorbuit." *Bulletin du Comité historique des monuments écrits de l'histoire de France* 1 (1849): 178–83.

Hausrath, August. "Das Problem der äsopischen Fabel." *Neue Jahrbücher für das klassische Altertum* 1 (1898): 305–22.

Häussler, Reinhard, ed. *Nachträge zu A. Otto, Sprichwörter und sprichwörtlichen Redensarten der Römer*. Hildesheim: Olms, 1968.

Hávamál. Ed. and trans. David A. H. Evans. Text Series 7. London: Viking Society for Northern Research, 1986.

Head, Thomas. *Hagiography and the Cult of the Saints: The Diocese of Orléans, 800–1200*. Cambridge Studies in Medieval Life and Thought, 4th ser., 14. Cambridge: Cambridge University Press, 1990.

———. "Letaldus of Micy and the Hagiographic Traditions of Selles-sur-Cher." *Analecta Bollandiana* 107 (1989): 393–414.

———. "Letaldus of Micy and the Hagiographic Traditions of the Abbey of Nouaillé: The Context of the *Delatio corporis S. Juniani*." *Analecta Bollandiana* 115 (1997): 253–67.

Head, Thomas, and Richard Landes, eds. *The Peace of God: Social Violence and Religious Response in France around the Year 1000*. Ithaca, NY: Cornell University Press, 1992.

Healey, Antonette Di Paolo, ed. *Dictionary of Old English: Old English Corpus*. Ann Arbor: University of Michigan, Humanities Text Initiative, 1998.

Hearne, Betsy. *Beauty and the Beast: Visions and Revisions of an Old Tale*. Chicago: University of Chicago Press, 1989.

Hélin, Maurice. *A History of Medieval Latin Literature*. Trans. Jean Chapman Snow. 2nd ed. New York: William Salloch, 1949.

Henderson, George. "The Fionn Saga." *Celtic Review* 2 (1905–6): 150–51.

Henningsen, Gustav. "The Art of Perpendicular Lying: Concerning a Commercial Collecting of Norwegian Sailors' Tall Tales." Trans. Warren E. Roberts. *Journal of the Folklore Institute* 2 (1965): 180–219.

Henssen, Gottfried. "Deutsche Schreckmärchen und ihre europäischen Anverwandten." *Zeitschrift für Volkskunde* 51 (1953): 84–97.

Herder, Johann Gottfried. *Ideen zur Philosophie der Geschichte der Menschheit*. 4 vols. Riga and Leipzig: Bey Johann Friedrich Hartknoch, 1784–91.

———. *Volkslieder*. 1st ed. 2 parts. Leipzig: Weygand, 1778–79. Retitled in 2nd ed. as *Stimmen der Völker in Liedern*, ed. Johannes von Müller (1807).

———, ed. *Von deutscher Art und Kunst: Einige Fliegende Blätter.* Hamburg: Bey Bode, 1773.

Hindley, Alan, Frederick W. Langley, and Brian J. Levy. *Old French-English Dictionary.* Cambridge: Cambridge University Press, 2000.

The Hisperica famina. Ed. F. J. H. Jenkinson. Cambridge: Cambridge University Press, 1908.

Historia Augusta. Ed. and trans. David Magie. 3 vols. Loeb Classical Library 139–40, 363. Cambridge, MA: Harvard University Press, 1921–32.

Hoffman, Daniel. *Paul Bunyan: Last of the Frontier Demigods.* Philadelphia: University of Pennsylvania Press for Temple University Publications, 1952. Repr., East Lansing: Michigan State University Press, 1999.

Holbek, Bengt. "Hans Christian Andersen's Use of Folktales." *Merveilles et contes* 4 (1990): 220–32.

———. *Interpretation of Fairy Tales: Danish Folklore in a European Perspective.* FFC 239. Helsinki: Suomalainen Tiedeakatemia, Academia scientiarum fennica, 1998.

Hollis, Susan Tower. *The Ancient Egyptian "Tale of Two Brothers": The Oldest Fairy Tale in the World.* Norman and London: University of Oklahoma Press, 1990.

The Holy Bible: Douay-Rheims Version. Baltimore, MD: John Murphy, 1899.

Honemann, Volker. "Unibos und Amis." In *Kleinere Erzählformen im Mittelalter: Paderborner Colloquium 1987,* ed. Klaus Grubmüller, L. Peter Johnson, and Hans-Hugo Steinhoff, 67–82. Paderborn: Schöningh, 1988.

Hoops, Johannes. "Rübe." In Johannes Hoops, ed., *Reallexikon der Germanischen Altertumskunde,* ed. Johannes Hoops, 4:1–2. Strasbourg: Karl J. Trübner, 1918–19.

Horovitz, Chaim M. *Agudat agadot: O, Kovets midrashim ketanim.* Berlin: Bi-defus Ts. H. Ittskovski, 1881.

Hrotsvit of Gandersheim. *Opera omnia.* Ed. Walter Berschin. Munich and Leipzig: K. G. Saur, 2001.

Hugo of Trimberg. *Registrum multorum auctorum.* In *Das "Registrum multorum auctorum" des Hugo von Trimberg: Untersuchungen und kommentierte Textausgabe,* ed. Karl Langosch, 160–95. Germanische Studien 235. Berlin: Verlag Dr. Emil Ebering, 1942.

Imperato, Ferrante. *Dell'historia naturale.* Naples: Costantino Vitale, 1599.

Innocent III, Pope. *Mysteriorum evangelicae legis et sacramenti eucharistiae libri sex.* In *PL* 217.773–915.

Irwin, Bonnie D. "What's in a Frame? The Medieval Textualization of Traditional Storytelling." *Oral Tradition* 10 (1995): 27–53.

Isidore of Seville. *Etymologiae.* Ed. W. M. Lindsay. 2 vols. Oxford Classical Texts. Oxford: Clarendon, 1911.

It's the Great Pumpkin, Charlie Brown. Directed by Bill Melendez. Released in 1966.

Jacoby, Felix, ed. *Die Fragmente der griechischen Historiker.* Vol. 1. 2nd ed. Leiden: E. J. Brill, 1957.

Jaeger, C. Stephen. *The Origins of Courtliness: Civilizing Trends and the Formation of Courtly Ideals, 939–1210.* Philadelphia: University of Pennsylvania Press, 1985.

Jakobson, Roman, and Petr Bogatyrev. "Die Folklore als eine besondere Form des Schaffens." In *Selected Writings,* ed. Roman Jakobson, 4:1–15. The Hague and Paris: Mouton, 1966. Translated by Manfred Jacobson as "Folklore as a Special Form of Creativity," in *The Prague School: Selected Writings, 1929–1946,* ed. Peter Steiner (Austin: University of Texas Press, 1982), 32–46.

Jason, Heda, and Aharon Kempinski. "How Old Are Folktales?" *Fabula* 24 (1983): 1–27.

Jauss, Hans Robert. *Untersuchungen zur mittelalterlichen Tierdichtung.* Beihefte zur Zeitschrift für romanische Philologie 100. Tübingen: Max Niemeyer, 1959.

Jean Renart. *Galeran de Bretagne.* Ed. Lucien Foulet. Classiques Français du Moyen Age 37. Paris: Honoré Champion, 1925.

Jeremias, Alfred. *Das alte Testament im Lichte des alten Orients.* 4th ed. Leipzig: J. C. Hinrichs'sche Buchhandlung, 1930.

Jerome. *Commentarius in Ionam prophetam.* In *Jérôme, Commentaire sur Jonas,* ed. and trans. Yves-Marie Duval. Sources chrétiennes 323. Paris: Les Éditions du Cerf, 1985.

Jesi, F. "Sul mito e la fiaba." In *"Tutto è fiaba": Atti del Convegno internazionale di studio sulla Fiaba,* ed. G. Cusatelli et al., 43–53. Milan: Emme Edizioni, 1980.

John Chrysostom, pseudo-. *De jejunio.* In *PG* 62:731–38.

John of Alta Silva. *Dolopathos sive De rege et septem sapientibus.* Ed. Alfons Hilka. Sammlung mittellateinischer Texte 5. Heidelberg: Carl Winter, 1913.

John the Deacon [Johannes Hymmonides]. *Cena Cypriani.* Ed. Karl Strecker. *MGH Poetae* 4, no. 2 (1923): 872–900.

Jolles, André. *Einfache Formen: Legende/Sage/Mythe/Rätsel/Spruch/Kasus/Memorabile/Märchen/Witz.* Halle an der Salle: Max Niemeyer, 1930.

Josephus, Flavius. *Jewish War.* Ed. and trans. H. St. J. Thackeray. 3 vols. Loeb Classical Library 203, 210, 487. Cambridge, MA: Harvard University Press, 1997.

Jung, Marc-René. *Hercule dans la littérature française du XVI siècle: De l'Hercule courtois à l'Hercule baroque.* Geneva: Droz, 1966.

Juvenal. *Satires.* In *Juvenal and Persius,* ed. and trans. G. G. Ramsay, 1–307. Loeb Classical Library 91. Cambridge, MA: Harvard University Press, 1940.

Kamenetsky, Christa. *The Brothers Grimm and Their Critics: Folktales and the Quest for Meaning.* Athens: Ohio University Press, 1992.

Keller, Ernst, and Marie-Luise Keller. *Miracles in Dispute: A Continuing Debate.* Trans. Margaret Kohl. Philadelphia: Fortress, 1969.

Keller, Walter, and Lisa Rüdiger, trans. *Italienische Märchen.* Düsseldorf and Cologne: Eugen Diederichs Verlag, 1959.

Kennedy, Louise. "New Storybook Reopens Old Wounds." *Boston Globe,* 14 December 2003.

Kiefer, Emma Emily. *Albert Wesselski and Recent Folktale Theories.* Indiana University Publications: Folklore Series 3. Bloomington: Indiana University, 1947.

Kinzer, Stephen. "America Yawns at Foreign Fiction." *New York Times,* late edition-final, section B, 26 July 2003.

Klein, Thomas. "'Versus de Uniboue': Neuedition mit kritischem Kommentar." *Studi medievali,* 3rd ser., 32 (1991): 843–86.

Der kleine und der große Klaus [Little Claus and Great Claus]. Produced by Fernsehen der DDR. Directed by Celino Bleiweiß. First broadcast on television on 25 December 1971.

Klopsch, Paul. *Einführung in die mittellateinische Verslehre.* Darmstadt: Wissenschaftliche Buchgesellschaft, 1972.

Klotz, Volker. *Das europäische Kunstmärchen: Fünfundzwanzig Kapitel seiner Geschichte von der Renaissance bis zur Moderne.* Munich: Deutscher Taschenbuch Verlag, 1987.

Knauf, Christiane, and Fredrik Vahle. *Die Rübe: Kinderliederarbeitsheft (ab 6 J.).* Kleine Rote Reihe 18. Dortmund: Weltkreis-Verlags-GmbH, 1974.

Knuf, Joachim. *Unsere Welt der Farben: Symbole zwischen Natur und Kultur.* Cologne: Dumont, 1988.

Koegel, Rudolf. *Geschichte der deutschen Litteratur bis zum Ausgange des Mittelalters.* 2 vols. in 3 parts. Strasbourg: Karl J. Trübner, 1897.

Kofod, Else Marie. *De vilde svaner og andre folkeeventyr: Sidestykker til syv af H. C. Andersens eventyr.* Foreningen Danmarks Folkeminders Skrifter 86. Copenhagen: Foreningen Danmarks Folkeminder, 1989.

Köhler, Ines. "Hans mein Igel." In *EM* 6:494–98.

Koppenfels, Werner von. *Esca et Hamus: Beitrag zu einer historischen Liebesmetaphorik.* Bayerische Akademie der Wissenschaften, philosophisch-historische Klasse, Sitzungsberichte. Munich: Verlag der Bayerischen Akademie der Wissenschaften, 1973.

Koszinowski, Ingrid, and Vera Leuschner. *Ludwig Emil Grimm: Zeichnungen und Gemälde.* 2 vols. Quellen zur Brüder Grimm-Forschung 3, nos. 1–2. Marburg: Dr. Wolfram Hitzeroth Verlag, 1990.

Kramer, Karl-S. "Bauer." In *FM* 1:1317–38.

Krapp, George Philip, and Elliott Van Kirk Dobbie, eds. *The Exeter Book.* Anglo-Saxon Poetic Records 3. New York: Columbia University Press, 1936.

Kratz, Dennis. "*Fictus lupus:* The Werewolf in Christian Thought." *Classical Folio* 30 (1976): 57–79.

Krohn, Kaarle. *Folklore Methodology Formulated by Julius Krohn and Expanded by Nordic Researchers.* Trans. Roger L. Welsch. Publications of the American Folklore Society: Bibliographical and Special Series 21. Austin: University of Texas Press, 1971.

Kutzer, Elizabeth. "Das indische Märchen." In *BP* 4:286–314.

Lacarra, María Jesús. *Cuentística medieval en España: Los orígenes.* Zaragoza: Departamento de literatura española, Universidad de Zaragoza, 1979.

———. *Cuentos de la edad media.* Madrid: Editorial Castalia "Odres nuevos," 1986.

Lamma, Ernesto, ed. *El dyalogo di Salomon e Marcolpho.* Bologna: Gaetano Romagnoli, 1885.

Langosch, Karl. "Asinarius." In *VL*[1] 1:509–10.

———, ed. *Asinarius und Rapularius.* Sammlung mittellateinischer Texte 10. Heidelberg: Carl Winter, 1929.

———. "Rapularius." In *VL*[1] 5:927–31.

———. "Unibos." In *VL*[1] 4:634–38.

———, ed. and trans. *Waltharius-Ruodlieb-Märchenepen: Lateinische Epike des Mittelalters mit deutschen Versen.* Darmstadt: Wissenschaftliche Buchgesellschaft, 1956.

Lapidge, Michael. "Aldhelm's Latin Poetry and Old English Verse." *Comparative Literature* 31 (1979): 209–31.

La Placa, Gabriella. "I Versus de Unibove, un poema dell'XI secolo tra letteratura e folklore." *Sandalion* 8–9 (1985–86): 285–306.

Lapucci, Carlo, ed. *Fiabe toscane.* Milan: Arnoldo Mondadori, 1984.

Latham, R. E., and D. R. Howlett, eds. *Dictionary of Medieval Latin from British Sources.* Fascicule 1–. London: Oxford University Press, 1975–.

Lavesne, Douin de. *Trubert, fabliau du XIIIe siècle.* Ed. Guy Raynaud de Lage. Textes littéraires français 210. Geneva: Droz, 1974.

Lawrence, Marion. "Ships, Monsters, and Jonah." *American Journal of Archaeology* 66 (1962): 289–96.

Leclercq, Jean. *The Love of Learning and the Desire for God: A Study of Monastic Culture.* Trans. Catharine Misrahi. 3rd ed. New York: Fordham University Press, 1982.

Lecouteux, C. "Introduction à l'étude du merveilleux médiéval." *Etudes germaniques* 36 (1981): 2763–90.

Lecoy, F. "La Farce de *Cauteleux, Barat et le Vilain.*" In *Mélanges de langue et de littérature du moyen âge et de la Renaissance offerts à Jean Frappier,* 2:595–602. Publications romanes et françaises 112. Geneva: Droz, 1970.

Lesky, Albin. "Herakles und das Ketos." In *Österreichische Akademie der Wissenschaften, Philosophisch-historische Klasse, Anzeiger (1967),* 1–6. Graz, Vienna, and Cologne: Hermann Böhlaus Nachfolger, 1967.

Lestocquoy, J. "Baleine et ravitaillement au Moyen Age." *Revue du Nord* 30 (1948): 39–43.

Letaldus of Micy. *Delatio corporis sancti Juniani in synodum Karoffensem.* In *PL* 137.823C–826B (*BHL* 4565).

———. *De quodam piscatore quem ballena absorbuit.* Tours, Bibliothèque Municipale, MS 890, fols. 45r–48v; Paris, Bibliothèque Nationale, MS lat. 5230A, fols. 156v–158v.

———. *De quodam piscatore quem ballena absorbuit: Il pescatore Within.* Ed. and trans. Feliciana L. Pennisi. Libellus 1. Reggio Calabria: Giuseppe Pontari Editore, 1997.

———. *Letaldo di Micy, Within piscator.* Ed. and trans. Ferruccio Bertini. Biblioteca del Medioevo latino. Florence: Giunti, 1995.

———. *Liber miraculorum sancti Maximini abbatis Miciacensis.* In *PL* 137.795B–824B (*BHL* 5820).

———. *Miracula Martini abbatis Vertavensis.* Ed. Bruno Krusch. *Passiones vitaeque sanctorum aevi Merovingici et antiquiorum aliquot.* MGH Scriptores rerum Merovingicarum 3 (1896), 567–75.

———. *Miracula sancti Martini Vertavensis.* (*BHL* 5667–68).

———. *Vita et miracula sancti Eusicii.* BHL 2754, 2756. Ed. Philippe Labbé. In *Nouae bibliothecae manuscript[orum] librorum.* 2:463–66. Paris: Apud Sebastianum Cramoisy, 1657.

———. *Vita sancti Juliani Cenomannensis.* In *PL* 137.781B–796A (*BHL* 4544).

Levine, Lawrence W. "How to Interpret American Folklore Historically." In Dorson, *Handbook of American Folklore,* 338–44.

Lewis, Bernard. *The Muslim Discovery of Europe.* New York: W. W. Norton, 1982.

Leyen, Friedrich von der. "Märchen und Spielmannsdichtung." *Germanisch-romanische Monatsschrift* 10 (1922): 129–38.

———. "Zur Entstehung des Märchens." *Archiv für das Studium der neueren Sprachen und Literaturen* 116 (1906): 282–300.

Liljeblad, Sven. *Die Tobiasgeschichte und andere Märchen mit toten Helfern.* Lund: P. Lindstedts Univ.-Bokhandel, 1927.

Lindahl, Carl, John McNamara, and John Lindow, eds. *Medieval Folklore: An Encyclopedia of Myths, Legends, Tales, Beliefs, and Customs.* 2 vols. Santa Barbara, CA: ABC-CLIO, 2000. Reprinted in abridged ed. in 1 vol. as *Medieval Folklore: A Guide to Myths, Legends, Tales, Beliefs, and Customs* (New York: Oxford University Press, 2002).

Lindquist, O. "Whaling by Peasant Fishermen in Norway, Orkney, Shetland, the Faeroe Islands, Iceland, and Norse Greenland: Medieval and Early Modern Whaling Methods and Inshore Legal Régimes." In *Whaling and History: Perspectives on the Evolution*

of the Industry, ed. B. Basberg, J. E. Ringstad, and E. Wexelsen, 17–54. Sandefjord: Sandefjord Museum, 1995.

Little, Lester K. *Religious Poverty and the Profit Economy in Medieval Europe.* Ithaca, NY: Cornell University Press, 1978.

Lixfeld, Hannjost. "Bolte, Johannes." In *EM* 2:603–5.

Lontzen, Günter. "The Earliest Version of the Chinese 'Little Red Riding Hood.'" *Merveilles et contes* 7 (1993): 513–15.

———. "Das Gedicht 'De puella a lupellis servata' von Egbert von Lüttich: Eine Parabel zum Thema der Taufe." *Merveilles et contes* 6 (1992): 20–44.

Lopez, Barry Holstun. *Of Wolves and Men.* New York: Scribner, 1978.

Lord, Albert Bates. *Epic Singers and Oral Tradition.* Ithaca, NY: Cornell University Press, 1991.

Lucian. *Lucian.* Ed. and trans. A. M. Harmon, K. Kilburn, and M. D. Macleod. 8 vols. Loeb Classical Library 14, 54, 130, 162, 302, 430–32. New York: Putnam; Cambridge, MA: Harvard University Press, 1913–67.

———. *A True History.* In *Lucian,* vol. 1, ed. and trans. A. M. Harmon, 247–357. Loeb Classical Library 14. New York: Putnam, 1913.

Lucian, pseudo-. "Lucius, or The Ass." In *Lucian,* vol. 8, ed. and trans. M. D. Macleod, 47–145. Loeb Classical Library 432. Cambridge, MA: Harvard University Press, 1967.

Lugli, Adalgisa. *Wunderkammer.* Turin: Umberto Allemandi, 1997.

Lund, Niels, ed. *Two Voyagers at the Court of King Alfred: The Ventures of Ohthere and Wulfstan, together with the Description of Northern Europe from the Old English Orosius.* Trans. Christine E. Fell. York, UK: William Sessions, 1984.

Lüthi, Max. *Die Gabe im Märchen und in der Sage: Ein Beitrag zur Wesenerfassung und Wesensscheidung der beiden Formen.* Bern: Buchdruckerei Büchler, 1943.

———. *Once upon a Time: On the Nature of Fairy Tales.* Trans. Lee Chadeayne and Paul Gottwald. Bloomington: Indiana University Press, 1976.

Lutz, Cora E. "Letaldus, a Wit of the Tenth Century." *Viator* 1 (1970): 97–107.

Lycophron, pseudo-. *Alexandra.* Ed. Lorenzo Mascialino. Bibliotheca scriptorum graecorum et romanorum teubneriana. Leipzig: B. G. Teubner, 1964.

Lynch, Joseph H. *Godparents and Kinship in Early Medieval Europe.* Princeton, NJ: Princeton University Press, 1986.

Maaz, Wolfgang. "Märchen und Märchenmotive im MA." In *LdM* 6:224–26.

Makaryk, Irena R., ed. *Encyclopedia of Contemporary Literary Theory: Approaches, Scholars, Terms.* Toronto, Buffalo, and London: University of Toronto Press, 1993.

Malson, Lucien. *Wolf Children.* London: NLB, 1972.

Mandeville, John. *Mandeville's Travels.* Ed. and trans. Malcolm Letts. 2 vols. Hakluyt Society, 2nd ser., 101–2. London: Hakluyt Society, 1953.

Mann, Jill. *Chaucer and Medieval Estates Satires: The Literature of Social Classes and the "General Prologue" to the "Canterbury Tales."* Cambridge: Cambridge University Press, 1973.

Map, Walter. *De nugis curialium.* Ed. and trans. M. R. James. Rev. C. N. L. Brooke and R. A. B. Mynors. Oxford: Clarendon, 1983.

Marchand, Alfred. *Le siège de Strasbourg, 1870: La Bibliothèque, la Cathédrale.* Paris: Librairie de J. Cherbuliez, 1871.

Marie de France. *Fresne.* In *Les lais de Marie de France,* ed. Jean Rychner, 44–60. Classiques Français du Moyen Age 93. Paris: Honoré Champion, 1973.

Marrou, H. I. *A History of Education in Antiquity.* Trans. George Lamb. Madison: University of Wisconsin Press, 1982.

Marsan, Rameline E. *Itinéraire espagnol du conte médiéval, VIIIe–XVe siècles.* Témoins de l'Espagne: Série historique 4. Paris: Klincksieck, 1974.

Matthews, Leonard Harrison, ed. *The Whale.* New York: Simon and Schuster, 1969.

Mavrogenes, Nancy A., and Joan S. Cummins. "What Ever Happened to Little Red Riding Hood? A Study of a Nursery Tale." *Horn Book* 55 (1979): 344–49.

Mayer, Mathias, and Jens Tismar. *Kunstmärchen.* 3rd ed. Sammlung Metzler 155. Stuttgart and Weimar: J. B. Metzler, 1997.

Mazzacurati, Giancarlo. *All'ombra di Dioneo: Tipologie e percorsi della novella da Boccaccio a Bandello.* Ed. Matteo Palumbo. Biblioteca di cultura 211. Serie Teoria e analisi dei testi letterari 2. Scandicci [Florence]: La Nuova Italia, 1996.

McConnell, Winder. "Medieval German Heroic Epic." In *A Companion to Middle High German Literature to the 14th Century,* ed. Francis G. Gentry, 151–213. Leiden: E. J. Brill, 2002.

McCulloch, Florence. *Mediaeval Latin and French Bestiaries.* University of North Carolina Studies in Romance Languages and Literatures 33. Chapel Hill: University of North Carolina Press, 1960.

McGlathery, James M., ed. *The Brothers Grimm and Folktale.* Urbana and Chicago: University of Illinois Press, 1988.

———. *Fairy Tale Romance: The Grimms, Basile, and Perrault.* Urbana: University of Illinois Press, 1991.

Meletinsky, Eleazar. "Marriage: Its Function and Position in the Structure of Folktales." In *Soviet Structural Folkloristics,* ed. Pierre Maranda, 1:61–72. Approaches to Semiotics 42. The Hague and Paris: Mouton, 1974.

———. "Problem of the Historical Morphology of the Folktale." In *Soviet Structural Folkloristics,* ed. Pierre Maranda, 1:53–59. Approaches to Semiotics 42. The Hague and Paris: Mouton, 1974.

Mendelson, Kathy. "Giant Vegetables: Weigh-Off Winners from Way Back When." *Pacific Northwest Garden History.* http://www.halcyon.com/tmend/giants.htm (accessed 13 August 2005).

Mesnil, Marianne. "Saintyves, Pierre." In *EM* 11:1050–53.

Meyer, Maurits de. *Vlaamsche sprookjesthema's in het licht der Romaansche en Germaansche Kultuurstroomingen.* Koninklijke Vlaamsche Academie voor Taal- en Letterkunde, 6th ser., 63. Leuven: De Vlaamsche Drukkerij, 1942.

Michaelsen, O. V. *Words at Play: Quips, Quirks, and Oddities.* New York: Sterling, 1997.

Michel, A. "Miracle." In *Dictionnaire de théologie catholique,* ed. Alfred Vacant and E. Mangenot, vol. 10, part 2, 1803. Paris: Letouzey et Ané, 1927.

"Midrasch Jona." In *Aus Israels Lehrhallen,* trans. August Wünsche, 2:39–56. Leipzig: E. Pfeiffer, 1907–8. Repr., Hildesheim: Georg Olms, 1967.

Mieder, Wolfgang. "Modern Anglo-American Variants of the Frog Prince (AT 440)." *New York Folklore* 6 (1980): 111–35.

———. "Survival Forms of 'Little Red Riding Hood' in Modern Society." *International Folklore Review* 2 (1982): 23–40.

Minghella, Anthony. *Jim Henson's "The Storyteller."* New York: Knopf, 1991.

Mitius, Otto. *Jonas in der altchristlichen Kunst.* Freiburg: C. A. Wagner, 1897.

Modesto, Christine. *Studien zur "Cena Cypriani" und zu deren Rezeption.* Classica Monacensia 3. Tübingen: Gunter Narr Verlag, 1992.

Morgan, Jeanne. *Perrault's Morals for Moderns.* American University Series II, Romance Languages and Literatures 28. New York: Peter Lang, 1985.

Moser, Dietz-Rüdiger. "Alterbestimmung des Märchens." In *EM* 1:407–19.

Mosetti Casaretto, Francesco. "Il tempo curvo del contadino: Per una lettura qohèletica dei 'Versus de unibove.'" *Studia monastica* 42 (2000): 65–112.

Müller, Josef. *Das Märchen vom Unibos.* Deutsche Arbeiten der Universität Köln 7. Jena: Eugen Diederichs Verlag, 1934.

Müller, Karl Otfried, Theodor Müller, and Charles Victor Langlois, ed. *Fragmenta Historicorum Graecorum.* 5 vols. Paris: Firmin Didot, 1848–78. Repr., Frankfurt am Main: Minerva, 1975.

Müller-Bahlke, Thomas J. *Die Wunderkammer: Die Kunst- und Naturalienkammer der Franckeschen Stiftungen zu Halle (Saale).* Halle an der Saale: Verlag der Franckeschen Stiftungen, 1998.

Musset, Lucien. "Raoul Glaber et la baleine: Les sources d'un racontar du XIe siècle." *Revue du Moyen Age latin* 4 (1948): 167–72.

Navigatio sancti Brendani. Ed. Giovanni Orlandi. Vol. 1. Testi e documenti per lo studio dell'antichità 38. Milan: Istituto editoriale cisalpino, 1968.

———. Ed. Carl Selmer. Publications in Medieval Studies 16. South Bend: University of Notre Dame Press, 1958. Repr., Kill Lange, Blackrock County, Dublin: Four Courts, 1989.

Neumann, Erich. *Amor and Psyche: The Psychic Development of the Feminine; A Commentary on the Tale by Apuleius.* Trans. Ralph Manheim. Bollingen Series 54. New York: Pantheon, 1956.

Neumann, Siegfried. "The Brothers Grimm as Collectors and Editors of German Folktales." In Zipes, *Great Fairy Tale Tradition,* 969–80.

Neustadt, Heinrich von. *"Apollonius von Tyrland" nach der Gothaer Handschrift, "Gottes Zukunft" und "Visio Philiberti" nach der Heidelberger Handschrift.* Ed. Samuel Singer. Deutsche Texte des Mittelalters 7. Berlin: Weidmann, 1906.

Newall, Venetia. "Lang, Andrew." In *EM* 8:766–70.

Niermeyer, J. F., and C. van de Kieft. *Mediae Latinitatis Lexicon Minus.* Rev. J. W. J. Burgers. 2nd ed. 2 vols. [Darmstadt]: Wissenschaftliche Buchgesellschaft, 2002.

Nikiforov, Alexksandr Isaakovich. *K voprosu o zadachakh i metodakh nauchnogo sobiraniia.* Leningrad: G.R.G.O., 1928.

Nivardus. *Ysengrimus.* Ed. and tran. Jill Mann. Mittellateinische Studien und Texte 12. Leiden: E. J. Brill, 1987.

Nixdorff, Heide, and Heidi Müller. *Weisse Westen, rote Roben: Von den Farbordnungen des Mittelalters zum individuellen Farbgeschmack.* Berlin: Staatliche Museen Preussischer Kulturbesitz, Museum für Völkerkunde und Museum für Deutsche Volkskunde, 1983.

Nordström, Carl-Otto. "Rabbinic Features in Byzantine and Catalan Art." *Cahiers archéologiques* 15 (1965): 179–205.

———. "Some Jewish Legends in Byzantine Art." *Byzantion* 252–57 (1955–57): 487–508.

Nörtersheuser, Hans-Walter. "Arm und reich." In *EM* 1:789–94.

Nykrog, Per. *Les Fabliaux.* 2nd ed. Publications romanes et françaises 123. Geneva: Droz, 1973.

Oberfeld, Charlotte, ed. *Wie alt sind unsere Märchen?* Regensburg: Erich Röth, 1990.

Oesterley, Hermann, ed. *Gesta Romanorum.* Berlin: Weidmann, 1872.

Oesterreicher-Mollino, Marianne. *Herder Lexikon Symbole.* 6th ed. Freiburg: Herder, 1978.

Ogilvy, J. D. A. *"Mimi, Scurrae, Histriones:* Entertainers of the Early Middle Ages." *Speculum* 38 (1963): 603–19.

O'Kearney, Nicholas, ed. *Feis tighe Chónain: The Festivities at the House of Conan of Ceann-Sleibhe, in the County of Clare.* Vol. 2. Transactions of the Ossianic Society for the Year 1954. Dublin: John O'Daly, 1855.

Olrik, Axel. "Märchen in Saxo Grammaticus." *Zeitschrift für Volkskunde* 2 (1892): 117–23, 252–58, 367–74.

———. *Principles for Oral Narrative Research.* Trans. Kirsten Wolf and Jody Jensen. Bloomington and Indianapolis: Indiana University Press, 1992.

Ong, Walter J. "Latin Language Study as a Renaissance Puberty Rite." *Studies in Philology* 56 (1959): 103–24. Reprinted in *Rhetoric, Romance, and Technology: Studies in the Interaction of Expression and Culture* (Ithaca, NY: Cornell University Press, 1971), 113–41.

———. *Orality and Literacy: The Technologizing of the Word.* London and New York: Methuen, 1982.

Opie, Iona, and Peter Opie. *The Classic Fairy Tales.* Oxford and New York: Oxford University Press, 1974.

Orenstein, Catherine. *Little Red Riding Hood Uncloaked: Sex, Morality, and the Evolution of a Fairy Tale.* New York: Basic, 2002.

Osgood, Charles G., trans. *Boccaccio on Poetry: Being the Preface and the Fourteenth and Fifteenth Books of Boccaccio's "Genealogia Deorum Gentilium."* Princeton, NJ: Princeton University Press, 1930.

Otten, Charlotte. *A Lycanthropy Reader: Werewolves in Western Culture.* Syracuse, NY: Syracuse University Press, 1986.

Otter, Monika. *Inventiones: Fiction and Referentiality in Twelfth-Century English Historical Writing.* Chapel Hill and London: University of North Carolina Press, 1996.

Otto, August. *Die Sprichwörter und sprichwörtlichen Redensarten der Römer.* Leipzig: B. G. Teubner, 1890.

Ovid [P. Ovidius Naso]. *Amores, Medicamina faciei femineae, Ars amatoria, Remedia amoris.* Ed. E. J. Kenney. Oxford Classical Texts. Oxford: Clarendon, 1961.

Ozawa, Toshio. "Das Märchen von Unibos." *Doitsu Bungaku* 46 (1971): 35–43.

Page, R. I. *An Introduction to English Runes.* London: Methuen, 1973.

Paladini, Virgilio, and Maria De Marco, eds. *L'Epica post-Carolingia.* Bari, 1966.

Paris, Gaston. Review of *Egberts von Lüttich Fecunda Ratis,* ed. Ernst Voigt. *Journal des savants,* 1890, 559–72.

Parkes, M. B. "Tachygraphy in the Middle Ages: Writing Techniques Employed for *Reportationes* of Lectures and Sermons." In *Grafia e interpunzione del latino nel medioevo: Seminario internazionale, Roma, 27–29 settembre, 1984,* ed. Alfonso Maierù, 15–29. Rome: Edizioni dell'Ateneo, 1987. Reprinted in M. B. Parkes, *Scribes, Scripts, and Readers: Studies in the Communication, Presentation, and Dissemination of Medieval Texts* (London and Rio Grande, OH: Hambledon, 1991), 19–33.

Parkinson, Kathy. *The Enormous Turnip.* Morton Grove, IL: Albert Whitman, 1986.

Pascal, Paul. "The Poem of Letaldus: A New Edition." In *Hrotsvit of Gandersheim: "Rara avis in Saxonia?"* ed. Katharina M. Wilson, 211–28. Medieval and Renaissance

Monograph Series 7. Ann Arbor: Published for M.A.R.C./Medieval and Renaissance Collegium, 1987.

Pastoureau, Michel. *Couleurs, images, symboles: Etudes d'histoire et d'anthropologie.* Paris: Le Léopard d'Or, 1989.

Patience. Ed. J. J. Andersen. Manchester: Manchester University Press, 1969.

Pausanias. *Description of Greece.* Ed. and trans. W. H. S. Jones. 5 vols. Loeb Classical Library 93, 188, 272, 297–98. Cambridge, MA: Harvard University Press, 1918–35.

Peeters, K. C. "De oudste West-Europese sprookjetekst: Unibos-problemen." *Volkskunde* 71 (1970): 8–24.

Perrault, Charles. "Le Petit Chaperon rouge." Trans. Maria Tatar. In Tatar, *Annotated Classic Fairy Tales,* 371–73.

———. *Perrault's Complete Fairy Tales.* Trans. A. E. Johnson et al. New York: Dodd, Mead, 1961.

Perry, B. E., ed. and trans. *Babrius and Phaedrus.* Loeb Classical Library 436. Cambridge, MA: Harvard University Press, 1965.

Peßler, Wilhelm, ed. *Handbuch der deutschen Volkskunde.* 3 vols. Potsdam: Akademische Verlagsgesellschaft, 1934.

Petrini, Mario. *La fiaba di magia nella letteratura italiana.* Udine: Del Bianco, 1983.

Petrus Alfonsi. *Disciplina clericalis.* Ed. Alfons Hilka and Werner Söderhjelm. Vol. 1. Acta Societatis Scientiarum Fennicae 38, no. 4. Helsinki: Druckerei der Finnischen Litteraturgesellschaft, 1911.

Pipping, Rolf. *Oden i galgen.* Studier i nordisk filologi 18, no. 2. Skrifter utgivna av Svenska literatursällskape i Finland 197. Helsinki: Mercator tryckeri, 1928.

Plato. *The Collected Dialogues of Plato.* Ed. Edith Hamilton and Huntington Cairns. Bollingen Series 71. Princeton, NJ: Princeton University Press, 1963.

Pliny the Elder. *Natural History.* Ed. and trans. H. Rackham, W. H. S. Jones, and D. E. Eichholz. 10 vols. Loeb Classical Library 330, 352–53, 370–71, 392–94, 418–19. Cambridge, MA: Harvard University Press, 1949–62.

Plummer, Charles, ed. *Vitae sanctorum Hiberniae.* 2 vols. Oxford: Clarendon, 1910.

Plutarch. "Sayings of Romans." In *Moralia,* vol. 3, ed. and trans. Frank Cole Babbitt, 154–237. Loeb Classical Library 245. Cambridge, MA: Harvard University Press, 1931.

Preller, Ludwig. *Griechische Mythologie.* Vol. 2, *Die greichische Heldensage.* Rev. Carl Robert. 4th ed. Berlin: Weidmann, 1920.

Prinz, Otto, et al., eds. *Mittellateinisches Wörterbuch bis zum ausgehenden 13. Jahrhundert.* Munich: C. H. Beck, 1960–.

Propp, Vladimir IAkovlevich. *La fiaba russa: Lezioni inedite.* Ed. and trans. Franca Crestani. Turin: Giulio Einaudi editore, 1990.

———. *Morphology of the Folktale.* Trans. Laurence Scott. Rev. Louis A. Wagner. 2nd ed. Publications of the American Folklore Society, Bibliographical and Special Series 9. Indiana University Research Center in Anthropology, Folklore, and Linguistics 10. Austin and London: University of Texas Press, 1968.

———. *Le radici storiche dei racconti di fate.* 2nd ed. Turin: Boringhieri, 1985.

———. *Russkaia skazka.* Leningrad: Izdatelstvo Leningradskogo universiteta, 1984.

———. *Theory and History of Folklore.* Trans. Ariadna Y. Martin and Richard P. Martin. Ed. Anatoly Liberman. Theory and History of Folklore 5. Minneapolis: University of Minnesota Press, 1984.

Prudentius. *Psychomachia* 231. In *Prudentius,* ed. and trans. H. J. Thomson, 2 vols., Loeb Classical Library 387 and 398, 1:274–343. Cambridge, MA: Harvard University Press, 1949–53.

Pugliarello, Mariarosaria. *Le origini della favolistica classica.* Brescia: Paideia, 1973.

Pulmer, Karin. "Vom Märchenglück zum Bürgeridyll: Zu H. C. Andersens Volksmärchenbearbeitungen." *Skandinavistik: Zeitschrift für Sprache, Literatur und Kultur der nordischen Länder* 10 (1980): 104–17.

Quintilian. *Institutio oratoria.* Ed. M. Winterbottom. 2 vols. Oxford Classical Texts. Oxford: Clarendon, 1970.

Radermacher, Ludwig. *Mythos und Sage bei den Griechen.* Darmstadt: Wissenschaftliche Buchgesellschaft, 1968.

———. "Walfischmythen." *Archiv für Religionswissenschaft* 9 (1906): 248–52.

Radin, Paul. *The Trickster: A Study in American Indian Mythology.* New York: Schocken, 1972.

Rager, Catherine. *Dictionnaire des fées et du peuple invisible dans l'occident païen.* Turnhout: Brepols, 2003.

Rahner, Hugo. *Symbole der Kirche: Die Ekklesiologie.* Salzburg: Müller, 1964.

Rank, Otto. *Art and Artist: Creative Urge and Personality Development.* Trans. C. F. Atkinson. New York: Tudor, 1932.

———. *The Myth of the Birth of the Hero, and Other Writings.* Ed. Philip Freund. New York: Knopf, 1932.

Ranke, Kurt, ed. *Folktales of Germany.* Trans. Lotte Baumann. Chicago: University of Chicago Press, 1966.

Raspe, Rudolph Erich. *The Surprising Adventures of Baron Munchausen.* With an introduction by Thomas Secombe. Illustrated by William Strang and J. B. Clark. London: Lawrence and Bullen, 1895.

Rattunde, Eckhard. *Li Proverbes au Vilain: Untersuchungen zur romanischen Spruchdichtung des Mittelalters.* Studia Romanica 11. Heidelberg: Carl Winter, 1966.

Rausmaa, Pirkko-Liisa. "Größe: Die ungewöhnliche G." In *EM* 6:239–49.

Reich, Hermann. *Der Mann mit dem Eselskopf: Ein Mimodrama vom klassischen Altertum verfolgt bis auf Shakespeares Sommernachtstraum.* Separat-Abdruck aus dem Jahrbuch der Deutschen Shakespeare-Gesellschaft 40. Weimar: R. Wagner Sohn, 1904.

Riché, Pierre. "La Renaissance intellectuelle du Xe siècle en Occident." *Cahiers d'histoire* (Lyon) 21 (1976): 27–42.

Riddler, Ian. "Worked Whale Vertebrae." *Archaeologia Cantiana* 118 (1998): 205–15.

Riedel, Ingrid. *Hans mein Igel: Wie ein abgelehntes Kind sein Glück findet.* Weisheit im Märchen. Zurich: Kreuz Verlag, 1984.

Ritz, Hans. *Die Geschichte vom Rotkäppchen: Ursprünge, Analysen, Parodien eines Märchens.* 1st ed. Emstal: Muriverlag, 1981. 12th ed., Göttingen: Muriverlag, 1997.

Rizzardi, Simona, ed. and trans. *Asinarius.* In *Commedie latine del XII e XIII secolo,* 4:137–251. Università di Genova, Facoltà di lettere, Pubblicazioni dell'Istituto di filologia classica e medievale 79. Genoa: Istituto di filologia classica e medievale, 1983.

———. "Le *Piacevoli notti* di Giovan Francesco Straparola e le 'commedie elegiache' latine medievali." In *Moving in Measure: Essays in Honour of Brian Moloney,* ed. Judith Bryce and Doug Thompson, 63–77. Hull: Hull University Press, 1989.

Robert, Raymonde. *Le Conte de fées littéraire en France de la fin du XVIIe à la fin du XVI-IIe siècle.* Nancy: Presses universitaires de Nancy, 1982. Repr., Paris: Honoré Champion, 2002.

Rodulfus Glaber. *Historiarum libri quinque.* Ed. and trans. John France. Oxford: Clarendon, 1989.

Rodulfus Tortarius. *Rodulfi Tortarii Carmina.* Ed. Marbury B. Ogle and Dorothy M. Schullian. Papers and Monographs of the American Academy in Rome 8. Rome: American Academy in Rome, 1933.

Röhrich, Lutz, ed. *Erzählungen des späten Mittelalters und ihr Weiterleben in Literatur und Volksdichtung bis zur Gegenwart: Sagen, Märchen, Exempel und Schwänke.* 2 vols. Bern and Munich: Francke Verlag, 1962–67.

———. *Folktales and Reality.* Trans. Peter Tokofsky. Bloomington and Indianapolis: Indiana University Press, 1991.

———. *Das große Lexikon der sprichwörtlichen Redensarten.* 2nd ed. 3 vols. Freiburg, Basel, and Vienna: Herder, 1990–92.

———. *Wage es, den Frosch zu küssen: Das Grimmsche Märchen Nummer Eins in seinen Wandlungen.* Cologne: Eugen Diederichs Verlag, 1987.

Rölleke, Heinz, ed. *Die älteste Märchensammlung der Brüder Grimm: Synopse der handschriftlichen Urfassung von 1810 und der Erstdrucke von 1812.* Texte: Bibliotheca Bodmeriana 1. Cologny-Geneva: Fondation Martin Bodmer, 1975.

———. "New Results of Research on *Grimms' Fairy Tales.*" In McGlathery, *The Brothers Grimm and Folktale,* 101–11.

Le Roman de Thèbes. Ed. Guy Raynaud de Lage. 2 vols. Les classiques français du moyen âge 94, 96. Paris: Honoré Champion, 1967–68.

———. Trans. John Smartt Coley. Garland Library of Medieval Literature 44. New York: Garland, 1986.

Le Roman de Thèbes, Publié d'après tous les manuscrits. Ed. Léopold Constans. 2 vols. Société des Anciens Textes Français. Paris: Firmin Didot, 1890.

Rosenberg, Bruce A. *Folklore and Literature: Rival Siblings.* Knoxville: University of Tennessee Press, 1991.

———. "Oral Literature in the Middle Ages." In *Oral Traditional Literature: A Festschrift for Albert Bates Lord,* ed. John Miles Foley, 440–50. Columbus, OH: Slavic, 1981.

Rosenberg, Rainer. *Literaturwissenschaftliche Germanistik: Zur Geschichte ihrer Probleme und Begriffe.* Berlin: Akademie Verlag, 1989.

———. *Zehn Kapitel zur Geschichte der Germanistik: Literaturgeschichtsschreibung.* Berlin: Akademie Verlag, 1981.

Rosenmeyer, Patricia A. "The Unexpected Guests: Patterns of *Xenia* in Callimachus' 'Victoria Berenices' and Petronius' *Satyricon.*" *Classical Quarterly* 41 (1991): 403–13.

Rothmann, Michael. "Mirabilia vero dicimus, quae nostrae cognitioni non subiacent, etiam cum sint naturalia: 'Wundergeschichten' zwischen Wissen und Unterhaltung; der 'Liber de mirabilibus mundi' ('Otia Imperialia') des Gervasius von Tilbury." In *Mirakel im Mittelalter: Konzeptionen, Erscheinungsformen, Deutungen,* ed. Martin Heinzelmann, Klaus Herbers, and Dieter R. Bauer, 399–432. Beiträge zur Hagiographie 3. Stuttgart: Franz Steiner Verlag, 2002.

Rotunda, D. P. *Motif-Index of the Italian Novella in Prose.* Bloomington: Indiana University Press, 1942.

Die Rübe: Magazin für kulinarische Literatur. Ed. Vincent Klink and Stephan Opitz. Zurich: Haffmans Verlag, 1988–.

Rumpf, Marianne. *Rottkäppchen: Eine vergleichende Märchenuntersuchung.* Artes populares: Studia ethnographica et folkloristica 17. Frankfurt am Main: Peter Lang, 1989.

———. "Ursprung und Entstehung von Warn- und Schreckmärchen." FFC 160 (1955): 3–16.

Runeberg, J. "Le conte de l'Ile-poisson." *Mémoires de la Société néo-philologique à Helsingfors* 3 (1902): 345–95.

Rupert of Deutz. *In Jonam prophetam.* In *Commentariorum in duodecim prophetas minores libri XXXI,* in *PL* 168.399C–440B.

Sabadino degli Arienti, Giovanni. *Novelle Porretane.* Ed. Bruno Basile. Rome: Salerno Editrice, 1981.

Saintyves, Pierre [Émile Nourry]. *Les contes de Perrault et les récits parallèles.* Paris: Émile Nourry, 1923.

Salomon et Marcolfus. Ed. Walter Benary. Sammlung mittellateinischer Texte 8. Heidelberg: Carl Winter, 1914.

Sands, Donald B., ed. *Middle English Verse Romances.* New York: Holt, Rinehart, and Winston, 1966.

Scheer, Eduard, ed. *Lycophronis Alexandra.* 2 vols. Berlin: Weidmann, 1881–1908.

Scheiber, Alexander. "Motivgeschichte des Gedichts von Ady An den grossen Walfisch." *Fabula* 12 (1971): 229–38.

Schenda, Rudolf. *Von Mund zu Ohr: Bausteine zu einer Kulturgeschichte volkstümlichen Erzählens in Europa.* Göttingen: Vandenhoeck und Ruprecht, 1993.

———. "Walfisch-Lore und Walfisch-Literatur." In *IV. International Congress for Folk-Narrative Research in Athens (1.9–6.9 1964),* ed. Georgios A. Megas, 431–48. Laographia 22. Athens, 1965.

Scherf, Walter. *Lexikon der Zaubermärchen.* Kroners Taschenausgabe 472. Stuttgart: Kroner, 1982.

———. *Das Märchenlexikon.* 2 vols. Munich: C. H. Beck, 1995.

Schier, Kurt. "Leyen, Friedrich von der." In *EM* 8:1005–11.

Schmeidler, B. "Ein bisher nicht verwertetes Zeugnis zur Verfassungs- und Wirtschaftsgeschichte des 11. Jahrhunderts." *Historische Vierteljahrschrift* 20 (1920–21): 129–38.

Schmidt, Gary D. *The Iconography of the Mouth of Hell: Eighth-Century Britain to the Fifteenth Century.* Selinsgrove, PA: Susquehanna University Press, 1995.

Schmidt, Hans. *Jona: Eine Untersuchung zur vergleichenden Religionsgeschichte.* Forschungen zur Religion und Literatur des Alten und Neuen Testaments 9. Göttingen: Vandenhoeck und Ruprecht, 1907.

Schmidt, Paul Gerhard. *Proverbia sententiaeque latinitatis medii aevi: Lateinische Sprichwörter und Sentenzen des Mittelalters in alphabetischer Anordnung.* Carmina medii aevi posterioris latina, part 2, vols. 7–9. Göttingen: Vandenhoeck und Ruprecht, 1982–86.

Schmitt, Jean-Claude. *Medioevo "superstizioso."* Universale Laterza 743. Bari: Editori Laterza, 1992.

Schmook, Reinhard. *Gesunkenes Kulturgut, primitive Gemeinschaft: Der Germanist Hans Naumann (1886–1951) in seiner Bedeutung für die Volkskunde.* Beiträge zur Volkskunde und Kulturanalyse 7. Vienna: Helmut-P.-Fielhauer-Freundeskreis, 1993.

Schröder, E. "Zum Text des Unibos." *Zeitschrift für deutsches Altertum und deutsche Literatur* 68 (1931): 152.

Schweizer, Werner R. *Münchhausen und Münchhausiaden: Werden und Schicksale einer deutsch-englischen Burleske*. Bern and Munich: Francke Verlag, 1969.

Scobie, Alexander. *Apuleius and Folklore: Toward a History of ML3045, AaTh567, 449A*. London: Folklore Society, 1983.

———. *Apuleius Metamorphoses (Asinus Aureus) I: A Commentary*. Beiträge zur Klassischen Philologie 54. Meisenheim am Glan: Verlag Anton Hain, 1975.

Searle, William George. *Onomasticon Anglo-Saxonicum*. Cambridge: Cambridge University Press, 1897.

Sedgwick, W. B. "Coniecturae in poetas aliquot medii aevi." *Bulletin Du Cange: Archivum Latinitatis Medii Aevi* 5 (1929–30): 215–25.

Seifert, Lewis. "The Marvelous in Context: The Place of the *Contes de Fées* in Late Seventeenth-Century France." In Zipes, *Great Fairy Tale Tradition*, 902–33.

Seneca the Younger. *Dialogorum Liber XII*, "Ad Helviam matrem De consolatione." In *L. Annaei Senecae Dialogorum libri duodecim*, ed. L. D. Reynolds, 291–317. Oxford Classical Texts. Oxford: Clarendon, 1977.

Sercambi, Giovanni. *Novelle*. Ed. Giovanni Sinicropi. 2 vols. Filologia: Testi e studi 5. Florence: Casa Editrice Le Lettere, 1995.

[Sextus Aurelius Victor, pseudo-]. *De viris illustribus*. Ed. Franciscus Pichlmayr. In *Sexti Aurelii Victoris Liber de Caesaribus, praecedunt Origo gentis romanae et Liber de viris illustribus urbis Romae*, 23–74. Stuttgart and Leipzig: B. G. Teubner, 1911. Repr., 1993.

Sextus Empiricus. *Adversus mathematicos*. Ed. Hermann Mutschmann. Rev. Jürgen Mau and Karel Janáček. Bibliotheca teubneriana 3. Leipzig: B. G. Teubner, 1954.

Shamy, Hasan El-. "Gesunkenes Kulturgut." In *Folklore* 1:419–22.

Shepherd, G. T. "The Emancipation of Story in the Twelfth Century." In *Medieval Narrative: A Symposium*, ed. Hans Bekker-Nielsen, 44–57. Odense: Odense University Press, 1979.

Sigebert of Gembloux. *Catalogus de viris illustribus*. Ed. Robert Witte. Lateinische Sprache und Literatur des Mittelalters 1. Bern: Herbert Lang; Frankfurt am Main: Peter Lang, 1974.

Simon, Marcel. *Hercule et le Christianisme*. Paris: Belles Lettres, 1955.

Simpson, William. *The Jonah Legend: A Suggestion of Interpretation*. London: Grant Richards, 1899. Repr., Detroit: Grand River, 1971.

Simson, Georg von. "Benfey, Theodor." In *EM* 2:102–9.

Singer, Samuel. *Sprichwörter des Mittelalters*. 3 vols. Bern: Herbert Lang, 1944–47.

Singh, J. A. L., and Robert M. Zingg. *Wolf-Children and Feral Man*. Contributions of the University of Denver 4. New York: Harper, 1942.

Slier, Debby. *The Enormous Turnip*. Illustrated by Thomas Sperling. Domino Readers. New York: Star Bright, 1998.

Smith, Sarah Stanbury. "'Game in myn hood': The Traditions of a Comic Proverb." *Studies in Iconography* 9 (1983): 1–12.

Soriano, Marc. *Les Contes de Perrault: Culture savante et traditions populaires*. Paris: Gallimard, 1968.

Spearing, A. C. *The Medieval Poet as Voyeur: Looking and Listening in Medieval Love-Narratives*. Cambridge: Cambridge University Press, 1993.

Speculum sacerdotale. Ed. Edward H. Weatherly. Early English Text Society, o.s., 200. London: Humphrey Milford, Oxford University Press, 1936.

Spies, Otto. *Orientalische Stoffe in den Kinder- und Hausmärchen der Brüder Grimm.* Beiträge zur Sprach- und Kulturgeschichte des Orients 6. Walldorf: H. Vorndran, 1952.

Steffen, Uwe. *Das Mysterium von Tod und Auferstehung: Formen und Wandlungen des Jona-Motives.* Göttingen: Vandenhoeck und Ruprecht, 1963.

Storer, Mary Elizabeth. *Un Episode littéraire de la fin du XVIIe siècle: La mode des contes de fées (1685–1700).* Bibliothèque de la Revue de littérature comparée 48. Paris: Honoré Champion, 1928. Repr., Geneva: Slatkine, 1972.

Storia di Campriano contadino. Ed. Albino Zenatti. Bologna: Gaetano Romagnoli, 1884.

Strabo. *Geography.* Ed. and trans. Horace Leonard Jones. 8 vols. Loeb Classical Library 49–50, 182, 196, 211, 223, 241, 267. Cambridge, MA: Harvard University Press, 1960–70.

Straparola, Gianfrancesco [Giovanni Francesco]. *Le piacevoli notti.* Ed. Donato Pirovano. Rome: Salerno Editrice, 2000.

———. *Le piacevoli notti. The Facetious Nights of Straparola,* Trans. W. G. Waters. 4 vols. London: Privately Printed for Members of the Society of Bibliophiles, 1898.

Strayer, Joseph R., ed. *Dictionary of the Middle Ages.* 13 vols. New York: Charles Scribner's Sons, 1982–89.

Strecker, Karl, ed. *Die Cambridger Lieder: Carmina Cantabrigiensia.* MGH Scriptores rerum Germanicarum in usum scholarum separatim editi 40. Berlin: Weidmann, 1926.

———, ed. *Ecbasis cuiusdam captivi per tropologiam.* MGH Scriptores rerum Germanicarum in usum scholarum separatim editi 69. Hanover: Impensis Bibliopolii Hahniani, 1935.

Stricker, Der. *Pfaffe Amis.* Ed. K. Kamihara. 2nd ed. Göppinger Arbeiten zur Germanistik 233. Göppingen: Kümmerle Verlag, 1990.

Suchier, Walther, ed. *Das mittellateinische Gespräch Adrian und Epictitus nebst verwandten Texten (Joca Monachorum).* Tübingen: Max Niemeyer, 1955.

Suchomski, Joachim. *"Delectatio" und "Utilitas": Ein Beitrag zum Verständnis mittelalterlicher komischer Literatur.* Bern: Francke Verlag, 1975.

Sudre, Léopold. *Les Sources du Roman du Renart.* Paris: Université de Paris, 1892; Paris: E. Bouillon, 1893. Repr., Geneva: Slatkine, 1974.

Sulzer, Johan Georg. *Zum Gebrauch der letzten Classe des Königl. Joachimsthalischen Gymnasium.* Part 1 of *Vorübungen zur Erweckung der Aufmerksamkeit und des Nachdenkens,* rev. Johann Heinrich Ludwig Meierotto. 3rd ed. Berlin: Friedrich Nicolai, 1780.

Swahn, Jan-Öjvind. *The Tale of Cupid and Psyche (Aarne-Thompson 425 & 428).* Lund: CWK Gleerup, 1955.

Sydow, Carl Wilhelm von. "Folktale Studies and Philology: Some Points of View." In Dundes, *The Study of Folklore,* 219–42.

———. *Selected Papers on Folklore.* Copenhagen: Rosenkilde and Bagger, 1948.

Szabo, Vicki Ellen. "The Use of Whales in Early Medieval Britain." *Haskins Society Journal* 9 (1997): 137–57.

Tatar, Maria, ed. *The Annotated Classic Fairy Tales.* New York and London: W. W. Norton, 2002.

———, ed. *The Classic Fairy Tales.* New York and London: W. W. Norton, 1999.

———. *The Hard Facts of the Grimms' Fairy Tales.* Princeton, NJ: Princeton University Press, 1987.

Tegethoff, Ernst, trans. *Märchen, Schwänke und Fabeln.* Bücher des Mittelalters. Munich: F. Bruckmann, 1925.

———. *Studien zum Märchentypus von Amor und Psyche.* Rheinische Beiträge und Hülfsbücher zur germanischen Philologie und Volkskunde 4. Bonn and Leipzig: Kurt Schroeder, 1922.

Tenèze, Marie-Louis. "Bédier, Joseph." In *EM* 2:21–25.

Terentianus Maurus. *De syllabis.* In *Grammatici latini,* ed. Heinrich Keil, 6:334–63. Leipzig: B. G. Teubner, 1874. Repr., Hildesheim and New York: Georg Olms Verlag, 1981.

Theophylaktos of Ohrid. *Expositio in prophetam Ionam.* In *PG* 126:906–68.

Thesaurus Proverbiorum Medii Aevi: Lexikon der Sprichwörter des romanisch-germanischen Mittelalters. 13 vols. with an additional index vol. Berlin and New York: Walter de Gruyter, 1995–2002.

Thiel, Helmut van. *Der Eselroman.* 2 vols. Zetemata: Monographien zur klassischen Altertumswissenschaft 54, nos. 1–2. Munich: C. H. Beck, 1971–72.

The Thirteenth Warrior. Directed by John McTiernan. Touchstone Pictures, 1999.

Thompson, Stith. *The Folktale.* New York: Holt, Rinehart, and Winston, 1946. Repr., Berkeley and Los Angeles: University of California Press, 1977.

Thys, Walther. *Andre Jolles (1874–1946): Gebildeter Vagant; Brieven en documenten bijeengebracht, ingeleid en toegelicht door Walter Thys.* Amsterdam: Amsterdam University Press; Leipzig: Leipziger Universitätsverlag, 2000.

Timm, Werner. "Der gestrandete Wal, eine motivkundliche Studie." *Staatliche Museen zu Berlin, Forschungen und Berichte* 3–4 (1961): 76–93.

Tolstoy, Aleksei. *The Gigantic Turnip.* Illustrated by Niamh Sharkey. New York: Barefoot, 1999.

———. *The Great Big Enormous Turnip.* Illustrated by Helen Oxenbury. New York: Franklin Watts, 1968.

Tomkowiak, Ingrid. *Lesebuchgeschichten: Erzählstoffe in Schullesebüchern 1770–1920.* Berlin and New York: Walter de Gruyter, 1993.

Tonnelat, Ernest. *Les contes des frères Grimm: Étude sur la composition et le style du recueil des "Kinder- und Hausmärchen."* Paris: Armand Colin, 1912.

Toussaint-Samat, Maguelonne. *A History of Food.* Trans. Anthea Bell. Cambridge, MA, and Oxford: Blackwell Reference, 1992.

"The Trial of Joseph and Mary." In *Ludus Coventriae, or The Plaie Called Corpus Christi: Cotton MS. Vespasian D. VIII,* ed. K. S. Block, 124–35. Early English Text Society, extra ser., 120. London: Oxford University Press, 1922.

Tubach, Frederic C. *Index Exemplorum: A Handbook of Medieval Religious Tales.* FFC 204. Helsinki: Suomalainen Tiedeakatemia, Academia scientiarum fennica, 1981.

Tylor, Edward Burnett. *Primitive Culture: Researches into the Development of Mythology, Philosophy, Religion, Language, Art, and Custom.* Vol. 1. 7th ed. New York: Brentano's, 1924.

Uther, Hans-Jörg. *Märchen vor Grimm.* Munich: Eugen Diederichs, 1990.

———. "Ranke, Kurt." In *EM* 11:207–13.

Valerius Maximus. *Memorable Doings and Sayings.* Ed. and trans. D. R. Shackleton Bai-

ley. 2 vols. Loeb Classical Library 492–93. Cambridge, MA: Harvard University Press, 2000.

Vàrvaro, Albert. *Apparizioni fantastiche: Tradizioni folcloriche e letteratura nel medioevo; Walter Map.* Bologna: Il Mulino, 1994.

Veillodter, Valentin Karl. *Lieder, Erzählungen und Fabeln für Kinder zur Uibung im Lesen und Deklamiren.* Nuremberg: Bauer und Mann, 1797.

Velay-Vállantin, Catherine. "From 'Little Red Riding Hood' to the 'Beast of Gévaudan': The Tale in the Long Term Continuum." In *Telling Tales: Medieval Narratives and the Folk Tradition,* ed. Francesca Canadé Sautman, Diana Conchado, and Giuseppe Carlo Di Scipio, 269–95. New York: St. Martin's, 1998.

———. "Little Red Riding Hood as Fairy Tale, *Fait-divers,* and Children's Literature: The Invention of a Traditional Heritage." In Canepa, *Out of the Woods,* 306–51.

Verbaal, W. "Amys and Amelis." In *A Dictionary of Medieval Heroes,* ed. Willem P. Gerritsen and Anthony G. van Melle, trans. Tanis Guest, 24–26. Woodbridge, UK: Boydell, 1998.

Verdier, Yvonne. "Little Red Riding Hood in Oral Tradition." *Marvels and Tales: Journal of Fairy-Tale Studies* 11 (1997): 101–23. Originally published as "Le Petit Chaperon rouge dans la tradition orale." *Le Débat* 3 (1980): 31–61.

Vergil. *Opera.* Ed. R. A. B. Mynors. Oxford Classical Texts. Oxford: Clarendon, 1969.

Vezin, Jean. "Leofnoth: Un scribe anglais à Saint-Benoît-sur-Loire." *Codices manuscripti* 3 (1977): 109–20.

Vigfusson, Guðbrandr, and C. R. Unger, eds. *Flateyjarbók: En samling af norske kongesagaer med inskudte mindre fortællinger.* 3 vols. Christiania: P. T. Malling, 1860–68.

Virtanen, Leea. "Historic-Geographic Method." In *Folklore* 1:442–48.

Vita sancti Albei archiepiscopi de Imlech. In *Vitae sanctorum Hiberniae,* ed. Charles Plummer, 1:46–64. Oxford: Clarendon, 1910.

Vogel, Martin. *Onos lyras: Der Esel mit der Leier.* 2 vols. Orpheus-Schriftenreihe zu Grundfragen der Musik 13–14. Düsseldorf: Verlag der Gesellschaft zur Förderung der systematischen Musikwissenschaft, 1973.

Vollmann, Benedikt Konrad. "Lantfrid und Cobbo." In *VL*² 5:610–11.

———. *Ruodlieb.* Wiesbaden: Dr. Ludwig Reichert Verlag, 1985.

———. "Unibos." In *VL*² 10:80–85.

Wagner, Fritz. "Asinarius." In *EM* 1:865–67.

Wailes, Stephen L. "Fortuna and Social Anomaly: Principles of Mediaeval Humour in *Rapularius* and *Asinarius.*" *Seminar* 9 (1973): 87–96.

Waldemarson-Rooth, Anna Birgitta. "Kung Lindorm, en orientalisk saga i Danske-Skånsk Sagotradition." *Folkkultur,* 1942, 176–245.

Walther, Hans. *Proverbia sententiaeque latinitatis medii aevi: Lateinische Sprichwörter und Sentenzen des Mittelalters in alphabetischer Anordnung.* Carmina medii aevi posterioris latina, part 2, vols. 1–6. Göttingen: Vandenhoeck und Ruprecht, 1963–69.

Ward, Benedicta. *Miracles and the Medieval Mind: Theory, Record, and Event, 1000–1215.* 2nd ed. Philadelphia: University of Pennsylvania Press, 1987.

Ward, Donald, trans. and ed. *The German Legends of the Brothers Grimm.* 2 vols. Philadelphia: Institute for the Study of Human Issues, 1981.

———. "New Misconceptions about Old Folktales: The Brothers Grimm." In McGlathery, *The Brothers Grimm and Folktale,* 91–100.

Warner, Marina. *From the Beast to the Blonde: On Fairy Tales and Their Tellers.* New York: Farrar, Straus, and Giroux, 1994.

Weber, Albrecht. "Ueber den Zusammenhang indischer Fabeln mit griechischen." *Indische Studien: Beiträge für die Kunde des indischen Alterthums* 3 (1855): 327–73.

———. "Ueber die Siṅhâsanadvâtriṅçkâ." *Indische Studien: Beiträge für die Kunde des indischen Alterthums* 15 (1878): 185–453.

Weber, Max. *Wirtschaft und Gesellschaft.* Tübingen: J. C. B. Mohr, 1922.

Wegehaupt, Heinz. *Hundert Illustrationen aus anderthalb Jahrhunderten zu Märchen von Hans Christian Andersen.* Hanau: Verlag Dausien, 1990.

Weinhold, K. "Über das Märchen vom Eselmenschen." *Sitzungsberichte der Königlich Preussischen Akademie der Wissenschaften zu Berlin* 29 (plenary session of June 15, 1893): 1–14.

Weinreich, Otto. "Antiphanes und Münchhausen: Das antike Lügenmärlein von den gefrornen Worten und sein Fortleben im Abendland." *Akademie der Wissenschaften in Wien, Philosophisch-historische Klasse, Sitzungsberichte* 220. Band, 4. Abhandlung (Vienna and Leipzig: Hölder Pichler Tempsky, 1942): 17–21.

Welkenhuysen, Andries. *Het lied van boer eenos (uersus de uniboue): Kluchtig versverhaal uit de elfde eeuw (inleiding, facsimile-weergave, teksteditie, metrische vertaling, bijlage ter verantwoording en duiding).* 2 vols. [text volume and "Bijlage" with commentary]. Louvain: Acco, 1975.

Wells, David A. "Die biblischen Wörter im 'Unibos': Ein Beitrag zum Verständnis des Antiklerikalismus im Frühmittelalter." In *Kleinere Erzählformen im Mittelalter: Paderborner Colloquium 1987,* ed. Klaus Grubmüller, L. Peter Johnson, and Hans-Hugo Steinhoff, 83–88. Paderborn: Schöningh, 1988.

Wendland, Johannes. *Miracles and Christianity.* Trans. H. R. Mackintosh. New York: Hodder and Stoughton, 1911.

Werber, Gertrud. "Frazer, James George." In *EM* 5:220–27.

Wesselski, Albert. *Märchen des Mittelalters.* Berlin: H. Stubenrauch, 1925.

———. *Mönchslatein: Erzählungen aus geistlichen Schriften des XIII. Jahrhunderts.* Leipzig: Wilhelm Heims, 1909.

———, ed. *Die Schwänke und Schnurren des Pfarrers Arlotto.* 2 vols. Berlin: Alexander Duncker Verlag, 1910.

———. *Versuch einer Theorie des Märchens.* Prager Deutsche Studien 45. Reichenberg i. B.: F. Kraus, 1931.

Whitaker, Edward C., trans. *Documents of the Baptismal Liturgy.* Rev. Maxwell E. Johnson. 3rd ed. Alcuin Club Collections 79. London: SPCK, 2003.

Whiting, Bartlett Jere. *Proverbs, Sentences, and Proverbial Phrases from English Writings Mainly before 1500.* Cambridge, MA: Harvard University Press, Belknap, 1968.

Wilmart, André. "Le florilège de Saint-Gatien: Contribution à l'étude des poèmes d'Hildebert et de Marbode." *Revue Bénédictine* 48 (1936): 3–40, 147–81, 235–58.

———. "Le poème héroïque de Létald sur Within le pêcheur." *Studi medievali,* n.s., 9 (1936): 188–203.

Wilson, Ambrose John. "The Sign of the Prophet Jonah and Its Modern Confirmations." *Princeton Theological Review* 25 (1927): 630–42.

Wilson, R. M. *The Lost Literature of Medieval England.* 2nd ed. London: Methuen, 1970.

Wilson, William A. "Herder, Folklore, and Romantic Nationalism." *Journal of Popular Culture* 6 (1973): 819–35.

———. "Richard M. Dorson as Romantic-Nationalist." *Journal of Folklore Research* 26 (1989): 36–42.

"The Wish-Goat." In *Carmina sangallensia*, ed. Ernst Dümmler, 474–75. MGH Poetae Latini Aevi Carolini 2. Berlin: Weidmann, 1884.

Woestijne, Paul van de. *De Klucht van boer Eenos naar een latijnsch gedicht uit de 11e eeuw: Versus de Unibove.* Antwerp: N. V. Standaard-Boekhandel, 1944.

Wolterbeek, Marc. *Comic Tales of the Middle Ages: An Anthology and Commentary.* Contributions to the Study of World Literature 39. New York: Greenwood, 1991.

Wood-Martin, W. G. *Traces of the Elder Faiths of Ireland, a Folklore Sketch: A Handbook of Irish Pre-Christian Traditions.* 2 vols. London: Longmans, Green, 1902.

Worstbrock, F. J. "Rapularius." In *VL*² 7:1000–1002.

Wührl, Paul-Wolfgang. *Das deutsche Kunstmärchen: Geschichte, Botschaft und Erzählstrukturen.* Heidelberg: Wuelle und Meyer, 1984.

Wunderlich, Werner. "Gabe." In *EM* 5:625–37.

Wundt, Wilhelm. *Völkerpsychologie: Eine Untersuchung der Entwicklungsgesetze von Sprache, Mythus und Sitte.* Vol. 5, part 2. 2nd ed. Leipzig: Alfred Kröner, 1914.

Wyss, Ulrich. *Die wilde Philologie: Jacob Grimm und der Historismus.* Munich: C. H. Beck, 1979.

Xenophon of Ephesus. *An Ephesian Tale of Anthia and Habrocomes.* Trans. Graham Anderson. In *Collected Ancient Greek Novels*, ed. B. P. Reardon, 125–69. Berkeley: University of California Press, 1989.

Young, Karl. *The Drama of the Medieval Church.* 2 vols. Oxford: Clarendon, 1933.

Zellinger, Johannes. "Der geköderte Leviathan im Hortus deliciarum der Herrad von Landsperg." *Historisches Jahrbuch* 45 (1925): 161–77.

Ziefert, Harriet. *The Turnip.* Illustrated by Laura Rader. New York: Puffin, 1996.

Ziolkowski, Jan M. "Always Beyond Compare: The Past, Present, and Future of Comparative Literature." *Journal X: A Journal in Culture and Criticism* 8 (2004): 115–35.

———. "The Beast and the Beauty: The Reorientation of 'The Donkey,' from the Middle Ages to the Brothers Grimm." *Journal of Medieval Latin* 5 (1995): 53–94.

———. "Cultural Diglossia and the Nature of Medieval Latin Literature." In *The Ballad and Oral Literature*, ed. Joseph Harris, 193–213. Harvard English Studies 16. Cambridge, MA: Harvard University Press, 1991.

———. "The Deeds and Words of Aesop and Marcolf." In *Scripturus vitam: Lateinische Biographie von der Antike bis in die Gegenwart Festgabe für Walter Berschin zum 65. Geburtstag*, ed. Dorothea Walz, 105–23. Heidelberg: Mattes Verlag, 2002.

———. "Ernst Robert Curtius (1886–1956) and Medieval Latin Studies." *Journal of Medieval Latin* 7 (1997): 147–67.

———. "A Fairy Tale from Before Fairy Tales: Egbert of Liège's 'De puellis a lupellis seruata' and the Medieval Background of 'Little Red Riding Hood.'" *Speculum* 67 (1992): 549–75.

———. "Folklore and Learned Lore in Letaldus's Whale Poem." *Viator* 15 (1984): 107–18.

———. "Folktales in Medieval Latin Poetry, 1000–1300." In *Poesía latina medieval (siglos V–XV): Actas del IV Congreso del "Internationales Mittellateinerkomitee" (Santiago*

de Compostela, 12–15 de septiembre de 2002), ed. Manuel C. Díaz y Díaz and José M. Díaz de Bustamante, 75–91. Millennio Medievale 55. Atti di Convegni 17. Florence: SISMEL, 2005.

———. Introduction to *Obscenity: Social Control and Artistic Creation in the European Middle Ages*, ed. Jan M. Ziolkowski. Leiden: E. J. Brill, 1998.

———. "A Medieval 'Little Claus and Big Claus': A Fabliau from Before Fabliaux?" In *The World and Its Rival: Essays on Literary Imagination in Honor of Per Nykrog*, ed. Kathryn Karczewska and Tom Conley, 1–37. Amsterdam: Rodopi, 1999.

———. "Metaphilology." *Journal of English and Germanic Philology* 104 (2005): 239–72.

———. "Old Wives' Tales: Classicism and Anticlassicism from Apuleius to Chaucer." *Journal of Medieval Latin* 12 (2002): 90–113.

———, ed. *On Philology.* University Park, PA: Penn State Press, 1990.

———. "The *Rapularius* and 'The Turnip' in *Grimms' Fairy Tales:* A Comparative Study with Translations." *Journal of Medieval Latin* 13 (2003): 61–126.

———. "The Spirit of Play in the Poetry of St. Gall." In *Sangallensia in Washington: The Arts and Letters in Medieval and Baroque St. Gall Viewed from the Late Twentieth Century*, ed. James C. King, 143–69. New York: Peter Lang, 1994.

———. *Talking Animals: Medieval Latin Beast Poetry.* Philadelphia: University of Pennsylvania Press, 1993.

———. "Towards a History of Medieval Latin Literature." In *Medieval Latin: An Introduction and Bibliographical Guide*, ed. F. A. C. Mantello and A. G. Rigg, 505–36. Washington, DC: Catholic University of America Press, 1996.

———. "Vergil as Shahrazad: How an Eastern Frame Tale Was Authorized in the West." In *Studies for Dante: Essays in Honor of Dante Della Terza*, ed. Franco Fido, Rena A. Syska-Lamparska, and Pamela D. Stewart, 25–36. Florence: Edizioni Cadmo, 1998.

———. "What Is Philology? Introduction." *Comparative Literature Studies* 27 (1990): 1–12.

Zipes, Jack, trans. *Beauties, Beasts, and Enchantment: Classic French Fairy Tales.* New York: Meridian, 1991.

———. *Breaking the Magic Spell: Radical Theories of Folk and Fairy Tales.* Austin: University of Texas Press, 1979. Repr., New York: Routledge, 1992.

———. *The Brothers Grimm: From Enchanted Forest to the Modern World.* New York and London: Routledge, 1988.

———, ed. *The Great Fairy Tale Tradition: From Straparola and Basile to the Brothers Grimm.* New York and London: W. W. Norton, 2001.

———. "The Origins of the Fairy Tale for Children, or How Script Was Used to Tame the Beast in Us." In *Children and Their Books: A Celebration of the Work of Iona and Peter Opie*, ed. Gillian Avery and Julia Briggs, 119–34. Oxford: Clarendon, 1989.

———, ed. *The Oxford Companion to Fairy Tales.* Oxford: Oxford University Press, 2000.

———. *Spells of Enchantment: The Wondrous Fairy Tales of Western Culture.* New York: Penguin, 1991.

———. *The Trials and Tribulations of Little Red Riding Hood: Versions of the Tale in Sociocultural Context.* South Hadley, MA: Bergin and Garvey, 1983.

———. *The Trials and Tribulations of Little Red Riding Hood: Versions of the Tale in Sociocultural Context.* 2nd ed. New York: Routledge, 1993.

Zumwalt, Rosemary Lévy. *American Folklore Scholarship: A Dialogue of Dissent.* Bloomington and Indianapolis: Indiana University Press, 1988.

Zwetsloot, H. "De Iconographie van Pinksteren." *Het Gildeboek* 34 (1952): 33–39.

———. "De Iconographie van Pinksteren (II): Het uitgangspunt der stralen of tongen." *Het Gildeboek* 34 (1952): 68–73.

General Index

Numerals referring to appendixes of translations are italicized.

chest, 158, 161, *272, 301–3, 308–9, 313–15.*
 See also barrel; cask; sack
chiasmus, 124, 192
Child, Francis James, 27
childlessness, 222. *See also* barrenness;
 sterility
children, feral, 108
children's legends, 18
children's literature, 236
Child Who Was Melted in the Sun, The
 (*De L'enfant que fu remis au soleil*), 135
Chiron, 217
Chrétien de Troyes, 40
Christ. *See* Jesus Christ
Christian elements and Christianization,
 104–7, 109, 110, 196
Christian Hebraism, 86
Cicero, Marcus Tullius, 57
Cinderella, 62, 64
Cinderella (film), 65
Cistercian, 234
classic, 8, 36
"classic" fairy tales, 37, 67, 144, 179,
 368n9; in collections, 25–26, 44, 230;
 and medieval stories, 6, 27; as oxy-
 moron, 8
classics (field of study), 1–2
Clausen-Stolzenburg, Maren, 377n107
cleric (clerk), 106, 128, 186, 207; and
 courtliness, 42, 174–75; and folk litera-
 ture, 40, 53, 124; and peasant, 32, 193;
 in tales, *246, 306, 313–15*
clothes: loss of, 85; red, 108, 111–12. *See
 also* nakedness
Clouds, The, 188
Clouston, William Alexander, 371n20
Cockaigne, land of, 145, 154, *294–95, 307,
 322*
coins. *See* defecation and coins; donkey
 (mare) that defecates coins
collecting, collectors, and collections, 21,
 29, 43–44, 55, 104, 167, 191, 225, 231–38
Collodi, Carlo (pseudonym of Carlo
 Lorenzini), 6, 65–66
Columella, Lucius Junius Moderatus,
 421nn78, 83
comedia, 40, 134, 221, 235. *See also* com-
 edy: Medieval Latin

comedy: Medieval Latin, 40, 175. See
 also *comedia*
comparative literature, 1–2
composition in performance, 40, 49,
 375n87
conception, miraculous, 144
conduit theory, 202, 203
Congress of Vienna, 166
Conon, 180, 181
Constance, 257
conte de fées, 45, 46
coracle, 67, *244*
Cormac, 108
"cornice." *See* frame tale
Cosquin, Emmanuel, 202, 371n20
court, 42, 175, 193, 208–9, 213; in tales,
 323, 345, 362–63
courtier, 5, 42, 175, 181, *342*
courtliness, 141, 429–30n23, 431n37
Coyote, 134
Creusa, 68
Crichton, Michael, 71
Croce, Benedetto, 7, 13–14
Croce, Giulio Cesare, 157, 183–84
Cross, Holy, *289*
crucifixion, 82
Crusades, 219
cumulative tales, 178
Cupid and Psyche, 26, 44, 58, 62, 91, 161,
 162, 209, 221
Curius Dentatus, Manius, 182
Curtius, Ernst Robert, 28, 166
Cyprian's Banquet. See *Cena Cypriani*
Cyril of Alexandria, 75, 76

Daniel, 109
Danish literature, 125–26
Dante, 145
Darwin, Charles, 28. *See also* Darwinism
Darwinism, 39
Daston, Lorraine, 423–24nn99–105
deacon, 153, 160. *See also* priest; sexton
death, simulated, *271*
decorum, 192
Deeds of the Romans, 26, 55, 79
defecation and coins, 132, 137–39, 146–
 47, 157, 158, *266. See also* donkey
 (mare) that defecates coins

wedding, 206, 209, 215, 227, *364. See also* marriage

werewolf, 108, 110, 223

Wesselski, Albert, 25, 45, 53, 55, 59, 60, 95, 113–14, 130, 144, 373n57, 396n29

whale, 76, 78–79, 81–85, 89–90. *See also* great fish

whaling, 70–72

white, 115–16, 118

wife, 63, 154, 195–96; in tales, *268, 286–93, 323, 325, 333;* killed and revived, 132, *271–76;* wears breeches and is slain, *309*

Willems, J. F., 126

William of Malmesbury, 234

William of Newburgh, 234

wind, 193, 426n134

wine, 116, *261, 301–2, 304–5, 313–14*

wisdom, 189

"Wish-Goat, The," 33, 56, 143, 145, 207, *253–55*

Within, 67–70, 76, 82–83, *244–48,* 383n17

wizard, 153

wolf, 103, 105, 107, 109, 110, 112, 116, 120, 149, 232, *262–63;* suckling human being, 399n67; tamed by saint, 106, 109

Wolf, Friedrich, 17

"Wolf and the Kids, The" (*KHM* 5), 67

wolf children, 107, 108

Wolfdietrich, 107–8

women, 51, 53, 61; old, 5, 57, 62, 63; representation of, 180–81, 195, 208; in tales, *273, 275–76*

wonder: and miracles, 232–33; as circum-

scribed in childhood, 8; in *The Donkey Tale,* 213, 224; as fundamental to fairy tales, 64; in Letaldus, 48; nature of, 45; in *One-Ox,* 50, 145, 146, 163, *267, 268;* in *The Turnip Tale,* 184–86, 189, 196, 197

wonder chambers, 185–86

wonders of the East, 234

wonder tale, 235–39; *The Donkey Tale* as, 57, 200, 224, 230; and magic tale, 47, 62; Medieval Latin examples of, 34, 44–45; and miracle, 144–46; and novelistic folktale, 49; as technical term for fairy tale, 19, 55, 64, 370n14; and trickster tale, 162; *The Turnip Tale* as, 57, 172; and wonder, 184, 196–97, 232, 418n30;

woodcutter, 119

woods, 108, 110, 119

wordplay, 229. *See also* paronomasia

"world literature," 3

Wunderkammer, 185–86

"Wunschbock," 33. *See* "Wish-Goat, The"

Xenophon of Ephesus, 109

Yalqut Shim'oni, 86

Ysengrimus, 24, 150, 160

Zeman, 78

Zeus, 75

Zingerle, Ignaz Vinzenz, 17

Zingerle, Joseph, 17

Zipes, Jack, 25–26, 96, 368n9, 431n44, 437n5

Index of Tale Types and Motifs

This index identifies only places where specific tale types or motifs are explicitly identified by their ATU or *MI* designations

ATU 123: 67, 115, 403n113
ATU 156: 400n77
ATU 300–749: 46
ATU 328A: 62
ATU 333: 67, 93–124, 403n113
ATU 410: 62
ATU 425–49: 209
ATU 425: 213, 214, 431n42
ATU 425A: 431n40
ATU 425B (AT 428) 431n42
ATU 425C: 62, 201, 210, 431n40
ATU 430: 33, 200, 213, 214, 341, 428n6
ATU 433B: 212
ATU 440: 23, 62
ATU 441: 214, 432n57
ATU 510–510A: 62
ATU 563: 146
ATU 709: 62
ATU 852: 42, 376n94
ATU 973: 80
ATU 1362: 42, 376n92
ATU 1525: 162
ATU 1525A: 131, 187
ATU 1535: 33, 130–31, 187, 408n31

ATU 1539: 187
ATU 1689A: 33, 162, 176, 322
ATU 1737: 162, 187
ATU 1775–99: 160
ATU 1889: 77
ATU 1889G: 78, 241
ATU 1960: 420n61
ATU 1960A: 56
ATU 1960D: 176, 177

MI A535: 384n37
MI B103: 320
MI B103.1.1: 146
MI B641.4: 213
MI B641.5: 214
MI B771: 108
MI C31.1.2: 435n94
MI C758.1: 213, 214
MI D132.1: 213, 428n7
MI D361.1: 435n94
MI D457.13: 320
MI D563: 320
MI D721.3: 213, 214, 434n90
MI D963: 213